Legal Information
How to Find It, How to Use It

by

Kent C. Olson

Oryx Press
1999

The rare Arabian Oryx is believed to have inspired the myth of the unicorn. This desert antelope became virtually extinct in the early 1960s. At that time, several groups of international conservationists arranged to have nine animals sent to the Phoenix Zoo to be the nucleus of a captive breeding herd. Today, the Oryx population is over 1,000, and over 500 have been returned to the Middle East.

© 1999 by The Oryx Press
4041 North Central at Indian School Road
Phoenix, Arizona 85012-3397

Published simultaneously in Canada
Printed and bound in the United States of America

∞ The paper used in this publication meets the minimum requirements of
American National Standard for Information Science—Permanence
of Paper for Printed Library Materials, ANSI Z39.48, 1984.

Library of Congress Cataloging-in-Publication Data

Legal information : how to find it, how to use it / by Kent Olson.
    p. cm.
    Includes biblographical references and index.
    ISBN 0-89774-961-8 Case 0-89774-963-4 Paper (alk. paper)
    1. Legal research—United States—Popular works. 2. Law—United
States—Popular works.
    I. Title.
    KF240.O365   1999
    340'.07'2073—dc21   98-46517
                                                                CIP

Contents

List of Exhibits

List of Tables

Preface

To many people legal information is an isolated body of knowledge, locked away in a formidable law library with its own inscrutable and idiosyncratic means of access. But the law is not the exclusive province of lawyers and law students, of interest only to those who must work within the legal system. Legal literature has much to tell us about our society and our history, and it can be valuable to researchers from a wide range of disciplines.

This book is part of the "How to Find It, How to Use It" series of reference works published by the Oryx Press; its general framework is modeled on the format used by Michael R. Lavin in the two editions of his *Business Information: How to Find It, How to Use It* (1987, 1992). This imitation has a purpose. Most books on legal information are designed for law students or for people handling their own legal affairs, and they focus on the skills needed to determine what laws govern particular situations. This is an important role for legal resources, of course, but people seek legal information for other reasons as well. This book looks not only at "the law," but also at other aspects of the legal system, such as the history, politics, and structure of lawmaking institutions. Following a pattern familiar to other disciplines will help make legal literature more accessible and less mysterious.

Although "How to Find It, How to Use It" makes a fine subtitle, it is in some ways antithetical to the purpose of this book. This volume aims to explain where legal information is located, whether in general libraries, in law libraries, or electronically, and to provide the background knowledge necessary to make effective use of that information. How you use legal information depends on your needs and interests, but the subtitle "How to Find It, What You Do with It Is Up to You" just didn't have the right ring.

A substantial number of books have been published recently about legal information on the Internet. These are valuable guides, but most focus on the Internet to the exclusion of other, more traditional information sources. This book recognizes that the Internet may work best as one of several search options, along with library books and other electronic resources. The Internet is fine for some purposes, inadequate for others. Consideration of the Internet and other approaches is therefore integrated into the discussion throughout the book. To the extent possible, resources available in general libraries or at free Internet sites are emphasized. In many instances, however, important materials may be available only in law libraries or through commercial legal databases.

The 12 chapters of *Legal Information* are divided into four parts. Part 1 provides a brief introduction to the legal system and to basic reference works that can help make some sense of it. Part 2 focuses on sources that explain and discuss legal matters, such as reference works, treatises, and journals, as well as the catalogs, indexes, and directories needed to learn more. With this background, the text moves on to examine the primary sources of the law. Part 3 looks at federal law, beginning with the Constitution and the Supreme Court, and then the work of Congress, the lower federal courts, and administrative agencies. It examines such reference resources as guides and directories, means of access to the laws, cases, regulations, and the tools needed to make sense of this vast body of material. Part 4 provides similar coverage of state law, but in more general terms, due to variations among the states.

Research often follows the course outlined by this organization. The first step is to find an overview placing a legal issue in its doctrinal or historical context. The next step is to search for relevant books focusing on the area and explaining the background, and for recent journal articles to gain a current perspective. Telephone calls or e-mail inquiries may provide missing information or enlist professional assistance. With this background knowledge, a researcher is prepared to delve into the statutes and case law needed to fully understand an issue.

The most difficult step is often the first—determining how an issue is classified in legal literature and finding relevant explanations. As evidenced by the large number of legal dictionaries available, legal terminology is complex and often confusing. Using the indexes in many publications can be frustrating. Full-text electronic access does not eliminate the frustration because a poorly worded search is likely to elicit a glut of marginally relevant documents.

This is why a basic understanding of the legal system and its classifications and categories is essential. Determining whether an issue is one of state or federal law can narrow the focus of inquiry considerably. Identifying an issue as one of tort law or of civil procedure can lead to the resources that are most relevant.

At this point, the research path generally becomes easier. Most legal literature provides extensive citations to other resources, usually the primary statutes and cases involved but also other books and articles. One document leads to several more, and those in turn provide further research leads.

Web site addresses are provided throughout the book, even though the volatility and pace of Internet development ensures that some of these sites have already moved or disappeared. References to individual sites do not indicate the dates on which they were visited, but each address was rechecked during the editing process and verified as of September 1998.

This book is limited in scope to the law of the United States. Although legal issues often cross national boundaries, the legal systems of other countries and international law have their own distinct literatures and research approaches. Discussion of these sources could easily fill a volume larger than this one.

ACKNOWLEDGMENTS

Several people have helped bring this book into existence. Michael Lavin provided the example and Lynn Foster the initial push. Dean Robert E. Scott and Librarian Larry B. Wenger of the University of Virginia School of Law generously allowed me the time needed to focus on this work. Anne Gaulding and Laura Skinner tracked down a number of sources that would otherwise have remained out of reach. They also serve who handle the other work left neglected, and the people covering for me with grace and skill have been Michael Klepper, Xinh Luu, Cathy Palombi, Barbie Selby, Susan Tulis, and Joe Wynne. I am grateful to all of them. My wife, Marsha, abided my long hours at the computer with patience and good humor. Finally, my loyal assistant Allie has helped with every sentence, lying on the floor under my desk since she was a small pup. I think we can take that walk now, girl.

PART 1
Introduction

CHAPTER 1
Overview

The law is a complex field of study covering an incredibly wide range of human activity, from marriage and child raising to mergers of multinational corporations. Even when we are unaware of it, the law affects our day-to-day lives in such matters as freedom to discuss political issues, standards for disabled access to buildings, or job safety requirements. For those involved in disputes with their neighbors or with the government, the law has a definite presence and must be understood and interpreted.

Access to the law is any citizen's right, and much legal information is available in general libraries and through electronic sources. The collections of major public and academic libraries can address most questions of constitutional law or public policy. Even if a general library is only a starting point, beginning with familiar resources may provide the confidence needed to tackle the specialized materials designed for the legal profession.

These specialized materials are found in libraries at law schools, courthouses, and bar associations. Law libraries can be intimidating places to the uninitiated, with row upon row of court reports accompanied by complex digests and impenetrable texts. Although most law libraries are open to the public, their books are generally written for people with extensive legal training. Few resources are designed to help nonlawyers find and interpret the law. However, if the need for legal information arises from a complicated real-life dilemma rather than a scholarly interest, only the resources in a law library are apt to provide an adequate answer because these resources are designed to help lawyers, and others, find the legal doctrines that are applicable to specific situations.

Finding the applicable law can be a simple matter of locating a relevant statute, for example, to learn the requirements for changing one's name. At other times, the endeavor is so complicated, requiring interpretation of complicated statutes and conflicting court decisions, that only a lawyer specializing in the particular area will be able to perform adequate research.

This book discusses both resources found in law libraries and those available more readily to other researchers. Its goal is to help make legal information more accessible to anyone needing it. In part, it seeks to help people who need to find the law that applies to their situation. This type of research requires some commitment in time and patience while learning how to use a new set of unfamiliar tools. Legal resources generally follow a few basic patterns, however, and can be mastered with study and practice.

Some researchers can use legal information but do not need to determine what the law is. These people are not seeking to learn the law, but are instead looking for factual information about the legal system. Some researchers may seek background information on a historical court decision, while businesspeople may need to contact a county court for lien information or to find an attorney in another state. The legal information discussed here includes not only the constitutions, statutes, and cases that affect our lives, but analysis of these sources and of guides to legal statistics; directories of lawyers, courts, and legislatures; and historical information about legal developments and institutions.

THE AMERICAN LEGAL SYSTEM

Successful use of legal information resources requires a basic understanding of the nature of the American legal system and its major institutions. The term *legal system* has several meanings. To a person involved in a lawsuit, the legal system can refer to the courts involved in resolving the dispute through fact-finding, trial, and appeal. To someone facing criminal charges, the legal system is a broader array of institutions and agencies involved in enforcing the law—police, courts, correctional institutions, and parole or probation agencies.

More generally, however, legal system means the methods by which rules are established and enforced in a society. This process involves broader issues, such as the organization of government and the ways that laws are created, as well as the specific means for enforcing rules and settling controversies. The legal system governs the effect of a contract, even if no dispute arises leading to litigation, because it creates an understanding of the contract's terms with which both parties usually can agree. This broader definition of legal system is the focus of this section.

Four major aspects of our legal system are important to understand when seeking legal information.

- Legal rules come from several sources. A constitution determines the legal framework, and laws are created by legislatures, courts, and executive agencies.
- The law created by the courts, the common law, can be particularly complex and confusing.
- The United States does not have one legal system. Although some matters are governed by federal law, each state also has its own body of laws which controls most issues affecting legal rights.
- Lawyers view legal issues in rigid categories: tort or contract, substance or procedure. A large part of finding an answer to a legal question is knowing how the question is classified.

Sources of Law

Several major sources determine U.S. law, including federal and state constitutions, legislative acts, and court decisions. Although tensions exist among these institutions, they work in conjunction with each other. At the top of the hierarchy is the United States Constitution. Article VI of the Constitution declares it to be the "supreme Law of the Land" and binding on all judges. The meaning of the Constitution's provisions has been subject to considerable discussion over the past two centuries, and this debate will continue. The terms of the Constitution, however, govern any issue to which they apply.

The Constitution established a system of federal government with three distinct branches, creating institutions that would exercise legislative, executive, and judicial powers. These branches work together to create and interpret the law, with the separation of their powers designed to provide a balance between the branches and to prevent any one of them from becoming too powerful.

In addition, each state has its own constitution and a legal system created by that constitution. Although differences characterize the framework of state legal systems, all reflect the three-part division of powers of the federal Constitution.

Legislative Powers

The Constitution vests all legislative powers that it creates in the United States Congress. Article I, section 8, lists several specific areas over which Congress has the power of regulation, including taxation, immigration, bankruptcy, and interstate commerce. The Constitution also provides that Congress shall have power "To make all Laws which shall be necessary and proper for carrying into Execution the foregoing Powers, and all other Powers vested by this Constitution in the Government of the United States, or in any Department or Officer thereof." Congressional action now covers everything from telecommunications to school lunch programs to importation of endangered animals.

The Constitution leaves most of the details associated with determining governmental structure to Congress. The positions of president and vice president are established in the Constitution, but Congress creates federal departments and executive agencies and determines the scope of their power. Congress also has the power to create and abolish federal courts (other than the Supreme Court) and to determine the scope of their jurisdiction. The legislative branch creates the framework under which the other two branches of government operate.

The Executive Power

Federal executive power is vested in a president and, by delegation, in a host of executive departments and agencies. The president has few powers expressly listed in the Constitution: Presidents serve as commander of the armed forces, make treaties with other countries, and name ambassadors, judges, and executive officers. In addition, the president "shall take care that the laws are faithfully executed," a phrase providing the president with extensive power to implement the laws and manage the government.

In carrying out these duties, the executive departments and agencies do more than simply enforce congressional acts. As part of their mission, they interpret those statutes through extensive regulations. Within the scope of their field of expertise, executive agencies have wide powers to create rules defining responsibilities and permissible actions. Some congressional statutes are specific, but others leave it to executive agencies to determine appropriate standards. These agency rules have the same force of law as the congressional acts under which they were created, unless Congress or the courts determine that they conflict with the legislative mandate.

The Judicial Power

The judicial power is vested in the Supreme Court and "such inferior courts as the Congress may from time to time ordain and establish." This phrase has led to an extensive system of trial and appellate courts.

One purpose of courts is to resolve disputes between litigants. An impartial court system ensures that the law is applied equally to all citizens. However, other aspects of the judicial power make the courts an important force in our legal and political systems. The courts have the responsibility for determining the scope and meaning of the Constitution and of statutes. The protections of the Bill of Rights, for example, are general and vague; it is up to the courts to apply them to specific situations. The courts act as arbiter when disputes arise between the legislative and executive branches, or between federal and state governments. Under the doctrine of *judicial review*, the courts also have the power to invalidate statutes that are found to conflict with the Constitution.

The Common Law and the Role of the Courts

Besides establishing the basic constitutional powers of the branches of government, the Constitution governs relations between the people and their government. Many other areas of human activity are subject to the legal system's rules and resolution processes. For example, the courts interpret statutes and administrative regulations. Courts also respond to conflicts by creating legal rules through judicial decisions. This body of decisions is known as the *common law*. The United States inherited the common law system from England, where it evolved over the course of several centuries. The common law as it relates to a particular issue de-velops gradually; one decision is used as a guide to aid in resolving future disputes. Contrast common law with *civil law*, in which rules are articulated in a code of written laws; judges in civil law systems apply and interpret these rules, but they do not create new legal rights, and their decisions have little influence in later conflicts.

Precedent

Two important aspects characterize common law: (1) stability and (2) flexibility. Judicial decisions provide stability, while at the same time allowing flexibility to adapt interpretation of laws to changing conditions in society. The stability provided by judicial decisions comes from the doctrine of precedent, or *stare decisis* (Latin for "let the decision stand"). This doctrine means simply that past decisions guide determination of later disputes. The *holding* of a decision, or the legal principle decided, is followed in other cases with similar circumstances. (One of the first skills new law students must master is the ability to read a case and determine its holding.) People can study published decisions with an eye toward evaluating the probable consequences of actions they have undertaken or are planning. Relying on precedent allows them to act with knowledge of how the legal system will respond.

On the other hand, the common law system reacts to developments in society and technology, adapting legal rules to changed circumstances. Early in the twentieth century, for example, negligence law had to adapt to a change from horse-drawn carriages to automobiles. At first, the old rules were extended to the new horseless carriages, but gradually a new law of automobile liability was developed. As another example, in 1969, a released mental patient in California killed a woman with whom he was obsessed; he had told his doctors of his plans, but they had done nothing to protect the woman. Seven years later, in the famous case of *Tarasoff v. Regents of the University of California*, the state supreme court created a new common law duty for therapists to warn potential victims of a patient's violent intentions.

The doctrine of precedent extends beyond common law doctrine—tort law, contract law, property law—to the Constitution and statutes. Courts are asked to determine the meaning of constitutional and statutory provisions, and those judicial interpretations become part of the law. One of the most famous examples of changing interpretations of the Constitution concerns the equal protection clause of the Fourteenth Amendment. In *Plessy v. Ferguson* (1896), the Supreme Court ruled that racial segregation in railroad compartments did not violate the equal protection clause. This doctrine of "separate but equal" became the law of the land and was used to justify segregation in other forms of public accommodation and services until 1954, when the Court, in *Brown v. Board of Education*, ruled that separate school systems were unconstitutional and brought an end to the "separate but equal" era.

The common law continues to evolve, as courts grapple with such emerging legal issues as surrogate motherhood and electronic invasions of privacy. More and more matters are covered by statutes and regulations, but the role of the courts remains the same: To apply the Constitution, statutes, and existing judicial doctrines to new situations as they arise.

Court Systems

Understanding the importance of judicial decisions requires a familiarity with the basic organization of the court system and its strict hierarchy of trial and appellate courts. The average person is most familiar with the trial courts because these are where most disputes between litigants are resolved. However, a party who disputes a trial judge's ruling can ask an appellate court to review it. Appellate courts do not hold trials or hear evidence; instead, lawyers debate the legal principles in written briefs and oral arguments. Three or more judges then decide which lawyer's interpretation of the law is correct, usually *affirming* or *reversing* the trial court's judgment. Most jurisdictions contain two appellate tiers, an intermediate appellate court and a court of last resort. Names for these courts vary from state to state. At the federal level, the United States District Courts hold trials and issue decisions that can be reviewed by the United States Courts of Appeals. The court of last resort is the Supreme Court of the United States.

A court's lawmaking power depends largely on its place in this hierarchy. The published opinions that guide the law are generally the products of appellate courts. Trial courts have grave responsibilities in deciding conflicts before them, but their decisions on points of law are not binding on any other tribunal. The decisions of appellate courts, however, are binding on all trial courts within their jurisdiction, and decisions from the court of last resort are binding on all trial and appellate courts within the system.

The decisions of appellate courts not only determine the rights of individual litigants but set policy for the jurisdiction. For example, a trial judge may allow a prosecutor to tell a jury of statements a defendant made after being forcibly deprived of sleep for several days; these statements may influence the jury to reach a guilty verdict unsupported by other evidence. If this decision is reversed on appeal, it means a new trial for the defendant and an admonition to trial judges and prosecutors that coerced confessions cannot be used in a criminal trial. The appellate court decision thus has helped to define the scope of individual rights under the Constitution.

Federal and State Jurisdictions

Each of the 50 states has its own legal system. Although similarities exist among the states, each has its own constitution creating a distinct system of government. Each state also has its own body of statutes and common law. Most issues affecting day-to-day life are governed by state law. Among the major areas of state law are domestic relations (marriage and divorce, parental rights, custody of children); property law (real estate, inheritance, landlord–tenant issues); tort law (negligence, personal injury); commercial law; and criminal law.

The Constitution limits the power of the federal government to specifically enumerated areas, leaving most matters in the states' hands. The Constitution establishes exclusive federal jurisdiction in areas such as admiralty, bankruptcy, copyright, and immigration. In other areas, such as consumer protection, environmental law, and labor relations, Congress has determined that there is an overriding national concern and has legislated extensively. Congress has used its commerce clause powers, for example, to pass laws barring discrimination in employment or public accommodations. In many areas, both federal and state laws may apply.

Determining whether an issue involves federal or state law, or both, is not always easy. It is one of the many reasons that most research begins not with federal or state statutes or decisions, but with reference materials and commentaries that provide an explanation of such matters.

Legal Taxonomy

First-year law students throughout the country start their legal education with courses in civil procedure, contracts, criminal law, property law, and torts. In studying these topics, they learn how to analyze and categorize legal issues, using a framework that applies not only in law school classes but throughout the legal literature.

Legal issues are highly compartmentalized. Thus, although a few law books for consumers focus on "real-life" concerns, such as homeownership or legal liability involving pets, most legal writing focuses on specific areas of legal doctrine. The distinction between federal and state legal systems is one such example. Is an issue one of federal or state law? The answer determines where to look for more information.

The law contains several other basic dichotomies. Is an action criminal or civil? If civil, does it involve contract or tort law? Is an issue one of substantive or procedural law? Some of these distinctions are, over time, growing less distinct, but they have shaped the way lawyers have thought about legal issues for centuries.

The answers are not always simple; law students take three years to learn how to analyze legal questions. For the rest of us, the books discussed in the following section can provide a sense of how legal information is organized and a framework within which to approach legal literature and ask intelligent questions.

Background Reading on the Legal System

Several books provide overviews of the U.S. legal system. Some, designed for foreign lawyers, assume a general knowledge of legal structures and systems, but most are written as well for a general U.S. audience. These volumes are *not* designed to answer specific questions about a neighbor's fence or an airline's liability for lost luggage; works attempting this task are discussed in Chapter 3, "General Reference Sources."

Fundamentals of American Law (Oxford University Press, 1996) is one of the newest works of this sort and one of the most ambitious. Edited by Alan B. Morrison with contributions from two dozen faculty members at the New York University School of Law, it is designed for four distinct audiences: foreign lawyers, businesspeople and others working with legal issues, college students considering legal careers, and general readers interested in American law. The book begins with several chapters on general principles (common law systems, litigation, an overview of the Bill of Rights, the American legal profession), then moves on to its substantive chapters, divided into "State Based Laws" (contract law, torts, property law, criminal law and procedure, corporate law, commercial law, family law) and "Federal Law" (antitrust law, bankruptcy, environmental law, intellectual property, labor and employment law, banking, securities, and taxation). The

chapters provide footnotes to major cases and secondary sources, but not bibliographies or recommendations for further reading. The book also includes an extensive subject index as well as tables of cases and legislation discussed.

E. Allan Farnsworth's *An Introduction to the Legal System of the United States* (Oceana Publications, 3d ed., 1996) is a more established, highly regarded work. This brief volume (under 200 pages) provides a much more concise summary while still managing to cover quite a bit of territory. Part 1, "Sources and Techniques," has eight chapters, covering historical background, legal education, the legal profession, the judicial system, case law, the legislative system, statutes, and secondary authority. Part 2, "Organization and Substance," has chapters on classification (law and equity, substance and procedure, public and private law), procedure (civil, criminal, evidence, conflict of laws), private law (contracts, torts, property law, family law, commercial law, business enterprises), and public law (constitutional law, administrative law, trade regulation, labor law, tax law, and criminal law). Like *Fundamentals of American Law*, this work provides a useful outline that can be employed to clarify and sort legal issues.

Two other recent works round out this genre. In *Introduction to the Law and Legal System of the United States* (West Publishing, 1995), William Burnham explains basic legal concepts, provides a background of the common law and the adversary system, and summarizes several basic areas of legal doctrine: civil procedure, criminal procedure, constitutional law, contract law, tort law, property law, family law, criminal law, and business law (including such matters as bankruptcy and antitrust). Somehow taxation appears to have eluded Burnham's notice in this introductory survey. An index, not listed in the table of contents, is tucked away before several appendixes. *Introduction to the Law of the United States*, edited by David S. Clark and Tuğrul Ansay (Kluwer Law and Taxation Publishers, 1992), contains chapters on specialized topics written by 15 American law professors, again covering such issues as the sources of law, constitutional law, labor law, contracts, and torts. These overviews are designed primarily for a foreign audience, but according to the preface, the book is also intended for American students desiring "a reliable overview of the American system of law."

American Law by Lawrence M. Friedman (Norton, 2d ed., 1998) provides a broader, more interdisciplinary introduction to the legal system. Rather than organizing his discussion around the various fields of legal doctrine, Friedman examines the nature of legal systems and the structure of government, looking at such topics as federalism, civil liberties, and law and social change. A noted legal historian and author of *The History of American Law* (Simon & Schuster, 2d ed., 1985), Friedman provides a thorough examination of the historical developments that have created the U.S. legal system and the forces involved in the administration of justice today. The book is written for a general audience, rather than for potential lawyers or foreign lawyers seeking to adapt to the U.S. system. Just one chapter, "Inside the Black Box," covers standard legal doctrines such as contract, tort, and family law. Although not the best source for an overview of such doctrines, the book is an excellent place to begin for those curious about the role of the U.S. legal system in society.

Several books on the legal system are designed for undergraduate "introduction to law" courses. Most provide excerpts from court decisions for class discussion. James V. Calvi and Susan Coleman's *American Law and Legal Systems* (Prentice Hall, 3d ed., 1997) is a straightforward work outlining court organization, procedures, and topical areas such as constitutional law, criminal law, administrative law, torts, contracts, property law, and family law. Each chapter contains notes citing major cases, constitutional provisions, and other texts, and the volume includes a brief glossary.

Finally, several volumes focus specifically on court systems and procedures. Lawrence Baum's *American Courts: Process and Policy* (Houghton Mifflin, 4th ed., 1998) provides a straightforward overview of court systems and the way they work. Chapters cover court organization, selection of judges, the work of judges, trial court processes in criminal and civil cases, the appellate process, and the policy role of appellate courts. Each chapter includes a brief "For Further Reading" bibliography and extensive endnotes.

Daniel John Meador's *American Courts* (West Publishing, 1991) is a small volume outlining the nature of the state and federal court systems. It discusses the business of the trial and appellate courts, notes several circumstances—such as overlapping state and federal jurisdiction—that complicate the picture, and explains the roles of judges, clerks, support staff, and lawyers. A companion volume by Meador and Jordana Simone Bernstein, *Appellate Courts in the United States* (West Publishing, 1994), focuses on the functions and structures of appellate courts, and includes discussion of rules governing access to the courts, appellate procedures, and decision-making processes.

Law and the Courts: A Handbook about United States Law and Court Procedures (American Bar Association, 1995) is a volume in the ABA's "You and the Law" series. It explains the nature of the adversary system, the structure of court systems, the roles of lawyers and judges, and the different types of courts, such as family, probate, and small claims. It then outlines the procedures in civil and criminal cases, from pretrial proceedings through settlement or trial to appeals. This handy pamphlet also includes suggestions for further reading and a useful glossary of about 300 legal terms.

FORMS OF LEGAL INFORMATION

As we have seen, the law derives from several branches of government in each of several jurisdictions. The various forms of law interact and sometimes conflict with each other. Distinctions in the forms of legal information must also be considered. Understanding these distinctions is essential to conducting successful research. A variety of primary and secondary sources in legal literature, print and electronic sources, and current and historical materials address this issue.

Primary and Secondary Sources

In law, the terms *primary source* and *secondary source* have somewhat different meanings than they do in fields such as history or business. Primary does not simply mean "firsthand," as in the original manuscript of a contemporary observer or a corporate report generated for a specific purpose. Instead, the designation primary refers to the lawmaking power of its source. Simply put, primary sources are the law. Only a lawmaker such as a legislature or court can produce a primary source.

Within the world of primary sources exists a wide variation in legal force. In most instances, the Constitution, federal statutes, and Supreme Court decisions are the law throughout the country. Some statutes and Supreme Court decisions, however, apply only to the way business is conducted in the federal government or by the federal courts, and have no effect in state court proceedings. In interpreting state law, the acts of the state legislature and the decisions of the highest state court have the greatest authority. Decisions from courts in other states may be *persuasive*, if they deal with similar issues and provide a well-reasoned analysis, or they may be ignored altogether.

A secondary source describes or analyzes the law, but it has no official legal status. Secondary sources are prepared by scholars, attorneys, and other commentators. Their work may be highly persuasive, but it has no direct legal force. Secondary sources embody a wide range of scholarly treatises, journal articles, self-help manuals, government reports, and monographs. These sources can explain the law, clarify legal situations, and provide easy access to the ruling doctrines in the primary sources. Some secondary sources, such as the *Restatements of the Law*, are produced by committees of leading scholars and are highly esteemed, but they are not the law unless a legislature or court expressly adopts their position.

Although secondary sources do not have the same official status as primary sources, they are usually the better place to start a search for legal information. Primary sources are published chronologically and can be a bewildering, contradictory mass. Secondary sources organize and make sense of this mass. For this reason, they are discussed in Part 2 of this book, before the discussions of federal and state primary sources in Parts 3 and 4.

Print and Electronic Sources

Can you find legal information from the comfort of your home office with a few keystrokes or mouse clicks? Certainly. The amount of legal resources available electronically is vast and continues to grow rapidly. For many people, particularly those without convenient access to a law library, this is the primary means of accessing information.

Electronic resources have a number of advantages over printed books and journals. An electronic text can be searched by any combination of keywords, so that a query can match a very individual and specific need. The information retrieved can be downloaded, manipulated, and used in other documents. In addition, resources can be updated daily or weekly with no delays for printing and postal delivery.

On the other hand, no electronic database is extensive enough to include all the published primary and secondary sources dating back hundreds of years. A large law library has thousands of volumes that may never be available in a digital form. In addition, the legal literature that has developed over the past century comprises a highly sophisticated system for providing subject access to the statutes and court decisions needed in most research situations. The editorial enhancements of the major legal publications are important aids to research. These are available to anyone in a public law library; some are available online for those with access to expensive fee-based systems, but few are available through free electronic sites.

This book discusses both print and electronic sources. Neither form can be neglected by someone seeking thorough, effective access to legal information.

Law Books

Legal literature includes a wide variety of books, journals, and other printed material. Some, but not all, of the primary sources, such as statutes and court decisions, are published by the federal and state governments. University presses and other general publishers issue a number of monographs on legal topics. To a large extent, however, the world of legal information is dominated by a small number of specialized publishing companies.

The largest of these, West Group, a subsidiary of Thomson Corporation, consists of several formerly independent publishers that have been consolidated as product lines within one corporate umbrella. Among these is West Publishing Company, the largest publisher of American legal material. West publishes not only texts and other secondary sources, but also the most frequently used sources for both statutes and court decisions. Its primary source publications are important because they provide a uniform editorial treatment of a wide range of legal matters on diverse topics and from numerous jurisdictions.

The person seeking to become familiar with legal information sources should be aware that the dominance of West Group and a small group of other legal publishing companies has influenced the field in two ways. First, the literature of the law has become highly standardized and systematic; although there are numerous obscure, idiosyncratic publications, many of the most significant resources follow a standard paradigm. Second, the growth of publishing companies specializing in materials for lawyers has contributed to the compartmentalization of information and the fact that many major legal resources are found only in law libraries. Because most nonlawyers seeking legal information have easier access to general libraries, more widely available materials are emphasized in this book to the extent possible.

Commercial Electronic Sources

The electronic resources most frequently used by the legal profession are the two major commercial online services: LEXIS-NEXIS, a service of Reed Elsevier, Inc., and WESTLAW, a service of West Group. These services provide the most extensive electronic access to legal information available. They are also among the most expensive. Subscribers using LEXIS-NEXIS or WESTLAW databases can pay up to $100 per search or $500 per hour of online time. On the other hand, law school libraries generally have flat-rate subscriptions permitting unlimited use but restricting access to law school faculty and students. Many university libraries also subscribe to one service or the other, particularly the Web-based LEXIS-NEXIS Academic Universe. Even so, these databases may be inaccessible for many researchers.

Despite their high costs, LEXIS-NEXIS and WESTLAW are covered extensively in this volume because of their pervasive role in disseminating legal information. No other resources provide such extensive and convenient access to statutes, cases, legal periodical literature, directories, and news sources. Each service contains thousands of databases and millions of documents. Both also provide sophisticated search interfaces allowing either Boolean searching, a method requiring use of logical connectors specifying combination and proximity of particular terms, or natural language searching, through which the computer system accepts simple phrases or questions, weighs terms, and provides a result based on statistical relevance.

Although LEXIS-NEXIS and WESTLAW are the ubiquitous players in legal information, other more specialized electronic services, such as Legi-Slate or CQ Washington Alert, are also discussed. A few databases covering legal materials are also available through general electronic services such as DIALOG.

Legal publishers are also turning to CD-ROM technology for both primary and secondary sources. Although CD-ROM is not as comprehensive or as frequently updated as an online database, it allows full-text keyword searching without hourly or per-search charges. For many lawyers, CD-ROM is the most cost-effective method of accessing legal information because it eliminates both the need to maintain large book collections and the cost of online access. Most legal CD-ROM products, however, are still expensive materials designed for specialized professional markets, and are not as widely or freely accessible as the books on library shelves.

The Internet

The Internet, of course, is the hottest information source around. Gallons of ink have been spilled writing about the Internet generally, and about the Internet as a source for legal information in particular. This attention is justified because governments, institutions, and individuals have all put legal resources on the World Wide Web.

The number of statutes, court decisions, and other legal documents available on the Internet grows daily.

Some sources are subscription-based commercial sites. LEXIS-NEXIS and WESTLAW, for example, are both accessible through Web sites: <http://www.lexis-nexis.com> and <http://www.westlaw.com>. More important for most people, however, are the free Internet sites maintained by government agencies and law schools to provide free access to primary sources. Most states now have sites with statutes and pending legislation, and the Library of Congress and U.S. Government Printing Office provide access to federal acts and regulations. Courts from practically every jurisdiction now have recent opinions available on the Internet. These sites have dramatically increased access to information that has always been "public" in theory but has not always been so widely disseminated.

The Internet can perform several other valuable functions in a search for legal information. It can be an excellent source for information about an agency or institution, providing background data, important documents, and contact names and e-mail addresses. It can provide information about law firms and lawyers, through directories and Web sites. Through e-mail and listservs, it can provide a forum for sharing information.

As of this writing, the Internet is not yet a viable alternative to more comprehensive resources. Its collections are not as comprehensive as those of the commercial databases or law libraries. Many of the more sophisticated information sources are proprietary and may never be available at free Web sites. Sometimes, information on the Internet is outdated or less reliable than information available commercially. On the other hand, the Internet is an ideal and cost-effective place to find a recent court decision, to track current legislative developments, or to find out about any agency's activities.

It has been said of the Internet that change is the only constant. Anything written on the subject is immediately outdated. Nonetheless, we will discuss a few valuable Web sites that may be with us for a while—or may at least provide a starting point for watching the medium grow and develop.

Current and Historical Sources

In most instances, researchers need to know about the law today. They need to know what statutes are in force, whether a court case has been overruled, or who now administers a federal program. Because the law can change rapidly, an important consideration in judging the value of a resource is the speed and accuracy with which it is updated. If a resource is not updated on a regular basis, the value of its information diminishes rapidly. An outdated book or Web site can become dangerously misleading. It is therefore essential that books be updated with supplements, that CD-ROMs be replaced periodically, and that electronic databases and Web sites be updated frequently with new information.

Many times, however, historical information is needed. The documents surrounding the enactment of a law are useful in interpreting its provisions, even decades later. A case may turn on the precise statute or regulation that was in effect on a particular date several years ago. Researchers may also wish to study legislative activity in a particular era, trace the development of a judicial doctrine, or examine the life and work of a nineteenth-century jurist. For these reasons, even older legal resources have continuing research value. Although many legal resources are regularly updated, others (such as monographs and journals) provide snapshots of the time when they were published.

The following chapters, then, are written not just for those who need to know what the law is, but for anyone seeking to learn more about the purpose, the functions, or the history of the complex U.S. legal system.

CHAPTER 2
Understanding Legal Information

This chapter discusses resources that are often needed to understand legal information. Legal dictionaries interpret the language in legal documents. Citation guides and abbreviations dictionaries aid in identifying sources and provide a standard means of referring to materials. Legal research guides can further explain the intricacies of a complex body of literature. Although these resources are seldom the first works consulted by researchers, it is important to be aware of their existence because they can be invaluable in deciphering legal literature and helping chart a research course.

DICTIONARIES AND GUIDES TO LEGAL LANGUAGE

Legal terms often appear foreign to the lay reader, an occurrence not unusual in a specialized area monopolized by an organized and powerful profession. For example, not all doctors communicate in terms their patients can understand. Few people can understand articles in *JAMA* or the *New England Journal of Medicine* without the help of a medical dictionary. Physicians at least have the excuse that their primary focus is fighting disease rather than explaining its causes and solutions in an easily intelligible manner.

Lawyers have no such excuse. Words are the primary tools of legal work. Legislators create statutes; judges write court opinions; and lawyers draft contracts and letters for their clients. These documents should communicate their meaning to any intelligent reader, clarifying and illuminating complex legal issues. Far too often, the opposite is true. Lawyers communicate in a stylized language comprehensible only to other lawyers. Legal writing is full of arcane terminology and convoluted phrases. In a famous article, "Goodbye to Law Reviews," 23 Va. L. Rev. 38 (1936), Professor Fred Rodell of the Yale Law School noted that legal writing is full of "the kind of sentence that looks as though it had been translated from the German by someone with a rather meager knowledge of English."

Sixty years later most legal writing still arouses the same sense of dismay and revulsion, despite repeated urgings for lawyers to express themselves in "plain English." In 1978, President Jimmy Carter even issued an executive order declaring that government regulations "shall be as simple and clear as possible" and ordered that agencies ensure that each new regulation "is written in plain English and is understandable to those who must comply with it." Little has changed. Nonetheless, readers need not be unduly intimidated. Anyone armed with a good dictionary can grapple with legal documents.

In many instances, a good general dictionary will serve as well as a specialized legal dictionary. Comprehensive works such as *Webster's Third New International Dictionary of the English Language* (Merriam-Webster, 1961) or *The Random House Dictionary of the English Language* (Random House, 2d ed., 1987) include such terms as *amicus curiae* or *nolle prosequi*; even a good college dictionary such as *Merriam-Webster's Collegiate Dictionary* (Merriam-Webster, 10th ed., 1993) provides definitions for most common legal terminology. General dictionaries are cited as often as specialized legal dictionaries by judges seeking to determine the legal meaning of particular terms.

In legal writing, however, many everyday words and phrases assume different meanings. In general use, for example, the word *infant* means a very small child. In legal terminology, however, *infant* traditionally refers to anyone under the age of majority. Its use has diminished in favor of more common terms such as minor, but infant is still used as a classification in case names and in legal reference works. (In this instance, the general dictionaries cited above serve us well; all note these different meanings, and *Random House* prefaces the legal meaning with the signal *"Law."*)

Some terminology appears in legal literature because it has been used for decades or centuries by lawyers, without much notice of the changing world. Older court opinions in particular are full of Latin phrases such as "Reversed with a procedendo" (order to proceed to judgment) or "Reversed, and a venire facias de novo awarded" (new trial). These may be impressive stylistic flourishes, but they mean little to an uninitiated reader.

Other terms are made up of common words but have specialized meanings in the law. A *next friend* is a person acting in a court proceeding on behalf of a child (or infant). A person applying an everyday understanding to such a phrase (something like *best friend*?) would make little sense of its legal significance.

To confuse matters further, some terms with traditional meanings in law are changing as the law evolves. In laws of succession, for instance, *issue* refers to direct descendants. The term is traditionally limited to legitimate, natural children, but recent decisions have extended its meaning to include illegitimate children, and many states have enacted legislation to include adopted children within the definition.

A good legal dictionary can eliminate much confusion in the examination of legal documents. Fortunately, there are several to choose from—ranging from comprehensive works designed for legal practitioners to shorter volumes written specifically for general audiences. No matter the audience, a good legal dictionary should do the following:

- Be comprehensive enough to include most terms encountered in modern legal writing. You should be able to rely on one dictionary most of the time, rather than needing to turn from one to another whenever an unfamiliar word appears. If judges continue to use an archaic term, such as *procedendo*, it should be included.

- Be straightforward enough for a general audience to use. It should note differences between general and legal usage for terms such as infant, and define terminology that may be familiar to lawyers but would help others understand the way the legal system works. (What does the *holding* of a case mean? What is an *advance sheet*?) A dictionary that simply defines one legalism with another is of little use to nonlawyers.

- Note changes in legal usage over time. This is not always a simple matter, but a dictionary must serve readers of both nineteenth-century court opinions and contemporary journal articles. A dictionary that simply explains what words meant 200 years ago will be misleading if those terms are still in use.

- Provide pronunciations of less familiar terms. Legal language is full of Latin and pseudo-Latin terminology, and much of it is easier read than said. Dictionaries use a wide variety of methods to indicate sounds, some more straightforward than others. Consider, for example, the range of pronunciations indicated for *cy pres*, the legal doctrine that wills or other documents should be construed to carry out their creators' intentions: see-pray / sē prā' /ˌsē-prā / sē'-prĕ / sìpréy / sī-**pray** *or* see- / sie pray / sī-**pray**. Although part of the problem here is that there is disagreement whether the first syllable has a long *i* or a long *e*, there is also a wide range of ways to display the pronunciations. Obviously, ones that seem more intuitive will make life easier.

When seeking to determine the legal meaning of a word, it may help to remember what Justice Oliver Wendell Holmes wrote 70 years ago in *Towne v. Eisner*, 245 U.S. 418, 425 (1918): "A word is not a crystal, transparent and unchanged, it is the skin of a living thought and may vary greatly in color and content according to the circumstances and the time in which it is used." In one sense, this means that the law is not stuck in the past. In another, it can mean that a precise legal definition may be hard to pin down, no matter how good a dictionary is available.

Black's Law Dictionary

Black's Law Dictionary (West Publishing, 6th ed., 1990) is considered the leading modern U.S. work in this area. It is certainly the most extensive legal dictionary commonly available, heir to the three-volume classic *Bouvier's Law Dictionary and Concise Encyclopedia* (West Publishing, 8th ed., 1914). *Black's* contains more than 30,000 entries, as well as appendixes providing the text of the Constitution and a 16-page table of abbreviations (mostly journals and law reports, although a few governmental and organizational acronyms also appear). It is far and away the law dictionary most relied on by lawyers and judges.

Black's was first published in 1891, and, unfortunately, its age shows in many of its entries. The latest edition claims to include more than 5,000 new or revised entries, but the dictionary is still full of archaic definitions of obsolete terms—and lacking in modern terminology that arises in legal proceedings. Consider the term *paraphernalia*, which generally refers to equipment and supplies needed for a particular activity and most often appears in the context of "drug paraphernalia." *Black's* makes no mention of either of these meanings. Instead it defines *paraphernalia* as "the separate property of a married woman, other than that which is included in her dowry, or dos," and goes on to explain the distinction in the civil law between dotal and extradotal, or paraphernal, property.

How useful is this definition of paraphernalia in modern legal discourse? Paraphernalia, in the sense of a woman's separate property, is mentioned in but a handful of twentieth-century court opinions. Paraphernalia in the sense of drug equipment and supplies, on the other hand, has appeared in thousands of cases in the past 40 years. One court even put the editors of *Black's* on notice that its definition was obsolete. In 1973, an Oklahoma appellate court overturned a conviction for unlawful possession of paraphernalia on the grounds that the statute was too vague in proscribing "any paraphernalia used by abusers of controlled dangerous substances for administering a controlled dangerous substance" (*Cole v. State*, 511 P.2d 593 [Okla. Crim. App. 1973]). The court quoted the definition from the 4th edition of *Black's* (1968), referring only to the separate property of a married woman, and *Webster's Third*, which included the additional definition "articles of equipment." The court held that "a person of ordinary intelligence, using the above definitions of paraphernalia, could not determine what items he could or could not possess lawfully." Yet in an edition published 17 years later, *Black's* definition of paraphernalia remains untouched—pure, obsolete, and practically useless.

Some of the older references in *Black's* offer fascinating glimpses of bygone eras. Consider, for example,

the entry under *attaint*, which refers to William Blackstone's discussion in *Commentaries on the Laws of England* (1765) of a proceeding used to inquire whether a jury had given a false verdict. If a jury of 24 knights found the verdict to be false, "the judgment was that the jurors should become infamous, should forfeit their goods and the profits of their lands, should themselves be imprisoned, and their wives and children thrust out of doors, should have their houses razed, their trees extirpated, and their meadows plowed up, and that the plaintiff should be restored to all that he lost by reason of the unjust verdict."

Many *Black's* entries provide cryptic references to old cases from which its definitions are drawn, but rarely indicate that reading these cases would be particularly helpful. The definition of *holding*, for example, includes the following:

> The legal principle to be drawn from the opinion (decision) of the court. Opposite of dictum (*q.v.*). It may refer to a trial ruling of the court upon evidence or other questions presented during the trial. Edward L. Eyre & Co. v. Hirsch et al., 36 Wash.2d 439, 218 P.2d 888. . . .

A terse general statement is followed by a minor clarification reprinted from a 1950 Washington Supreme Court case. The space could more profitably have been used to expand a bit on the primary meaning of this important legal concept.

Black's definition for *infancy* explains the legal meaning ("Minority; the state of a person who is under the age of legal majority,—at common law, twenty-one years; now, generally 18 years. . . .") but makes no comment on the origins of this confusing legal usage or on its conflict with everyday understanding. On the other hand, *Black's* does sometimes get it right. The definition for *issue* notes that this legal term for descendants traditionally was limited to legitimate children but has in recent cases been applied to illegitimate children as well, and that "many state intestacy statutes provide that an adopted child is 'issue' of his or her adopted parents."

Black's includes pronunciations of many terms, although it uses an unusual phonetic system that may take some getting used to. *Amicus curiae,* "friend of the court," refers to persons or organizations advising the court in an action to which they are not a party. According to *Black's*, it is pronounced əmáykəs kyúriyiy. The plural of this term, *amici curiae*, is even more troublesome to pronounce, but *Black's* does not mention it at all.

Black's is available not only in print, but also on disc and as a database in WESTLAW. The online version does not include pronunciations and has no table of abbreviations, but it does include links to cases cited. An electronic version of *Black's* can also be loaded onto a computer to provide pop-up access while using word processing software.

In 1994, Bryan Garner, author of the *Dictionary of Modern Legal Usage*, was named editor-in-chief of *Black's*. Perhaps he may be able to breathe some new life into a new edition. A paperback "pocket edition" (discussed below) was published in 1996, with new terms and streamlined definitions. The fully revised 7th edition is not expected until 2000.

Ballentine's Law Dictionary

The traditional rival to *Black's* is *Ballentine's Law Dictionary* (Lawyers Cooperative, 3d ed., 1969). This dictionary has some advantages, including a slightly larger number of definitions than *Black's*, but it has fallen considerably out of date in the three decades since its most recent edition.

Some parts of *Ballentine's* rival *Black's* in obscurity, like the following definition of *paraphernalia*:

> At common and civil law, the apparel and ornaments of the wife, suitable and appropriate to her station, which, although being the subject of the husband during his life and subject to the claims of his creditors for the satisfaction of such claims and subject to disposal by the husband except by his will, became, upon his death, the exclusive property of the widow as against all persons other than the husband's creditors.

Perhaps there is no mention of drug paraphernalia because that use was relatively new when *Ballentine's* was published. Similarly, the entry for *issue* may make no mention of recent changes because it predates many of these decisions and statutes.

On the other hand, at times *Ballentine's* is more modern and straightforward than *Black's*. The definition of *infant* draws the helpful distinction between English and legalese: "In ordinary usage, a child of a tender and helpless age. In law, a person who has not reached the age of majority, usually 21 years, at which the law recognizes a general contractual capacity." While *Black's* explains the technical differences between *venire facias de novo* and *new trial* at some length, the *Ballentine's* entry for *venire facias de novo* notes in simple English, "In modern terminology, the same as new trial."

For pronunciations *Ballentine's* uses a phonetic system that is easier to understand at a glance than *Black's*. *Amicus curiae* is shown as "a-mī´kus kū´ri-ē" (which puts it at odds with the pronunciations in *Black's*

and other more modern dictionaries). Like *Black's*, however, *Ballentine's* neglects the pronunciation of the plural *amici*.

The major law dictionaries, *Black's* and *Ballentine's*, are the most comprehensive law dictionaries generally available, and they are certainly the best places to check when attempting to decipher an obscure term in an older court opinion. For most present-day needs, however, shorter dictionaries may provide quicker access to the meaning of modern legal terminology.

Shorter Law Dictionaries

Several less comprehensive law dictionaries are available in paperback editions; one or more of these may be the wisest purchase for people needing to understand legal terminology.

One of the best of the paperbacks is *Oran's Dictionary of the Law* by Daniel Oran (West Publishing, 2d ed., 1991). This straightforward dictionary defines more than 5,000 terms for a general audience, with no references to outdated cases. An abridged version with 2,500 frequently used terms has been published as *Law Dictionary for Nonlawyers* (West Publishing, 3d ed., 1991). Both editions of Oran's dictionary include a useful list of "The Basic 50," terms with which any reader of legal writing should be familiar. The larger volume also includes a helpful 40-page appendix summarizing legal research concepts, techniques, and sources.

Oran's definitions are generally clear and helpful. He has one of the most useful definitions of *holding* available.

> The core of a judge's **decision** in a case. It is that part of the judge's written **opinion** that applies the law to the facts of the case and about which can be said "the case means no more and no less than this." When later cases rely on a case as **precedent**, it is only the *holding* that should be used to establish the precedent. A *holding* may be less than the judge said it was. If the judge made broad, general statements, the holding is limited to only that part of the generalizations that directly apply to the facts of that particular case. Compare with "**dicta**."

Without unduly belaboring the point, Oran explains this important concept in plain English and clarifies distinctions between related concepts. He does not provide definitions of more obscure terms such as *procedendo* but does include more common terms such as *next friend* or *advance sheet*. The definition for *issue* is straightforward but does not mention any recent legal developments. Oran does not provide many pronunciations, although stress syllables are sometimes underlined. The pronunciation of *amicus curiae* is shown as "a-<u>me</u>-kus <u>cure</u>-e-eye," a simple and straight-forward method.

Steven H. Gifis's *Law Dictionary* (Barron's, 4th ed., 1996) may be more widely available in bookstores than Oran's work. Gifis defines more than 3,000 terms in a straightforward manner, with references to cases, statutes, and treatises. He includes only a few pronunciations. The book is published in two sizes, a cramped 4¼ by 7 inches and a much more readable and easily handled 6 by 9 inches. The smaller edition may be handier for those who want to keep a legal dictionary in their pocket, but the larger type and easier handling of the larger version more than justify the difference in price. An abridged version of the 1991 third edition, with no references to other sources and defining only 2,000 terms, is *Dictionary of Legal Terms: A Simplified Guide to the Language of Law* (Barron's, 3d ed., 1998).

Gifis's work is generally clear. The dictionary includes *procedendo*, noting that "it is more frequently called a remand." Some definitions are more troublesome. *Holding*, for instance, is defined as follows: "In procedure, any ruling of the court, including rulings upon the admissibility of evidence or other questions presented during trial, may be termed a 'holding.' See 218 P.2d 888, 893. Compare dictum." How is it that Gifis needs to make the same marginal clarification as *Black's*, with a reference to the same Washington case that was cited in the larger work? Gifis also follows *Black's* lead in his definition of *infant*, providing only the legal definition. The treatment of *issue* makes no mention of recent changes and introduces a confusing digression about whether terms appearing in a will are "words of limitation."

The Gifis work is part of a series of small dictionaries from Barron's. Others in related fields include *Dictionary of Accounting Terms* (2d ed., 1995), *Dictionary of Banking Terms* (3d ed., 1997), *Dictionary of Finance and Investment Terms* (5th ed., 1998), *Dictionary of Insurance Terms* (3d ed., 1995), *Dictionary of International Business Terms* (1996), and *Dictionary of Real Estate Terms* (4th ed., 1997).

Robert E. Rothenberg's *The Plain-Language Law Dictionary* (Signet) also came out with a new edition in 1996; an electronic version is available from Parsons Technology. This work is expressly designed for the general public. Rothenberg, editor of a "bestselling dictionary of medical terms," has a lawyer, Stephen A. Gilbert, as assistant editor. The book contains 7,000 entries and includes appendixes containing the texts of the Declaration of Independence and the Constitution, as well as brief summaries of legal issues related to social security, immigration, customs, and divorce laws, among others.

Rothenberg provides no pronunciations, and his definitions are short—perhaps a bit too short and full of cross-references to be illuminating. The definition of *holding*, for instance ("The JUDGE'S RULING or DECISION in a CASE") provides four cross-references in an eight-word definition. Actually, there are only three cross-references because the dictionary has no entry under *ruling*. The same blind lead appearing in the 1981 first edition goes uncorrected even after 15 years. In some instances, there is confusion about whether the dictionary is providing legal or general definitions. *Infancy*, defined as "the age prior to the attainment of legal majority. A minor may still be liable to meet his/her obligations," is followed by a definition of *infant* as "a very young child." Why does one definition provide a strictly legal meaning while the other ignores it altogether?

A new entrant, *Merriam-Webster's Dictionary of Law* (Merriam-Webster, 1996), is somewhat larger than the other paperback dictionaries, with more than 600 pages and 10,000 entries. It includes appendixes containing the Constitution; an outline of the judicial system; and annotated lists of major Supreme Court cases, statutes, and agencies. Edited by Linda Picard Wood, a lawyer, the work combines a familiar and comforting *Merriam-Webster's* style with references to various legal sources, such as the Federal Rules of Appellate Procedure, the Uniform Commercial Code, and major legal treatises.

Merriam-Webster's has clear, concise definitions, but perhaps relies too heavily on cross-references. *Holding*, for example, is defined as "a ruling of a court upon an issue of law raised in a case: the pronouncement of law supported by the reasoning in a court's opinion—compare DECISION, DICTUM, DISPOSITION, FINDING, JUDGMENT, OPINION, RULING, VERDICT." This is a bit more page-turning than most readers will probably care to indulge. *Infancy* makes no mention of the general usage but features two clear definitions: "**1 :** the legal status of an infant: MINORITY **2 :** the affirmative defense of lacking legal capacity (as to make a contract or commit a crime) because of being too young and esp. because one's age is below an age set by statute." The definition of *issue* makes no mention of current law, but *child* mentions both adoption and illegitimacy. The dictionary also provides good coverage of older terms such as *procedendo* ("an extraordinary writ ordering a lower court to proceed to or execute a judgment") and provides the Latin origin of *venire facias*. *Merriam-*

Webster's only shows pronunciations for some terms. Its format will appear familiar to users of other Merriam-Webster products but a bit foreign to others. This dictionary does show two choices for pronouncing the elusive *amici*: ə-ˈmē-ˌkē, ə-ˈmī-ˌsī.

Another recent publication, *Real Life Dictionary of the Law: Taking the Mystery Out of Legal Language*, by Gerald N. Hill and Kathleen Thompson Hill (General Publishing Group, 1995), is an attractive work with useful explanations of legal concepts. It is written specifically for a general audience by a lawyer and political psychologist team. It only contains about 3,000 definitions—including just two under *Y* (*your honor* and *youthful offenders*) and one under *Z* (*zoning*). The few entries provide even fewer cross-references. There is, for example, an entry under *release on one's own recognizance*, but nothing under *recognizance*, where someone may well look first in seeking to understand this expression. The most unfortunate aspect of the book, given its ambitious subtitle, is that it explains less than it could and confuses more than it should. *Holding* is simply defined as "any ruling or decision of a court," and the entry for *certiorari* states, "By denying such a writ the Supreme Court says it will let the lower court decision stand, particularly if it conforms to accepted precedents (previously decided cases)." The Supreme Court has stated time and again that its refusal to hear a case makes no comment on the correctness of the lower court's ruling. This book, however, reinforces the common misperception that a denial of *certiorari* puts a stamp of approval on the lower court decision. The *Real Life Dictionary* includes several useful appendixes, including a copy of the Constitution, information on court systems, and addresses of state bar associations.

Finally, there are recent paperback dictionaries bearing the illustrious names of *Black's* and *Ballentine's*. Although not as thorough as their comprehensive hardcover counterparts, these works are useful, handy sources for quick reference.

Black's Law Dictionary: Pocket Edition (West Publishing, 1996), under the editorship of Bryan A. Garner, provides definitions for more than 7,500 terms. Its entries are generally clear but rather terse. For example, the definition of *infant*, "**1.** A newborn baby. **2.** MINOR," hints at the discrepancy between general and legal usage without wasting a single word. Some entries provide examples of usage, although not all of these appear to have a legal context. Review, for instance, the following definition for *abide*: "To obey <try to abide the doctor's orders to quit smoking>." A fair number of Latin phrases and more obscure terms such as *proce-*

dendo and *venire facias de novo* are included. Pronunciations accompany a relatively small number of words.

Two paperback dictionaries bearing the *Ballentine's* name have appeared recently, although neither makes any mention of the comprehensive 1969 third edition. Both are copublished by Lawyers Cooperative Publishing and Delmar Publishers Inc. *Ballentine's Law Dictionary: Legal Assistant Edition* (1994), by Jack G. Handler, includes more than 10,000 entries. Some definitions of older terms (such as *procedendo*) come straight from the 1969 edition, but most are concise and helpful. *Holding* is defined as follows: "The proposition of law for which a case stands (*see* precedent); the 'bottom line' of a judicial decision. *Compare* opinion. *Also compare* dicta. *Also see* held; hold." *Infancy* includes definitions for both legal and general usages, and the definition of *issue* nicely states that it "may or may not include adopted children, depending on state law." This is also one of the few legal dictionaries to mention both a woman's separate property and drugs in its definition of *paraphernalia*:

> 1. At common law, the property of a wife which she had a right to possess separately from her husband. EXAMPLES: clothing; jewelry. 2. *Drug paraphernalia* are articles used in connection with the taking of illicit drugs. (EXAMPLE: hypodermic syringes; opium pipes.) Possession of drug paraphernalia is illegal in most states. 3. Equipment; accessories; miscellaneous articles.

A final enhancement to this dictionary's utility is that almost every word has pronunciation indicated. The form used may seem a bit simplistic (e.g., *hole · ding*), but it is certainly easier to grasp than obscure typographical symbols.

Ballentine's Legal Dictionary and Thesaurus (1995), by Jonathan S. Lynton, is remarkably similar to Handler's 1994 publication. It contains exactly the same definitions, word for word, supplemented by synonyms taken from Lynton's earlier *Ballentine's Thesaurus for Legal Research & Writing* (1994). Under *paraphernalia*, for example, the definition is followed by "gear, property, furnishings, accessories, supplies, equipment, accessories, articles." Just as neither Handler nor Lynton mentions his relationship to the standard *Ballentine's Law Dictionary*, Lynton makes no mention whatsoever of Handler's work. The copyright in both instances is held by the publishers, but it makes one wonder what an author's role in preparing a dictionary is if an entire volume can be transplanted without even a passing acknowledgment. Nonetheless, the *Ballentine's* paperbacks are useful volumes, with some of the handiest and clearest definitions available.

In addition to the dictionaries discussed here, several other reputable law dictionaries are published in England, Canada, and other countries. Because these works provide definitions based on the law in other countries, however, they are rarely the first place an American researcher should check. Most are not widely available in this country.

Internet Legal Dictionaries

Several Internet sites provide access to definitions of legal terms. The most comprehensive of these sites is West's Legal Directory, which provides free access to *Oran's Dictionary of the Law* <http://www.wld.com/client/clawinfo/orans.asp>.

None of the other dictionary sites are as comprehensive as the published dictionaries, but they can be useful for quick checks of unfamiliar terminology. At least two focus specifically on terms used in American law. Nolo Press, the leading publisher of self-help law books, features "Shark Talk: Everybody's Law Dictionary" on its Web site <http://www.nolo.com/dictionary/>. The dictionary provides plain-English definitions of nearly 1,000 legal terms, phrases, and acronyms, and can be searched or browsed by topic. To date, the dictionary lacks many standard terms, such as *infant* or *issue*, but the site includes a form for suggesting words to add. One impressive feature is that the definitions make no attempt whatsoever to sell Nolo books or software.

Another American site, the 'Lectric Law Library, includes a 'Lectric Legal Lexicon <http://www.lectlaw.com/ref.html> with straightforward definitions of legal terms, such as *reasonable doubt, recognizance,* and (oddly) *regicide*. Coverage is limited. There is no entry for *infant*, and the *issue* definition makes no mention of descendants. The 'Lectric site is packed with irreverent asides (such as "We all know it's only coincidence that *'attorney'* is Etruscan for *'Secret Minion of Satan'"*), which would be more amusing in smaller doses.

The World Wide Legal Information Association (WWLIA), based in Canada, also provides a Web dictionary. The WWLIA Legal Dictionary <http://wwlia.org/diction.htm>, is not written with U.S. law in mind and is limited in coverage. (There is no entry for *infant* or *issue*, just two terms beginning with the letter *Y*, and only *zipper* under *Z*). But it covers a number of basic terms, including Latin phrases, and provides hypertext cross-reference links between entries.

Dictionaries of Legal Usage

The dictionaries discussed to this point are written for the reader who needs to make sense of legal writing. Usage dictionaries serve a somewhat different function. They are written more for the writer, and are designed to encourage clear and literate prose. Two recent works in this genre are *Mellinkoff's Dictionary of American Legal Usage* and *Dictionary of Modern Legal Usage*. Despite their similar titles, the two works have distinct uses and purposes.

Mellinkoff's Dictionary of American Legal Usage (West Publishing, 1992) was written by David Mellinkoff, author of several books on legal writing, including *The Language of the Law* (Little, Brown, 1963). In a law review article, "The Myth of Precision and the Law Dictionary," 31 UCLA L. Rev. 423 (1983), Mellinkoff complained about the arcane and obsolete terminology found in *Black's* and *Ballentine's*, and proposed a dictionary of the type he proceeded to publish nine years later.

Mellinkoff's dictionary clearly defines legal terms and illustrates usage. However, coverage is hardly as comprehensive as a regular dictionary, and many older terms such as *procedendo* and *venire facias de novo* are omitted. Most valuable are Mellinkoff's distinctions among related terms. He devotes almost three pages, for example, to a discussion of the uses of *child, infant,* and *minor*. He begins with an explanation of why three different terms exist to refer to someone who is not an adult (child comes from Old English, infant from French, and minor from Latin). Similar helpful distinctions are provided among other related terms such as *lease, rent,* and *hire*.

At times, however, Mellinkoff seems to be dashing off definitions too quickly. Under *whistleblower*, he includes the shorthand note "To detractors, here is a troublemaker—makes waves." He includes an entry for *trustee in bankruptcy* but defines it only as "special usage in the bankruptcy laws of the United States." Why have an entry with no definition? (Oran does better by the term: "A *trustee in bankruptcy* is a person appointed by a court to manage a bankrupt person's property and to decide who gets it.") On the other hand, the volume is peppered with delightful asides that make it worth browsing. The entry for *meaningful* notes: "Once upon a time, *meaningful* was a natural antonym for *meaningless;* it now approaches the role of synonym."

Mellinkoff provides the best coverage yet of the elusive term *amici curiae*. His entry explains, "The

Latin plural *amici curiae* is only occasionally spoken, and as a result, pronunciation of *amici* is not uniform. Variants are uh-MY-sigh, uh-MEE-chee, uh-MEE- kee, and uh-MEE-kai. The problem disappears with *friends of the court.*"

The deepest mystery about *Mellinkoff's Dictionary* is the section of 96 green pages at the front, listing every term and every cross-reference in the volume. Because the dictionary is itself arranged alphabetically (like most dictionaries), why have a separate listing that simply duplicates the entries in the main listing?

Although *Mellinkoff's Dictionary* has its charms and is useful at times, it unfortunately falls between two genres. It is not extensive enough to take the place of a law dictionary, but its focus on definitions and etymology prevents it from serving as a guide to usage. A much more thorough work is Bryan A. Garner's *Dictionary of Modern Legal Usage* (Oxford University Press, 2d ed., 1995). Based on the model of H.W. Fowler's *Modern English Usage* (1926), Garner's dictionary combines entries on specific terms with more than 200 essays on usage, grammar, and related issues.

Garner's entries explain legal terminology and attempt to eliminate some of the more obfuscatory aspects of legal writing. His entry for *infant,* for example, both points out the special legal meaning and suggests using a different term to avoid confusion.

> **infant** (= a minor) is peculiar to legal language; in nonlegal contexts, *infant* means "a small child, a baby." But in law it is quite possible to write of, say, a *17-year-old infant.* E.g., "An exception was made for the time of filing for *infants,* incompetents, and nonresidents." The more usual—and less confusing—term is *minor.* Cf. **infanticide.** See **minority** (A) & **age of capacity.**

Although designed primarily as a tool for those who write legal documents, Garner's book can also be a useful guide to the twists and turns of legal language. It has numerous amusing entries and a far more arch, hard-nosed tone than Mellinkoff. Garner has strongly held opinions on what is correct in legal writing and provides numerous examples of poor drafting both in individual entries and in essays such as "Biblical Affectations" or "Flotsam Phrases." Many entries focus on the misuse of the English language, with quotations from a wide range of famous legal scholars and judges.

Garner's work does not seek to replace a general dictionary of legal terms. Terms that are not subject to misuse do not interest him. For example, the focus of the entry for *venire* is that the word means "jury" and that therefore *jury venire* and *venire panel* are both re-

dundancies. Nearly a page is spent on *amicus curiae,* once again pointing out mistakes in usage—such as using the singular *amicus* instead of the plural *amici.* This section concludes with one of Garner's infrequent notes on pronunciation: "The singular is PRONOUNCED /ə-*mee*-kəs-*kyoor*-ee-ɪ/ and the plural /ə-*mee*-kee-*kyoor*-ee-ɪ/ or /ə-*mee*-see/. Another acceptable pronunciation of the first word—a common pronunciation in AmE—is /*am*-ə-*kəzs*/." Apparently there is little need to worry, as almost any possible pronunciation could be considered correct.

As Garner notes, "The best legal writers attempt to formulate their thoughts anew. Their writing is fresh and original. And it is rare." His *Dictionary of Modern Legal Usage* is probably not the first place to look for a definition, but it's one of the best places to browse to develop a cogent and powerful writing style.

Legal Thesauri

A thesaurus is most useful in the writing process, but it may also be of assistance to a researcher because it can provide alternate terminology needed for finding information in indexes and through electronic searches. For example, a person looking for information on the effect of a failure to take action may not think to search such related terms as *dereliction*, *nonfeasance*, *nonperformance*, or *omission*.

The major work in this area is William C. Burton's *Legal Thesaurus* (Macmillan, 2d ed., 1992). The book contains 521 pages of main entries and a 487-page index. The main entries collect related terms under major headings, providing synonyms, associated concepts (phrases and contexts in which the term commonly appears), and foreign phrases, such as Latin maxims. If an entry appears more than once, the variant meanings are indicated in parentheses, as in "inform *(Betray)*" and "inform *(Notify)*." Some of the entries cover related topics, such as those for *child* (27 synonyms), *infant* (18 synonyms), and *minor* (23 synonyms). Remarkable dissimilarities characterize these three lists. *Toddler* and *little one* are listed under *infant*, while *newborn* appears under *child*. *Baby* is listed under *infant* and *minor*, but not under *child*. It appears as if the listings were compiled separately and never cross-checked.

West's Legal Thesaurus/Dictionary: A Resource for the Writer and Computer Researcher (West Publishing, 1985), by William P. Statsky, is a less extensive work than Burton's. As its title indicates, it attempts to combine thesaurus and dictionary functions. At times it is quite successful, as in its treatment of *paraphernalia,* noting first drug paraphernalia and then the obsolete definition of a woman's separate property. Much space, however, is wasted on entries that have little to do with legal usage. Do we need to know that *kilowatt* means "1,000 watts," particularly if there is no entry under *watt*? Other entries do not provide definitions, only cross-references to entries where the words appear as synonyms. Thus, the dictionary aspect of this work is less than successful when looking up terms such as *zombie* ("See corpse, boor") or *zoo* ("See confusion"). This is another work that tries to be too many things and doesn't quite succeed at any of them.

Encyclopedic Dictionaries

In seeking definitions of some terms, particularly basic legal concepts, a companion or encyclopedic work may be more useful than one of the standard legal dictionaries. A more encyclopedic treatment provides not just a definition but the background necessary to provide context for the terminology.

The standard work in this genre is David M. Walker's *Oxford Companion to Law* (Oxford University Press, 1980). Walker provides short definitions, biographies, and longer essays on legal institutions and legal history. The book focuses on British law, but it includes some coverage of American topics, such as brief articles on Congress and the Supreme Court, entries for major cases, and a 10-page general survey of U.S. law. Walker's coverage overlaps with that of a law dictionary. He includes definitions for terms such as *paraphernalia* ("In older law, jewellery and ornaments given by a husband to his wife. . . . The concept is now obsolete"), *holding* ("in relation to a judgment of a court, the view adopted on a point of law disputed in the case"), and *infant* ("In English law an infant is a person of either sex under the age of 21, or since 1970, of 18. The term minor is now used alternatively. Certain statutes also use the terms 'child' and 'young person' for those under 14 and aged 14-17 respectively. . . ."). Like the *infant* entry, much of the book focuses specifically on the U.K., so it is best used by an American audience for a broader view of legal institutions and history.

The nearest American counterpart to Walker's book is the *Oxford Companion to the Supreme Court of the United States,* edited by Kermit L. Hall (Oxford University Press, 1992). Less oriented toward definitions than Walker, this volume provides some background on basic terms that may arise in Supreme Court jurisprudence, such as *amicus brief* or *res judicata.* Its focus, however, is specifically on the Court, and basic definitions are only included by chance.

Peter G. Renstrom's *The American Law Dictionary* (ABC-Clio, 1991) is another work focusing on judicial matters. It contains 323 articles on major concepts in the judicial system, but its arrangement by subject rather than alphabetically minimizes its use as a ready reference tool. Jay M. Shafritz's *The HarperCollins Dictionary of American Government and Politics* (HarperPerennial, 1992) is much broader in scope, containing short definitions of more than 5,000 terms and phrases used in political science. Although the book does not cover simple legal terminology, it includes entries for Supreme Court cases, major congressional acts, and federal agencies.

Statutory and Judicial Definitions

A legal dictionary is always useful for determining the general meaning of a term, but sometimes a lawmaking body will supply an official legal definition. Terms may be defined in statutes or regulations, and court decisions often define words in issue to resolve disputes. The dictionary definition of a term may not matter if a legislature or appellate court has determined its legal meaning.

Drug paraphernalia is now defined by statute in 47 states. Most of these statutes are based on the Model Drug Paraphernalia Act, drafted by the Drug Enforcement Administration in 1979. The act defines *drug paraphernalia* as "all equipment, products, and materials of any kind which are used, intended for use, or designed for use in planting, propagating, cultivating, growing, harvesting, manufacturing, compounding, converting, producing, processing, preparing, testing, analyzing, packaging, repackaging, storing, containing, concealing, injecting, ingesting, inhaling, or otherwise introducing into the human body a controlled substance . . ." and then goes on to note that the term includes, but is not limited to, such objects as kits, scales and balances, balloons, syringes, and a variety of pipes.

Federal and state legislatures have enacted laws defining thousands of specific terms. Those defined in current federal statutes can be found in the *United States Code* index under "Definitions," a list that takes up almost 400 pages. Statutory definitions by state legislatures can be found in the indexes to each state's statutes, usually under the heading "Defined terms" or "Words and phrases."

Remember that most statutory definitions apply only to a specific context. Be careful to note qualifying language such as "For purposes of this act" at the beginning of a section. The word *manufacturer* means something quite different under the Fastener Quality Act, 15 U.S.C. § 5402(10) (1994), than it does under the Gun Control Act of 1968, 18 U.S.C. § 921(a)(10) (1994). A definition in one act has no legal effect in another context. One state's definition has no bearing in another state.

Other terms have been defined in court decisions. Courts often must interpret the language of statutes, determining whether the statutory provisions apply to the particular circumstances of the cases they hear. If a definition is part of a court's holding, it may be binding precedent in future cases. Even in other jurisdictions, judicial definitions may be persuasive because they show how courts have interpreted confusing or ambiguous language.

Judicial definitions are compiled in a 90-volume set known as *Words and Phrases* (West Publishing, 1940-date). Arranged alphabetically, *Words and Phrases* provides a vast array of definitions dating back to the seventeenth century, some of which are essential to deciding cases. Others are less useful. The first and last definitions in Volume 30A, "Ostracized to Ozark Hillbilly," show the range of material in the set. The volume begins with the following entry for *ostracized*: "Ostracized is a word which has been said to have no place in the vocabulary of American jurisprudence" (*U.S. v. Greene*, 146 F. 803 [D. Ga. 1906]). This may be a noble thought, but it doesn't really help us understand the term *ostracized*. (The opinion itself goes on to explain the word's origin in the Greek *ostrakon*, the shell with which Athenians voted to expel citizens.)

At the end of the volume, following definitions for terms such as *oyster*, *oyster bar*, *oyster bed*, *oyster industry*, and *oyster spat*, comes *Ozark hillbilly*. This term arose in a Missouri divorce case, *Moore v. Moore*, 337 S.W.2d 781 (Mo. App. 1960), in which the husband complained of various indignities, including the fact that his wife had referred to his family as "hillbillies." The judge explained that in southern Missouri "hillbilly" is an expression of envy, not an insult. As the *Words and Phrases* entry puts it,

> An "Ozark hillbilly" is an individual who has learned the real luxury of doing without the entangling complications of things which the dependent and over-pressured city dweller is required to consider as necessities, and who foregoes [sic] the hard grandeur of high buildings and canyon streets in exchange for wooded hills and verdant valleys.

This is a bucolic aside, but not a judicial definition of lasting legal significance.

The most recent volumes in the *Words and Phrases* set were published in 1972, but each of the 90 volumes is updated with an annual supplement kept in a pocket inside the back cover. These *pocket parts* are often the first place to look because they cover more modern cases and include coverage of new terminology such as *ostrich instruction* (used to describe a jury instruction about a defendant who deliberately avoids learning about the nature of a criminal transaction). The *Words and Phrases* pocket part is definitely the place to go for judicial interpretations of the term *drug paraphernalia*. Eight definitions are provided, mostly determining whether certain items fit within the meaning of the term. If so, then possession can form the basis of criminal conviction. (Instructions for making LSD, yes; plastic containers and notebooks, no; triple beam scales, maybe.) As in this instance, *Words and Phrases* is most useful when it is necessary to determine whether something is included within the scope of a term's meaning. It is less a dictionary of definitions than a compendium of nuances and interpretations.

None of the Above

Even the best and most up-to-date collection of dictionaries will not contain every term that arises in legal literature. Take, for example, the phrase *hostis humani generis* as it appears in a Supreme Court case, *Sentell v. New Orleans & C. R. Co.*, 166 U.S. 698, 702 (1897): "Laws for the protection of domestic animals are regarded as having but a limited application to dogs and cats; and, regardless of statute, a ferocious dog is looked upon as *hostis humani generis*, and as having no right to his life which man is bound to respect."

The expression is difficult to find in any of the legal dictionaries examined here. The venerable *Black's* and *Ballentine's* both include entries under *hostes* (half a column before the point where *hostis* would appear), and both define the phrase *Pirata est hostis humani generis* ("A pirate is an enemy of the human race"). But there is no entry under *hostis*, and someone reading about dogs would have little reason to look under *pirata*.

It turns out, however, that this eighteenth-century doctrine, which subjects pirates to trial wherever they are captured, has been used recently in several court cases involving human rights violations in Paraguay, Nicaragua, Guatemala, and Bosnia. Its first appearance was in *Filartiga v. Pena-Irala*, 630 F.2d 876, 890 (2d Cir.1980): "Indeed, for purposes of civil liability, the torturer has become—like the pirate and slave trader before him—*hostis humani generis*, an enemy of all mankind." Since 1980, *hostis humani generis* has appeared in several other cases and in dozens of law review articles, several of which explain not only its meaning but its history. In 1995, *Newsweek* reported that "FBI Director Louis Freeh called the Oklahoma bombers 'hostis humani generis'—enemies of mankind."

Almost every time that *hostis humani generis* appears in a recent case or article, its meaning is explained. All that is needed is the ability to find where the phrase appears, and a definition will be provided. This, of course, is what keyword searching can do, and it makes the online databases and the Internet invaluable tools in deciphering confusing terms. It is possible to find not only occurrences of an unusual term but the context in which it appears. Searches in LEXIS-NEXIS turn up the references mentioned above, while an Internet search engine such as Altavista <http://altavista.digital.com/> can retrieve a variety of material: course readings, Latin texts, briefs filed in federal court cases, even an Australian government report.

Most of the time a good law dictionary is a quick and systematic source for locating definitions and background information on legal terminology. Keyword access to electronic resources, however, provides the opportunity to do independent research on the meaning and scope of any term appearing in the legal literature.

LEGAL CITATIONS AND ABBREVIATIONS

Legal literature has a citation form all its own, with concise and sometimes cryptic abbreviations for sources and a particularly terse method of indicating volume and page numbers. To find legal information one must be able to use these citations as tools for accessing resources without feeling intimidated or stymied by them. Several guides can make the task easier.

Legal Citation Form

Most legal publications follow a standard form that lists the volume number immediately before an abbreviation for the publication, followed by the page number and then the date in parentheses. Already in this chapter we have seen the citation form for several cases.

Towne v. Eisner, 245 U.S. 418 (1918)

Cole v. State, 511 P.2d 593 (Okla. Crim. App. 1973)

U.S. v. Greene, 146 F. 803 (D. Ga. 1906)

Moore v. Moore, 337 S.W.2d 781 (Mo. App. 1960)

The *Towne v. Eisner* citation provides the names of the parties, the reporter volume (245), the source of the opinion (*United States Reports*), the page number (418) on which the case begins, and the date of the decision. The other cases add more parenthetical information identifying the court, because in each instance the publication (*Pacific Reporter, Second Series*; *Federal Reporter*; and *South Western Reporter, Second Series*) covers more than one court, and it is essential that researchers know what jurisdiction is involved. To a lawyer in Alabama, *Smith v. Jones*, 153 So.2d 226 (Ala. 1963) is usually a far more important case than *Smith v. Jones*, 654 So.2d 480 (Miss. 1995). Both deal with child custody issues, but the first is controlling precedent from the Alabama Supreme Court while the second is a case from a neighboring state that may or may not have persuasive value in Alabama.

If the information in parentheses is simply the abbreviation for the state, as in both *Smith v. Jones* cases, the case cited is a decision of the state's court of last resort. For a decision from an intermediate appellate court or trial court, a designation of the court must be included as well, as in "Okla. Crim. App. 1973" or "D. Ga. 1906."

The basic citation form has changed little in hundreds of years. It was developed because lawyers' briefs and judges' opinions include numerous references to support each legal proposition. Brevity kept the references from completely swamping the document. The citation form in a 1794 Supreme Court opinion ("1 Sid. 367, 3 T. Rep. 323, 1 Dall. Rep. 105") is quite familiar to today's lawyers, even if they may have difficulty finding these particular sources.

Deciphering older case citations such as these is more difficult because the abbreviations are unfamiliar and the jurisdictions are not always indicated. Early court reports were published privately and were known by the name of their compiler rather than the court. These *nominative* reporters were prevalent well into the nineteenth century.

Although citations to cases in nominative reporters were more prevalent in older cases, they are still found today because many older cases, including English decisions predating American independence, are still part of the common law of most U.S. jurisdictions and can still influence court decisions. The Supreme Court in *Heck v. Humphrey*, 512 U.S. 477 (1994), included a reference to "Burt v. Place, 4 Wend. 591

(1830)" without indicating what or where "Wend." was (*Wendell's Reports* from New York). An uninitiated researcher will usually need to check a dictionary or list of abbreviations to find such a case.

A similar format is used for journal articles. Thus the articles cited earlier in this chapter, at 23 Va. L. Rev. 38 (1936) and 31 UCLA L. Rev. 423 (1983), are found in volume 23 of the *Virginia Law Review* and volume 31 of the *UCLA Law Review*, at pages 38 and 423, respectively.

This is the citation form found in legal journals. It provides the key elements needed to find an article: volume, publication, page, and year. There are certainly other ways to present these elements, and journals in other disciplines generally do not follow the legal format. In 1964, Charles A. Reich published in the *Yale Law Journal* an influential article, "The New Property," on government entitlements. In law journals, this article is invariably cited as "73 Yale L.J. 733 (1964)."

This same information can be presented in other ways. Thus, *American Economic Review* cites "*Yale Law Journal*, April 1964, *73*, 733-87," and *Socialist Review* cites "*The Yale Law Journal*, vol. 73, no. 5 (April 1964) pp. 733-787." Both forms provide the information needed to find the article. Including the date in a citation not only provides important information about an article's currency, but also serves as a check against errors in the volume number, as in *American Political Science Review*'s "*Yale Law Journal*, 63 (April 1964), 733-787."

Citation forms that are less standardized and rigorous are less helpful. Omitting the volume number, as in *Western Political Quarterly*'s "*Yale Law Journal* 733 (1964)," shouldn't be too problematic. On the other hand, a laconic citation that provides neither volume nor page number, as in *Policy and Politics*'s "(1964) *Yale Law Journal*" can be a nuisance because it requires a good table of contents or index in the volume—and sometimes there is more than one volume per year. The worst-case citation form, from *Social Problems*, alters the name of the journal, gets the volume number completely wrong, and provides no page number: "1964 'The New Property.' Yale Law Review 93 (April)." Compared with that citation, legal form begins to make some sense.

One major difference between legal citation form and the forms used in other disciplines, as seen in the examples above, is that legal literature heavily abbreviates the names of journals. Doing so can save considerable space because some journals have rather long names. For someone unfamiliar with legal citations, however, it adds another layer of inaccessibility.

Several standard abbreviating conventions appear in legal literature. Some make sense: *Law* is abbreviated as *L*, *Journal* as *J*, and *Review* as *Rev*. Words such as *College* and *University* are reduced to initials, and noise words such as *of* and *the* are eliminated to save space. This yields abbreviations like *U. Chi. L. Rev.* for *University of Chicago Law Review* and *Det. C.L. Rev.* for *Detroit College of Law Review*. Most abbreviations are relatively easy to decipher, but following these conventions does lead to some bizarre results. How else to account for *J.C. & U.L.*, the abbreviation for *Journal of College and University Law*?

The *Bluebook*

Although the basic structure of legal citation form goes back centuries, the blame for its continued survival generally falls on the shoulders of *The Bluebook: A Uniform System of Citation* (Harvard Law Review Association, 16th ed., 1996). The *Bluebook* is the legal counterpart of such style manuals as the *Chicago Manual of Style* (University of Chicago Press, 14th ed., 1993) or Kate L. Turabian's *Manual for Writers of Term Papers, Theses, and Dissertations* (University of Chicago Press, 6th ed., 1996). The first edition of *A Uniform System of Citation* was prepared and printed in the summer of 1926 by Harvard law student Erwin Griswold, who would later become dean of the Harvard Law School and Solicitor General of the United States. It is still prepared by editors from the *Harvard Law Review*, in conjunction with the *Columbia Law Review*, *University of Pennsylvania Law Review*, and *Yale Law Journal*. The *Bluebook* is a required purchase for most first-year law students, and it determines how most legal journals cite material.

Much of the *Bluebook* contains rules for citing material to support or rebut a point of law, covering such matters as when to indent quotations, how to use introductory signals such as *Cf.* or *But see*, and whether to italicize case names. The more important rules for researchers' purposes are those that provide the forms by which legal publications are designated.

These forms are explained throughout the *Bluebook*, but the most convenient portion of the volume is the second half, consisting of tables printed on blue paper. Table T.1 lists materials for each jurisdiction in the United States, showing the major sources for cases, statutes, and regulations, and providing the standard abbreviation for each. Tables T.2 and T.3 provide similar information for two dozen other countries and for intergovernmental organizations. Tables T.6 to T.8 display abbreviations commonly appearing in case citations or court documents. The most extensive table, T.13, covers periodicals and lists abbreviations for individual words appearing in periodical titles as well as the full citations of most law reviews published in the United States.

The *Bluebook* is not without its critics. Reviews in legal journals rail about its constrictive rules each time a new edition is published. Others complain that it does not convey enough information for those outside the legal community. In *A Handbook for Scholars* (Oxford University Press, rev. ed., 1992), Mary-Claire van Leunen writes, "The forms described in *A Uniform System* are slick, sophisticated, clean as a whistle—and utterly unsuited to lay use." She speculates that lawyers may not want other people to look at court cases, but her solution is for "the rest of us to work out our own way of writing references to court cases, a way that will permit us to march boldly up to the desk in a law library and look the librarian in the eye." Instead of the *Bluebook*'s concise *Green v. State*, 484 S.W.2d 517 (Ark. 1982), her suggested citation is:

Green v. Arkansas.
Supreme Court of Arkansas, 18 September 1982.
Volume 484 South Western Reporter (second series),
    page 517.

This may be suitable for someone looking to fill as much space as possible, but most people would do better to learn the rudiments of legal citation form instead.

Although the *Bluebook* dominates the field, it is not the only source for citation rules in legal writing. A rival publication, *The University of Chicago Manual of Legal Citation* (Lawyers Cooperative, 1989), provides simpler rules for authors but makes few changes in basic citation formats. Many court opinions do not follow *Bluebook* form for frequently used documents. The Nevada Supreme Court, for example, cites *Nevada Revised Statutes* as "NRS," not "Nev. Rev. Stat." The *Bluebook*'s rules are the most prevalent citation system in legal literature, however, and its forms are generally used throughout this book.

Legal Abbreviation Dictionaries

Besides the tables of abbreviations in the *Bluebook*, other convenient sources can help find and decipher legal citations. The *Index to Legal Periodicals and Books*, one of the leading journal indexes, uses standard *Bluebook* abbreviations in its entries and includes a table of citations at the front of each issue. (Its com-

petitor, the *Current Law Index*, uses the full names of journals instead of abbreviations; this may make it more accessible to a researcher new to the field.) As noted earlier, *Black's Law Dictionary* includes a table of abbreviations listing a number of journals and court reports.

Sometimes, however, a more extensive listing is needed, particularly when trying to track down material cited in older court reports, which often use formats that may have been common at the time but appear cryptic today. Two major dictionaries focus specifically on legal abbreviations. Their coverage is similar, although one is American and the other British. The American dictionary, Mary Miles Prince's *Bieber's Dictionary of Legal Abbreviations* (William S. Hein & Co., 4th ed., 1993), contains more than 30,000 abbreviations. Donald Raistrick's *Index of Legal Citations and Abbreviations* (Bowker-Saur, 2d ed., 1993), less widely seen in this country, includes more than 25,000 entries.

Although Raistrick does not claim as many entries, there are several reasons why his is the stronger work. *Bieber's* lists the jurisdiction for most older court reports, an important clue in finding the source; Raistrick adds the dates of coverage as well. This can be of considerable help in determining which choice is indeed the correct one. For example, under "O.A.R.," Raistrick lists "Ohio Appellate Reports. 1913-" and "Ontario Appeal Reports. 1876-1900." If the year of a case is known, it is immediately clear which reporter is the source.

Raistrick also has an edge in accuracy. Consider the following entries in *Bieber's*: "Hill & Den./Lalor's Supplement to Hill & Denio's Reports, New York (1842-44)," "Vin. Abr./Supplement to Vineer's Abridgment of Law and Equity (Eng.)," and "Vin. Supp./ Supplement to Vner's Abridgment of Law and Equity." The first two are said to be references to supplements, for no apparent reason. In the second and third, Charles Viner's name is mangled. These errors seem to be the result of sloppy transcription, perhaps from some other list of abbreviations.

Another difference between the two works is the method of alphabetization. While Raistrick alphabetizes by word, *Bieber's* alphabetizes letter by letter. This puts *Vr.* between *V.R.* and *V.R.Adm.* An experienced or intellectually curious researcher would normally try to guess what an abbreviation stood for, but alphabetization by letter reduces the opportunity to browse and ponder nearby entries. Alphabetization by word makes it easier to spot a slightly different abbreviation if the one being checked is not quite correct. (Raistrick's alphabetization has its own idiosyncrasies. He puts & at the end of the alphabetized arrangement, so that *Hill & Den.* follows such entries as *Hill Real Prop.* and *Hill S.C.*)

Finally, Raistrick's major advantage is that he includes abbreviations in other languages. One might be reading a United States source on international law and see a citation to a treaty or article in *R.G.D.I.P.* It is not always clear from the context what language these initials represent, but Raistrick explains that this stands for "Revue générale de droit international public (Fr.) 1894-." Such foreign abbreviations have unfortunately been excluded from the latest edition of *Bieber's.* (On the other hand, *Bieber's* does include some Americanisms lacking in Raistrick, such as the signals used in *Shepard's Citations* to indicate that a case has been distinguished or overruled.)

It appears that abbreviations in other languages have been excluded from *Bieber's* to accommodate a related publication, *World Dictionary of Legal Abbreviations*, by Igor I. Kavass and Mary Miles Prince (William S. Hein & Co., 1991-date). This loose-leaf work is now in two volumes and includes abbreviations in six foreign languages—French, German, Hebrew, Italian, Portuguese, and Spanish, as well as sections of abbreviations appearing in Australian and English sources. The sections vary widely in scope, from the brief Hebrew section to almost 900 pages of Spanish abbreviations, which are listed both alphabetically and by country.

The *World Dictionary* can be useful when working with the legal literature of a particular country or language. Because each language has its own section, however, knowing the language of an abbreviation is a necessary first step. If an abbreviation is taken out of context, or for some reason its language is not immediately apparent, it may be easier to begin with Raistrick or with one of the general abbreviation dictionaries discussed below.

General Abbreviation Dictionaries

It is possible to decipher most legal abbreviations without the help of specialized dictionaries found only in law libraries because legal materials are well represented in standard reference works. *Periodical Title Abbreviations*, edited by Leland G. Alkire, Jr. (Gale, biennial), contains an extensive subtitle listing of the fields of study it encompasses, including law, and it does indeed provide coverage of many legal periodicals. This publication is multinational in scope and includes numerous foreign-language journals. *Periodical Title Abbreviations* is simply descriptive and does not prescribe a correct form. *Harvard Law Review*, for example, is listed under *HALRA, Har LR, Harvard Law R, Harvard L Rev, Harv Law R, Harv Law Rev, Harv L Rev*, and *HLR*—every possible abbreviation for the journal and then some. (Raistrick only provides *Harv. L. Rev.* and *H.L.R.*; *Bieber's* adds *Har. L.R., Harvard L. Rev.,* and *Harv LR*; neither includes the mysterious *HALRA*.) Volume 1 of the *Periodical Title Abbreviations* set, *By Abbreviation*, is the key source for deciphering a mysterious citation.

The *Acronyms, Initialisms & Abbreviations Dictionary*, edited by Mary Rose Bonk (Gale, annual), covers more than just periodicals; it includes abbreviations for organizations, scientific terms, and military technology. It too covers numerous fields, including law. The scope of this dictionary can be overwhelming at times. *ABA*, for example, is an abbreviation commonly seen in legal literature, usually standing for American Bar Association. However, Bonk's dictionary provides 80 other possibilities that *ABA* might represent. The extensive coverage of legal publications includes many of the same *Harvard Law Review* abbreviations listed in *Periodical Title Abbreviations*. This dictionary draws abbreviations from a wide variety of sources, including the *Bieber's* and Raistrick dictionaries, so a variety of other legal publications are also included, including court reports and statutory codes. The user will learn here that *USC* means *United States Code*, as well as Under Separate Cover, United Survival Clubs, and 25 other possibilities.

The *Acronyms, Initialisms & Abbreviations Dictionary* is limited to English-language abbreviations, with abbreviations from other countries listed in a separate *International Acronyms, Initialisms & Abbreviations Dictionary* (Gale, 4th ed., 1997). This source includes more than 150,000 abbreviations from around the world, including such standard foreign-language legal terms as *BGB* for the *Buergerliches Gesetzbuch* (the German civil code) and *RGDIP* for the *Revue Generale de Droit International Public.*

Another work, *Abbreviations Dictionary*, by Ralph De Sola, Deal Stahl, and Karen K. Kerchelich (CRC Press, 9th ed., 1995), is far less useful for deciphering legal abbreviations. The acronym *ABA* has a mere 28 entries, most duplicated in the Gale dictionaries. There is a *Harv* entry for Harvard, but no further guide to periodical titles such as the *Harvard Law Review*. The same page includes the entry "Harare, Zimbabwe," noting that it was formerly Salisbury, Rhodesia. With so many abbreviations and so little time, it's hard to warm to a work that wastes space on meaningless entries such as this.

Other Tools for Deciphering Abbreviations

It is not always necessary to refer to an abbreviations dictionary to understand a citation. One of the simplest ways is to check the source being consulted. Many legal publications include a table of frequently used or specialized abbreviations. A quick check of a table of contents for such a feature can save considerable time and frustration.

Sometimes an abbreviated reference to a source eludes even the most extensive dictionary. In nineteenth-century cases, books were frequently cited by author and topic. For example, "Taylor's Landlord and Tenant" is not pithy enough to be listed in an abbreviations dictionary, but it does not contain enough information to find the book. One handy publication that can be invaluable in such detective work is the *Catalogue of the Library of the Law School of Harvard University* (Harvard Law School, 1909). This catalog represented the holdings of the country's largest law library before the boom in legal publishing rendered a simple listing unmanageable. With a listing limited to pre-1909 publications, it is possible to look up an author's name and decipher many older references. A quick scan of the listings under *Taylor* in the Harvard catalog reveals John N. Taylor, *American Law of Landlord and Tenant*, which went through nine editions between 1844 and 1904. With the author's full name and the complete title, it is now easy to determine where the book can be found. In a way modern online catalogs offer similar possibilities for searching with less-than-complete information through the use of title keywords, delimiters by date, and other features.

Just as with definitions of legal terminology, the full-text databases and Internet search engines can be of assistance in trying to track down the meaning of an abbreviation. A legal periodical article may explain an obscure abbreviation the first time it is used, or, by offering a better sense of an abbreviation's context, may provide a lead to making sense of it.

Finally, it is sometimes necessary to ask for help. Some decisions from the National Oceanic and Atmospheric Administration are cited to a publication abbreviated as *O.R.W.* This term appears in none of the dictionaries. A full-text search of legal journals provides a few citations but no further leads, and the NOAA Web site <http://www.noaa.gov> isn't much help. But a call to the NOAA library in Washington quickly reveals that this is *Ocean Resources and Wildlife Reporter,* an obscure agency publication distributed to a handful of libraries.

RESEARCH GUIDES

This book focuses on a variety of legal information available for many research purposes. Numerous books have been written specifically for those people who need to use legal resources to resolve legal issues. Most of these are written for law students and are designed for the first-year legal research and writing curriculum.

In this genre, two of the standard texts are Morris L. Cohen, Robert C. Berring, and Kent C. Olson's *How to Find the Law* (West Publishing, 9th ed., 1989), and J. Myron Jacobstein, Roy M. Mersky, and Donald L. Dunn's *Fundamentals of Legal Research* (Foundation Press, 7th ed., 1998). Both include several appendixes providing useful information, and *Fundamentals* includes a glossary of terms used in legal research and a table of abbreviations. Each is thoroughly indexed. A shorter work by Morris L. Cohen and Kent C. Olson, *Legal Research in a Nutshell* (West Publishing, 6th ed., 1996), provides a more succinct summary.

The Process of Legal Research (Little, Brown, 4th ed., 1996), by Christina L. Kunz et al., is a thorough and well-illustrated guide featuring an extensive series of problem sets covering a variety of research situations. This excellent teaching tool is designed more for use in law school legal research classes than as a reference volume.

A work designed specifically for nonlawyers is Stephen Elias and Susan Levinkind's *Legal Research: How to Find and Understand the Law* (Nolo Press, 6th ed., 1998). It includes numerous straightforward explanations and useful asides on a process that can be frustrating to the uninitiated. Portions of the book have been adapted and posted on Nolo's Web site <http://www.nolo.com/ChunkLR/LR.index.html>.

In addition, a number of useful research guides focus on more specific topics. *Specialized Legal Research* (Little, Brown, 1987-date), edited by Leah Chanin, contains chapters covering primary sources and secondary literature on such topics as admiralty law, banking law, copyright, customs, environmental law, federal employment law, government contracts, immigration, income tax, military and veterans law, patents and trademarks, securities regulation, and the *Uniform Commercial Code*. The volume includes a bibliography of specialized legal research sources and a subject index.

Tax research is the subject of Gail Levin Richmond's *Federal Tax Research: A Guide to Materials and Techniques* (Foundation Press, 5th ed., 1997) and Robert L. Gardner and Dave N. Stewart's *Tax Research Techniques* (AICPA, 4th ed., 1993). Richmond's book is more useful for finding sources for obscure tax publications, while the AICPA volume provides a more thorough discussion of the entire research process, from gathering facts to communicating results.

Research in a number of specialized areas is covered in Julius J. Marke and Richard Sloane's *Legal Research and Law Library Management* (Law Journal Seminars-Press, rev. ed., 1990-date). In more than 70 chapters, this work covers a wide range of subjects, from techniques of research instruction to protection against library disasters. Chapters 22 through 32 cover research in particular legal subjects, including AIDS, copyright law, criminal law, environmental law, food and drug law, health care, sports and recreation law, sex discrimination, and trademarks. Chapters vary in organization and scope. Other research guidance (such as "Research in American Indian Law," Chapter 54) can be found throughout this substantial and regularly updated volume.

Numerous guides to legal research in specialized areas appear as articles in journals, such as *Law Library Journal* and *Legal Reference Services Quarterly,* accessible through the standard legal periodical indexes.

Finally, one of the most useful sources may be a guide to legal materials in a particular state. Such a guide will explain the sources available in that jurisdiction and go into much greater depth than possible in a more general treatment. Research guides have been published for many of the larger states, and an extensive series of state bibliographies has been published by the Government Documents Special Interest Section of the American Association of Law Libraries. Occasional guides to the practice materials and treatises in particular states appear as articles in *Law Library Journal* and other periodicals. Lists of these publications appear in numerous sources, such as the appendixes in *Legal Research in a Nutshell* and *Fundamentals of Legal Research*, and Chapter 27, "State Legal Publications and Information Sources," in Kendall F. Svengalis's *Legal Information Buyer's Guide & Reference Manual* (Rhode Island LawPress, annual). Nancy Adams Deel and Barbara G. James's "An Annotated Bibliography of State Legal Research Guides," 14 (nos. 1-2) *Legal Reference Services Q.* 23-77 (1994), is a useful descriptive guide to sources available as of 1994.

PART 2
Getting Started

CHAPTER 3
General Reference Sources

TOPICS COVERED

Libraries
Encyclopedias
   Interdisciplinary Encyclopedias
   Legal Encyclopedias
Consumer Guides

Web Sites
   Directories and Compilations
   Search Engines
   Mailing Lists and Newsgroups
   Published Guides
Legal Compendia
Formbooks

The first step in locating legal information is to determine how and where to begin. Some people will turn immediately to a lawyer for assistance. Others will search for answers at a local law library, or at a general public or academic library. More and more people are turning to the Internet. This chapter presents various reference tools, both print and electronic, that attempt to provide comprehensive coverage of legal issues.

Deciding which tools to use will depend on the type of information needed. Such tools include

- encyclopedic works that explain the role of legal institutions in society or summarize legal doctrines
- consumer guides to the law, designed to answer everyday legal questions
- World Wide Web sites providing electronic access to a broad range of legal information
- legal compendia providing addresses, statistics, and other data
- formbooks to assist in drafting documents and following legal procedures

LIBRARIES

Several of the resources discussed in this chapter are widely and easily available. The consumer guides and some of the encyclopedias are designed for general audiences, and can be found in most larger academic and public libraries. The World Wide Web sites to be discussed are available to anyone with access to a computer and the Internet.

For many patrons needing legal information, the public library is the first stop. It may be the only library nearby, or it may simply be a more comfortable setting than an unfamiliar and intimidating law library. Many public libraries, however, house limited collections of resources for legal information. Most have a few basic reference works such as *West's Encyclopedia of American Law* and legal dictionaries, and many have good collections of self-help law books. Larger collections usually have current sets of federal and state statutes and an extensive collection of reference materials.

Some material, however, will generally be found only in specialized law libraries. This is particularly true of the voluminous collections of statutes and cases required for extensive legal research, as well as the legal treatises and journals discussed later in this book. If no law library is nearby, a university library may have a fairly large legal collection to support the needs of its students and community. Most general libraries, however, do not purchase much legal material. Finding a law library and gaining access to it are therefore necessary steps in most research endeavors.

Law libraries are of a variety of types. The largest are generally the academic law school libraries. Most of these are open to the public, although some private institutions restrict access to their students and paid subscribers. Many larger communities have public law libraries supported by court fees. Smaller communities may have a bar association library that is open to the public, although some of these limit access only to lawyers. In addition, most law firms and many corporations have law libraries, but these are usually not easily accessible to outside researchers.

Thus, an essential step on the road to legal research is to find a law library and to determine whether and to what extent its facilities are available. Academic law libraries may be the easiest to find, through any of the numerous directories and Internet lists of law schools described in Chapter 6. In addition, several general directories list law libraries of all kinds.

The most comprehensive of these sources is the *AALL Directory and Handbook*, published annually by the American Association of Law Libraries. The directory portion of this volume has two major components: a list of individual association members and a geographical listing of law libraries. The geographical listing includes a wide range of public, academic, court, and private libraries. Entries include mailing addresses, phone and fax numbers, and names of librarians belonging to the association. In the near future, the directory will undoubtedly include Web site addresses as well.

Unfortunately the *AALL Directory* listings provide little information about the library collections. Some indicate the number of lawyers or students served, and some include an estimate of the number of volumes in the library (e.g., ">200,000" or "<10,000"). Many entries, however, provide neither of these details, and none contain any information about access policies or library hours.

Law libraries are also listed in the *American Library Directory* (Bowker, annual). This standard directory includes more than 1,700 law libraries in the United States. The directory is arranged geographically, making it relatively easy to scan entries looking for a law library. Each separately listed law library entry appears with the letter *L* in the margin. Simply scanning a page for those entries with marginal *L* notations, however, will not catch every law library listed. Many law libraries affiliated with general libraries have no notation in the margin. This is a valuable directory, but uniform treatment of l libraries and other specialized libraries would make it even more useful.

The *American Library Directory* provides more information about the scope of most law libraries than the *AALL Directory*. Besides addresses and telephone numbers, most entries indicate the number of book volumes, periodical subscriptions, and CD-ROM titles; staff size; and specialized subject interests. Perhaps most important for the potential researcher are notes indicating if access is restricted or available by appointment only.

Two other library directories provide some coverage of law libraries, but neither is entirely satisfactory for finding a general law library. Both are better suited to searches for more specialized resources.

The *Directory of Special Libraries and Information Centers* (Gale, annual) includes most major law libraries and provides information about staffing, holdings, subscriptions, and services (including whether the library is open to the public). Its only drawback is that the entries are arranged alphabetically by institution name rather than geographically, so finding an appropriate library may require checking first in the subject index. This index is detailed but provides only state abbreviations and references to entry numbers. A general category such as "Law—United States" contains almost a full page of listings. These begin with Alaska law libraries: "AK 247, 248, 256, 18506, 18518." From there one must check each of these entries for more information. The index is more useful for finding specialized collections in areas such as military law or water law, where there are not so many listings in each state.

The law library listings from *Directory of Special Libraries and Information Centers* are reprinted in a separate Gale publication, *Subject Directory of Special Libraries and Information Centers* (Gale, annual). Volume 1 of this set, *Business, Government and Law Libraries*, contains a section of almost 200 pages of law library listings. Although it is helpful to have law libraries concentrated in one section, the individual listings are merely reprinted from the general publication, in alphabetical order using the same indexing method. The only advantage is that someone looking for law libraries in a particular state has fewer pages to flip through.

The other specialized directory, *Subject Collections* (Bowker, 7th ed., 1993), is best suited to searches for special collections, such as rare books and manuscript materials. Because it is based on information reported by the libraries themselves, however, it includes entries for just enough general law libraries to be confusing. Under the index heading "Law," for example, more than three pages of libraries are listed geographically. Some of these, such as the Native American Rights Fund, have specialized collections. Others are general law libraries, but the listings for this category are short and misleading. The University of Georgia is listed, but none of the other law schools in Georgia appear. For Florida, no law schools are listed, and just two listings appear: Florida State Hospital in Chattahoochee, and Union Correctional Institution Library in Raiford. Most researchers in Florida can probably find legal information without having to enter a state hospital or correctional institution.

Law libraries are also listed in *Law and Legal Information Directory* (Gale, biennial). This volume contains information on a wide range of legal institutions, and is discussed in greater detail in Chapter 6. It is noteworthy here that section 12, "Special Libraries," is a useful list of law libraries arranged geographically. This listing provides addresses, telephone and fax numbers, and number of volumes held and subscriptions. It contains no information on personnel, but it does provide a quick summary of each library's restrictions on use (ranging from "None" to "Library not open to public"). The information in this directory is drawn primarily from Gale's directories of special libraries and information centers.

When using a law library, be aware that its librarians often perform a slightly different function than general librarians. A general reference librarian can resolve many queries, in person or by telephone, such as the pronunciation of a term or the date of a historical event. Questions on legal topics, however, often require determining the applicable law and applying it to a particular set of circumstances. Because interpreting legal doctrines is considered practicing law, law librarians are more likely to direct you to an appropriate resource and assist you in learning how to use it, but then leave it up to you to decide what provisions apply to your situation. Some librarians are overly concerned with unauthorized-practice-of-law constraints and hesitate even to answer factual questions; almost any librarian is wary of telling someone which particular state statute applies to a specific situation. When using a law library, be prepared to use your own judgment and take an active role in finding your own answers.

ENCYCLOPEDIAS

Two distinct types of encyclopedias cover legal issues. The first is the *interdisciplinary encyclopedia* that is often found in general reference collections. These encyclopedias provide a narrative summary of legal matters, generally covering such issues as legal history, institutions, famous jurists and lawyers, and leading Supreme Court cases. They are written for a broad audience with a wide variety of research needs. These works are somewhat similar to specialized encyclopedias in other areas, such as the *McGraw-Hill Encyclopedia of Science & Technology* (McGraw-Hill, 8th ed., 1997) or the new *Dictionary of Art* (Grove, 1996).

The second type of encyclopedia, usually found in law libraries, is a much different resource. A *legal encyclopedia* features little historical or biographical background but provides detailed explanations of legal doctrines. This type of encyclopedia is useful for finding case law and for understanding quickly an area of law. It is of little value, however, in researching issues such as jury psychology or Supreme Court history.

Interdisciplinary Encyclopedias

General interest encyclopedias do not ignore legal topics. The *New Encyclopædia Britannica* (Encyclopædia Britannica, 15th ed., revised annually), for example, has hundreds of articles on legal subjects. The Macropædia contains extensive treatments of such topics as constitutional law, criminal law, business law, family law, and property law. As an example, the property law article is 26 pages long, concluding with an entire page of bibliographic references. The *Britannica*'s Micropædia contains short articles on legal concepts (e.g., alimony, bailment, escheat) and institutions. Interestingly, the Supreme Court of the United States gets rather short shrift with but one column, but there are longer articles on individual justices. John Marshall, for example, merits four columns, and Roger Taney has two columns written by his biographer, A. J. Schumacher. Even newer justices, such as Clarence Thomas and Ruth Bader Ginsburg, have brief articles.

Other encyclopedias, although less extensive, also cover legal issues. The *Encyclopedia Americana* (Grolier, revised annually) has articles on a variety of legal institutions and topics. A nine-page overview article on law provides basic information, although the only changes in the past 10 years appear to be a change from "West Germany" to "Germany" and an updated bibliography. Similarly, the Supreme Court of the United States article has an updated listing of justices and a revised bibliography, but the history of the Court stops in the 1970s, with the most recent "landmark cases" from 1976. There is no mention at all of the tumultuous Bork or Thomas nomination hearings.

The *Columbia Encyclopedia* (Columbia University Press, 5th ed., 1993) covers legal topics in a more terse yet conscientious fashion. It has nearly two pages on the Supreme Court, brief articles on Supreme Court justices and nominees (including Robert Bork and Clarence Thomas), and coverage of major legal doctrines and issues.

West's Encyclopedia of American Law

Two encyclopedias dealing specifically with legal topics are published for a general audience. *West's Encyclopedia of American Law* (West Group, 12 vols., 1997-98) is the more substantial work. Successor to *The Guide to American Law: Everyone's Legal Encyclopedia* (West Publishing, 12 vols., 1983–85, with 7 supplement vols.), it has articles on a wide range of issues, covering legal history, doctrines, and institutions. Included are definitions of legal concepts; biographies of Supreme Court justices, presidents, and legislators; and discussions of controversial legal issues.

The set includes more than 4,000 entries, ranging in length from a paragraph to three or four pages. Unlike most legal publications, *West's Encyclopedia of American Law* is packed with illustrations, including photographs of major historical figures and events. Some of the illustrations seem a bit superfluous, such as the photograph for the "Warranty" article of a car buyer and salesperson shaking hands, but others are fascinating glimpses of people whose names have become linked with legal doctrines. One welcome feature in *West's Encyclopedia of American Law* that is missing from the general encyclopedias is the inclusion of citations for cases and statutes, making it possible to go straight from an encyclopedia article to the text of the document discussed.

Sidebars accompany many of the articles, along with "in focus" pieces examining particular issues in greater detail. Graphic timelines for the lives of major legal figures, such as Thomas Hobbes and Jimmy Hoffa, provide quick glimpses of their careers in relation to major milestones, such as world wars. Special sections at the end of several volumes, "Milestones in the Law," trace major cases, such as *Roe v. Wade* and *Brown v. Board of Education*, providing the text of court opinions and briefs. At the back of each volume is a list of abbreviations, a bibliography for each article, a table of cases, and an index by name and subject.

Exhibit 3-1 shows a sample page from *West's Encyclopedia of American Law* featuring the end of the article on "Jurisprudence" and the beginning of the "Jury" article. The page includes definitions of three terms (set off by small book symbols), cross-references to other articles (in the text in small capital letters and in a list at the end of an article), and references to two Supreme Court decisions.

At first glance, it appears that the bibliographies, listing both books and articles, would be more useful if they accompanied the articles. But journal articles are cited without the page references needed to find them, and some entries are peculiar enough—*The Law in Classical Athens* for the "Judiciary" article, a telephone interview with a reference librarian, and one constitutional law text listed again and again for articles ranging from "Korean war" to "Parties"—that they really can't be used as recommended readings.

The alphabetical sequence of articles occupies 10 volumes. Volume 11 is an appendix volume containing a variety of historical legal documents. These are divided into three sections: "Foundations of U.S. Law" (24 documents ranging in time from Magna Carta through the writing of the Constitution to the Monroe Doctrine); "Civil Rights" (24 documents showing milestones in slavery, racial equality, women's rights, and Native American rights); and "Reflections on Law and Society" (presidential speeches and examples of legal scholarship, beginning with Alexis de Tocqueville). Each group of documents is prefaced with an introduction explaining its importance and placing it in historical context. Some of the documents, such as the Stamp Act or the Missouri Compromise, may seem dry but cover events that had dramatic impacts on society. The volume concludes with a few miscellaneous reference items, such as lists of Supreme Court justices and U.S. attorneys general.

Volume 12 contains a dictionary and indexes. The dictionary simply duplicates the definitions provided in the main body of the work; the value of this feature is questionable because here the defined words are stripped of the supporting explanation provided in the encyclopedia articles. This might make a handy pocket dictionary, if it were a handy pocket size. Finally, a table of cases, a name index, and a subject index each cumulate the information in the first 10 individual volumes. The name index is useful, but the subject index is rather unsatisfactory, with numerous references to detailed concepts and events but few cross-references or broader entries to tie related material together. (In the earlier *Guide to American Law*, for example, the article on "Embracery," or attempting to influence a jury, was indexed under both "Jury—Corruption" and "Jury—Influence." In this edition, there are no leads from "Jury" to the related article.)

American Justice

The other general interest encyclopedia of legal matters is the much shorter three-volume set entitled *American Justice*, edited by Joseph M. Bessette (Salem, 1996). This work does not take as broad a view of legal topics as *West's Encyclopedia of American Law*; although it includes articles on such historical figures as mination. The Allies relied in part on the natural-law principle that human dignity is an inviolable right that no government may vitiate by written law. See also NUREMBERG TRIALS.

Positivists and naturalists tend to converge in the area of historical jurisprudence. Historical jurisprudence is marked by judges who consider history, tradition, and custom when deciding a legal dispute. Strictly speaking, history does not completely fall within the definition of either positivism or natural law. Historical events, like the Civil War, are not legislative enactments, although they may be the product of governmental policy. Nor do historical events embody eternal principles of morality, although they may be the product of clashing moral views. Yet, historical events shape both morality and law. Thus, many positivists and naturalists find a place for historical jurisprudence in their legal philosophy.

For example, Justice Holmes was considered a positivist to the extent that he believed that courts should defer to legislative judgment unless a particular statute clearly violates an express provision of the Constitution. But he qualified this stance when a given statute "infringe[s] on fundamental principles as they have been understood by the traditions of our people and our law" (*Lochner v. New York*, 198 U.S. 45, 25 S. Ct. 539, 49 L. Ed. 937 [1905]). In such instances, Holmes felt, courts were justified in striking down a particular written law. See also LOCHNER V. NEW YORK.

BENJAMIN N. CARDOZO, considered an adherent of sociological jurisprudence by some and a realist by others, was another Supreme Court justice who incorporated history into his legal philosophy. When evaluating the merits of a claim brought under the Due Process Clauses of the Fifth and Fourteenth Amendments, Cardozo denied relief to claims that were not "implicit in the concept of ordered liberty" and the "principle[s] of justice [that are] so rooted in the traditions and conscience of our people as to be ranked as fundamental" (*Palko v. Connecticut*, 302 U.S. 319, 58 S. Ct. 149, 82 L. Ed. 288 [1937]).

Each school of jurisprudence is not a self-contained body of thought. The lines separating positivism from realism and natural law from formalism often become blurry. The legal philosophy of Justice Holmes, for example, borrowed from the realist, positivist, pragmatic, and historical strains of thought.

In this regard, some scholars have observed that it is more appropriate to think of jurisprudence as a spectrum of legal thought, where the nuances of one thinker delicately blend with those of the next. Professor Harold Berman, of Harvard Law School, for example, has advocated the development of an integrative jurisprudence, which would assimilate into one philosophy the insights from each school of legal theory. The staying power of any body of legal thought, Berman has suggested, lies not in its name but in its ability to explain the enterprise of law.

CROSS-REFERENCES

Anarchism; Chicago School; Feminist Jurisprudence; Judicial Review; Law; Legal Education; Legal History; Roman Law; Socialism.

JURIST ◙ A JUDGE or legal scholar; an individual who is versed or skilled in law. ◙

The term *jurist* is ordinarily applied to individuals who have gained respect and recognition by their writings on legal topics.

JURISTIC ACT ◙ An action intended and capable of having a legal effect; any conduct by a private individual designed to originate, terminate, or alter a right. ◙

A court performs a juristic act when it makes a decision and hands down a JUDGMENT. An individual who enters into a contractual agreement is also performing a juristic act because of the legal ramifications of his or her agreement.

JURY ◙ In trials, a group of people selected and sworn to inquire into matters of fact and to reach a VERDICT on the basis of the EVIDENCE presented to it. ◙

In U.S. law, decisions in many civil and criminal trials are made by a jury. Considerable power is vested in this traditional body of ordinary men and women, which is charged with deciding matters of fact and delivering a verdict of guilt or innocence based on the evidence in a case. Derived from its historical counterpart in English COMMON LAW, trial by jury has had a central role in U.S. courtrooms since the colonial era, and it is firmly established as a basic guarantee in the U.S. Constitution. Modern juries are the result of a long series of Supreme Court decisions interpreting this constitutional liberty and, in significant ways, extending it.

History The historical roots of the jury date to the eighth century. Long before becoming an impartial body, during the reign of Charlemagne juries interrogated prisoners. In the twelfth century, the Normans brought the jury to England, where its accusatory function remained: citizens acting as jurors were required to come forward as witnesses and give evidence before the monarch's judges. Not un-

EXHIBIT 3-1

John Marshall, it accords far more text to contemporary social issues, such as homelessness. Articles cover Supreme Court cases, federal legislation, types of crimes, legal terminology, historical events, famous people, organizations, and agencies. The 843 articles are arranged alphabetically. Articles more than 1,000 words in length conclude with annotated bibliographies. These longer articles are the only ones that are signed, although an extensive group of scholars contributed to the work. Unlike many other legal works, the contributors are predominantly college professors rather than law school professors, so their writing may be more accessible to a general audience.

Each volume begins with an alphabetical list of articles and ends with a topical list arranging the articles in a dozen broad categories. One nice feature in each article is a short introductory sentence providing the term's definition (or in the case of a court decision or person, the court/date or identification, and significance). The coverage is thinner than that of *West's Encyclopedia of American Law*; there is but one entry under Y (*Yates v. United States*) and one under Z (zoning). The work has more than 270 photographs; one, accompanying the two-paragraph article "Lying to Congress," is a full-page shot of Oliver North testifying. The Declaration of Independence and the Constitution are included in appendixes, along with a brief glossary and bibliography.

Of the Supreme Court cases discussed, more than two-thirds were decided since 1960. Major cases omitted include *Martin v. Hunter's Lessee*, *Gibbons v. Ogden*, and *Erie Railroad Co. v. Tompkins*. These, of course, did not address such divisive modern issues as race discrimination or equal protection, but they did determine the nature and scope of federal judicial authority.

Major Supreme Court decisions are listed chronologically (a list that is largely replicated in a separate timeline of major legal events). The chronological listing, but not the encyclopedia articles or the timeline, provides citations to the *United States Reports* for researchers who wish to read the text of the Court's decisions.

On the whole, the topics covered by *American Justice* appear to be chosen not for their lasting historical significance but for their relevance to current social concerns. Oliver Wendell Holmes merits one column, while "King, Rodney, case and aftermath" has two and a half pages, including photographs and a bibliography. This focus means that the set is best used for researching areas of current interest; researchers working on less "hot" legal topics will have to look elsewhere.

It also means that *American Justice* will need to be revised frequently, or it will rapidly become dated.

Other Works

A handy one-volume summary of legal history and legal institutions would be useful. Two volumes that almost fill this need have already been mentioned in Chapter 2. One is David M. Walker's *Oxford Companion to Law* (Oxford University Press, 1980), which includes short explanations of legal terms and institutions, biographical information on major historical figures, and longer essays on legal doctrines and history (12 pages, for example, on medieval law). It is a British work, but it covers a number of famous American cases and jurists, along with articles on "United States law" and "Legal education and training (United States)." Most of the topical essays, however, focus on British law. The freedom of expression and freedom of speech articles, for example, make no mention of the First Amendment. The longer essays provide references to a few major texts.

The second title (and the closest American counterpart) is *Oxford Companion to the Supreme Court of the United States* (Oxford University Press, 1992), edited by Kermit L. Hall. This is a delightful and useful volume, but its scope is limited to the Supreme Court and constitutional issues. It covers specialized matters such as "Cert pool" or "Exhaustion of remedies," and provides some general background; "Tort," for example, begins with a paragraph explaining what the term means before focusing on the Court's role in creating that definition.

For issues of criminal law, *Encyclopedia of Crime and Justice* (Free Press, 4 vols., 1983), edited by Sanford H. Kadish, provides an extensive scholarly and interdisciplinary survey. Its 286 entries cover both legal and behavioral aspects of such subjects as criminal law, criminal procedure, criminal justice systems, causes of crime, criminal behavior, and social responses. Articles are arranged alphabetically and are generally well written, avoiding legalese and technical language. (The book's foreword notes, "Indeed, it is regrettable that when lawyers talk law, they talk mainly to themselves. One usually looks in vain for discussions of legal subjects that are neither wrapped in inscrutable legalisms nor so diluted that they fail to convey a sense of the real issues and problems the law confronts.") Most entries conclude with cross-references and a short, unannotated bibliography of books and articles. The final volume includes a glossary; two "legal indexes," one listing cases by name and the other providing a subject list of statutes and constitutional provisions discussed; and a general subject index. Unfortunately, the encyclopedia has not been supplemented and is becoming dated.

Two encyclopedias also cover aspects of American government, both federal and state. *Encyclopedia of the American Judicial System* (Scribner, 3 vols., 1987), edited by Robert J. Janosik, and *Encyclopedia of the American Legislative System* (Scribner, 3 vols., 1994), edited by Joel H. Silbey, are both arranged by subject rather than alphabetically. Each has just under 100 lengthy articles, divided into six broad sections. The judicial system set covers legal history, substantive law, institutions and personnel, process and behavior, constitutional law and issues, and methodology. The legislative system set has sections on the American legislative system in historical context; legislative recruitment, personnel, and elections; legislative structure and processes; legislative behavior; legislatures and public policy; and legislatures within the political system. The articles in both sets conclude with helpful bibliographies; instead of simply listing sources, they explain the importance and the purposes of the works mentioned. These encyclopedias are useful for background reading, but their subject arrangements make them less convenient for ready reference than alphabetically arranged works.

A number of encyclopedias cover specialized aspects of law. Several focus on civil rights issues. *Encyclopedia of Civil Rights in America* (Sharpe, 1998), edited by David Bradley and Shelley Fisher Fishkin, is a three-volume work with 677 entries on a wide range of human rights and civil liberties issues. Two similar works, each with a more specific focus, are *Encyclopedia of African-American Civil Rights: From Emancipation to the Present* (Greenwood Press, 1992), edited by Charles D. Lowery and John F. Marszalek, and *Encyclopedia of American Indian Civil Rights* (Greenwood Press, 1997), edited by James S. Olson. Each contains several hundred entries on major historical figures, issues, and court cases. Most entries are brief, but each includes a bibliography of suggested readings. Both volumes feature chronologies of major civil rights landmarks.

Legal Encyclopedias

If the focus of a research inquiry is what the law is, rather than Chief Justice Marshall's impact on judicial power or the political aftermath of *Brown v. Board of Education*, then a legal encyclopedia may be a useful starting place.

Although multidisciplinary encyclopedias are designed for a wide audience, legal encyclopedias are definitely written for lawyers. The language is technical, and the treatment of legal issues is exhaustive but narrowly focused. Legal encyclopedias tend to focus on case law and its impact on the evolving common law.

Two major encyclopedias of national scope and several encyclopedias focusing on the law of particular jurisdictions govern this category of resources. A researcher seeking information about a specific state would be wise to begin with that state's encyclopedia; the national encyclopedias provide an overview of general legal principles applicable throughout the country.

National Encyclopedias

The two national encyclopedias are now both published by West Group. *Corpus Juris Secundum (C.J.S.)* (1936-date) was originally published by West Publishing Company, and *American Jurisprudence 2d (Am. Jur. 2d)* (1962-date) was originally published by Lawyers Cooperative Publishing Company. Each is a massive set of well over 100 volumes. *C.J.S.* was originally published in 101 volumes between 1936 and 1958; gradual expansion and replacement of volumes have resulted in the current 154 volumes. *Am. Jur. 2d* was published between 1962 and 1976 in 82 volumes; it now has expanded to 123 volumes. Both sets are successors to earlier encyclopedias, *Corpus Juris* (1911-37) and *American Jurisprudence* (1936-60).

The encyclopedias seek to outline legal doctrine systematically and thoroughly, explaining general legal principles that apply throughout the United States. Their source and focus are almost exclusively case law. *C.J.S.* originally claimed to be a "complete restatement of the entire body of American Law" based on "all the reported cases," but reconciling conflicting cases from 50 states into a coherent summary of the law proved an impossible task. In the 1980s, *C.J.S.* finally abandoned this unrealistic goal and now calls itself "a contemporary statement of American law as derived from reported cases and legislation." Volumes of *C.J.S.* published since this change in mission are still comprehensive but have a more streamlined and less unwieldy format.

American Jurisprudence 2d is a newer work and is generally regarded as a clearer and more authoritative statement of the law. Perhaps the fact that its development is more recent has helped keep it from becoming bogged down in obscure, archaic doctrines. Like *C.J.S.*, it focuses primarily on case law, but it also pays more attention to federal statutes and regulations.

The text is decidedly focused on practical legal doctrine. Major decisions in constitutional and political history are mentioned only in their doctrinal context. A brief section in the *Am. Jur. 2d* "Constitutional Law" article, "Broad Philosophies of Supreme Court Justices," § 133, is simply part of an explanation of various factors affecting interpretation of constitutions. Three paragraphs provide a cursory discussion of justices' value systems, using John Marshall's views on property rights and federal power as one example. A rare mention of scholarship in other disciplines is found in the next section, § 134, but only as an explanation that social science data have had an impact on such Court decisions as *Brown v. Board of Education*. Major constitutional crises like Franklin Roosevelt's court-packing controversy go practically unnoticed in *Am. Jur. 2d* except for references to law review articles in notes to § 4 of the "Judges" article, "Constitutional or Legislative Power to Create Judge's Office." (One of the few examples of a historical treatment is the curious article, "Slaves," in a 1953 *C.J.S.* volume.)

Am. Jur. 2d and *C.J.S.* are not held in high esteem by legal scholars, but they are frequently cited by the courts. Judges may cite *Webster's* as much as *Black's Law Dictionary* when seeking to define terms, but they cite legal encyclopedias far more often than any general encyclopedic source when explaining doctrine. Together the two titles have been cited in well over 100,000 opinions, compared to a mere thousand or so for the *Encyclopedia Britannica* and fewer than a dozen for such respected reference works as the *Encyclopedia of Crime and Justice*. These are works designed for practicing lawyers, not to explain the legal system but to articulate and classify legal doctrines.

Format and Scope. Entries in *Am. Jur. 2d* and *C.J.S.* are arranged alphabetically by topic but cover such broad areas of law as "contracts" or "trade regulation." Unlike a general encyclopedia, which may have thousands of relatively brief entries, each of the legal encyclopedias has under 500 articles. Some of these are extensive. The "Constitutional Law" and "Criminal Law" articles each cover five volumes and well over 1,000 sections in *C.J.S.*

Each article includes cross-references to topics treated elsewhere in the encyclopedia. *Am. Jur. 2d*'s cross-references are generally more specific and therefore more helpful. While *C.J.S.* simply notes related titles, *Am. Jur. 2d* provides lists of specific issues indicating the exact topic and section where they are discussed. In addition, it provides research references to texts, formbooks, and other practice materials. Most *Am. Jur. 2d* articles, and some *C.J.S.* articles, also include a table providing references to statutes and regu-

lations discussed. Some of these tables can be found at the beginning of the articles, while others appear in the back of the volumes.

Each topical article is divided into numbered sections and begins with a detailed table of contents. In *C.J.S.*, but not *Am. Jur. 2d*, almost every section begins with a brief summary of its legal principles in bold type (known generally as "black letter" law). This is followed by a detailed discussion of the legal principles.

One important feature of both encyclopedias is the inclusion of extensive footnotes—often a dozen or more per page—providing references to the cases from which the issue's principles are drawn. An encyclopedia article thus serves both as an explanation and as a tool for finding cases on a specific topic. Neither encyclopedia, unfortunately, indicates the dates of decisions it cites, so it may be unclear at first whether a case cited is a modern statement of the law or an obscure nineteenth-century decision.

Almost all the legal sources cited in the encyclopedias are court decisions. Some federal statutes and constitutional provisions are cited, as are uniform laws and model acts (legislation adopted by several jurisdictions in much the same format), but there are no references to statutes from individual states. This deliberate exclusion can lead to odd results, such as text discussing provisions of state statutory law accompanied by footnote references only to cases decided under those provisions. To find the relevant statutes, the reader must go first to the cases cited to find the necessary references.

Exhibits 3-2 and 3-3 show pages from *Am. Jur. 2d* and *C.J.S.*, discussing the right to trial by jury. These are both from recent volumes (1995 and 1997, respectively), so they reflect newer trends in format and style. Note that both encyclopedias provide references to the U.S. Constitution and numerous court opinions. The statement in *C.J.S.*, for example, that "the Seventh Amendment right to a jury trial should be liberally construed" contains a footnote referring to a 1992 opinion from a federal bankruptcy court. This is an odd choice for expertise on this topic because a bankruptcy court judge has no statutory power to conduct a jury trial. An overreliance on court opinions pervades the encyclopedias, leading to a rather stilted, patchwork writing style, with each proposition supported by one or more cited cases.

Some legal principles vary little from state to state and thus make good subjects for general encyclopedias such as these. Other topics are heavily dependent on state law, making the generalizations in *Am. Jur. 2d* or *C.J.S.* less than helpful. Some sections merely point out that some courts hold one way and others another way, with footnotes referencing a few selected cases. In areas where differences among states are distinct, there is no comprehensive summary of these state rules. For example, some states require two witnesses to sign a will while others require three witnesses. *C.J.S.* merely points out that statutory requirements must be met; *Am. Jur. 2d* notes the distinction, but its footnotes only provide case references to 6 states requiring three witnesses and 18 states requiring two. The other 26 states remain a mystery.

Some volumes in each encyclopedia are more than 30 years old—volume 33 of *C.J.S.* was published in 1942—but they are all kept up-to-date by means of annual supplements inserted into pockets in the back of each volume. These pocket parts include some new text but mostly provide references to new cases. This limits the utility of older volumes in areas where the law is changing. For more than a dozen years after *Roe v. Wade,* the "Abortion" articles in both encyclopedias continued to discuss criminal penalties, with *Roe* and subsequent cases mentioned only in the pocket parts. The current volume 58 of *C.J.S.,* published in 1948, includes an article on "Miscegenation"; the pocket part includes a brief note that the Supreme Court has held that miscegenation statutes violate the U.S. Constitution.

The age of many *C.J.S.* volumes hampers the encyclopedia's utility. Not only do old topics such as "Miscegenation" linger, but the older volumes, in attempting to summarize "all the reported cases," are densely footnoted with references to old and obscure cases. Some pages provide references to hundreds of cases. These older volumes also include brief entries providing judicial definitions, most of which are simply clutter. The entry for "Millwork," for example, says only, "As applied to window sash it includes ordinary glass properly set into the sash and ready to be placed in position in the building."

The times are gradually changing, however, for *C.J.S.* volumes published since 1986 have a cleaner, more readable format. The definitions are gone. A few older topics, such as "Barratry," "Blasphemy," and "Livery Stable Keepers," have disappeared or have been subsumed in other topics. Certain topics have been reworded to be less offensive to the modern ear. "Bastards" are now "Children Out-of-Wedlock," and "Drunkards" are now "Chemical Dependents"; the encyclopedia now contains a "Mental Health" article rather than one on "Insane Persons." Yet most of the 412 topics are the same as in 1936; only a handful of new articles covering recently created or rapidly developing areas of law, such as "Products Liability," "RICO (Racketeer Influenced and Corrupt Organizations)," or "Right to Die," appear.

Am. Jur. 2d and *C.J.S.* cover much the same ground. The majority of titles cover straightforward areas of discrete legal doctrine and appear in both works, e.g., "Adjoining Landowners," "Adverse Possession," and "Alteration of Instruments." Among *Am. Jur. 2d*'s 427 articles are a few titles that appear more responsive to recent changes in the law, such as "Advertising," "Alternative Dispute Resolution," and "Habitual Criminals and Subsequent Offenders."

The set arrangement of articles in both encyclopedias, however, means that they are slow to recognize new areas of law. *Am. Jur. 2d* does have a "New Topic Service" binder for subjects not yet covered in the main volumes, including "Americans with Disabilities Act" and "Real Estate Time-Sharing." It rarely contains more than a handful of articles, however. Generally the encyclopedias are the place to look for information on settled doctrine rather than developing areas.

When a volume approaches obsolescence or its pocket part grows too large, the editors rewrite the text of its articles and issue a replacement volume. By now, many volumes in both sets have been replaced at least once; a few volumes have been replaced more than once. The original *Am. Jur. 2d* volume covering "Bankruptcy," published in 1963, was replaced in 1980 by two new volumes, which in turn were replaced in 1991 by three volumes. (Because federal taxation changes so frequently, and because it is so important to keep abreast of new developments, the volumes in both sets covering this topic are replaced every year.) The age of the volume covering a particular subject is an important factor to consider in determining whether *Am. Jur. 2d* or *C.J.S.* provides a more worthwhile treatment. Other factors may influence a preference for one set or the other. For example, older volumes in each encyclopedia provide references to its publisher's other publications. Thus, *C.J.S.* includes corresponding West key numbers, which can be useful for finding cases in West's digests, while *Am. Jur. 2d* provides references to *American Law Reports (ALR)*, as well as Lawyers Cooperative's sets of formbooks and practice materials.

When a topic is revised and republished in a new edition, the publisher provides a conversion table in the new volume showing the location of topics discussed in the previous version. This is an important

1. OVERVIEW [§§ 3-12]

§ 3. Generally

The right to have a trial by jury is a fundamental right in our democratic system,[28] and is recognized as such in the Federal Constitution,[29] the constitutions of the various states,[30] state statutes[31] and procedural rules.[32]

The local law of the forum determines whether an issue shall be tried by the court or by a jury.[33] A refusal to grant a jury trial is harmless error only if the record shows that no material issues of fact exist and an instructed verdict would have been justified.[34]

While the denial of a jury demand is a nonappealable interlocutory order,[35] the Supreme Court has stated that a writ of mandamus is the appropriate remedy to require a jury trial where it has been improperly denied.[36] The failure to take an immediate appeal from a denial of right to jury trial does not result in a waiver of the right to appeal such determination.[37]

§ 4. Federal constitutional provisions, generally

The Seventh Amendment to the Constitution provides that in suits at common law, where the value in controversy shall exceed $20, the right of trial by jury shall be preserved, and no fact tried by a jury shall be otherwise re-examined in any court of the United States, than according to the rules of the common law.[38]

The Seventh Amendment, under which a jury trial is preserved in suits at common law, was designed to preserve the basic institution of jury trials only in its most fundamental elements, not the great mass of procedural forms and details which, even in 1791, varied widely among common-law jurisdictions.[39] The Seventh Amendment preserves to litigants the right to jury trial not merely in suits which the common law recognized among its old and settled

---

28. § 13.

29. § 4.

30. § 6.

31. Usner v Strobach (La App 1st Cir) 591 So 2d 713, cert den (La) 592 So 2d 1289.

32. Mountain States Tel. & Tel. Co. v Di Fede (Colo) 780 P2d 533; Lum v Sun, 70 Hawaii 288, 769 P2d 1091.

Forms: Orders granting a jury trial. 15 Am Jur Pl & Pr Forms (Rev), Jury, Forms 61-65.

33. Vanier v Ponsoldt, 251 Kan 88, 833 P2d 949, 19 UCCRS2d 90.

34. Grossnickle v Grossnickle (Tex App Texarkana) 865 SW2d 211.

35. Cochran v Birkel (CA6 Ohio) 651 F2d 1219, 32 FR Serv 2d 958, cert den 454 US 1152, 71 L Ed 2d 307, 102 S Ct 1020.

36. Beacon Theatres, Inc. v Westover, 359 US 500, 3 L Ed 2d 988, 79 S Ct 948, 2 FR Serv 2d 650.

As to trial by jury as subject of mandamus, generally, see 52 Am Jur 2d, Mandamus § 329.

Annotations: Mandamus or prohibition as remedy to enforce right to jury trial, 41 ALR2d 780.

37. EEOC v Corry Jamestown Corp. (CA3 Pa) 719 F2d 1219, 33 BNA FEP Cas 871, 32 CCH EPD ¶ 33860, 37 FR Serv 2d 1216.

38. US Const. Amend 7.

For discussion of the right to jury trial in criminal cases, see 21A Am Jur 2d, Criminal Law §§ 672-691, 890-900.

39. Galloway v United States, 319 US 372, 87 L Ed 1458, 63 S Ct 1077, reh den 320 US 214, 87 L Ed 1851, 63 S Ct 1443.

715

EXHIBIT 3-2

The right should not be lightly denied.[79] The law favors a trial by a jury,[80] and the right to such trial is carefully guarded against infringement,[81] particularly in criminal cases,[82] and cannot be taken away by implication.[83] However, the jury is not invariably a necessary component of accurate factfinding.[84]

Speaking generally, and subject to many exceptions and qualifications, the parties to a civil action usually have the right to a jury trial.[85]

It has been broadly stated that one accused of crime is entitled to a trial by a jury of his or her peers.[86]

§ 8.   Federal Constitution in General

   The Seventh Amendment to the federal Constitution provides that in suits at common law, where the value in controversy shall exceed twenty dollars, the right of trial by jury shall be preserved.

Library References

   Jury ⊜9, 10.

The Seventh Amendment to the federal Constitution provides that in suits at common law, where the value in controversy shall exceed twenty dollars, the right of trial by jury shall be preserved.[87] Neither the courts nor Congress can deprive a litigant of the right to a jury trial guaranteed by that provision.[88]

The Seventh Amendment right to a jury trial should be liberally construed.[89]

In order to ascertain the scope and meaning of the Seventh Amendment, resort must be had to the rules of the common law as of the time the amendment was adopted,[90] and the principle that the common law may be adapted to meet varying conditions does not apply in determining the scope and meaning of the amendment.[91] The amendment guarantees the right only as it existed at common law,[92] and it neither enlarged nor abridged the right.[93]

§ 9.   —— Criminal Cases in General

   Article III of the federal Constitution provides that the trial of all crimes, except in cases of impeachment, shall be by jury. The Sixth Amendment provides that, in all criminal prosecutions, the accused shall enjoy the right to a trial by an impartial jury of the state and district wherein the crime shall have been committed.

Library References

   Jury ⊜9, 10, 21.1.

Article III of the federal Constitution provides that the trial of all crimes, except in cases of impeachment, shall be by jury.[94] The Sixth Amendment to the federal Constitution provides that, in all criminal prosecutions, the accused shall enjoy the right to a trial by an impartial jury of the state and district wherein the crime shall have been committed.[95] Thus, trial by jury has been established by the Constitution as the normal and preferable mode of disposing of issues of fact in a

---

79. Fla.—Nunn v. Florida Air Conditioning and Refrigeration Corp., 197 So. 388, 143 Fla. 648.

Ill.—People ex rel. Barrett v. Fritz, 45 N.E.2d 48, 316 Ill.App. 217.

80. Ill.—People v. Jameson, 56 N.E.2d 790, 387 Ill. 367.

81. Ill.—Stephens v. Kasten, 48 N.E.2d 508, 383 Ill. 127.

Ind.—Kettner v. Jay, 26 N.E.2d 546, 107 Ind.App. 643.

Okl.—Graham v. State, 121 P.2d 308, 73 Okl.Cr. 337.

Wash.—Watkins v. Siler Logging Co., 116 P.2d 315, 9 Wash.2d 703.

82. Ga.—Flint River Steamboat Co. v. Foster, 5 Ga. 194.

83. Va.—W.S. Forbes & Co. v. Southern Cotton Oil Co., 108 S.E. 15, 130 Va. 245.

84. U.S.—McKeiver v. Pennsylvania, Pa., 91 S.Ct. 1976, 403 U.S. 528, 29 L.Ed.2d 647 (per Mr. Justice Blackmun with the Chief Justice and two Justices concurring, one Justice concurring in the judgments and one Justice concurring in the judgment in No. 322 and dissenting in No. 128).

85. Ill.—North American Provision Co. v. Kinman, 6 N.E.2d 235, 288 Ill.App. 414.

Kan.—Loveless v. Ott, 250 P. 324, 121 Kan. 728.

N.Y.—Jackson v. Jackson, 7 N.Y.S.2d 407, 255 A.D. 812.

N.C.—Grantham v. Nunn, 124 S.E. 309, 188 N.C. 239.

86. Fla.—State v. Lewis, 11 So.2d 337, 152 Fla. 178.

Ind.—Niemeyer v. McCarty, 51 N.E.2d 365, 221 Ind. 688, 154 A.L.R. 115.

N.Y.—People v. Hines, 12 N.Y.S.2d 454.

Tex.—In re Dendy, Civ.App., 175 S.W.2d 297, affirmed Dendy v. Wilson, 179 S.W.2d 269, 142 Tex. 460, 151 A.L.R. 1217.

87. U.S.C.A. Const.Amend. VII.

U.S.—Baltimore & Carolina Line v. Redman, N.Y., 55 S.Ct. 890, 295 U.S. 654, 79 L.Ed. 1636.

88. U.S.—Raytheon Mfg. Co. v. Radio Corporation of America, C.C.A.Mass., 76 F.2d 943, affirmed 56 S.Ct. 297, 296 U.S. 459, 80 L.Ed. 327.

89. U.S.—In re Beeline Engineering & Const., Inc., Bkrtcy.S.D.Fla., 139 B.R. 1025.

90. U.S.—Baltimore & Carolina Line v. Redman, N.Y., 55 S.Ct. 890, 295 U.S. 654, 79 L.Ed. 1636—Dimich v. Schiedt, Mass., 55 S.Ct. 296, 293 U.S. 474, 79 L.Ed. 603, 95 A.L.R. 1150.

   Deoorah Leslie, Ltd. v. Rona, Inc., D.R.I., 63 F.Supp. 1250.

91. U.S.—Dimick v. Schiedt, Mass., 55 S.Ct. 296, 293 U.S. 474, 79 L.Ed. 603, 95 A.L.R. 1150.

92. U.S.—Martin v. C.I.R., C.A.6, 756 F.2d 38.

93. U.S.—Fitzpatrick v. Sun Life Assur. Co. of Canada, D.C.N.J., 1 F.R.D. 713.

94. U.S.C.A. Const. art. 3, § 2.

95. U.S.C.A. Const.Amend. VI.

EXHIBIT 3-3

tool for readers who are tracking references found in an older case or other document. Without the conversion table, it could be difficult to find the current treatment of the subject matter. Of course, because a revised volume does not reprint outdated material from an earlier edition, it may occasionally be necessary to find the discussion in the superseded volume itself.

Coverage in *Am. Jur. 2d* and *C.J.S.* of minor topics affords some sense of comparison. "Common scold" is an obsolete (and now offensive) term applied to women who habitually quarreled with neighbors and committed breaches of the public peace. Both encyclopedias still contain articles on this topic. The *C.J.S.* article, published in 1967, is a mere page and a half; in 20 footnotes, it cites 13 cases from 5 jurisdictions (7 of them from Pennsylvania). The text concludes by noting that the traditional punishment by the ducking stool is obsolete, citing an 1825 case in which such a sentence was overturned. The only notes that the entire doctrine has been discredited are found in a brief "Now obsolete" footnote and in the pocket part, which cites a 1972 New Jersey case with the note "No longer an offense." *Am. Jur. 2d*'s treatment, published in 1975, is longer, with 3 pages and 27 footnotes. It only cites 12 cases, but covers 6 jurisdictions rather than 5. The more recent *Am. Jur. 2d* treatment has the benefit of the 1972 case, which pointed out that the offense is not only obsolete but unconstitutionally discriminatory, as by definition only a woman could be indicted as a common scold. *Am. Jur. 2d* directs readers to the more equitable topic "Breach of Peace and Disorderly Conduct."

Next, compare the encyclopedias' treatment of the now obscure topic of "Embracery," or corruptly influencing a juror or jury. Each encyclopedia has an article of about three pages in length. The *C.J.S.* article, published in 1992, has more extensive footnotes, citing 33 cases from 20 jurisdictions. *Am. Jur. 2d*'s 1996 treatment cites only 18 cases from 13 jurisdictions, but 8 of its cases (and one state) are not mentioned in *C.J.S.* (On the other hand, *C.J.S.* provides references to 23 cases and 8 states not in *Am. Jur. 2d*.) The odd thing is that neither embracery article explains the difference between the old common law crime of embracery and its modern equivalent, jury tampering. Both have notes pointing out that jury tampering is treated in the "Obstructing Justice" article, but why are they discussed separately? Although a dozen states and the federal government have laws against jury tampering, two states (Georgia and Maryland) use the term embracery for substantially the same offense. Yet even in the 1990s,

neither encyclopedia has managed to coordinate the old with the new and modernize its treatment. Deleting the obsolete parts of the "Embracery" article and incorporating the rest with the "Obstructing Justice" discussion would clear up some confusion.

Indexes and Electronic Access. Because legal encyclopedias contain so few articles and cover such broad topics, it is generally not possible to locate the relevant discussion simply by using the alphabetical arrangement. Instead, it is necessary to start in the general index at the end of the set.

Aware that their users need access to highly specific discussions within the encyclopedias, the publishers of *C.J.S.* and *Am. Jur. 2d* provide extensive indexes. These indexes are recompiled and reissued annually in softcover volumes. *Am. Jur. 2d* has a five-volume index with nearly 6,000 pages. The *C.J.S.* is only three volumes and almost 4,000 pages. A heading in the index may go on for a dozen pages, with detailed subheadings and sub-subheadings.

One aspect of the indexes that may be confusing at first is the reliance on extensive cross-references to keep from increasing the total number of pages far beyond reason. Looking under "Trial" for information on the right to trial by jury, one is led in *C.J.S.* to "Juries, generally, this index"; and in *Am. Jur. 2d* to "Jury and Jury Trial (this index)." In both cases, "this index" means to check under that heading in the general index. Once there, the reader finds 8 pages in *C.J.S.* and 14 pages in *Am. Jur. 2d*, with fine subdivisions of jury issues. (One subheading, "Sleeping—New Trial," leads to a note that a juror's falling asleep is not grounds for a new trial.)

Am. Jur. 2d also includes cross-references within a particular subject heading, by use of *supra* (above) and *infra* (below). It may not be immediately apparent that *supra* and *infra* refer to subheadings within the same subject heading, unless one has already seen the "this index" cross-references.

C.J.S. avoids the use of *supra* and *infra*, but it provides confusing cross-references of its own. In addition to references to other points in the general index, it includes cross-references to the title indexes found in the backs of some text volumes. These individual title indexes, also found in *Am. Jur. 2d* volumes, may be handy for people who know what general subject area they need, or to check related topics in a volume already in hand. Generally, however, the general index covering the entire set is the most thorough and up-to-date index available.

Sometimes the cross-references between headings and indexes are combined in ways designed to drive even experienced researchers crazy. In the *C.J.S.* general index under "Wills," the subheading "Witnesses" refers to "Subscribing witnesses, generally, this index." But when one turns to that heading, there is merely a second referral, this time to the title index for the "Wills" article.

When using an index to an encyclopedia or other legal work, patience is an invaluable virtue. Although the indexes are extensive, they cannot possibly cover every way in which an issue can be phrased. For example, in the case of right to trial by jury, it may take some hunting to find information. *Am. Jur. 2d* has nothing at all under "Right to Trial by Jury" or "Trial by Jury," although there is a page of listings under "Trial by Court." "Trials" refers only to the "Job Discrimination" article, but finally the singular noun "Trial" provides a cross-reference to "Jury and Jury Trial." *C.J.S.* does better. It too has nothing under "Trial by Jury," but "Right to Jury Trial" and "Trial" both provide cross-references to the "Juries" heading.

Other problems with the indexes may arise from a lack of familiarity with legal terminology. As noted above, both *Am. Jur. 2d* and *C.J.S.* contain brief articles on embracery, or attempting to influence a jury. But a reader who did not know the term embracery might never find those articles because there are no cross-references in either index under "Juries—Corrupting" or "Juries—Bribery." *C.J.S.* has nothing under "Juries—Influencing," while *Am. Jur. 2d* sends readers to the "Criminal Law" and "Obstructing Justice" articles.

The editors at *Am. Jur. 2d* are aware that their index is a formidable tool. The bottom of each page contains a note, "For assistance using this Index, call 1-800-527-0430." Even though help is available, it is worth investing the time to learn to navigate these complex indexes. The skill gained will prove valuable in using other legal resources, such as statutory codes and case digests, which also have detailed multivolume indexing systems.

An indexing problem may arise if a subject is covered in a brand-new volume, reissued since the most recent index. Now that *Am. Jur. 2d* and *C.J.S.* indexes are republished every year, this is not a frequent problem, but it can occur. The 1997 *C.J.S.* volume containing the "Juries" article, for example, does not match the index references in the 1997 index, published earlier that year. If an index reference produces a lead that appears to make no sense, check the publication date of the volume in question. If it is very recent, remem-

ber to check the section-to-section conversion table showing where material in the older volume now appears.

The final volume in the *Am. Jur. 2d* index includes a short Popular Names Table, an alphabetical list of federal statutes discussed in the set. In addition, the *Am. Jur. 2d* set includes a *Table of Statutes, Rules, and Regulations Cited* volume, listing these sources numerically by citation. This table can be useful to a researcher looking for an explanation of a particular federal law or regulation. Because the encyclopedia does not discuss statutes from individual states, however, the only state law sources listed are uniform laws and model acts.

Am. Jur. 2d is available on CD-ROM as *Am. Jur. 2d on LawDesk* and can be found on both LEXIS-NEXIS and WESTLAW under the name AMJUR. One can either search for a particular term, or browse through the table of contents of an article. An advantage of using *Am. Jur. 2d* online is that you can use hypertext links to jump immediately to the text of cases cited in the encyclopedia. The electronic versions are updated once a year with information from the annual pocket parts, although for some reason online updating lags several months behind issuance of the printed pocket parts.

WESTLAW also has two *C.J.S.* articles, "Insurance" (CJS-INS) and "Internal Revenue" (CJS-FTX). The insurance volumes were published in 1993, but WESTLAW presents material in the volume and in the latest pocket part as separate documents, rather than integrated into one document. This means that it would be easy to retrieve the main text using a keyword search and never realize that there may be relevant supplementary information. This is not a problem with CJS-FTX because West revises the internal revenue volumes annually.

State Encyclopedias

A state encyclopedia is a work much like *Am. Jur. 2d* or *C.J.S.*, but focusing on the law of a particular jurisdiction. Where the national encyclopedias must deal in general terms with legal principles applicable in numerous states, a state encyclopedia can cite specific statutes and discuss a discrete (and perhaps coherent) body of case law. A national encyclopedia can provide helpful background, but a state encyclopedia is able to outline the actual rules of law in force in that state. This can make a state encyclopedia much more useful than its national counterpart.

Generally, the state encyclopedias follow the format of *Am. Jur. 2d* or *C.J.S.*, with somewhat shorter articles and a slightly smaller number of topics. These are still substantial multivolume sets; *New York Jurisprudence 2d*, for example, has well over 100 volumes. The sets are also updated the same way as the general encyclopedias, with annual pocket part supplements and replacement volumes published on an irregular basis. A few of the sets include deskbooks, court rules pamphlets, or other materials.

Although the list of topics is fairly uniform, there are some differences among the states. Material under "Poisons and Drugs" in Michigan appears under "Food, Drugs, Poisons and Hazardous Substances" in Ohio. "Trailer and Mobile Home Parks" in New York becomes "Manufactured Housing and Mobile Homes" in Texas. The differences in terminology are rarely a barrier, however, because the usual place to begin research in a state encyclopedia is its index. Each set has an extensive index, usually consisting of several volumes, which provides a detailed analysis of its contents.

More important, obviously, are the substantive differences. Each encyclopedia discusses its own state's body of law. The number of witnesses needed for a valid will can be stated with specificity. Community property is discussed at length in the encyclopedias for California and Texas, but receives little notice in most other jurisdictions.

One other distinction among state encyclopedias is the other publications to which they provide cross-references. Encyclopedias generally include references to other works from the same publisher. West Publishing and Lawyers Cooperative are now both part of West Group, but most volumes predate the merger of these former competitors. Lawyers Cooperative encyclopedias include footnotes referring to *American Jurisprudence 2d* and *American Law Reports (ALR)*, while West encyclopedias provide digest key numbers for finding cases in West resources.

Unfortunately, state encyclopedias are available only for 17 states (listed in Table 3-1). There may be few advantages to living in a large state heavily populated with lawyers, but one is having a large enough market to support state-specific legal publications. The smaller states generally have a few resources focusing on their laws, such as practice guides, treatises, or continuing legal education materials. Most, however, do not have works providing comprehensive coverage of substantive and procedural matters in an alphabetical arrangement, thoroughly indexed.

Only the largest law libraries contain encyclopedias from other states, but the local encyclopedia will be found in most public and court law libraries, as well as in larger general collections. Many of the state encyclopedias are available on CD-ROM as well as in print, often as part of products that include access to state codes and court decisions as well; several are available online through LEXIS-NEXIS or WESTLAW.

CONSUMER GUIDES

Legal encyclopedias attempt to provide a comprehensive overview of the law, from antitrust enforcement to adoption of zoning regulations. Another type of publi-

---

TABLE 3-1

STATE LEGAL ENCYCLOPEDIAS

California Jurisprudence 3d	(Lawyers Cooperative [now West Group], 89 vols., 1972-date)
Florida Jurisprudence 2d	(Lawyers Cooperative [now West Group], 80 vols., 1977-date)
Encyclopedia of Georgia Law	(Harrison, 53 vols., 1977-date)
Illinois Law and Practice	(West [now LEXIS Law Publishing], 51 vols., 1953-date)
Indiana Law Encyclopedia	(West, 36 vols., 1957-date)
Maryland Law Encyclopedia	(West, 31 vols., 1960-date)
Michigan Civil Jurisprudence	(Lawyers Cooperative [now West Group], 31 vols., 1957-date)
Michigan Law and Practice	(West [now LEXIS Law Publishing], 31 vols., 1955-date)
Dunnell Minnesota Digest, 3d/4th eds.	(Butterworth [now LEXIS Law Publishing], 51 vols., 1989-date)
Summary of Mississippi Law	(Lawyers Cooperative [now West Group], 4 vols., 1969-date)
New York Jurisprudence 2d	(Lawyers Cooperative [now West Group], 138 vols., 1979-date)
Strong's North Carolina Index 4th	(Lawyers Cooperative [now West Group], 42 vols., 1989-date)
Ohio Jurisprudence 3d	(Lawyers Cooperative [now West Group], 108 vols., 1977-date)
Pennsylvania Law Encyclopedia	(West [now LEXIS Law Publishing], 53 vols., 1957-date)
Tennessee Jurisprudence	(Michie [now LEXIS Law Publishing], 29 vols., 1982-date)
Texas Jurisprudence 3d	(Lawyers Cooperative [now West Group], 96 vols., 1979-date)
Michie's Jurisprudence of Virginia and West Virginia	(Michie [now LEXIS Law Publishing], 48 vols., 1948-date)

cation, the consumer guide, covers a much narrower gamut of legal issues relevant to the average person. Such works summarize issues that arise in everyday life and provide a general overview of the law. In many instances, they may provide all the information that is needed.

There are, however, two major drawbacks to these self-help guides. Like *Am. Jur. 2d* and *C.J.S.*, they are written for a national audience and therefore cannot focus on the specific legal doctrine of any particular jurisdiction. Unlike the encyclopedias and most other legal publications, the consumer guides provide few (if any) references to cases, statutes, and other sources. Therefore, they can rarely be used as springboards to further research.

A large number of books provide consumers with information on legal topics. They are all written for much the same audience and seek to explain legal issues in everyday language. They cover such basic concerns as marriage and divorce, buying and selling a home, consumer credit, automobiles, and workplace rights. Although coverage is similar, differences exist among these books both in style and scope.

The most extensive of the consumer works is the American Bar Association's *Family Legal Guide* (Times Books, 1994). The guide is written by lawyers but is designed to be free of legalese. Each chapter was written by a specialist in the area and reviewed by several practicing attorneys. The entire volume is written in a question-and-answer format, a useful way to raise legal issues, although one that can eventually grow tiresome. The book features numerous sidebars and boxes that summarize specific issues, as well as several charts that compare state laws on such topics as the factors considered in awarding alimony or spousal support.

One disadvantage of *Family Legal Guide* is that the chapters are based on classifications of legal principles (tort, contract, etc.) rather than real-life concerns, so coverage of some issues is scattered among several chapters. For example, various aspects of pet ownership are discussed throughout the volume. Purchasing a pet appears under "Contracts and Consumer Law," damages for injury to a pet are discussed under "Personal Injury," and restrictions on pets in rental leases are treated in "Renting Residential Property." Liability for dog bites and problems of vicious dogs are covered in chapters on homeownership and personal injury. The homeownership treatment discusses ways to prevent injuries, while the personal injury section focuses solely on liability (post-bite) issues.

One of the most user-friendly of the guides is produced by Nolo Press, a leading publisher of legal information for consumers. *Nolo's Everyday Law Book: Answers to Your Most Frequently Asked Legal Questions* (1996) is edited by Shae Irving, but it includes chapters by more than a dozen other Nolo authors and editors. The coverage is not as extensive as that found in the *Family Legal Guide*. The only aspect of pet ownership discussed is what to do about a neighbor's dog that barks all the time. This is, however, one of the few works in this genre to survey the laws of all 50 states. It includes such helpful features as a list providing citations to landlord–tenant statutes in each state and comparative tables of each state's approach to such topics as common-law marriages and joint custody. The volume also includes references to other publications (both Nolo and non-Nolo) and Web sites.

Nolo's Everyday Law Book also provides a focus on how *not* to become involved in the legal system. Features such as ways to make your home safer are helpful. Even more refreshing are notes such as "A Little Common Sense" in the section on property boundaries: "If a problem exists on your border, keep the lines of communication open with the neighbor, if possible . . . . Boundary lines simply don't matter that much to us most of the time; relationships with our neighbors matter a great deal." The note advises people who are having no trouble with their neighbors to consider the time, money, and hostility that might be involved in rushing out to determine their exact boundaries.

Another clearly written and helpful work is Jill Rachlin's *Kiplinger's Handbook of Personal Law* (Kiplinger Books, 1995). Rachlin's book is practically organized, written in a straightforward manner, and includes useful examples and entertaining cartoons. It also provides references to more detailed books from the ABA, Nolo Press, and other publishers. Again, however, coverage is limited, and the only discussion of animals addresses liability issues in cases of dog bite. The *Handbook of Personal Law* is also available electronically as a component of *Kiplinger's Home Legal Advisor* (Block Financial Corp., 1996), a software product containing a variety of contracts and other documents.

Carol Haas et al.'s *The Consumer Reports Law Book: Your Guide to Resolving Everyday Legal Problems* (Consumer Reports Books, 1994) also has much valuable information, but it may be more difficult to use because it has only a one-page table of contents with broad chapters such as "Contracts" and "Civil Rights and Personal Freedoms." There is no indication of what specific topics these chapters cover. The text itself is helpful, with clear explanations and numerous examples illustrating appropriate actions to take to minimize legal difficulties. *Consumer Reports* provides one of the best treatments of topics related to pets of any of these books. The first chapter, "The Family," includes a problems with pets section covering not only dog bites but such issues as buying a pet, licenses, vaccinations, leash laws, and cruelty to animals. The treatment is concise but thorough, addressing related issues that arise in the course of pet ownership.

One of the newer consumer reference guides is John Ventura's *Law for Dummies* (IDG Books, 1996). Part of the popular *Dummies* series that began with computer software programs but has expanded to cover such topics as golf and sex, this book follows the same format as its predecessors. It is written in the conversational *Dummies* tone, with many of the same icons found in the computer titles—such as a bull's-eye for "tip" and a bomb for "warning." Icons point out other publications and Web sites with further information, and chapters list such information as "ten great free and almost-free sources of information" and "top ten law-related home pages." The *Dummies* book provides a brief introduction to the legal system, with nine chapters covering "laws that affect your daily life" and five chapters on "tough stuff: being sick, getting older, dying." Coverage extends to immigration, juvenile laws, criminal law, and privacy. Here, the only mention of animals is a note that many states prohibit leaving property to pets in wills. This is one of the most readable of the self-help law books; like other *Dummies* books, it packs a lot of information into a format that is user friendly but gets a bit too cute at times.

The CourtTV Cradle-to-Grave Legal Survival Guide: A Complete Resource for Any Question You Might Have About the Law (Little, Brown, 1995), by the editors of CourtTV and the *American Lawyer*, has an interesting approach, with chapters tracking legal questions chronologically from birth (covering birth certificates and names), to being a kid and going to school, to owing money, retiring, and dying. After the chapter on dying, rather ominously, come chapters on the legal system, suing and being sued, and finding and using a lawyer. This book contains much useful information, although, again, coverage of animal issues is limited, with treatment only of dog-bite and testamentary issues. Like the ABA *Family Legal Guide*, this work uses a question-and-answer approach. Each section of questions is preceded by an example from the lives of a hypothetical family. This unfortunate family is faced

with almost every possible legal dilemma, from custody battles to criminal charges. (Beatrice and Max, for example, divorce in Chapter 12 but are expecting a baby in Chapter 24.)

Melvin M. Belli, Sr., and Allen P. Wilkinson's *Everybody's Guide to the Law* (Harcourt Brace Jovanovich, 1986) is the oldest guide discussed in this section, but it is still found in many libraries and contains much useful information. It has, for example, the best coverage of animal issues of any of the guides. An entire chapter on animals covers most of the issues found in the other guides and discusses liability issues at some length (including such variations as injury to a visitor who leaps back to avoid a snarling dog and is injured in a fall). A section on veterinarians explains that pet owners are generally *not* liable if their dog bites its doctor but that the veterinarian can hold the dog if the owner does not pay its bill.

One final volume worth mentioning is Steven Mitchell Sack's *The Lifetime Legal Guide* (Book-of-the-Month Club, 1996). This guide is arranged differently from the others, with 74 alphabetical entries from "Abuse" to "Zoning Laws." Numerous cross-references punctuate the book, but it contains neither a table of contents nor an index. It does include a number of sample forms of letters and contracts, as well as boxes showing the elements of various causes of action and the ways these elements are proved. This is a serious tome, with no mention of dog bites or other animal issues.

Other similar volumes include George Gordon Coughlin's *Your Handbook of Everyday Law* (Harper Perennial, 5th ed., 1993); Alice K. Helm's *E Z Legal Advisor* (E Z Legal Books, 1995); Daniel Johnson's *The Consumer's Guide to Understanding and Using the Law* (Betterway Books, 1994); and Robert D. Rothenberg and Steven J. Blumenkrantz's *Personal Law: A Practical Legal Guide* (Wiley, 1986). Each offers slightly different features but covers much the same territory. Any might be useful in answering basic legal questions.

As noted at the outset, one major shortcoming of all these books is that they provide few research leads. Although most include addresses and telephone numbers for agencies that can provide further assistance (the *CourtTV Cradle-to-Grave Legal Survival Guide* and *Kiplinger's Handbook of Personal Law* include helpful sidebars with addresses, while the *Consumer Reports Law Book* and ABA's *Family Legal Guide* include "Where to Go for Help" or "Where to Get More Information" sections at the end of each chapter), there is little direction for a person eager to take the next step in learning more. None provide citations for the major federal statutes they discuss, such as the Civil Rights Act of 1964 or the Americans with Disabilities Act, so that readers can find the text of the statute and cases that interpret it. *The CourtTV Cradle-to-Grave Legal Survival Guide* discusses leading "Cases in Point" but does not even provide their names. Where differences exist in state laws, most of these books fail to indicate which state falls into which category, let alone provide references to state statutory codes or cases. Only Nolo's *Everyday Law Book* includes a brief discussion of how to find a law library and do your own legal research.

WEB SITES

The Internet is at once the most accessible and the most chaotic of legal sources. Thousands of Internet sites provide access to legal information, but it is not always clear which sites are worthwhile and which contain misleading information or are primarily marketing ploys.

Some of the most valuable legal resources on the Web are the government sites providing access to primary sources that had in the past been available only in law libraries or through commercial online services at considerable expense. Sites such as those sponsored by state legislatures or the U.S. Government Printing Office are making primary materials more widely accessible than ever before.

In addition to sites from specific agencies or jurisdictions, a growing number of sites can be used as starting points in finding legal information. These sites allow the researcher to view information from a variety of sources, usually by providing links to other Web pages.

As with any Internet research, the two basic approaches to finding legal information are through directories and search engines. This section focuses on a few of the more comprehensive resources. Anything written about the Internet is obsolete long before the ink dries, but these resources have been around for a long time (months, even years), and chances are that they will improve with age rather than wither away and be supplanted by new entrants.

When using legal information from the Internet, it is always important to determine the authority and timeliness of the source. Some pages are produced by government agencies; others are provided by individuals or organizations. Private sites provide useful information, but one should evaluate them before taking their

information at face value. A site may advocate only one side of a controversial issue and omit important information, or it may simply be out of date. A Web site that is not regularly updated may provide dangerously misleading information. Tread carefully if a site does not clearly indicate when it was most recently updated—or if it includes notes of material that is expected to be added in 1996 or 1997. The Internet is littered with abandoned sites that are not tended on a regular basis.

Directories and Compilations

The best Internet directories arrange resources by subject into a coherent body of information. A simple alphabetical list of resources may be useful for someone searching for a specific known item, but it provides precious little information about the range of resources available. Alphabetization has its purposes, of course, as in indexes, but it is best used in conjunction with other, thematic approaches. A list in which *Anarand* (a Supreme Court case) is followed alphabetically by "Arkansas" and "Australia" is of little use to someone needing an introductory overview or an orientation to available resources.

The archetypal subject site on the Internet, familiar to many, is Yahoo <http://www.yahoo.com>. This interdisciplinary site features extensive coverage of legal matters and is often the first stop for legal researchers new to the Internet. In the "Government" category, the subheading "Law" leads to a number of additional categories, including specific jurisdictions and more than two dozen legal subject categories. Some of the links include Yahoo ratings and reviews. In addition to using the hierarchical index, it is possible to keyword search either in all of Yahoo or in a particular section or subsection. Yahoo's searching is not as sophisticated as other search engines, however; its strength is in its indexing and organization of resources.

Because Yahoo is a general interest resource, its legal resources are not as thoroughly organized as those of commercial sites and law school research homepages that focus specifically on legal information. A Web site's strength lies in the breadth of material to which it provides access, the ways it organizes this access to make relevant information easy to find, and the accuracy with which it is updated and maintained.

One of the best legal sites is FindLaw <http://www.findlaw.com>. FindLaw not only provides access to law school Web sites, legal journals, and government sources, but it organizes sites and resources into subject pages so that a searcher can survey the major sites in more than 35 topical areas. One of the most valuable aspects of these subject pages is that their links are organized into major classes of material. One can browse through links to the major primary sources available on the Net, as well as specialized electronic publications or mailing lists. These links are followed by an alphabetical list of other relevant Web sites. Exhibit 3-4 is a printout of the introductory screen for FindLaw, showing the range of material and subjects available.

FindLaw has several other interesting features. Users are not limited to the categories of legal topics; they can also search an index for sources matching particular keywords. More extensive search capabilities include a feature for searching the full text of online legal journals, and a search engine, LawCrawler, which uses AltaVista software to search legal sites.

Other commercial sites also worth noting include the following:

- American Law Sources On-line (ALSO!) <http://www.lawsource.com/also> provides information for each jurisdiction (federal and state), with links organized into *law* (cases, statutes, and other primary authorities), *commentary* (law reviews, newsletters, and other articles), and *practice* (various resources, including court information and topical Web sites).

- CataLaw <http://www.catalaw.com>, a meta-index, provides access to information from more than 100 legal indexes on the Internet. It calls itself a "catalog of catalogs of law on the Internet" and provides lists of sites by topic or by region. These topical lists indicate focused sites (resources dedicated to that particular subject) and "usual suspects" (more comprehensive sites that include information on the given topic), as well as cross-references to related topics of interest.

- Hieros Gamos <http://www.hg.org> is a comprehensive legal site produced by Lex Mundi, an international association of law firms. It offers a wide range of information, including links organized into more than 200 different subject areas. Hieros Gamos also includes an extensive directory of law-related organizations.

- The Internet Legal Resource Guide <http://www.ilrg.com> is an index of selected legal Web sites with substantive information. ILRG is organized into sections for academia (including course outlines and information on law school rankings), the legal profession (legal forms, law firms, legal associations, and a topical index of resources), and legal research (search engines and indexes). A sis-

ter site, LawRunner, provides a search engine for finding information on other Web sites.

Several law schools have also done excellent jobs of organizing legal material and presenting links to pertinent sites. Almost every law school library provides this service to some extent. Among the leaders in providing subject access are the following:

- Cornell Law School's Legal Information Institute <http://www.law.cornell.edu>, which provides links to "Legal Material Organized by Topic" and "Legal Material Organized by Type and Source." The topical list is organized into 18 broad categories, with more than 100 subtopics, providing links to federal and state statutes, case law, and other Internet sources. One resource available through Cornell is its library's Cornell Legal Research Encyclopedia <http://www.law.cornell.edu/library>, a directory of sources available through various print and electronic formats. Subjects covered include traditional doctrinal areas such as torts, and social issues such as the death penalty; religion and law; and sexuality and law. The listings include primary sources available through the Internet and through the online systems LEXIS-NEXIS and WESTLAW; major treatises; topical journals; and links to organizations, topical Web sites, and Internet discussion groups. Coverage of print resources is limited to those materials available at Cornell.

- WashLaw WEB <http://lawlib.wuacc.edu> is one of the most comprehensive law school sites, with access to U.S. and foreign materials, legal organizations, law journals, discussion groups, and many other categories of information. Full-text searching of many of its resources is available.

- The University of Southern California Law Library <http://www.usc.edu/dept/law-lib>, which has a topic list of legal resources on the Internet, with mostly annotated links, as well as listings of electronic journals, law schools, and organizations.

- The World Wide Web Virtual Library: Law at the University of Indiana <http://www.law.indiana.edu/law/v-lib> is a component of the World Wide Web Consortium. It provides access to legal information by organization type (law schools, law firms, government servers) and topic, along with an extensive list of other comprehensive sites, including many of those already mentioned in this section.

LegalMinds
Community

Laws
Cases & Codes

FindLaw
Internet Legal Resources

LegalNews
Today's News

LawCrawler
Web Search

US Supreme Court
Cases 1893+ Free!

Build your practice with a home page from West Group. Click Here

Antitrust, Microsoft and
the USDOJ

1997 US Federal and State Tax Forms

| | Search | FindLaw Guide | ▼ | [options] |

LawCrawler - LegalMinds - Supreme Court Opinions - Law Reviews - Bookstore - **Free Web Sites**
Message Boards - Chat - Online CLE - Career Center - Legal Jobs - Legal News

Legal Subject Index
Constitutional, Intellectual Property Labor...

Law Schools
Law Reviews, Outlines, Student Resources...

Professional Development
Career Development, CLE, Employment...

Legal Organizations
National Bars, State Bars, Local Bars ...

Law Firms & Lawyers
Lawyers WWW sites, NLJ 250...

Consultants & Experts

Directories
Government, Yellow Pages, Phone, Maps...

Laws: Cases & Codes
Supreme Court Opinions, Constitution, State Laws...

U.S. Federal Government Resources

State Law Resources
California, New York, Texas...

Foreign & International Resources
Country Pages, Int'l Law, Int'l Trade...

News & Reference
Legal News, Library Information...

Legal Practice Materials
Forms, Publishers, Software & Technology...

LegalMinds - Community
Message Boards, Mailing List Archives, Chat...

FINDLAW

EXHIBIT 3-4

In addition, the American Bar Association provides LAW*link* <http://www.abanet.org/lawlink>, designed to be a starting point for legal research. It has a list of links to government resources organized by jurisdiction and branch, as well as law schools and other Internet research points. The ABA's list is not the most thorough or up-to-date, but it does provide a view of what the nation's leading organization of lawyers considers to be useful resources.

A number of Web sites provide information on consumer legal issues. Although most are not extensive, they can provide a starting place for legal research. For example, the self-help department of Legal Pad <http://www.legalpad.com/self-help/> includes information on a dozen different areas, including bankruptcy, taxes, employment law, and family law. Legal Pad also specializes in providing legal information for children and teenagers.

The CourtTV homepage <http://www.courttv/com> is a rather claustrophobic site with lots of promotional material. Its focus is on trials in the news (and broadcast on CourtTV) and on promoting opportunities to buy trinkets such as pencils with erasers shaped like gavels. But the site also includes a short glossary of legal terms and consumer legal information from *The CourtTV Cradle-to-Grave Legal Survival Guide*.

Search Engines

The technology of search engines continues to develop, as services such as AltaVista <http://altavista.digital.com> and HotBot <http://www.hotbot.com> fine-tune their ability to zero in on documents matching queries. A number of search engines exist, each with different strengths. No single search engine can find everything on the Web, so it is important to be familiar with more than one. Even more important is learning one well enough to take advantage of its advanced search techniques to focus retrieval.

One way to decide on the best search engine for a specific purpose may be to begin with a site that uses several of them. MetaCrawler <http://www.metacrawler.com>, for example, uses several of the major search engines, including AltaVista and HotBot, and its retrieval ranks material for relevance and indicates which search engine is responsible for finding each item. A meta-search site cannot take advantage of the advanced techniques of an individual engine, but its broader net may turn up material that might otherwise be missed.

One thing that search engines are not good at is distinguishing between substantive legal sources and tangential information. A search for "sexual harassment," for example, may turn up a list of Texas attorneys working in the area and information about assistance programs at the University of Toronto. (A search in Excite <http://www.excite.com> for "sexual harassment" found well over 1,000 documents, but these were shown on a screen advertising an all-XXX search engine—perhaps raising a new set of harassment concerns.) Using a search engine may require one to scan through many entries to find those few that can provide background information on a topic.

The general search engines are far more useful when searching for specific information. Using names or other unique terms allows them to zero in on organizational Web pages, biographical information, or postings by a particular person.

Subject searches for legal information are generally more effective with search engines limited to legal sites, such as FindLaw's LawCrawler <http://www.lawcrawler.com> or ILRG's LawRunner <http://www.lawrunner.com>. Both LawCrawler and LawRunner use AltaVista software to create searches automatically limited to sites with legal information. These search engines allow the user to restrict a query to information from particular jurisdictions or specific agencies of government. The results through LawCrawler and LawRunner are similar because they both use AltaVista; one difference is that LawRunner shows the advanced AltaVista syntax it uses to narrow a search to specific sites. This can be helpful for someone interested in learning how to structure more effective searches.

Mailing Lists and Newsgroups

Among the most valuable sources for information on the Internet are other Internet users. Material on Web pages is minuscule compared with what is available in the minds of scholars and researchers. Besides personal e-mail, two simple ways that interested persons can share ideas through the Internet are through mailing lists and newsgroups. A mailing list, or listserver, is a discussion group in which subscribers share messages through e-mail. Newsgroups serve a similar function but operate more like bulletin boards; messages are read and postings are accepted through newsreader or Web browser software. Monitoring the messages in a specialized list or newsgroup is one of the easiest ways to develop a familiarity with basic terminology and current concerns.

Several hundred mailing lists and newsgroups focus on legal topics. The most extensive listing of these sources is Law Lists <http://www.lib.uchicago.edu/cgi-bin/law-lists>, maintained by Lyonette Louis-Jacques at the University of Chicago Law School. Law Lists is searchable for list names or summaries containing particular terms. Search results provide information about the scope of a list and instructions for subscribing, with hypertext links for sending subscription requests.

The University of Oklahoma's Directory of Law-Related Discussion Groups <http://www.law.ou.edu/lists/> also provides convenient access to subscription information and addresses for more than 200 lists. The Oklahoma site simply lists groups by name. A disadvantage of this is that although the focus of some groups (such as Cong-Reform or Dispute-Res) will be self-evident, it may not immediately be apparent that a discussion group called Dirt is about real estate law.

The information shared in mailing lists and newsgroups can have continuing value if older messages are archived and available to researchers. Scanning through a list of subject lines of old messages is seldom productive, but archives searchable by keyword can form a substantial body of accumulated knowledge. Both LawLists and the Oklahoma directory include links to sources for list archives.

Another collection of information on mailing lists is available in the "Legal Minds" service of FindLaw <http://www.legalminds.org>. This service lists groups by subject and by professional interest (judges, lawyers, law librarians, students). Summary pages for each list indicate how many messages there are per month (which may be an important consideration in deciding whether to subscribe), provide subscription instructions, and present a sampling of recent messages.

Deja News <http://www.dejanews.com> and AltaVista both allow keyword searching of the archives of thousands of newsgroups. The articles retrieved may be useful in their own right, and they can also provide clues to which newsgroups are most likely to discuss a topic (and perhaps be most likely to answer a query or provide research leads). Results may even suggest approaches that would not otherwise be considered. A search for "sexual harassment," for example, retrieves not only messages from groups such as *alt.feminism* and *misc.legal*, but also discussion in *rec.arts.sf.tv. babylon5* and *misc.fitness.weights*.

Published Guides

Although printed directories of Web sites tend to grow rapidly out of date, they may be useful as starting points in determining what is available.

One of the most extensive printed sources on Internet legal information is James Evans's *Law on the Net* (Nolo Press, 2d ed., 1997). This book provides little background information or instruction on the Internet generally, but it lists more than 2,000 resources, beginning with general collections and search engines. Sources of federal and state law are followed by law schools and other institutions, legal organizations, publications, and discussion groups. The final section, spanning nearly 250 pages, is a topical listing with nearly 80 subject headings. This arrangement is a substantial improvement over the first edition, which lumped the major comprehensive and primary resources into the same alphabetical listing with the specialized topical sites. The entries for all these resources provide access information, but little description. A "What's There" section simply lists the contents as they appear on the listed sites' screens, and only a few sites have additional editorial comments. The volume includes an extensive keyword index; even better, it is published with a searchable CD-ROM containing the same information as the printed volume. Using the CD-ROM in conjunction with an Internet browser eliminates the need to copy long URLs from the printed page.

Several other books list Internet sites and also provide background information on using the Internet. Because they are more expensive than *Law on the Net*, however, they are likely to be found in fewer libraries and bookstores. Ultimately, determining which title is most useful at any given time may depend on which was most recently published.

Yvonne J. Chandler's *Neal-Schuman Guide to Legal and Regulatory Information on the Internet* (Neal-Schuman, 1998) is one of the most extensive of the guides. Six chapters list sites and cover guides and meta-indexes; judicial materials; government information generally; legislative information; administrative law; and secondary reference sources. Each chapter or section begins with a brief introduction explaining the types of resources under discussion, and Web sites are listed alphabetically or by jurisdiction with brief annotations. Each chapter concludes with a list of "best bets," but these don't narrow the wide field of choices much. The volume includes indexes by subject and by Web site name.

Don MacLeod's *Internet Guide for the Legal Researcher* (Infosources Publishing, 2d ed., 1997) devotes one page to each major federal Internet site and two pages to sites from each state. The federal section mostly reproduces each site's main page; the limitation to one page means that there can be little discussion of major sites, such as the Library of Congress's THOMAS, or extensive agency sites, such as that of the Environmental Protection Agency. Even worse, pages are wasted on sites with little legal content, such as the Marines and Coast Guard. The treatment of states is more descriptive and is better served by such even-handedness; each section discusses access to executive, legislative, and judicial materials, as well as sites for the state library, state bar association, and local resources. The book begins with introductory chapters on how such Internet functions as listservs, Usenet, and HTML work. The volume includes useful chapters on indexes and search engines and on general reference sources on the Web.

Josh Blackman's *How to Use the Internet for Legal Research* (Find/SVP, 1996) provides a brief and readable introduction to the Internet and its use in legal practice. Despite its title, the book provides only limited information on legal research techniques. However, Chapter 5, "Legal Research on the Internet," provides some helpful tips and illustrations of Internet sites, as well as an interesting discussion of the reliability and accuracy of information obtained from the Internet. More than half of Blackman's book consists of a directory of Internet sites. Substantive resources are listed by jurisdiction, with federal material followed by individual states, foreign countries, and other sources of international legal information. These are followed by more than 20 pages of discussion lists and by publications available online, such as journals, newsletters, and directories. The final section lists several centralized legal servers that provide links to other sites, such as those discussed earlier in this section.

The Legal List: Research on the Internet by Diana Botluk (West Group, 1997) also includes lists of Web sites and discussion groups. The first three chapters provide an introductory overview of Internet basics and techniques for finding legal information, and are followed by eight chapters on different types of sources, such as legislative material, judicial opinions, and secondary authority. Each contains a useful introduction and lists of sources.

LEGAL COMPENDIA

A legal compendium serves a different purpose than the other resources discussed in this chapter. This is the place to go not for a summary of the law but for addresses, statistical data, or organizational charts. Compendia provide a broad range of information about the legal system, usually reprinted from a variety of sources. Their value is as a one-stop resource for locating a variety of information.

One of the handiest works in this genre is Arlene L. Eis's *The Legal Researcher's Desk Reference* (Infosources Publishing, biennial). This volume includes a diverse collection of information in 12 chapters and just over 400 pages. The texts of the Declaration of Independence and the Constitution are followed by directories of all three branches of the federal government, tables of presidents and Supreme Court justices, and outlines of the *United States Code* and the *Code of Federal Regulations*. State information includes directories of governors, attorneys general, secretaries of state, and other major officials; charts showing the court structure of each state; and a handy list of state codes, reporters, and regulatory publications, showing names and publishers, number of volumes, and frequency of publication. The book also contains directories of embassies, consular offices, legal publishers, bar associations, law schools, and legal newspapers. It concludes with a brief miscellany of economic and reference data. A detailed table of contents and a three-page index provide convenient access.

The Lawyer's Almanac (Aspen Law & Business, annual) is a much thicker volume, well over 1,000 pages, but does not yield its information as conveniently as *The Legal Researcher's Desk Reference*. The book has a detailed table of contents, but no index. It focuses on information on the legal profession, with profiles of the nation's largest law firms (from the newsletter *Of Counsel*), statistics on lawyer compensation and bar examinations, and continuing legal education requirements for each state. This material takes up more than half the volume, with the remainder including directory information on court and executive personnel in federal and state jurisdictions (reprinted from the *United States Court Directory* and other sources), and summaries of state laws governing motorist liability and handguns (courtesy of the American Automobile Association and the National Rifle Association).

The Lawyer's Almanac is a rather unwieldy tome with a discordant variety of typographical arrangements. Almost everything is photocopied directly from other sources. Some material is printed sideways to fit the pages, while other pages are nearly blank. Some pages from the *United States Court Directory* list just one telephone number. Would it have been that much more expensive to scan the information and reset it in a more economical format? A typical example of the volume's problems is its three lists of abbreviations: acronyms reprinted from the *United States Government Manual*; a list of reporters and texts reprinted from *Corpus Juris Secundum*; and a list of journal abbreviations from the *Index to Legal Periodicals*. If you're unfamiliar with an abbreviation, which list do you check? The book does have some useful features, such as a good, up-to-date annotated list of more than 100 legal Web sites.

West's Legal Desk Reference (West Publishing, 1991), compiled by William P. Statsky, Bruce L. Hussey, Michael R. Diamond, and Richard H. Nakamura, is an even larger volume (more than 1,500 pages); several major sections could well have been published as separate works. These include a legal dictionary spanning more than 200 pages, a lengthy list of federal statutes, and charts of state judicial systems. One of the most useful sections is "Research by Subject," almost 500 pages listing basic resources by topic as well as by state or country. The subject entries provide references to specialized journals, treatises and loose-leaf services, and subject headings in legal encyclopedias, digests, and periodical indexes. The state entries list research guides, statutory sources, administrative regulations, court reports, journals focusing on state law, and treatises (listed alphabetically by title). Directory information is provided in a "Useful Addresses" section. The volume contains no preface or explanation of how its contents were chosen or in what ways they are expected to work together.

American Jurisprudence 2d (discussed earlier in this chapter) is accompanied by a *Deskbook* with a variety of documents, tables, and statistics. It is divided into four sections: "Federal Matters," "International

Matters," "National and State Matters," and "Research and Practice Aids." Some directory information is included, but the *Deskbook* tends to focus more on charts and tables reprinted from sources such as the *United States Government Manual,* the *Statistical Abstract*, or the *Book of the States*. The volume is an odd assortment of material ranging from statistics on immigration to medical diagrams of wrist fractures and a "helicopter accident glossary." Like the rest of *Am. Jur. 2d*, the *Deskbook* is updated each year with a cumulative pocket part supplement. Unfortunately, the supplement's table of contents lists only items added in the latest update. Useful items carried over from previous supplements, such as an environmental law glossary and a list of legal abbreviations, are not listed. There is no index to the supplement, so these items are effectively hidden from view unless one happens upon them.

Lawyer's Desk Book (Prentice Hall, 10th ed., 1995, with 1997 supp.) is a different type of compendium, providing concise summaries of 45 areas of law. It functions as a quick review, answering questions such as "Who is a principal?" in the "Agents, Principals and Independent Contractors" chapter. References are provided to relevant law review articles and, less frequently, to treatises and hornbooks. The volume also includes a variety of statistical tables and charts.

FORMBOOKS

Finally, we turn to a group of often overlooked resources. Formbooks provide examples of contracts, leases, court pleadings, and other documents. They are an essential practice tool for many lawyers, and can also be a valuable resource for nonlawyers trying to draft a lease, prepare a service agreement, or file a complaint.

The best formbook publications contain more than just sample documents. In addition, they provide background information on the legal issues involved, checklists of actions to take and points to consider, and cross-references to legal encyclopedias and other publications. Several comprehensive sets of forms are published in print and CD-ROM, as well as a number of smaller works designed for consumer use and a growing number of forms collections on the Internet.

The formbooks discussed in this section are designed for use throughout the United States. Formbooks are also published for individual states and for federal practice. These may include insights and local court specifications that the national publications cannot provide. (On the other hand, few jurisdiction sets contain as extensive a variety of forms as these comprehensive collections.)

One of the most readily accessible of the multivolume sets is *American Jurisprudence Legal Forms 2d* (Lawyers Cooperative [now West Group], 46 vols., 1971-date). As is apparent from its title, this is an adjunct to *American Jurisprudence 2d*; the encyclopedia includes footnote cross-references to relevant forms, and the formbook provides references to legal discussions in *Am. Jur. 2d*. The set is organized by subject into nearly 300 chapters paralleling many of the article topics in the encyclopedia. Sections include drafting guides and checklists as well as sample forms.

Am. Jur. Legal Forms contains such documents as contracts, wills, and other transactional instruments. Documents to be filed in court or with administrative agencies are contained in a separate set, *American Jurisprudence Pleading and Practice Forms,* (Lawyers Cooperative [now West Group], 57 vols., rev. ed., 1967-date). This set includes a vast array of possible complaints (Damaged your car swerving to avoid a dog? Sue its owner!), as well as motions, affidavits, jury instructions, and judgments. It too is arranged alphabetically, with more than 300 chapters. Some chapters present the litigation side of topics also presented in *Am. Jur. Legal Forms*; others, such as "Mobs and Riots," may be the subject of litigation but rarely arise in contracts or deeds. Both *Am. Jur.* form sets are available on CD-ROM as well as in printed volumes. The electronic forms can be downloaded and manipulated using word processing software, but the print volumes are found in more libraries to which the general public has access.

West's Legal Forms (West Publishing, 2d ed., 36 vols., 1981-date) is arranged into 14 broad topics rather than in alphabetical chapters. Volumes 16 to 18, for example, cover various aspects of estate planning, while volume 18A focuses on elderlaw and deals with issues ranging from living wills to consumer fraud. The set provides introductory explanations, as well as a large number of detailed clauses and provisions that can be added to standard forms (such as possession of a pet in a prenuptial agreement). The focus is on contracts and transactional forms, but some complaints and other litigation forms are included.

It's hard to say whether *Am. Jur. Legal Forms* or *West's Legal Forms* is the better publication. Because *Am. Jur. Legal Forms* is organized alphabetically by factual situation, it may be easier for someone unfamiliar with the law to find a form applicable to a specific problem. *West's* topical organization, on the other hand, may provide more legal context once the appropriate heading is found. Each set has some forms not found in the other. The "Animals" chapter in *Am. Jur. Legal Forms*, for instance, includes 60 pages on contracts for the fattening of cattle and other livestock. *West's Legal Forms* includes, in its "Aviation & Airline Services" section, a sample contract for transportation of an animal, reptile, or bird in which the carrier reserves the right to "refuse to carry said animal, reptile, or bird and to discharge it at any point enroute, to the extent of throwing same overboard, if it becomes incorrigible or dangerous to the lives, health or comfort of passengers, by reason of illness, disposition or other similar or dissimilar causes." The best route is to check the softcover, annually revised index volumes that accompany each set to see if it provides relevant forms. The forms themselves are kept up to date, with new forms added through annual pocket parts and periodically revised volumes.

Another major set of forms, Jacob Rabkin and Mark H. Johnson's *Current Legal Forms with Tax Analysis* (Bender, 34 vols., 1948-date), is published in a looseleaf format for quarterly updating. This is one of the most highly esteemed formbook sets, but as it is designed for lawyers drafting complicated documents, it may be the least accessible for a new researcher. Like *Am. Jur. Legal Forms*, its scope is limited to contracts and transactional forms. The set is divided by subject into 39 broad chapters. Some chapters, such as "Pension Plans and Other Exempt Employees' Plans" and "Real Estate Securities," occupy as much as two volumes. Each chapter begins with an extensive discussion of the tax background; some chapters also include discussions of practice issues and checklists indicating matters to consider and steps to take in preparing documents. Explanatory comments precede the forms. The index is thorough and provides references to both background discussions and forms.

A fourth comprehensive set, *Nichols Cyclopedia of Legal Forms Annotated* (Clark Boardman Callaghan, 36 vols., 1936-date), most closely resembles the scope and format of *Am. Jur. Legal Forms,* with more than 200 chapters of transactional forms. The *Nichols* set is not as widely available in law libraries as *Am. Jur. Legal Forms*, *West's Legal Forms,* and *Current Legal Forms with Tax Analysis.* It is, however, also available on CD-ROM.

Besides these mammoth sets of forms designed for professional use, several publications with basic forms are available for consumer use. Stephen Elias and Marcia Stewart's *Simple Contracts for Personal Use* (Nolo Press, 2d ed., 1991) contains about three dozen forms for matters such as leases and home repair contracts, and includes instructions and explanations. Nolo also publishes several books with forms in more specialized areas, such as estate planning and bankruptcy.

Other self-help publications that may be available in bookstores or public libraries include Carl W. Battle's *Legal-Wise: Self-Help Legal Forms for Everyone* (Allworth Press, 3d ed., 1996) and *Complete Legal Kit* (Running Press, 1988). The latter volume contains about 150 forms but little explanation or background. Still other products are available on CD-ROM, including *Quicken Family Lawyer* (Parsons Technology, 1997) and *Kiplinger's Home Legal Advisor* (Block Financial Corp., 1996).

Forms are also available from numerous sites on the Internet. Lists of forms collections and indexes are available from comprehensive sites such as FindLaw <http://www.findlaw.com/16forms/>, which provides links to nearly 100 sites, including general collections, specialized resources, and government agencies. The Internet Legal Resource Guide <http://www.ilrg.com/forms/> also provides links to sources for forms, and includes its own archive of about 70 forms for starters.

CHAPTER 4
Law Books

Chapter 3 examined resources that seek to span a wide area of legal information. We now turn to more specialized materials dealing with particular areas of legal doctrine.

A vital first step in locating specialized legal resources is to have a clear understanding of how the legal research issue is classified in legal literature—whether the question would be covered, for example, in books on constitutional law or torts. The guides and reference works discussed in the preceding chapters of this book can be helpful in making this determination.

Once you have assigned your research question to the appropriate area of law, you must then differentiate among law books with a variety of styles and purposes. Some sources are much too technical for anyone but specialists to use. Others provide an unrealistically simplistic view of legal problems and do not even cite the statutes and cases necessary to pursue further research.

A major concern in evaluating legal books is age. A book written 10 or 20 years ago can still be valuable if used for its scholarly or historical insights. It cannot, however, present the current state of the law. To be of practical value as a guide to legal doctrine, a book must be updated on a regular basis.

Books are updated in a number of ways.

- Some are revised and republished on a regular basis. A number of books are reissued in new paperback editions each year. Frequent new editions may cut into a library's book budget, but researchers appreciate their currency.

- Many law books contain "pocket part" supplements in the back of each volume. The new pocket part cumulates new information and replaces its predecessor. These pocket parts are usually published annually.

- Other books are updated by freestanding pamphlets that serve the same purpose as pocket parts. Some books are updated with pocket parts until the supplement becomes too large to fit in the volume, at which point a separate pamphlet is published instead. With either method, the format can become unwieldy if one must constantly check back and forth between main volume and supplement. Before a supplement gets too large, however, most publishers issue a newly revised volume incorporating the more recent information.

- Many legal publications are issued in binders, with supplementary material inserted on a quarterly or annual basis. For some publications, an insert at the front or back of the volume serves the same purpose as a pocket part; other works are updated with replacement pages or chapter pamphlets. Just because a publication appears in binders, however, does not mean that it is regularly updated; it is important to check the date on the title page or the latest insert to determine how current a work is.

If a book is used simply for background research or historical information, the date of publication or updating is not particularly vital. But if a text is to be relied on as a correct and current statement of the law, it is essential that it be as up-to-date as possible.

TYPES OF LAW BOOKS

A broad range of texts and treatises encompass legal literature. Some are written for specialists in particular areas and are virtually impenetrable to outsiders, while others are published specifically for general audiences. Some books for the legal market are scholarly, abstract treatments designed for student use in learning broad, substantive doctrines. Others are filled with examples and practical tips because they are designed for practicing attorneys, who need to know not only the substance of the law but how to apply it in their day-to-day practices.

Sometimes a book's audience is mentioned in its subtitle or preface. A publisher's reputation can also indicate a work's scope and intended market. Some companies, such as CCH or Matthew Bender, specialize in materials for lawyers and assume more specialized background from their readers. West Group and Aspen Law & Business publish a broad range of legal materials, with many designed specifically for law students. Works from general publishers such as Macmillan or Oxford University Press are geared toward a broader scholarly market. Nolo Press publishes specifically for the self-help legal market.

The user of specialized legal resources should take into account several considerations when evaluating law books: the reputations of the author and the publisher; timeliness, accuracy, and scope of updating; and the extent to which the book is cited in other publications.

Book reviews are a useful evaluative tool, but it is relatively difficult to find helpful reviews of legal publications. Standard texts are reviewed less frequently in legal periodicals than specialized monographs, and many book reviews in academic legal journals simply use the book as a springboard for the reviewer to expand on related issues. Reviews in legal newspapers and bar journals tend to be shorter and more helpful, focusing more on the book's practical applications.

Different texts, of course, have different purposes. To evaluate the value of a text to your work, look at such factors as whether the index is easy to use; whether the text is clear and instructive, neither too detailed nor too superficial; and whether the volume includes such features as tables and illustrations that can help clarify complex issues. Even factors such as volume size and typeface can affect a book's practical value. A book that lies flat when opened and has legible print is easier to use and is likely to be used more often than a tightly bound, overweight tome that causes backaches and eyestrain.

With these general guidelines for evaluation in mind, let's consider the differences among several distinct types of law books, discussed below roughly in increasing order of complexity.

Consumer Books

Most law books are written for lawyers. A few books, however, are expressly designed to make legal topics understandable to persons without legal training. Some of the works discussed in Chapter 3, such as *West's Encyclopedia of American Law* or the ABA's *Family Legal Guide*, are examples of this genre. In some ways, however, general treatments such as these are poor representatives because they attempt to do too much. Consumer-oriented law books that focus on specific areas of law or a particular state's legal system are often more successful.

The leading publisher of self-help law books is Nolo Press. Nolo began in the early 1970s with the publication of *How to Do Your Own Divorce in California* and *California Tenants' Handbook*. It now publishes more than 100 titles, covering legal issues of interest to consumers and small business. Topics range from bankruptcy and incorporation to laws concerning neighbors and dogs. Some of Nolo's publications are still specifically designed for use in California, but most are written for a national market. Three of Nolo's publications, *Legal Research: How to Find and Understand the Law*, *Nolo's Everyday Law Book*, and *Law on the Net*, have already been discussed in the preceding chapters.

Nolo's law books are user-friendly but not condescending. They include drawings and humorous asides, along with the step-by-step legal information and forms necessary to handle one's own legal affairs. In addition, they generally include citations for the cases and statutes they discuss. Many Nolo books include "Help Beyond the Book" sections discussing more detailed legal treatises and other information sources.

Nolo books provide an excellent introduction to legal issues and are widely available in public libraries and bookstores. At least they *should* be widely available in libraries, if they were not among the items most frequently stolen. That they often disappear from libraries is a testament to their popularity. Most Nolo titles are revised frequently to reflect changes in the law, so a new edition may soon be published to replace a stolen volume.

Nolo publishes a quarterly newsletter, *Nolo News*, highlighting its publications and containing features on legal topics, including a regular column of lawyer jokes. Similar coverage is provided by Nolo's Web page <http://www.nolo.com>.

Another extensive series designed for general use is the American Civil Liberties Union's series on civil rights, listed below. Titles in this series are thorough and clearly written, with footnotes at the end of each chapter providing references to federal and state cases and statutes. These footnotes to laws in each state, rare in texts written for a general audience, will facilitate further research. Many chapters also provide addresses and telephone numbers for organizations and agencies working to protect civil rights.

Until 1995, each book was subtitled *The Basic ACLU Guide*, but recent books feature the subtitle *The Authoritative ACLU Guide*. The series has had several publishers since the first volumes appeared in the early 1970s, but since 1988 it has had a home at the Southern Illinois University Press. SIU has published every title except those few that have not been revised since 1984 or 1985, which are published by Bantam Books.

David Rubin & Steven Greenhouse, *The Rights of Teachers* (2d ed., 1984)

Mitchell Bernard et al., *The Rights of Single People* (1985)

Martin Guggenheim & Alan Sussman, *The Rights of Young People* (1985)

Christine M. Marwick, *Your Right to Government Information* (1985)

James H. Stark & Howard W. Goldstein, *The Rights of Crime Victims* (1985)

Janet R. Price, Alan H. Levine, & Eve Cary, *The Rights of Students* (3d ed., 1988)

David Rudovsky et al., *The Rights of Prisoners* (4th ed., 1988)

George J. Annas, *The Rights of Patients* (2d ed., 1989)

Robert N. Brown, *The Rights of Older Persons* (2d ed., 1989)

David Carliner et al., *The Rights of Aliens and Refugees* (2d ed., 1990)

Evan Hendricks, Trudy Hayden, & Jack D. Novick, *Your Right to Privacy* (2d ed., 1990)

Joel M. Gora et al., *The Right to Protest* (1991)

Nan D. Hunter, Sherryl E. Michaelson, & Thomas B. Stoddard, *The Rights of Lesbians and Gay Men* (3d ed., 1992)

Kenneth P. Norwick & Jerry Simon Chasen, *The Rights of Authors, Artists, and Other Creative People* (2d ed., 1992)

Stephen L. Pevar, *The Rights of Indians and Tribes* (2d ed., 1992)

Laughlin McDonald & John A. Powell, *The Rights of Racial Minorities* (2d ed., 1993)

Robert M. O'Neil, *The Rights of Public Employees* (2d ed., 1993)

Susan Deller Ross et al., *The Rights of Women* (3d ed., 1993)

Wayne N. Outten, Robert J. Rabin, & Lisa R. Lipman, *The Rights of Employees and Union Members* (2d ed., 1994)

Barry Lynn, Marc D. Stern, & Oliver S. Thomas, *The Right to Religious Liberty* (3d ed., 1995)

Martin Guggenheim, Alexandra Dylan Lowe, & Diane Curtis, *The Rights of Families* (1996)

Robert M. Levy & Leonard S. Rubenstein, *The Rights of People with Mental Disabilities* (1996)

William B. Rubenstein, Ruth Eisenberg, & Lawrence O. Gostin, *The Rights of People Who Are HIV Positive* (1996)

Helen Hershkoff & Stephen Loffredo, *The Rights of the Poor* (1997)

A new series of consumer guidebooks has recently been launched by the American Bar Association. To date, the series consists of six titles, each covering in greater detail a specific topic presented in the ABA's *Family Legal Guide* (discussed in Chapter 3). The specialized works, however, abandon the constricting question-and-answer format for a more straightforward narrative style that allows for more background and explanation. Each includes numerous sidebars highlighting specific issues, and some volumes include charts, sample forms, and sources for further information. Each volume was reviewed by more than a dozen practicing attorneys and law professors to ensure its accuracy. Titles available, all published by Times Books, are

The American Bar Association Guide to Home Ownership (1995)

The American Bar Association Guide to Wills and Estates (1995)

The American Bar Association Guide to Family Law (1996)

The American Bar Association Guide to Consumer Law (1997)

The American Bar Association Guide to Workplace Law (1997)

The American Bar Association Legal Guide for Older Americans (1998)

Among the most prolific publishers of legal information designed for consumers are federal and state government agencies. Their works are often available free or at low cost. Some titles provide a general introduction to a state's constitution or its court system, while others detail specific policies or programs. Some are simple brochures providing brief overviews, while others are useful research tools. The Environmental Protection Agency, for example, publishes numerous guides to environmental issues, from the broad *Everything You Wanted to Know about Environmental Regulations—But Were Afraid to Ask: A Guide for Small Communities* (rev. ed., 1993) to more specific *Citizen's Guides* to issues such as groundwater pollution, pesticides, and radon. As another example, the U.S. Senate's Special Committee on Aging has published a number of guides and "information papers" on issues concerning the elderly, such as health care and taxation. These and other government publications vary widely in comprehensiveness and value.

Books for Law Students

More than 40,000 students enter American law schools each year. This creates a substantial market for legal publishers, who have responded by designing several types of publications specifically for law students. These works vary in their research value.

Casebooks

The books most commonly used in law school courses are casebooks. Most are designed to be used with a teaching method in which students read and analyze court opinions. Casebooks contain edited versions of the opinions, usually followed by notes and questions. Although they can be a handy source for abridged versions of significant decisions, it must be remembered that cases are chosen for inclusion because they make good teaching tools—not necessarily because they represent current legal doctrines.

Casebooks generally have titles such as *Criminal Law: Cases and Comments* or *Cases and Materials on Constitutional Law*. Some titles do not make the works' classroom purpose so obvious, but they are published as part of casebook series from one of the major law school publishers, such as Aspen Law & Business, Foundation Press, or West.

Although some people find casebooks to be useful overviews of legal subject areas, they are designed to deliver information gradually, in small drips, over the course of a law school semester and in conjunction with classroom discussion. Their purpose is not only to teach the subject but to train law students to think like lawyers. Simple explanations are few and far between, while open-ended questions are common. How useful this approach will be to someone seeking immediate and straightforward answers to legal questions is debatable.

Hornbooks

Because the casebooks used in courses can be somewhat opaque, law students often turn to other sources for help in understanding the law. The most important of these other sources are hornbooks, one-volume textual summaries of specific areas of legal doctrine. Instead of reprinting cases and posing questions, hornbooks explain legal rules in relatively straightforward terms. They also provide footnote references to cases, journal articles, and other sources, making them valuable research tools. Most are also well indexed, making it relatively easy to pinpoint a particular legal issue in the discussion.

Although hornbooks are designed for student use, many are written by leading scholars and have become highly respected. Works such as W. Page Keeton et al.'s *Prosser and Keeton on the Law of Torts* (West Publishing, 5th ed., 1984) and Charles Alan Wright's *Law of Federal Courts* (West Publishing, 5th ed., 1994) are frequently cited by the courts not only as summaries of existing legal doctrine but as persuasive authorities on how the law should be interpreted.

Unlike casebooks and many other law school publications, hornbooks are available in most law library collections as part of a variety of series, with West's Hornbook Series the best known and most extensive. Foundation Press publishes a University Textbook Series of about two dozen titles, and Matthew Bender publishes about 20 paperbacks in a Legal Text Series designed to be thorough but not as extensive as the hardbound hornbooks.

Study Aids

Law students also provide an extensive market for relatively simple, straightforward summaries of the law. Unlike the more scholarly and extensive hornbooks, these volumes generally provide few footnote references to other sources. They can be useful, however, for someone seeking a quick overview of a subject area.

The most extensive series of study aids is known as Nutshells. This series of small paperback volumes from West Group contains almost 100 titles. They are specifically designed to have a footnote-free, clear text focusing on the major issues in a particular area of law. Some cover rather specific issues, such as employee benefit plans or white-collar crime, while others discuss more general topics, such as constitutional law or contracts. Several of the Nutshells focus not on legal doctrines but on legal processes and skills, such as appellate advocacy, legal interviewing, or legal writing.

Most Nutshells are written by law professors, including some leading authorities in their subject fields. A few are even cited occasionally by the courts as persuasive authority, so they might also be considered small-scale texts as well as study aids.

Outlines, the other major study aids, are more expressly designed with one particular purpose in mind: to help students prepare for law school exams. There are several competing series, including *Casenote Law Outlines*, *Emanuel Law Summaries*, *Legalines*, and *West's Black Letter Series*. The most extensive is *Gilbert Law Outlines*, with more than three dozen titles. With titles such as *Contracts* and *Torts*, these works are specifically designed to match courses in the law school curriculum. Straightforward definitions are accompanied by examples of the application of rules.

A few outlines are written by leading law professors in the subject fields and may provide a more authoritative tone than a work prepared by a publisher's editorial staff. On the other hand, there is something peculiar about a law professor writing an outline to clarify matters that the same professor's casebook has obfuscated, and a fresh nonacademic perspective may be more helpful.

Outlines are found in relatively few law libraries. They are designed for purchase by distraught law students as talismans against poor grades, and the place to find them is in bookstores serving law school populations.

Practice Manuals and Continuing Legal Education (CLE) Material

Books published for practicing lawyers are often different from hornbooks prepared for educational use. Of course, practitioners need to know basic legal doctrine and often turn to hornbooks and legal texts for such information. Yet they also have access to an extensive literature of practice handbooks containing tips, checklists, and forms. While law school publications tend to match closely the focus of law school courses, many practitioners' works focus on much narrower subjects or address problems that cross doctrinal frontiers. They tend to be much more functional and focused on issues that arise in legal practice. Three particular kinds of publications are worth noting.

Trial handbooks and other materials designed for litigators provide practical guidance on proceedings before, during, and after trial. These often contain step-by-step guidelines and include the texts of relevant statutes and court rules.

Books devoted to the law of a particular state can be extremely helpful to someone researching a state-specific legal question. These volumes are similar to the state encyclopedias discussed in Chapter 3, but with a focus on specific subjects, such as family law or workers' compensation. Larger states, particularly California and New York, generally have a more extensive literature of such works. States like Vermont, with fewer than 2,000 lawyers, have few state-specific works. Even so, obtaining just one of these works, such as Kimberly B. Cheney's *Labor and Employment in Vermont* (Michie Butterworth, 1994), can be a godsend.

One particular type of state-specific practice guide deserves special mention. Model jury instructions are developed by judiciary or bar committees for use in summarizing the law to jurors. They are designed to explain legal issues to a lay audience and, therefore, seek to be as clear as possible. A jury instruction in a criminal case, for example, spells out the specific elements that the state must prove for the jury to convict a defendant. As an official statement of the law, a jury instruction is no substitute for the actual statutes and cases on which it is based. Most sets of instructions do, however, cite these sources and provide a good, concise introduction. Model jury instructions do not cover all situations, however; most sets are limited to issues that frequently arise in civil and criminal trials.

A third type of publication worth noting are handbooks published by bar associations and continuing legal education (CLE) groups. Two organizations of national scope providing CLE programs are the American Law Institute-American Bar Association Committee on Continuing Professional Education (ALI-ABA) and the Practising Law Institute (PLI). Both present courses of study and conferences throughout the year and publish handbooks to accompany these courses. Similar materials are published by bar associations in most states. Some state CLE organizations, such as California Continuing Education of the Bar, are major publishers of state-specific texts. Smaller jurisdictions may have less elaborate and extensive materials, but because they also have fewer commercial publications, these CLE materials can provide valuable insights.

CLE programs often center on new areas of growing concern to the bar and include contributions from attorneys whose practices focus in these areas. Some are unique resources in developing areas. On the other hand, course materials for CLE programs can vary widely in quality. Some chapters are polished works, while others are little more than outlines. For example, the first page of a chapter in a 1996 PLI handbook, *What Lawyers Need to Know About the Internet: Basics for the Busy Professional*, has just two lines: "The Problem with Lawyers / · Individually our clients love us." Over the next several pages these phrases are repeated, each time with one or two new lines added. This material obviously was designed to accompany a presentation and means little standing on its own.

Finding relevant discussions in continuing legal education handbooks can be difficult because the volumes are often not indexed. It may be necessary to peruse the table of contents or to page through a volume to search for a specific topic. Researchers with access to WESTLAW, which has ALI-ABA Course of Study materials since 1988 and PLI course handbooks since 1984, may find the search easier. The full texts of these materials can be searched using particular keyword combinations in the ALI-ABA or PLI databases or in the more general JLR (journals and law reviews) and TP-ALL (all texts and periodicals) databases.

Treatises

The traditional hallmark of legal scholarship is the treatise. No hard and fast line distinguishes treatises from other forms of legal publication such as hornbooks and practice manuals. Generally, the term *treatise* is applied to a multivolume work exploring a particular doctrinal area in exhaustive depth.

Legal treatises seek to clarify legal doctrine by ordering the variety of rules and decisions into a coherent body of law. Like the legal encyclopedias discussed in Chapter 3, some achieve this goal while taking little account of aspects of the law beyond narrow legal rules. In his *A History of American Law* (Simon & Schuster, 2d ed., 1985) leading legal historian Lawrence M. Friedman has called one of the first major multivolume treatises of this century, Samuel Williston's *The Law of Contracts* (Baker, Voorhis, 5 vols., 1920-22), "volume after volume of a heavy void" and "a monumental fortress . . . solid, closely knit, fully armored against the intrusion of any ethical, economic, or social notions whatsoever" (pp. 626, 629).

The exhaustive depth of a legal treatise is unnecessary for many inquiries but may be invaluable for someone trying to work out a thorny legal issue. It explains the law, and its extensive footnotes provide references to cases from throughout the country. It is helpful to note several facts about legal treatises.

Most of the major treatises were originally produced by individual scholars, with whose names they are forever linked. In some instances, the author associated with the title has long since left the project. Some have long since left the earth. Erastus C. Benedict, of *Benedict on Admiralty*, died in 1880. Other "names above the title" have not been around for some time: George J. Couch, of *Couch on Insurance*, died in 1936, and William Miller Collier, of *Collier on Bankruptcy*, died in 1956. (The posthumous longevity award in American treatises may go to Francis Wharton, who published a first edition of a treatise on criminal law in 1846. The 15th edition of *Wharton's Criminal Law* began publication in 1993. The British author Joseph Chitty died in 1838, but a 27th edition of *Chitty on Contracts* was published in 1994.)

The demise of some authors is hard to ascertain. Neither George W. Thompson (1864-?) of *Thompson on Real Property* or Philip Nichols (1875-?) of *Nichols' The Law of Eminent Domain* is mentioned in the current editions, nor do they appear in standard biographical reference works. (On the other hand, the preface in the new edition of *Appleman on Insurance* by Eric Mills Holmes includes a moving tribute to the late John Appleman, as well as to his daughter and successor, Jean Appleman.) And some authors never really die. A new fourth edition of Samuel Williston's *A Treatise on the Law of Contracts* began publication in 1990; despite Williston's death in 1963 at the age of 101, he is still listed on the title page as "Dane Professor of Law Emeritus, Harvard University."

Some treatises continue with scholars with visions as strong as the original authors. Many works are carried on, however, by publishers' editorial staffs or teams of authors. Perhaps the task has become too large for any one person. Arthur L. Corbin published an 11-volume treatise on contracts in the early 1950s. A new edition is in the process of publication; three law professors have worked on the first three volumes, with the pocket part supplements prepared by two more professors. The involvement of multiple authors may not necessarily diminish a treatise's value as a research tool, but it is less likely to be a coherent and focused interpretation of legal doctrine.

One intriguing feature of several treatises is that they have been carried on by offspring of the original author. As noted above, *Insurance Law and Practice* was originally by John Alan Appleman (1912-1982) and was then revised by his daughter Jean Appleman (1939-).

Other family businesses that children have joined include *The Law of Trusts and Trustees*, with a first edition by George Gleason Bogert (1884-1977) and a second edition coauthored with his son George Taylor Bogert (1920-); *The Law of Workmen's Compensation*, originally written by Arthur Larson (1910-1993) and now by his son Lex K. Larson (1939-); and *Nimmer on Copyright*, by Melville B. Nimmer (1923-1985) and David Nimmer (1955-).

In recent years, it has become hard to keep track of who publishes a treatise. Several legal publishing companies have merged, and some product lines have shifted from one imprint to another. When Clark Boardman Callaghan and Lawyers Cooperative merged, the general works from both companies received the Lawyers Cooperative imprint and the specialized treatises received the CBC imprint. These companies have since merged with West Publishing to form West Group, and product lines have been shuffled further. Meanwhile, Shepard's/McGraw-Hill sold its treatise line to Clark Boardman Callaghan, and Little, Brown sold its treatise line to Aspen Publications. So a treatise may have one imprint on early volumes, another on later volumes, and a third on the latest supplementation.

One effect of such mergers is that a single publisher may produce several competing treatises. Before Lawyers Cooperative, Clark Boardman, and Callaghan & Co. merged, each published a treatise on zoning law. Lawyers Cooperative published *American Law of Zoning* by Robert M. Anderson; Clark Boardman published *The Law of Zoning and Planning* by Arden H. Rathkopf; and Callaghan & Co. published *American Planning Law* by Norman Williams, Jr. These three rather similar works all appeared for a time under the Clark Boardman Callaghan imprint; they are now West Group publications.

Treatises are published in both bound volumes and loose-leaf binders. The format is not significant; what matters is that the treatise is supplemented in one form or another to provide information about recent changes in the law. Treatises in bound volumes are supplemented either with pocket parts in the back of each volume or separate pamphlets or volumes updating the entire set. From time to time revised volumes are published. Treatises in loose-leaf format are updated with revised pages or chapters, as well as supplementary pamphlets filed at the front or back of each volume.

The nature and quality of the supplements vary from treatise to treatise. Some merely provide new footnotes citing or summarizing new cases, while others contain extensive analysis of recent developments. One unfortunate trend in recent treatise supplementation is the inclusion of footnotes listing cases in which the treatise itself is cited, as in "*Garlotte v. Fordice*, 515 U.S. 39 (1995) (citing **Treatise**)." It is hard to see the value of this boldface bloat other than puffery. The importance of a case is not enhanced simply because it cites a particular secondary source.

In many instances, the supplementation to treatises is expensive. Legal publishers cater to a relatively small, professional market, one that can often bear exorbitant costs. The impact on researchers is that a treatise found in an academic or public law library may not be fully up-to-date, simply because the library cannot afford to keep pace with the cost of supplementation.

Table 4-1 provides a selected list of legal treatises designed to identify the most authoritative works in particular subject areas. It is limited to multivolume works and therefore excludes important one-volume works such as Wayne R. LaFave and Jerold H. Israel's *Criminal Procedure* (West Publishing, 2d ed., 1992) and Laurence H. Tribe's *American Constitutional Law* (Foundation Press, 2d ed., 1988). The works listed have been cited in more court opinions than other works in their field, particularly in recent years. In addition, they are owned by a large number of libraries, a fact that in itself may not indicate a work's value but does reflect the esteem with which it is generally viewed. With few exceptions, they are regularly supplemented to provide a reasonably current perspective.

Many of the works listed in Table 4-1 have experienced changes of both authors and publishers since they were first published. Such changes are indicated in the entries. It may be necessary to locate the identities of the initial authors and publishers to find the treatises in most library catalogs, whereas the current names are used in publishers' catalogs as well as in some recent citations to the works. The entire list reflects only eight current imprints, and these are actually the products of just four companies. Because publications and publishing houses continue to change hands, perhaps the best way to get up-to-date contact and product information for these and other legal publishers is through their homepages, listed on the Web at <http://www.findlaw.com/04publications/>.

Restatements

Similar to treatises but of a slightly different cast is a series of works known as restatements of the law. Like treatises, restatements attempt to clarify legal doctrines. They are not as comprehensive as most treatises because their purpose is not to summarize and reconcile conflicting case law but to articulate the basic principles guiding legal decision-making. The restatements

TABLE 4-1	

MAJOR LEGAL TREATISES

Administrative Law	Kenneth Culp Davis & Richard J. Pierce, Jr., *Administrative Law Treatise,* 3d ed. Little, Brown [now Aspen], 1994, 3 bound vols. with annual supp. pamphlet
Admiralty	Erastus C. Benedict [1800-80], *Benedict on Admiralty,* 7th ed. Bender, 1958-date, 27 loose-leaf vols. updated three times a year
	Thomas J. Schoenbaum, *Admiralty and Maritime Law,* 2d ed. West Publishing, 1994, 3 bound vols. with annual pocket part supps.
Antitrust	Phillip Areeda [1930-95] & Donald F. Turner [1921-94] [recent volumes by Areeda & Herbert Hovenkamp], *Antitrust Law: An Analysis of Antitrust Principles and Their Application.* Little, Brown [now Aspen], 1978-date, 12 bound vols. to date, with revised vols. and annual supp. volume
Bankruptcy	*Collier on Bankruptcy,* 15th ed. rev. Lawrence P. King, editor-in-chief. Bender, 1996-date, 22 loose-leaf vols. updated three times a year
	Norton Bankruptcy Law and Practice 2d. William L. Norton, Jr., editor-in-chief. Clark Boardman Callaghan [now West Group], 1993-date, 12 loose-leaf vols. updated bimonthly
Civil Rights	Sheldon H. Nahmod, *Civil Rights and Civil Liberties Litigation: The Law of Section 1983,* 4th ed. West Group, 1997-date, 2 loose-leaf vols. updated annually.
Commercial Law	Ronald A. Anderson, *Anderson on the Uniform Commercial Code,* 3d ed. Lawyers Cooperative [now West Group], 1981-date, 18 bound vols. with revised vols. and annual pocket part supps.
	James J. White & Robert S. Summers, *Uniform Commercial Code,* 4th ed. West Publishing, 1995, 4 bound vols. with annual pocket part supps.
Constitutional Law	Ronald D. Rotunda & John E. Nowak, *Treatise on Constitutional Law: Substance and Procedure,* 2d ed. West Publishing, 1992, 4 bound vols. with annual pocket part supps.
Contracts	Arthur L. Corbin [1874-1967], *Corbin on Contracts,* rev. ed. by Joseph M. Perillo. West Publishing [now LEXIS Law Publishing], 1993-date, 3 bound vols. to date with annual pocket part supps. Gradually replacing first ed., West Publishing, 1950-64, 11 bound vols. with annual pocket part supps.
	E. Allan Farnsworth, *Farnsworth on Contracts.* Aspen, 1998, 3 bound vols. with annual supp. pamphlet
	Richard A. Lord, *A Treatise on the Law of Contracts* by Samuel Williston [1861-1963], 4th ed. Lawyers Cooperative [now West Group], 1990-date, 8 bound vols. to date with pocket part supps. Gradually replacing 3d ed. by Walter H.E. Jaeger [1902-82]. Baker, Voorhis/Lawyers Cooperative, 1957-79, 22 bound vols. with pocket part supps.
Corporations	William Meade Fletcher [1870-1943], *Cyclopedia of the Law of Private Corporations.* Callaghan [now West Group], 1931-date [current vols. 1987-date], 35 bound vols. with revised vols. and annual pocket part supps.
Criminal Law and Procedure	Wayne R. LaFave, *Search and Seizure: A Treatise on the Fourth Amendment,* 3d ed. West Publishing, 1996, 5 bound vols. with annual pocket part supps.
	Wayne R. LaFave & Austin W. Scott, Jr., *Substantive Criminal Law.* West Publishing, 1986, 2 bound vols. with annual pocket part supps.
	Charles E. Torcia, *Wharton's Criminal Law,* 15th ed. Clark Boardman Callaghan [now West Group], 1993-96, 4 bound vols. with annual pocket part supps.
	Charles E. Torcia, *Wharton's Criminal Procedure,* 13th ed. Lawyers Cooperative [now West Group], 1989-92, 4 bound vols. with annual pocket part supps.

TABLE 4-1 (continued)

MAJOR LEGAL TREATISES

Employment Law	*The Developing Labor Law: The Boards, the Courts, and the National Labor Relations Act,* 3d ed. Patrick Hardin, editor-in-chief. BNA, 1992, 2 bound vols. updated by annual supp. pamphlet
	Arthur Larson [1910-93] & Lex K. Larson, *Larson's Workers' Compensation Law* [formerly *The Law of Workmen's Compensation].* Bender, 1952-date, 11 loose-leaf vols. updated semiannually
	Lex K. Larson, *Employment Discrimination,* 2d ed. Bender, 1994-date, 8 loose-leaf vols. updated three times a year
Environmental Law	William H. Rodgers, Jr., *Environmental Law.* West Publishing, 1986-92, 4 bound vols. with annual pocket part supps.
Evidence	Barbara Bergman & Nancy Hollander, *Wharton's Criminal Evidence,* 15th ed. West Group, 1997-date, 1 vol. to date. Gradually replacing 14th ed. by Charles E. Torcia. Lawyers Cooperative [now West Group], 1985-87, 4 bound vols. with annual pocket part supps.
	Charles T. McCormick [1889-1963], *McCormick on Evidence,* 4th ed. John William Strong, general editor. West Publishing, 1992, 2 bound vols., no supp. to date
	Christopher M. Mueller & Laird C. Kirkpatrick, *Federal Evidence,* 2d ed. Lawyers Cooperative [now West Group], 1994, 5 bound vols. with annual pocket part supps.
	The New Wigmore: A Treatise on Evidence. Richard D. Friedman, general editor. Little, Brown [now Aspen], 1996-date, 1 vol. to date. Gradually replacing John Henry Wigmore [1863-1943], *Evidence in Trials at Common Law,* 4th ed. by John T. McNaughton [1921-67], James H. Chadbourn [1905-82], and Peter Tillers. Little, Brown, 1961-88, with annual supp. pamphlet
	Weinstein's Federal Evidence: Commentary on Rules of Evidence for the United States Courts, 2d ed. Joseph M. McLaughlin, general editor. Bender, 1997-date, 6 loose-leaf vols. updated three times a year
Family Law	Homer H. Clark, Jr., *The Law of Domestic Relations in the United States,* 2d ed. West Publishing, 1987, 2 bound vols., no supp. to date
Federal Practice	*Moore's Federal Practice,* 3d ed. James William Moore [1905-94], original author. Bender, 1997-date, 31 loose-leaf vols. updated quarterly
	Herbert B. Newberg [1937-92] & Alba Conte, *Newberg on Class Actions,* 3d ed. Shepard's/ McGraw-Hill [now West Group], 1992-date, 6 loose-leaf vols. updated semiannually
	Charles Alan Wright [with Arthur R. Miller and other coauthors], *Federal Practice and Procedure.* West Publishing, 1969-date, 48 bound vols. to date, with revised vols., annual pocket part supps., and monthly pamphlet
Immigration	*Immigration Law and Procedure,* rev. ed. by Charles Gordon, Stanley Mailman, & Stephen Yale-Loehr. Bender, 1966-date, 20 loose-leaf vols. updated quarterly
Insurance	*Holmes's Appleman on Insurance, 2d.* Eric Mills Holmes, general editor. West Publishing [now LEXIS Law Publishing], 1996-date, 3 bound vols. to date. Gradually replacing John Alan Appleman [1912-82] & Jean Appleman, *Insurance Law and Practice, with Forms.* West Publishing, 1941-87, 56 bound vols. with revised vols. and annual pocket part supps.
	Lee R. Russ & Thomas F. Segalla, *Couch on Insurance 3d.* Clark Boardman Callaghan [now West Group], 1995-date, 6 loose-leaf vols. to date with semiannual supplements. Gradually replacing George J. Couch [1881-1936], *Couch Cyclopedia of Insurance Law,* 2d ed. by Ronald

TABLE 4-1 (continued)

MAJOR LEGAL TREATISES

	A. Anderson; rev, by Mark S. Rhodes. Lawyers Cooperative, 1959-88 [current vols. 1981-88], 33 bound vols. with semiannual pocket parts
Intellectual property	Rudolf Callmann [1892-1976], *The Law of Unfair Competition, Trademarks and Monopolies,* 4th ed. by Louis Altman. Callaghan [now West Group], 1981-date, 9 loose-leaf vols. updated three times a year
	Donald S. Chisum, *Patents: A Treatise on the Law of Patentability, Validity, and Infringement.* Bender, 1978-date, 13 loose-leaf vols. updated quarterly
	J. Thomas McCarthy, *McCarthy on Trademarks and Unfair Competition,* 4th ed. Clark Boardman Callaghan [now West Group], 1996-date, 5 loose-leaf vols. updated semiannually
	Melville B. Nimmer [1923-85] & David Nimmer, *Nimmer on Copyright.* Bender, 1978-date, 6 loose-leaf vols. updated three times a year
Local Government	Eugene McQuillin [1860-1937], *The Law of Municipal Corporations,* 3d ed. Callaghan [now West Group], 1949-date [current vols. 1987-date], 30 bound vols. with revised vols. and annual pocket part supps.
Products Liability	*American Law of Products Liability* 3d. Lawyers Cooperative [now West Group], 1987-date, 19 loose-leaf vols. updated quarterly
	Louis R. Frumer [1918-87] & Melvin I. Friedman, *Products Liability.* Bender, 1960-date, 11 loose-leaf vols. updated three times a year
Property	*Nichols on Eminent Domain* [formerly *Nichols' The Law of Eminent Domain*], rev. 3d ed. by Julius L. Sackman. Bender, 1964-date, 18 loose-leaf vols. updated semiannually
	Richard R. Powell [1890-1982], *Powell on Real Property* [formerly *The Law of Real Property*]. Patrick J. Rohan, revision editor. Bender, 1949-date, 16 loose-leaf vols. updated quarterly
	Thompson on Real Property. David A. Thomas, editor-in-chief. Michie [now LEXIS Law Publishing], 1994, 15 bound vols. with annual pocket part supps.
Remedies	Dan B. Dobbs, *Dobbs Law of Remedies: Damages, Equity, Restitution,* 2d ed. West Publishing, 1993, 3 vols., no supp. to date
Securities	Thomas Lee Hazen, *Treatise on the Law of Securities Regulation,* 3d ed. West Publishing, 1995, 3 bound vols. with annual pocket part supps.
	Louis Loss [1914-97] & Joel Seligman, *Securities Regulation,* 3d ed. Little, Brown [now Aspen], 1989-date, 11 bound vols. with revised vols. and annual supp. vol.
Taxation	Boris I. Bittker & Lawrence Lokken, *Federal Taxation of Income, Estates, and Gifts,* 2d ed. Warren, Gorham & Lamont, 1989-93, 5 bound vols. with quarterly supp. pamphlets
	Jacob Mertens, Jr. [1896-1990?], *The Law of Federal Income Taxation.* Callaghan [now West Group], 1942-date, 19 loose-leaf vols. updated monthly
Torts	Fowler V. Harper [1897-1965], Fleming James, Jr. [1904-81], & Oscar S. Gray, *The Law of Torts,* 3d ed. Little, Brown [now Aspen], 1996-date, 1 vol. to date. Gradually replacing 2d ed., Little, Brown, 1986, 6 bound vols. with semiannual supp. pamphlets
	Ronald E. Mallen & Jeffrey M. Smith, *Legal Malpractice,* 4th ed. West Publishing, 1996, 4 bound vols. with annual pocket part supps.
	Stuart M. Speiser, Charles F. Krause, & Alfred W. Gans [1907-92], *The American Law of Torts.* Lawyers Cooperative [now West Group], 1983-93, 10 bound vols. with annual pocket part supps.

TABLE 4-1 (continued)	
MAJOR LEGAL TREATISES	
Trusts	George G. Bogert [1884-1977] and George T. Bogert, *The Law of Trusts and Trustees,* rev. 2d ed. West Publishing, 1977-date, 23 bound vols. with revised vols. and annual pocket part supps.
	Austin W. Scott [1884-1981] & William F. Fratcher [1913-92], *The Law of Trusts,* 4th ed. Little, Brown [now Aspen], 1987-91, 12 bound vols. with annual supp vol. by Mark L. Ascher
Zoning and Planning	*Anderson's American Law of Zoning,* 4th ed., revisions by Kenneth H. Young. Clark Boardman Callaghan [now West Group], 1996-date, 3 bound vols. to date. Gradually replacing Robert M. Anderson, *American Law of Zoning,* 3d ed. Lawyers Cooperative, 1986, 5 bound vols. with annual pocket part supps.
	Arden H. Rathkopf & Daren A. Rathkopf, *Rathkopf's The Law of Zoning and Planning,* 4th ed. Edward H. Ziegler, Jr., principal author for revision. Clark Boardman [now West Group], 1975-date, 5 loose-leaf vols. updated quarterly

attempt to define and codify the rules of common law doctrines. They cover 11 discrete areas of law: agency, conflict of laws, contracts, foreign relations law, judgments, property, restitution, security, torts, trusts, and unfair competition.

In some ways, the restatements might be thought of as treatises by committee. They are prepared under the auspices of the American Law Institute, an organization of judges, lawyers, and law professors from around the country founded in 1923 "to promote the clarification and simplification of the law and its better adaptation to social needs." The process of creating a restatement is a laborious one. Generally a legal scholar is appointed as reporter and works with a small group of advisers to create an initial draft. Eventually a series of tentative drafts and a proposed final draft go to the entire membership for consideration and approval.

The first series of restatements was completed between 1923 and 1944, covering the subjects of agency, conflict of laws, contracts, judgments, property, restitution, security, torts, and trusts. A second series was begun in 1952, updating most of these earlier restatements and adding coverage of foreign relations law. The third series of restatements was launched in 1987. Five topics have been completed: *Foreign Relations Law of the United States* (1987); *Trusts: Prudent Investor Rule* (1992); *Unfair Competition* (1995); *Suretyship and Guaranty* (1996); and *Torts: Products Liability* (1998). A new restatement on the law governing lawyers is also nearing completion. Several *Restatement 3d* projects are in the tentative draft stage now, including property (donative transfers, mortgages, and servitudes), torts (apportionment of liability), and trusts. Note that a *Restatement 3d* need not have a predecessor in the first or second series, and that some topics,

such as restitution and security, were covered in the first series but have not been updated.

Each restatement is divided into sections, which contain black-letter statements of the law followed by comments and illustrations. The black-letter statements spell out basic principles, such as "A contract is a promise or a set of promises for the breach of which the law gives a remedy, or the performance of which the law in some way recognizes as a duty." The comments explain the context and application of this rule, while the illustrations provide examples of the rule's application ("A orally agrees to sell land to B . . .").

Each restatement includes an index providing references not only to sections but to specific comments. Most of these indexes are cumulative for an entire restatement, but a few cover only individual volumes. Christina L. Kunz et al.'s *The Process of Legal Research* (Little, Brown, 4th ed., 1996) includes useful tables at pages 99-101 showing the location and coverage of restatement indexes, tables of contents, and other features.

The restatements create a neat world that does not match the complicated jumble of case law that actually makes up the body of precedent. Nonetheless, they are the work of highly respected scholars, and their reasoning is often persuasive in the courts. They are among the most frequently cited secondary sources.

As an example of how influential the restatements are, the American Law Institute (ALI) publishes appendixes to each set compiling annotations of cited cases. The annotations summarize the cases and note the use to which the restatement section is put, as in "cit. and quot. in ftn. and com. (a) cit. in disc." (cited and quoted in footnote and comment (a) cited in discussion). Like the notes in a treatise supplement of cases that cite it, these appendixes must do wonders for the fragile egos of the scholars responsible for the restatements. For major provisions, these annotations may occupy several hundred pages in two or more bound volumes and a pocket part supplement. The notes for each section are organized by court (federal appellate courts, then federal district courts, then state courts alphabetically), providing quick access to cases from a particular jurisdiction. Because they are not arranged topically, however, they are of little help in determining the scope and application of restatement principles.

The current editions of all restatements are online in both WESTLAW (REST database) and LEXIS-NEXIS (RESTAT file). The ALI Web site <http://www.ali.org> provides brief summaries of each restatement and forms for ordering copies at $60 or more per volume. It does not include the text of any of the restatements. Free public access apparently is not yet considered a component of the ALI's mission to promote the law's "better adaptation to social needs."

Scholarly Monographs

Relatively few scholarly monographs exist in the legal field. To some extent, the law reviews have been traditionally seen as the primary repository of legal scholarship. Most legal academics served as law review editors as students, and it is a publication form with which they are familiar. The standard product of most other graduate students, the dissertation, is rarely required in legal education. Without a dissertation, a new law professor must start from scratch rather than revising an already substantial tome for publication.

Nonetheless, many authors have produced influential and informative monographs on legal topics. A major advantage of these books is that they are written for the broader scholarly community and are often published by general trade and university presses. They are, therefore, more often found in general academic libraries than are books from publishers focusing on specifically legal markets.

Unlike many other legal publications, monographs are rarely supplemented on a regular basis. (The absence of steep updating costs is another reason why they may be found in more libraries.) Revised editions do appear, but a monograph's purpose is not to present a current statement of the law but to provide policy arguments or historical analysis.

A scholarly monograph can provide an interdisciplinary perspective lacking in strict legal publications. Treatises and law review articles are largely the work of lawyers and law professors, but monographs (and dissertations) discussing legal matters come from a variety of related disciplines, such as history, political science, and psychology. These can be valuable starting places for research because they place legal issues in a broader context. They generally do not, however, provide as many leads to cases and other primary sources as hornbooks or treatises.

Electronic Texts

Most of the other chapters in this book incorporate discussion of electronic and print resources. This chapter, however, shows a decided bias toward print resources. By and large, a book is still a book. The printed format offers several advantages, such as browsability and portability, that make it ideal for comprehensive coverage of a specific topic.

Nonetheless, a number of texts and treatises are available online, adding the advantage of keyword searching to other means of access. In addition, a number of electronic treatises include hypertext links from the commentary to the texts of the cases and statutes they discuss.

Several treatises are available through the online databases in WESTLAW. Its TEXTS and TP-ALL (all texts and periodicals) databases provide access to more than 100 texts and treatises. Each title is also accessible as a separate database; these include the following works from Table 4-1:

Couch on Insurance 3d	COUCH
LaFave, *Search and Seizure*, 3d ed.	SEARCHSZR
LaFave & Scott, *Substantive Criminal Law*	SUBCRL
Mertens, *The Law of Federal Income Taxation*	MERTENS
Newberg on Class Actions, 3d ed.	CLASSACT
Norton Bankruptcy Law and Practice 2d	NRTN-BLP
Rodgers, *Environmental Law*	ENVLAW
Wright & Miller, *Federal Practice and Procedure*	FPP

LEXIS-NEXIS has fewer treatises than WESTLAW, but it too has several titles from Table 4-1 (showing library and file).

Chisum, *Patents*	PATENT/CHISUM
Collier on Bankruptcy	BKRTC/COLBKR
Loss & Seligman, *Securities Regulation*, 3d ed.	FEDSEC/LOSS
Moore's Federal Practice, 3d ed.	GENFED/MOORES
Nimmer on Copyright	COPYRT/NIMMER
Norton Bankruptcy Law and Practice 2d	BKRTCY/NORTON
Weinstein's Federal Evidence, 2d ed.	GENFED/WEUSR

Although the online treatises offer the advantages of keyword searching and hypertext links, they are not necessarily more up-to-date than their print counterparts. Most are simply updated each time a new supplement is published.

Even more texts are published on CD-ROM. Most of the treatises published by Matthew Bender, for instance, are available as part of CD-ROM products containing a number of texts and primary sources. Although most CD-ROM texts are expensive, some may be available for use at law school libraries that subscribe to the print counterparts. To determine what is available on CD, consult the *Directory of Law-Related CD-ROMs* (Infosources Publishing, annual). This directory provides contact information, prices, and descriptions for more than 1,000 CD-ROM products, and is indexed by publisher and subject. Information on CD publications is also available through publishers' homepages.

Matthew Bender also markets the information on its CD-ROM treatises in an "Authority-On-Demand" program through its Web site <http://www.bender.com>. Users select a subject area or a particular treatise and then can either browse tables of contents or search for particular keywords. They can subscribe to specific titles or purchase individual sections, and download the information from the Web site. This service is not cheap—its value depends on the ability to identify a particular section of a treatise as the one that is needed—but it may be one of the quickest ways to obtain needed information.

FINDING LAW BOOKS

Having surveyed the range of law books published, we can now examine ways to find books that would be useful and appropriate resources in a research project. Many legal texts are written for a specialized audience, and they can be expensive to purchase and maintain. If a law library is nearby, the holdings of many general libraries will in all likelihood be limited to materials needed to support interests in current affairs or courses in political science and history. On the one hand, it may have an excellent collection for answering legal questions involving constitutional issues or public policy; on the other hand, it may have little to support research on questions such as the rights of a landowner to an easement on a neighbor's property. Depending on the nature of the inquiry, then, one of the first research steps may be to find the nearest law library (see Chapter 3).

Local Law Library Resources

Although it is possible to use Internet resources and bibliographies to look for law books, one of the best places to begin is with a visit to the local law library. It is far easier to evaluate resources by scanning their tables of contents and perusing their text than by examining a list or online catalog record. Obviously, and just as important, materials you are looking at are available immediately. An item found in a list may take days or weeks to track down.

As in any library, there are three major ways to find material in a law library: using the card or online catalog, browsing the shelves, or asking a librarian.

The library catalog organizes materials by author, title, or subject. The problem with this approach is that someone who doesn't already know of a relevant work to search by author or title must predict the subject headings that librarians have assigned to a topic. Legal subject headings can be long and obtuse, and irregularities abound. The subheading "Law and legislation" is often used, but a search for "Education—Law and legislation" would come up empty; the correct heading turns out to be "Educational law and legislation." Similarly, "Advertising laws" is used instead of "Advertising—Law and legislation."

Once the user has determined the relevant legal subject heading, he or she must then go to the "United States" geographic subheading to find materials on U.S. law. Otherwise, the books listed will probably be international in scope. Materials on state law will be found under specific states, as in "Contracts—Michigan," but works covering more than one state feature yet another subdivision, as in "Commercial law—United States—States" or "Taxation—Law and legislation—United States—States." Patience is required to wade through these layers of subject headings.

One advantage of online catalogs is that they also permit searches for keywords appearing in titles. It is far easier for most people to think like an author than to think like a librarian. A book about the Equal Protection Clause can be found using the words *equal* and *protection* instead of the subject headings "Equality before the law" or "United States—Constitutional law—Amendments—14th."

A keyword search is a great beginning point, but it is only a first step. Once an appropriate book is found using a keyword search, it is important to use its subject headings to search for other works that may use different title words altogether. By using subject headings, you get expert assistance in finding analogies and related ideas. Stick to keyword searches, and you're limited to your own terminology and concepts.

In using law library catalogs it can be difficult to separate the helpful introductory texts from highly technical monographs or congressional hearings. All may be assigned the same subject heading. "Environmental law—United States" covers *Environmental Law in a Nutshell* as well as *Icons and Aliens: Law, Aesthetics, and Environmental Change* and hearings on the National Ground Water Research Act of 1989. Some factors to consider in determining whether a book is worth pursuing are its age, its length, and whether it appears that the work is updated. Many online catalogs allow the searcher to limit retrieval to books in a reserve collection. This often eliminates older and specialized works and zeroes in on books helpful for students trying to understand a legal topic.

Of the various subheadings assigned to subjects in law library catalogs, one that sounds promising but should usually be avoided is "Cases," as in "Constitutional law—United States—Cases" or "Trade regulation—United States—Cases." This is the subheading used for casebooks. Despite their value as teaching tools, few casebooks provide an easily accessible summary of law that the researcher can put to quick use.

Most academic and law libraries use the Library of Congress classification system, which arranges material roughly by subject. Legal materials are in the classification K, separated from more general historical (D-F), social science (H), or political science (J) treatments. Once you have determined the appropriate classification for your subject area, you can browse the shelves looking for useful resources.

Legal materials are arranged geographically, with KF used for United States law generally and KFA to KFZ used for materials on the laws of specific states and territories. This geographic arrangement is useful for people looking for the laws governing a particular state or country. One unfortunate side effect is its impact on the treatment of legal topics in *Library of Congress Subject Headings* (Library of Congress, annual). This valuable resource's primary purpose is to help catalogers determine the proper terms under which to classify books. It can, however, also be used by researchers looking for appropriate subject headings. For practically every discipline but law, the guide also provides Library of Congress classification numbers in brackets after headings. Because a book on a legal topic can be classed in K or KF or KFA, depending on the

jurisdiction it covers, *Library of Congress Subject Headings* lists no call numbers at all for most legal topics.

The classification system, like the subject headings, generally does not distinguish among treatises, monographs, or shorter works. KF1524, the LC classification for "Bankruptcy—General works," includes treatises such as *Collier on Bankruptcy* and scholarly policy analyses such as Thomas H. Jackson's *The Logic and Limits of Bankruptcy Law* (Harvard University Press, 1986). At least popular works such as *How to File for Bankruptcy* (Nolo Press, 7th ed., 1998) are separated a bit, at KF1524.6.

Finding the classification for a specific subject generally requires locating one or two works in the area and then using those as a springboard to further browsing, rather than scanning detailed classification lists. But some familiarity with the classification system can help, at least in understanding that there is some method to the madness of the library shelves. Table 4-2 presents some of the major areas within the KF classification. Each of these areas, of course, is further subdivided into narrower classifications based on subject and type of material.

TABLE 4-2	
LIBRARY OF CONGRESS CLASSIFICATIONS FOR LAW	
KF 501-553	Family law
KF 560-720	Property
KF 801-1241	Contracts
KF 1246-1327	Torts
KF 1384-1480	Corporations
KF 1501-1548	Bankruptcy
KF 1601-1666	Trade regulation
KF 1971-3192	Intellectual property
KF 3301-3580	Labor law
KF 4501-5130	Constitutional law
KF 8700-9075	Courts; Procedure
KF 9201-9760	Criminal law and procedure

Although most academic libraries use the LC system, the call numbers most often found in public libraries belong to the Dewey Decimal classification. The Dewey system accommodates the entire range of legal information at 340 to 349. These 10 numbers rather neatly divide the entire field of legal literature, as shown in Table 4-3.

TABLE 4-3
DEWEY DECIMAL CLASSIFICATIONS FOR LAW

340	Works on legal philosophy and legal systems generally
341	International law
342	Constitutional and administrative law
343	Miscellaneous public law (tax, trade regulation, public utilities)
344	Social law (labor, welfare, public health, environment, education)
345	Criminal law
346	Private law (domestic relations, contracts, torts, property)
347	Civil procedure (including courts and judicial administration)
348	Statutes, regulations, cases (including works such as digests and encyclopedias)
349	Laws of other countries

In a Dewey Decimal library, the bankruptcy books mentioned above would be found within the "Private law" heading at either 346.078 (bankruptcy) or 346.73078 (with the ".73" indicating that these works focus on the law of the United States). Again, it is not necessary for a library user to study the classification system—simply to be aware that it can be used as an aid in finding related resources.

The third path to finding books in a law library leads directly to the reference librarian's desk. The online catalog or the shelves may have hundreds of books on trademark law, but the librarian knows which source is the leading treatise in the area. Most librarians are wary of interpreting patrons' legal issues and giving what may be considered legal advice, but they are happy to assist in finding resources that can help people help themselves. Know when to turn to the librarian for help. Don't use up your goodwill by leaning on the librarian instead of looking up your own call numbers, but rely on the expertise of the person who has worked most closely with the law library collection and has probably assisted with issues similar to yours in the past.

Internet Online Catalogs

A researcher with access to the Internet is not limited to the resources in a local law library. Online catalogs can be used not only for finding materials readily at hand but can serve as bibliographic guides to the range of available materials. Through interlibrary loan and other resource sharing programs, even books from distant libraries can be obtained if time is not of the essence.

Numerous online catalogs are available over the Internet. One of the leading access points for legal collections is the American Association of Law Libraries' collection of law library catalogs <http://lawlib.wuacc.edu/washlaw/lawcat/lawcat.html>. This site provides links to more than 100 library catalogs, most of which belong to law school libraries. The list does, however, also include several state libraries and library networks, the Library of Congress, the New York Public Library, and even a few Canadian and British libraries. A growing number of the catalogs are accessible through Web interfaces, but many still require access through Telnet software. (Researchers without Telnet can use the University of Saskatchewan's WebCats collection of library catalogs on the World Wide Web <http://www.lights.com/webcats/>. From there, links to library catalogs are listed geographically and by type of library.)

One difficulty in using remote online catalogs is the number of software systems in use; accessing each new catalog may require learning a new set of commands. Whatever system a library catalog uses, it should provide some sort of on-screen assistance in entering searches and finding information. One way to avoid facing a new learning curve each time you search a catalog is to stick to one type of software. Many (but certainly not all) law libraries use the INNOPAC system from Innovative Interfaces, Inc., a rather straightforward, menu-driven system providing simple author/title/subject/keyword choices and several ways to limit retrieval. Its use in so many law library catalogs makes it easy to jump from one catalog to another, using one set of commands.

Another approach to finding law school library catalogs is to use the law schools' homepages. These may provide more up-to-date links that have not yet been added to the American Association of Law Libraries (AALL) site, and they include access to other Web-based information about the libraries and the institutions. The quickest route to a law school site is often to guess the URL for an institution, e.g., <http://www.georgetown.edu> or <http://www.gwu.edu>, <http://www.howard.edu> and then follow the path to the law school and its library. Some law school aliases are easy to guess; others are not. A University of California graduate may guess at <http://www.cal.edu> or <http://www.uc.edu> instead of <http://www.berkeley.edu>. The first leads nowhere, and the second turns out to be the University of Cincinnati. Several lists of law school homepages are available, including the American Bar Association's list of ABA-approved schools <http://www.abanet.org/legaled/approved.html>. FindLaw provides convenient access to law schools <http://www.findlaw.com/02lawschools/>. Like the ABA site, it lists schools both alphabetically and by state, and it also includes links to law school homepages, library Web sites, library Telnet servers, journals, and university homepages. For a broader view of academe beyond law schools, a list of American universities is maintained at <http://www.clas.ufl.edu/CLAS/american-universities.html>.

Two major research libraries merit special mention. The Harvard University HOLLIS system includes coverage of the largest law library in the world, with nearly two million volumes. The HOLLIS system covers the entire Harvard library system, not just the law library, and is available at <telnet://hplus.harvard.edu>. The Web address <http://hplus.harvard.edu> provides a link to the Telnet site. Even if Cambridge, Massachusetts, is far away, most items found through HOLLIS are also available in other, more accessible libraries.

The Library of Congress is the library of record for the United States, and its online catalog includes comprehensive coverage of law books. One can search the LC catalog in several ways, as the library explains on its Web site <http://lcweb.loc.gov/catalog/>. Simple word and browse searches are available through the Web, with more powerful and flexible searching done using the library's LOCIS system through Telnet <telnet://locis.loc.gov>. LOCIS is unfortunately not the world's most user-friendly online catalog, and a fairly complex and inscrutable set of commands is required for advanced searching.

Another online approach to finding bibliographic information is to use a bibliographic utility such as OCLC or RLIN to search the cataloging information of thousands of libraries. Such a search has the advantage of reaching many more publications, although it does not provide information on the specific holdings of a particular library. OCLC's WorldCat system, available through its member libraries, includes more than 36 million records from 12,000 libraries around the world, and provides bibliographic information and lists of holding libraries for each record.

Bibliographies

A variety of bibliographies of law books are published. Some, which seek to list all law books available, are most useful for librarians in making purchasing decisions. They are simply too comprehensive to provide much guidance for most researchers. An ideal bibliographic guide for a researcher's needs highlights the most informative and influential works, and provides annotations explaining the contents and value of specific publications. This section therefore begins with such works and then moves on to more comprehensive titles.

Selective Bibliographies

Some of the most useful bibliographies are the simplest. They provide the necessary foot in the door, identifying the first place to go with a question on antitrust law or torts.

E. Allan Farnsworth's *An Introduction to the Legal System of the United States* (Oceana Publications, 3d ed., 1996), discussed in Chapter 1, is one of the best guides to basic sources. Each section discussing basic areas of legal doctrine ends with a paragraph or two of suggested readings. These provide not just references but brief descriptive comments. For constitutional law, for example, Farnsworth writes, "Treatises include J. Nowak & R. Rotunda, *Handbook on Constitutional Law* (4th ed., 1991), also in a multivolume edition. A more ambitious and idiosyncratic work is L. Tribe, *American Constitutional Law* (2d ed., 1988). For a brief treatment, see J. Peltason, *Corwin & Peltason's Understanding the Constitution* (10th ed., 1985)." He then goes on to recommend helpful monographs and collections of constitutions.

Some of the other works discussed in Chapter 1 also provide references to texts and treatises, but they are not as user-friendly. William Burnham's *Introduction to the Law and Legal System of the United States* (West Publishing, 1995) includes footnotes at the beginning of each section providing references to hornbooks and treatises. These are useful, although the footnotes are sometimes hard to find and the references seem to lean toward other books from the same publisher. *Introduction to the Law of the United States* (Kluwer Law and Taxation Publishers, 1992), edited by David S. Clark and Tuğrul Ansay, includes a selected bibliography at the end of each chapter, but the references are unannotated and generally not as helpful.

Another useful work, which unfortunately is growing increasingly out of date, is *Recommended Law Books* (ABA, 2d ed., 1986), edited by James A. McDermott. This small volume of 152 pages provides references to the most respected works in 70 legal categories. Its valuable references include excerpts from book reviews and lawyers' comments. Some of the best and most succinct comments are from the editor himself. Where Farnsworth called Tribe on constitutional law "more ambitious and idiosyncratic" than Nowak and Rotunda, McDermott refers to the latter work as "more straightforward and matter-of-fact, albeit less scintillating." *Recommended Law Books* is a convenient source for learning what have been considered the most important works in each field; unfortunately, the editor of the 1986 edition has retired from the practice of law and the ABA has announced no plans to publish a new edition.

Subject Bibliographies

From highly selective listings, such as those provided by Farnsworth and McDermott, we move to more extensive bibliographic treatments. The most helpful of these is found in Kendall F. Svengalis's *Legal Information Buyer's Guide & Reference Manual* (Rhode Island LawPress, annual). This work, first published in 1996, is designed for attorneys and librarians responsible for purchasing legal materials. Much of it discusses acquisition strategies. Some sections, however, are useful for researchers. In particular, the "Legal Treatises" chapter provides informative annotations on materials in nearly 50 subject categories. This chapter runs nearly 200 pages, about a third of the entire volume. It covers both multivolume treatises and smaller works, such as hornbooks and Nutshells, providing price information, frequency of supplementation, summaries of contents, and analyses of the style and value of publications. The section on constitutional law, for example, covers eight works, including the oft-mentioned treatments by Tribe and Nowak and Rotunda.

A more extensive work, but one without annotations, is *Encyclopedia of Legal Information Sources* (Gale, 2d ed., 1993), edited by Brian L. Baker and Patrick J. Petit. The subtitle, *A Bibliographic Guide to Approximately 29,000 Citations for Publications, Organizations, and Other Sources of Information on 480 Law-Related Topics*, indicates the ambitious nature of this volume. Baker and Petit cover a broader range of topics than the other works and include far more references. At times this can be helpful, but often it is simply bewildering. Under constitutional law, for example, the editors include more than 50 "textbooks and general works." This alphabetical list of titles ranges from general treatments of the subject to books on James Madison and William Rehnquist.

The value of *Encyclopedia of Legal Information Sources* lies in its extensive range of topics covered and its classification within each topic by material type. Besides textbooks, subsections include loose-leaf services and reporters; handbooks, manuals, formbooks; law reviews and periodicals; newsletters and newspapers; bibliographies; directories; associations and professional societies; and online databases. The distinctions between some of these categories are not always clear, but together they provide references to a significant number of legal publications. The unannotated entries, however, provide little information about the scope of publications or the frequency of supplementation, making it difficult to distinguish between a serious, regularly updated treatise and an aging monograph. Exhibit 4-1 shows a representative page from this work, covering basic works and organizations in the field of housing discrimination.

Baker and Petit provide brief coverage of state-specific materials in a "states" section listing resources for each jurisdiction. More extensive coverage of state texts and treatises is provided in Francis R. Doyle's *Searching the Law: The States* (Transnational Publishers, 2d ed., 1994, with 1996 and 1997 supplements). Separate sections for each state list materials in 75 different subjects. Coverage includes not just major texts but a broad range of continuing legal education materials and other rather obscure sources. Because the entries are unannotated, it may be difficult to identify the more important and useful works. Appendixes in the main volume and the supplements provide addresses for the publishers of most of the works listed.

Searching the Law: The States first appeared as a companion volume to Edward J. Bander, Frank Bae, and Francis R. Doyle's *Searching the Law* (Transnational Publishers, 1987, with supplements in 1989, 1990, and 1992). This volume provides similar coverage of works of national scope. Individual items are not annotated, but brief introductory explanations cover most subjects and references to sources for further information.

Another source listing materials by topic and by state is "Research by Subject" in *West's Legal Desk Reference* (West Publishing, 1991), discussed in Chapter 3. Like *Encyclopedia of Legal Information Sources*, this work lists specialized journals, treatises, and looseleaf services by subject. The state sections list primary sources, research guides, journals, and treatises on state law. This volume has not been updated since its 1991 publication, however, and its unannotated entries provide no information on the scope or supplementation of cited works.

Jean Sinclair McKnight's *Law for the Layperson: An Annotated Bibliography of Self-Help Law Books* (Rothman, 2d ed., 1997) is a more tightly focused work. It contains only books published specifically for nonlawyers and excludes as too outdated most titles published before 1990. (A few exceptions are included if nothing newer is available in an area.) Entries include descriptive annotations summarizing the contents

DISCRIMINATION, EMPLOYMENT

Encyclopedia of Legal Information Sources • 2nd Ed.

REPORT TO THE ATTORNEY GENERAL: REDEFINING DISCRIMINATION: "DISPARATE IMPACT" AND THE INSTITUTIONALIZATION OF AFFIRMATIVE ACTION. U.S. Department of Justice, Office of Legal Policy. Superintendent of Documents, United States Government Printing Office, Washington, D.C. 20402. 1988.

DISCRIMINATION, HOUSING
See also: CIVIL RIGHTS AND LIBERTIES; DISCRIMINATION, RACE; SEGREGATION AND INTEGRATION

LOOSELEAF SERVICES AND REPORTERS

FAIR HOUSING - FAIR LENDING CASES. Prentice-Hall, Incorporated, Route 9W, Englewood Cliffs, New Jersey 07632. 1989- .

HOUSING DISCRIMINATION: LAW AND LITIGATION. Robert G. Schwemm. Clark Boardman Company, Limited, 435 Hudson Street, New York, New York 10014. 1990- .

TEXTBOOKS AND GENERAL WORKS

A DECENT HOME: A REPORT ON THE CONTINUING FAILURE OF THE FEDERAL GOVERNMENT TO PROVIDE EQUAL HOUSING OPPORTUNITY. Citizens Commission on Civil Rights, 2000 M Street, Northwest, Washington, D.C. 20036. 1983.

DIVIDED NEIGHBORHOODS: CHANGING PATTERNS OF RACIAL SEGREGATION. Gary A. Tobin. Sage Publications, 2455 Teller Road, Newbury Park, California 91320. 1987.

THE FAIR HOUSING ACT AFTER TWENTY YEARS: A CONFERENCE AT YALE LAW SCHOOL. Robert G. Schwemm. Yale Law School, New Haven, Connecticut. 1989.

FAIR HOUSING AND COMMUNITY DEVELOPMENT DISCRIMINATION LAW AND PRACTICE. Shepard's Citations, Incorporated. Shepard's/McGraw-Hill, P.O. Box 1235, Colorado Springs, Colorado 80901. 1983.

FAIR HOUSING COMES OF AGE. George R. Metcalf. Greenwood Publishing Group, Incorporated, 88 Post Road West, P.O. Box 5007, Westport, Connecticut 06881. 1988.

FAIR HOUSING: DISCRIMINATION IN REAL ESTATE, COMMUNITY DEVELOPMENT, AND REVITALIZATION. James A. Kushner. Shepard's/McGraw-Hill, P.O. Box 1235, Colorado Springs, Colorado 80901. 1983- . (Annual Supplements).

THE HIGH COST OF HOUSING DISCRIMINATION: A REPORT ON DISCRIMINATION CASES IN NEW YORK METROPOLITAN AREA 1981-1985. Open Housing Center of New York, 150 Fifth Avenue, New York, New York 10011. 1986.

HOUSING DISCRIMINATION LAW AND LITIGATION. Robert G. Schwemm. Bureau of National Affairs, Incorporated, 1231 Twenty-fifth Street, Northwest, Washington, D.C. 20037. 1990.

THE LEGACY OF JUDICIAL POLICY-MAKING: GAUTREAUX V. CHICAGO HOUSING AUTHORITY: THE DECISION AND ITS IMPACTS. Elizabeth Warren. University Press of America, 4720 Boston Way, Lanham, Maryland 20706. 1988.

RESIDENTIAL SEGREGATION, THE STATE AND CONSTITUTIONAL CONFLICT IN AMERICAN URBAN AREAS. R.J. Johnston. Academic Press, Incorporated, 1250 Sixth Avenue, San Diego, California 92101. 1984.

SHELTERED CRISIS: THE STATE OF FAIR HOUSING IN THE EIGHTIES. United States Commission on Civil Rights. Superintendent of Documents, United States Government Printing Office, Washington, D.C. 20402. 1984.

LAW REVIEWS AND PERIODICALS

HARVARD CIVIL RIGHTS -- CIVIL LIBERTIES LAW REVIEW. Harvard Law School, Harvard University Press, 79 Garden Street, Cambridge, Massachusetts 02138. Biannual.

LAW BULLETIN. National Housing Law Project, 1950 Addison Street, Berkeley, California 94704. Bimonthly.

BIBLIOGRAPHIES

AN ANNOTATED BIBLIOGRAPHY OF HOUSING AND SCHOOL SEGREGATION ARTICLES AND DOCUMENTS, WITH ADDITIONAL MATERIAL FOR RESEARCH. Housing Advocates, Incorporated and Edward G. Kramer. Vance Bibliographies, P.O. Box 229, 112 North Charter Street, Monticello, Illinois 61856. 1980.

FAIR HOUSING AND FAMILIES: DISCRIMINATION AGAINST CHILDREN. Jim Buchanan. Vance Bibliographies, P.O. Box 229, 112 North Charter Street, Monticello, Illinois 61856. 1985.

RESIDENTIAL SEGREGATION BY RACE AND CONSTITUTIONAL CONFLICT IN THE UNITED STATES: A BIBLIOGRAPHY. Lorna Peterson. Vance Bibliographies, P.O. Box 229, 112 North Charter Street, Monticello, Illinois 61856. 1986.

DIRECTORIES

DIRECTORY OF STATE AND LOCAL FAIR HOUSING AGENCIES. United States Commission on Civil Rights. Superintendent of Documents, United States Government Printing Office, Washington, D.C. 20402. 1985.

ASSOCIATIONS AND PROFESSIONAL SOCIETIES

LAWYERS COMMITTEE FOR CIVIL RIGHTS UNDER LAW. 1400 I Street, Northwest, Suite 400, Washington, D.C. 20005. (202) 371-1212.

NATIONAL ASSOCIATION FOR THE ADVANCEMENT OF COLORED PEOPLE. 4805 Mt. Hope Drive, Baltimore, Maryland 21215. (212) 481-4100.

NATIONAL HOUSING LAW PROJECT. 1950 Addison Street, Berkeley, California 94704. (415) 548-9400.

OPEN HOUSING CENTER. 594 Broadway, Suite 608, New York, New York 10012. (212) 941-6101.

272

ENCYCLOPEDIA OF LEGAL INFORMATION SOURCES

EXHIBIT 4-1

and features of the books. Items are listed under about 70 subjects. General works are followed by titles written specifically for individual states. The number of works available for a given state varies widely, from 31 California titles to just one title for each of 14 states (Karen A. Shaw, Michael D. Jenkins, and Anthony J. Walters, *Starting and Operating a Business in _____*, published by Oasis Press). More than 160 publishers are represented, from small, specialized firms to general publishing houses. Nolo Press is extensively represented, as are legal guides from organizations such as the American Bar Association and the American Management Association. The volume includes indexes by author, title, and jurisdiction, and a list of publishers' addresses and phone numbers.

One of the most convenient sources for lists of basic legal texts is available in the front of most volumes in West Group's Hornbook and Nutshell series. Under about 70 subjects, these lists provide the titles of works in these series as well as West's Black Letter series of study aids. Coverage is limited to West books, of course, but the result is a rather extensive list of nearly 200 titles from the country's largest publisher of legal texts. Unfortunately, these convenient lists have been discontinued in new editions published since early 1994, so they are gradually becoming outdated. West now lists its books, including practitioners' works and educational texts, on the Internet <http://www.westgroup.com/products/store/>.

Comprehensive Bibliographies

Comprehensive works listing all available legal publications are too unwieldy to be of much assistance to researchers. Even when arranged by subject, they combine coverage of treatises, monographs, and other books with little indication of each work's application or scope. They can be useful aids, of course, in purchasing law books, and they may come in handy when attempting to verify the title or publisher of an elusive work.

Legal materials are covered in the general *Books in Print* (Bowker, 9 vols., annual) and *Subject Guide to Books in Print* (Bowker, 5 vols., annual), but two other publications focus specifically on law. *Bowker's Law Books and Serials in Print* (Bowker, 3 vols., annual) lists works from more than 3,000 publishers, with brief annotations accompanying some entries. Books are indexed by subject, author, and title. The set is updated with a quarterly supplement. Nicholas Triffin's *Law Books in Print: Law Books in English Published Throughout the World and in Print through 1993*

(Glanville Publishers, 6 vols., 7th ed., 1994) provides similar coverage by author, title, and subject, but is less frequently revised. Both of these works include not just books but such other materials as microforms, videotapes, and software. They also include extensive listings for contacting publishers of legal material.

Other works focus on listing new legal publications, which makes them useful for library acquisitions purposes but poorly suited for research use. Because many law books are regularly updated, a work first published 15 or 20 years ago may be as current as a brand new title. A list of recent publications may be of use for a specialist wishing to stay abreast of developments in a particular field, but it is less helpful to a researcher seeking to find the standard works.

The two most comprehensive listings of new books are *Law Books Published* and *Catalog of Current Law Titles*. *Law Books Published* (Glanville, semiannual with annual cumulations) serves as an update to *Law Books in Print*, listing new publications by author, title, subject, publisher, and series. *Catalog of Current Law Titles* (Ward and Associates, bimonthly with annual cumulations) is a list of works acquired by some 60 major U.S. law libraries. General materials are arranged by subject, followed by state-specific materials listed by state. Separate sections list reference materials and new journal subscriptions. Each issue includes author and title indexes, and the annual cumulations add subject indexes. Many obscure publications acquired by just one or two libraries are included; a "Hot Sheets" section at the front of each issue lists material acquired by 25 percent or more of the contributing libraries.

More selective coverage is provided by Oscar J. Miller and Mortimer D. Schwartz's *Recommended Publications for Legal Research* (Rothman, annual). Books are listed under about 50 subjects, with marginal notes indicating whether they are recommended for basic collections (A), intermediate collections (B), or in-depth research collections (C). Twenty-five individual volumes have been published covering the years 1970-95. A cumulation of the "A" list recommendations from these volumes would be a valuable guide to basic legal resources, but none has yet been published.

Launched in 1998, IndexMaster <http://www.indexmaster.com> is a subscription Web site offering a new way to find legal treatises and monographs. It provides searchable access to the table of contents and index of each publication in its database. Searches often retrieve a large number of titles, but results are ranked and the tables of contents and indexes can be displayed in PDF format. Materials from several dozen publishers are represented, but IndexMaster's effectiveness may depend on the participation of West Group and other major legal publishing houses.

Finally, since 1994, selected new books have been included in *Index to Legal Periodicals & Books* (H.W. Wilson, monthly with annual cumulations). Coverage appears to be sporadic, so this is best seen as a place to bump fortuitously into book references while looking for journal articles.

References in Other Works

Despite the number and variety of online catalogs and legal bibliographies, the easiest way to find reliable texts is to bypass all these bibliographic tools and follow research leads gathered from other materials. Most catalogs and bibliographies are simply too comprehensive to provide much guidance in choosing helpful and informative resources.

As you pursue other aspects of your research, be aware of references to texts. To support their decisions or provide explanatory background, most judges include citations to leading scholarly authorities. Frequent citation in court opinions is a good indication that a work provides a correct and coherent statement of legal doctrine.

Even more than court opinions, law review articles are excellent bibliographic resources. Most articles include hundreds of footnotes citing not only cases and statutes but also legal texts and books from other disciplines. A footnote in an article's introductory section may provide convenient citations to the basic works in an area, and scattered throughout may be references to a broad range of literature. Follow a reference to "the leading text" or "a major treatise," and you can be assured that you are turning to a reliable work.

Finding these law review articles from which to work is the subject of the next chapter.

CHAPTER 5
Journals and Periodicals

TOPICS COVERED

Law Reviews
Bar Journals
    American Bar Association (ABA)
    State Bar Associations
Directories of Law Reviews and Journals
Legal Newspapers
Newsletters

Loose-Leaf Services
Access to Articles
    Full-Text Searches
    Legal Periodical Indexes
    Comprehensive Indexes
    Current Awareness Sources
    Other Indexes
    Citators

Journal literature is often the best place to begin a research project in law, particularly a project involving recent developments or rapidly growing areas of law. Periodicals generally respond more quickly to new developments than encyclopedias and texts, and they provide extensive references to the statutes, cases, and other sources needed to analyze a legal problem.

Legal periodical literature is a broad field, encompassing hundreds of scholarly journals, lawyers' magazines and newspapers, and specialized newsletters. These types of periodicals have different audiences, and their articles are useful for different purposes. A law review article may provide an extensive historical background, while a newsletter provides information on the latest developments in litigation.

This chapter looks first at the nature of legal periodicals, then at ways to find articles in them. This will involve using paper and electronic indexes as well as full-text databases and Web sites. Increasingly, legal periodical information is disseminated electronically as well as in print. Although there is much duplication, many sources are still available only in print—and a growing number of sources are available only online. A thorough researcher needs to be able to use both means of access to information.

LAW REVIEWS

Academic law reviews are the most serious and scholarly of the legal periodicals. Edited by law students,

they are an institution unique to legal education. In other disciplines, the leading journals are edited by established scholars, and potential articles are subject to peer review. In the field of law, articles in the most prestigious law reviews are selected and edited by law students. Scholars in other disciplines may shake their heads in wonder, but the law review continues to be an integral part of the law school experience. Most law reviews exist as much for the training of their editors as for the edification of their readers.

Student-edited law reviews are produced at nearly every American law school. Most are based on the model of the *Harvard Law Review*, founded in 1887. They generally contain lead articles written by established scholars (usually law professors, although academics from other disciplines, judges, and practicing lawyers are also represented), and comments or notes written by students. The term *article* is generally used only for nonstudent work, although in many instances the practical differences between articles and student comments are few.

Because law reviews are edited by students and serve as educational tools, much of what they publish is student work. Traditionally, there has been a sharp distinction between the lead articles by established scholars and the student comments. When Sandra Day and William Rehnquist were editors at the *Stanford Law Review* in 1951, student work was published anonymously. This was the norm until the 1960s, when some journals began adding students' names to the end of their pieces. The *Bluebook*, arbiter of legal citation form, continued to insist that student work be cited anonymously. In 1986, the *Stanford Law Review* took the giant leap of putting students' names at the beginning of articles and citing their work by name with the parenthetical note "student author." Finally, in 1991, the *Bluebook* changed its rule to include student authors' names in citations—as long as the name is immediately followed by the word "Note" or "Comment" to denote its author's lower status. Now most student authors receive full credit—except in the *Harvard Law Review*, which continues to publish student work anonymously. Even at Harvard, however, things are better than they once were. Until 1968, student work was also published in a smaller, more cramped typeface than lead articles.

Academic law reviews have produced much of the most influential legal writing in this century. Unfortunately, they are also home to some of the longest and most tedious journal literature in any discipline. A recent article focusing on the nature of student-edited reviews, Rosa Ehrenreich's "Look Who's Editing," *Lingua Franca,* Jan./Feb. 1996, at 58, quotes the dean of Yale Law School, Anthony Kronman, as summarizing current law journal literature as "unreadable junk that goes on endlessly." Not much has changed in the 60 years since another Yale Law School professor, Fred Rodell, wrote that law reviews reminded him of "an elephant trying to swat a fly" ("Goodbye to Law Reviews," 23 Va. L. Rev. 78 [1936]).

Some law review articles are helpful in researching a legal problem. They discuss issues currently confronting the courts, summarize and criticize the approaches taken by different jurisdictions, and propose judicial or legislative solutions. Some law review articles survey practices in each state, providing references to statutory provisions and cases throughout the country.

In the early decades of this century, the law was an isolated world of its own, and law review articles made reference to little outside the insular world of court opinions, legal treatises, and other law review articles. Today, law reviews are increasingly interdisciplinary. Sometimes this manifests itself in a new level of empirical research previously unseen in legal literature. At other times, it only serves to remove law reviews from practical legal concerns. Increasingly, law review articles are written on academic topics for a narrow audience. "Impractical" scholarship was one of the complaints about law schools raised by Judge Harry T. Edwards of the U.S. Court of Appeals for the District of Columbia Circuit in a recent influential article, "The Growing Disjunction Between Legal Education and the Legal Profession," 91 Mich. L. Rev. 34 (1992). Edwards hit a nerve in the legal and academic communities, and his article caused considerable discussion (but relatively little change).

One thing almost all law review articles have in common is that they are heavily footnoted. Unlike journals in many disciplines that simply list references alphabetically at the end of an article, law reviews have numbered footnotes at the bottom of each page. Many articles have hundreds of footnotes, sometimes thousands. (The unchallenged record holder is a nearly 500-page article by securities attorney Arnold S. Jacobs, "An Analysis of Section 16 of the Securities Exchange Act of 1934," 32 N.Y. L. Sch. L. Rev. 209 (1987), with 4,824 footnotes.) Exhibit 5-1 shows the first page from a recent law review article, Thomas A. Schweitzer, "Hate Speech on Campus and the First Amendment: Can They Be Reconciled?," 27 Conn. L. Rev. 493 (1995), with 10 Supreme Court cases and a treatise cited in the first paragraph.

Law review footnotes can go off on tangents, sometimes for a page or more of tiny type. This discursive tendency drives some people crazy and has led to a strident campaign against footnotes by some judges and legal scholars. (It should come as no surprise that the nature of the law review article is a leading topic of discussion in law reviews.) But the value of footnotes, even long discursive ones, is that they provide extensive references to cases, statutes, and secondary literature. Law review editors are notorious for finding authority to support any proposition. Here, for example, are the first two sentences and accompanying footnotes from Mark Kadish's "Behind the Locked Door of an American Grand Jury: Its History, Its Secrecy, and Its Process," 24 Fla. St. U.L. Rev. 1 (1996).

The purpose of our Constitution is to create a government that protects people from each other.[1] The purpose of our Bill of Rights is to protect each of us from our government.[2]

1. *See generally* THOMAS HOBBES, LEVIATHAN (Cambridge Univ. Press 1991) (1651) (asserting that freedom requires relinquishment of power to avoid pitting each person against the other).

2. *See e.g.,* Hugo L. Black, *The Bill of Rights*, 35 N.Y.U. L. REV. 865, 870-73 (1960); Loren A. Smith, *Introduction to Symposium on Regulatory Takings*, 46 S.C.L. REV. 525, 526 (1995) (stating that the very purpose of the Bill of Rights is to protect citizens from government).

HATE SPEECH ON CAMPUS AND THE FIRST AMENDMENT: CAN THEY BE RECONCILED?

Thomas A. Schweitzer[*]

I. INTRODUCTION

Protection of expression from infringement by governmental authority was enshrined in the First Amendment to the United States Constitution[1] in 1791. Since the 1920's, the United States Supreme Court, under the influence of such jurists as Justice Louis D. Brandeis,[2] Justice Oliver Wendell Holmes, Jr.,[3] and Judge Learned Hand,[4] has developed from this constitutional guarantee what is perhaps the most far-reaching system of protection of free expression of any country in the world. Although there are a number of traditional exceptions to this protection, such as libel[5] and fraudulent misrepresentation,[6] strict requirements

---

[*] Associate Professor of Law, Touro College, Jacob D. Fuchsberg Law Center; J.D., Yale Law School. Professor Schweitzer served as Reporter for the conference.

1. The First Amendment states in relevant part: "Congress shall make no law . . . abridging the freedom of speech, or of the press . . . ." U.S. CONST. amend. I. The United States Supreme Court has held that the First Amendment's prohibitions are binding as well on state governments, *see* Gitlow v. New York, 268 U.S. 652 (1925), and that, of course, includes public, but not private, colleges and universities.

2. *See* Whitney v. California, 274 U.S. 357, 372 (1927) (Brandeis, J., concurring).

3. *See* Abrams v. United States, 250 U.S. 616, 624 (1919) (Holmes, J., dissenting).

4. *See* Masses Publishing Co. v. Patten, 244 F. 535 (S.D.N.Y. 1917) (Opinion of Hand, J.), *rev'd*, 246 F. 24 (2d Cir. 1917).

5. Actions for libel or slander were long thought to be immune to any First Amendment limitations. *See, e.g.*, Roth v. United States, 354 U.S. 476, 483 (1957); Chaplinsky v. New Hampshire, 315 U.S. 568 (1942); Near v. Minnesota, 283 U.S. 697, 719 (1931). But the Supreme Court, in New York Times Co. v. Sullivan, 376 U.S. 255 (1964), and its progeny imposed significant First Amendment restrictions on the law of defamation in cases brought by public officials and public figures. Defamation actions brought by other private plaintiffs, however, were unaffected. *See* Dun & Bradstreet v. Greenmoss Builders, 472 U.S. 749 (1985); *see also* RODNEY A. SMOLLA & MELVILLE B. NIMMER, SMOLLA AND NIMMER ON FREEDOM OF SPEECH: A TREATISE ON THE FIRST AMENDMENT § 6.02(1)(b) (1994).

6. The prevailing view is that factually false statements are not entitled to First Amendment protection. The Supreme Court has stated that "there is no constitutional value in false statements of fact," Gertz v. Robert Welch, Inc., 418 U.S. 323, 340 (1974), and that "[a]dvertising that is false, deceptive, or misleading of course is subject to restraint." Bates v. State Bar Ass'n, 433 U.S. 350, 383 (1977). *See also* SMOLLA & NIMMER, *supra* note 5, § 11.01(4)(b) (sec-

493

EXHIBIT 5-1

Note that the first footnote provides a reference to a classic work, albeit one predating the Constitution by 136 years and hence perhaps a bit remote; and that the second footnote simply provides references to other law review articles making the same point—although one is written by an influential Supreme Court justice.

To someone unfamiliar with the style of law reviews, a page with three or four lines of text and 50 lines of footnote can seem confusing, oppressive, or downright absurd. But these footnotes are what can make even a mediocre article a valuable research tool. They provide jumping-off points to a broad range of sources—not simply the court opinions cited in legal encyclopedias and treatises, but books, articles from the scholarly and popular press, government reports, working papers, even occasional dust jacket blurbs.

As noted earlier, student-edited law reviews are published at every accredited U.S. law school. (The final holdout, the CUNY School of Law, began publishing the *New York City Law Review* in 1996.) Most schools have a general interest law review simply named after the school and publishing articles on a wide variety of legal topics. A few schools have chosen instead to focus their attention on a specialized journal rather than add yet another general law review to the pile. Notable among these are the *University of Louisville Journal of Family Law*, Lewis & Clark's *Environmental Law*, and the Franklin Pierce Law Center's *IDEA: The Journal of Law and Technology*.

In addition, a growing number of student-edited specialized law reviews are popping up at schools that already publish general law reviews. This increases the number of students who are able to participate in the editing experience, which is seen as both educational and resume-enhancing. To some extent, these specialized journals are useful sources for information on particular topics, but they have multiplied to such a degree that demand has long since been outstripped by supply.

Harvard Law School, home of the first modern law review, now publishes 12 student-edited journals. In the olden days, when there were just a few dozen law reviews published in the country, the *Harvard Law Review* was Harvard's only publication. In recent decades, however, it has been joined at an ever speedier pace by new titles.

1887 *Harvard Law Review*
1959 *Harvard International Law Journal* (originally *Bulletin of the Harvard International Law Club*)
1964 *Harvard Journal on Legislation*
1966 *Harvard Civil Rights-Civil Liberties Law Review*
1976 *Harvard Environmental Law Review*
1978 *Harvard Journal of Law and Public Policy*
1978 *Harvard Women's Law Journal*
1984 *Harvard Blackletter Law Journal* (originally *Harvard Blackletter Journal*)
1988 *Harvard Human Rights Journal*
1988 *Harvard Journal of Law and Technology*
1994 *Harvard Latino Law Review*
1996 *Harvard Negotiation Law Review*

Believe it or not, Harvard is not the only law school with 12 journals. Columbia Law School also publishes

12 journals, which cover several of the same topics as Harvard's. It also publishes journals on arts law, business law, international arbitration, Asian law, and European law. Several other schools have six or more journals. Even Lewis & Clark, which forwent a general interest review to focus on *Environmental Law*, has added two other titles, *International Legal Perspectives* and *Animal Law*. In all, more than 240 specialized law reviews complement the 172 general interest law reviews in existence. By far the most popular specialty is international and comparative law, with more than 70 journals. But there are also 28 journals specializing in environmental law and a dozen or more in entertainment, sports, and the arts. This glut of journals may reduce the overall quality of articles, but it means that there is probably an article out there of some use on just about any issue being researched.

A second trend in recent years is the development of journals edited by faculty—the norm elsewhere in academia, but still a relative rarity in law. These journals provide peer review and a more experienced editorial hand. Articles often are shorter, filled less with publish-or-perish tenure pieces than with an exchange of ideas between scholars. The University of Chicago is a leading center of faculty-edited journals, with four publications: *Journal of Law and Economics* (1958-date), *Supreme Court Review* (1960-date), *Journal of Legal Studies* (1972-date), and *Crime and Justice: A Review of Research* (1979-date). Other leading faculty-edited journals include *Law and Contemporary Problems* (1933-date), *Tax Law Review* (1945-date), *American Journal of Legal History* (1957-date), *Law and History Review* (1983-date), *Constitutional Commentary* (1984-date), *Journal of Law, Economics and Organization* (1985-date), and *Florida Tax Review* (1992-date).

A newer development, paralleling trends in other disciplines, is the appearance of several journals published only electronically. The first of these was the *National Journal of Sexual Orientation Law* <http://sunsite.unc.edu/gaylaw/>; most of the others focus on technology issues. *Michigan Telecommunications and Technology Law Review* is available both on the Internet <http://www.law.umich.edu/mttlr/> and on LEXIS-NEXIS, while several publications, such as *Journal of On-line Law* <http://www.wm.edu/law/publications/jol/> and *Richmond Journal of Law and Technology* <http://www.richmond.edu/~jolt> are available only on the Internet. Without the need to consume a certain amount of paper for each volume, online journals may not produce as steady a stream of articles as printed journals. *Journal of On-line Law*, for example, published just two articles in 1996 and none in 1997.

Many of the traditional, print-based law reviews are moving to electronic publication as well. The first step in this process has been inclusion in the subscription-based online services of LEXIS-NEXIS and WESTLAW. Both services began providing access to law review articles in the early 1980s. LEXIS-NEXIS began with full coverage of about 50 journals in 1982, while WESTLAW chose to provide selected articles from a much broader range of journals. WESTLAW's selective approach proved problematic, as it was never clear whether valuable articles had been excluded, so a decade later it switched to a predominantly full-coverage system.

Both online systems now provide access to hundreds of law reviews and tens of thousands of articles. LEXIS-NEXIS offers full-text coverage of more than 400 journals and law reviews in its LAWREV library, although coverage extends back beyond 1993 for only about 100 of these journals. WESTLAW provides full or selected coverage of more than 600 journals. Some 475 of them have full coverage, with nearly 300 beginning full coverage in 1993 or later. The majority of the journals WESTLAW now covers in full include material from earlier volumes on a selective basis.

Each system has individual files for specific titles and comprehensive databases covering all available law reviews. The ALLREV file on LEXIS-NEXIS combines the contents of almost all journals in the LAWREV library. WESTLAW's journals are in the JLR (journals and law reviews) and TP-ALL (all texts and periodicals) databases. Although law reviews are in both databases, TP-ALL also includes coverage of bar journals and more than 100 texts and treatises.

The online systems also have subject-specific databases for articles in specialized areas. WESTLAW, for example, has practice area databases in three dozen areas, including civil rights (CIV-TP), criminal justice (CJ-TP), the First Amendment (CFA-TP), jurisprudence and constitutional theory (JCT-TP), and Native American law (NAM-TP). These specialized databases can cost less than the larger ones but may omit relevant articles. WESTLAW's ED-TP database, for example, includes several articles on campus speech codes but neglects others found in the JLR database, such as Stephen Fleischer's "Campus Speech Codes: The Threat to Liberal Education," 27 J. Marshall L. Rev. 709 (1994), and the Schweitzer article shown in Exhibit 5-1.

Law reviews are appearing more slowly on the Web than through LEXIS-NEXIS and WESTLAW. Although a large number of journals have Web sites of one sort or another, relatively few provide the full text of recent articles—and fewer still include access to older issues. Gradually, however, law schools are committing resources to Web publication, and access is increasing. The Duke University School of Law is a leader in this trend, with all six of its journals available through a common site <http://www.law.duke.edu/journals/>. The Duke site includes links between text and footnotes, references within articles to the corresponding pages in the print versions, and a procedure for ordering Portable Document Format (PDF) versions that duplicate the exact format of the printed pages.

Of several lists of online law journals, two of the most extensive are maintained by law schools. The University of Southern California's "Legal Journals on the Web" <http://www.usc.edu/dept/law-lib/legal/journals.html> has separate lists of general law reviews, subject-specific law reviews, commercial law journals, foreign law journals, and ABA journals and newsletters, with notes indicating whether sites contain full text, abstracts, or just tables of contents. Washburn University <http://lawlib.wuacc.edu/washlaw/lawjournal/lawjournal.html> lists all journals alphabetically, with brief notes but a less consistent method for indicating which journals actually feature material on the Web and which simply have informational homepages. FindLaw <http://www.findlaw.com/03journals> lists general law reviews and specialized journals under 18 topics. FindLaw's lists do not include descriptive annotations, but they do indicate which journals have articles in full text and which have abstracts.

One attractive feature of publication in a hypertext medium is the way that footnotes drop into the background. The notes may be just as extensive, providing irrelevant discursions as well as valuable research leads, but they are merely marked by underlined or highlighted text instead of occupying half or more of each page and causing consternation in some readers. Those who wish to follow the narrative of the article are not disturbed, and those interested in using the notes as guides for further research can click on the numbers to follow the hypertext trail.

BAR JOURNALS

Law reviews are published principally for an academic audience. Another genre of legal periodical, the bar journal, is published specifically for practicing lawyers.

Generally published on a more frequent schedule than law reviews, bar journals tend to focus on areas of current concern to practitioners and contain news about recent legal developments. Their articles are shorter than those in law reviews and are usually written by practicing lawyers rather than academics. They are valuable for monitoring current issues but are less productive for further research than the lengthier and more heavily footnoted law review sources.

Journals for the practicing bar are issued by national, state, and local bar associations; by a variety of specialized organizations of lawyers; and by commercial publishers. The following discussion focuses on materials from the major national organization of lawyers and from state bar associations.

American Bar Association (ABA)

The leading producer of bar journals is the American Bar Association. Its flagship publication is the *ABA Journal*, a glossy monthly magazine with brief articles, notes of recent books of general interest, and columns on matters ranging from the Supreme Court to office technology. The *ABA Journal* is a news magazine; unlike its counterpart from the American Medical Association, *JAMA*, it is not a forum for controversial or groundbreaking new research.

The ABA is a wide-ranging organization with several dozen specialized sections for lawyers interested in particular legal topics. Many of these sections also issue periodicals. Several of these are magazines similar in style to the *ABA Journal*, with short, nontechnical articles on topics in their fields. Topical magazines that may be of interest to nonlawyers include *Criminal Justice*, *Family Advocate*, and *Natural Resources and Environment*. There are also magazines for general practitioners (*Compleat Lawyer*), law students (*Student Lawyer*), new attorneys (*Young Lawyer*), and senior attorneys (*Experience*).

Generally of more research value are the quarterly journals published by a number of ABA sections. These titles include the following:

Administrative Law Review
Antitrust Law Journal
Business Lawyer
Family Law Quarterly
International Lawyer
Journal of Affordable Housing and Community
  Development Law
Jurimetrics: Journal of Law, Science and
  Technology
Labor Lawyer

Public Contract Law Journal
Real Property, Probate and Trust Journal
Tax Lawyer
Tort and Insurance Law Journal
Urban Lawyer

In some ways, these journals find a valuable middle ground between the academic and practice worlds. The articles are scholarly and well documented, but they generally focus on more practical issues than the articles published in most law reviews. The journals are edited by lawyers and professors, but law student staffs assist in the editorial process. This process has worked for years with some titles, such as *Tax Lawyer* (Georgetown University) and *Urban Lawyer* (University of Missouri-Kansas City), and in recent years more and more ABA journals have become affiliated with law schools. *Business Lawyer*, for example, teamed up with the University of Maryland in 1991, and *Public Contract Law Journal* with George Washington University in 1995. Only *Antitrust Law Journal* and *Tort and Insurance Law Journal* continue to publish without student editorial staffs.

Access to articles in ABA publications is possible through several means. The *ABA Journal*, the specialized journals, and most of the magazines are covered in the major legal periodical indexes discussed later in this chapter. LEXIS-NEXIS and WESTLAW provide online access to many of these publications. WESTLAW covers more than three dozen ABA journals and magazines. Each has its own database, and they can all be searched together in the AMBAR-TP database—as well as with hundreds of other journals in the TP-ALL database. The date of coverage varies, with several journals online as far back as 1982. In most instances, however, WESTLAW contains only selected articles. LEXIS-NEXIS's ABA library includes coverage of about 18 journals, both in separate files and in the ALLABA file. Some access to ABA periodicals is provided on the Internet <http://www.abanet.org/store/periodicals.html>; a few titles, such as *Compleat Lawyer*, are covered extensively, while others just have sample articles or tables of contents on the Web.

State Bar Associations

Most state bar associations publish magazines similar in design to the *ABA Journal*. These contain short articles on current legal topics and developments of interest to lawyers, usually with a few footnote references to statutes and cases. These magazines can be useful sources for practical information on legal issues in a particular state. Some state bars also publish scholarly

journals (*Connecticut Bar Journal, Pennsylvania Bar Association Quarterly*) or bulletins containing new court decisions (*Ohio State Bar Association Report*), and a few publications for lawyers in specific states are issued by commercial publishers (*California Lawyer*) or other organizations (*Delaware Lawyer*, published by the Delaware Bar Foundation).

State bar magazines are not as widely accessible as ABA publications. Some, but not all, are covered by the legal periodical indexes, and only a few are available in full text through online databases and state bar Web sites. A list of these appears in Table 5-1; notes at the end of the list indicate whether the title is covered in the major legal periodical indexes and databases.

In addition to publications from state bars, a number of local bar associations publish journals or magazines. The most prominent of these, such as the *Boston Bar Journal* and the *Record of the Bar Association of the City of New York*, are also covered in the periodical indexes and online databases.

TABLE 5-1

STATE BAR ASSOCIATION PERIODICALS

Alabama Lawyer	(Alabama State Bar, bimonthly) [IAC, ILP, L, W]
Alaska Bar Rag	(Alaska Bar Association, bimonthly)
Arizona Attorney	(State Bar of Arizona, 11 issues per year) [IAC, L, W]
Arkansas Lawyer	(Arkansas Bar Association, quarterly) [IAC, W]
California Bar Journal	(State Bar of California, monthly)
Colorado Lawyer	(Colorado Bar Association, monthly) [IAC, ILP, W]
Connecticut Lawyer	(Connecticut Bar Association, 9 issues per year)
In Re	(Delaware State Bar Association, monthly)
Washington Lawyer	(District of Columbia Bar, bimonthly) [IAC]
Florida Bar Journal	(Florida Bar, monthly) [IAC, ILP, L, W]
Georgia Bar Journal	(State Bar of Georgia, bimonthly) [IAC, ILP]
Hawaii Bar Journal	(Hawaii State Bar Association, monthly) [L, W]
Advocate	(Idaho State Bar, monthly) [IAC, W]
Illinois Bar Journal	(Illinois State Bar Association, monthly) [IAC, ILP, W]
Res Gestae	(Indiana State Bar Association, monthly) [IAC, ILP, W]
Iowa Lawyer	(Iowa State Bar Association, monthly)
Journal of the Kansas Bar Association	(Kansas Bar Association, 10 issues per year [IAC, ILP, W]
Kentucky Bench & Bar	(Kentucky Bar Association, quarterly) [IAC]
Louisiana Bar Journal	(Louisiana State Bar Association, bimonthly) [IAC, ILP, L, W]
Maine Bar Journal	(Maine State Bar Association, bimonthly) [IAC, ILP, L, W]
Maryland Bar Journal	(Maryland State Bar Association, bimonthly) [IAC, ILP]
Massachusetts Law Review	(Massachusetts Bar Association, quarterly) [IAC, ILP, W]
Michigan Bar Journal	(State Bar of Michigan, monthly) [IAC, ILP, L, W]
Bench & Bar of Minnesota	(Minnesota State Bar Association, 11 issues per year) [IAC]
Mississippi Lawyer	(Mississippi Bar, bimonthly)
Journal of the Missouri Bar	(Missouri Bar, bimonthly) [IAC, ILP, L, W]
Montana Lawyer	(State Bar of Montana, 11 issues per year) [L, W]
Nebraska Lawyer	(Nebraska State Bar Association, monthly)
Nevada Lawyer	(State Bar of Nevada, monthly) [IAC, L, W]
New Hampshire Bar Journal	(New Hampshire Bar Association, quarterly) [IAC, ILP]
New Jersey Lawyer	(New Jersey State Bar Association, 8 issues per year) [ILP, W]
Bar Journal	(State Bar of New Mexico, bimonthly)
New York State Bar Journal	(New York State Bar Association, 8 issues per year) [IAC, ILP, W]
North Carolina State Bar Journal	(North Carolina State Bar, quarterly)
Gavel	(State Bar Association of North Dakota, bimonthly)
Ohio Lawyer	(Ohio State Bar Association, bimonthly)

TABLE 5-1 (continued)	

STATE BAR ASSOCIATION PERIODICALS

Oklahoma Bar Journal	(Oklahoma Bar Association, weekly)
Oregon State Bar Bulletin	(Oregon State Bar, 10 issues per year) L, W
Pennsylvania Lawyer	(Pennsylvania Bar Association, bimonthly) L, W
Rhode Island Bar Journal	(Rhode Island Bar Association, 9 issues per year) L, W
South Carolina Lawyer	(South Carolina Bar, bimonthly) L, W
Newsletter	(State Bar of South Dakota, monthly)
Tennessee Bar Journal	(Tennessee Bar Association, bimonthly) IAC, ILP, W
Texas Bar Journal	(State Bar of Texas, 11 issues per year) IAC, ILP, L
Utah Bar Journal	(Utah State Bar, monthly) IAC, ILP, L, W
Vermont Bar Journal and Law Digest	(Vermont Bar Association, bimonthly) L, W
Virginia Lawyer	(Virginia State Bar, monthly)
Washington State Bar News	(Washington State Bar Association, monthly) IAC, ILP
West Virginia Lawyer	(West Virginia State Bar, monthly) W
Wisconsin Lawyer	(State Bar of Wisconsin, monthly) IAC, ILP, W
Wyoming Lawyer	(Wyoming State Bar, bimonthly)

IAC = Information Access Co. indexes, including *Current Law Index* and *LegalTrac*; ILP = *Index to Legal Periodicals & Books*; L = LEXIS-NEXIS; W = WESTLAW

DIRECTORIES OF LAW REVIEWS AND JOURNALS

Most law journals, including both academic law reviews and bar journals, are listed in comprehensive works such as *Ulrich's International Periodical Directory* (Bowker, 5 vols., annual). *Ulrich's* provides a good deal of information, such as the date a periodical began, frequency of publication, subscription cost, addresses and telephone numbers, and indexing and abstracting services that cover the title. Many entries also include a brief description of the journal's focus or purpose. The "Law" section of *Ulrich's* stretches for more than 200 pages; although there are subheadings for topics such as estate planning and family law, most titles are simply listed in alphabetical sequence. A few legal topics are covered elsewhere in the directory; tax journals are listed under "Business and Economics—Public Finance, Taxation," and labor and employment law journals are listed under "Business and Economics—Labor and Industrial Relations." The whereabouts of a specific journal can be found by referring to the title index in Volume 4.

Standard Periodical Directory (Oxbridge, annual) also lists journals by subject, but its coverage is less extensive than *Ulrich's*. A 60-page "Law" section includes addresses, telephone and fax numbers, a brief summary of editorial focus, and subscription costs. The listings include a variety of journals, legal newspapers, law school alumni publications, and other materials such as court reports.

Two extensive directories focus specifically on law journals: *Hein's Legal Periodical Check List*, 3d revision (William S. Hein & Co., 3 vols., 1991-date) and Eugene M. Wypyski's *Legal Periodicals in English* (Glanville Publishers, 5 vols., 1976-date). These two resources are designed primarily for library staff needs in cataloging and processing periodicals, but they contain some useful reference information. The Hein checklist provides a detailed record of exactly what issues have been published and includes a publishers directory with subscription addresses. The Wypyski set includes a 64-page subject index, last updated in 1995, that may be useful in finding topical journals.

Michael H. Hoffheimer's *Anderson's Directory of Law Reviews and Scholarly Legal Publications* (Anderson Publishing Co., annual) is a much smaller, more specialized directory published as a service for legal scholars. This thin paperback volume contains names, frequency of publication, addresses, and phone and fax numbers for three groups of journals: general student-edited law reviews, special focus student-edited law reviews, and non-student-edited peer review and trade journals. Together these total nearly 600 entries. The second and third sections are each divided into 30 or more subject areas, making this a convenient source for finding journals on specialized topics. The directory is designed for use by authors, so it excludes jour-

nals that publish only student work and journals that do not accept unsolicited contributions. The volume includes an alphabetical index and an extensive bibliography of law review articles written *about* law review articles. *Anderson's Directory* is also available on the Web <http://www.andersonpublishing.com/lawschool/directory/directory.html>.

Another work designed for authors, recently updated, is Al Joyner's *Directory for Successful Publishing in Legal Periodicals* (Qucoda Publishing, 2d ed., 1997). This directory covers nearly 500 journals, with information on manuscript submission and the review process, such as preferred page length, number of copies to submit, and percentage of manuscripts accepted (*Harvard Law Review* accepts 1.5 percent). One of several appendixes lists journals by subject. This is a useful directory, although it omits journals such as *Cornell Law Review* and *Minnesota Law Review* that apparently did not return questionnaires.

Two convenient sources for contact information for large numbers of journals are the front pages of any issue of the major periodical indexes *Current Law Index* and *Index to Legal Periodicals & Books*. These alphabetical lists of the journals and magazines covered in the indexes are in both cases more extensive than *Anderson's Directory of Law Reviews and Scholarly Legal Publications*. Neither list includes telephone numbers, but both provide ISSN numbers and subscription costs if available. The *Index to Legal Periodicals & Books* list also indicates frequency of publication.

LEGAL NEWSPAPERS

Like bar journals, legal newspapers are published for practicing lawyers and are designed to provide information on current developments. They usually contain short articles on such topics as new legislative actions or Supreme Court decisions. Articles in legal newspapers are generally briefer and less thoroughly documented than articles in monthly or quarterly journals. In many instances, however, they are written by journalists rather than lawyers, so they may be less laden with legal jargon and provide a more accessible introduction to a topic.

Local legal newspapers serve other functions for the legal community. Many report new decisions from local courts, either abstracted or in full text, and they are often filled with classified legal notices on such matters as lost property and wills, and divorces, which are published to satisfy statutory notice requirements. These materials are the bread and butter of local legal newspapers. For some, which have no reporters and no news articles, they are the entire diet.

Many legal newspapers are published weekly, but a few in larger cities are published daily. Some of these have been around for some time. The *Legal Intelligencer*, a daily newspaper in Philadelphia, was established in 1843, and the *Chicago Daily Law Bulletin* first appeared in 1854. Two of the most widely read and respected dailies, *Los Angeles Daily Journal* and *New York Law Journal*, were both first published in 1888.

A newer breed of newspaper has sprung up since the 1970s—glossier weekly papers with more regional news and fewer local notices. One of the most respected of these is *Legal Times* (1982-date), covering developments in Washington, D.C. Lawyers Weekly Publications in Boston publishes newspapers in seven states (*Massachusetts Lawyers Weekly* and similar publications in Michigan, Missouri, North Carolina, Ohio, Rhode Island, and Virginia), covering news of the local bar and local federal and state court decisions. In 1993, Lawyers Weekly launched a national edition, *Lawyers Weekly USA*, which, despite its title, is published every two weeks. Other state-based weekly newspapers include *Connecticut Law Tribune* (1975-date), *New Jersey Law Journal* (1878-date), *Pennsylvania Law Weekly* (1977-date), and *Texas Lawyer* (1985-date).

Most legal newspapers limit their coverage to particular states or regions, but the weekly *National Law Journal* (1978-date) covers events throughout the country and is widely circulated. It includes news of recent court cases, a "Washington Brief" section focusing on legislative and regulatory developments, announcements of recent verdicts and settlements, and regular op-ed columns on legal topics. *American Lawyer* (1979-date, monthly) is a tabloid-style magazine that first became known for its exposés of law firm life but over time has established its reputation with investigative reports and in-depth articles on such topics as jury deliberations in important cases.

Most of these papers are available online in the LEGNEW and NEWS libraries on LEXIS-NEXIS. The LEGNEW library contains information from 20 daily and weekly legal newspapers, as well as a number of newsletters and other legal news sources. Most of the legal newspapers in LEGNEW are also in the NEWS library, as separate files, combined in a LGLNEW file, or in larger files with general newspapers, magazines, and wire services. The overlapping coverage of LEGNEW and LGLNEW sounds confusing, but it just reflects two paths to the same information sources.

WESTLAW has a LEGALNP database with coverage of about a dozen legal newspapers. Online coverage of most newspapers begins in the early to mid-1990s, although LEXIS-NEXIS coverage of *Legal Times* begins in 1982 and of *National Law Journal* in 1983.

Several Web sites feature legal news. Perhaps the leading source is Law Journal Extra! <http://www.ljx.com> from the publisher of *National Law Journal* and *New York Law Journal*. Extra! offers current legal news as well as a variety of other resources, including topical sections with news stories in about three dozen practice areas. It also provides links to online versions of its print publications, although some material is restricted to paid subscribers. Lawyers Weekly also has an online news site <http://www.lawyersweekly.com> with stories from *Lawyers Weekly USA* and its local legal newspapers. FindLaw provides links to these and other legal news sites, including several sources for news on specialized topics <http://www.findlaw.com/15reference/legalnews.html>.

Legal newspapers are included in most directories of newspapers and periodicals. Those listing publications geographically are the most useful because legal newspapers carry court notices and articles of local concern. Differentiating directory listings for legal newspapers from those for other newspapers is not always easy; not all legal newspapers are thoughtful enough to include the word *Law* in their title.

The most extensive of these directories, *Gale Directory of Publications and Broadcast Media* (Gale, annual), includes numerous legal newspapers, but unfortunately they can be hard to find because there is little consistency in the way they are identified. *New York Law Journal* and *Recorder* (San Francisco) are called "Legal newspapers," but the *Los Angeles Daily Journal* is called a "Newspaper for the legal community" and *National Law Journal* a "Tabloid focusing on the practice of law and trends in law." A subject index includes entries under "Law," but its listings are hardly comprehensive. For the District of Columbia, a dozen publications are listed, but there is no sign of either *Daily Washington Law Reporter* or *Legal Times*. For some reason, however, the "Law" index does include the *Chadron Record*, a weekly newspaper for a Nebraska town of 6,000 people. The Gale directory is available electronically as part of the *Gale Database of Publications and Broadcast Media*, which also includes coverage of *Directories in Print* and *Newsletters in Print*. Among the means through which the database is available are CD-ROM, DIALOG (File 469), and WESTLAW (GALE-DPBM database).

The *Newspaper Directory* volume of *The Working Press of the Nation* (National Research Bureau, annual) has a "Special Interest Newspapers" section listing fewer than a dozen papers under "Legal" but about 50 under "Court and Commercial," including *American Lawyer* and the *New York Law Journal*. The *Los Angeles Daily Journal*, on the other hand, is listed with general daily newspapers, with little indication of its legal focus.

Editor & Publisher International Year Book (Editor & Publisher Co., annual) has a slightly more extensive listing of specialized papers at the end of its section 1, "Daily Newspapers Published in the United States." The "Court, Law, Business, Commerce and Finance" section lists about 70 newspapers alphabetically by city. The *Year Book* also lists weekly newspapers, but with no comparable subject listing.

Although this section has focused on newspapers with a specific legal focus, the legal coverage of general interest newspapers has grown increasingly extensive and sophisticated in recent years. In addition to covering such news as Supreme Court decisions, major newspapers also cover the world of legal practice in such regular features as the daily "Legal Beat" column in the *Wall Street Journal* and the "Washington Hearsay" page in the *Washington Post*'s weekly "Washington Business" section. For several years, the *New York Times* published a law page every Friday, featuring an "At the Bar" column, but this was discontinued in 1995.

FindLaw Legal News <http://legalnews.findlaw.com> presents stories on legal topics from the Reuters news service, updated several times a day. A table of contents presents these stories under more than a dozen subject headings, such as "White House Affairs," "Tobacco Litigation," and "US Supreme Court." The text of the stories is searchable, and it is possible to receive news updates by e-mail.

NEWSLETTERS

Legal newsletters are published on a wide variety of topics. Some are distributed at little or no cost by government agencies or public interest groups, while others are expensive services written for a highly specialized audience.

Newsletters are often the best place to track current developments in specialized areas because they serve as the forum for area practitioners to share news. New court decisions on an issue such as tobacco products liability may circulate among lawyers but never be published in the court reports or other regular sources. A newsletter can quickly provide its subscribers with a simple photocopy of an unpublished decision without worrying about typesetting, editorial enhancements, or subject indexing.

Most of the time, however, this information does not come cheap. Monthly publications may be $150 to $200, and subscriptions to weekly or biweekly newsletters can run more than $1,000; a few daily newsletters cost more than $5,000 per year. As a result, many newsletters have limited circulation and may be hard to find in libraries open to the public.

Several publishers produce newsletters on a wide variety of legal topics. Chief among these is the Bureau of National Affairs (BNA), a company based in Washington, D.C. BNA's weekly flagship publication, *The United States Law Week*, provides information on a broad range of current legal developments. *Law Week* is published in several sections and shelved in two loose-leaf binders. The second binder, covering the Supreme Court, will be discussed in Chapter 7. The first part, "General Law," consists of two sections: "Case Alert," summarizing recent decisions from federal and state courts; and "Legal News," providing stories about other developments, such as newly introduced legislation, settlements, administrative actions, and judicial appointments. Items in each issue are arranged by subject, and indexes are published every three months.

BNA also publishes dozens of more specialized weekly newsletters, such as *Criminal Law Reporter*, *Family Law Reporter*, and *Health Law Reporter*, which track developments in the legislatures, the administrative agencies, and the courts. Some BNA newsletters are published every day: *Daily Environment Report*, *Daily Labor Report*, *Daily Report for Executives*, and *Daily Tax Report*. Twenty other daily BNA reports are available electronically through LEXIS-NEXIS and WESTLAW.

Other publishers focus on topics that are the subject of current litigation. Mealey Publications produces about two dozen reports in such areas as insurance law, products liability, and toxic torts. Some are highly specialized, such as *Mealey's Litigation Reports: Lead* or *Mealey's Litigation Reports: Pedicle Screws*. These newsletters summarize new case developments and reproduce current court documents that may never be published in the standard sources.

Andrews Publications produces more than 50 biweekly or monthly newsletters, including such titles as *Electromagnetic Field Litigation Reporter*, *Repetitive Stress Injury Litigation Reporter*, and *Sexual Harassment Litigation Reporter*. Other publishers include

Leader Publications, a division of New York Law Publishing Company, which produces more than two dozen newsletters on aspects of legal practice management and litigation; and LRP Publications, with about 16 reporters and bulletins covering such topics as AIDS policy, immigration, and workplace substance abuse. The National Association of Attorneys General publishes about a dozen newsletters on issues of concern to state policymakers, such as civil rights, consumer protection, environmental law, gaming, military base closures, and state constitutional law. In addition, a number of state-specific newsletters publish in such areas as employment and environmental law.

All these series of newsletters are available online through LEXIS-NEXIS. Each Mealey's and Andrews newsletter appears in a separate file; combined MEALEY and ANDRWS files can be found in the BKRTCY, INSURE, LEGNEW, NEWS, and TORTS libraries. The LEGNEW library contains collected newsletters in 20 practice areas (asbestos, banking law, bankruptcy, computer law, corporate law, employment/labor law, energy and utility law, entertainment law, environmental law, health care law, human resources, insurance law, international law, intellectual property law, litigation/tort, realty law, securities law, school law, tax law, and telecommunications law). Hundreds of legal and business newsletters are included in the NEWS library.

WESTLAW coverage of newsletters is less extensive, but it does provide access to numerous BNA, Mealey's, and Andrews titles. The Mealey's and Andrews newsletters, but not those from BNA, are included in the comprehensive TP-ALL database.

Law firms produce a large number of newsletters as a means of keeping clients informed on developing topics and attracting new business. Some are informative, while others are little more than sales pitches for their services. Most of these have a limited circulation, but a growing number are available on the Internet and can be found through search engines or links from subject sites. The Arent Fox Web site, for example, <http://www.arentfox.com> includes the texts of eight newsletters in such areas as employment law, environmental law, health law, and antitrust. It also provides a form to be submitted by those who wish to receive any of these newsletters by regular mail.

The leading directory of newsletters is *Legal Newsletters in Print* (Infosources Publishing, annual), edited by Arlene L. Eis, covering more than 2,200 newsletters published in the United States. Entries in the main alphabetical listing indicate the publisher;

contact information by mail, phone, fax, URL, and e-mail; date of first publication; frequency; issue size; subscription cost; and online availability. Each entry also includes a short summary of the newsletter's focus or contents. The major accent point to the directory is the subject index, listing newsletters under some 300 headings.

Two general directories of newsletters also include coverage of legal publications, although neither is as extensive as *Legal Newsletters in Print*. *Oxbridge Directory of Newsletters* (Oxbridge Communications, annual) lists more than 1,600 newsletters alphabetically under "Law," with some law-related items found elsewhere ("Business and Industry," "Consumer Interests," "Taxes") and numerous cross-references. The entries list publisher, personnel, editorial description, year established, frequency, number of pages per issue, and subscription cost. There is a title index, but no subject index or further subdivision under the topic "Law."

Newsletters in Print (Gale, annual) lists more than 11,500 newsletters altogether, with extensive coverage of legal material. One of its 33 chapters is "Law and the Administration of Justice," but several other chapters include topical legal materials dealing with such issues as commerce, human resources, public affairs, and the environment. Entries provide contact, descriptive, and pricing information similar to the other newsletter directories. *Newsletters in Print* includes a title keyword index. It is also available electronically as part of the *Gale Database of Publications and Broadcast Media*.

LOOSE-LEAF SERVICES

One final form of legal periodical publication remains to be considered in this chapter—the loose-leaf service. Unlike journals, newspapers, and newsletters, which are found in a variety of specialized areas, the loose-leaf service is a distinctly legal form of publication. It is designed to provide comprehensive and current access to legal information. In some respects, it is similar to a newsletter in that it is usually published weekly or biweekly with news of court decisions and regulatory developments. Yet many people consider it more akin to a treatise than a periodical because it contains basic information and often serves as the first reference point for specialists in an area of law.

A loose-leaf service serves these purposes by virtue of its publication format, which consists of binders containing individual loose pages. Updated information is issued on pages that are interfiled with and re-place existing pages. These updates contain the text of amendments to statutes and regulations, new court decisions, and editorial material explaining and providing access to these developments. A user need not flip between a main volume and a separate supplement because the volume itself is continually being updated.

Loose-leaf services are designed to be one-stop research sources containing everything a lawyer working in a particular area would need to analyze a legal issue. The first services were developed in 1913 to cover the newly enacted federal income tax, but they have expanded since to cover many other specialized areas. The leading publisher of loose-leaf services is CCH (formerly Commerce Clearing House), which produces *Federal Securities Law Reports, Standard Federal Tax Reports, Trade Regulation Reports,* and dozens of other titles. Other publishers include the Bureau of National Affairs (BNA) (*Environment Reporter, Labor Relations Reporter*) and the Research Institute of America (RIA) (*United States Tax Reporter*). Some loose-leaf services are contained in one or two binders, but many are extensive and occupy several volumes. The major tax loose-leaf services, CCH's *Standard Federal Tax Reporter* and RIA's *United States Tax Reporter*, each consist of more than a dozen volumes.

Many loose-leaf services include not only material generally available in other sources, such as statutes, regulations, and court decisions, but other more specialized documents that might otherwise be hard to obtain, such as agency opinion letters or guidance documents. More important for most researchers are the editorial commentary and organization that help make sense of a complex area of law.

Nonetheless, loose-leaf services can be intimidating to the new researcher. Many have an idiosyncratic organization that makes sense only to experienced specialists. Because it is often not clear where to begin, it is helpful to keep in mind several features shared by most loose-leafs that can make the task of using them less daunting.

- In the front of the first volume is usually a guide to the service, with a title such as "How to Use This Reporter." If clearly written, this brief section explains the various features and can save considerable time.

- Most services have several series of indexes and tables that can be used for finding material. The most commonly used is the *topical index*, listing references by subject. To keep this topical index up-to-date, supplements are frequently issued with such names as "Current Topical Index" or "Latest

Additions to Topical Index." Be aware when using a loose-leaf service that it may be necessary to check more than one index.

- In addition to providing a topical index, most loose-leaf services issue *finding lists* that provide direct access to particular regulations, forms, or other documents. Some services, such as those on federal income tax, are arranged by code section, making finding lists unnecessary for locating particular statutory sections or regulations.

In many loose-leaf services, particularly those published by CCH, references in the indexes and finding lists are to paragraph numbers rather than page numbers. A "paragraph" in loose-leaf terminology is a specific document, which may be up to several pages in length. Each new court decision, for example, is assigned a paragraph number. This format can often be confusing, particularly because pages have both page numbers and paragraph numbers. The page numbers, however, are used only for filing purposes, while the paragraph numbers are the key to finding information.

Many CCH services include a feature known as a *cumulative index*. Despite its name, this is not the place to begin research in the service. Instead, it is a means of providing links from the main body of the work to a section summarizing recent developments. With the cumulative index providing references to new court decisions and other actions, the pages in the main body need not be replaced as often. However, having to check a separate section for supplementation makes using the service more cumbersome, reducing its advantages over other texts. Nevertheless, the device is employed in several major services, and it is important to recognize how to use it to find the latest available information.

Loose-leaf services in such areas as taxation or securities law are research tools that specialists in these areas swear by. They are, however, complex and dense resources that often take time and practice to use effectively. They may not be the simplest means for getting quick information, but they are well worth considering for extensive research projects.

The leading directory of loose-leafs is Arlene L. Eis's *Legal Looseleafs in Print* (Infosources Publishing, annual), a companion volume to *Legal Newsletters in Print*. For purposes of these directories, any material requiring interfiling is considered a loose-leaf rather than a newsletter. *Legal Looseleafs in Print* lists more than 3,800 publications alphabetically, with information about publisher, number of volumes, price, and frequency of supplementation. Access by topic is through an extensive subject index. The directory is

not limited to services that are updated weekly, bi-weekly, or monthly. It also includes treatises and other materials that are published in binders but are supplemented annually or "periodically," and even some publications that have never been supplemented. Because a major purpose of a loose-leaf service is to provide notice of current developments, frequency of updating is an important consideration in evaluating a publication's research value.

Encyclopedia of Legal Information Sources (discussed in Chapter 4) includes loose-leaf services under many of its 480 topics, although it doesn't provide much information about the sources it lists. Few entries indicate the frequency of updating or the number of volumes in a set. Shorter subject listings of major loose-leaf services are found in legal research guides such as *Fundamentals of Legal Research* and *Legal Research in a Nutshell*. These can be useful as a quick check to see if a loose-leaf service covers a particular area. In many law libraries, loose-leaf services are shelved together in a separate area, so the simplest way to determine what services are available may be to browse the library shelves or ask a librarian.

Increasingly, the function of loose-leaf services is being taken over by electronic products, which can provide the same mix of primary sources and commentary without the labor-intensive cost of interfiling new material. Many of the CCH services, for example, are also available on CD-ROM, and most BNA services are available on LEXIS-NEXIS and WESTLAW. These electronic services are keyword searchable, obviating the need to be familiar with such complex indexing; however, familiarity with the scope and attributes of the printed counterpart makes it easier to determine the context of bits of information retrieved electronically.

ACCESS TO ARTICLES

Four distinct methods allow the researcher to find law journal articles: full-text searches, periodical indexes, citation searching, and following leads in other works or bibliographies. Each has its strengths.

Full-Text Searches

To a traditionalist, it may seem heretical to discuss full-text keyword searching for journal articles before periodical indexes. The indexes are the most comprehensive and systematic resources, and they continue to provide broader, more comprehensive coverage than is possible through the more limited number of journals available in full text. Yet the ease of full-text searching, and the immediate gratification of going directly to the relevant section of text, make it the first choice for growing numbers of researchers. Sometimes a quick look at an article provides all the information needed, either to answer a question or to evaluate whether it is worth reading in full. We'll discuss full-text searching first but attempt to keep in mind its shortcomings and the indexes' advantages.

The major sources for online legal materials in full text are LEXIS-NEXIS and WESTLAW. Business journals and academic literature in other disciplines are available through a variety of sources, such as Data-Star, DataTimes EyeQ, Dialog, and Ovid. All these systems carry such journals as *ABA Banking Journal*, *National Petroleum News*, or *Vaccine Weekly*, but they have ceded most of the lengthy and voluminous legal literature to the law systems.

Well over 1,000 legal periodicals are available online in full text, including most—but not all—of the academic law reviews published in the United States, several bar magazines, and hundreds of legal newspapers and newsletters.

Searching full text has several advantages. It allows one to search the details of an article, find any mention of a particular case or concept, or zero in on a discussion that is only part of a more general article. An article may discuss a topic briefly and provide useful insights, but if that topic is not the focus of the article, there will be no mention of it in an index. A full-text search can use any combination of words, rather than the limited number of terms available to an indexer. These words can include case names, authors, or literary quotations as well as legal subjects. Articles on developing topics can be found by keyword before the index services have had a chance to develop new subject headings to keep up with the changes.

On the other hand, lack of indexing can lead to a less focused inquiry. If you are looking for articles on campus speech codes, for instance, finding every article that mentions these words may produce far too many irrelevant and time-wasting citations. An index search would immediately lead to articles directly on point. The subject headings assigned by an index can better ensure that an article is indeed on the issue being researched.

When searching full text, there are ways to narrow retrieval to eliminate articles that only make passing reference to a topic.

- In either LEXIS-NEXIS or WESTLAW, you can limit a search to terms that appear in the title of an article by specifying the title field and putting the terms in parentheses, as in *title(hate speech)*. This will retrieve only articles that use that phrase in the title, but it will miss related articles with "campus speech" or "speech codes" in their title. In addition, student-edited law reviews are infamous for articles with "cute" titles that provide little information about their subject.

- LEXIS-NEXIS allows the use of an "atleast" command, specifying that a particular term appear a certain number of times in a document to be retrieved. A search for *atleast10(hate speech)* will quickly zero in on relevant documents while eliminating less pertinent ones.

The full-text databases can also be used to find articles by particular authors, although coverage is rarely as extensive as the indexes. This search in WESTLAW is *author(robert /2 berring)* or *au(robert /2 berring)*. On LEXIS-NEXIS, the *author* segment includes any information in a footnote after the author's name. These footnotes normally include not just the author's affiliation, but acknowledgment for comments received from colleagues. A search for *author(berring)* retrieves not just any article *by* Berring but any article in which he is thanked by the author in an introductory footnote. The *name* segment is the author's name without the footnote, so the search *name(robert w/2 berring)* will find only articles written by Berring.

One advantage of full-text searching is the ability to delve directly into the articles' footnotes. The lengthy footnotes that cause many to cringe at law review literature can be a trove of obscure references and citations. Although few law review articles address a topic such as blood feuds (an ancient system of settling disputes), several articles provide quick references to books tracing the history and development of this custom.

Because some topics are not the focus of articles, they cannot be found in indexes. Nonetheless, they are discussed in the literature. A search for *dormitory w/ 20 search* will turn up several articles on the law of search and seizure in the college context. Of course, a full-text search can also lead to false drops, such as this article about something quite different: M. Kathleen Price, "Technology and Law Library Administration," 70 St. John's L. Rev. 145, 156 (1996). ("If collections of primary source government materials are made available to our students in their *dormitory* rooms, will dial up access have to be provided to our public patrons if they want to *search* our collections?")

Although LEXIS-NEXIS and WESTLAW are by far the most extensive sources for full-text journal searches, the Internet does provide some access to recent articles. Its searches are free, so even a less extensive body of literature and a less flexible search engine may be a more preferable research option than an expensive or unavailable commercial database.

The major source for Web searching of journal texts is the University Law Journal Project <http://www.lawreview.org/> and <http://www.findlaw.com/lawreviews/>. Search results provide the titles and a brief introduction of articles retrieved. Information shown varies between sources, but anything is helpful when a search for "hate speech" turns up an article on the Belarus constitution in addition to articles on free speech in the workplace. Washburn University also provides searching of law reviews <http://lawlib.wuacc.edu/washlaw/lawjournal/lawjournal. html>. As of this writing, the Washburn retrieval produces a list that provides the URLs of the documents found but little indication of the articles' titles or authors. Full-text searching of journals is still in its infancy, with relatively few articles to choose from. Those few, however, may well be enough to get started and find references to other sources.

Legal Periodical Indexes

Once they have experienced the wonders of full-text searching, many researchers never look back at periodical indexes. This is a pity, for indexes are still an essential part of any research process. They are necessary not only for finding articles that were published before electronic access became widespread, but also for finding the thousands of recent articles that are not available online and for pinpointing retrieval to articles that most closely match research needs.

Two general indexes cover legal periodicals. Both are available in monthly printed issues that cumulate in annual bound volumes, on CD-ROM, and through online databases. The older publication is the *Index to Legal Periodicals & Books*, which was launched in 1908 by the fledgling American Association of Law Libraries. Since 1914 it has been published by the H.W. Wilson Company. Electronic coverage extends back to mid-1981, and selected indexing of books began in 1994, causing the title change from *Index to Legal Periodicals*. The index is available online through LEXIS-NEXIS, OCLC, Ovid, WESTLAW, and WILSONLINE.

As an H.W. Wilson publication, *Index to Legal Periodicals & Books (ILP)* has a style that should be familiar to users of *Reader's Guide to Periodical Literature* or *Social Sciences Index*. It covers almost 700 legal periodicals, most from the United States but also including titles from Australia, Canada, Ireland, New Zealand, and the United Kingdom. Exhibit 5-2 shows a page from *ILP* including a reference to the article shown in Exhibit 5-1 under the subject heading "Academic freedom—Students."

The newer index, from Information Access Co., is known by several names, depending on format: the printed *Current Law Index (CLI)*, the CD-ROM *LegalTrac*, and the online *Legal Resource Index (LRI)*, available through DataStar, DIALOG, Knowledge Index, LEXIS-NEXIS, and WESTLAW. The index covers more than 800 titles; like *ILP*, its coverage extends beyond the United States to Australia, Canada, Ireland, New Zealand, and the United Kingdom.

Current Law Index (CLI) and its electronic counterparts are similar, but the electronic *LegalTrac* and *LRI* provide more extensive coverage in two ways. In 1992, they began including abstracts for some articles. These can be useful because they provide quick summaries as well as more searchable terms. *LegalTrac* and *LRI* also include coverage of several legal newspapers omitted from *CLI*. *Los Angeles Daily Journal, Legal Times, National Law Journal, New Jersey Law Journal*, and *New York Law Journal* are indexed from January 1980; *Pennsylvania Law Journal-Reporter*, now *Pennsylvania Law Weekly*, was added in 1981, and *Chicago Daily Law Bulletin* was added in 1984.

The newspaper coverage provides a significant portion of the articles indexed. Thirty percent of articles retrieved by most searches may be from newspapers. These can be useful for finding information on legal events, but for researchers looking for scholarly analysis of legal issues they produce a lot of noise—particularly if one is not aware that a publication such as *New York Law Journal* is a daily newspaper rather than a law review. One way to distinguish newspaper listings is that such entries indicate the length of each article in column inches, a useful means of evaluating the depth of a newspaper article and screening out the newspapers when they are not wanted. In the online versions one simply adds *and not col* or *% col* to a search string to eliminate newspaper articles.

The CD-ROM versions of the indexes may be the ones most frequently encountered by researchers in general university libraries. The *ILP* CD is part of the *Wilsondisc* system and uses its search methods. One can browse subject headings or authors, combine subject headings using the Wilsearch mode, or do sophis-

4   INDEX TO LEGAL PERIODICALS & BOOKS

ticated command searches using Wilsonline syntax. Extensive on-screen help explains these processes.

The *LegalTrac* CD is related to other *InfoTrac* products, such as *Academic Index* and *Business Index*. It has two search modes: EasyTrac, which uses either a subject index or keyword searching; and PowerTrac, which allows the user to search specific fields (such as author or title) and to combine retrieval sets. (In neither search mode, unfortunately, does adding *not col* to a search string eliminate references to newspaper articles.) Two useful features in EasyTrac are "explore," which can be used to find articles with the same subject headings as those already found, and "narrow," which limits a search further by adding new keywords. *LegalTrac* offers less on-screen guidance than *Wilsondisc*, but extensive help screens are available.

Both indexes provide access to articles by subject and by author. *ILP* combines the two in one index while *CLI* provides separate subject and author/title indexes. Treatment of subject headings is one of the major distinguishing characteristics between the two indexes. Information Access Co. uses specific Library of Congress subject headings, adapted somewhat for use in periodical literature. This can be helpful in narrowing a search, but it also tends to atomize articles. Most articles are assigned to three or four subject headings, from the broad "Freedom of speech" to the narrow "Hate speech." The indexers then assign a subheading, such as "Analysis" or "Laws, regulations, etc.," to every heading. Some of these subheadings ("Moral and ethical aspects" or "Public opinion") can be useful, but many are hard to distinguish and seem arbitrarily assigned. These subheadings appear in the printed *CLI* only if there are 16 or more entries under the heading. Users of *LegalTrac* can choose either to view all articles under a heading in reverse chronological order or to sort the articles by subheading.

The main problem with Information Access's subject classifications is that there appears to be little consistency between articles. For articles on campus speech codes, coverage is all over the map. More than 25 different subject headings are used, with the only constant being "Freedom of speech," which is used for nearly all of them. When we look for a more specific heading, we have articles classed under "Universities and colleges," "College students," "College discipline," and "Academic freedom," as well as "Hate speech," "Racism," "Political correctness," and "Censorship." Deborah R. Schwartz's "A First Amendment Justification for Regulating Racist Speech on Campus," 40 Case W. Res. L. Rev. 73 (1990) is indexed under "Invective"

as well as "Racism" and "Freedom of speech," but there is no subject heading indicating that the article deals with college or university issues.

Take as another example the subject of employment discrimination based on weight. For most articles, Information Access uses the subject headings "Obesity" and "Employment discrimination." Occasionally, however, it uses "Discrimination against overweight persons" instead of "Obesity." So a search for the term *obesity* would turn up most of the relevant literature, but it would miss the pertinent article by Jane Byeff Korn, "Fat," 77 B.U. L. Rev. 25 (1997).

The easiest way to verify that subject headings are handled inconsistently by Information Access is to look at two treatments of the same article. When Patricia M. Wald's lecture "Thoughts on Decisionmaking" was published in 87 W. Va. L. Rev. 1 (1984), it was assigned the subject headings of "Business judgment rule," "Judicial process," and "Products liability." These headings appear helpful, because it is not clear from the title that Judge Wald discusses these issues. The next year, the same lecture was reprinted in 27 Corp. Practice Commentator 460 (1985) and assigned the subject headings "Corporations," "Decision-making," "Judicial process," and "Political science." A few years later, Pamela S. Karlan's "Bringing Compassion into the Province of Judging: Justice Blackmun and the Outsiders," 97 Dick. L. Rev. 527 (1993) was classified under Blackmun's name and "Sociological jurisprudence." When the article was reprinted in 71 N.D. L. Rev. 173 (1995), two more headings were added, "United States. Supreme Court—Officials and employees" and "Judges—Criticism, interpretation, etc." These may all be valid choices, but shouldn't there be more consistency in their application?

ILP, on the other hand, uses a smaller number of broader subject headings, which are listed in the front of each bound volume. This list includes extensive cross-references to related topics. The limitation to a more controlled list of subjects can result in a long entry under some headings. Wilson's indexing, however, is more standardized in its assignment of headings. Nearly all relevant articles on campus speech codes have the subject heading "Hate speech," and most are also assigned to "Academic freedom," as shown in Exhibit 5-2. A handful of other headings show up ("Paternalism," "Politically correct movement," "Student speech"), but the overbroad headings of "Colleges and universities" and "Freedom of speech" are generally avoided in favor of more specific headings. Information Access's headings may be more readily familiar to librarians, but Wilson indexers seem to better understand the need for specificity and consistency.

In addition to subject and author access, both indexes include tables of statutes and cases useful for finding articles written on specific legislative acts and court decisions. These tables do not include every article that discusses a statute or case; they are limited to those that focus specifically on these materials. *ILP* also contains a separate book review section, while *CLI* incorporates book reviews into its main author/title listing. The titles of books reviewed are the *only* titles appearing in this index; despite its name, it does not list articles indexed by title.

For articles published before 1980, the printed *ILP* was for years the only available source. Besides the claustrophobic old H. W. Wilson typeface, older volumes of *ILP* (up to 1982-83) include another problematic feature. Subject searching is fairly standard, but anyone searching by author is in for a struggle. Under authors' names, the index only provides cross-references to the subject headings under which articles are listed—followed by the first letter of the article's title in parentheses. The Schweitzer article shown in Exhibit 5-1, for example, might have been listed this way under the old system:

SCHWEITZER, Thomas A.
Academic freedom (H)
Colleges and universities (H)
Hate speech (H)

According to this entry, one or more articles by Schweitzer are indexed under these subject headings and all of the entries begin with the letter H. Unfortunately, it is impossible to tell from this list how many articles are represented. The only shortcut is to turn to one of the subject headings, find an entry for the hate speech article, and evaluate whether the other subject headings apply to the same article. If the letters in parentheses are different, it usually means there is more than one article—but sometimes an article is listed under one subject by its title and under another subject as part of a group entry for a symposium of which it is a part. Occasionally an author may have written two articles beginning with the same letter classified under the same subject heading—but the listing "Internat law (P)" under Richard B. Lillich's name in the 1970-1973 volume gives no indication that it covers two articles: "The Procedural Aspects of International Law Institute," 4 Int'l Law. 741 (1970), and "The Proper Role of Domestic Courts in the International Legal Order," 11 Va. J. Int'l L. 9 (1970).

Most research for current articles may be conducted by subject, but a search for articles 20 or 30 years old is likely to be for a specific work by a particular author, so the *ILP* indexing system continues to cause annoyance. Some cross-references are easy to find, but others, such as "Constitutional law (C)" may require scanning dozens of listings. Fortunately, the older indexes are most frequently used by librarians, who are accustomed to handling hardships of this sort.

Even though the older *ILP* indexes are not available electronically, there are alternatives to hunting through the volumes. One is to search the more current articles online in full text in the hope of finding a footnote reference to a particular older article. Even though the online journals only go back 10 or 15 years, a search for *hohfeld w/10 yale* will turn up numerous references to Wesley N. Hohfeld, "Some Fundamental Legal Conceptions as Applied in Judicial Reasoning," 23 Yale L.J. 16 (1913). Another possibility for finding articles in major law reviews is the author and keyword searching now possible through the electronic *Periodical Contents Index,* discussed below.

Another difference between the Information Access indexes and *ILP* is the way that works written by law students are treated. The Information Access indexes do not differentiate between articles by professionals and students, except for those pieces with obvious student titles such as "Case Note." Since 1992, *ILP* has identified student work by appending the parenthetical note "student author" after a name, following the lead of the 1991 change in *Bluebook* citation form. Earlier *ILP* listings followed the earlier *Bluebook* rule and did not provide the names of student authors at all. This is one indication of *ILP*'s closer identification with the rules of the law review world. The printed *ILP* uses *Bluebook* citation form for the names of journals, while Information Access uses full journal titles. The index's use of the *Bluebook* forms may help researchers learn how to cite articles, and how to find other articles cited in law review footnotes. Some unfamiliar citations may be confusing, but the front of each volume and issue includes a table of the periodical abbreviations used. (The electronic *ILP*, with no need to conserve space and no abbreviation table handy, uses full names of journals.)

ILP contains some entries not appearing in *CLI* or *LegalTrac,* despite the fact that Information Access covers more journals. A few journals are indexed by *ILP* but not *CLI.* More common are the journal issues that the Information Access indexers apparently never received. A *LegalTrac* user would never learn of the

Schweitzer article in Exhibit 5-1 or of Ronald J. Rychlak, "Civil Rights, Confederate Flags, and Political Correctness: Free Speech and Race Relations on Campus," 66 Tul. L. Rev. 1411 (1992). (This may change once the publishers are notified of these omissions.) The few articles missing from *LegalTrac*, of course, are balanced by the dozens of journals that *ILP* doesn't even cover. Either index is good enough to provide several research leads, but the thorough researcher will not rely exclusively on one or the other.

Even though *LegalTrac/CLI* and *ILP* both index several hundred journals and regularly expand coverage to include new publications, the continued growth of new specialized journals outstrips their ability to keep up. No single index can cover everything, particularly when law school students and commercial publishers launch dozens of new journals every year.

Among the several other legal literature indexes that may be of use are the following:

- The series called *Index to Legal Periodical Literature* (Boston Book Co., 6 vols., 1888–1939) is a predecessor of *Index to Legal Periodicals,* which did not begin until 1908. The first volume, compiled by Leonard A. Jones, indexes articles in 158 journals dating back to 1770. The subject indexing will seem inadequate to the modern reader, but the work was clearly a prodigious feat; the compiler tallied in his introductory notes the 5,807 volumes (1,373 volumes of legal periodicals and 4,434 of general periodicals) he examined in preparing the index. Jones prepared a second volume covering the years 1887-98, and Frank E. Chipman carried on with four more volumes for articles from 1898 to 1937.

- *Index to Foreign Legal Periodicals* (University of California Press, quarterly) is an invaluable source for any research involving issues of international or foreign law. This index covers more than 450 periodicals from around the world, as well as essay collections and *festschriften.* The periodicals indexed are mostly from countries outside the common law system, but about three dozen U.S. journals on international and comparative law are included. The major index is by subject, with cross-references listed in an author index and a geographic index (listing subject headings with articles about specific countries). Articles from some journals in other common law countries are indexed in *ILP* and *CLI,* but more extensive coverage is available in indexes published in those countries, such as *Index to Canadian Legal Literature* (Carswell,

eight times per year) or the British *Legal Journals Index* (Legal Information Resources, monthly).

- Specialized indexes to legal journals provide useful information. In taxation, for example, *Federal Tax Articles* (CCH, monthly) contains abstracts of journal articles arranged by Internal Revenue Code section; and *Index to Federal Tax Articles* (Warren Gorham & Lamont, quarterly) provides retrospective subject indexing back to 1913.

- Roy M. Mersky, J. Myron Jacobstein and Donald J. Dunn's *Index to Periodical Articles Related to Law* (Glanville Publishers, quarterly) features law-related articles in other journals. Older coverage is contained in four volumes covering the years 1958-88, a five-year cumulation for the years 1989-93, and annual cumulations. This index provides selective coverage of law-related issues in nearly 300 journals and periodicals that are *not* covered in the standard legal indexes. Before the days of electronic indexing, this was a valuable means of providing an interdisciplinary perspective in the study of legal issues. Now its coverage is largely duplicated by comprehensive multidisciplinary indexes, but it may still be useful because it brings a specifically legal focus to the inquiry and because it covers some periodicals (such as *Antishyster* or *Hustler*) that may not be regularly indexed elsewhere.

- Finally, the magazines that law schools publish for their alumni frequently have brief articles on legal topics of interest. Many of these magazines may be hard to find, but nearly 120 are indexed by author and title in Mary D. Burchill's *Index to Law School Alumni Publications* (Rothman, 1985-date, 2 vols. and semiannual updates).

Comprehensive Indexes

While *Index to Legal Periodicals & Books* and *Current Law Index/LegalTrac/Legal Resource Index* are the leading indexes focusing specifically on legal materials, more general indexes provide coverage of legal sources in a broader context. These may be available to many researchers who do not have convenient access to the legal indexes.

The most extensive and most easily accessible of the comprehensive indexes is *UnCover*, from CARL Corporation. *UnCover* indexes nearly 17,000 periodicals, with a database of seven million articles. *UnCover*'s coverage of legal journals is impressive. It indexes nearly 1,000 law-related titles, including some journals that have not been picked up by either of the major legal indexes, such as *International Bulletin of*

Law and Mental Health (1989-date), *Quinnipiac Health Law Journal* (1996-date), and *San Joaquin Agricultural Law Review* (1991-date). *UnCover* covers almost every major scholarly journal and magazine, but many of its 17,000 titles are obscure. The nonlegal titles include *Friends of Financial History*, for collectors of stock certificates; *Haliotis*, a French journal on mollusks; *Pizza Today*; and a few family newsletters.

UnCover is available free through the Internet, on the Web <http://uncweb.carl.org>, or by telnetting to *database.carl.org*. A charge is incurred only if copies of articles are ordered. The disadvantages to using *UnCover*'s huge database are that it extends back only to 1988 and that searching is largely limited to author and title keywords. A few records also include keywords from abstracts, but there is no subject indexing. With *UnCover*'s extensive database, however, even a keyword search can yield impressive results. In addition to many of the articles in legal journals found using *LRI* and *ILP*, a "hate speech" search in *UnCover* turned up articles from sources such as the *Howard Journal of Communications* and the *Review of Higher Education*. Even in research focused on the legal aspects of an issue, articles from other disciplines can provide valuable new perspectives.

ArticleFirst, accessible through OCLC FirstSearch, is not as broad as *UnCover*, but it provides similar coverage of the tables of contents of more than 13,000 journals beginning in 1990. Its coverage of law reviews is limited, but it can be used to find law-related articles in other disciplines. Like *UnCover*, there is no subject indexing, so it is necessary to rely on author or title keywords in searching.

UnCover and *ArticleFirst* are limited to recent literature, but another index fills some of the earlier gap. *Periodical Contents Index* (*PCI*), from Chadwyck-Healey, is designed to provide electronic access to journals from the dark age of print. It offers the tables of contents of thousands of journals from their first issues to 1990/91. *PCI*, available on the Web by subscription <http://pci.chadwyck.com/>, is in the process of providing retrospective coverage of more than 3,000 journals. Although there is no subject indexing of articles, it is possible to search by author or title keywords or browse the journal tables of contents. Legal coverage is considerably less extensive than *UnCover*'s, with about 60 U.S.-based legal journals and another 35 from other countries, but most major law reviews are included.

PCI is obviously of little use for research in developing areas (such as hate speech), but it can be of great value in historical research. Remember that the only general index to legal journals before 1980 is the rudimentary print *Index to Legal Periodicals*. *PCI* provides a way to do a keyword search and find articles such as those in the 1966 *California Law Review* symposium "Student Rights and Campus Rules," as well as intriguing older articles such as Kenneth L. Daughrity's "Handed-Down Campus Expressions," 6 Am. Speech 129 (1930/31).

The print *Social Sciences Citation Index* (Institute for Scientific Information, three times per year), and its electronic counterpart *Social Scisearch*, available on CD-ROM and online through Data-Star, DIALOG, and OVID, covers 1,400 social science journals extending back to 1972. Legal coverage is not as extensive as *UnCover*'s and is focused primarily on interdisciplinary journals such as *Behavioral Sciences and the Law* and *Journal of Health Politics, Policy and Law*. But its scope does include about 50 law reviews, and the database includes more than 120,000 articles in the journal subject category "law." Some article records include abstracts, and "keywords plus" indexing provides improved access by subject since 1991.

Current Awareness Sources

The legal and general periodical indexes just discussed are the tools of choice for searches spanning several years. A different set of resources provides ways of keeping up with the latest literature in areas of interest.

The leading source for indexing of new law review issues is the *Current Index to Legal Periodicals* (*CILP*), published weekly by the Gallagher Law Library at the University of Washington. *CILP* provides both the tables of contents of new issues and a subject index, using about 100 broad subject headings. It does an excellent, quick job of providing subject access to the latest literature, covering about 475 journals within two or three weeks of their arrival in most libraries. *CILP* is available in print in many law libraries, and the most recent eight issues can be searched on WESTLAW. Subscribers can also sign up for *SmartCILP*, a service providing customized e-mail delivery of indexing in specific subject areas. Information about *CILP* and *SmartCILP* is available on the Web <http://lib.law.washington.edu/cilp/cilp.html>.

The Tarlton Law Library at the University of Texas also provides table of contents access to recent journals. Its service is less sophisticated than the University of Washington's, but it is available free on the Internet <http://tarlton.law.utexas.edu/tallons/content_search.html>. More than 750 law reviews and other journals from around the world are covered. There is no subject indexing, but the files can be searched by keyword. Like *CILP*, this site is limited to recently received issues and is designed to provide interim coverage until the regular indexes are published.

UnCover Reveal is a current awareness service that provides the tables of contents from new issues of any of *UnCover's* 17,000 journals, and can automatically run searches on a weekly basis and deliver the results by e-mail. It is available by institutional or individual subscription. Information is available on the Web <http://uncweb.carl.org/reveal/index.html>.

The Institute for Scientific Information (ISI) publishes seven weekly editions of *Current Contents*, providing access to the tables of contents of new journals. The *Social & Behavioral Sciences* edition covers a number of specialized interdisciplinary journals (*Issues in Law and Medicine*, *Law and Human Behavior*, *Law and Philosophy*) as well as about three dozen general law reviews. *Current Contents* is also available in electronic formats, which provide keyword searching and access to author abstracts.

Other Indexes

Legal researchers often make the mistake of limiting their inquiry to legal literature, forgetting that resources from other disciplines may offer valuable perspectives on legal issues. This section briefly covers a few indexes that do not focus specifically on law but that include coverage of legal matters. Many of these indexes are available not only in print but through a variety of online vendors, including DIALOG, Ovid, DataStar, and OCLC FirstSearch.

PAIS International in Print (Public Affairs Information Service, monthly) covers public policy literature and indexes selected articles from about 1,600 journals, as well as books, government documents, and international organization documents. Coverage includes articles from more than 100 law-related journals, most of which focus on issues of public policy or international law. About 40 general interest law reviews are represented, although the selection seems arbitrary—*Northern Kentucky Law Review* is included, but not *Texas Law Review* or *University of Chicago Law Review*. Because PAIS is international in scope, the subject descriptors for U.S. domestic articles specify the jurisdiction (e.g., "Freedom of speech—United States"; "United States—Constitution—First amendment"; "Colleges and universities—United States").

Coverage in *Social Sciences Index* (H. W. Wilson, quarterly) includes issues of public policy and govern-

ment in more than 350 scholarly journals and magazines. It indexes several criminology journals but few other legal sources—notably *American Journal of International Law*, *Law and Contemporary Problems*, and *Law and Society Review*. Descriptive abstracts are available in an online version, *Social Sciences Abstracts*.

Indexes to business literature such as *Business Periodicals Index* (H.W. Wilson, monthly) or the electronic-only *Business Index* (Information Access) and *ABI Inform* (University Microfilms) include coverage of specialized legal journals focusing on issues such as corporate law, employee relations, communications law, and securities regulation. The journals covered in *Psychological Abstracts* (American Psychological Association, monthly) or its online counterpart, *PsycINFO*, can be valuable resources on such issues as the credibility of child witnesses.

Several indexes cover the criminal justice field. *Criminal Justice Periodicals Index* (University Microfilms, 3 times per year) provides subject and author indexing of more than 100 U.S., British, and Canadian journals in corrections, criminology, juvenile justice, and police studies. It focuses on journals specifically in criminal justice and excludes coverage of general law reviews. *Criminal Justice Abstracts* (Willow Tree Press, quarterly) and *Criminology, Penology, and Police Science Abstracts* (Kugler Publications, bimonthly) both cover books and articles in this area, with abstracts arranged by subject. Neither is comprehensive, but they may provide a few good starting points for research.

Guides to general literature such as *Readers' Guide to Periodical Literature* (H.W. Wilson, 15 times per year) and *Periodical Abstracts* (University Microfilms, electronic only) are geared to the popular press but may provide journalism perspectives on legal issues. *Periodical Abstracts* is so focused on short magazine pieces that anything more than 31 column inches is classified as "long," but it includes descriptors and helpful abstracts covering a wide range of material, from the *Chronicle of Higher Education* to *Playboy* (even including a few legal sources such as *California Law Review* and *National Law Journal*).

Indexes in the humanities, such as *Humanities Index* (H.W. Wilson, quarterly) or *Arts & Humanities Citation Index* (ISI, semiannual), are less likely to cover legal topics, but they may lead to articles that aren't included in the social science indexes, such as Catherine R. Stimpson's "Dirty Minds, Dirty Bodies, Clean Speech," 32 Mich Q. Rev. 317 (1993). *Arts & Humanities Citation Index* even covers some legal literature through such interdisciplinary journals as *Law and Philosophy* and *Law and Social Inquiry,* along with a handful of major law reviews. Unfortunately, it has yet to take notice of the increasing number of law school journals dealing specifically with the humanities, such as *Cardozo Studies in Law and Literature* and *Yale Journal of Law and the Humanities.*

Dozens of other specialized indexes may be useful. One of the newest, *Family Index* (Human Sciences Publications, 1995-date, annual), covers an interesting grab bag of specialized journals on family and gender issues, including *Cornell Journal of Law and Public Policy, Elder Law Journal, Georgetown Immigration Law Journal,* and *Yale Journal of Law and Feminism.*

Citators

A final way to find articles of interest is through citation searching, or retrieving articles that refer to an article or other document known to be relevant to a particular research situation. This type of searching has been used in other aspects of legal research for more than a century, with the help of a series of tools known as *Shepard's Citations. Shepard's* lists every time a decision is cited in subsequent court opinions and is used to determine whether the decision can still be cited as good law. It can also be used to find law review articles that cite specific cases, statutes, or other periodical articles.

Using *Shepard's Citations* to find journal articles may involve one of several different publications, depending on the nature of the source being cited. Articles citing court decisions can be found using *Shepard's* jurisdictional publications, such as *Shepard's United States Citations* (for the Supreme Court), *Shepard's Federal Citations* (for the lower federal courts), and *Shepard's Alabama Citations, Shepard's Alaska Citations,* etc. (for state courts). The *Shepard's* citators for the federal courts include references found in 19 leading law reviews. For the state courts, coverage is broader and includes law reviews and journals published in that state. Coverage varies from state to state, and does not necessarily include *every* law review published in the state. *Shepard's California Citations,* for example, includes citing references in journals from 17 California schools, as well as a bar magazine and the same 19 leading law reviews covered in the federal series. It does not include any of the specialized journals published at the California law schools. Maryland does not have so many law schools, so *Shepard's Maryland Citations* includes only *Maryland Law Review, University of Baltimore Law Review,* and the 19 usual suspects. A few citators for smaller states include law reviews from neighboring states; *Shepard's*

West Virginia Citations, for example, includes citing references in four Virginia law reviews as well as *West Virginia Law Review.* (References to law review articles citing state cases are *not* listed in regional reporter editions of *Shepard's,* such as *Shepard's Southeastern Reporter Citations.* For this purpose, it is necessary to use the state *Shepard's* and the official state case citation if one exists. "Shepardizing" state cases is discussed more fully in Chapter 12.

Articles citing state constitutional provisions and statutes can also be found in these same state *Shepard's* publications. To find articles citing federal constitutional provisions or statutes, however, it is necessary to use a separate publication called *Shepard's Federal Law Citations in Selected Law Reviews* (3 vols., 1994, with bimonthly supplements). This set covers citations to federal law in the 19 major law reviews. For cases from the Supreme Court and the lower federal courts, it duplicates the law review coverage in *Shepard's United States Citations* and *Shepard's Federal Citations.* Just to make things confusing, however, law review citations to constitutional provisions and statutes appear only in *Shepard's Federal Law Citations in Selected Law Reviews* and not in *Shepard's Federal Statute Citations.* (Those who Shepardize electronically should note that the law review citations have been incorporated into the listings for federal statutes in LEXIS-NEXIS but do not appear at all in WESTLAW.)

Law review articles citing other articles can be found using *Shepard's Law Review Citations* (2 vols., 1986, with bimonthly supplements). This source lists citations to articles appearing in about 160 legal publications since 1957. Coverage includes most of the general interest academic law reviews published in the United States, but only about a dozen specialized journals such as *Banking Law Journal* and *Business Lawyer.* Citations to law review articles in federal or state court cases are also listed, so this can be a tool for finding court decisions as well as subsequent articles. *Shepard's Law Review Citations* can be used to find that the Schweitzer article in Exhibit 5-1 has been cited in S. Douglas Murray's "The Demise of Campus Speech Codes," 24 W. St. U. L. Rev. 247 (1997).

Shepard's can be a rather confusing tool at first because all it contains are lists of numbers and abbreviations, indicating the publication, volume, and exact page where a reference to the cited source appears. Law reviews have terse abbreviations unique to *Shepard's,* such as "30VLP494" for an article in *Valparaiso University Law Review,* or "39VR58" for *Villanova Law Review.* A table in the front of each volume and pamphlet helps decipher these abbreviations. This extremely compressed style is designed to save space in print; in its electronic formats, *Shepard's* is not so telegraphic. For many researchers, however, the printed volumes of *Shepard's Citations* remain the most readily available format for this resource.

Like *Shepard's*, WESTLAW's KeyCite citation system serves primarily as a means of tracking the validity of judicial decisions. In addition to subsequent cases, however, it also lists articles citing these decisions. KeyCite encompasses all articles in WESTLAW's full-text law review databases, and its coverage for recent years is far more extensive than *Shepard's* limited stable of major and local law reviews. It is, however, available only for cases, and cannot be used to find articles discussing constitutional provisions, statutes, or other documents.

The *Shepard's* approach to citation searching has been applied in other disciplines by the Institute for Scientific Information (ISI) in its three major sets of citation indexes, *Arts and Humanities Citation Index*, *Science Citation Index*, and *Social Sciences Citation Index*. Although these indexes' coverage of law reviews as *citing* sources is not extensive, they can be used to find a broad range of articles that cite legal scholarship. Thus, references to a *Duke Law Journal* article on campus speech can be found in *Ethics*, *Journal of Higher Education* or *Philosophy & Public Affairs* by using *Arts and Humanities Citation Index* or its electronic counterparts. *Social Sciences Citation Index* covers these same sources, as well as several law journals. Some of these are also covered in *Shepard's Law Review Citations*, but others are not. We can learn from the *Social Sciences Citation Index* but not *Shepard's*, for example, that Schweitzer's article was also cited in J. B. Jacobs and K. A. Potter's "Hate Crimes: A Critical Perspective," 22 Crime & Justice 1 (1997). The ISI citation indexes can also be used to find journal references to monographs and other sources that *Shepard's* has no way to cover.

With full-text searching, it is also possible to search law review databases for the names or citations of any article or other document of interest. An online search reveals a third citation to Schweitzer's article in Jonathan M. Holdowsky, Note, "Out of the Ashes of the Cross: The Legacy of R.A.V. v. City of St. Paul," 30 New Eng. L. Rev. 1115 (1996), a journal not covered by ISI or *Shepard's*.

A full-text search may be an expensive way to find references, but it is certainly the quickest, easiest, and most flexible way. A full-text retrieval zeroes in immediately on that portion of the document citing the text in question, and can be used to find references to any sort of document, from journal articles to books to Shakespearean sonnets.

CHAPTER 6
Finding Lawyers and Institutions

Most of this book covers resources with which you can help yourself—and *to* which you can help yourself. You may need assistance finding material in a library or gaining access to an electronic resource, but most research is a solitary pursuit. It is up to you to find the relevant information, analyze its value, and draw your own conclusions.

This chapter, however, covers a different style of research that cannot be conducted on your own, one used more commonly by journalists than by academic researchers. It involves contacting people by telephone or e-mail, and can lead to information ranging from simple facts or leads to published sources to inside knowledge that may not appear anywhere in print. This type of research requires a set of skills somewhat different from other research—knowing whom to contact and how to ask questions to get information that is complete and reliable.

Like other aspects of research, finding and using people contacts is a skill that can be developed. It is important to know when to turn to the telephone or e-mail, and how to elicit a positive response. Demonstrating "people skills" such as politeness and the ability to ask engaging questions is important, but it is just as essential to do your homework before contacting individuals. Most people are much more likely to share information if they know that the person calling or writing has exhausted library sources and is turning to them with questions that are not so easily answered.

The more you know, the more focused your inquiry can be and the better use you can make of the information you receive. You'll know what follow-up questions to ask, and you may learn of related issues you hadn't considered. You may even have information you can share with the person you call, creating a contact that could be of mutual benefit in the future.

To some extent, inquiries posted to Internet mailing lists and newsgroups serve the same function as telephone calls: Both seek advice from others with expertise in an area. A direct telephone or e-mail contact poses the question to one person, whereas a posting to a group throws it open to all comers. This approach is recommended if you're seeking a variety of opinions ("Has anyone used this new product?") or want to poll the collected wisdom of a larger group. It can also be highly effective if it is unclear who may have experience with a particular issue. Throwing a question out to hundreds of people, however, should rarely be a first resort. If possible, it is usually more effective to identify an individual likely to be knowledgeable and make direct contact. If nothing else, this may keep your goodwill with the Internet group from dissipating through overuse.

This chapter focuses on ways to find lawyers, bar associations, law schools, and other sources of legal information. It does not include sources in Congress, state legislatures, courts, or government offices. People in government can be among the most valuable information sources, but they are covered by directories and Web sites discussed in Chapters 8 through 13. The resources discussed here can be used not only by people seeking information, but by those seeking to hire lawyers or other legal experts.

LAWYERS

If institutions such as legislatures and courts are the gears of the legal system, lawyers are the oil that lubricates those gears—and they are most people's most direct contact with the legal system. Information on practicing lawyers is not only sought by people seeking representation, but also by those interested in finding out about the parties to a lawsuit or looking for experts in particular legal fields. In addition, background information on law firms is highly sought by students looking for employment as associates or paralegals. This section focuses primarily on sources for consumers seeking information about attorneys.

Virtually all consumer guides to the law advise that the best way to find a lawyer is through recommendations from friends or colleagues, or by word of mouth from people who have been confronted with similar legal issues. Most guides also list as sources lawyer referral services and advertisements in local yellow pages, with the warning that they provide little quality control. These are the only suggestions that most guides offer. Even the American Bar Association's pamphlet *The American Lawyer: When and How to Use One* (1993) limits itself to these three approaches, except for people eligible for legal aid, a prepaid legal service plan, or a legal clinic. (Another ABA publication, *Finding the Right Lawyer* by Jay G. Foonberg (1995), is one of the few consumer guides that suggests doing research to find a lawyer.)

Personal recommendations may certainly be the most reliable means for finding competent, knowledgeable attorneys, but other tools are available if that approach proves ineffective. These include numerous directories, a growing number of Web sites with information about lawyers and their practices, and such sources as news stories and case reports.

Directories

Many directories of lawyers are published, but few provide much information beyond names, addresses, and telephone numbers. Most include a tiny bit of biographical background, such as law school attended and date admitted to practice law, but some don't even go that far. Few directories provide information such as narra-

tive descriptions of practices or objective evaluations of lawyers' expertise and skill. Those with more detailed information often focus on large corporate law firms rather than smaller firms with consumer-oriented practices.

No single directory covers all 950,000 lawyers licensed to practice in the United States, but two directories offer reasonably comprehensive coverage. Only one is available in print, but both are accessible online and through the Internet. The older, published work is the *Martindale-Hubbell Law Directory*, and its electronic-only competitor is *West's Legal Directory*.

Martindale-Hubbell Law Directory

The annual *Martindale-Hubbell Law Directory* was first published in 1931 as the successor to *Martindale's American Law Directory* (1874-1930) and *Hubbell's Legal Directory* (1868-1930). Now published by Reed Elsevier Inc., *Martindale-Hubbell* appears in 19 volumes. The directory is part of a 25-volume set that also includes the *Martindale-Hubbell Corporate Law Directory* (1 volume), *Martindale-Hubbell Law Digest* (2 volumes), *Martindale-Hubbell International Law Directory* (3 volumes), and *Martindale-Hubbell International Law Digest* (1 volume).

The first 16 volumes of the *Martindale-Hubbell Law Directory* list attorneys geographically, with each volume covering up to eight states. California covers almost two volumes, and New York City has a volume of its own. Two index volumes list attorneys alphabetically and by area of practice, and include sections covering state bar associations and law schools.

Martindale-Hubbell covers more than 900,000 lawyers and law firms. Each of the geographical volumes consists of three parts: blue pages, "Practice Profiles," listing lawyers alphabetically (like the white pages in a telephone book); white pages, "Professional Biographies," containing longer paid listings for law firms; and yellow pages, containing advertisements for court reporters, process servers, and other legal service companies.

The first section, the blue pages, is the most comprehensive listing of attorneys. Listings within each state are arranged by city or town, with an introductory list of counties indicating which cities and towns are included in the directory. Thus, someone looking for an attorney in Trinity County, California, would know to look only under "Weaverville," while someone seeking an attorney in neighboring Humboldt County would know to check under 14 listed cities and towns.

Martindale-Hubbell entries have a telegraphic format that conveys a fair amount of information in a small space. Typical listings look like this:

Olson, Daniel M. .... '56 '92 C.350 B.S. L.352 J.D. 4111 18th St.
Olson, James C. ...... '54 '79 C.390 B.A. L.902 J.D. [Pillsbury M.&S.]
Olson, Karl (AV) ... '52 '82 C.1078 B.A. L.1065 J.D. [Cooper,W.&C.]
    *PRACTICE AREAS: Litigation; Media Law; First Amendment Law; Insurance Coverage Law; Intellectual Property Law.
Olson, Lamont R. ------------------------ '37 '71 C.351 .B.A. L.352 J.D.
                        (adm. in IA; not adm. in CA) I.R.S.

This information indicates the date of birth, date of admission to the bar, college, law school, and address. A key to the academic institution codes appears in the front of each volume. "L.352," for example, stands for the University of Iowa, the law school attended by two of these four attorneys. Instead of an address, many entries give an abridged cross-reference to an entry for a law firm, where contact information can be found. Two of the attorneys shown are partners at firms, the names of which are given in abbreviated form. One attorney works for the federal government, while the other appears to be in solo practice. Note that the listings include neither telephone numbers nor zip codes. They provide some of the information needed to find attorneys, but not enough to make contact.

A basic listing without a telephone number or full address is free to any licensed attorney. More extensive listings are available for a price. The boldface type used for the names of two of the attorneys means simply that their firms subscribe to the directory. Subscribers' listings include telephone and fax numbers, areas of specialization, and names of representative clients; some also include e-mail and Web site addresses.

The accuracy and completeness of *Martindale-Hubbell*'s free listings are dependent on lawyers responding to questionnaires and notifying the publisher of changes. One recent study estimated that 16 percent of Florida lawyers were missing from the directory (Manuel R. Ramos, "Legal Malpractice: No Lawyer or Client is Safe," 47 Fla. L. Rev. 1, 25 n. 132 [1995]). Entries for large, established firms are regularly updated, but many solo practitioners have no office staff to take care of matters such as inquiries from directories. If they fail to respond to an inquiry from *Martindale-Hubbell* or change office locations, they may be lost to the system. Conversely, sometimes entries linger well after they become obsolete. George R. Moscone, mayor of San Francisco, was assassinated in 1978 but continued to be listed in *Martindale-Hubbell* for six more years. As of 1997, Charles H. Whitebread II was still listed as professor of law at the University of Virginia, despite having moved to the University of Southern California in 1981.

At the end of one attorney's name in the sample listings above is the abbreviation "AV." These letters indicate the attorney's rating for legal ability (A) and general recommendation (V). The legal ability rating considers experience, nature of practice, and qualifications, while the general recommendation rating covers ethical matters such as adherence to professional standards of conduct and reliability. For legal ability, lawyers are rated A (Very High to Preeminent), B (High to Very High), or C (Fair to High). The only time these legal ability ratings are published is if they are accompanied by a general recommendation rating of V (Very High). No general recommendation ratings lower than V are published.

This rating system is one of the most important features of *Martindale-Hubbell*, for it is the only evaluation widely applied to the legal profession. The ratings are based on questionnaires sent to attorneys asking them to rate colleagues with whose work they are familiar. The responses are evaluated by Martindale-Hubbell staff, and every year more than 50,000 ratings are reviewed. Ratings are not given lightly; most lawyers with legal ability ratings of A have many years of experience.

Not every lawyer has a rating in *Martindale-Hubbell*, but the publisher warns that no adverse conclusions can be drawn from the absence of a rating. Insufficient information may be available because a lawyer is new in a community or has a highly specialized practice, and some lawyers are rated but have asked that their ratings not be published. (Presumably many of these are CV lawyers who think that rating looks less than impressive.)

Older volumes of *Martindale-Hubbell* and its predecessor, *Martindale's American Law Directory*, had a much more extensive rating system. Legal ability ratings included d (medium) and e ("We decline to rate"), and there were five steps of recommendations from v (very high) to z (rating declined). In addition, lawyers' estimated net worth was graded from 1 to 9, and they were rated on their promptness in paying bills from g (good) to m (medium). Numerous attorneys in older directories were saddled with ratings of "e z 9 m"—the lowest in each category, and a net worth of under $1,000. These other ratings gradually disappeared from the directory. The lower recommendations of x, y, and z departed in the 1930s, while the estimated worth and promptness ratings lingered until the 1970s but were used less and less.

The ratings of AV, BV, and CV don't convey a lot of information about lawyers, but they provide more than is available elsewhere. Just remember that AV is the highest rating available and not an abbreviation for "average." *The Economist* made this mistake in discussing Stephen Jones, attorney for Oklahoma City bomber Timothy McVeigh. A July 1, 1995, article about Jones mentioned that a survey had ranked him "as merely an 'average' lawyer." Two weeks later, the magazine issued an apology and explained the correct interpretation of Jones's AV rating.

It is important to recognize that individual lawyers, not law firms, are evaluated. Ratings are listed for law firms, but these are generally just the ratings assigned to a firm's highest-rated partner. A law firm with one "AV" star and dozens of disreputable, unrecommended lawyers would still receive an "AV" rating. To get a better sense of the firm, it is necessary to check the ratings of individual attorneys.

The second part of the directory, the "Professional Biographies" white pages, contains paid advertisements for law firms. It occupies the largest part of each volume but covers far fewer lawyers than the blue pages. The typeface is much larger than in the first section, and the range of information provided is more extensive. Unlike advertisements in telephone yellow pages, these entries follow a standardized form, providing contact information, a brief summary of the firm's area of practice, and biographical data on attorneys. These biographies can be extensive, with some going on for a page or more. Space in this part of the directory costs about $1,000 per page, however, so an increasing number of firms have reduced the length of their lawyer biographies, limiting partners to three or four lines and simply listing associates' names with no further information.

The summaries of firms' practices can sometimes be helpful in finding firms in particular specialties. Too often, however, they provide only vague catchall phrases like "General civil and trial practice in all state and federal courts," with little indication where their expertise may lie. For further information it may be necessary to parse individual lawyers' biographies for such clues as membership in specialized bar associations or publications in particular areas.

Until the Supreme Court decision in *Bates v. State Bar of Arizona*, 433 U.S. 350 (1977), these *Martindale-Hubbell* biographies were the most extensive lawyer advertisements permitted by law. Lawyers now advertise in the yellow pages and on television, but *Martindale-Hubbell*'s subdued treatment remains the standard for the more traditional wing of the legal profession. Many law firms dealing with corporate clients have extensive listings in *Martindale-Hubbell* but simple one-line entries in the local yellow pages. On the other hand, personal-injury lawyers know that *Martindale-Hubbell* is not the best way to reach their potential clients and may choose to spend their marketing budget on television and billboard ads rather than directory space. The Albuquerque firm of Ronald Bell & Associates was featured in the *New York Times* as the first law firm to advertise on MTV, but it has only a simple one-line listing in *Martindale-Hubbell*.

Martindale-Hubbell also contains information on state bar associations and listings for corporate law departments and law schools. Lawyers working for corporations are listed in the geographical volumes, but only the *Martindale-Hubbell Corporate Law Directory* volume has information on their corporate legal departments. As in the other volumes, there are both simple "Practice Profiles" listings and more extensive "Professional Biographies" entries. Although many corporations purchase entries to display the qualifications of their legal staff, some—including major corporations such as American Airlines and Johnson & Johnson—are content simply to list their attorneys. The law school section was introduced in 1992, but it still does not cover all law schools. Nearly two-thirds of the ABA-accredited schools, however, include a narrative description, contact information for administrative offices, and biographies of professors.

For many years it was virtually impossible to find attorneys in *Martindale-Hubbell* without knowing the cities in which they practiced because there was no general alphabetical listing. Finally, in 1992, an alphabetical index was introduced, for the first time providing a single listing of all lawyers and firms included in the directory. This index provides just two pieces of information: a cross-reference to the city and state where further information can be found, and a nine-digit International Standard Lawyer Number (ISLN), a numbering system developed to assist state bars in tracking lawyers who have faced disciplinary proceedings in other states.

The areas of practice index (first introduced in 1993) covers hundreds of subjects, listing attorneys' names geographically under each heading. This is a useful resource, although it is based on the descriptions provided by subscribers and therefore excludes the thousands of attorneys listed in the blue pages who do not pay for subscriptions. It is also based on the attorneys' own descriptions of their practices. The result is a certain amount of inconsistency in listings. For example, headings for "Criminal Law—Burglary" and "Criminal Law—Forgery" list just one Albuquerque attorney. On the other hand, broad categories like "Litigation" and "Real Estate" have more than 100 pages of listings. A few cross-references are provided, but hardly enough to cover the variety of terminology used.

Martindale-Hubbell is available in several electronic versions: on CD–ROM, through LEXIS-NEXIS, and on the Internet. The electronic versions eliminate the print version's awkward and confusing abbreviations, such as "L.352" for the University of Iowa. Because space is not an issue, the names of colleges and universities can be spelled out in full. More important, electronic access makes keyword searches possible. Thus, all attorneys who graduated from a particular college or who speak a specific language can be found. Keywords can be used to identify lawyers who practice in or have written articles about a specialized area beyond those identified in the areas of practice index. Because the database contains the same information as the printed directory, however, only lawyers who pay the subscription fee have extensive entries providing detailed information beyond education and address.

The *Martindale-Hubbell Law Directory* is found in almost all law libraries and in many larger general libraries, but its information is most widely accessible through the *Martindale-Hubbell Lawyer Locator* on the Internet <http://www.martindale.com>. The *Lawyer Locator* has a form allowing searchers to find lawyers by name or to create lists combining such criteria as area of practice, location, and language. The form lists 50 areas of practice, but more specialized terminology can be used as part of a keyword search. Through keyword searching it is possible to find attorneys specializing, for example, in age discrimination litigation. Remember, however, that terms assigned to entries are the result of attorneys' self-categorization, and some attorneys claim a number of areas of expertise. One solo practitioner, for example, lists age discrimination among more than two dozen areas of expertise, including ERISA, ADA, medical malpractice, toxic torts, trade secrets, contract disputes, insurance fraud, construction industry litigation, blasting litigation, and maritime law.

The major drawback to the *Martindale-Hubbell Lawyer Locator* is that it does not include the lawyer ratings found in the other versions. According to a notice at the Web site, these ratings "have been designed for use by lawyers, and are not intended for use by the general public." As these are the only general ratings covering lawyers, members of the general public may wish to know about them whether the legal profession wants to share them or not. To find them, however, they may need to visit a local library.

LEXIS-NEXIS provides access to the complete *Martindale-Hubbell Law Directory,* including ratings, in its MARHUB library. Within this library are a comprehensive file (ALLDIR) containing all listings, as well as separate files for each state (ALDIR, AKDIR, etc.) and for corporate legal departments, government attorneys, and patent and trademark attorneys. The 35 practice areas can also be searched as separate files (e.g., MHADMR for admiralty lawyers).

West's Legal Directory

The other major directory of attorneys, *West's Legal Directory* (WLD), is not published in book form but is available on CD-ROM, through WESTLAW, and on the Internet <http://www.wld.com>. WLD began in 1990 and contains profiles of more than 800,000 lawyers and law firms. Like *Martindale-Hubbell,* it provides basic listings for free but charges attorneys and firms for more extensive profiles. WLD's major advantage over *Martindale-Hubbell* is that it includes telephone numbers in its basic listings.

On the Internet, the introductory WLD page offers a choice of "The Informed Client" and "Attorney Resources." Both provide templates for finding lawyers by location, name, and area of practice, and "Attorney Resources" includes further directories of government attorneys, corporate law departments, courts, and law students. WLD includes a few practice areas not found in Martindale-Hubbell, such as agriculture, education, and workers' compensation.

For some lawyers, WLD provides even less information than *Martindale-Hubbell*: simply an address and a date of admission to practice. But lawyers who have answered West's surveys have more extensive listings, indicating law school attended and practice areas. Some listings indicate percentage of time spent in each practice area—a useful piece of information when an attorney claims to specialize in a dozen or more fields of law.

WLD entries for law firms provide contact information, a list of attorneys' names (with links to pages for biographical information for individual attorneys), and, in many instances, a narrative summary of the firm's practice, including discussion of major cases and representative clients. These narratives often focus on recruiting and training programs for new attorneys, perhaps an indication that many of WLD's users are law students looking for jobs.

The WESTLAW version of WLD can be searched in its entirety, or by state (e.g., WLD-AL for Alabama attorneys) or specialty (WLD-ADMIR for admiralty attorneys). WESTLAW users can either use a template to fill in blanks or perform a free-text search.

Both *Martindale-Hubbell* and WLD are available free on the Internet. Which one is better? There is no right answer because as each includes some listings that are not in the other. Which should you use if you are looking for a lawyer in a particular location or subject area, or with a particular background or language skill? Here there is a right answer: Use both. As long as both sites are available without charge, the benefit of having information from both directories certainly outweighs the small amount of additional time needed to search two sites.

Because the information in both directories is based on responses to surveys, each includes some attorneys not in the other, and each is first to note some changes in address or affiliation. *Martindale-Hubbell* has been around much longer, and it is therefore more likely to include older attorneys with inactive practices who may not have seen the need to return a WLD survey form. In both directories, the attorneys most likely to be missing are solo practitioners or attorneys in small firms.

Either directory can be useful when looking for attorneys with specific characteristics. A lawyer need not have attended the same college as a client to provide effective representation, but it is important that they speak the same language. Simple keyword searches turn up several attorneys who claim that they speak Tamil or Urdu. In both instances, *Martindale-Hubbell* returns a larger result, but each time WLD includes several names that don't make the *Martindale-Hubbell* list. A search for an Uzbek-speaking attorney turns up just one lawyer in *Martindale-Hubbell* and none in WLD.

For attorneys who subscribe or purchase advertising space, there is little difference between the two directories. For those who do not subscribe, *Martindale-Hubbell* is more likely to provide information about age and education, while WLD is the only site to include telephone numbers in its basic listings.

The one area where there is a clear winner between *Martindale-Hubbell* and WLD is historical research. Anyone looking for information on the lawyers in a decades-old court case or doing genealogical research should turn to *Martindale-Hubbell* and its predecessors. WLD, like most electronic sources, focuses on current information, while *Martindale-Hubbell* is preserved in annual volumes providing a wealth of data about the changing face of the country's legal profession over the past century.

State and Local Directories

Besides the two directories of national scope, numerous directories of lawyers are published for particular states or regions. Some are published by state bar associations, and some by private companies. Some provide simple lists of attorneys' names and addresses, while many are similar in scope to *Martindale-Hubbell*, with biographical information on attorneys in private practice. In addition, a number of state and local directories provide information on government offices and courts in the area.

Legal Directories Publishing Company, based in Dallas, issues the most extensive series of directories for individual states. It publishes annually revised directories for 32 states and the District of Columbia, each in a separate volume except for a combined *Virginias Legal Directory* covering Virginia and West Virginia. Legal Directories Publishing does not cover several of the largest states (including California, Florida, and New York), but in more than a dozen states its publication serves as the official directory of the state bar association.

Legal Directories' works do not provide as much biographical detail as *Martindale-Hubbell*, but they include a variety of useful information on government offices and bar associations. Each directory includes an introductory section on federal government offices and national professional associations, followed by contact information for law schools, state government officials and courts, and state professional associations. (These sections for all 50 states—including those for which separate directories are not published—are reprinted in an annual six-volume set, *United States Lawyers Reference Directory.*) Alphabetical listings of attorneys in each directory indicate only city, county, and telephone number, but these are followed by geographic rosters with full mailing addresses, as well as fax numbers for a number of entries. The geographic rosters also include directories of county officials, including judges, prosecuting attorneys, school superintendents, and coroners.

The Legal Directories volumes generally conclude with sections listing specialists by field of practice and a biographical section providing *Martindale-Hubbell*-type profiles of a few firms. These sections are often too brief to be of any use; for West Virginia, for example, the fields of practice index has just one listing each under "criminal law," "family law," "personal injury," and "real estate"—all for the same three-person firm in Grantsville (population: 825); the biographical section for West Virginia covers five firms. *Martindale-*

Hubbell, on the other hand, provides biographical information on attorneys in nearly 300 West Virginia firms. (Only in the publisher's home state of Texas is there an extensive biographical section.)

Despite these minor shortcomings, the Legal Directories Publishing volumes are handy sources for information on a state's attorneys and government offices. The inclusion of telephone numbers is a feature notably lacking in basic *Martindale-Hubbell* listings. There is substantial overlap in coverage of attorneys between *Martindale-Hubbell* and a state Legal Directories work, but each has a few listings that the other has missed. *Martindale-Hubbell* tends to include more people who are not actively practicing law, both older attorneys and those who have moved from the state in which they were admitted. Solo practitioners, on the other hand, sometimes appear in a state directory but not in *Martindale-Hubbell*.

Other state bar directories include *Lawyers Diary and Manual*, published for five states by Skinder-Strauss Associates of Newark, New Jersey. Each of the directories, covering Florida, Massachusetts, New Hampshire, New Jersey, and New York, varies slightly but generally contains an alphabetical list of lawyers admitted in the state, with telephone numbers, date of admission, affiliation, address, and fax number; and a geographical directory listing lawyers by city. The volumes include a variety of useful features, including directories of federal and state courts in the state, federal and state agencies, law libraries, prosecutors' offices, and legal aid offices; summaries of court costs and fees; digests of federal and state procedural rules; and surveys of state marriage and divorce laws.

Many bar associations publish state and local directories. For example, both the *Florida Bar Journal* and the *Michigan Bar Journal* publish annual directory issues, listing lawyers admitted in the state alphabetically and geographically. These directory issues also include information on courts, government offices, bar associations, lawyer referral services, and legal aid offices. Because these are official bar lists, they include licensed attorneys who do not actively practice law and who may never have been included in the commercial directories.

Selective Directories

Comprehensive directories are useful for finding information on any lawyer in a particular area, but other than *Martindale-Hubbell*'s rating system they provide little information about the reputation or expertise of lawyers listed. Other directories may be more helpful

in this regard. Several focus on law firms, while others offer selective listings of individual lawyers.

Law Firms. The most extensive printed competitor to *Martindale-Hubbell* is *The American Bar* (Forster-Long, annual). This two-volume set is a "prestigious directory of the leading attorneys, the most competent and the most capable in the profession." Like *Martindale-Hubbell*, its selections are based on confidential surveys and interviews. Listings provide a brief description of a firm's practice, short biographies of attorneys, a list of representative clients, and contact information. Volume 1 includes an alphabetical index of attorneys listed, indicating firm and city, and an index of firm names and locations. An intriguing little feature, following these indexes, is a table indicating the number of partners at listed law firms who attended each U.S. law school.

Martindale-Hubbell publishes a similar work of its own, the *Bar Register of Preeminent Lawyers* (annual). This one-volume publication lists "firms and attorneys of significant stature" in general practice and in about three dozen specialized areas. It is limited to attorneys who receive AV ratings from Martindale-Hubbell, but the "Subscriber Index" in the front of the volume gives away another criterion for inclusion: Virtually every firm listed subscribes to this volume and purchases advertising space in the *Martindale-Hubbell Law Directory*. Nonetheless, the subject listings may be useful for people looking for reputable firms in specialized areas of practice. Like *The American Bar*, its focus is law firms rather than individual attorneys.

Another volume focusing on larger law firms is *Law Firms Yellow Book* (Leadership Directories, semi-annual). Like the other volumes in the publisher's *Yellow Books* series, this work is designed to provide the names and numbers of specific administrative personnel. It covers more than 700 firms, listing members of management committees, heads of practice area departments, and firm administrators. Biographical information is limited to name, law school, year of graduation, and telephone number. The volume includes indexes by department, law school, city and state, and individual name. It is available on WESTLAW as the LAWFRMYB database.

The *Of Counsel 700*, an annual special issue of Aspen Law & Business's biweekly newsletter *Of Counsel*, provides comparative information on the nation's largest law firms, including staffing levels, hiring practices, and billing rates. It also includes the names of department heads and administrators for most firms.

Two Web sites use different approaches to focus on large firms. The *National Law Journal*'s Top 250 Database <http://www.ljextra.com/lf250/nlj250index.html> contains information about the 250 largest firms in the United States, including statistics on the number of lawyers and links to *National Law Journal* stories about the firm. Hieros Gamos <http://www.hg.org/lawfirms.html> presents lists of the largest law firms in each state, with addresses, telephone and fax numbers, and the name of a contact person.

The Insider's Guide to Law Firms (Mobius Press, 4th ed., 1998), edited by Francis Walsh and Sheila Malkani, is a descriptive work focusing on large law firms for a law student audience. The guide profiles nearly 200 firms in 12 major cities, explaining what a new associate should expect in terms of workload, training, salary, diversity, atmosphere, and social life. Its entries are insightful and well written, but they offer little information for nonattorneys or potential clients. This book is definitely about working *at* these law firms rather than working *with* them.

Information about law firm practices is also available from the National Association for Law Placement's *National Directory of Legal Employers* (Harcourt Brace, annual). Like *The Insider's Guide*, this volume's primary audience is law students seeking employment. It provides basic information on the demographics and practice of more than 1,000 law firms, as well as a few corporations and nearly 100 public interest organizations and government agencies. Each employer has one page, with tabular information on the firm's attorneys, showing numbers of partners and associates by race and gender; employment information, such as recruiting practices, salary, and average number of hours worked annually; and narrative sections on the firm's practice, representative clients, and recruiting and training programs for new lawyers. Listings are arranged geographically, with an alphabetical index and a practice area index listing firms under more than 100 topics. The directory is available electronically on CD-ROM and through LEXIS-NEXIS.

Another perspective on large law firms is offered by *Minority Partners in Majority/Corporate Law Firms Directory* (American Bar Association, 4th ed., 1995). Because this loose-leaf directory does not cover a large number of partners, it dedicates an entire page to each profile, providing a photograph as well as information on background and professional experience. The directory is organized alphabetically, with indexes by location, law school, and practice area.

Lawyers. The leading source for finding highly esteemed individual attorneys is probably *The Best Lawyers in America* (Woodward/White, biennial), by Steven Naifeh and Gregory White Smith (coauthors of *How to Make Love to a Woman*, *Why Can't Men Open Up?*, and a series of *The Best Doctors in America* volumes). This volume lists nearly 14,000 lawyers chosen by their colleagues as the leading practitioners in their areas of expertise. Its selections are based on the responses of more than 11,000 attorneys to the question "If you had a close friend or relative who needed a [insert a category] lawyer, and you couldn't handle the case yourself—for reasons of conflict of interest or time, to whom would you refer them?" Inclusion thus depends on a lawyer being visible to colleagues and likable, or at least respected. Lawyers are listed by state under two dozen specialized categories, such as banking law, business litigation, family law, First Amendment law, labor and employment law, and personal injury litigation. The only information provided is the attorney's name, law firm, address, and telephone number. The volume includes an alphabetical index of attorneys listed. Because this is a directory of individual lawyers, not law firms, there is no index of firms.

Who's Who in American Law (Marquis, biennial) is one of a dozen specialized works by the publisher of the general *Who's Who in America*. It covers about 22,000 lawyers and professionals in law-related areas, including federal and state judges, attorneys general, law school deans and professors, general counsel of major corporations, and bar association officials, as well as "highly rated lawyers in private practice." The criteria for selection are not altogether clear, at least to someone who has been listed in the 6th (1990-91) and 8th (1994-95) editions but omitted from the 7th (1992-93) and 9th (1996-97).

Information in *Who's Who in American Law* is similar to that in the general *Who's Who in America*, with data on birth, family, education, and professional positions. Practicing lawyers have been asked to identify up to three fields in which they practice; the volume has a "Fields of Practice Index" covering more than 70 areas of specialization. Educators, judges, and others outside private practice are listed in a separate "Professional Index." Within each field of practice or profession, names are listed geographically, but there is no comprehensive geographical index covering everyone in the volume.

Who's Who in America, the annual flagship publication from the same publisher, includes a number of lawyers and legal professionals missing from *Who's*

Who in American Law. Who's Who in America lacks the indexing of lawyers' fields of practice, but it does include a general index of lawyers by city and state. Perhaps the best way to find someone who might appear in either publication is electronically through the Marquis Who's Who database on CD-ROM or online through DIALOG (File 234) or WESTLAW (database MARQUIS).

Attorneys also use a number of smaller directories for referral purposes. Most of these "law lists" purport to limit their coverage to highly esteemed practitioners, but because they contain little editorial matter or description, it is hard to see what sets the listed attorneys apart. The *National Law Network Legal Desk Reference* (Professional Information Corp., semiannual) is one of the most interesting of this lot. It includes useful information, such as law firm narratives and hourly billing rates, but it covers few firms: only two in San Francisco, for example, and two in the entire state of Virginia.

Some of the other referral directories are downright strange. Both *International Lawyers Referral Directory* (International Lawyers Co., annual) and *United States Bar Directory* (Attorneys' National Clearing House Co., annual) are arranged geographically, listing attorneys by city and town. These attorneys serve the cities and towns for which they are listed, but they are not necessarily based there. Scan a page in one of these directories and you will see the same names appearing over and over. *International Lawyers* has just four Wyoming lawyers, including 11 listings for one in Lander. *United States Bar Directory* has 25 listings in Alaska, all for the same Anchorage attorney, and more than 80 percent of its 145 Kentucky listings are for a Newport attorney specializing in commercial and retail collections. Directories such as these are best left for the use of listed attorneys as a source for sharing business.

A far more promising series of directories, *Guidebooks to Law & Leading Attorneys*, is available only for a few areas, although its publisher, American Research Corp., once announced plans to expand to nearly 40 states. Consumer guidebooks have been published only in three states, each with a slightly different title: *Minnesota Consumer Guidebook to Law & Leading Attorneys* (1994), *Law & Leading Attorneys: Florida Consumer Guidebook* (1995), and *Leading Illinois Attorneys: Consumer Law Guidebook* (1996); Minnesota is the only state to have a *Business Guidebook to Law & Leading Attorneys* (1994). These works outline basic legal matters, explain the structure of the legal sys-

tem, and summarize specialized areas of law. The guidebooks cover such topics as accidents, divorce, child custody, bankruptcy, taxes, and wills. These summaries are accompanied by biographical information on leading attorneys, chosen by surveyed attorneys in the state. The listings include descriptive text, employment history, representative clients, community involvement, and background on the attorney's law firm. These guides reflect a growing recognition that consumers of legal services need to be able to make informed hiring decisions. They are a model for other states, but it is not yet clear whether additional volumes will be published.

Another source for "best" lawyer recommendations may be articles in local newspapers or magazines. These articles are usually based on interviews with other lawyers and can provide some helpful insider information. Recent examples include "Hawai'i's Top Lawyers" and "567 Top Lawyers," in the February 1997 issues of *Honolulu* and *The Washingtonian,* respectively.

Specialized Directories

Numerous directories address specialized areas of legal practice. Some simply cover law firms working in these areas, with the customary lists of attorneys, but others focus on individual attorneys with specialized practices.

Corporate Counsel. Several directories cover attorneys working for corporate legal departments, including the *Martindale-Hubbell Corporate Law Directory.* Another leading work is *Directory of Corporate Counsel* (Aspen Law & Business, 2 vols., annual), covering more than 7,000 corporations, with contact information and brief biographical entries on attorneys. A separate section in Volume 2 covers nonprofit organizations. Corporations and organizations are listed alphabetically, with indexes in each volume by individual attorneys' names and by city and state. Volume 2 also contains a subject index to the nonprofit organizations and a law school alumni index. The directory is also available on CD-ROM and on WESTLAW as the CORP-DIR database.

Another work focusing on corporate counsel is *Lawyer's Register International by Specialties and Fields of Law, Including a Directory of Corporate Counsel* (Lawyers Register Publishing Co., annual). The list of corporations is extensive and includes telephone and fax numbers, but little information is provided on attorneys other than job title and law school. The first tenth of the directory is a small section of specialty law firms listed by field. A new *National Directory of Women Corporate Counsel* (Fulcrum Information Services, annual) began publication with a 1997 edition. It lists women attorneys alphabetically, with address, telephone and fax numbers, law school attended, and practice areas. Not included is information on age, year of graduation, or year of admission to the bar.

Criminal Law. Attorneys working in criminal defense are featured in the *National Directory of Criminal Lawyers* (Gold Publishers, 3d ed., 1991), edited by Barry Tarlow. This highly selective directory is based on responses from attorneys asked about whom they would retain in a serious criminal matter. There are, for example, just 11 Cleveland criminal lawyers listed, and only four in Cincinnati. In all, about 800 lawyers are listed and given a rating of I (highly competent and experienced) or II (a slight notch lower). The listings contain straightforward biographical profiles similar to those in *Martindale-Hubbell*, with no narrative information or data on cases handled. To avoid potential bias, the California-based editor has omitted his home state altogether. Unfortunately, this work is irregularly updated and has not been published in a new edition for several years.

Other Specialties. Directories focusing on specific practice areas include *American Bank Attorneys* (Capron Publishing, 2 vols., semiannual), *Best's Directory of Recommended Insurance Attorneys and Adjusters* (A. M. Best Co., 2 vols., annual), and *Markham's Negligence Counsel* (Markham Publishing, annual). Although coverage is more selective, entries in these volumes are generally similar to those in *Martindale-Hubbell*. Several specialized, annual *Law & Business Directories* were published by Prentice Hall Law & Business (now Aspen Law & Business), covering attorneys practicing in bankruptcy, environmental law, intellectual property, and litigation, but these were discontinued in the mid-1990s.

Many of the lawyers and law firms listed in general directories specialize in defending lawsuits and do not represent injured consumers or other plaintiffs. The Association of Trial Lawyers of America (ATLA) is an organization whose membership consists primarily of plantiffs' attorneys. ATLA publishes a biennial *Desk Reference* listing its members geographically, with names, addresses, and telephone numbers. This may be a useful starting place for someone seeking an attorney to take on a products liability or negligence lawsuit.

Dispute Resolution. The *Martindale-Hubbell Dispute Resolution Directory* (annual) lists individuals and organizations active in this rapidly growing area. It is organized geographically like the *Martindale-Hubbell Law Directory*, with biographical information for some people and simply a name and address for others. Entries are indexed alphabetically, by services offered, and by practice area. Introductory sections profile major ADR organizations; explain the procedures of various ADR approaches such as arbitration, mediation, and private judging; and discuss the applications of ADR in several major practice areas. A reference section at the end of the volume includes the texts of arbitration statutes and rules, sample forms, and a brief glossary. This directory is available on LEXIS-NEXIS, in the MARHUB library, DRD file. The American Bar Association also publishes a more concise *Dispute Resolution Program Directory* (1993), providing information about programs but lacking the biographical data found in the Martindale-Hubbell volume.

Legal Aid. Several directories cover lawyers and organizations involved in public interest and legal aid work, although none provide the extensive biographical information available for law firms and corporate counsel. *Directory of Legal Aid and Defender Offices in the United States* (National Legal Aid & Defender Association, biennial) contains three sections, listing civil legal aid offices, public defender offices, and special programs in about 20 categories, such as AIDS/HIV law, immigration law, and veterans legal assistance. Entries provide contact information, locations of branch offices, and names of executive directors. The section listing special programs may be the most useful because local legal aid offices can usually be found through the phone books or referral services, and clients needing public defender services are already in touch with the legal system. The *Directory of Legal Aid and Defender Offices* is available on LEXIS as the CAREER library, NLADA file.

Many local areas publish directories of free and low-cost legal services, usually listing agencies and explaining the types of cases handled, fees (if any), and procedures. These directories often include lists of frequently used numbers for government offices. A list of these local directories appears in the "Annotated Bibliography" chapter of the Harvard Law School's *Public Interest Job Search Guide*, an annual publication for law students.

Some directories of legal aid organizations cover relatively narrow ground. For example, the American Bar Association publishes the *Directory of Legal Resources for People with AIDS & HIV* (2d ed., 1997) and the *Directory of Pro Bono Legal Service Providers for Environmental Justice* (1996). Services for prisoners are covered in Anthony J. Bosoni's *Legal Resource Directory: A Guide to Free or Inexpensive Assistance for Low Income Families, with Special Sections for Prisoners* (McFarland, 1992), and in *Directory: Law Libraries Offering Services to Prisoners* (American Association of Law Libraries, Contemporary Social Problems Special Interest Section, rev. ed., 1993).

Public Interest. A number of organizations provide legal advocacy for a wide range of political and public interest causes. Harvard's *Public Interest Job Search Guide* includes an extensive directory of these organizations, briefly summarizing the services each provides. *Directory of Public Interest Law Centers* (Alliance for Justice, 1996) is a simple alphabetical listing of addresses and telephone numbers with indexes by program emphasis and location. The Meiklejohn Civil Liberties Institute's *Human Rights Organizations & Periodicals Directory* (8th ed., 1996) includes a large number of public interest legal organizations, with brief descriptions, addresses, and telephone numbers, as well as a subject index.

Two works provide more extensive coverage of selected organizations. The Foundation for Public Affairs' *Public Interest Profiles, 1996-97* (Congressional Quarterly, 1996) covers several major legal advocacy organizations, including descriptions of each group's purpose, staffing, and publications. Quotations from news sources provide perspectives on each group's effectiveness and political orientation. Karen O'Connor and Lee Epstein's *Public Interest Law Groups: Institutional Profiles* (Greenwood, 1989) provides descriptive summaries of about 175 organizations. Entries, ranging from two paragraphs to five pages, discuss each group's history, major cases, and ongoing projects. The book provides mailing addresses but includes few names and no telephone numbers. A few entries include references to sources for further information, and a brief index provides some subject access.

Nonprofit programs operated by law firms and bar associations can be found in the American Bar Association publications *Directory of Pro Bono Programs* (annual) and *Directory of State Bar Public Service Activities and Programs* (1992). These may be useful resources for someone seeking an attorney interested in taking on a specific public interest cause. Another ABA work, *Law School Public Interest Law Support Programs: A Directory* (1995), is designed for students, not potential clients. It is arranged by school and has no subject access, but it may be helpful in indicating what programs exist in a particular metropolitan area or region.

Web Sites

Like other businesses, a growing number of lawyers and law firms have discovered the Internet as a way to disseminate information and market their services. Law firm Web sites vary from simple directories listing firm members to elaborate resources with detailed information on specialized topics and links to related resources.

Yahoo has the largest collection of links to law firm homepages <http://www.yahoo.com/business_and_economy/companies/law/firms>. More than 3,000 firms are represented, with separate listings for firms in about 20 specialized areas. Also accessible is a complete listing of all law firms, mostly in alphabetical order. Users can browse these lists or search the subdirectory for particular names or terms.

Several other lists of law firm links exist on the Internet. As with any discussion of Web resources, access will obviously change and grow as more law firms join the Internet.

- The Internet Legal Resource Guide <http://www.ilrg.com/lawyers.html> has two extensive lists, one of law firms and one of solo practitioners, but it provides no information beyond the firm or lawyer's name. ILRG also provides convenient forms for accessing the *Martindale-Hubbell* and WLD Web sites.

- The Emory Law Library Electronic Reference Desk has separate alphabetical listings of law firms and solo practitioners <http://www.law.emory.edu/LAW/refdesk/lawyers/>. It includes fewer entries than ILRG but provides some information about most, such as geographical location or field of practice.

- Indiana University School of Law—Bloomington offers one alphabetical listing of lawyers and firms <http://www.law.indiana.edu/law/v-lib/lawfirms.html>. This list is searchable and includes annotations for most entries, showing the location and nature of practice.

- Washburn University School of Law's WashLaw Web law firm page <http://lawlib.wuacc.edu/washlaw/lawfirms.html> is arranged geographically. Instead of one alphabetical list, firms are listed in separate pages for each state. Most entries include annotations, but many of these are simply blurbs—such as "Proficiency is the hallmark of Conkle & Olesten's representation of clients"—from the firms' homepages.

- The Internet Lawyer provides a selective site of Profiled Law Firms, <http://www.internetlawyer.com/firms.htm> with reviews of several law firm

Web pages added each month. These reviews, by a lawyer/Web site designer, range from raves to scathing critiques, and provide tips on getting the most from Web pages as a user or a designer.

- "Lawyer Search" <http://www.counsel.com/lawyersearch/> is a directory of lawyers who subscribe to Counsel Connect's online service for attorneys. It seeks to compete with *Martindale-Hubbell* and WLD, but because its coverage is limited to subscribers, it is not nearly as comprehensive as either of those works. This may be one of the best sources for finding electronic contacts, however, because everyone listed has an e-mail address. The database can be searched by name or location. Although some lawyers' entries include lengthy narratives on their background and expertise, as well as links to related sites, most entries provide little information.

Several Web sites offer the Internet version of the "law lists" discussed earlier—referral choices among a small number of lawyers who happen to subscribe to the service. These services generally allow searching based on a locality and a specialized area of law, but most searches turn up just one or two lawyers per state. Still, access is free and useful referrals can be found, often with links to lawyers' homepages and e-mail addresses. These services include AttorneyFind <http://www.attorneyfind.com>, Attorney Locate <http://www.attorneylocate.com>, and LawInfo <http://www.lawyersource.com>. Law Journal Extra! <http://www.ljextra.com/firms/lfonline.html> includes a Law Firm Finder, which is also limited in scope but at least acknowledges it in a notice on its search page: "Also, please remember the practice area database is in its infancy. As more firms contact us this will become a much more valuable resource."

Other Sources of Information

The first place most people turn for information about attorneys is their local telephone books. Advertising by lawyers in the yellow pages grows each year, but most ads do not provide much descriptive information about lawyers' experience or the quality and nature of legal services offered. Areas of practice are usually indicated.

Referral Services

Another way to find lawyers is through referral services, usually operated by state and local bar associations. However, using a lawyer referral service does not guarantee finding someone particularly qualified

and experienced because it is often younger lawyers looking for new clients who subscribe to these services. The simplest way to find a referral service for a particular area is to check the local yellow pages under a heading such as "Lawyers Referral Service" or "Attorney Referral Service." In addition, the American Bar Association publishes an annual *Directory of Lawyer Referral Services*, listing some 300 lawyer referral programs throughout the country, with brief information on the scope of services provided. This information is also available on the Internet <http://www.abanet.org/referral/home.html> with links to homepages.

Articles

Further information about lawyers and law firms can be found in a variety of sources available in law libraries, in both print and electronic forms. The legal newspapers discussed in Chapter 5 frequently include articles on developments in the legal profession, including occasional profiles of specific firms or lawyers. Research on a particular topic can lead to articles written by practitioners, who can then be found in directories such as *Martindale-Hubbell* or WLD.

Cases

Published case law can also provide information because almost all reported decisions identify the attorneys representing the parties. Researching a legal issue thus can provide the names and addresses of attorneys with experience in that area. Keep in mind two points when using published cases as a means to find attorneys in a particular area of law. First, attorneys who represent parties before appellate courts may be specialists in appellate practice rather than in the subject area; they might nonetheless make worthwhile first contact points in searching for a subject specialist. Relatively few trial court decisions are published, so the cases are less useful in finding attorneys who specialize in trial litigation. Verdict reporters such as *National Jury Verdict Review and Analysis* and *Verdicts, Settlements & Tactics* (both monthly) can provide the names of trial lawyers, but these publications are not as widely accessible as court decisions. In addition, attorneys who successfully advise clients how to *avoid* litigation may not be represented in these sources at all.

Second, because the cases indicate which attorneys won and which lost, it may be tempting to use such "boxscores" as an indicator of the attorneys' professional skills. A lawyer's winning percentage, however, is not a foolproof yardstick. As one lawyer recently wrote, "With notable exception lawyers do not win cases. Cases win cases. Lawyers who never lose are mostly skilled at picking winners" (C. M. Steve Aron, Defining the Ultimate Lawyer, 30 Land & Water L. Rev. 515, 526 [1995]).

Electronic access makes court decisions a far more flexible and valuable resource for obtaining background information on attorneys. Published cases are not indexed by attorney, so in print it is only possible to stumble on a specific attorney's name while looking for cases by subject. Electronically, on the other hand, you can search for any word appearing in a document—including the names of lawyers or law firms. Both LEXIS-NEXIS and WESTLAW provide specific procedures to facilitate such searches by designating specific parts of case documents for identification of the attorneys. Searches in the *counsel* segment in LEXIS-NEXIS or the *attorneys* field in WESTLAW will focus in on the names of attorneys or law firms listed.

Statistics

Statistics on the legal community are of widespread interest, but they can be hard to find. Some are available in *The Lawyer Statistical Report: The U.S. Legal Profession in the 1990s*, by Barbara A. Curran and Clara N. Carson (American Bar Foundation, 1994). This is the 10th in a series of statistical reports issued by the Foundation, beginning in 1956. For the national lawyer population and for each state, this volume provides tables indicating demographics by sex, age, and employment status (private practice, government, private industry, legal aid, education, etc.). It also includes data on the size and characteristics of law firms, and provides state population/lawyer ratios. (In 1991, the District of Columbia had one lawyer for every 15 people, while South Carolina was the most lawyer-free state with one lawyer for every 592 people.) An introductory section surveys overall characteristics of the lawyer population. The statistics are based on data supplied by Martindale-Hubbell, with no attempt to take into account lawyers omitted from that publisher's directory.

Although *The Lawyer Statistical Report* compares male and female lawyer populations, it does not consider race or ethnicity in its tables. Summary information on these aspects of the legal profession is available from the U.S. Bureau of Labor Statistics. Table 11 in each year's January issue of *Employment and Earnings* includes the number of lawyers in the country, as well as a combined total of lawyers and judges, and the female, black, and Hispanic percentages of this total. This information is reprinted in the federal government's annual *Statistical Abstract* volume.

From time to time legal newspapers and state bar journals feature surveys on minority representation in the legal profession. Most of these cover specific states or metropolitan areas. The *National Law Journal* has on occasion surveyed minority employment practices on a nationwide basis, most recently in Ann Davis's "Big Jump in Minority Associates, But . . . ." *National Law Journal*, Apr. 29, 1996, at A1.

The Lawyer Statistical Report includes no treatment of lawyer incomes. The major source for this information is an annual "What Lawyers Earn" survey published as a supplement to a *National Law Journal* issue in early summer. The survey includes a summary of salary trends, usually showing the rise in law firm compensation and the stagnation in government and public interest salaries. Tables list representative salaries from cities across the country for various positions, including judges, prosecutors, public defenders, law clerks, and law school professors.

EXPERTS AND CONSULTANTS

The law puts food on the table for other professionals besides attorneys. Any major lawsuit involves a corps of expert witnesses and consultants. A major source for finding experts is the *Forensic Services Directory* (National Forensic Center, annual), which provides information on about 5,000 specialists in scientific, medical, and technical areas. The directory is arranged topically, with several hundred classifications of expertise. Entries provide the experts' specialties, affiliations, and qualifications; a few include more extensive biographical information. A subject index running well over 100 pages precedes the listings. The index simply uses the terminology from the entries (is there a difference between "lightning damage analysis" and "lightning damage assessment"?), but it does provide extensive keyword access. A useful feature in this directory is an extensive list of associations and agencies that can provide information on specialized subjects. Entries describe areas of interest and the scope of information services. Another lengthy subject index precedes these listings. The *Forensic Services Directory* is available online on LEXIS/NEXIS (LEXREF library, EXPERT file) and WESTLAW (FSD database).

The Best Lawyers in America: Directory of Experts (Woodward/White, 1992) lists expert witnesses nominated by attorneys in the publisher's *Best Lawyers in America* volume. It covers 1,200 experts in nearly 200 subject areas; some entries include background information, but most simply provide contact information. The experts are indexed geographically and by name.

This directory has not been updated in several years, and its information is gradually becoming less reliable.

Chapter 1 of Harry M. Philo and Harry M. Philo, Jr.'s *Lawyers Desk Reference* (Clark Boardman Callaghan, 8th ed., 1993) lists more than 400 pages of expert witnesses by subject, followed by about 30 organizations that provide a range of consulting and advisory services. Each entry includes a brief summary of areas of expertise. Additions and changes are provided in an annual pocket part supplement.

There are other directories of expert witnesses, but most have limited listings. For example, *The LeMark Directory: A Comprehensive Guide to Expert Witnesses* (LeMark Publishing Co., 1996) provides little more than names supplied by universities trying to promote their faculties. In Mississippi, 136 of 161 listings are from the University of Southern Mississippi. The Massachusetts section is dominated by faculty at Boston University and the University of Massachusetts, with no mention of other local schools such as Harvard or M.I.T. Another recent work, *The National Directory of Expert Witnesses* (Claims Providers of America, 1998), also claims to be comprehensive but is similarly limited in scope.

The same problem plagues Web sites listing expert witnesses. LawInfo.com's expert witness database <http://www.lawinfo.com> lists experts in more than 100 categories, but most categories feature only one or two listings. Links are provided, however, to experts' homepages. The Los Angeles County Bar Association sponsors expert4law <http://www.expert4law.org>; this is a more extensive, searchable directory, but most of its listings are limited to California. Several other directories and referral services are available through the Internet; the growing list can be tracked through FindLaw's Experts and Consultants page <http://www.findlaw.com/13experts/>.

Specialists in such areas as jury selection, juror psychology, and trial strategy are listed in the American Society of Trial Consultants' annual *Membership Directory*. This small volume lists consultants alphabetically, indicating their areas of specialty, and includes indexing by subject and by state.

ORGANIZATIONS AND INSTITUTIONS

There is more to the legal system than lawyers and law firms. A broad range of organizations and institutions focus on legal issues. Many of these have staff who can provide information on legal topics, usually at no charge.

Among the most important institutions in the legal system are the legislatures, courts, and administrative agencies. Directories covering these lawmaking entities are discussed in separate chapters, along with other sources for information about their work. This section discusses more general resources and information on organizations, such as bar associations and academic institutions.

One of the broadest directories of legal organizations is *Law and Legal Information Directory* (Gale, biennial). This directory provides contact information for more than 34,000 organizations, institutions, and services, with material compiled from a wide range of sources. Coverage includes law-related organizations, state and local bar associations, requirements for admission to practice in federal and state courts, federal and state regulatory agencies, law schools, paralegal programs, law libraries, legal publishers, lawyer referral services, and legal aid offices. Much of the directory's impressive heft comes from its section on law enforcement agencies, which covers more than 600 pages. There is no index for the directory as a whole, but some chapters have alphabetical or keyword indexes. One of the handiest aspects of this publication is the introductory "Section Descriptions," providing references to the sources for information in each of the book's 41 sections. The *Law and Legal Information Directory* may not be as current or as comprehensive as these more specialized works, but it is a handy compilation that may be more readily available than many of its sources.

Because Washington, DC, is the center of so much legal activity, a number of directories focus on finding information in and around the capital. Most of these list federal government offices, but two directories combine coverage of the government with a variety of organizations, institutes, and businesses—making them excellent places to check, in part because they may lead to avenues of inquiry that might not have been considered.

The more widely found volume, the *Washington Information Directory* (Congressional Quarterly, annual), is also the more useful. This directory is organized by subject into 19 chapters, each of which is further subdivided. The "Law and Justice" chapter, for example, includes sections on "Business and Tax Law," "Constitutional Law and Civil Liberties," "Law Enforcement," and "Legal Professions and Resources." Each subsection contains listings of government agencies, congressional committees, and nongovernmental organizations working in the area, with brief descriptions and contact information. The subject sections are followed by reference sections covering Congress, federal agencies, regional information sources (contact points outside Washington for federal agencies), state governments, and foreign embassies. The volume includes a name index and an extensive subject index with listings for all agencies and organizations covered. Exhibit 6-1 shows a sample page from this directory, listing organizations active in constitutional law and civil liberties.

Washington: A Comprehensive Directory of the Key Institutions and Leaders of the National Capital Area (Columbia Books, annual) covers the same territory in a different manner. Its 17 chapters are arranged by type of organization, such as businesses, national associations, labor unions, and foundations. Some of its sections, covering local educational, religious, and cultural institutions may be useful for some purposes, but they are not of much value for research on public policy or legal issues. The listings in this volume tend to provide more detailed information on staff names and positions than the *Washington Information Directory*. They are not, however, easily accessible by subject, due to the arrangement and the absence of a topical index. There is, however, an extensive index of listed organizations and individuals.

Although CQ's *Washington Information Directory* is a unique resource, directories similar to the Columbia Books *Washington* are available for many state capitals and other major cities.

Associations

As in any other professional field, the law has a wealth of organizations representing particular interests or working to effect changes in the legal system. The first place to look for any nonprofit organization is the well-known *Encyclopedia of Associations* (Gale, annual). The most common, and for most purposes the most valuable, component of this work is Volumes 1 and 2, *National Organizations of the U.S.*, but the set also includes two volumes of *International Organizations* and five regional volumes of *Regional, State and Local Organizations*.

Encyclopedia of Associations: National Organizations of the U.S. has a section on legal, governmental, public administration, and military organizations, which is subdivided into specific areas; but organizations with legal interests are found throughout the encyclopedia. Civil rights and liberties groups are listed under "Public Affairs Organizations," and associations of legal educators appear under "Educational Organizations." The

"Health and Medical Organizations" section includes the American Association of Nurse Attorneys, while "Religious Organizations" includes the Christian Legal Society. Entries explain a group's purpose and activities, list its publications, and provide other basic information. An extensive name and keyword index provides several points of access for most organizations, and entries for full names include addresses and telephone numbers.

Information from the *Encyclopedia of Associations* is available from Gale in a variety of electronic formats. *Associations Unlimited*, on CD-ROM and as a fee-based Internet service <http://galenet.gale.com>, includes information about national, international, and regional associations, as well as entries on 300,000 other nonprofit entities and full-text brochures and pamphlets from major national associations. The data are also available online through DIALOG (File 114), LEXIS-NEXIS (BUSREF, LEGIS, or MARKET library, ENASSC file) and WESTLAW (EOA database).

Less extensive directories of associations are also available. *National Trade and Professional Associations of the United States* (Columbia Books, annual) provides similar listings for a more select group of organizations. The entries are listed alphabetically, but a subject index includes more than 150 listings under "Law." A handful of legal organizations are represented in *The Associations Yellow Book* (Leadership Directories, semiannual), which provides more detailed staff information for major trade and professional associations than the other directories. Like the other Leadership *Yellow Books*, it is available on WESTLAW as the ASSOCYB database.

The most prominent legal organizations, of course, are associations of lawyers, or bar associations. These provide a wide variety of useful services, not just for lawyers but for the public as well. Most have lawyer referral services, and many publish common sense guides to legal topics. In many jurisdictions the state bar association assumes primary responsibility for fielding complaints about lawyers and handling disciplinary cases.

The most well-known association of lawyers is the American Bar Association; its many activities include the publication of several of the sources we have already discussed, including practical legal manuals, journals, and directories. The ABA is a voluntary organization with some 360,000 members and a large number of specialized sections, commissions, committees, and task forces. It has a thorough Web page <http://www.abanet.org> that provides information on its or-

JUDICIARY

Supreme Court of the United States, *1 1st St. N.E. 20543; 479-3000. William H. Rehnquist, chief justice; William K. Suter, clerk, 479-3011. Library, 479-3037. Supreme Court opinions and information, 479-3211. Internet, http://www.law.cornell.edu/lii.table.html.*

Highest appellate court in the federal judicial system. Interprets the U.S. Constitution, federal legislation, and treaties. Provides information on new cases filed, the status of pending cases, and admissions to the Supreme Court Bar. *(For complete list of justices, see chap. 12.)*

NONGOVERNMENTAL

American Civil Liberties Union (ACLU), *122 Maryland Ave. N.E. 20002; 544-1681. Laura W. Murphy, director, Washington office. Fax, 546-0738. Internet, http://www.aclu.org.*

Initiates test court cases and advocates legislation to guarantee constitutional rights and civil liberties. Focuses on First Amendment rights, minority and women's rights, gay and lesbian rights, and privacy; supports legalized abortion, opposes government-sponsored school prayer and legislative restrictions on television content. Washington office monitors legislative and regulatory activities and public policy. Library open to the public by appointment. (Headquarters in New York maintains docket of cases.)

Center for Individual Rights, *1233 20th St. N.W., #300 20036; 833-8400. Michael S. Greve, executive director. Fax, 833-8410. Internet, cir@wdn.com or http://www.wdn.com/cir.*

Public interest law firm that supports reform of the civil justice system on the basis of private rights and individual responsibility. Interests include economic regulation, freedom of speech, and libel law.

Ethics and Public Policy Center, *Law and Society Program, 1015 15th St. N.W., #900 20005; 682-1200. Elliott Abrams, president. Fax, 408-0632. Internet, ethics@eppc.org.*

Examines current issues of jurisprudence, especially those relating to constitutional interpretation.

Institute for Justice, *1717 Pennsylvania Ave. N.W., #200 20006; 955-1300. Chip Mellor, president. Fax, 955-1329. Internet, general@instituteforjustice.org or http://www.instituteforjustice.org.*

Sponsors seminars to train law students, grass-roots activists, and practicing lawyers in applying advocacy strategies in public interest litigation. Seeks to protect from arbitrary government interference free speech, private property rights, parental school choice, and economic liberty. Litigates cases.

Legal Affairs Council, *3554 Chain Bridge Rd., #301, Fairfax, VA 22030; (703) 591-7767. Richard A. Delgaudio, president. Fax, (703) 273-4514.*

Provides conservative activists with financial and legal assistance for court challenges of alleged violations of human and civil rights, especially First Amendment rights.

NAACP Legal Defense and Educational Fund, *1275 K St. N.W., #301 20005; 682-1300. Penda Hair, director, Washington office. Fax, 682-1312.*

Civil rights litigation group that provides legal information on civil rights issues, including employment, housing, and educational discrimination; monitors federal enforcement of civil rights laws. Not affiliated with the National Assn. for the Advancement of Colored People (NAACP). (Headquarters in New York.)

National Assn. for the Advancement of Colored People (NAACP), *1025 Vermont Ave. N.W., #1120 20005; 638-2269. Harold McDougall, director, Washington bureau. Fax, 638-5936. Internet, http://www.nvi.net/naacp_washington_bureau/.*

Membership: persons interested in civil rights for all minorities. Works for the political, educational, social, and economic equality of minorities through legal, legislative, and direct action, and educational programs. (Headquarters in Baltimore.)

National Committee Against Repressive Legislation, *3321 12th St. N.E., 3rd Floor 20017-4008; 529-4225. Kit Gage, Washington representative.*

Educational organization that seeks to protect First Amendment rights of free speech and association. Interests include privacy, protection of due process rights, government secrecy and surveillance, and control of federal intelligence agencies; sponsors educational programs; organizes grass-roots political activities; maintains speakers bureau. (Headquarters in Los Angeles.)

National Organization for Women (NOW), *1000 16th St. N.W., #700 20036; 331-0066. Patricia Ireland, president. Fax, 785-8576. TDD, 331-9002. Internet, now@now.org or http://www.now.org/now.*

Membership: women and men interested in civil rights for women. Works to end discrimination based on gender, to preserve abortion rights, and to pass an equal rights amendment to the Constitution.

See also Lawyers' Committee for Civil Rights Under Law (p. 36) ganization and services, and it publishes an annual *American Bar Association Directory* listing the leaders of its various boards, committees, sections, and divisions. The *ABA Directory* also includes listings for state and local bar associations as well as several dozen other national legal organizations. It is available on WESTLAW as the ABA-DIR database.

Although the ABA is the largest association of attorneys and certainly wields an influential voice in national legal matters, it does not have the official weight of state bar associations, which bear the responsibility for licensing and disciplining attorneys. More than two-thirds of the states have *integrated* or *unified* state bars, which means that membership in the state bar is required for all practicing attorneys.

State bar associations are covered in several directories. The ABA publishes an annual *Directory of Bar Associations*, providing brief profiles indicating membership figures and contact information for officers. (Each year the ABA also publishes a similar but more specialized *Directory of Associations for Women Lawyers*.) The *Directory of State Bar Associations* (Raven Research and Library Services, 1995) provides more in-depth information in a standardized questionnaire format (contact information, staffing, publications, sources of ethics opinions, meeting date, referral services, etc.). As noted earlier, the *Martindale-Hubbell Law Directory* also includes profiles of state bar associations. These vary from state to state, but most include a brief history of the organization and names and addresses of officers and committee chairs.

On the Web, Martindale-Hubbell's state bar association profiles are available in "The Profession" section of its Web site <http://www.martindale.com/profession/statebarmap.html>. A number of state bar homepages are useful sources of information for both lawyers and members of the public. Two that have been praised for providing consumer information are the State Bar of Wisconsin <http://www.wisbar.org>, and the State Bar of California <http://www.calbar.org>. Lists of bar associations, with links to their homepages, are also available through FindLaw <http://www.findlaw.com/06associations>, as well as through the international legal site Hieros Gamos <http://www.hg.org/northam-bar.html>. These lists also cover local bar associations, national associations for attorneys with particular interests, and other legal organizations.

The definitive source on the standards for membership in a state bar is the *Comprehensive Guide to Bar Admission Requirements*, an annual publication of the ABA Section on Legal Education and Admission to the Bar and the National Conference of Bar Examiners. The guide contains a number of charts and lists summarizing such matters as educational requirements, bar examinations, and fees. Other sources of information on bar admission and exams include the annual *BAR/BRI Digest*, a state-by-state guide by a leading bar preparation company, providing data on the procedure, format, and grading for each state's exam; a guide in every March issue of *Student Lawyer*, with addresses, application procedures, dates and locations of exams, and fees; and *The Bar Guide: Attorney's Guide to State Bar Admission Requirements* (Federal Reports, 2d ed., 1995), written for experienced lawyers interested in moving from one state to another.

Law Schools

Several directories of law schools are published. Most are designed for prospective law students. The simplest and most straightforward is *The Official Guide to U.S. Law Schools*, published annually by Broadway Books for the Law School Admission Council, in cooperation with the American Bar Association and the Association of American Law Schools. Introductory chapters cover such matters as applying to law school and financial aid, and include tables providing information on minority representation, school size, programs, library, and tuition; maps show the location of each accredited law school. Each law school has a two-page entry in a standardized format, discussing its facilities, curriculum, special programs, admission requirements, and expenses. Most entries include a chart indicating the acceptance rate for applicants.

The Official Guide to U.S. Law Schools contains some statistical information on the student body, faculty, and library facilities as well as admissions, but it has recently been joined by a new publication, the *Official American Bar Association Guide to Approved Law Schools* (Macmillan, annual). This title replaces the less extensive ABA publication *A Review of Legal Education in the United States*, which was issued annually through 1995. Although the ABA guide has introductory chapters on admission rates, expenses, and related issues, most of the book consists of tables. Thirty pages of subject tables provide comparative information on career placement, bar passage rates, expenses, faculties, student bodies, and admissions. Following these are two pages of tabular data for each school, with detailed information on the faculty, library, student body, curriculum, admission rates, expenses, and placement. This is the place to learn how many hours per week the library is open, how many students are involved in law journals, or how many graduates are employed in foreign countries. The standardized format makes it easy to flip back and forth to compare schools.

Several other directories of law schools are designed for prospective students. These generally combine descriptions of individual schools with introductory sections on the law school experience, the admission process, financial aid, and employment prospects. One of the most widely available, *Barron's Guide to Law Schools* (Barron's Educational Series, biennial), provides a simple, straightforward summary of each school. *REA's Authoritative Guide to Law Schools* (Research and Education Association, 1997) has similar information and includes a few photographs of law school buildings. *The Princeton Review Student Advantage Guide to the Best Law Schools* (Random House, annual) covers every ABA-accredited law school, and includes useful comparative graphs on such issues as the quality of the curriculum, the teaching, and the facilities.

Other guides cover a smaller number of schools but provide more opinionated entries based on comments from students. S.F. Goldfarb's *Inside the Law Schools: A Guide by Students for Students* (Plume, 7th ed., 1998) covers about 110 schools, and Bruce S. Stuart and Kim D. Stuart's *Top Law Schools* (Prentice-Hall, 1990) covers 56 schools; the most selective guide is Cynthia L. Cooper's *The Insider's Guide to the Top Fifteen Law Schools* (Doubleday, 1990).

In addition to these narrative directories are several rankings of law schools. The most influential is *U.S. News and World Report*'s annual "America's Best Graduate Schools" issue. This and a variety of other rankings are available on the Internet through Wehrli's Graduate School Rankings, part of the Internet Legal Resource Guide <http://wehrli.ilrg.com/>.

One of the best law school guides is written by law professors from 16 schools, but it does not discuss specific institutions. *Looking at Law School: A Student Guide from the Society of American Law Teachers* (Meridian, 4th ed., 1997), edited by Stephen Gillers, discusses reasons for attending law school and aspects of the law school experience. It includes brief over-

views of the issues addressed in such major law school courses as criminal law, property law, and torts. Several chapters include recommendations for additional reading.

Information on law schools and their faculties can also be found in two standard biographical directories. These can be useful because many law professors are willing to share their expertise with researchers and the press as well as with their classes. The Association of American Law Schools publishes an annual *Directory of Law Teachers*. A list of teachers by school, with mailing addresses, direct dial numbers, and e-mail addresses, is followed by a biographical section, arranged alphabetically and providing information on academic degrees, positions held, memberships, subjects taught, and publications. An index by subject covers nearly 90 topics and lists professors by the number of years they have been teaching in the area of expertise. The *Directory of Law Teachers* is available on WESTLAW as the WLD-AALS database.

As noted earlier, the *Martindale-Hubbell Law Directory* includes coverage of about 120 law schools, including narrative descriptions, telephone numbers of administrators, and brief biographies of professors. These biographies are shorter than those in *Directory of Law Teachers* and are limited to birth date, bar membership, education, and courses taught. This information is also available through LEXIS-NEXIS in the MARHUB library, LAWDIR file, and on the Web at <http://www.martindale.com/profession/schools/>, which includes a clickable U.S. map and keyword searching.

In many cases, the most thorough (if not the most impartial) source of information on a law school is the school itself. Catalogs listing courses and describing the program are available from admission offices, and most law schools have extensive homepages on the Internet. Two convenient lists of these homepages are provided by the ABA <http://www.abanet.org/legaled/approved.html>, and by FindLaw <http://www.findlaw.com/02lawschools/fulllist.html>.

PART 3
Federal Law

CHAPTER 7
The Constitution and the Supreme Court

The Constitution is a vital legal document for all Americans, even for those of us who never step into a courtroom or never have need to read a statute or court decision. It affects our daily lives because it establishes many of the basic rules governing society. It creates the political framework, limits the government's powers, and ensures that citizens have fundamental freedoms. For a short document that has changed little in more than 200 years, the Constitution is often at the center of debates about the structure and values of our culture.

The Supreme Court is the ultimate arbiter of the meaning and scope of the Constitution. Each year it hears difficult cases in which it must apply constitutional principles to such new concerns as physician-assisted suicide or Internet censorship. These decisions from the Supreme Court are as much a part of the Constitution as the text itself. To understand the Constitution, it is also necessary to understand how its provisions have been interpreted and applied by the Supreme Court.

The Supreme Court has other responsibilities as the court of last resort in the federal system. It also must interpret federal statutes and court rules, and mediate conflicts between the legislative and executive branches of government or between the federal and state governments. But it is not solely responsible for interpreting the Constitution. Congress and the executive branch are charged with carrying out their duties within the scope of the Constitution, and the lower federal courts make the initial determination on whether government action is constitutional. One might even say that the Supreme Court's decisions are not really final, for they can be overturned by subsequent decisions, by constitutional amendment, or, as in the case of *Dred Scott v. Sandford*, by civil war.

REFERENCE WORKS

Generally in approaching an unfamiliar issue of constitutional law it is best to begin with a reference work to obtain the background information necessary to understand this complicated field. Several reference resources focus on the Constitution and the Supreme Court. Almost all include the text of the Constitution as well. Although individual tastes vary, many people find an alphabetically arranged encyclopedia to be the most convenient starting point for learning about a particular constitutional subject.

Encyclopedia of the American Constitution

The grandest reference work on the Constitution, in scope and design, is the *Encyclopedia of the American Constitution* (Macmillan, 1986), edited by Leonard W. Levy, Kenneth L. Karst, and Dennis J. Mahoney. The original set was published in four blue volumes; a 1990 reissue on thinner paper condensed it to two volumes with red bindings. Both sets use the same attractive and easily readable typeface and spacious layout. This is a serious and stately work, with no photographs or other illustrations.

The encyclopedia contains more than 2,100 articles by 262 scholars in law, history, and political science. The articles cover not only constitutional doctrines and issues, but historical periods, persons (not just Supreme Court justices but other major figures such as presidents, members of the Constitutional Convention, and constitutional theorists), legislative acts, and major decisions of the Supreme Court. The entries contain cross-references, indicated by the setting off of words in small capitals, and most include brief but useful bibliographies listing books and articles for further study.

The writers were encouraged to express their own views in addition to describing and analyzing their subjects, and the editors sought contributors with a range of viewpoints. As the preface notes, "Readers should be alert to the likelihood that a cross-referenced article may discuss similar issues from a different perspective, especially if the issues have been the subject of recent controversy." This can make for interesting reading, although readers should expect an encyclopedia to provide as impartial an authoritative analysis as possible even when dealing with controversial issues.

On the other hand, a valuable reference work goes beyond bare historical facts to provide some critical perspective on the events and people of constitutional law. A good test case for this is the treatment of Charles Whittaker, perhaps the least distinguished Supreme Court justice of the twentieth century. Some works provide simple biographical outlines, but this encyclopedia's treatment is unsparing: After comparing Whittaker to T. S. Eliot's Mr. Prufrock ("Full of high sentence, but a bit obtuse"), Michael E. Parrish goes on to note that Whittaker's tenure on the Court "was distinguished only by its brevity and by his own inability to develop a coherent judicial philosophy."

Appendixes contain the text of the Constitution and several other major documents, as well as chronological information and a brief glossary. Three indexes cover court cases, individual names, and subjects. The most useful is the case index, which provides page ref-

erences in the encyclopedia and citations to the opinions themselves for further study. The name index is useful for references to minor figures, but its treatment of important justices is frustrating—names are simply followed by long lists of page numbers, with no subdivision by case or subject. The subject index is also disappointing, with most of its main entries merely duplicating the terminology used for the titles of the alphabetically arranged articles.

The writing in this work is first-rate, but the editorial apparatus could have been better. The indexes are substandard and the cross-references between articles are numerous but incomplete. The article on the First Amendment doctrine of "Clear and Present Danger," for example, neglects the "Subversive Advocacy" article about the context in which the clear and present danger test was developed. Gerald Gunther's article on "Judicial Review" makes no reference to the one immediately following it, Robert H. Bork's "Judicial Review and Democracy," which offers a different perspective on essentially the same topic.

The *Encyclopedia of the American Constitution* is current only through July 1985, but *Supplement I* (1992) updates material to mid-1991. The supplement includes 320 articles, including treatment of nearly 250 new topics. Some gaps in the original work were filled, covering topics that had been neglected or assigned to authors who didn't produce articles. Other articles were updated, not by the original contributors but by authors "of different constitutional persuasions." Some topics, such as "Abortion and the Constitution," have two updates with different perspectives on recent developments. Cross-references in the supplement note in which volume or volumes a subject appears; this is helpful, but some readers may find the bracketed additions to a sentence about "Justice SANDRA DAY O'CONNOR [3, I] and Justice BYRON R. WHITE [4, I]" a bit too intrusive. One helpful feature of the supplement is that its indexes are cumulative and cover all five volumes.

The *Encyclopedia of the American Constitution* does not reflect the most recent constitutional developments, but it is still one of the most important of all legal reference sources. Despite its hefty price tag, it will be found in any substantial public or educational library collection.

Oxford Companion to the Supreme Court

The Oxford Companion to the Supreme Court of the United States (Oxford University Press, 1992), edited by Kermit L. Hall, is similar to the *Encyclopedia of the*

American Constitution but in a more compact and handy format. Instead of four large tomes, the *Companion* is one volume of just more than 1,000 pages. Its type is much smaller than the *Encyclopedia,* but it includes a variety of photographs and other illustrations, including a portrait of each justice. The *Oxford Companion's* primary focus is how the Supreme Court performs its role as "the preeminent guardian and interpreter of the Constitution." It also includes articles on other aspects of the Court, covering such diverse matters as sculpture in the Supreme Court building, judicial salaries, and the nomination process. Like the *Encyclopedia*, the *Oxford Companion* is full of cross-references, indicated by asterisks, as in "John *Marshall."

The *Companion's* almost 300 contributors include scholars, lawyers, and journalists. To reach a wide range of readers, they were asked to avoid arcane legal terminology and to provide historical and interpretive background in their entries. Generally, the articles are clear and thorough, and tend to be more neutral than those in the *Encyclopedia of the American Constitution*. The article on Justice Whittaker, for example, contains no literary references and simply notes that his brief tenure on the court was "undistinguished."

Many *Companion* articles provide leads for further reading, but only to books. It contains no references to journal articles, which can often provide more concise and focused treatments of specific topics. The index entries for justices are more helpful than the *Encyclopedia's* because they include subheadings for names of major cases. A separate case index includes citations for opinions. The volume includes the Constitution in an appendix, as well as several chronological charts on the appointment and tenure of the justices.

Other Encyclopedic Works

Although *Encyclopedia of the American Constitution* and the *Oxford Companion to the Supreme Court* are the preeminent encyclopedic works on the Supreme Court and the Constitution, several other alphabetically arranged resources on the subject may be of use. In addition, numerous other reference works cover these subjects, including excellent and scholarly narrative guides to the Court.

Jethro K. Lieberman's *The Evolving Constitution: How the Supreme Court Has Ruled on Issues from Abortion to Zoning* (Random House, 1992) is a less wideranging work than the *Encyclopedia* or the *Oxford Companion*, focusing specifically on constitutional doctrines as interpreted by the Supreme Court, rather than the history, personnel, and politics of the Court. As the work of one person rather than hundreds of contributors, its style is somewhat more consistent and informal. The volume begins with three brief, informative essays: "The Constitution: A Guided Tour," "Some Thoughts on Interpreting the Constitution," and "How the Supreme Court Hears and Decides Cases." These are followed by nearly 1,000 alphabetically arranged articles, ranging in length from one paragraph to three pages. Some entries are too terse to be of much value, as in: **domestic tranquillity** In the words of the Preamble, one of the major purposes of the Constitution was 'to insure domestic tranquility.' " There is no further discussion, no definition, and no agreement in whether to spell the noun with one *l* or two.

The Evolving Constitution is an interesting, wellwritten, but rather idiosyncratic work. Although specifically designed for a nonlawyer audience, it is not a particularly accessible or comprehensive reference source. There is no index, so it may be difficult at first to find an appropriate entry. Another frustrating aspect of this work is that cases are generally not indicated by name but by footnote number. All cases discussed in the text are listed alphabetically at the back of the volume and numbered from 1 to 2291 (*Zwickler v. Koota*). This was done to streamline the text, but it makes it difficult to match cases with historical or legal developments—particularly in sentences such as "In a number of cases during the 1960s, [1645, 265, 123] the Court held . . . ." The list of cases indicates name, date, citation, author of the opinion, and the vote of the Court. It does not show where the case is discussed in *The Evolving Constitution*, so one cannot use it as an index, beginning with a case name to find an appropriate article.

Like the other volumes discussed in this section, *The Evolving Constitution* contains appendixes featuring the text of the Constitution and background information on the Supreme Court. One appendix contains 52 articles covering the 1991-92 term, the last before the book's publication. Apparently it was too late to include this material in the body of the text, but the unintended result of this appendix is to give the book a transitory and outdated appearance. An "updated and expanded" edition is expected, however, in 1999.

The Supreme Court A to Z: A Ready Reference Encyclopedia (Congressional Quarterly, rev. ed., 1994), Volume 3 of CQ's *Encyclopedia of American Government*, may be the most accessible of the encyclopedias. It almost seems designed for browsing—entries such as "Background of justices" or "Housing the court" make for fascinating reading, even if these subject headings are seldom the focus of much research. The volume contains a much smaller number of entries—under 350—and includes an article on each justice. Coverage of constitutional issues is not particularly deep. There is, for example, neither article nor index entry under "Clear and present danger." On the other hand, the book includes a six-page article on "Constitutional law," succinctly explaining the Supreme Court's role, methods of interpretation, and historical watersheds. Entries are straightforward and uncritical; the article on Whittaker, for example, makes no mention of his indecisiveness or failures.

This book has a fascinating range of illustrations, not limited to portraits of major jurists. These include buildings, editorial cartoons, and individuals who have become synonymous with doctrines of constitutional law. There is a photograph of nine-year-old Linda Carol Brown in 1952, two years before her name would stand for the end of the separate-but-equal doctrine in public education. These features are helpful in humanizing what some may consider to be abstract legal principles. The Constitution is included in an appendix, along with charts of justices and nominations. Unfortunately, *A to Z* contains no guides to further reading other than a brief, unannotated bibliography at the end of the volume. Its references to Supreme Court cases do not even provide citations indicating where the opinions can be found.

John J. Patrick's *The Young Oxford Companion to the Supreme Court of the United States* (Oxford University Press, 1994) may not be found in many academic libraries, due to the limiting nature of its title. This is a shame because the book should not be dismissed so quickly. At 368 pages, it is almost as long as *The Supreme Court A to Z*. Although the volume contains plenty of fascinating photographs and other illustrations, this is no picture book; the illustrations are small and do not distract from the text. Entries are arranged alphabetically and include coverage of each justice and of 100 major cases. Most are brief but insightful. The Whittaker article, for example, notes, "He wrote few opinions, none of them memorable, and he was generally viewed as the weakest thinker on the Court." Unlike *The Supreme Court A to Z*, this volume provides *United States Reports* citations for researchers who want to find the texts of decisions discussed. "Further reading" suggestions for many entries provide references to books, magazine articles, and book chapters. A brief appendix explains procedures for visiting the Court.

Not all reference works, of course, are arranged alphabetically. For many purposes a thematic organization, which places issues in broader contexts, can be more useful. David P. Currie's *The Constitution of the United States: A Primer for the People* (University of Chicago Press, 1988) is a small book outlining major constitutional precepts. In under 100 pages of text, Currie covers judicial review, federalism, separation of powers, due process of law, equality, freedom of speech, freedom of the press, and church and state. The book also includes a chronology, the text of the Constitution, and an index.

Two major reference works on the Court, *Guide to the U.S. Supreme Court*, by Joan Biskupic and Elder Witt (Congressional Quarterly, 3d ed., 1996), and *A Reference Guide to the United States Supreme Court* (Facts on File, 1986), contain chapters covering the Constitution and the Court's activities in several major areas. Both works also include biographical information on Supreme Court justices and data on major decisions of the Court, as well as a variety of portraits, cartoons, and other illustrations.

Guide to the U.S. Supreme Court is the more highly esteemed work, providing comprehensive coverage of a wide range of issues. It consists of two volumes and more than 1,200 pages, arranged by subject into six major parts. Part 1, "Origins and Development of the Court," briefly traces its history. Part 2, "The Court and the Federal System," contains four sections focusing at length on the Court's role in determining the scope of the powers of Congress, the president, the federal judiciary, and the states. Each of these sections is extensively subdivided by topic. Part 3, "The Court and the Individual," contains five sections covering individual rights, First Amendment freedoms, rights of political participation, due process and the protections accorded criminal defendants, and discrimination and the equal protection of the laws. Parts 2 and 3 provide a thorough background on constitutional issues, with occasional illustrations and sidebars highlighting specialized topics. Footnotes at the end of each chapter provide references to *United States Reports* citations and other sources.

Volume 2 begins with Part 4, "Pressures on the Court," which looks at the roles Congress and the president have played in the Court's development, as well as the Court's image in the press and public opinion. Part 5, "The Court at Work," outlines the procedures and personnel involved in the Court's operations. Part 6, "Members of the Court," contains brief biographies of every justice, with data about their personal lives, education, public careers, and service on the Court. This section is arranged chronologically, so it may be necessary to check the index first to find a particular justice's biography. Biographies and index entries are both much improved from the 1990 second edition. The earlier biographies included no discussion of justices' Supreme Court careers, and index entries for biographies were hard to pick out from strings of page references after justices' names. Now the biographies discuss major cases and each justice's impact, and "biography" subheadings in the index make these entries much easier to find.

Appendixes in *Guide to the U.S. Supreme Court* provide a variety of reference material. Appendix A reproduces several documents, including the Constitution, rules of the Supreme Court, and five major cases. Appendix B includes a chronology of several hundred major decisions, historical tables of justices and nominations, and a brief glossary. Both volumes include cumulative case indexes and subject indexes. This extensive and valuable guide is useful for gaining an overview of broad areas of Supreme Court jurisprudence and politics.

A Reference Guide to the United States Supreme Court is less up-to-date than its CQ counterpart, and has a more cramped, pedestrian feel. Its organization is similar, however, with sections on the Court's role, governmental powers, federal–state relations, and individual rights. The discussion of individual rights is not as extensive as the treatment in the *Guide to the U.S. Supreme Court* (which spends four pages on *Brown v. Board of Education* alone), but it may be easier to find a topic because the text tracks the rights amendment by amendment from the First (freedom of speech and religion) to the Twenty-Fourth (prohibition of poll taxes). The listing of landmark cases is alphabetical, making it a convenient source for locating information on particular decisions. Most of the biographies of justices are brief (one-half page or so), but major figures, such as John Marshall, Roger Taney, and Earl Warren, are given four or more pages. The biographies include discussion of opinions and judicial philosophies, but they generally do not delve deeply or critically into the justices' characters or importance. Appendixes provide data on justices, list landmark cases chronologically, and reprint the text of the Constitution. A single index provides references to names, cases (without citations), and subjects. This is a utilitarian but somewhat dated work.

Lisa Paddock's *Facts About the Supreme Court of the United States* (H. W. Wilson, 1996) is also a handy source for basic historical information. It is arranged chronologically, with a separate chapter on each chief justice's court providing background on important historical events, summaries of prominent cases, and biographies of justices. The case summaries outline the facts, explain major legal issues, and list participating judges, but give short shrift to the historical significance of most cases. The one- or two-page biographies appear in a convenient, standardized format, with entries for items such as date of birth, education, length of service, and place of burial. What the book lacks in all these details is a sense of the broader picture of the Court's political and social significance, not a surprise given the fact that its title acknowledges that this is a source for facts, not analysis. Appendixes provide the text of the Constitution, *United States Code* sections concerning Supreme Court jurisdiction, and the Court's procedural rules. A glossary and a bibliography are included. An index of cases and a general index round out the volume, but each has some unfortunate aspects. The index of cases lists all references to a particular decision, with no means for distinguishing which entry is for the case summary; a reference such as "*Furman v. Georgia*, 329, 330, 390, 400" does not lead readily to the *Furman* summary. The general index includes boldface references for justices' biographies, but justices' entries also list every case in the volume in which they participated, whether or not they wrote the opinion. The biographies list significant opinions by each justice, so it's hard to see the value of these lists in the index.

Another chronologically arranged work, similar in style to *Facts About the Supreme Court of the United States*, is *The United States Supreme Court* (Grolier, 10 vols., 1995). Most volumes in this set cover the term of one specific chief justice. All but the most recent were previously published as *The Supreme Court in American Life* (Associated Faculty Press, 1986-87). Each volume has three major parts: a chronology of the period, including both legal and general developments (such as the invention of the telephone or dedication of the Washington Monument); "decisions and documents," providing excerpts from major opinions and other important sources; and biographies of justices. This is a rather disappointing work, with little narrative to tie things together. A brief foreword in each volume is the only thing providing an overview of each era. The bibliographies, however, are annotated with insightful comments, such as "sometimes unfair, but never dull" or "despite its age, still an immensely valuable work."

A narrower work focusing on major Supreme Court cases, rather than the members of the Court or the institution itself, is *Historic U.S. Court Cases, 1690-1990: An Encyclopedia* (Garland, 1992), edited by John W. Johnson. Contributions to this volume, written by historians and political scientists, are designed for a general audience and provide an excellent introduction to each case's background and significance. Each includes a selected bibliography of further readings. Although some of this volume's 171 chapters cover cases from other courts (including colonial courts, state courts, and the U.S. Senate), 120 chapters discuss Supreme Court decisions. The work is arranged by subject in six parts ("Crime and Criminal Law"; "Governmental Organization, Power, and Procedure"; "Economics and the Law"; "Race and Gender in American Law"; "Civil Liberties"; and "Law in Critical Periods of American History"). An index of cases and a general index of names and subjects complete the work.

Historic U.S. Court Cases is part of Garland's American Law and Society series. Other volumes in this series use a similar format to focus on specific subject areas. Richard F. Hixson's *Mass Media and the Law: An Encyclopedia of Supreme Court Decisions* (1989) is the only volume limited to cases from the Supreme Court. Arthur S. Leonard's *Sexuality and the Law: An Encyclopedia of Major Legal Cases* (1993) and Charles E. Quirk's *Sports and the Law: Major Legal Cases* (1996) both discuss some Supreme Court cases, but their coverage includes a higher percentage of cases from other courts.

Another source for summaries of major Supreme Court cases is Ralph C. Chandler, Richard A. Enslen, and Peter G. Renstrom's *Constitutional Law Dictionary* (ABC-Clio). Together, Volume 1, *Individual Rights* (1985), and Volume 2, *Governmental Powers* (1987), cover more than 300 decisions, following each summary with a paragraph explaining the case's significance. The volumes are arranged by subject, each with a table of cases at the beginning and an index that includes case names. Both volumes have introductory chapters on concepts and figures in constitutionalism generally (Bill of Rights, Separation of Powers, John Rawls) and a closing chapter defining a small number of legal words and phrases. Volume 2 also includes a chapter with brief entries on 35 leading Supreme Court justices. Volume 1 has been supplemented three times (1987-95) to cover new cases through 1994.

Lee Epstein et al.'s *The Supreme Court Compendium: Data, Decisions, and Developments* (Congressional Quarterly, 2d ed., 1996) can be a valuable reference work for someone seeking statistics on the Court. It includes 160 tables, with material covering topics ranging from Court pensions to public opinion. Except for chapter introductions, everything is presented in tabular format. Some tables are helpful, while others seem of dubious utility. Table 2-13, displaying opinions that have held state constitutional and statutory provisions or municipal ordinances unconstitutional, is a 37-page chronological list, with no indication of subject matter or even what states are represented. The tables with background information on the justices are arranged alphabetically, making it easy to find a particular person but difficult to discern trends over time. The information comes from a wide variety of sources, and footnotes for each table provide references to these sources.

Since 1991, Congressional Quarterly has published an annual *Supreme Court Yearbook*. The volume discusses the major news of the term (such as the appointment of a new justice), summarizes all the year's decisions by subject, provides excerpts from major opinions, and previews the upcoming term. An appendix contains a description of the Court's procedures and brief biographies of the current justices, as well as a short glossary of legal terms and the text of the Constitution.

Robert J. Wagman's *The Supreme Court: A Citizen's Guide* (Pharos Books, 1993) provides a brief general introduction to the Court. The first chapter shows how the Court operates by following one case through the judicial system, from the event that led to the filing of criminal charges to the decision by the Supreme Court. This is followed by a historical overview and brief descriptions of the author's choices for the 100 most important, and 10 worst, Supreme Court decisions. The summaries of the cases omit such information as who wrote the Court's opinion, but they do include citations for further study. The volume also includes short biographies of the justices and chapters on rejected nominees and the Court as an institution. This book has some handy features, but it provides little information that isn't more thoroughly presented elsewhere.

Ellen Greenberg's *The Supreme Court Explained* (Norton, 1997) is another straightforward but slight guide to understanding what the Supreme Court does. It begins with a helpful explanation of the courtroom's accoutrements and personnel. A glossary defines some terms unique to the Supreme Court (*bench opinion, riding circuit*) but is also padded with numerous terms in general legal parlance (*accessory, prosecutor, wit-*

ness). Brief chapters discussing how cases are chosen and decided are followed by an explanation of procedures for visiting the Court and finding further information. Nearly half the book consists of appendixes reprinting the Supreme Court's rules and the Constitution.

Basic Texts

A vast literature is available on the Constitution and the Supreme Court, with dozens of books added each year by historians, political scientists, and lawyers. Although most books draw upon all three of these disciplines to some extent, the distinctions among them provide a framework for looking at works on the Constitution and the Court.

History

Several valuable works focus on the history of the Supreme Court and its handling of constitutional issues. Many of these, such as William E. Leuchtenburg's *The Supreme Court Reborn: The Constitutional Revolution in the Age of Roosevelt* (Oxford University Press, 1995), cover specific periods, but several works attempt to survey the entire 200-year history of the Constitution and the Supreme Court.

The best one-volume general history of the Court may be Bernard Schwartz's *A History of the Supreme Court* (Oxford University Press, 1993). Schwartz's book contains 16 chapters: 12 cover chronological periods, and 4 discuss "watershed cases"—*Dred Scott, Lochner v. New York* (which invalidated state regulation of working conditions in 1905), *Brown v. Board of Education*, and *Roe v. Wade*. Schwartz includes interesting asides on issues such as the difficulties early justices faced traveling each year to sit in the circuit courts, and the modern rise of law clerks. The volume contains extensive notes and an unannotated bibliography.

Robert G. McCloskey's *The American Supreme Court*, revised by Sanford Levinson (University of Chicago Press, 2d ed., 1994), is a shorter work originally published in 1960. It provides a chronological survey of the Court's history, but it is too brief to provide extensive coverage of most issues. One of the best aspects of the book is the excellent 24-page bibliographical essay, which does not just list books but explains their value.

David P. Currie, a leading scholar of constitutional history and author of *The Constitution of the United States: A Primer for the People,* discussed earlier in this chapter, has also written two volumes tracing the history of the Supreme Court's constitutional jurisprudence: *The Constitution in the Supreme Court: The First Hundred Years, 1789-1888* (University of Chicago Press, 1985) and *The Constitution in the Supreme Court: The Second Century, 1886-1986* (University of Chicago Press, 1990). Both volumes have detailed and clear tables of contents providing convenient access to particular decisions and issues.

The most extensive and systematic scholarly treatment of the Court's history is the *Oliver Wendell Holmes Devise History of the Supreme Court of the United States*, created by Congress after Justice Holmes bequeathed $250,000 to the United States government. All but two volumes of this massive work have been published. Although the early volumes have been criticized as being too exhaustive for general readers, recent additions to the series have provided a more accessible narrative for the nonspecialist. The following volumes have been published to date:

> Julius Goebel, Jr., *Antecedents and Beginnings to 1801* (Macmillan, 1971)
> George Lee Haskins & Herbert A. Johnson, *Foundations of Power: John Marshall, 1801-15* (Macmillan, 1981)
> G. Edward White, *The Marshall Court and Cultural Change, 1815-35* (Macmillan, 1988)
> Carl Brent Swisher, *The Taney Period, 1836-64* (Macmillan, 1974)
> Charles Fairman, *Reconstruction and Reunion, 1864-88* (Macmillan, 2 vols., 1971-87)
> Charles Fairman, *Five Justices and the Electoral Commission of 1877* (Macmillan, 1988)
> Owen M. Fiss, *Troubled Beginnings of the Modern State, 1888-1910* (Macmillan, 1993)
> Alexander M. Bickel & Benno C. Schmidt, Jr., *The Judiciary and Responsible Government, 1910-21* (Macmillan, 1984)

The two volumes still in progress are *Constitutional Rights and the Regulatory State, 1921-30*, by Robert C. Post, and *The Crucible of the Modern Constitution, 1930-41*, by Richard D. Friedman.

Robert Shnayerson's *The Illustrated History of the Supreme Court of the United States* (Abrams, 1986), sponsored by the Supreme Court Historical Society, is hardly as authoritative as the Holmes devise, but it does have nice color photographs. In addition to its historical survey, the volume includes a tour of the Court building, including the barbershop, cafeteria, and police room. The Historical Society also publishes a semi-annual *Journal of Supreme Court History*, successor to a *Yearbook* that was published from 1976 to 1989. Both publications contain brief but scholarly articles on the Court's history, accompanied by numerous illustrations. Articles in the *Yearbook* and *Journal* are indexed in *Current Law Index/Legal Resource Index* (from 1980) and *Index to Legal Periodicals and Books* (from 1985).

Two standard constitutional histories discussing both political and judicial developments are Alfred H. Kelly, Winfred A. Harbison and Herman Belz's two-volume *The American Constitution: Its Origins and Development* (Norton, 7th ed., 1991) and Melvin I. Urofsky's *A March of Liberty: A Constitutional History of the United States* (Knopf, 1988). Access to these works is available through tables of cases and subject indexes. Neither includes many footnotes, although both have useful descriptive bibliographies. *The American Constitution* has an 82-page bibliography, printed at the end of each volume, while *A March of Liberty* includes a "For further reading" section at the close of each chapter.

Politics

The decision-making processes of the Supreme Court, and the impact of those decisions, are the subject of hundreds of books. Two leading introductions to the way the Court works are David M. O'Brien's *Storm Center: The Supreme Court in American Politics* (Norton, 4th ed., 1996), and Lawrence Baum's *The Supreme Court* (Congressional Quarterly, 6th ed., 1998). These and similar works pay less attention to Supreme Court history than to the politics of the appointment process, the process by which cases reach the Court, the way in which the Court's agenda is set, the justices' decision-making process, and the Court's impact on politics and society. These works usually include tables and charts on various characteristics of nominations and decisions.

A number of accounts by journalists detail the inner workings of the Court. The most famous is Bob Woodward and Scott Armstrong's *The Brethren: Inside the Supreme Court* (Simon & Schuster, 1979), legendary for the cracks it showed in the Court's wall of secrecy. Notable recent contributions include David Savage's *Turning Right: The Making of the Rehnquist Supreme Court* (Wiley, expanded ed., 1993) and James F. Simon's *The Center Holds: The Power Struggle Inside the Rehnquist Court* (Simon & Schuster, 1995).

Jurisprudence

Works designed for lawyers and law students working in areas of constitutional law can be helpful in understanding how courts have interpreted the Constitution. Such books generally focus on the legal effect of the Supreme Court's decisions, rather than the historical or political significance of those decisions.

The most influential modern commentary is generally considered to be Laurence H. Tribe's *American Constitutional Law* (Foundation Press, 2d ed., 1988). This volume is growing increasingly out of date, but a third edition is expected soon. A similar but more even-handed work, Ronald D. Rotunda and John E. Nowak's *Treatise on Constitutional Law: Substance and Procedure* (West Publishing, 4 vols., 2d ed., 1992), has the advantage of being updated by annual pocket part supplements in each volume. Nowak and Rotunda have also written an abridged, one-volume edition for student use, *Constitutional Law* (West Publishing, 5th ed., 1995), and an "expanded edition" of their treatise is published on CD-ROM with hypertext links to the texts of all cases cited.

A number of shorter works designed for student use have also been published. West's Nutshell series contains the following several works on constitutional issues:

Jerome A. Barron & C. Thomas Dienes, *Constitutional Law in a Nutshell* (3d ed., 1995)

Jerome A. Barron & C. Thomas Dienes, *First Amendment Law in a Nutshell* (1993)

David E. Engdahl, *Constitutional Federalism in a Nutshell* (2d ed., 1987)

Jerold H. Israel & Wayne R. LaFave, *Criminal Procedure: Constitutional Limitations in a Nutshell* (5th ed., 1993)

Norman Vieira, *Constitutional Civil Rights in a Nutshell* (3d ed., 1998)

Jerre S. Williams, *Constitutional Analysis in a Nutshell* (1979)

A competing, somewhat more substantial work, *Understanding Constitutional Law* (Matthew Bender/ Irwin, 1995), by Norman Redlich, Bernard Schwartz, and John Attanasio, covers a wider range of constitutional issues, from judicial review, the federal system, and congressional powers to equal protection and First Amendment rights.

The law reviews and journals discussed in Chapter 5 are filled with extensive discussions of constitutional issues. Two journals that focus specifically on this area are the University of Minnesota's *Constitutional Commentary* (1984-date) and the University of California's *Hastings Constitutional Law Quarterly* (1974-date). The University of Chicago Law School produces an annual *Supreme Court Review* (1960-date), edited originally by the late Philip B. Kurland and now by other members of the Chicago faculty, with 5 to 12 scholarly articles per year on recent or historical constitutional developments.

Of the numerous law review commentaries covering the Supreme Court, one of the most influential is the *Harvard Law Review*'s annual survey of the Court's previous term. This survey appears in the first issue of each volume and has been an annual feature since 1949, picking up an earlier series of articles by Felix Frankfurter and colleagues covering the 1928-38 terms. Each survey includes a foreword by a leading scholar. The first foreword, by Louis L. Jaffe, was published in 1951 and was eight pages long; these days many forewords exceed 100 pages. The foreword is followed by a shorter, but still substantial "comment" by another law professor, and then student analyses of the decisions. The survey closes with a statistics section, including tables showing voting alignments, action by individual justices, and disposition of cases in total and by subject. Periodic multiyear statistical summaries are published, most recently at 104 Harv. L. Rev. 367 (1990), covering the years 1980 to 1989, and 109 Harv. L. Rev. 349 (1995), covering the years 1990 to 1994.

Biographical Sources

As we have already seen, most reference works on the Supreme Court include biographical information on the justices. Information on justices can also be found in general works such as the *Dictionary of American Biography* (Scribner, 1928-58 and quinquennial supplements) and *Current Biography* (H. W. Wilson, monthly, 1940-date). Brief biographical entries on justices are also available at several sites on the Internet. Cornell's Legal Information Institute <http://supct.law.cornell.edu/supct/justices/fullcourt.html> and the CourtTV library <http://www.courttv.com/library/supreme/justices/> cover the current members of the Court, while Northwestern University has biographies of every justice since 1789 <http://court.it-services.nwu.edu/oyez/justices/justice.pl>, including photographs and links to summaries of cases in which the justice participated.

A convenient source of biographical information on current justices is the first section of Volume 2 of the *Almanac of the Federal Judiciary* (Aspen Law & Business, updated semiannually). Its biographies include not only the standard information available elsewhere but extensive lists of publications by and about each justice, an overview of media coverage of each justice, and sketches by Tony Mauro, Supreme Court correspondent for *Legal Times* and *USA Today*. These sketches include an interesting section on what to talk about upon meeting each justice. For William Rehnquist, Mauro writes, "Don't be fazed by his sometimes shy, awkward manner"; recommended topics of conversation include opera with Ruth Bader Ginsburg, and the Dallas Cowboys, cigars, or Corvettes with Clarence Thomas.

Several reference works focus specifically on biographical coverage of Supreme Court justices. The most extensive treatment in one publication is found in *The Justices of the United States Supreme Court: Their Lives and Major Opinions* (Chelsea House, 5 vols., 1997), edited by Leon Friedman and Fred L. Israel. As originally published in 1969, this was a thorough and scholarly treatment of each justice, with biographical sketches accompanied by bibliographies and representative opinions. The new 1997 edition, unfortunately, simply adds new biographies on recent justices. The earlier work is virtually unchanged, despite nearly 30 years of intervening scholarship. The opinions have been omitted, and some of the bibliographies are updated—inadequately, for several recent biographies of Oliver Wendell Holmes are ignored. The text of the articles, however, is untouched. The biography of Earl Warren, for example, was written by Anthony Lewis in 1969, the year Warren retired. In the new edition, this entry is unchanged, with no historical perspective and no new information from the Thurgood Marshall papers or any other source. (At least this edition has a new Marshall biography by Mark Tushnet.)

A shorter publication, *The Supreme Court Justices: A Biographical Dictionary* (Garland Publishing, 1994), edited by Melvin I. Urofsky, provides coverage in one volume of all members of the Court from John Jay through Ruth Bader Ginsburg. Its entries, ranging from a few paragraphs for minor figures to 11 pages for William Brennan, were written by a distinguished group of law professors and historians. The contributors were asked to focus specifically on their subjects' judicial careers, and to evaluative their importance. The articles thus lack some general biographical details, but they are critical and often insightful. Although illustrations accompany only some of the entries, they include some interesting choices, such as Owen Roberts sitting in a garden wearing knickers and reading *Vogue*, or a young Byron White walking down the steps of the Supreme Court building. Excellent bibliographies for each entry include information on the location of the justice's papers, if available, and provide suggestions for further reading.

A less critical perspective is found in *The Supreme Court Justices: Illustrated Biographies, 1789-1995*

(Congressional Quarterly, 2d ed., 1995), edited by Clare Cushman and issued by the Supreme Court Historical Society. Designed for a general audience, this volume is so evenhanded that it gives exactly five pages to each justice, no matter how illustrious or obscure a career each had. Photographs, cartoons, and other illustrations accompany the biographies. A bibliography lists general sources and works on individual justices. Major Supreme Court cases are mentioned by name, but no citations are provided.

Far simpler—too simple to deserve mention if it were not found in so many libraries—is *The Supreme Court of the United States: Its Beginnings & Its Justices, 1790-1991* (Commission on the Bicentennial of the United States Constitution, 1992). This glossy work includes full-page color portraits of each justice but just one large-type page of biographical information. None of the biographies discuss a justice's importance on the Court, except for one sentence on John Marshall: "During his tenure, he helped establish the Supreme Court as the final authority on the meaning of the Constitution."

Digressing into picture books allows us to take a quick look at an excellent new photographic treatment of a significant symbolic aspect of the institution, the Supreme Court building. Fred J. Maroon's *The Supreme Court of the United States* (Thomasson-Grant & Lickle, 1996) is packed with color photographs of the monumental exterior and lavish marble halls. The most fascinating parts of the book, however, are those dedicated to areas of the building the public never sees, such as the justices' conference room and chambers. A glimpse of individual personalities is found in the details: Ruth Bader Ginsburg's beige furniture is a pleasant contrast to the black leather dominating most of the chambers, while one of Clarence Thomas's chairs sports a "He Ain't Heavy, He's My Brother" throw pillow. Maroon also produced an earlier volume on the legislative branch's headquarters, *The United States Capitol* (Stewart, Tabori, & Chang, 1993).

A major source for information on justices' lives and work *before* they joined the Court is often the hearings and reports issued by the Senate Judiciary Committee in considering their nominations. Although some nominees have sailed through the Senate with little notice, recent nominations have usually been the subject of much scrutiny and debate. These hearings and reports are published by the Government Printing Office; material on all nominees from Louis D. Brandeis to Stephen G. Breyer has also been commercially published in *The Supreme Court of the United States: Hear-*

ings and Reports on Successful and Unsuccessful Nominations of Supreme Court Justices by the Senate Judiciary Committee (William S. Hein & Co., 1975-date), compiled by Roy M. Mersky and J. Myron Jacobstein.

Finally, the papers of many justices are available at libraries or archives for in-depth research. These can be a treasure trove of information on the workings of the Court. Although the availability of papers of recent justices may be limited (particularly after the uproar caused in 1993 by *Washington Post* stories based on the Thurgood Marshall papers at the Library of Congress), most older collections allow unrestricted access. Alexandra K. Wigdor's *The Personal Papers of Supreme Court Justices: A Descriptive Guide* (Garland, 1986) provides information on collections ranging from a few scattered letters to the 700,000-item William Howard Taft papers at the Library of Congress.

Bibliographies

With so many publications about the Constitution and the Supreme Court, it would be helpful if library catalogs provided a way to distinguish general overviews useful for obtaining background information from narrowly focused monographs of value only to specialists. Unfortunately, the major subject headings such as "Constitutional history—United States," "Constitutional law—United States," and "United States. Supreme Court" are used for a wide range of material, and it may be necessary to turn to a bibliography for guidance in finding appropriate sources. As we have seen, many of the encyclopedias and other sources already discussed include bibliographies and lists of recommended readings. Several resources also are available specifically for this purpose.

Kermit Hall's *A Comprehensive Bibliography of American Constitutional and Legal History, 1896-1979* (Kraus International, 5 vols., 1984), with a *Supplement, 1980-1987* (2 vols., 1991) is an unannotated listing of books and articles dealing with legal history. (The *1896* in the title refers to the date of publication of listed works, not the date of their subject matter.) The bibliography has several sections, with materials listed under biographical, chronological, and geographical headings as well as by subject. Chapter 3, "Constitutional Doctrine," covers 49 areas, such as judicial review and separation of powers; Chapter 4, "Legal Doctrine," encompasses 59 other legal subjects, such as corporations and procedure. Each subject covers a rather broad area, and the best approach to the work is through the extensive index in Volume 5.

One unfortunate aspect of Hall's bibliography is that it lists each item several times, making the work far more cumbersome than it need be. Most articles are assigned to a subject *and* a chronological period *and* a geographical area, whether or not they have a specific focus in time or place. This leads to a fair amount of bloat, with more than 3,000 entries assigned to a chronological "General" heading and more than 9,000 entries, nearly 400 pages, listed alphabetically under a geographical "United States (General)." Worse, this practice carries over to the index, which lists all these locations for the same item. Fortunately, one entry is chosen as the "primary location" and is printed in boldface. This simply means that the bulk of entries in the index, those in italics, can be ignored. A listing such as "Supremacy clause **5954**, *29139, 33455, 54957*" provides four references to one article.

Research references on the Supreme Court can be found in Fenton S. Martin and Robert U. Goehlert's *The U.S. Supreme Court: A Bibliography* (Congressional Quarterly, 1990). This volume lists more than 9,000 references to books and articles about the Court and about individual justices. The bibliography covers books, journal articles, and dissertations, but no magazine articles or government publications. An introductory survey on ways to research the Court provides annotated lists of reference works, but the listings in 14 subsequent subject areas are unannotated. The final and most extensive chapter is arranged alphabetically by justice, and lists works by and about members of the Court. The book includes author and subject indexes. A smaller (and far less expensive) publication by Martin and Goehlert, *How to Research the Supreme Court* (Congressional Quarterly, 1992), is basically a reworking of parts of the larger work.

Albert P. Melone's *Researching Constitutional Law* (Scott, Foresman, 1990) provides an overview of legal research processes, surveys basic works on constitutional law and the Supreme Court, and provides guidance on briefing cases and writing research papers. The volume also includes brief summaries of landmark cases and a glossary of terms and phrases. The survey of books in Chapter 2 includes helpful annotations; a more extensive bibliography at the end of the volume is arranged by subject but is unannotated.

One of the most helpful and recent of several bibliographies on the Constitution generally is Robert J. Janosik's *The American Constitution: An Annotated Bibliography* (Salem Press, 1991). Janosik limits coverage to books, but he provides helpful, lengthy annotations. The bibliography is divided into more than 30 sections, covering such topics as the framing and ratification of the Constitution, the institutions of national government (including the history and processes of the Supreme Court), and specific areas of constitutional law.

THE TEXT OF THE CONSTITUTION

The United States Constitution is one of the most widely available documents in any library's reference collection. As we have seen, it is reprinted in numerous publications about constitutional law and the Supreme Court. It also appears in a variety of standard reference works from the *World Almanac* to encyclopedias, including the one-volume *Columbia Encyclopedia* (5th ed., 1993) as well as multivolume works. Larger general dictionaries usually include copies of the Constitution, as do most legal dictionaries and a number of legal compendia and guides.

The Constitution is also published in a variety of pamphlet formats. The National Archives and Records Administration issues a pocket-sized version, *We the People: The Constitution of the United States of America* (1986). At 7 by 4 inches, it looks huge next to the 6-by-3-inch *The Constitution of the United States and the Declaration of Independence* (Commission on the Bicentennial of the United States Constitution, 18th ed., 1992). (The Bicentennial Commission was a prodigious publisher, issuing 18 editions over the course of just seven years.) A slightly larger version, including unratified amendments and an extensive index, is published periodically by the Judiciary Committee of the House of Representatives, most recently in 1992 as House Document 102-188. The Law Library of the Library of Congress joined in the bicentennial spirit by reprinting and updating several translations as a series of pamphlets, *The Constitution of the United States of America in Various Foreign Languages*. Nine languages were published in 1987-88, with an Arabic edition added in 1994.

Of commercially published editions, one of the most convenient is *CQ's Guide to the U.S. Constitution*, by Ralph Mitchell (Congressional Quarterly Inc., 2d ed., 1994), which includes some historical background, an index, and a glossary of terms. Less utilitarian but more intriguing is Sam Fink's *The Constitution of the United States of America: To Honor the Two-Hundredth Anniversary, September 17, 1987* (Random House, 1985), an oversize volume lettered by hand and illustrating each provision with elaborate drawings. Marginal asides add a few interesting historical notes.

The U.S. Constitution is also available at several locations on the Internet. The Library of Congress's THOMAS site also provides the text <http://lcweb2.loc.gov/const/const.html>. The Bill of Rights and other amendments are included as separate files, as well as other historical documents, such as the Declaration of Independence, the *Federalist* Papers, and materials from the Continental Congress and constitutional convention. The Constitution and other documents can be searched together or separately, and background information is provided.

Numerous other sites are available. Yahoo lists more than a dozen <http://www.yahoo.com/Government/Law/Constitutional/Constitutions/United_States>. The U.S. House of Representatives also has a copy <http://www.house.gov/Constitution/Constitution. html>. The Constitution Society, a private non-profit organization, provides several versions as well as scanned copies of the original four-page document <http://www.constitution.org/cs_found.htm>.

Finding the simple text of the Constitution, of course, is merely the first step in making sense of its provisions. More extensive versions provide explanations as well as guides to the drafting and adoption of the original document and its amendments.

Annotated Constitutional Texts

Several publications track the Constitution section by section, providing explanation and commentary on each provision's background and the court cases in which it has been applied. These range from simple paperback editions to multivolume comprehensive works.

J. W. Peltason's *Corwin & Peltason's Understanding the Constitution* (Harcourt Brace, 13th ed., 1994), is one of the best of the shorter works. It begins with a bit of historical background and discussion of basic features of the American constitutional system, such as federalism, separation of powers, and judicial review. The book then discusses the Constitution and the amendments, clause by clause. Explanations range from one line (e.g., the provision allowing the president to adjourn Congress if the Houses of Congress disagree on when to adjourn: "The president has never been called upon to exercise this duty.") to 36 pages for the Fourteenth Amendment's equal protection clause. A few Supreme Court cases are mentioned in the text, and others are cited in footnotes.

The Constitution of the United States of America: Analysis and Interpretation

Every 10 years the Congressional Research Service of the Library of Congress prepares an authoritative edition of the Constitution accompanied by discussion of Supreme Court decisions, *The Constitution of the United States of America: Analysis and Interpretation*. The current edition was published in 1996 as Senate Document 103-6, edited by Johnny H. Killian and George A. Costello. It covers cases decided by the Supreme Court through June 1992. At nearly 2,500 pages, the discussion is thorough, scholarly, and extensive.

The Library of Congress's *Constitution of the United States of America* provides the text of each provision of the Constitution, then follows with an explanation of its history and development, focusing specifically on interpretation by the Supreme Court. References to a few lower court decisions, to congressional reports, and to other sources are included. Appendixes include lists of statutes and ordinances that have been held unconstitutional and of Supreme Court cases that have been overruled. The emphasis on case law is evident from the fact that the volume's 148-page table of cases is four times as long as its subject index. This is one of the most useful starting points for understanding how the Supreme Court has interpreted the Constitution.

Pocket part supplements are prepared periodically to summarize new developments. The first supplement to the 1992 edition, Senate Document 104-14, covers developments through July 1, 1996, including 8 more acts of Congress held unconstitutional and 11 more Supreme Court cases overruled in full or in part. Successor updates are scheduled to be issued at two-year intervals, until the time comes for the next complete revision as of 2002.

The current edition of the Library of Congress's *Constitution of the United States of America* is available on the Internet <http://www.access.gpo.gov/congress/senate/constitution/>. It is possible to view the discussion of particular sections or amendments by choosing chapters from the table of contents, or to search the entire document for keywords, including names of Supreme Court cases. Brief searching instructions are provided, and results are weighted for relevance. Sections can be downloaded in either plain text or Adobe Acrobat's PDF format, which provides an exact replica of the pages in the published volume. Exhibit 7-1, for example, shows the first page of the discussion of the Fourth Amendment, as downloaded from the Internet and printed through Adobe Acrobat.

FindLaw offers a modified version of the Library of Congress's *Constitution of the United States of America* at it's Web site <http://www.findlaw.com/casecode/constitution/>. FindLaw's version is also searchable, and it has hypertext links allowing a reader to skip back and forth between text and footnotes.

United States Code Annotated and *United States Code Service*

Two other annotated editions of the Constitution make the eight-pound Library of Congress edition look almost like a pocket book. These editions are published as parts of *United States Code Annotated (USCA)* (West Group) and *United States Code Service (USCA)* (LEXIS Law Publishing, formerly Lawyers Cooperative), the two major commercial publications of federal statutes, which will be discussed at greater length in Chapter 8. This section focuses briefly on their treatment of the Constitution.

Both *USCA* and *USCS* provide the text of each clause of the Constitution, along with references to cases. Unlike the cases cited in the Library of Congress's *Constitution of the United States of America*, these cases come not just from the Supreme Court but from the lower federal and state courts as well. This means that some provisions have notes of thousands of cases following the text.

These extensive notes make these annotated versions of the Constitution anything but terse. The *USCS* Constitution occupies six volumes published between 1984 and 1997, while *USCA* uses 10 volumes published for the Constitution's bicentennial in 1987. Each volume is updated with an annual supplement; the 1997 supplements for the 10 *USCA* volumes contain well over 6,000 pages. As these supplements get too cumbersome, the volumes will be replaced by recompiled new editions incorporating the new cases and clearing out some of the older, less important references.

The Library of Congress's *Constitution of the United States of America* devotes 63 pages to the Fourth Amendment, summarizing Supreme Court doctrine on searches and seizures. In contrast, the Fourth Amendment in either *USCA* or *USCS* occupies an entire volume. Even that pales in comparison with *USCA*'s two volumes covering the 17 words of the Fourteenth Amendment's Due Process Clause.

What fills these volumes? Thousands of cases, summarized and organized into elaborate subject classifications. For the Due Process Clause, *USCA* uses 90 subdivisions and 7,389 sections. Cases about the rights of teachers, for example, appear at sections 5121-5230;

section 5131 specifically includes notes of cases about whether graduate students have a property right in teaching assignments.

Although the case notes in *USCA* and *USCS* are extensive, they are not woven together into a cohesive narrative, but simply summarize each case. These sources are *not* the place to look for a coherent restatement of constitutional doctrine. Doing so would not only be overwhelming but counterproductive, as the notes do not provide the background necessary to understand how the cases fit together. Instead, the *USCA* and *USCS* Constitutions are useful for finding cases that apply constitutional provisions to specific situations. For this purpose, they are two of the best resources available.

To find cases on a specific issue, one must work from the topical outline at the beginning of the notes. Here *USCS* has a distinct advantage, for it provides not only a detailed table of contents but an alphabetical index at the beginning of each clause's notes. *USCA* provides only a summary table of contents of the broad subdivisions; it is then necessary to turn to a particular subdivision for an alphabetical index of individual sections.

On the other hand, even though *USCA* does not provide a general index or detailed table of contents, its notes are generally more extensive and more finely subdivided than those in *USCS*. Unlike *USCA*, for example, *USCS* does not have a section dealing specifically with the rights of graduate student instructors. Each publication has its strengths, and it pays to be familiar with both.

The *USCA* and *USCS* Constitution volumes have other useful features. In addition to the thousands of casenotes, they include references to legal encyclopedias, treatises, formbooks, and law review articles. For some provisions, the list of articles is extensive. Neither title, unfortunately, organizes its lists of articles in a thematic or otherwise useful format. The law review articles in *USCA* are simply listed alphabetically by title; *USCS*'s approach is even more arbitrary and pointless, with references arranged alphabetically by the name of the journal.

To further supplement the annual pocket parts for each *USCA* and *USCS* volume, periodic pamphlets are published to provide updated information for the entire code. These pamphlets (those for *USCS* are called *Cumulative Later Case and Statutory Service*, while the *USCA* pamphlets are untitled) include notes of new decisions. Because the pocket parts are generally issued in the spring, these supplementary pamphlets may

SEARCH AND SEIZURE

FOURTH AMENDMENT

The right of the people to be secure in their persons, houses, papers, and effects, against unreasonable searches and seizures, shall not be violated; and no Warrants shall issue but upon probable cause, supported by Oath or affirmation, and particularly describing the place to be searched, and the persons or things to be seized.

SEARCH AND SEIZURE

History and Scope of the Amendment

History.—Few provisions of the Bill of Rights grew so directly out of the experience of the colonials as the Fourth Amendment, embodying as it did the protection against the utilization of the "writs of assistance." But while the insistence on freedom from unreasonable searches and seizures as a fundamental right gained expression in the Colonies late and as a result of experience,[1] there was also a rich English experience to draw on. "Every man's house is his castle" was a maxim much celebrated in England, as was demonstrated in *Semayne's Case*, decided in 1603.[2] A civil case of execution of process, *Semayne's Case* nonetheless recognized the right of the homeowner to defend his house against unlawful entry even by the King's agents, but at the same time recognized the authority of the appropriate officers to break and enter upon notice in order to arrest or to execute the King's process. Most famous of the English cases was *Entick v. Carrington*,[3] one of a series of civil actions against state officers who, pursuant to general warrants, had raided many homes and other places in search of materials

---

[1] Apparently the first statement of freedom from unreasonable searches and seizures appeared in The Rights of the Colonists and a List of Infringements and Violations of Rights, 1772, in the drafting of which Samuel Adams took the lead. 1 B. SCHWARTZ, THE BILL OF RIGHTS: A DOCUMENTARY HISTORY 199, 205–06 (1971).

[2] 5 Coke's Rep. 91a, 77 Eng. Rep. 194 (K.B. 1604). One of the most forceful expressions of the maxim was that of William Pitt in Parliament in 1763: "The poorest man may in his cottage bid defiance to all the force of the crown. It may be frail— its roof may shake—the wind may blow through it—the storm may enter, the rain may enter—but the King of England cannot enter—all his force dares not cross the threshold of the ruined tenement."

[3] 19 Howell's State Trials 1029, 95 Eng. 807 (1705).

1199

EXHIBIT 7-1

be the first place to learn of Supreme Court decisions handed down at the end of the Court's term in late June. Because these decisions can dramatically affect the interpretation of a constitutional provision, it is important that research be as up-to-date as possible. Even though the text of the Constitution changes little, judicial interpretations are constantly evolving.

The *USCA* and *USCS* editions of the Constitution are available online through WESTLAW and LEXIS-NEXIS, respectively, as part of the federal statutory databases. The online versions for heavily litigated sections and amendments can be cumbersome, occupying thousands of screens with annotations of court cases. The advantage to these online versions is that they allow for keyword searching of the annotations for specific fact situations. Thus, it is a simple matter to find cases applying the due process clause to graduate students, for example, or to teachers' aides.

Historical Sources

To interpret constitutional provisions, it may also help to refer to the documents in which its framers defined and debated the words they used. For this purpose, one of the most useful resources is *The Founders' Constitution* (University of Chicago Press, 5 vols., 1987), edited by Philip B. Kurland and Ralph Lerner. This set contains excerpts from documents ranging from Magna Carta to court decisions as late as 1835, providing background on constitutional issues and provisions. Volume 1 covers "major themes," such as republican government, bicameralism, and separation of powers, while the remaining volumes track the Constitution and the first 12 amendments, provision by provision. The documents include letters, debates, and contemporary articles. Each volume includes an index of constitutional provisions, identifying the article, clause, and section of specific subjects. This is followed by a table of cases and an index of authors and documents, with references to provision and document numbers (rather than to volume and page numbers).

A similar compilation of sources focusing in depth on the first 10 amendments is *The Complete Bill of Rights: The Drafts, Debates, Sources, and Origins* (Oxford University Press, 1997), edited by Neil H. Cogan. For each clause, this volume presents the text of proposals in Congress and from the state conventions; earlier and contemporaneous state law provisions on related issues; other relevant texts, including treatises and cases; and discussion of drafts and proposals in Congress, conventions, newspapers, and letters. Coverage is thorough, and excerpts are well documented.

The only omission is an index, which would make it easier to trace the influence of a particular author or source.

The standard source on the drafting of the original Constitution is *The Records of the Federal Convention of 1787* (Yale University Press, 4 vols., rev. ed., 1937), edited by Max Farrand. A 1987 supplement to Farrand's work, edited by James H. Hutson, contains newly discovered material and an index to the entire set. Farrand's traditional counterpart covering ratification is Jonathan Elliot's, *The Debates in the Several State Conventions on the Adoption of the Federal Constitution* (Lippincott, 5 vols., 2d ed., 1836-45), but a more ambitious work, *The Documentary History of the Ratification of the Constitution* (State Historical Society of Wisconsin, 1976-date), is in the process of being published. Materials on conventions in six states have thus far been published, as well as six volumes of contemporary commentaries in newspapers, pamphlets, and letters. One or two volumes yet to be published will cover the proposal and ratification of the Bill of Rights. *The Debate on the Constitution: Federalist and Antifederalist Speeches, Articles, and Letters During the Struggle over Ratification* (Library of America, 2 vols., 1993), edited by Bernard Bailyn, provides a chronological compilation of the debates in the press, in private correspondence, and in the state ratifying conventions. This set also includes biographical information on speakers, writers, and letter recipients; a chronology; notes explaining references in the texts; and a detailed index.

Thurston Greene's *The Language of the Constitution: A Sourcebook and Guide to the Ideas, Terms, and Vocabulary Used by the Framers of the United States Constitution* (Greenwood Press, 1991) is an intriguing volume providing examples of the usage of 85 key constitutional terms in earlier and contemporary documents that would have been familiar to the constitutional framers. Sources include state constitutions, letters, *The Federalist,* and other contemporary commentaries and newspaper accounts. These are not definitions but simply examples of the contexts in which the constitutional terminology had been used. Unfortunately, but as might be expected, some of the more controversial terms have the fewest entries. "Due process of law" has just one precursor, the 1628 English Petition of Right, while entries for "republican form of government" cover nearly 30 pages.

John R. Vile's *Encyclopedia of Constitutional Amendments, Proposed Amendments, and Amending Issues, 1789-1995* (ABC-Clio, 1996) is an intriguing work focusing not on the Constitution per se but on amendments, and attempts to amend, over the past 200 years. It includes articles on court cases considering the scope or application of the amendments, major figures involved in disputes leading to amendments, and issues in constitutional law. The volume contains more than 400 entries, alphabetically arranged, including brief coverage of amendments by number. The focus is on the process of amendment rather than the substantive impact of the amendments; no entries appear for issues such as freedom of speech, due process, and equal protection. Appendixes provide information on proposed and approved amendments. A lengthy bibliography cites a wide range of sources but is unannotated and simply arranged alphabetically. The index includes names of cases as well as subjects, and a list of cases provides citations to the *U.S. Reports*.

SUPREME COURT OPINIONS

Eventually a researcher studying constitutional law must turn to the opinions of the Supreme Court. Journalists and scholars comment extensively on the Court's work, but the Supreme Court itself speaks only through its opinions. Justices do not hold press conferences or issue supplementary reports explaining their decisions.

Finding Supreme Court opinions is usually a simple, straightforward matter, but reading them is not always so easy. Judicial opinions can be long, complicated, and full of obscure footnotes. Even worse is the confusion caused when the nine justices do not speak with one voice. Occasionally, a Supreme Court decision is unanimous. More often than not, however, the result is a majority opinion, to which five or more justices subscribe, and one or more dissenting opinions. Sometimes it is even more complicated, in cases where a majority of the justices cannot agree on the grounds for a decision. In such instances, one justice announces the Court's judgment and delivers a *plurality opinion*, one without majority support. Perhaps the most famous of these cases is *Regents of the University of California v. Bakke*, 438 U.S. 265 (1978), in which a plurality of four justices went one way, another plurality of four went the other way, and Justice Louis Powell was left in the middle to agree with some of each plurality opinion and to decide what the law should be. Rest assured that decisions such as this are as confusing to constitutional scholars and lawyers as they are to anyone else.

The Supreme Court knows that its opinions can be hard to understand, so it issues each one with an official *syllabus* prepared by the Reporter of Decisions.

The syllabus summarizes the facts of the case and the Court's holding. Exhibit 7-2 shows the syllabus of a recent Supreme Court case, *Garlotte v. Fordice*, 515 U.S. 39 (1995). In this case, a prisoner serving a three-year sentence for marijuana possession followed by life sentences for two murders won the right to petition for a writ of habeas corpus to challenge the fairness of his drug conviction. This syllabus is just over one page. In more complicated cases, even the syllabus can go on for three or more pages. The second page of Exhibit 7-2 shows the names of the attorneys who filed briefs and argued the case, and the beginning of the Court's opinion by Justice Ginsburg.

Major opinions of the Supreme Court are excerpted in various locations, including course texts on constitutional law. They have even been translated from legalese into English, in a series of books edited by Maureen Harrison and Steve Gilbert. Their *Landmark Decisions of the United States Supreme Court* (Excellent Books, 1991), and several successor volumes covering decisions on abortion, civil rights, and First Amendment freedoms, remove some legal terms and provide bracketed translations for others. The latter approach is more helpful, because it allows the reader to learn, for example, that "granted certiorari" means "agreed to review the case," or that "inter alia" means "among other things." Also missing are footnotes, procedural details, and most concurring and dissenting opinions, but citations to the full texts are provided. Thomas E. Baker's *"The Most Wonderful Work . . .": Our Constitution Interpreted* (West Publishing, 1996) also provides edited versions of nearly 100 cases, shortened and free of technical language. Each of its five chapters begins with an essay outlining the cases' historical contexts and issues.

United States Reports

An opinion of the Supreme Court is officially published by the government in three successive versions. It first appears as a *slip opinion* on the day that the decision is announced. This is an individual, separately paginated pamphlet containing just the decision. About two years later several cases are published together in a paperback *preliminary print*. Typographical errors are corrected, the names of the attorneys are added, and, most important, the decisions are assigned the volume and page numbers by which they are cited. After two more years, two or three of these preliminary prints are combined into a bound volume of the *United States Reports*. In recent years, four *U.S. Reports* volumes have been published for each annual term of the Court. Each volume includes a table of cases and a brief index.

OCTOBER TERM, 1994   39

Syllabus

GARLOTTE *v.* FORDICE, GOVERNOR OF MISSISSIPPI

CERTIORARI TO THE UNITED STATES COURT OF APPEALS FOR THE FIFTH CIRCUIT

No. 94–6790.   Argued April 24, 1995—Decided May 30, 1995

A Mississippi trial court ordered that petitioner Garlotte serve, consecutively, a 3-year prison sentence on a marijuana conviction, followed by concurrent life sentences on two murder convictions. State law required Garlotte to serve at least 10 months on the first sentence and 10 years on the concurrent sentences. Garlotte unsuccessfully sought state post-conviction collateral relief on the marijuana conviction. By the time those proceedings ended, he had completed the period of incarceration set for the marijuana offense, and had commenced serving the life sentences. The Federal District Court denied his subsequent federal habeas petition on the merits, but the Court of Appeals dismissed the petition for want of jurisdiction. The Court of Appeals adopted the State's position that Garlotte had already served out the prison time imposed for the marijuana conviction and, therefore, was no longer "in custody" under the conviction within the meaning of the federal habeas statute, 28 U. S. C. §2254(a). The court rejected Garlotte's argument that he remained "in custody" because the marijuana conviction continued to postpone the date on which he would be eligible for parole.

Held: Garlotte was "in custody" under his marijuana conviction when he filed his federal habeas petition. Pp. 43–47.

(a) In *Peyton* v. *Rowe,* 391 U. S. 54, this Court allowed two prisoners incarcerated under consecutive sentences to apply for federal habeas relief from sentences they had not yet begun to serve. Viewing consecutive sentences in the aggregate, the Court held that a prisoner serving consecutive sentences is "in custody" under any one of them for purposes of the habeas statute. A different construction of the statutory term "in custody" will not be adopted here simply because the sentence imposed under the challenged conviction lies in the past rather than in the future. *Maleng* v. *Cook,* 490 U. S. 488—in which the Court held that a habeas petitioner could not challenge a conviction after the sentence imposed for it had fully expired—does not control this case, for the habeas petitioner in *Maleng,* unlike Garlotte, was not serving consecutive sentences. Pp. 43–46.

(b) Allowing a habeas attack on a sentence nominally completed is unlikely to encourage delay in the assertion of habeas challenges. A

40 GARLOTTE *v.* FORDICE

Opinion of the Court

prisoner naturally prefers release sooner to release later, and delay is apt to disadvantage a petitioner—who has the burden of proof—more than the State. Moreover, under Habeas Corpus Rule 9(a), a district court may dismiss a habeas petition if the State has been prejudiced in its ability to respond because of inexcusable delay in the petition's filing. Pp. 46–47.

29 F. 3d 216, reversed and remanded.

GINSBURG, J., delivered the opinion of the Court, in which STEVENS, O'CONNOR, SCALIA, KENNEDY, SOUTER, and BREYER, JJ., joined. THOMAS, J., filed a dissenting opinion, in which REHNQUIST, C. J., joined, *post,* p. 47.

Brian D. Boyle, by appointment of the Court, 513 U. S. 1125, argued the cause for petitioner. With him on the briefs were *James R. Asperger* and *Matthew B. Pachman.*

Marvin L. White, Jr., Assistant Attorney General of Mississippi, argued the cause for respondent. With him on the brief were *Mike Moore,* Attorney General, and *Jo Anne M. McLeod* and *John L. Gadow,* Special Assistant Attorneys General.*

JUSTICE GINSBURG delivered the opinion of the Court.

To petition a federal court for habeas corpus relief from a state-court conviction, the applicant must be "in custody in violation of the Constitution or laws or treaties of the United States." 28 U. S. C. §2254(a); see also 28 U. S. C. §2241(c)(3). In *Peyton* v. *Rowe,* 391 U. S. 54 (1968), we held that the governing federal prescription permits prisoners incarcerated under consecutive state-court sentences to apply for federal habeas relief from sentences they had not yet begun to serve. We said in *Peyton* that, for purposes of habeas relief, consecutive sentences should be treated as a continuous series; a prisoner is "in custody in violation of the

---

*Harold J. Krent filed a brief for the Post-Conviction Assistance Project of the University of Virginia et al. as *amici curiae* urging reversal.

Kent S. Scheidegger filed a brief for the Criminal Justice Legal Foundation as *amicus curiae* urging affirmance.

EXHIBIT 7-2 (continued)

More than 500 volumes of *U.S. Reports* have been published since the Supreme Court's first term in 1790. Since 1874, these have simply been cited by U.S. volume number; the earlier volumes were originally known by the names of their reporters. Like other reporters in England and America in the seventeenth and early eighteenth centuries, the first volumes of Supreme Court opinions were privately published. Even though the series became an official publication in 1817, the practice of referring to the volumes by their reporters' names continued for almost 60 more years. Long ago, these early volumes were incorporated into the series of U.S. volumes and assigned volume numbers 1-66. Tradition dies hard in the law, however, and it is still common to find citations to *Marbury v. Madison*, 1 Cranch 137 (1803). The modern trend, and the practice in law reviews, is to provide both abbreviations, as in "*Marbury v. Madison*, 5 U.S. (1 Cranch) 137 (1803)."

The reporters cited by name are

Dallas	1-4 U.S. (1-4 Dall.) (1790-1800)
Cranch	5-13 U.S. (1-9 Cranch) (1801-15)
Wheaton	14-25 U.S. (1-12 Wheat.) (1816-27)
Peters	26-41 U.S. (1-16 Pet.) (1828-42)
Howard	42-65 U.S. (1-24 How.) (1843-60)
Black	66-67 U.S. (1-2 Black) (1861-62)
Wallace	68-90 U.S. (1-23 Wall.) (1863-74)

The *United States Reports* is a handsomely designed, punctilious publication of the opinions of the Supreme Court. It has just two problems. First, it is not published in a timely manner, which means that it cannot be relied on for recent opinions. A *U.S. Reports* citation is not even available for two years or more. Second, it provides no comprehensive means of finding the opinions it contains. The case tables and indexes in each individual volume are not cumulated into publications covering an entire term, let alone the complete 500-volume set. Researchers looking for cases by name or by subject must therefore use other sources.

Commercial Publications

Although Supreme Court cases are cited to the official *United States Reports*, many libraries have one of two commercial series of volumes containing these same cases. These commercial series are published much sooner than the official series, with pamphlets providing access to new decisions within four to six weeks. Of more importance in the long run is that each decision is accompanied by editorial analysis using numerical classification systems that can provide subject access to the entire body of Supreme Court decisions.

These two publications are *Supreme Court Reporter* (West Group) and *United States Supreme Court Reports, Lawyers' Edition* (LEXIS Law Publishing; published by Lawyers Cooperative until 1997). *Lawyers' Edition* contains cases all the way back to the first volume of *U.S. Reports*, while *Supreme Court Reporter* coverage begins in 1882 with cases appearing in Volume 106 of *U.S. Reports*. After 100 volumes, *Lawyers' Edition* started a second series of volume numbers in 1956. *Garlotte v. Fordice*, the case shown in Figure 7-2, is also published at 115 S.Ct. 1948 and 132 L.Ed.2d 36.

Somewhat like *U.S. Reports*, both *Supreme Court Reporter* and *Lawyers' Edition* are published in three successive formats. The first version is pamphlets known as "advance sheets," published biweekly while the Court is in session. There is a delay of several weeks before new cases appear because the publishers' staffs prepare summaries and notes for each decision. At the end of the annual Supreme Court term, decisions are then published in temporary hardcover "interim editions."

The final, permanent volumes are published only after the official *U.S. Reports* volume is also available. The reason for this is that the commercial publications add *star paging*, a feature indicating on exactly what page of the *U.S. Reports* a given piece of text appears. This is done by showing the precise location of the first word of each new page, by means of a small symbol and number ($\perp$43) in *Supreme Court Reporter*, and by a bracketed notation **[515 US 43]** in the text of *Lawyers' Edition*. This is an important feature because it allows a reader to use the commercial version but still cite a particular discussion or quotation to the official source.

Both commercial editions make it easy for people with official *U.S. Reports* citations to find cases in their sets. Each volume indicates on its spine which *U.S. Reports* volumes it covers, and tables at the beginning of each volume provide cross-references from the official citations to the location of cases in the volume in hand.

The commercial editions reprint the official syllabus from the Reporter of Decisions but supplement it with their own editorial matter. Both publishers prepare their own summaries of each case, which may be clearer than the official statement. *Supreme Court Reporter*'s summary is a short, one-paragraph synopsis that explains succinctly the issue in the case and the holding. *Lawyers' Edition* provides a somewhat longer, more descriptive summary followed by a "Research References" section, citing relevant sections of legal encyclopedias, formbooks, and other sources. Other features at the end of each *Lawyers' Edition* volume are annotations categorizing and explaining Supreme Court cases in specific areas, and concise summaries of the briefs submitted. These summaries of briefs are too short to offer much insight, but they identify major themes and provide the names of the lawyers. Neither annotations nor briefs are in the biweekly pamphlets; the annotations are included in the interim editions, but the briefs do not appear until the permanent bound volumes are published.

Each reporter also includes in the biweekly advance sheets summaries of recent developments. This feature, called "Current Awareness Commentary" in *Lawyers' Edition* and "United States Supreme Court Actions" in *Supreme Court Reporter*, provides news of cases pending on the docket and recent decisions.

Because *Supreme Court Reporter* and *Lawyers' Edition* take several weeks to reach subscribers, yet another commercial source is used for the fastest print access to new opinions. This is *The United States Law Week* (Bureau of National Affairs, weekly), which publishes the official slip opinions in a reformatted, smaller typeface. Decisions announced on Mondays are included in *Law Week*'s regular weekly mailing, while decisions from later in the week are sent out in separate "extra editions" to reach subscribers as soon as possible. For the first month or two after a decision comes down, this is its most widely available source of information and is the version to which new decisions are usually cited. *Law Week* also provides valuable information about cases pending on the Court's docket, as will be discussed later in this chapter.

Electronic Sources

Supreme Court opinions are among the most widely disseminated electronic sources in the law. The Court itself has been distributing its opinions electronically since 1990, through a program known as Project Hermes, and earlier decisions are also available through a number of electronic sources.

The most comprehensive electronic suppliers of legal information in general are the major database services LEXIS-NEXIS and WESTLAW; likewise, they are the most comprehensive electronic suppliers of Supreme Court opinions. Both services include the Court's opinions since its beginning. LEXIS-NEXIS stores these opinions in the GENFED library, US file, while WESTLAW uses the SCT database for opinions since 1945 and SCT-OLD for pre-1945 decisions. The Supreme Court decisions are also included in broader case law databases on both systems.

Supreme Court opinions are also available on CD-ROM from several publishers. Coverage and price vary dramatically, as do ease of use and availability of hypertext links to other materials. Several CDs, including West's *Supreme Court Reporter*, *Lawyers' Edition* and *Lawyers' Edition 2d on LawDesk* (Lawyers Cooperative), and *Michie's Federal Law on Disc,* provide complete coverage from the Court's inception in 1790. These products require hefty licensing fees. Other products provide less extensive coverage but at a lower cost. *USSC+ CD-ROM* (Infosynthesis), for example, contains several hundred leading cases dating as far back as 1793 and complete coverage beginning in 1953, while coverage in *LOIS Professional Library: U.S. Reports Series* (Law Office Information Systems) goes back to 1899.

Until recently, the Internet was a viable source only for very recent Supreme Court decisions, but that has changed. Several free sites now provide valuable coverage.

- FindLaw <http://www.findlaw.com/casecode/supreme.html> provides access to Supreme Court decisions since 1893. The database is searchable by citation, by case name, or by keyword. *U.S. Reports* page breaks are indicated, just as in *Lawyers' Edition* and *Supreme Court Reporter*. Cited Supreme Court cases have hypertext links. A useful feature provides access to later Supreme Court decisions citing the one at hand. It is thus possible, for example, to read *Plessy v. Ferguson*, 163 U.S. 537 (1896) and then jump to *Brown v. Board of Education*, 347 U.S. 483 (1954).

- USSC+, from Infosynthesis, Inc. <http://www.usscplus.com/> contains selected leading cases dating back to 1793 and full coverage since 1938. Cases can be found by citation, name, or subject matter, as well as through a full-text keyword search.

- Cornell Law School's Legal Information Institute <http://supct.law.cornell.edu/supct/> provides convenient coverage of opinions since May 1990. It also offers access to more than 500 historic decisions dating back to 1803. These opinions can be retrieved by date or name, and keyword searching is possible either in the syllabi or in the full texts. Decisions from 1990 to 1997 are available in HTML or WordPerfect format. Opinions beginning with the October 1997 term are released in HTML or PDF format. The PDF versions are exact duplicates of the printed slip opinions distributed at the Court, and can be viewed, downloaded, or printed using Adobe Acrobat software.

- A complete collection of Supreme Court opinions from 1937 to 1975 (volumes 300 to 422 of *U.S. Reports*), originally a database maintained by the U.S. Air Force, is available from GPO Access <http://www.access.gpo.gov/su_docs/supcrt/>. The collection is searchable by name, citation, or keyword. Other sources for this archive are the Center for Information Law and Policy <http://www.cilp.org/Fed-Ct/sct.html>, and FedWorld <http://www.fedworld.gov/supcourt/>.

Internet access is also available through subscription-based commercial sites such as LOIS <http://www.pita.com> (coverage from 1899) and V. <http://www.versuslaw.com> (coverage from 1900).

Case-Finding Tools

The major Supreme Court case-finding resources are the digests published as accompaniments to *Lawyers' Edition* and *Supreme Court Reporter*. Both *Digest of United States Supreme Court Reports, Lawyers' Edition* (LEXIS Law Publishing, formerly Lawyers Cooperative Publishing, 42 vols., 1948-date) and *United States Supreme Court Digest* (West Group, 31 vols., 1943-date) provide access to Supreme Court decisions by name and by subject. The *Lawyers' Edition* digest also includes six volumes containing court rules annotated with notes of Supreme Court cases.

Although both digests began publication in the 1940s, the *Lawyers' Edition* version is considerably more modern, with no volume predating 1985. The West digest still includes two volumes from the original 1943 publication, as well as several volumes dating from the 1960s. These volumes still provide current information—all are updated with annual pocket part supplements—but may be less convenient to use than recently recompiled versions.

By Name

Finding the citation to a Supreme Court case if you know its name is a simple matter, whether using print or electronic resources. For one thing, almost all the encyclopedias and other reference works discussed earlier in this chapter include *United States Reports* citations for the cases they discuss. In addition, the *Lawyers' Edition* and West Supreme Court digests provide tables of cases listing every Supreme Court decision back to 1790.

The formats of the *Lawyers' Edition* and West tables are somewhat different, however. In five volumes (15 to 15D), *Lawyers' Edition* lists every case under the names of both petitioner (or appellant) and respondent (or appellee), with the latter entries providing only cross-references. West Volumes 14 and 14A list cases under petitioners' names, with cross-references in a separate Defendant-Plaintiff table in Volume 15. Both publications include in the tables thousands of cases in which the Supreme Court simply denied review. The full opinions are relatively easy to pick out, however, because these entries also list the relevant digest topics and numbers. The *Lawyers' Edition* table uses boldface type to distinguish entries for opinions.

Lawyers' Edition is also accompanied by a paperback *Quick Case Table with Annotation References*, which is recompiled annually. This one-volume table is more convenient to use than the comprehensive index because it includes only cases with opinions, excluding the large numbers of cases that the Supreme Court declined to review. As is apparent from its title, this table also includes notes of *Lawyers' Edition* and *American Law Reports* (*ALR*) annotations in which decisions are discussed.

The tables of cases in the digests are updated with annual pocket part supplements (although the West pocket parts do *not* include denials of certiorari and other memorandum orders). They are further updated by tables in recent advance sheets of *Lawyers' Edition* and *Supreme Court Reporter*. The tables in *Lawyers' Edition* are cumulative for each volume, but not for the entire term, while the *Supreme Court Reporter* table is cumulative for the term. Boldface type serves different purposes in these two sources. In *Lawyers' Edition,* it signifies the small minority of cases with opinions, while in *Supreme Court Reporter,* it indicates decisions in the latest pamphlet, whether full opinions or memorandum denials of certiorari.

Finding a Supreme Court case by name is one function in which the electronic sources have little advantage over the print sources. Nonetheless, the electronic means make name searches straightforward. A search for *name(garlotte)* on LEXIS-NEXIS or *title(garlotte)* on WESTLAW rapidly retrieves the decision shown in Exhibit 7-2. Several of the CD-ROM products offer similar capabilities, and each of the major Internet sites mentioned above provides a specific form for retrieving cases by using the names of the parties.

By Subject

The easiest way to find Supreme Court decisions on particular topics is to use the secondary sources discussed earlier in this chapter, such as encyclopedias or journal articles. These sources provide the background information needed to put decisions in context, and they focus on decisions that have proved to be most significant over time. In addition, however, there are several ways to search the entire collection of decisions for particular issues.

The standard print sources for subject searches of Supreme Court opinions are the digests accompanying *Lawyers' Edition* and *Supreme Court Reporter*. These digests are based on the headnotes the publishers prepare for each decision. In the *Garlotte* case, for example, each publisher assigned a headnote classified in the "Habeas Corpus" topic, with the specific subject identified by a numerical subdivision. West's subdivisions are known as "key numbers," but both systems work roughly the same way. *Garlotte* is a relatively simple case; more complex decisions may have dozens of headnotes assigned to several different topics and classifications.

To find cases in the digests, turn first to the "Descriptive-Word Index" in Volumes 1-1C of the West digest, or to the "Index to Decisions, Annotations, and Digest" in Volumes 16-16E of the *Lawyers' Edition* digest. These detailed indexes provide subject access to the classified system; to find cases, it is necessary to turn to the volume with the appropriate topic and section number. The *Lawyers' Edition* index also provides references directly to cases, but these references are not as helpful as they might appear. They indicate only the subject matter and citations of relevant cases, not the names or dates, which would help in identification and evaluation.

The *Lawyers' Edition* index also includes references to annotations, articles that summarize Supreme Court cases on particular topics and appear in the back of each reporter volume. These provide another means of finding Supreme Court cases by subject. A researcher working on habeas corpus issues, for example, could find a useful annotation in 104 L.Ed. 2d, "When is person 'in custody' in violation of Federal Constitution, so as to be eligible for relief under federal habeas corpus legislation–Supreme Court cases." This annotation predates the *Garlotte* decision by several years, but the volume includes a pocket part supplement with a reference to that case.

Another useful *Lawyers' Edition* feature, the "Citator Service," provides brief summaries of later Supreme Court cases that make reference to a particular decision, noting whether the decision was quoted, followed, distinguished, overruled, or merely cited. This feature is available for cases since 1 L. Ed. 2d (1956). It is found in separate *Later Case Service and Citator Service* volumes for 1 L.Ed.2d to 31 L.Ed.2d, and in pocket parts beginning with 32 L.Ed.2d. (This is but one of several ways to find more recent cases that cite

or affect the validity of a decision. Other sources used in legal research, including *Shepard's Citations*, will be discussed in Chapter 9.)

West's *Supreme Court Reporter* and its accompanying digest do not contain as many auxiliary features as *Lawyers' Edition*. Their major advantage is that the same classification system for headnotes is also used in the publisher's reporters and digests covering the lower federal and state courts. This allows one to integrate the search for Supreme Court cases into more general case research. Limiting research to the Supreme Court may be reasonable for historians or political scientists studying the Court's approach to a legal issue, but lawyers and legal researchers cannot ignore cases from other courts. A lower court's interpretation of a constitutional issue may be just as decisive and as illuminating as a Supreme Court case, particularly if it addresses issues that have not reached the Supreme Court. More general digests covering federal and state courts will be discussed in Chapters 9 and 12.

West's *Supreme Court Digest* is updated in advance sheets of its *Supreme Court Reporter*, with a cumulative digest in the final advance sheet and bound volume for each term. *Lawyers' Edition* advance sheets and volumes contain only a table of digest classifications for the cases they contain, indicating only digest section number and page. Each volume, however, has a cumulative index to its opinions by subject. This index is included in the advance sheets, and cumulates for the several pamphlets that make up each volume.

By Justice

One area in which the standard digests are of little help is in finding opinions written by a particular justice. Reference works and biographies, of course, discuss major opinions by a particular justice, but they are not comprehensive. One index, however, serves precisely this purpose: *Supreme Court of the United States, 1789-1980: An Index to Opinions Arranged by Justice* (Kraus International, 2 vols., 1983), edited by Linda A. Blandford and Patricia Russell Evans. Prepared under the sponsorship of the Supreme Court Historical Society, this work lists opinions written by each justice, separated by type (majority, concurrence, dissent). Justices are listed chronologically, but cases within each category are listed alphabetically. A supplement updating coverage to 1990 was published in 1994.

Access to electronic information makes this kind of search far easier. WESTLAW includes a "judge" field, so that a search for *judge(ginsburg)* retrieves all cases in which Justice Ginsburg wrote a majority or plurality opinion. LEXIS-NEXIS provides a series of similar features with more awkward names; *writtenby(ginsburg)* retrieves all cases in which Justice Ginsburg wrote an opinion, while *opinionby(ginsburg)* retrieves only opinions for the Court, and *concurby(ginsburg)* and *dissentby(ginsburg)* limit retrievals to those specific types of opinions. Most Internet sites do not provide searches specifically for authors of opinions, but the names of justices can be used in full-text searches.

Current Awareness Sources

The Supreme Court is both a lawmaker and a political institution, and it has a vital role in determining the course of public policy and discourse. Its choices in deciding which cases it will take and which arguments it will hear may have as much impact as the opinions it publishes. Several thousand petitioners ask the Court each year to hear their cases, but fewer than 100 are argued and decided in most years. The Court simply declines to hear most of the others.

Most cases reach the Supreme Court through petitions for certiorari, a writ to retrieve the record from the lower court for review. In a few narrow areas, such as legislative reapportionment or cases invalidating federal statutes as unconstitutional, the Court has mandatory jurisdiction and receives a notice of appeal rather than a certiorari petition. In such cases, the Court signals that it will hear the case by "noting probable jurisdiction" instead of granting a writ of certiorari. In practical terms, however, the certiorari and appeal procedures are similar and the Court exercises broad discretion over its docket.

It is often said that the Supreme Court's refusal to hear a case has no precedential effect—it is not to be taken as the Court's views on the issues in the case. But a denial of certiorari has an important legal effect, not only on the parties to a particular case, but in letting stand the lower court decision as binding precedent within its jurisdiction and as persuasive authority throughout the rest of the country.

The Supreme Court also has a small number of cases in which it has *original jurisdiction*, or acts as the trial court. In such instances, the Court generally appoints a *special master* to hear the evidence and prepare a report for the justices' consideration. Most of these are cases between states, often involving disputed ownership of land. In 1993, for instance, New Jersey filed suit against New York over ownership of Ellis Island.

The key to finding information on cases pending before the Supreme Court is the docket number, which is assigned when the initial petition is filed with the clerk's office. This number, which usually begins with the last two digits of the year of the term, is used throughout the process to identify the case. Cases in which filing fees have been paid begin each term with the number 1, while *in forma pauperis* petitions, for which filing fees and other requirements are waived, are numbered separately, beginning with 5001. Most *in forma pauperis* petitions are filed by indigent defendants and prisoners, such as Harvey F. Garlotte, whose case was assigned the docket number 94-6790. This number appears below the name of the case in all reported versions, as shown in Exhibit 7-2.

The United States Law Week (Bureau of National Affairs, weekly) is the leading source of information on developments pending before the court. The "General Law" sections of this publication have already been discussed in Chapter 5. Its most valuable features, however, are its rapid publication of new Supreme Court opinions and coverage of the Court's actions in pending cases in its "Supreme Court Today" section (called "Supreme Court Proceedings" before July 1997).

A case first appears in *Law Week* as a simple entry indicating its docket number, name, citation of the ruling below, and general subject. Within a few weeks, a much more thorough entry provides a summary of the ruling by the court below and of the specific questions that the Supreme Court has been asked to decide. This summary also includes the names and cities of the attorneys who filed the petition asking the Court to hear the case. The only cases that are not summarized are those in the 5000-series docket, *in forma pauperis* petitions such as *Garlotte v. Fordice*.

When the Court has decided whether or not to hear the case, it appears on another list, either the short "review granted" list or the much longer "review denied" list. A "Journal of Proceedings" section provides a simple list of actions taken, and a "Summary of Orders" section presents more information on cases acted on. If a 5000-series case is accepted for review, this is the first time *Law Week* presents a summary of the decision below and the issues presented. After the *Garlotte* summary appeared, *Law Week* then proceeded to note further developments in the case, including the appointment of counsel three weeks later and the scheduling of oral argument within a few months. For selected cases (not *Garlotte*), *Law Week* also provides narrative summaries of these arguments.

Access to all this information about the Supreme Court is available through a series of indexes. Cases can be found by subject in an "Index-Summary" and by name in a "Table of Cases." Both of these indexes, however, provide references to docket numbers, which must then be checked in a numerical "Case Status Report" for further information on developments in the case and page references to notices and summaries. Only if an opinion has been issued do the "Index-Summary" and "Table of Cases" provide page references directly; these entries are highlighted with a ▶ symbol.

Law Week indexes can take some getting used to. The vast majority of cases on the Supreme Court's docket, and listed in the indexes, have been denied review, but it can be difficult to determine from the subject entries those few cases that the Court has agreed to hear. Because listings in the "Index-Summary" refer simply to docket numbers and include neither case names nor page references, one must turn to the "Case Status Report" to differentiate between cases still pending and those in which review has been denied.

Law Week is also available online through LEXIS-NEXIS and WESTLAW, both in its weekly edition and in a daily electronic-only edition. Information on Supreme Court proceedings since July 1997 is available *only* in the daily version, USLWD on LEXIS-NEXIS and BNA-USLWD on WESTLAW. *Law Week*'s information on the Supreme Court is also available to subscribers on the Internet through BNA's *Supreme Court Today* <http://www.bna.com/newsstand>. Information on the status of cases before the court can be found using keywords, case names, or docket number.

Each July and August, *Law Week* publishes a series of articles summarizing the decisions of the just-ended term. Other regular summer features include statistical surveys of the term (showing the number of cases decided, opinion authorship, and voting relationships) and of the Court's workload over the preceding three years.

No other sources are as thorough as *Law Week* in presenting information about matters pending before the Court, but the calendar of arguments is also available on the Internet from Cornell's Legal Information Institute <http://supct.law.cornell.edu/supct/>. Cornell's list provides links to brief summaries of the cases, which in turn have links to cited cases and statutes.

One of the most valuable and accessible sources of background information on pending cases is *Preview of United States Supreme Court Cases*, published monthly during the term by the American Bar Association's Public Education Division. *Preview* provides analyses of pending cases by legal scholars, explaining the background and significance of each case and summarizing the arguments on each side. It also includes the names and telephone numbers of attorneys representing the parties and filing briefs. The final issue for each term compiles summaries of the year's decisions, including notes on their practical impact. (The *Garlotte* summary, for example, noted that the petitioner's victory hadn't affected the fact that he was still serving two life terms for murder convictions.) Unfortunately, the ABA does not provide access to *Preview* on its Web site, but it is available online through LEXIS-NEXIS (PRE-VU) and WESTLAW (SCT-PRE-VIEW).

Two electronic services are provided free of charge by the Supreme Court itself. Modem users can contact the U.S. Supreme Court Electronic Bulletin Board System for information on the Court's docket, argument calendar, and order lists, among other things, at (202) 554-2570. Anyone with a touch-tone telephone can learn the status of cases, using names or docket numbers, through the U.S. Supreme Court Clerk's Automated Response Systems (CARS) at (202) 479-3034. Updated information on these services is available from the U.S. Courts homepage <http://www.uscourts.gov/PubAccess.html>.

One easy way to keep tabs on new Supreme Court opinions is to subscribe to Cornell's LIIBulletin and automatically receive each new syllabus. You can then request that the full text of decisions of interest also be delivered by e-mail. To subscribe, send a message with "subscribe liibulletin" followed by your name all on one line to *listserv@listserv.law.cornell.edu*.

Major newspapers are leading sources of information on matters before the Supreme Court or recently decided. Newspapers such as the *New York Times* and *Washington Post* have Supreme Court reporters who provide insightful analyses of pending matters and new decisions, as well as occasional features on the justices or other aspects of the Court. Linda Greenhouse at the *Times* has covered the Supreme Court for 20 years, and Joan Biskupic began reporting on the Court for the *Post* in 1992 after several years covering Capitol Hill for *Congressional Quarterly*. The *Post* also provides extensive coverage of the Court on its Web site <http://www.washingtonpost.com/wp-srv/national/longterm/supcourt/supcourt.htm>.

Legal newspapers can often be useful as well. Stuart Taylor, Jr., who formerly covered the Court for the *New York Times*, now writes columns for several legal newspapers. Tony Mauro, who covers legal matters for *USA Today*, writes a biweekly "Courtside" column in *Legal Times*. The monthly *American Lawyer* features a column reporting on advocacy in the Supreme Court, "Courtly Manners," by Lyle Denniston, who is also the Supreme Court reporter for the *Baltimore Sun* and an adjunct professor at Georgetown University Law Center.

The *National Law Journal* features an annual summer survey of the Court's year in a special section appearing in late July or August. This section, "In Focus: Supreme Court Review," includes several articles, statistics, and summaries of each decided case. The *Journal* is also available online as the NTLAWJ file on LEXIS-NEXIS and the NLJ database on WESTLAW. Many of the *Journal's* articles on the Supreme Court are available on the Web <http://www.ljextra.com/courthouse/supindex.html>.

OTHER SUPREME COURT RESOURCES

Rules and Practice

Like other courts, the Supreme Court has specific rules to be followed by litigants appearing before it. These rules govern such matters as the filing of briefs and petitions for rehearing, and are found in a variety of publications and online databases. Sources such as the CQ *Guide to the Supreme Court* reproduce the rules, but because they are subject to revision, it is better to use a source that is updated regularly. The *Lawyers' Edition* Supreme Court digest includes the rules in Volume 17, annotated with Supreme Court cases. *United States Code Annotated* and *United States Code Service* also publish annotated versions, with references to a few cases from lower courts as well as the Supreme Court. Along with other sets of rules governing actions in lower federal courts, these are found after Title 28 (Judiciary and Judicial Procedure) in *USCA* and at the end of the set in *USCS*.

The standard and comprehensive guide to the practical aspects of arguing a case before the Court is Robert L. Stern et al.'s *Supreme Court Practice* (Bureau of National Affairs, 7th ed., 1993). This valuable volume has a wealth of procedural information, as well as background discussion of the Court's jurisdiction to hear cases. It includes forms and checklists spelling out the procedural steps in a Supreme Court action and the time allowed for each.

A more cursory discussion of procedures is available in a short pamphlet, *Guide for Counsel in Cases to Be Argued Before the Supreme Court of the United States,* issued by the Supreme Court Clerk's Office and available in WESTLAW's LAWPRAC database.

Most contact with the Supreme Court by people other than litigants begins with the Public Information Office, (202) 479-3211. Directories of the federal courts such as *Judicial Yellow Book* (Leadership Directories, Inc., semiannual) and *Judicial Staff Directory* (CQ Staff Directories, annual) include coverage of the Supreme Court, although neither provides an extensive listing of personnel. *Judicial Yellow Book* contains information on the educational backgrounds of the justices' clerks, and *Judicial Staff Directory* contains biographical information on several key members of the Court staff.

Briefs and Oral Arguments

A major source for background information on Supreme Court cases is the briefs filed by the parties, usually beginning with the petition for certiorari. If the Court agrees to hear a case, both sides file briefs on the merits, or substance, of the issue. Appendixes to the briefs provide the text of the lower court opinions, and may also include other such documents as pleadings and motions. In many cases, interested persons and organizations file amicus curiae, or "friend of the Court," briefs. As noted in the footnote in Exhibit 7-2, two amicus briefs were filed in the *Garlotte* case. Major cases affecting public policy may have dozens of amicus briefs.

The briefs often contain more factual background on the case than does the court's opinion. The brief for the losing party also presents an analysis of the issues with which the Supreme Court, obviously, did not agree. It is worth noting that most conflicts that make it to the Supreme Court are difficult and contentious, and a brief that did not persuade the Court this year may provide guidance in limiting or overruling a holding next year.

Most major law libraries carry Supreme Court briefs in microform editions, generally filed by *U.S. Reports* citation or docket number. Briefs from 1832 to 1896 are available on microfilm from Scholarly Resources, Inc., and, beginning in 1897, on microfiche from Congressional Information Service (CIS). Recent briefs are also available through LEXIS-NEXIS (BRIEFS file, since 1979) and WESTLAW (SCT-BRIEF database, since 1990). The online files are generally limited to briefs on the merits in cases for which oral argument has been scheduled. Certiorari petitions for cases in which review has been denied are not included.

Briefs are not generally available on the Internet, although interest groups often post briefs and other documents in cases they are following. The Web site of the United States Department of Justice includes briefs submitted since 1982 to the Supreme Court by the Solicitor General <http://www.usdoj.gov/osg/>.

Landmark Briefs and Arguments of the Supreme Court of the United States: Constitutional Law (University Publications of America, 1975-date), originally edited by Philip B. Kurland and Gerhard Casper, and now by Gerald Gunther and Casper, provides a convenient compilation of briefs in major cases. Coverage goes all the way back to *Chisholm v. Georgia*, 2 U.S. (2 Dall.) 419 (1793). The earliest cases simply have summaries of arguments reprinted from *U.S. Reports*, but briefs begin in the 1850s, just in time for *Dred Scott v. Sandford*, 60 U.S. (19 How.) 393 (1857). The set now has more than 250 volumes, with several new cases covered each term.

In addition to briefs, *Landmark Briefs and Arguments* includes transcripts of oral arguments. In many instances, the arguments show the attorneys under rapid-fire questioning; they are less valuable in obtaining the parties' perspectives than they are in illustrating the justices' thoughts. The oral argument transcripts generally do not identify the names of justices asking questions, but experienced attorneys often get this information in the record by prefacing their answers with the name of the justice to whom they are responding. (This approach can backfire badly when an attorney calls a justice by the wrong name. See, e.g., Tony Mauro, "Even Tribe Can Have a Bad Day," *Legal Times*, Jan. 13, 1997, at 7.)

Transcripts of arguments are also available from CIS on microfiche, beginning with the 1953 term, and are online through LEXIS-NEXIS and WESTLAW. LEXIS-NEXIS coverage in the USTRAN file begins earlier, in 1989, but its file is only updated once a year with the previous term's cases. WESTLAW's SCT-ORALARG database begins in 1990 and generally provides transcripts of new arguments within a week or two.

Two sources also provide recorded versions of arguments. *May It Please the Court: The Most Significant Oral Arguments Made Before the Supreme Court Since 1955* (Norton, 1993), edited by Peter Irons and Stephanie Guitton, caused a stir when it released edited audiotapes of arguments in 23 major cases without the Court's permission. That commotion passed without endangering the Republic, however, and audio versions of arguments are now available on the Internet at *Oyez Oyez Oyez: A Supreme Court Database* <http://oyez.nwu.edu/>. Arguments in more than 300 cases from 1956 to date are available, along with background information on the cases, the constitutional question, the Court's holding, and the names of attorneys arguing before the Court. The site also provides instructions for downloading the RealAudio software needed to listen to the arguments. Taped oral arguments in individual cases can also be purchased from the National Archives and Record Administration (NARA). For more information, contact NARA's Motion Picture, Sound, and Video Branch, 8601 Adelphi Rd., College Park, MD 20740-6001; (301) 713-7060.

CHAPTER 8
Federal Legislation

TOPICS COVERED

Statutes
  United States Code
  Annotated Codes
  Statutes at Large and Public Law Sources
  Other Statutory Research Tools
  Related Sources

Congressional Materials
  Reference Works on Congress
  Legislative History Documents
  Key Research Tools
  Information on Pending Legislation
  Guides for Further Research

This chapter is about Congress, but it does not attempt to address the full range of roles Congress plays in American government and society. It focuses instead on Congress as the creator of federal statutory law.

Federal law may have a less immediate impact in most people's lives than state law, which regulates such basic matters as driver's license issuance and child custody. There has always been considerable support for the view that each state has the power to establish its own social rules, free from federal interference. But the pervasive impact of modern federal law cannot be denied. Federal statutes have established basic legal protections in the workplace, with laws governing such issues as employment discrimination and occupational safety, and in the home, with legislation addressing such issues as consumer protection and safe drinking water. Although less directly felt by many people, federal laws governing such areas as antitrust or securities regulation affect business and the economy as well.

In researching issues of federal law, statutes are often the first place to turn after exploring the reference materials, books, and articles discussed in Part 2 of this book. It is important to use these secondary sources first because they explain whether an issue involves federal or state law, or both, and they also provide references to the specific statutes that may be pertinent.

Statutory law is relatively simple to research in some ways because all laws in force are arranged by subject in a compilation known as a code. Yet statutory language is notoriously difficult to comprehend. Some statutes are vaguely worded, while others are filled with complex distinctions and subclauses. Interpreting a statute may require consulting a wide range of judicial decisions and legislative documents. Other difficulties can arise if it is necessary to determine the terms and effect of a statute at a particular point in the past, rather than that currently in force.

The first half of this chapter looks at simpler statutory inquiries, primarily using publications and databases containing the texts of the statutes. Finding and reading federal statutes does not normally require a familiarity with the ways they are enacted by Congress. The second half of this chapter looks at the congressional materials necessary to research legislative intent and to analyze issues pending before Congress.

As in many other areas, research in federal legislation uses a variety of print and electronic resources. The Internet has revolutionized access to congressional information, but its reach extends back only to the mid-1990s. Many earlier documents needed to interpret statutes may never be available electronically. Legislative research thus requires access to large sets of published material, generally found in either law libraries or larger research libraries.

The publication and access procedures for federal law have set the paradigm for state laws. The codes, session laws, and legislative publications we will examine in this chapter are forms that are generally followed by the states. State publications are usually less voluminous, although in some cases they are also less thoroughly organized. An understanding of federal statutory and legislative research provides a solid basis for similar research on the state level.

STATUTES

Congress passes several hundred laws during each of its two-year terms. These are designated as either *public laws*, which are of general application, or *private laws*, which benefit particular people—compensating individuals for harm caused by the government, for example, or providing relief from immigration laws. Some public laws are simple, one-paragraph dedications of federal office buildings, while others span hundreds of pages and affect dozens of agencies and activities. Public laws and private laws are numbered in separate series indicating the term of Congress. Pub. L. 103-141, the Religious Freedom Restoration Act, for example, was the 141st public law passed in the 103rd term of Congress (1993-94).

New public and private laws are published in chronological order at the end of each session of Congress. These *session laws* are known as the *United States Statutes at Large*, and occupy more than 200 volumes going back to the first Congress in 1789. In most instances, however, researchers seek to determine the public laws currently in force in the country. Some of these acts were passed within the past year, while others have been in force for more than 100 years. For this purpose, the statutes in force are arranged by subject into a *compilation* or *code*. The official compilation of federal statutes is called the *United States Code*. Whether in print or electronic form, it is the basic source of most federal statutory research.

United States Code

The *United States Code*, commonly cited as "U.S.C.," is prepared by the Office of the Law Revision Counsel of the House of Representatives and is published in a new edition every six years. The current *U.S. Code* contains statutes in force as of January 4, 1995; it is called the 1994 edition because it includes statutes enacted through the end of 1994. The set was published in 35 volumes over the course of more than a year, with the final volume issued in late summer 1996.

Each new edition of the *U.S. Code* adds statutes enacted since the previous revision and removes material since repealed by Congress. Between revisions, the *Code* is updated by annual bound supplements. Each supplement cumulates information from its predecessors, so that only the most recent supplement is usually needed. The first supplement is relatively concise, but by the fifth year it may swell to 10 or more volumes. Like the *Code* itself, the supplement volumes are published gradually, so some parts may be more up-to-date than others.

Organization

The *United States Code* follows a format established for its first edition in 1926, with a division into 50 subject titles. These titles, generally arranged alphabetically, are listed in the front of each volume. (Actually, there are now 48 titles, as Title 6, Surety Bonds, was repealed in 1982, and Title 34, Navy, was incorporated into Title 10, Armed Forces, in 1956.) Each title covers a subject area, some more narrow than others. Title 9, Arbitration, is just seven pages in the 1994 edition, while Title 42, Public Health and Welfare, fills four volumes totaling nearly 6,000 pages.

Title can be a confusing word in statutory research, because it has two distinct meanings. The *U.S. Code* has 50 titles, but individual acts can also be divided into numbered titles. The Civil Rights Act of 1964, for example, has a Title VII prohibiting discrimination in employment. The provisions of this Title VII are not in Title 7 of the *U.S. Code*, Agriculture, but in Title 42, Public Health and Welfare. Title VII of an act is different from Title 7 of the *Code*. To find Title VII in the *U.S. Code*, it is necessary first to understand what act it is part of. This is not always clear in references to employment discrimination law in the press. The *New York Times* is more precise than most newspapers, and most of its articles cite "Title VII of the Civil Rights Act of 1964." But one recent article quotes a lawyer speaking about "Title VII, the really important Federal law, the one that prohibits job discrimination." Robert Lipsyte, "In the Gender Game, New Rules to Play By," *New York Times*, June 22, 1997, § 8, at 9. (This article is actually about Title IX of the Education Amendments of 1972, but that act is not identified either.)

Each *U.S. Code* title is divided into chapters covering more specific subjects, as is shown in the "Table of Titles and Chapters" that is also printed in the front of each volume. Generally, each chapter covers a discrete area, such as mail fraud, meat inspections, or control of coal mine fires. It is important to recognize the scope of the chapter with which one is working, and familiarity with the chapter structure is useful in understanding the organization of the statutes. The chapter, however, is not part of a code section's citation, as all sections in each title are numbered in one sequence. (Some titles also have additional sections in appendixes.) The title and section numbers are all that are needed to identify a section, and together they comprise a citation to a federal statute. The Religious Freedom Restoration Act, for instance, appears in chapter 21B of Title 42, but it is cited as 42 U.S.C. §§ 2000bb to 2000bb-4.

The "bb" and "bb-4" in these section numbers are an unfortunate, but not uncommon, result of trying to squeeze this act into its appropriate subject slot, following chapter 21, Civil Rights, and chapter 21A, Privacy Protection (ending at § 2000aa-12), before the subject shifts in chapter 22 to Indian Hospitals and Health Facilities (beginning with § 2001). The basic structure of the *U.S. Code* was established more than 70 years ago, and the committee that prepared the first edition could not have foreseen the dramatic increase in legislation in this area. The first Title 42 in 1926 had just 6 chapters and 106 sections on topics such as quarantines and communicable diseases. Title 42 now has more than 160 chapters and 7,000 sections, covering such matters as fair housing, disaster relief, and solid waste disposal. Any classification system, of course, can grow cumbersome and overcrowded as it adapts to accommodate new issues and additional material.

Exhibit 8-1 shows the page from the *U.S. Code* that contains 42 U.S.C. § 2000bb. Note that chapter 21B begins with a list of its sections, and that the text of section 2000bb is followed by a reference in parentheses to its original source: Pub. L. 103-141, § 2, Nov. 16, 1993, 107 Stat. 1488. This reference is an important feature because it is the key to tracing changes in the statute and to finding legislative history information.

Had this provision been amended, the parenthetical note would indicate these public laws as well. The text would also be followed by paragraphs explaining the precise nature of each amendment. This facilitates reconstructing the statute as it existed at a particular point in time, an exercise that has more than purely historical value. To interpret the terms of a contract or will, it may be necessary to refer to the statutes in force when it was written. Determining the law in force can sometimes be a matter of life and death; prosecutors can seek the death penalty only if a capital punishment law was in effect at the time a crime was committed.

Access

Although many people turn to the *U.S. Code* seeking a specific provision cited in an article or case, the set includes several means of access to its contents. The most frequently used is the general index, which occupies volumes 29 through 35. At seven volumes and nearly 9,000 pages, this is a rather detailed and extensive index. Exhibit 8-2 shows a page from this index, with references to religious freedom restoration under the heading "Religion."

The indexers are well aware that statutes can be hard to find, and their mission is to provide as many access points as possible without making the index bigger than the *Code* itself. The index is full of cross-references and permutations to accommodate the many ways people might seek particular statutes. Indexing can be a thankless task, and faults are easy to find no matter how thorough the work. In Exhibit 8-2, for example, note that "Religious Corporations" and "Religious Orders" both have cross-references to "Religious Organizations," while "Religious Group" refers only to "Genocide." (Because these are all on the same page, it is easy to find the right heading.) Using a code index is often frustrating. Statutory language is dense and difficult, and finding the right section is not always easy.

One difficulty in statutory indexing is that the language of a statute does not always reflect the full scope of its coverage. Some statutes are broadly worded. 42 U.S.C. § 2000e-2, for instance, prohibits employment discrimination on the basis of "race, color, religion, sex, or national origin." Court decisions have established that sexual harassment is a form of discrimination under this section, even though the term "sexual harassment" is not in the statute. References under "Sexual Harassment" were first added to the *U.S. Code* index in the 1992 supplement, perhaps in response to inquiries from people unable to find the appropriate section. In addition to references to § 2000e-2 under "Sexual Harassment—Employer and Sexual Harassment—Unlawful Employment Practices," dozens of other subheadings provide references to specialized provisions elsewhere in the *Code,* covering harassment in areas such as Clean Water Act programs or management of surplus federal property.

The fact that "Sexual Harassment" is found in the index, even though it is not explicitly in the *Code,* is an indexing triumph. There will always be work, however, in striving to create a more perfect index. The heading "Women" has a "Sexual Harassment" subheading, with a cross-reference to "Sex," but that entry is now a dead end, with nothing about harassment and no reference to § 2000-e2. Specific forms of sexual harassment, such as "Hostile Work Environment," are nowhere to be found in the index.

One useful part of the subject index is the "Definitions" section, which spans nearly 400 pages. It provides access to statutory provisions that define certain terms, from "a comparable facility" to "Yurok Tribe." It is important to remember, however, that these defi-

§ 2000aa-11   TITLE 42—THE PUBLIC HEALTH AND WELFARE   Page 572

(Pub. L. 96-440, title I, § 107, Oct. 13, 1980, 94 Stat. 1881.)

SUBCHAPTER II—ATTORNEY GENERAL GUIDELINES

§ 2000aa-11. Guidelines for Federal officers and employees

(a) Procedures to obtain documentary evidence; protection of certain privacy interests

The Attorney General shall, within six months of October 13, 1980, issue guidelines for the procedures to be employed by any Federal officer or employee, in connection with the investigation or prosecution of an offense, to obtain documentary materials in the private possession of a person when the person is not reasonably believed to be a suspect in such offense or related by blood or marriage to such a suspect, and when the materials sought are not contraband or the fruits or instrumentalities of an offense. The Attorney General shall incorporate in such guidelines—

(1) a recognition of the personal privacy interests of the person in possession of such documentary materials;

(2) a requirement that the least intrusive method or means of obtaining such materials be used which do not substantially jeopardize the availability or usefulness of the materials sought to be obtained;

(3) a recognition of special concern for privacy interests in cases in which a search or seizure for such documents would intrude upon a known confidential relationship such as that which may exist between clergyman and parishioner; lawyer and client; or doctor and patient; and

(4) a requirement that an application for a warrant to conduct a search governed by this subchapter be approved by an attorney for the government, except that in an emergency situation the application may be approved by another appropriate supervisory official if within 24 hours of such emergency the appropriate United States Attorney is notified.

(b) Use of search warrants; reports to Congress

The Attorney General shall collect and compile information on, and report annually to the Committees on the Judiciary of the Senate and the House of Representatives on the use of search warrants by Federal officers and employees for documentary materials described in subsection (a)(3) of this section.

(Pub. L. 96-440, title II, § 201, Oct. 13, 1980, 94 Stat. 1882.)

§ 2000aa-12. Binding nature of guidelines; disciplinary actions for violations; legal proceedings for non-compliance prohibited

Guidelines issued by the Attorney General under this subchapter shall have the full force and effect of Department of Justice regulations and any violation of these guidelines shall make the employee or officer involved subject to appropriate administrative disciplinary action. However, an issue relating to the compliance, or the failure to comply, with guidelines issued pursuant to this subchapter may not be litigated, and a court may not entertain such an issue as the basis for the suppression or exclusion of evidence.

(Pub. L. 96-440, title II, § 202, Oct. 13, 1980, 94 Stat. 1883.)

CHAPTER 21B—RELIGIOUS FREEDOM RESTORATION

CHAPTER REFERRED TO IN OTHER SECTIONS

This chapter is referred to in sections 1988, 1996a of this title; title 5 section 504.

§ 2000bb. Congressional findings and declaration of purposes

(a) Findings

The Congress finds that—

(1) the framers of the Constitution, recognizing free exercise of religion as an unalienable right, secured its protection in the First Amendment to the Constitution;

(2) laws "neutral" toward religion may burden religious exercise as surely as laws intended to interfere with religious exercise;

(3) governments should not substantially burden religious exercise without compelling justification;

(4) in Employment Division v. Smith, 494 U.S. 872 (1990) the Supreme Court virtually eliminated the requirement that the government justify burdens on religious exercise imposed by laws neutral toward religion; and

(5) the compelling interest test as set forth in prior Federal court rulings is a workable test for striking sensible balances between religious liberty and competing prior governmental interests.

(b) Purposes

The purposes of this chapter are—

(1) to restore the compelling interest test as set forth in Sherbert v. Verner, 374 U.S. 398 (1963) and Wisconsin v. Yoder, 406 U.S. 205 (1972) and to guarantee its application in all cases where free exercise of religion is substantially burdened; and

(2) to provide a claim or defense to persons whose religious exercise is substantially burdened by government.

(Pub. L. 103-141, § 2, Nov. 16, 1993, 107 Stat. 1488.)

REFERENCES IN TEXT

This chapter, referred to in subsec. (b), was in the original "this Act", meaning Pub. L. 103-141, Nov. 16,

EXHIBIT 8-2

nitions apply only to particular chapters or acts. The only reference to sexual harassment in the "Definitions" section leads to a provision in 38 U.S.C. § 1720D dealing with counseling programs for veterans who have experienced sexual trauma. Its definition has no bearing outside that limited context.

Another means of finding a particular act is the "Acts Cited by Popular Name" table in Volume 26. *Popular name* is a legal term that has little to do with popularity. A few acts have acquired names by which they are commonly known (such as the Hatch Act restricting political activities by government employees, named after Senator Carl A. Hatch), and Congress occasionally acknowledges these names. Pub. L. 103-355, 108 Stat. 3243 (1994), for example, officially recognized the popular names for several acts from the 1930s and 1940s, including the Miller Act, the Buy American Act, and the Walsh-Healey Act. But the popular name table mostly contains names that the acts themselves provide, such as Comprehensive Environmental Response, Compensation, and Liability Act of 1980 (CERCLA) or Federal-State Extended Unemployment Compensation Act of 1970. Some acronyms, such as CERCLA, are also listed; CETA (Comprehensive Employment and Training Act) appears, but FIFRA (Federal Insecticide, Fungicide, and Rodenticide Act) does not. The major omission is colloquial terms, such as Title VII or Title IX, which are used in everyday parlance. The table is of no help in figuring out to what acts these titles belong. (The best way to do that is to begin with a book or article that explains the law and provides citations to the relevant statutory provisions.)

The popular name table in the *U.S. Code* provides *Statutes at Large* citations for all acts, but it includes code citations only if an entire act is located in one specific location. The Religious Freedom Restoration Act includes amendments to 5 U.S.C. § 504 and 42 U.S.C. § 1988 as well as its five new sections, so the *U.S. Code* table provides no code listing, just a public law number and a *Statutes at Large* citation. To find the act in the *Code* requires another table.

The table to which we turn is one of several parallel reference tables in Volumes 27 and 28. The major table, spanning more than 2,200 pages, lists statutes chronologically by *Statutes at Large* citation and public law number, and indicates where each section appears in the *U.S. Code*. Some sections have never been codified and are not listed, but sections that appear only in notes to *U.S. Code* sections are included. Statutes that have been repealed or eliminated are listed, with a brief "Rep." or "Elim." in a "status" column to indicate that they are no longer on the books.

Among the other tables is one listing revised titles and providing information on the fate of older section numbers. Since 1947, nearly half of the *Code* titles have been revised and reorganized, so this table helps make sense of references found in older cases or texts.

The index and tables are updated in each annual *U.S. Code* supplement. Because these are published after a substantial delay, coverage never includes the most recent legislation.

Electronic Formats

The *U.S. Code* is also available on CD-ROM and through the Internet. The Government Printing Office publishes the code annually on CD-ROM for under $40, a savings of $2,000 over the 35-volume print publication. The CD-ROM is no more up-to-date than the most recent printed version, but material in the supplements is incorporated into each year's new edition. The CD also includes the tables and other documents in the printed code.

Searching the *Code* on CD-ROM is not intuitive, but its accompanying brochure explains that it "affords great savings in effort and money in return for a small investment in learning time." You can search by keyword (and find out immediately if a word is in the database), as well as browse through the *Code* by clicking open a title, then a chapter, and then a section.

Searching is reasonably straightforward, with the Boolean connectors *and*, *or*, *not*, *adj* (adjacent to), and *w/n* (within number of words of) acceptable. *Adj* is the default connector, so a term such as *religious freedom* can be searched without punctuation. Once a search is run, it is possible to move either to the next section matching the search criteria or to the next section in the *Code*.

A helpful "dictionary" feature shows the frequency of terms in the database. Some words are used thousands of times, and knowing how often they appear may be useful in structuring successful searches. Other features may be more intriguing than useful. A "fuzzy advisor" comes up with phonetically similar terms; for *freedom*, it suggests *freed*, *freedman*, *freedmen*, and *freedoms*. "Related terms" finds other words that appear near your term and are relatively unique to that situation. For *religious*, the top three terms listed are *peyote*, *abortion*, and *sterilization*. *Peyote* also tops the list for *freedom*, along with *Eurasian* and *Russia*; the leading terms for *restoration* are *boating*, *inpatient*, and *Yaquina*. In some situations, these alternate terms might suggest useful leads, but they are of little help in researching religious freedom restoration.

A "concept search" takes the "related terms" approach one step further and automatically looks for the appearance of these related terms as well as the search terms. This approach is recommended only if you are too unfamiliar with a topic to construct a sensible search. Using an exclamation point after a term creates a concept search, so *freedom!* finds any occurrence of *peyote* or *Eurasian*.

The Internet provides free access to the *United States Code* in two distinct versions, from the federal government itself and through the Legal Information Institute at Cornell Law School.

The House of Representatives Office of the Law Revision Counsel provides the *Code* <http://law.house.gov/usc.htm>; similar versions are also available from the Government Printing Office <http://www.access.gpo.gov/congress/cong013.html> and through GPO gateway sites. The currency matches the printed *U.S. Code*, which is usually one to two years out of date. As annual supplements are produced, some titles may be more current than others.

Search procedures vary slightly between the House and GPO sites, but the House version offers features similar to the CD-ROM. Boolean connectors can be used, as well as phrases ("religious freedom restoration") and truncation of words using asterisks, as in *religio** to retrieve "religion" or "religious." A "topical search" is the Web site's version of the CD-ROM's "concept search."

Although the Web code is not fully up-to-date, the Office of the Law Revision Counsel does offer a way to find amendments affecting a particular section. At <http://law.house.gov/uscct.htm>, it provides a classification table with references to newly passed legislation. For each *Code* section amended or repealed, this table lists the public law number, section, and *Statutes at Large* page for the amending act. It does not provide a hypertext link to the new law.

Cornell's version of the *Code* <http://www.law.cornell.edu/uscode> is based on the most recent CD-ROM version published by the Government Printing Office. It is no more current than the official site, but it includes several features that make it more accessible and useful. The search software accepts plain English queries without Boolean connectors, and results are ranked for relevance. A simple search for "religious freedom restoration" retrieves more than 1,000 sections, but the Religious Freedom Restoration Act is at the top of the list. *Code* sections can also be retrieved by citation or through a table of popular names. This table <http://www.law.cornell.edu/uscode/topn/> includes

links to the texts of acts—except for those (like the Religious Freedom Restoration Act) that are not codified in one specific location.

To speed processing and conserve resources, Cornell encourages limiting searches to individual code titles. It may not always be clear, however, what title would be relevant. Much of employment discrimination law, for example, is in Title 42 (Public Health and Welfare) rather than Title 29 (Labor); and many environmental laws are not in Title 16 (Conservation) but in Titles 33 (Navigation and Navigable Waters) and 42.

Cornell's version includes a table of contents like that for the CD-ROM. Hypertext links from the names of titles through chapters and subchapters to individual sections make it possible to browse from the table of titles to an appropriate section or to view the context of a retrieved section. Browsing is also facilitated by *Next* and *Previous* buttons, which provide a convenient means for viewing neighboring sections within the chapter. (It is also possible to move to adjacent sections in the House version of the *Code,* but no table of contents is displayed and no distinction is made between sections in the same chapter and those in unrelated chapters. At Cornell, the first section in a chapter has only a *Next* button and the last section only a *Previous* button.)

Cornell also provides a simple means to update a *Code* section. Clicking on an "update" button automatically runs a search in the Law Revision Counsel's table of revisions and provides a list of public laws affecting the section. The second part of this process, unfortunately, is not yet automatic; you must jot down or print out these public law numbers and then access the Library of Congress THOMAS Web site to find the appropriate act.

The Internet includes numerous other sources for federal laws in specific areas. None are as comprehensive as those discussed above, but they may be useful starting places for research in an area on which they focus. The Parental Kidnapping Prevention Act, for example, is available from DivorceNet <http://www.divorcenet.com/28uscode.html>, and the Commerce Department's U.S. Business Advisor <http://www.business.gov> provides links to statutes and explanations of various legal issues listed under subject headings such as "Environment," "Health," "Immigration," "Labor," and "Taxes." The House of Representatives Internet Law Library <http://law.house.gov/16.htm> provides an extensive list of sources for specific statutes and subject areas.

Annotated Codes

The official print and CD-ROM *United States Code*, and the Web sites based on it, are thorough and accurate sources, with just two problems: (1) they are not the most timely resources, and (2) they provide few research aids other than historical notes on the sources and development of *Code* sections. Some *Code* volumes are published more than a year after the close of the period covered, and the Web versions are no more up-to-date. The Web sites do provide means for updating a section, but this is a rather cumbersome process. There is no mention of articles analyzing the statute or court decisions interpreting its provisions. These court decisions play such a vital role in determining the scope and meaning of statutory provisions that few lawyers actually use the *U.S. Code* in their research. Instead, they rely on one of two commercially published editions that are more up-to-date and provide additional information needed in almost any statutory research. These commercial editions are both mammoth publications, but they can be found in almost every law library.

> *United States Code Annotated* (West Group [formerly West Publishing], 244 vols., 1927-date)
> *United States Code Service* (LEXIS Law Publishing [until 1997, Lawyers Cooperative], 215 vols., 1972-date)

These publications are commonly known as *USCA* and *USCS*. Exhibit 8-3 shows the first section of the Religious Freedom Restoration Act as printed in *USCS*.

Unlike the *U.S. Code*, these publications are not reissued periodically in new editions. Instead, each set contains volumes of varying ages, all supplemented with annual pocket parts. As the amount of material in the supplement grows, it may no longer fit in the volume's pocket and is instead published as a separate pamphlet. Eventually a revised volume is published, incorporating the supplementary material and replacing the older volume. Sometimes the material in one volume and supplement is split into two or more replacement volumes, and gradually the code grows larger. There is no regular or systematic revision schedule, but in each set several new volumes are published each year. *USCA* has been around for 70 years, but more than half of its current volumes are less than 10 years old. Only one original volume from 1927 (Title 27, Intoxicating Liquors) remains in the current set.

Unlike the official *U.S. Code*, which is published after a substantial delay, the commercial codes provide fairly current information about new statutory developments. The basic means of updating is the annual pocket part or pamphlet accompanying each volume. In addition, each set publishes supplementary pamphlets that contain new statutory provisions arranged by code section. The *USCS* pamphlets, published quarterly, are called *Cumulative Later Case and Statutory Service*; the bimonthly *USCA* pamphlets have no distinct title, but they are marked on the spine with large numerals and are generally shelved at the end of the set. These pamphlets generally provide the text of new code sections or amendments within two or three months of enactment.

Even more current information is provided in monthly pamphlets publishing new session laws in chronological order. The companion pamphlet for *USCS* is *USCS Advance*; for *USCA*, the companion pamphlet is *United States Code Congressional and Administrative News (USCCAN)*. To learn of developments during the current session of Congress, check the cumulative table of code sections affected in the most recent pamphlet. This table is called "Table of Code Sections Added, Amended, Repealed or Otherwise Affected" in *USCS*, and table 3, "U.S. Code and U.S. Code Annotated Sections Amended, Repealed, New, Etc." in *USCCAN*.

The most significant advantage of *USCA* and *USCS*, however, is not timeliness but the editorial material the publishers provide. Most sections conclude with summaries of court decisions interpreting and applying code sections. Just as the Constitution cannot be read without considering how the Supreme Court and other courts have interpreted its provisions, an essential part of understanding a statute is reading court decisions to determine how it has been applied. Some court decisions answer challenges to a statute's constitutionality, others clarify what is meant by its language, and the vast majority apply its provisions to particular situations. The annotated codes provide access to these decisions. Because current judicial developments are as important as amendments by Congress, the notes of decisions are updated in the annual pocket parts and in the interim pamphlets.

An analysis of 42 U.S.C. § 2000bb in *USCA* and *USCS* shows the importance of these notes. *USCA* publishes the text of the statute in a 1995 volume, with a note of just one case. By the time of the 1997 pocket part, 14 more cases were noted. The *USCS* volume containing the same section was published in 1996 and noted 10 cases. Three more appear in its 1997 pocket part. Exhibit 8-4 shows the notes of decisions following § 2000bb in the *USCS* volume. Note that the first two decisions consider whether the act is constitutional and reach opposite conclusions. The first case would

CHAPTER 21B.   RELIGIOUS FREEDOM RESTORATION

CROSS REFERENCES

This chapter is referred to in 5 USCS § 504; 42 USCS §§ 1988, 1996a.

§ 2000bb.   Congressional findings and declaration of purposes

(a) Findings. The Congress finds that—

(1) the framers of the Constitution, recognizing free exercise of religion as an unalienable right, secured its protection in the First Amendment to the Constitution;

(2) laws "neutral" toward religion may burden religious exercise as surely as laws intended to interfere with religious exercise;

(3) governments should not substantially burden religious exercise without compelling justification;

(4) in Employment Division v. Smith, 494 U.S. 872 (1990) the Supreme Court virtually eliminated the requirement that the government justify burdens on religious exercise imposed by laws neutral toward religion; and

(5) the compelling interest test as set forth in prior Federal court rulings is a workable test for striking sensible balances between religious liberty and competing prior governmental interests.

(b) Purposes. The purposes of this Act are—

(1) to restore the compelling interest test as set forth in Sherbert v. Verner, 374 U.S. 398 (1963) and Wisconsin v. Yoder, 406 U.S. 205 (1972) and to guarantee its application in all cases where free exercise of religion is substantially burdened; and

(2) to provide a claim or defense to persons whose religious exercise is substantially burdened by government.

(Nov. 16, 1993, P. L. 103-141, § 2, 107 Stat. 1488.)

HISTORY; ANCILLARY LAWS AND DIRECTIVES

References in text:

"This Act", referred to in this section, is Act Nov. 16, 1993, P. L. 103-

EXHIBIT 8-3

eventually reach the Supreme Court, which in 1997 ruled that the act did indeed exceed Congress's power (*City of Boerne v. Flores*, 117 S. Ct. 2157 [1997]). This Supreme Court decision was reached too late to make it into the 1997 pocket parts; it was first noted in interim pamphlets later that year.

For § 2000bb the two annotated codes have roughly the same number of notes, but generally *USCA* is more comprehensive and *USCS* more selective in providing casenotes. For the following section, § 2000bb-1, *USCS* provides a total of 21 casenotes in three topics ("Application," "Immunity," "Liability"), while the *USCA* notes have mushroomed to more than 100 cases in 18 topics (including detailed divisions such as "Prison Regulations" and "Drug Offenses"). The first notes always concern general issues about a statute, such as its constitutionality and construction with other laws; subsequent notes, arranged by subject, focus on its application to specific circumstances. These casenotes flesh out the statutory text and show how the courts have applied its provisions.

Although *USCA* generally provides more exhaustive notes of judicial decisions, *USCS* coverage is more extensive in one respect. Unlike *USCA*, it includes annotations of decisions from administrative agencies. These are usually less authoritative than court decisions, but they can be just as valuable in interpreting the scope of a statute's terms. In addition, *USCS* includes some court decisions not mentioned in *USCA*. In 1997, charges were made that Vice President Al Gore may have violated 18 U.S.C. § 607, which prohibits soliciting campaign contributions from any federal building. The *USCA* version of this section contains no annotations of court decisions. *USCS* includes notes of four cases, including two 1908 decisions under the section's predecessor statute. These cases may be old, but they could still be relevant in interpreting the scope of the current provision.

Not all sections in the annotated codes are followed by notes of court decisions. Some provisions have never been challenged or applied in court, and, thus, no annotations are available. Other code sections, on the other hand, are the subject of vast amounts of litigation. 42 U.S.C. § 1983, concerning actions for state deprivation of civil rights, appears in both publications in volumes published in 1994. The statute consists of two sentences and just 145 words. To cover the court decisions, *USCA* devotes an entire 1,100-page volume to the section, with over 250 more pages in the pocket part. *USCS* has two volumes for § 1983, with nearly 1,400 pages of annotations.

Differences in style characterize *USCA* and *USCS* annotations for § 1983. *USCA* uses a far more detailed classification system, with more than 5,000 numbered sections, as opposed to only 1,700 in *USCS*. It may be easier to find an appropriate section, however, in *USCS*, because it includes both a topical outline and an alphabetical index of all 1,700 sections. At the beginning of its notes, *USCA* provides only a brief outline of the 61 major divisions into which the 5,000 sections are divided. To obtain more detailed information one must turn to the beginning of one of these divisions, where its sections are listed alphabetically. This requires determining a broad area of inquiry first, rather than going directly from an index or table of contents to a specific section.

Other notes in the annotated codes may be as helpful as the notes of decisions. These include references to relevant regulations and secondary sources, such as texts and law review articles. Note in Exhibit 8-4 that *USCS* includes the citation of a law review article on the Religious Freedom Restoration Act. The later pocket part includes a reference to an annotation, "Validity, Construction, and Application of Religious Freedom Restoration Act," 135 ALR Fed. 121 (1996), which discusses and organizes the case law. The notes in *USCA* list more than two dozen law review articles and also provide references to congressional committee reports, which may be useful in interpreting the purpose and scope of the law, as reprinted in *United States Code Congressional and Administrative News*.

One other difference between the annotated codes is that *USCA* uses the same statutory language as the official *U.S. Code*, while *USCS* makes a point of using the exact language that appears in the original acts in the *Statutes at Large*. This is the authoritative text, as we shall see below, but usually the difference is a slight change in wording. In Exhibit 8-1 the *U.S. Code* refers to "the purposes of this chapter," while the *USCS* text in Exhibit 8-3 follows the *Statutes at Large* in referring to "the purposes of this Act."

Each annotated code is accompanied by a softcover, multivolume index that is updated and revised each year. Because these indexes are reissued annually, they are more current than the official edition's index. Otherwise, the nine-volume *USCA* index is virtually identical to the official *U.S. Code* index—which makes sense once you see the note in the official edition that its index has been "created and supplied by West Publishing Company." *USCA* has the same entries under "Religion and Sexual Harassment" and the same blind cross-reference from "Women" to "Sex" for sexual

42 USCS § 2000bb   PUBLIC HEALTH AND WELFARE

141, 107 Stat. 1488, popularly known as the Religious Freedom Restoration Act of 1993, which appears generally as 42 USCS §§ 2000bb et seq. For full classification of this Act, consult USCS Tables volumes.

Short title:

Act Nov. 16, 1993, P. L. 103-141, § 1, 107 Stat. 1488, provides: "This Act may be cited as the 'Religious Freedom Restoration Act of 1993'.". For full classification of this Act, consult USCS Tables volumes.

RESEARCH GUIDE

Law Review Articles:

Smolin. The free exercise clause, the Religious Freedom Restoration Act, and the right to active and passive euthanasia. 10 Issues L & Med 3, Summer 1994.

INTERPRETIVE NOTES AND DECISIONS

1. Constitutional issues
2. Application
3. Preliminary injunction

1. Constitutional issues

Religious Freedom Restoration Act (42 USCS §§ 2000bb et seq.) is unconstitutional, where Act purports to change burden of proof in Free Exercise Clause cases to "compelling interest," because Congress specifically sought to overturn Supreme Court precedent through passage of Act, in violation of doctrine of Separation of Powers. Flores v City of Boerne (1995, WD Tex) 877 F Supp 355.

Religious Freedom Restoration Act (RFRA) (42 USCS § 2000bb) is not unconstitutional on separation of powers grounds, where state prison was defending itself against Native-American prisoner's civil rights actions against state prison officials for allegedly violating his constitutional right to free exercise of religion on grounds that Congress had no authority to heightened degree of scrutiny regarding free exercise of certain religions, because Congress has broad authority to interpret Constitution and to expand fundamental rights such as free exercise of religion under § 5 of Fourteenth Amendment even in areas where Supreme Court has already ruled. Belgard v Hawaii (1995, DC Hawaii) 883 F Supp 510.

2. Application

Inmate's claim that prison regulations restricting practice of "Nahuatli religion" are too severe must fail, where inmate is allowed to possess in cell headband, shell, medicine pouch, 7 sacred stones, feather, and other objects, and to have access to drums, pipes, tobacco, gourd, sage, sweetgrass, and cedar for worship, because restrictions are justified by compelling interest in prison security, and do not amount to substantial burden on inmate's religion but rather reflect substantial effort to meet religious needs of Native American inmates. Diaz v Collins (1994, ED Tex) 872 F Supp 353.

Muslim inmates fail to make threshold showing of liability under either 42 USCS §§ 1983 or 2000bb, where they complain about unfair treatment in comparison to accommodations made for religious practices of Christian inmates, but have been allowed to pray 5 times daily, to maintain weekly worship services, and even to have statewide meetings for their 2 major holidays, because inmates cannot show that any actions by corrections officials placed substantial burden on their exercise of fundamental tenets of their religion. Woods v Evatt (1995, DC SC) 876 F Supp 756, affd without op (1995, CA4 SC) 68 F3d 463, reported in full (1995, CA4 SC) 1995 US App LEXIS 29657.

Inmate's claim against prison officials, alleging civil rights violation arising from his being prevented from attending services of Jewish congregation in prison, is denied summarily, where inmate was disruptive during congregational meetings and interfered with other inmates' rights of worship, because officials' actions served compelling interest in maintaining order and security at facility. Best v Kelly (1995, WD NY) 879 F Supp 305 (criticized in Francis v Keane (1995, SD NY) 888 F Supp 568, 66 CCH EPD ¶ 43690).

Inmate demonstrated that prison officials substantially burdened his religion in violation of Religious Freedom Restoration Act of 1993 (RFRA) (42 USCS § 2000bb), where inmate presented substantial documentation of legitimacy of his religious convictions and proof that prison officials prevented him from following his beliefs, which include maintaining kosher diet, taking vow of poverty, not cutting hair, and wearing headcovering of certain color, because prison officials failed to show that prison policies which precluded in-

140

EXHIBIT 8-4

harassment issues. *USCS* has its own four-volume index, which for some issues may provide approaches not found in the *U.S. Code* and *USCA* indexes. It has fewer headings—just "Religion and Religious Societies," for example, rather than the multiple entries in the other editions. "Sexual Harassment—Generally" leads directly to 42 U.S.C. § 2000e et seq., but "Sex Discrimination—Generally" refers only to provisions governing educational programs and makes no mention of employment discrimination. "Women" provides a cross-reference to "Females," which leads to nothing useful on discrimination or harassment laws.

In addition to their multivolume indexes covering the entire range of federal statutes, both *USCA* and *USCS* provide separate indexes for each individual code title. If it is clear which title would be of use, these indexes may be less complex and troublesome to use than the general indexes.

USCA and *USCS* also include tables similar to those in the *U.S. Code*. In both cases, the popular name tables are a considerable improvement over the official version. They include more acronyms for acts, such as FIFRA; more important, they both provide code references for acts that are codified in more than one location. The listings for the Religious Freedom Restoration Act, for example, lead to 5 U.S.C. § 504, 42 U.S.C. § 1988, and 42 U.S.C. § 2000bb to 2000bb-4. *USCA*'s popular name table is in the final index pamphlet (*U to Z*), while *USCS*'s shares the *Tables* volume covering the most recent volumes of the *Statutes at Large*. The index volume containing the *USCA* table is revised each year, while the *USCS* table is in a bound volume updated by an annual supplement. Both tables are further updated in the supplementary pamphlets accompanying each set.

Another source that can be used to find statutes by name is *Shepard's Acts and Cases by Popular Names: Federal and State* (3 vols., 1992, with bimonthly supplements). This table is similar to the popular name tables in the codes, but it also includes state statutes. It may be useful if you know the name of an act but not its jurisdiction. If, for example, you see a reference to the Hatch Act but are not aware that it is a federal law, *Shepard's Acts and Cases* could be of assistance. It also tends to include older, more obscure federal acts that may be omitted from *USCA* and *USCS*.

Both *USCA* and *USCS* are available online (*USCA* on WESTLAW and *USCS* on LEXIS-NEXIS and through Congressional Universe) and in CD-ROM. Unlike the GPO's electronic code, these are not products for the budget-conscious. Online, the CODES and

GENFED libraries on LEXIS-NEXIS have files named USCS, with just the annotated statutes, and USCODE, which combines the statutes with the Constitution, court rules, international conventions, and public laws. The online code is updated monthly, with amendments current within two or three months—about the same as the printed version. In WESTLAW's USCA database, new material is not incorporated into the text of code sections as quickly as it is for *USCS,* but notice of the latest developments is provided through a feature called "update." If a new public law affects a section, a notice appears on the screen to check this update feature. Clicking on this prompt automatically leads to the public law affecting the section. A third online service, LEGI-SLATE, offers the most frequently updated online code. Its "Current USC Service" is updated on a continuous basis, but it does not include the annotations in USCA or USCS. All three services also provide access to older editions of the code: LEXIS-NEXIS back to 1992, WESTLAW to 1990, and LEGI-SLATE to 1987.

The annotated code databases are large, with the full text of the notes of decisions as well as the statutory text. To find a relevant statute, it is often helpful to limit a search to the "text" segment or field, which excludes the notes. (For this purpose, WESTLAW also provides an unannotated version of the code as a separate database, USC.) On the other hand, in some instances the power to search the casenotes is just what is needed. The phrase *hostile work environment* appears in no code section, but a search for it in the casenotes leads directly to the relevant code provision, 42 U.S.C. § 2000-e2.

Both systems also offer other ways to approach the statutes. You can retrieve a particular section by typing *lexstat 42 usc 2000bb* (on LEXIS-NEXIS) or *find 42 usc 2000bb* (on WESTLAW). Tables of contents services similar to the one Cornell provides on the Internet are available and allow one to navigate through the titles and chapters to find an appropriate section. This feature is called USTOC on LEXIS-NEXIS and TOC USCA on WESTLAW. Also, separate databases contain the popular name and cross-reference tables. WESTLAW even has a database limited just to the code index, USCA-IDX.

One advantage of using a code section in a printed book is that you can survey neighboring sections to get a sense of its context. LEXIS-NEXIS and WESTLAW provide some browsing facility. When viewing a statute on LEXIS-NEXIS, you can type *b* for browse, then use Previous Document or Next Document commands to move from section to section. WESTLAW users can type *d* or click on "documents in sequence" to move between sections.

Although *USCA* and *USCS* are the only sources for comprehensive annotated coverage of federal statutes, other publications serve similar functions in specialized areas. The Internal Revenue Code is Title 26 of the *U.S. Code,* and both *USCA* and *USCS* publish versions full of annotations to court decisions. Few tax lawyers use these versions of Title 26, however, because even more extensive annotation, including excerpts from congressional committee reports, texts of relevant regulations, and notes of IRS actions, are available from the tax loose-leaf services *Standard Federal Tax Reporter* (CCH) and *United States Tax Reporter* (RIA).

Similar coverage is provided in some other specialized areas. *Federal Securities Law Reporter* (CCH) uses the same approach for the Securities Act of 1933, the Securities Exchange Act of 1934, and other major securities legislation. Other loose-leaf services, such as *Environment Reporter* (BNA) and *Labor Relations Reporter* (BNA), simply print the texts of statutes in separate sections from regulations, annotations, and commentary. These services provide frequent updating of federal statutes, but their versions are not conveniently annotated.

Statutes at Large and Public Law Sources

As we have seen, it is frequently necessary to consult recent public laws to update code references. In addition to finding new legislation, researchers also turn to the session laws to reconstruct the law in force at a particular point in time and to determine when specific provisions were added to the code. The most significant aspect of federal session laws is that they represent the *positive law*—the authoritative text—of most federal statutes. The code is merely prima facie evidence of the law, which means that it can be rebutted if incorrect. Differences between the code and the session laws seldom exist, but it does happen. The Supreme Court recently considered a case involving a provision that had been omitted from the *U.S. Code* since 1952 but that was, the Court held, still good law (*United States National Bank of Oregon v. Independent Insurance Agents of America*, 508 U.S. 439 [1993]).

Twenty-one titles of the *U.S. Code* have been enacted by Congress as positive law, meaning that they, and not the earlier session laws, are now the authoritative text of the law. Congress is slow and careful in enacting *U.S. Code* titles, perhaps because of past experience. In 1875, the *Revised Statutes of the United States,* the first official codification of federal law, was published as Volume 18, Part 1, of the *Statutes at Large.* Congress enacted the *Revised Statutes* and expressly repealed all earlier acts that came within its scope. Before long, however, enough errors and omissions were discovered that a second edition had to be published in 1878. That edition was not enacted as law. The earlier *Revised Statutes* remains the authoritative source for laws it contains, and citations to it still appear in court decisions today. Each edition of the *U.S. Code* contains a table providing cross-references from the *Revised Statutes* to successor provisions in the current code.

The official series of session laws, the *United States Statutes at Large,* covers the entire range of federal acts beginning with 1789. One numbered volume, which may have up to 6 physical parts and more than 5,000 pages, is now published each year. Exhibit 8-5 shows the page in Volume 107 of the *Statutes at Large* with the beginning of Pub. L. 103-141, the Religious Freedom Restoration Act of 1993. Note that the *U.S. Code* references appear in the left margin and that the text of section 2 is the same as that of section 2000bb in *USCS* in Exhibit 8-3. (It is also identical to the *U.S. Code* text in Exhibit 8-1, but for use of the word *Act* instead of *chapter.*)

Each volume of the *Statutes at Large* includes lists of acts by bill number and by public law number, a popular name index, and a subject index. Because these do not cumulate from year to year, they are of relatively little research value. Most people turning to the *Statutes at Large* do so with a particular citation already in hand.

New volumes of the *Statutes at Large* take more than a year to make it into print. The Government Printing Office, however, issues each new act individually as a *slip law* within a few weeks of enactment. Unlike separately paginated slip opinions from courts, these slip laws include the *Statutes at Large* page numbers for each act. They can usually be found in government depository libraries along with the *Statutes at Large* volumes.

Slip laws are also available on the Internet from GPO Access <http://www.access.gpo.gov/nara/nara005.html>. For current legislation, this is one of the quickest and most effective sources, with new laws appearing online within a few days of enactment. (For the latest laws, it may be necessary to check a legislative site such as THOMAS for the *enrolled bill,* or the version that was passed by both houses.) GPO Access coverage begins with the 104th Congress in 1995, so with time this will also become a more extensive repository. There is no convenient form for retrieving an act by public law number, but the database is searchable by keyword or phrase, which can include the title or public law number or bill number. Once you find an act, you can either view the ASCII text or retrieve the PDF document that reproduces the printed slip law, complete with *Statutes at Large* pagination.

The updating services that accompany the annotated codes provide the text of new laws, in a format virtually identical to the official *Statutes at Large*. Both *United States Code Congressional and Administrative News* and *USCS Advance* publish pamphlets with the text of new laws within a month or two. *USCS Advance* is published only as monthly pamphlets, but *USCCAN* is compiled into annual bound volumes. Since 1975, these volumes have reproduced the *Statutes at Large* pagination, so they can be used instead of the official text. Earlier *USCCAN* volumes back to 1941 (when it began publication as *United States Code Congressional Service*) also have the text of public laws but not the official *Statutes at Large* pagination.

Recent public laws are also available from the commercial databases. LEXIS-NEXIS coverage in the PUBLAW file begins with the 100th Congress, 2nd Session (1988). This file is found in several LEXIS-NEXIS libraries, including CODES and GENFED. WESTLAW's US-PL database contains laws from the current Congress, while older documents beginning with the 93rd Congress (1973) are in a separate database, US-PL-OLD. Both PUBLAW and US-PL are updated within a few days of the signing of new laws.

The only comprehensive electronic alternative to the volumes of the *Statutes at Large* is a CD-ROM product from Potomac Publishing Company, *United States Statutes at Large on CD-ROM*. This 33-CD set is a photo-reproduced copy; acts can be found by volume and page number, name, or public law number, but there is no full-text keyword searching.

Other Statutory Research Tools

Although this chapter focuses on the primary sources of statutory research, numerous other resources are available for analyzing questions involving federal statutes. Texts and journal articles include extensive discussion of issues of federal law. One convenient way to find relevant articles is to use the tables of statutes in the major periodical indexes. Of these, the tables in *Index to Legal Periodicals & Books* are arranged in a

more coherent fashion, with federal acts at the beginning of the section, followed by laws from individual states and then from foreign jurisdictions. *Current Law Index* simply lists all acts in one alphabetic sequence. *ILP*'s advantage, however, is more than offset by the fact that it only lists the citations of relevant articles without even providing their titles. *CLI* includes article titles, providing more information about whether an article is worth pursuing. "Why the Religious Freedom Restoration Act is Unconstitutional. 69 New York University Law Review 437-476 June '94" is more illuminating than just "69 N.Y.U. L. Rev. 437-76 Je '94." Neither index, unfortunately, includes authors' names in these tables.

Another resource worth mentioning is *Shepard's Federal Statute Citations* (7 vols., 1996, with semimonthly supplements). This publication contains lists of *U.S. Code* and *Statutes at Large* citations, followed by references to court decisions that have cited each specific provision. Although the annotated codes generally provide an excellent overview of citing cases, some decisions not listed in the codes may appear in *Shepard's*.

Shepard's is certainly not as easy to use as the annotated codes. It provides no summary of the citing case, just a citation and perhaps a one-letter signal such as *C* for "constitutional" or *U* for "unconstitutional"— and that only for cases with major relevance to the statutory provision. Other cases listed may simply make passing references. For example, 18 U.S.C. § 607, the law prohibiting solicitation of campaign contributions in federal buildings, is cited in *United States v. Palma-Ruedas*, 121 F.3d 841 (3d Cir. 1997). It turns out that *Palma-Ruedas* is a case about a drug conspiracy and kidnapping scheme, with § 607 among several code sections cited in one sentence: "There are a great many federal criminal statutes that are phrased along the following lines: It shall be unlawful to do x. See, e.g., 18 U.S.C. §§ 602, 603, 607(a), 795(a), 842, 922, 964(a), 1082(a), 1731, 1752(a), 1962, 2342." This would not be considered a productive lead on the issue of campaign finance law.

Another difficulty in using *Shepard's* is that statutes are listed exactly as they appear in the citing cases. The Religious Freedom Restoration Act can be cited as 42 U.S.C. §§ 2000bb et seq., §§ 2000bb to 2000bb-4, or simply § 2000bb. Each has an entry in *Shepard's*. If a specific subsection is cited, it too has an entry. In all, the five sections of the RFRA have a total of 30 separate listings. This scheme can be useful when looking for cases under a specific subsection of a lengthy

107 STAT. 1488   PUBLIC LAW 103-141—NOV. 16, 1993

Public Law 103-141
103d Congress

An Act

Nov. 16, 1993
[H.R. 1308]

To protect the free exercise of religion.

Religious
Freedom
Restoration Act
of 1993.
42 USC 2000bb
note.

Be it enacted by the Senate and House of Representatives of the United States of America in Congress assembled,

SECTION 1. SHORT TITLE.

This Act may be cited as the "Religious Freedom Restoration Act of 1993".

42 USC 2000bb.

SEC. 2. CONGRESSIONAL FINDINGS AND DECLARATION OF PURPOSES.

(a) FINDINGS.—The Congress finds that—

(1) the framers of the Constitution, recognizing free exercise of religion as an unalienable right, secured its protection in the First Amendment to the Constitution;

(2) laws "neutral" toward religion may burden religious exercise as surely as laws intended to interfere with religious exercise;

(3) governments should not substantially burden religious exercise without compelling justification;

(4) in Employment Division v. Smith, 494 U.S. 872 (1990) the Supreme Court virtually eliminated the requirement that the government justify burdens on religious exercise imposed by laws neutral toward religion; and

(5) the compelling interest test as set forth in prior Federal court rulings is a workable test for striking sensible balances between religious liberty and competing prior governmental interests.

(b) PURPOSES.—The purposes of this Act are—

(1) to restore the compelling interest test as set forth in Sherbert v. Verner, 374 U.S. 398 (1963) and Wisconsin v. Yoder, 406 U.S. 205 (1972) and to guarantee its application in all cases where free exercise of religion is substantially burdened; and

(2) to provide a claim or defense to persons whose religious exercise is substantially burdened by government.

42 USC
2000bb-1.

SEC. 3. FREE EXERCISE OF RELIGION PROTECTED.

(a) IN GENERAL.—Government shall not substantially burden a person's exercise of religion even if the burden results from a rule of general applicability, except as provided in subsection (b).

(b) EXCEPTION.—Government may substantially burden a person's exercise of religion only if it demonstrates that application of the burden to the person—

STATUTES AT LARGE

EXHIBIT 8-5

code provision, but in most instances it means that a lot of double-checking is necessary.

A third problem arises in that the 1996 bound volumes—but not the supplements—include notations of amendments to code provisions in the *Statutes at Large.* Only changes through 107 Stat. (1993) are included, so at best the information is incomplete. At worst it is misleading, particularly if one draws the reasonable but

erroneous conclusion that all amendments are listed. This is particularly easy to do when using the CD-ROM or online version of *Shepard's,* where there is no separation between material from the 1996 volumes and more recent additions. Older amendments are listed, but recent acts are omitted, with little notice of a change in policy. Suffice it to say that *Shepard's* is *not* the place to look for statutory amendments.

Why, then, is *Shepard's* worth knowing about? There are two major reasons. First, with biweekly updates it is more current than the code supplements. The latest pamphlet provides references to recent decisions well before they appear in code annotations. It even cites new decisions by docket number before they are published in the reporters. A table in the back of the pamphlet provides case names, dates of decision, and citations for retrieving documents on LEXIS-NEXIS. (As we shall see, most are available from noncommercial Internet sites as well.) These recent cases can be important in considering a statute. For example, *Shepard's* provided notice that the Religious Freedom Restoration Act had been held unconstitutional by the Supreme Court months before the codes included that information.

Second, *Shepard's* includes coverage of laws that do not appear in the current *U.S. Code*, with citations either to the *Statutes at Large* or to earlier code editions. The annotated codes are of little use in finding sources citing these laws. (*USCS* does include an *Annotations to Uncodified Laws and Treaties* volume with some coverage of these acts, but its coverage is far from comprehensive.) *Shepard's* can be used, for example, to find cases citing the Judiciary Act of 1789, 1 Stat. 70. This can be useful in historical research and in seeking to determine the scope or application of a provision that for one reason or another is not included in the current code.

Shepard's Federal Statute Citations lists references to statutes only in federal cases and in annotations in *American Law Reports* (*ALR*) and *Lawyers' Edition*. Federal statutes are also cited in state court decisions and in law review articles, but those references are found in *Shepard's* publications for individual states and in *Shepard's Federal Law Citations in Selected Law Reviews* (3 vols., 1994, with bimonthly supplements).

Researchers with access to the full-text databases of LEXIS-NEXIS and WESTLAW can replicate *Shepard's* work by using a statutory citation as a search term. This approach lacks the editorial control *Shepard's* provides, but it may turn up additional sources. *Shepard's Federal Law Citations in Selected Law Reviews* covers only 19 law reviews, and under 18 U.S.C. § 607 it cites only a *Northwestern University Law Review* article in which the section is mentioned in passing. A full-text search in a law review database finds an article specifically on campaign finance in the *Chicago-Kent Law Review*, a journal not covered in the *Shepard's* publication.

Related Sources

Several other sources of federal law are important to understand in conjunction with statutes. One of the most important of these, the Constitution, is included in each version of the *U.S. Code*. Decisions of the federal courts must be read to understand the scope and meaning of statutes. These decisions are cited in the annotated codes and in *Shepard's Federal Statute Citations*. Other sources worth noting appear below.

Treaties and Conventions

Under Article VI of the Constitution, treaties are part of the supreme law of the land, having the same legal effect as federal statutes. In considering federal legislation, it is important not to neglect the possible importance of an international convention or treaty.

Bilateral treaties, between two countries, and *multilateral treaties* or *conventions*, among several countries, can have a direct impact on everyday life. Important bilateral treaties cover issues such as double taxation and extradition. The Warsaw Convention provides many of the rules governing air travel, and the Convention on the Civil Aspects of International Child Abduction may influence child custody disputes.

The annotated codes provide the texts of a few major conventions. *USCA* includes some, such as the Universal Copyright Convention and the Convention on the Taking of Evidence Abroad, in notes following relevant code sections. *USCS* coverage of treaties is more extensive. An *International Agreements* volume contains about two dozen major conventions on matters such as air travel, civil litigation, intellectual property, and sales. The conventions are accompanied by references to texts, law review articles, and court decisions, and a separate index for each convention is included. Another *USCS* volume, *Annotations to Uncodified Laws and Treaties*, includes references to court decisions citing other multilateral treaties, as well as treaties with Native American nations and other countries.

A far more extensive source for information on international treaties and conventions is the Department of State's annual *Treaties in Force*, a guide listing both bilateral treaties, by country, and multilateral conventions, by subject. This volume, like other treaty research sources, also includes coverage of *executive agreements*, which are international accords made by the president without requiring Senate approval.

Beyond the few treaties reproduced in the annotated codes, treaty text can be found in the *Statutes at Large* (up to 1949) and in *United States Treaties and*

Other International Agreements (*UST*), beginning in 1950. The pre-1950 treaties have been published in an official compilation, *Bevans' Treaties and Other International Agreements of the United States of America 1776–1949* (13 vols., 1968–75).

Several volumes of *UST* are published each year, but there is a delay of several years before a new treaty appears in this set. Other sources for current treaties include the microfiche *UST Current Service* (William S. Hein & Co., 1990–date) and the print publication *Consolidated Treaties & International Agreements: Current Document Service* (Oceana, 1990–date, quarterly). Oceana also publishes *TIARA CD-ROM: Treaties and International Agreements Researchers Archive*, an electronic index and compilation of more than 9,000 treaties dating back to 1783. The treaties on the *TIARA* CD are also available to some subscribers on LEXIS-NEXIS as the USTRTY file and on WESTLAW as the TIA database. Another WESTLAW database, USTREATIES, has more than 3,700 treaties. It begins coverage in 1979 and is updated with new treaties within several weeks of their signature or entry into force.

The Internet does not yet have any comprehensive source for U.S. treaties, but it does have several sites featuring international conventions. The Multilaterals Project at the Fletcher School of Law & Diplomacy <http://www.tufts.edu/fletcher/multilaterals.html> is one of the most extensive and best-organized free sites.

Court Rules and Sentencing Guidelines

Rules that govern court procedures often have the same force and effect as statutes, even though they are usually prepared by advisory committees of judges rather than legislators. The Supreme Court submits amendments and new rules to Congress, and they take effect unless Congress expressly disapproves them. Similarly, Congress created the United States Sentencing Commission in 1984 to prepare sentencing standards; these Federal Sentencing Guidelines took effect in 1987 when Congress did not disapprove. One set of court rules, the Federal Rules of Evidence, was specifically enacted by Congress in 1975 because some of its provisions affect substantive rights and were therefore considered to be beyond the rulemaking power of the courts.

The major sets of rules are published in each set of the code, following Titles 18 (Crimes and Criminal Procedure) and 28 (Judiciary and Judicial Procedure) in the official *U.S. Code* and *USCA*, and in separate volumes at the end of the *USCS* set (except for the evidence rules, which are considered statutes and are published as an appendix to Title 28).

The Federal Sentencing Guidelines, which have been amended extensively since their initial adoption, are published by the U.S. Sentencing Commission in its *Guidelines Manual* (biennial) and are available on the Internet <http://www.ussc.gov/guidelin.htm>. They are also available from several commercial publishers. Among the more useful versions of the guidelines are two editions that combine the official text and commentary with their authors' analysis: Roger W. Haines, Jr., et al.'s *Federal Sentencing Guidelines Handbook: Text and Analysis* (West Group, annual) and Thomas W. Hutchison et al.'s *Federal Sentencing Law and Practice* (West Group, annual). The guidelines are not published with the official *U.S. Code*, but both annotated editions include versions of the guidelines accompanied by notes of court decisions. *USCA* has three hardcover volumes with pocket part supplements, and *USCS* publishes an annually revised paperback volume. Online versions can be found in WESTLAW's FCJ-FSG database and in the GLINE file in LEXIS-NEXIS's GENFED and CRIME libraries.

Executive Orders and Delegated Legislation

The president and the departments and agencies of the executive branch also have significant lawmaking functions. The president issues proclamations and executive orders that have the effect of law, and the departments and agencies provide detailed regulations that fill in vague congressional mandates. In analyzing the effect of a statute it is always important to consider related legal documents from the executive branch. All three editions of the *United States Code* include the texts of a few executive orders and regulations, and the two annotated editions provide references to relevant sections of the *Code of Federal Regulations*. This and other administrative law sources will be discussed in Chapter 10.

CONGRESSIONAL MATERIALS

Thus far this chapter has looked at the product of congressional labors but not the processes by which legislation is created. Finding a federal statute requires little understanding of Congress and its procedures. But to interpret that statute, it may be necessary to consult materials produced by Congress during its consideration and passage of the statute. Chief among these are reports from committees that studied the bill and recommended its passage, and transcripts of floor debates in which its scope and purpose were discussed.

Of the many reasons to study Congress and the political process, we focus here specifically on the procedures by which laws are considered and enacted. These procedures can vary dramatically from law to law, but a simplified overview may be helpful. A bill is introduced by a member of the House or Senate and referred to a committee with jurisdiction over its subject matter. There, it may languish, or it may be considered by the committee or by one of its subcommittees. The committee may hold hearings on the bill to evaluate its merits and then convene a markup session at which it analyzes and perhaps modifies the bill. If the committee decides that a bill should become law, it issues a report to the full house recommending passage and explaining the bill's purpose and provisions. The house then debates the bill, perhaps amending it further on the floor. If the bill comes to a vote and passes, it goes to the other chamber, where the same process begins again. If the versions of a bill passed by the House and Senate differ, and neither will acquiesce and accept the other's language, a conference committee of members of both houses works out differences and prepares a compromise bill that both houses must accept or reject without further amendment. A bill that passes both houses goes to the president and becomes law when signed. If the president vetoes the bill, it can still become law if the veto is overridden by a two-thirds majority in each house.

Reference Works on Congress

Several reference sources provide comprehensive coverage of Congress and its role in the enactment of federal laws. Most of these works discuss both the lawmaking function and other aspects of Congress. They are most useful for background information on the legislative process rather than for interpretation of specific federal statutes.

Encyclopedia of the United States Congress (Simon & Schuster, 4 vols., 1995), edited by Donald C. Bacon, Roger H. Davidson, and Morton Keller, is an extensive, current reference set. With more than 1,000 signed articles from more than 500 contributors, this is a major work covering all aspects of Congress. Articles, arranged alphabetically, include biographies of 247 major legislators, a series of 8 essays providing a history of Congress, and nearly 100 articles on specific acts. Useful features include tables of the sessions of Congress and holders of key offices since 1789, and a chart in the front of each volume indicating the years of each term of Congress. Volume 4 includes an extensive glossary of terms used in the legislative process, from *act* to *zone whip*, and a thorough index. The set is illustrated with 900 photographs, cartoons, and maps. Every article but one includes a bibliography of recommended readings.

Two shorter works with alphabetical entries, providing accessible information but fewer research leads, are Ann O'Connor's *Congress A to Z: A Ready Reference Encyclopedia* (Congressional Quarterly, 2d ed., 1993) and Donald A. Ritchie's *The Young Oxford Companion to the Congress of the United States* (Oxford University Press, 1993). *Congress A to Z* is part of CQ's *Encyclopedia of American Government* and combines longer essays on broad subject areas with briefer articles on major historical figures, institutional bodies such as committees, and significant terminology. The *Young Oxford Companion* may be hobbled by its juvenile name, but this work by the Senate's associate historian is actually a fair rival to *Congress A to Z* for accessibility and clear information. Coverage in the two books is similar, with each providing some entries missing from the other and a few leads for further research. Both include appendixes with various tables, including leaders of Congress and the dates of terms and sessions since 1789.

The most thorough single-volume overview of Congress, *Congressional Quarterly's Guide to Congress* (4th ed., 1991), is arranged by subject, rather than alphabetically, with eight sections covering various subjects. Parts 2, "Powers of Congress," and 3, "Congressional Procedures," are the most useful for studying Congress's lawmaking roles. Part 2 discusses Congress's role in taxing and spending, foreign policy, regulation of commerce, and other matters. Part 3 explains such issues as party leadership, parliamentary procedures, floor action, and the committee system. Appendixes include House and Senate rules, a glossary, various statistics and tables, and a list of all members of Congress from 1789 to 1991.

For background information on the legislative process, the Library of Congress THOMAS site provides access to two documents prepared by congressional parliamentarians—*How Our Laws Are Made*, revised by the House's Charles Johnson, <http://thomas.loc.gov/home/lawsmade.toc.html>, and *Enactment of a Law*, by the Senate's Robert B. Dove, <http://thomas.loc.gov/enactment/enactlawtoc.html>. Each emphasizes procedures, in its house; *Enactment of a Law*, for example, includes coverage of Senate procedures, such as treaty ratification and executive sessions. Older versions of these pamphlets are available in print as House Document 101-139 and Senate Document 97-20, respectively.

How Our Laws Are Made and *Enactment of a Law* are straightforward, official versions of congressional procedures, with little discussion of political realities and few anecdotes. Commercially published works on Congress provide a more thorough and realistic view of the lawmaking process. One of the most useful is Walter J. Oleszek's *Congressional Procedures and the Policy Process* (Congressional Quarterly, 4th ed., 1996). Oleszek, of the Congressional Research Service, explains the intricacies of the ways that legislation is introduced, referred to committee, and considered. Chapters cover the systems for scheduling legislation in each house, floor procedures, and conference committees. The volume includes a glossary of congressional terminology and several tables and illustrative sidebars.

Two books by former House staffers provide more detail on specific procedures. Lawrence E. Filson's *The Legislative Drafter's Desk Reference* (Congressional Quarterly, 1992) is a general guide to bill writing, but Part 7, "The Uniquely Federal Forms and Styles," includes a good deal of insider information on federal legislative action. A more exhaustive work, Charles Tiefer's *Congressional Practice and Procedure: A Reference, Research, and Legislative Guide* (Greenwood Press, 1989), provides extensive historical background and detailed information on legislative and parliamentary procedures.

The organizational and procedural terminology used in Congress can be a bit bewildering, but most reference works include glossaries. A few full-length dictionaries also define congressional terminology. Walter Kravitz's *Congressional Quarterly's American Congressional Dictionary* (Congressional Quarterly, 2d ed., 1997) provides a thorough guide to terms used in Congress, with clear explanations of parliamentary procedures, such as "laying on the table" and several entries on various aspects of "yielding." An abridged version has been published as *CQ's Pocket Guide to the Language of Congress* (1994). Paul Dickson and Paul Clancy's *The Congress Dictionary: The Ways and Meanings of Capitol Hill* (Wiley, 1993) is a more discursive work, with colloquialisms such as "the take" and "young Turk," historical entries such as "Watergate babies," and fewer insights on procedural details. Ellen Greenberg's *The House and Senate Explained: The People's Guide to Congress* (Norton, 1996) provides a briefer, more practical glossary, and also contains a guide to the House and Senate chambers, a chapter of "frequently heard phrases," and other features. Several glossaries of congressional terms are available on the Internet; the Library of Congress provides links to these and to guides to the legislative process <http://lcweb.loc.gov/global/legislative/legproc.html>.

Legislative History Documents

Legislative history research is made necessary by the ambiguity in the language of statutes. Lawyers and judges must determine whether a statute applies to a particular situation, and this inquiry often turns on the meaning of its words. One way to interpret statutes is to use the "plain meaning" of the words, applying common sense and dictionary definitions of terminology. Lawyers and judges use this and a variety of other rules and methods in interpreting statutes. These are summarized in the "Statutes" articles in *American Jurisprudence 2d* and *Corpus Juris Secundum*, and are the subject of a multivolume treatise, Norman J. Singer's *Statutes and Statutory Construction* (Clark Boardman Callaghan, 8 vols., 5th ed., 1992-94, with annual supplements). Successor to an 1891 work by J. G. Sutherland, and commonly known as *Sutherland Statutory Construction*, Singer's treatise covers legislative procedures, the various forms of statutory enactments, and policies guiding the interpretation of statutes. A shorter work written for law students is Abner J. Mikva and Eric Lane's *An Introduction to Statutory Interpretation and the Legislative Process* (Aspen Law & Business, 1997).

Among the resources used in interpreting federal statutes are the materials created while the statute was being drafted and considered by Congress. Committee reports are generally considered to be the most persuasive legislative history materials and are the sources most frequently cited by the courts. A statistical analysis of Supreme Court citations to legislative history materials found that almost half of all references were to committee reports. Floor debates were next in prominence, followed by hearings, bills, and other sources (Jorge L. Carro and Andrew R. Brann, "Use of Legislative Histories by the United States Supreme Court: A Statistical Analysis," 9 J. Legislation 282 [1982]).

Citations to legislative history of the Religious Freedom Restoration Act follow these general principles. The committee reports are by far the most frequently cited legislative materials in court decisions. Nearly one out of every five cases mentioning the act also cites at least one of the committee reports. Floor debates are cited far less frequently, almost always in conjunction with the reports. Few references are to hearings, and these usually focus on the sponsor's explanation of the act's scope.

Legislative documents, including bills and committee reports, are available in most government depository libraries. Recent material can also be found using several electronic sources. LEXIS-NEXIS and WESTLAW, familiar resources in many areas of legal research, have extensive collections of legislative materials, and two other commercial online systems specialize in this area: LEGI-SLATE, a service of the Washington Post Company, and Washington Alert, from Congressional Quarterly. Each of these services includes the text of major documents and provides a wealth of other information about Congress. Another commercial service, Congressional Universe, is also available on the Web <http://web.lexis-nexis.com/cis>. Access is limited to subscribers, but these include many university libraries. Congressional Universe is produced by Congressional Information Service (CIS), a sister company of LEXIS-NEXIS, and provides access to recent documents as well as indexes of congressional material.

Besides these commercial services, the federal government makes a great deal of information available on the Internet. Two major government sites, the Library of Congress's THOMAS system <http://thomas.loc.gov> and the Government Printing Office's GPO Access <http://www.access.gpo.gov/congress> (with the same material available through more than 20 mirror sites at universities and public libraries around the country) have overlapping coverage, but each has a distinct purpose. THOMAS is the major source for legislative information; it is the place to go for procedural details on a bill's passage through Congress. GPO Access focuses on documents; as the Web site of the government's publisher, it is the place to go for PDF files, which reproduce the exact format of the printed page. Both of these sites are fairly new, and consequently their materials do not extend as far back in time as those of the commercial services. For recent and pending legislation, however, they can be excellent, cost-effective places to begin research. Exhibit 8-6 shows the homepage for THOMAS, presenting an array of search options for congressional information.

Each house of Congress maintains a Web site <http://www.senate.gov> and <http://www.house.gov> providing information on its procedures as well as links to pages for individual members and committees. Some committee homepages are more extensive than others, with summaries of major pending legislation, background information, and schedules of upcoming hearings and meetings. In time more information will undoubtedly be available on these pages.

Numerous other Web sites provide access to congressional information. The Library of Congress provides links to many of these sites, arranged by subject, at <http://lcweb.loc.gov/global/legislative/congress.html>. One of the LC's offerings is an annotated list of "Congressional Mega Sites," which includes links to the major comprehensive sources discussed here. More specific links provide information on committees, schedules, floor proceedings, and voting records, as well as congressional news and analysis.

Bills

Legislative history research involves searching for information about a piece of legislation prior to its passage—and thus before it was cited by public law number or *United States Code* section. The first step, therefore, is often to find the bill number. This number does not appear in the code, but it is shown on the slip law and in the *Statutes at Large*. Note in Exhibit 8-5 that the bill number, H.R. 1308, is indicated in brackets in the left margin, below the date of passage. The *Statutes at Large* has included bill numbers at the beginning of each law enacted since 1903. Earlier bill numbers, while rarely needed, can be found using Eugene Nabors's *Legislative Reference Checklist: The Key to Legislative Histories from 1789-1903* (Rothman, 1982).

The early versions of bills that would later become law are not the most frequently consulted legislative history sources, but they are the focus of the process and key to finding other information. Changes in a bill's language can sometimes provide significant information about a statute's meaning. For example, if an early version of a bill is vaguely worded but a later version has a list of specific activities covered, the decision to identify these activities may indicate that Congress deliberately excluded coverage of other, similar activities.

Only a few hundred bills become laws during each term of Congress, but several thousand are introduced. These are issued in separate numbered series for each house. Numbering begins anew with each term of Congress, so it is important to know not only the bill number but the number of the Congress.

In the case of the Religious Freedom Restoration Act, bills were introduced in the 101st (1989-90) and 102nd (1991-92) Congresses before the act was finally passed in the 103rd Congress in 1993. Although the substance of the final act changed little from the first bill introduced, several minor modifications were made along the way. There were eight distinct versions of H.R. 1308, the bill that finally became law. In addition, in each of these terms of Congress bills were also introduced in the Senate, so that each chamber could

THOMAS — Legislative Information on the Internet

QUICK SEARCH TEXT OF BILLS 105th CONGRESS:

Search by Bill Number:

Ex: *s. 435, H.R. 842*
OR
Search by Word/Phrase:

Ex: *line item veto, tax reform*

[Search] [Clear]

Frequently Asked Questions (FAQs)

105th Congress:
House Directories
Senate Directories

Congressional Internet Services:
House - Senate
Library of Congress
GPO - GAO - CBO
AOC - OTA - More

Library of Congress Web Links:
Legislative
Executive
Judicial
State/Local

■ CONGRESS NOW

Congress in the News NEW

House and Senate: Floor Activities

House: Latest Floor Actions - Floor Activities This Week

National Bipartisan Commission on the Future of Medicare

■ BILLS

Bill Summary & Status: 105th (1997-98)
Previous Congresses (1973 - 1996)

Bill Text:
105th (1997-98) - 104th (1995-96) - 103rd (1993-94) - 102nd (1991-93) - 101st (1989-90)

House Roll Call Votes [Help]: 105th - 2nd (1998) - 105th - 1st (1997)
Previous Congresses (1990 - 1996)

Senate Roll Call Votes [Help]: 105th - 2nd (1998) - 105th - 1st (1997)
Previous Congresses (1989 - 1996)

Public Laws By Law Number: 105th (1997-98)
Previous Congresses (1973 - 1996)

Major Legislation: [Definition]
105th: By topic - By popular/short title - By bill number/type - Enacted into law
104th: By topic - By popular/short title - By bill number/type - Enacted into law

■ CONGRESSIONAL RECORD

***Congressional Record* Text:** Most Recent Issue
105th (1997-98) - 104th (1995-96) - 103rd (1993-94) - 102nd (1991-92)- 101st (1989-90)

***Congressional Record Index*:**
105th - 2nd (1998) - 105th - 1st (1997) - 104th - 2nd (1996) - 104th - 1st (1995) - 103rd - 2nd (1994)

***Résumés of Congressional Activity*:**
105th - 1st (1997) - Previous Congresses (1969 - 1996)

Annals of Congress (Precursor of the *Congressional Record*) [About]
1st Congress (1789-1791) - 2nd Congress (1791-1793)

■ COMMITTEE INFORMATION

Committee Reports: Congress: 105th (1997-98) - 104th (1995-96)

Committee Home Pages: House - Senate

House Committees: Today's Schedules - Schedules and Oversight Plans - Selected Hearing Transcripts

■ THE LEGISLATIVE PROCESS

How Our Laws Are Made (by Charles W. Johnson, House Parliamentarian)

Enactment of a Law (By Robert B. Dove, Senate Parliamentarian)

■ HISTORICAL DOCUMENTS

Historical documents including the Declaration of Independence, the Federalist Papers, early Congressional documents (Constitutional Convention and Continental Congress broadsides), and the Constitution. U.S. Congressional Documents and Debates: 1774 - 1873.

LIBRARY OF CONGRESS THOMAS WEB SITE

EXHIBIT 8-6

begin consideration of the legislation without waiting for the other to pass a version. Sometimes the House and Senate versions are identical *companion bills*; often, as in the case of RFRA, they are related but have slight differences.

Because the House and Senate must pass one bill for it to become law, eventually one chamber must vote on the other's bill. In doing so, it is free to amend the bill by changing its text to that of the version it had been considering. This is done by striking out everything after the initial enacting clause ("Be it enacted by the Senate and House of Representatives of the United States of America in Congress assembled") and substituting different language. For example, in 1993 the Senate considered and passed the Religious Freedom Restoration Act after the House, but its version, S. 578, provided that government could not "substantially burden" the exercise of religion without a compelling governmental interest. The House's version had a lower threshold that omitted the word *substantially*. When it came time for Senate consideration and passage, H.R. 1308 was amended by replacing everything after the enacting clause with the Senate language. The House then agreed to the Senate version, and the bill went to the president for his signature.

The Religious Freedom Restoration Act was a concise and relatively simple piece of legislation, but it shows some of the complexities of tracing the progress of a bill through Congress. Here, the bill that was considered by the Senate (S. 578) ended up being passed, but with a different number (H.R. 1308). Several bills may be introduced on related topics, with one approved by a committee but a different one passed on the floor. A number of bills may be combined into a comprehensive piece of omnibus legislation. Finding the bill number for the enacted law may only be the first step in tracking down the proposed legislation leading to a bill's passage.

Bills are not the only form of action introduced in Congress. A *joint resolution* usually concerns matters of a temporary nature, but it must be passed by both houses and signed by the president (or passed over his veto), just like a bill. If passed, it becomes a public law. Two other types of resolutions of lesser importance, because they do not have the force of law, are *concurrent resolutions,* expressing the opinion of both houses of Congress, and *simple resolutions,* concerning the procedures of just one house.

Although bills and resolutions currently pending in Congress may be available from legislators or committees, it is generally necessary to turn to microfiche or electronic sources for older bills. Microfiche sets are issued by the Government Printing Office and CIS. The CIS collection goes back to 1933, and bills from earlier Congresses dating back to 1789 are available on microfilm from the Library of Congress.

Fee-based online sources for bills include LEGISLATE (1985-date), Washington Alert (1987-date), and LEXIS-NEXIS/Congressional Universe (1989-date). Bills introduced since 1993 are available from GPO Access and THOMAS. GPO provides the PDF file, replicating the original typeset bill, but THOMAS has more sophisticated software, with several searching options and results ranking the relevance of documents retrieved. (Documents with the search terms in close proximity to each other are shown first, followed by those containing all the terms but not located near each other, and finally documents with one or more of the terms.)

Committee Reports

The most important documents for legislative history research are generally considered to be the reports in which committees considering a bill explain its provisions and purpose. These usually provide the most straightforward description of a bill's meaning. The Supreme Court accords a committee report the most weight because it "represents the considered and collective understanding of those Congressmen involved in drafting and studying proposed legislation. Floor debates reflect at best the understanding of individual Congressmen" (*Zuber v. Allen*, 396 U.S. 168, 186 [1969]).

The use of committee reports as indicators of legislators' intent has been challenged extensively by Justice Antonin Scalia. He points out that reports are prepared by staffers, not members of Congress, and may not even be read by committee members. In a concurring opinion in *Blanchard v. Bergeron*, 489 U.S. 87, 98 (1989), Justice Scalia argued that no heed should be paid to material that was included in a report "at best by a committee staff member on his or her own initiative, and at worst by a committee staff member at the suggestion of a lawyer-lobbyist."

Scalia's argument has been answered by Judge Patricia Wald of the D.C. Circuit:

> To disregard committee reports as indicators of congressional understanding because we are suspicious that nefarious staffers have planted certain information for some undisclosed reason, is to second-guess Congress' chosen form of organization and delegation of authority, and to doubt its ability to oversee its own constitutional functions effectively. It comes perilously close, in my view, to impugning the way a coordinate

branch conducts its operations and, in that sense, runs the risk of violating the spirit if not the letter of the separation of powers principle. (Patricia M. Wald, "The Sizzling Sleeper: The Use of Legislative History in Construing Statutes in the 1988-89 Term of the United States Supreme Court," 39 Am. U. L. Rev. 277, 306-307 [1990]).

It is important to remember that committee reports and other legislative history documents are not the law but are simply resources for interpreting ambiguous statutes. If the statute is clear, there is no need to consult congressional documents. If the statute and the committee report conflict, the statute is the law and will govern. Material in reports that seeks to express the will of Congress or of a committee, but does not interpret a specific statute, is not legislative history. Justice Scalia spoke for the Supreme Court when he wrote that "unenacted approvals, beliefs, and desires are not laws." (*Puerto Rico Dept. of Consumer Affairs v. Isla Petroleum Corp.*, 485 U.S. 495, 501 [1988]).

Reports usually include the text of a bill as passed by the committee, a general overview, and a section-by-section discussion. Some have additional material, such as dissenting views by individual legislators. The section-by-section analyses can be the most valuable portions of committee reports because they often explain the dry statutory language in something closer to comprehensible English.

Committee reports are numbered sequentially in one series for each house, for each term of Congress. Reports on the Religious Freedom Restoration Act, for example, were issued by the House Judiciary Committee, H.R. Rep. 103-88, and the Senate Judiciary Committee, S. Rep. 103-111. Each report includes some background information on the need for the legislation; discussion of its application to prisoners, the military, and abortion; and a section-by-section analysis of its provisions. The most frequently cited committee report is from the Senate, to accompany S. 578, not the House report accompanying H.R. 1308, because the language considered by the Senate committee is what became law. Exhibit 8-7 shows a page from the Senate report with an explanation of Congress's authority to pass this law (which would be refuted four years later by the Supreme Court), a record of the committee's vote, and the section-by-section analysis of the opening sections of the Religious Freedom Restoration Act.

Conference committee reports are issued when the two houses pass similar bills but do not agree on some provisions. Because these reports deal specifically with issues about which the two houses are in contention, they are among the most influential of legislative history sources. Conference reports are published as part of the *House Reports* series. Unlike other reports, they are also printed in the *Congressional Record*. In the case of the Religious Freedom Restoration Act, the House agreed to the Senate language, so there was no need to convene a conference committee.

Reports are issued by the Government Printing Office as separate pamphlets, and after the end of a session they are published in a bound compilation known as the *Serial Set* (although the GPO plans to discontinue publication of the bound volumes after the 104th Congress). The *Serial Set* dates back to 1817 and consists of more than 14,000 volumes; earlier reports are in a series known as the *American State Papers*. All reports in the *American State Papers* and *Serial Set* are also available on microfiche from CIS. In many libraries, however, the most convenient source is West's *United States Code Congressional and Administrative News (USCCAN)*, which reprints one or more committee reports for almost every public law.

WESTLAW offers the most extensive electronic access to committee reports, with the LH database containing reports printed in *USCCAN* back to 1948 and full coverage since 1990. Congressional Universe and the CMTRPT file on LEXIS-NEXIS also begin coverage in 1990, while LEGI-SLATE goes back to 1987 and Washington Alert to 1989. GPO Access provides access to reports beginning in 1993, and THOMAS coverage picks up in 1995.

Although the final committee reports are officially published and readily available online, documents from the markup sessions, which would show the committee's deliberative process, are much harder to obtain. Transcripts from House markup sessions are occasionally published, most often by the International Relations Committee, but most markups are unpublished and unavailable through the government Internet sites. LEGI-SLATE and Washington Alert, however, include information on markup sessions (from 1987 and 1989, respectively), and other news sources may report on these sessions as well.

Congressional Record

The *Congressional Record*, published each day when Congress is in session, is the source for proceedings on the floor of the House and Senate. It is the official record of debates, even though it is not a verbatim transcript. Representatives can amend their remarks, and some material in the *Record* is never even spoken on the floor. (Remarks inserted but not spoken are set off typographically, through the use of bullets in the Senate and a different typeface in the House.)

14

include a right to practice one's faith free of laws prohibiting the free exercise of religion.[40]

Section 5 of the 14th amendment provides that "Congress shall have power to enforce, by appropriate legislation, the provisions" of the amendment. Section 5 gives Congress "the same broad powers expressed in the necessary and proper clause" with respect to State governments and their subdivisions.[41] "Whatever legislation is appropriate, that is, adapted to carry out the objects the Amendments have in view," is within the power of Congress, unless prohibited by some other provision of the Constitution.[42]

Thus, congressional power under section 5 to enforce the 14th amendment includes congressional power to enforce the free exercise clause. Because the Religious Freedom Restoration Act is clearly designed to implement the free exercise clause—to protect religious liberty and to eliminate laws "prohibiting the free exercise" of religion—it falls squarely within Congress' section 5 enforcement power.[43]

VI. Vote of the Committee

On May 6, 1993, a reporting quorum being present, the Committee on the Judiciary ordered S. 578 reported to the full Senate by a rollcall vote of 15–1. Voting in favor of reporting the bill were the chairman and Senators Kennedy, Metzenbaum, DeConcini, Leahy, Simon, Kohl, Feinstein, Moseley-Braun, Hatch, Thurmond, Grassley, Specter, Brown, and Pressler. Voting against reporting the bill was Senator Simpson.

VII. Section-by-Section Analysis

Section 1. This section provides that the title of the act is the Religious Freedom Restoration Act of 1993.

Section 2. In this section, Congress finds that the framers of the Constitution recognized that religious liberty is an inalienable right, protected by the first amendment, and that government law may burden that liberty even if they are neutral on their face. Congress also determines that the Supreme Court's decision in *Employment Division* v. *Smith* eliminated the compelling interest test for evaluating free exercise claims previously set forth in *Sherbert* v. *Verner* and *Wisconsin* v. *Yoder*, and that it is necessary to restore that test to preserve religious freedom. The section recites that the act is intended to restore the compelling interest test and to guarantee its application in all cases where the free exercise of religion is substantially burdened.

Section 3. This section codifies the compelling interest test as the Supreme Court had enunciated it and applied it prior to the *Smith* decision. The bill permits Government to place a substantial burden on the exercise of religion only if it demonstrates a compelling

---

[40] *Cantwell* v. *Connecticut*, 310 U.S. 296 (1940).
[41] *Katzenbach* v. *Morgan*, 384 U.S. 641, 650 (1966).
[42] *Ex parte Virginia*, 100 U.S. 339, 345 (1879).
[43] While the act is intended to enforce the right guaranteed by the free exercise clause of the first amendment, it does not purport to legislate the standard of review to be applied by the Federal courts in cases brought under that constitutional provision. Instead, it creates a new statutory prohibition on governmental action that substantially burdens the free exercise of religion, except where such action is the least restrictive means of furthering a compelling governmental interest.

The *Congressional Record* began publication in 1873. It is published in a daily edition with separate sections of Senate and House pagination (as well as *E* pages containing "extensions of remarks," with such material as speeches, tributes, and reprints of newspaper editorials). Several years later, a final bound edition is published replacing the separate *S* and *H* paginations with one series. The *Record*'s privately published predecessors are the *Annals of Congress* (1789–1824), the *Register of Debates* (1824–37), and the *Congressional Globe* (1833–73).

Debates on the floor of the House and Senate are not as widely used for legislative history as committee reports, which represent the collected wisdom of those legislators assigned to study the bill. Statements by individual legislators, particularly those who are not sponsors of the legislation, are given little weight. The *Record* is, however, useful for several purposes. Statements by sponsors and floor managers (the committee members responsible for steering the bill through the process) may explain aspects of the bill that are not addressed in the committee reports. Occasionally, a floor manager will correct a misleading or erroneous statement in a report.

In addition, the *Congressional Record* may cover issues not addressed elsewhere. Sometimes amendments are introduced on the floor and important changes made that were not even considered in committee. For example, the inclusion of sex discrimination in Title VII of the Civil Rights Act of 1964, Pub. L. 88-352, 78 Stat. 241, 253, was a floor amendment introduced one day before the bill passed the House. Because the amendment was introduced by a representative who was against passage of the bill, it has been viewed as a means to block passage rather than an attempt to protect the rights of working women. There is no committee report discussing sex discrimination, and only nine pages of debate in the *Congressional Record,* providing few insights (110 Cong. Rec. 2577-2584 [1964]). Nonetheless, the text of the law clearly prohibits discrimination on the basis of sex, and the scope and application of that prohibition have been shaped by court decisions over the past 30 years.

Sometimes the rush to squeeze legislation through at the end of a session leads to shortcuts of the usual process. For example, the Bankruptcy Reform Act of 1994, Pub. L. 103-394, 108 Stat. 4106, was passed near the end of the 103rd Congress by the Senate. The House Judiciary Committee approved a bill different from the Senate's version, but there would not have been enough time to pass two bills and convene a conference committee. Senate and House members met informally and worked out differences before the bill went to the House floor, and the chairman of the House Judiciary Committee inserted a section-by-section description of the bill in the *Congressional Record* (140 Cong. Rec. 10,764-10,771 [Oct. 4, 1994]). Because neither Senate nor House committee report matches the bill that was passed, the *Congressional Record* description is considered the authoritative explanation of the bill.

In the case of the Religious Freedom Restoration Act, the debates in the House on May 11, 1993, and in the Senate on October 27, 1993, show the concerns of legislators about the potential abuse of religious liberty claims by federal and state prisoners. An amendment to prohibit the application of the act to prisoners was debated in the Senate and defeated, 58-41. Because the Senate amended the House bill to include the word "substantially," the bill went back to the House on November 3 for more debate and the House's concurrence in the Senate amendment.

For someone with a reference to a particular date of the *Congressional Record* but no specific page, the first stop is the "Daily Digest" in the back of each issue, which indicates the pages of particular measures considered and voted upon. Every two weeks an index is published, providing access by subject, name of legislator, and title of legislation, and including a "History of Bills and Resolutions" list with references by bill number. This provides a chronological record of activity on each bill, including introduction, committee referral, and floor consideration. It includes *Record* page references for each step, as well as committee report numbers.

The *Congressional Record* is available electronically, through WESTLAW (CR database), LEXIS-NEXIS (RECORD file), and Congressional Universe, beginning in 1985; LEGI-SLATE coverage begins in 1987 and Washington Alert in 1989. Full-text coverage through government Internet sites starts in 1993 with THOMAS, which provides extensive options for searching, including word or phrase, member of Congress, and date. GPO Access coverage picks up in 1994, and, beginning with 1995, pages can be viewed or downloaded in PDF format. GPO Access does not include as extensive a menu of searching options as THOMAS, but it provides access to the index and "History of Bills and Resolutions" lists back to 1983.

Hearings and Other Sources

Several other congressional publications are of occasional use in legislative history research, although they are not as important as committee reports or floor debates. *Hearings* are held by committees and subcommittees, and serve to gather information on areas of congressional concern. They are not limited to proposed legislation. The Senate Judiciary Committee's hearings on Robert Bork's nomination to the Supreme Court in 1987 filled five volumes, and records of the 1994 Whitewater hearings combined four volumes of hearings with two volumes of deposition transcripts and 17 volumes of documents. In April 1990, a subcommittee of the House Judiciary Committee held a hearing, *Statutory Interpretation and the Uses of Legislative History*, at which several judges and law professors testified. The published hearing also contains reprints of nearly 400 pages of articles and government reports.

Hearing transcripts generally contain opening remarks by legislators, prepared statements of witnesses, question-and-answer sessions, and material submitted for the record, such as journal articles and witnesses' responses to questions from committee members. Depending on the focus of the hearing, witnesses may include legislators; administration officials; academic scholars; representatives of local governments, industry, or professional organizations; or members of the public. The question-and-answer sessions are usually the most interesting part of hearings because they show the concerns of the legislators rather than simply the views of interested parties. The statements of witnesses are generally not persuasive legislative history sources, except for testimony by a bill's sponsor or by administration witnesses, if the executive branch proposed or assisted in drafting legislation. Although the value of hearings as legislative history is limited, they can provide useful background information on issues of public policy.

Hearings, including the prepared statements, transcripts, and submitted material, are published in separate pamphlets by the Government Printing Office and on microfiche by CIS. The numbering of hearings is not as systematic as that for reports, so the title on the cover, the name of the committee, and the date are usually used to identify a hearing.

Hearing testimony is reported by news services specializing in this area, such as Federal Document Clearing House and Federal News Service, and these transcripts are available through the commercial databases before the published GPO version is issued. Most often these reports contain the prepared statements of witnesses, although some transcripts of question-and-answer sessions are available. Hearing statements and transcripts are generally not available on the Internet from THOMAS or GPO Access, although a number of individual committees make prepared statements available on their homepages.

Committee prints contain a variety of materials prepared for the use of a committee. They can include studies by the committee staff or compilations of statutes in particular subject areas. The Joint Committee on Taxation, for example, publishes numerous descriptions and explanations of proposed and enacted tax legislation, such as *General Explanation of the Tax Reform Act of 1986* (1987) and *General Explanation of Tax Legislation Enacted in the 104th Congress* (1996). The House Committee on Ways and Means issues biennial editions of *Compilation of the Social Security Laws* and *Overview and Compilation of U.S. Trade Statutes*; another biennial publication is *A Compilation of Federal Education Laws*, for the House Committee on Economic and Educational Opportunities and the Senate Committee on Labor and Human Resources. Among the more prominent committee prints are the annual *Country Reports on Economic Policy and Trade Practices* and *Country Reports on Human Rights Practices*, both prepared for the House Committee on International Relations and the Senate Committee on Foreign Relations. For legislative research purposes, the most valuable are compilations of legislative history material by committee staff; these are discussed later in this chapter. Committee prints are distributed by the GPO and are issued on microfiche by CIS. They are less widely available online but can be found on Congressional Universe beginning in 1995.

Many committee prints are reports from the Congressional Research Service providing background information on areas of concern. Other CRS reports are available on microform from University Publications of America (UPA) as *Major Studies and Issue Briefs of the Congressional Research Service*. UPA publishes indexes to this series on paper and CD-ROM. Penny Hill Press publishes a monthly abstracting service, *Congressional Research Report*, and provides copies of individual reports.

House and Senate documents include presidential messages and communications from executive departments or agencies. These include annual reports, proposals for legislation, and veto messages. Like reports, they are published in a numbered series for each house and are reprinted in the official *Serial Set*.

The president frequently issues signing statements when approving legislation, and in recent years these statements have often provided his interpretation of the statutory language. Some commentators feel that these statements should be considered as legislative history sources, particularly when they clarify issues that are not discussed in congressional materials. Since 1986, they have been reprinted with the committee reports in *United States Code Congressional and Administrative News* (*USCCAN*). They are also available in the other sources of presidential documents discussed in Chapter 10.

Key Research Tools

Several resources aid in sorting through the mass of congressional material to find documents useful in interpreting statutes. These include lists of legislative history documents for particular acts, tables charting the path of legislation through Congress, and collections of source material.

One of the simplest and most widely available legislative history guides is the brief summary printed at the end of each public law, both in its slip law format and in the *Statutes at Large*. This summary provides citations of committee reports and lists the dates of consideration and passage in each house, thus providing quick access to the major sources. Exhibit 8-8 shows this summary in the *Statutes at Large* for the Religious Freedom Restoration Act. Summaries have appeared at the end of each law passed since 1975, and earlier *Statutes at Large* volumes from 1963 to 1974 include separate "Guide to Legislative History" tables.

Another convenient source for information on modern legislation is THOMAS, which includes legislative history summaries for laws enacted since 1973. For laws since 1995, this summary includes hot links to bills, reports, and *Congressional Record* debate. Summaries for earlier laws simply list these materials, but they provide a good head start. The THOMAS summary for the Religious Freedom Restoration Act, for example, has a list of floor actions, with *Congressional Record* references, as well as a chronology of actions in each house and a summary of the law. Information on an act can be retrieved by public law number or found through a keyword search of all the bills (not just enacted laws) for a particular Congress.

For laws enacted before the *Statutes at Large* and THOMAS summaries were prepared, one of the few available guides is the cumulative "History of Bills and Resolutions" in the index volume of the *Congressional Record*. This history goes all the way back to the 40th Congress in 1867, appearing in the final indexes of the *Congressional Globe* and in every volume of the *Congressional Record*. Earlier volumes of the *Globe*, as well as the *Annals of Congress* and the *Register of Debates*, did not include lists of bills but were indexed by subject. (The *Congressional Record* also includes an annual "History of Bills Enacted into Public Law" table, providing basic information on enacted bills. This less detailed table includes bill numbers, report numbers, and dates and pages of *Congressional Record* consideration. It has appeared since 1947 in the annual "Daily Digest" volume.)

United States Code Congressional and Administrative News (USCCAN)

As noted earlier, West Group's *United States Code Congressional and Administrative News* (*USCCAN*) reprints both public laws and committee reports. It is not the most comprehensive source of legislative history information, but because it gathers material in one publication, it is certainly one of the most convenient.

USCCAN is published in monthly pamphlets and in sets of bound volumes for each year. It has two separate series of page numbers, one for the laws (duplicating the *Statutes at Large* pagination since 1975) and another for legislative history documents. Both sets of material are presented in public law number order, with the first page of each law providing a cross-reference to the legislative history material.

LEGISLATIVE HISTORY—H.R. 1308 (S. 578):

HOUSE REPORTS: No. 103-88 (Comm. on the Judiciary).
SENATE REPORTS: No. 103-111 accompanying S. 578 (Comm. on the Judiciary).
CONGRESSIONAL RECORD, Vol. 139 (1993):
    May 11, considered and passed House.
    Oct. 26, 27, S. 578 considered in Senate; H.R. 1308, amended, passed in lieu.
    Nov. 3, House concurred in Senate amendment.
WEEKLY COMPILATION OF PRESIDENTIAL DOCUMENTS, Vol. 29 (1993):
    Nov. 16, Presidential remarks.

STATUTES AT LARGE LEGISLATIVE HISTORY SUMMARY

EXHIBIT 8-8

For most public laws, *USCCAN* reprints one committee report, usually that which most closely matches the bill that became law. For the Religious Freedom Restoration Act, for example, it reprints the report from the Senate Judiciary Committee, S. Rep. 103-111. The report is reprinted in full, with the original pagination indicated, except for the portion containing the text of the legislation. If there had been a conference committee report for this act, it too would have been reprinted in *USCCAN*.

USCCAN also provides references to reports it does not reprint in full. In the case of the Religious Freedom Restoration Act it includes the number of the House report, noting that the Senate language was adopted in the final version of the bill. In addition, it lists the dates of consideration in the *Congressional Record*, but not page numbers.

For a simple act such as the Religious Freedom Restoration Act, *USCCAN* may provide all the information needed for most inquiries. For laws with more complex legislative histories, it is not as satisfactory. Some acts are the combination of several bills. Reports for earlier bills are sometimes noted, but there are no annotations to indicate the subject matter of the bills or the scope of the reports. It may be necessary to track down each of the reports listed to determine which may be relevant. Reports from earlier terms of Congress may also be useful sources, but they are seldom mentioned by *USCCAN*. Material in the *Congressional Record* is not reprinted, even if (as in the case of the Bankruptcy Reform Act of 1994) it is more authoritative than a committee report.

An important feature of *USCCAN* is its monthly publication while Congress is in session, providing convenient access to reports on new legislation. Monthly issues also include a brief "Session Highlights" summary and "Major Bills Pending," a status table indicating bill numbers, House and Senate committees issuing reports, and dates of consideration in each chamber. If a bill has passed, this table shows the public law number, date of approval, and *Statutes at Large* citation. (This information also appears in the annual volumes as a "Major Bills Enacted" table. Another table, "Legislative History," lists acts by public law number and provides bill numbers, report numbers, and dates of consideration. This is simply the information from the *Statutes at Large* legislative summary reprinted in tabular format.)

The strength of *USCCAN* is simple: It publishes the text of laws and reports in one source, and it provides a quick start to legislative history research. Us-

ing this source can save considerable time in tracking down documents, particularly for acts before 1993, for which committee reports are not widely available on the Internet. With improved Internet coverage, *USCCAN* is becoming less essential, but it remains a convenient print resource.

Congressional Information Service (CIS)

The most comprehensive coverage available of legislative history sources is provided by the indexes and compilations of Congressional Information Service (CIS). CIS information is available in print, online through LEXIS-NEXIS, on CD-ROM as *Congressional Masterfile*, and on the Web as Congressional Universe <http://web.lexis-nexis.com/cis/>. As we have seen, CIS also provides access to congressional documents on microfiche and through Congressional Universe. Its great strength, however, is in organizing the mass of congressional documentation into a coherent and accessible body of information.

The major CIS print publication, *CIS/Index*, began in 1970. It is published monthly in separate index and abstract pamphlets, each of which cumulates in an annual bound volume (*CIS/Annual*). The index covers hearings, reports, prints, and documents by subject, name (including names of witnesses and of the organizations they represent), title, and bill number. The abstracts summarize the contents of each item and provide its Superintendent of Documents classification number. CIS arranges the abstracts by committee and assigns classification numbers based on the committee and the type of document. All material from the Senate Judiciary Committee, for example, is classified in the S520s; hearings are S521 and reports are S523. These are followed by item numbers beginning at 1 each year. In the CIS system, the report shown in Exhibit 8-7 is CIS93: S523-5. This number is the key to finding the abstract in *CIS/Index* and the full text of the report in the CIS microfiche set.

The annual bound *CIS/Annual* publication includes another valuable feature, a *Legislative Histories* volume containing extensive summaries of congressional materials leading to the enactment of each public law. CIS provides references to bills, hearings, reports, debates, and presidential documents, not only for the enacted law but for related bills as well. Unlike most other sources, coverage extends to related material from earlier terms of Congress. In the case of the Religious Freedom Restoration Act, for example, CIS notes that bills were introduced in earlier Congresses and that hearings were held by the House in 1990 and 1992, and by the Senate in 1992. Exhibit 8-9 shows the first page of the CIS Religious Freedom Restoration Act summary, listing the reports, the bills introduced in each Congress, and some of the references to floor debate in the *Congressional Record.*

The CIS legislative history summaries come in handy particularly when a number of bills cover the same subject or when several bills are combined and passed as one act. Some "comprehensive" or "omnibus" acts can be the product of numerous separate legislative history paths. The final bill number may bear no relation to the number associated with hearings and reports on a particular issue. Sources like *Statutes at Large*, THOMAS, and *United States Code Congressional and Administrative News (USCCAN)* focus on the final bill and usually neglect these earlier reports. In some instances, they report little or no legislative history. For the National Invasive Species Act of 1996, Pub. L. 104-332, 110 Stat. 4073, for example, none of these sources lists any reports because none were issued on the bill that finally passed. CIS lists two reports on earlier bills addressing the same issues, as well as six hearings.

In some instances, less comprehensive sources simply cannot provide access to the hundreds of relevant documents. For the 468-page Omnibus Trade and Competitiveness Act of 1988, Pub. L. 100-418, 102 Stat. 1107, the *Statutes at Large* summary lists just dates of floor consideration and a presidential statement. THOMAS contains a brief chronology of the bill that finally passed and mentions two related bills. *USCCAN* provides two reports from an earlier, substantially similar bill that had been vetoed. Those two reports take up more than 600 pages, but they are barely the tip of the iceberg. The CIS *Legislative Histories* entry for this act encompasses 117 pages, with abstracts of 55 reports and 251 hearings, as well as a list of 303 bills going back 15 years to the 93rd Congress. Pity the poor researcher who has to wade through all this material, but somewhere in this mass of documentation may be answers to specific questions.

CIS's *Legislative Histories* summaries are highly respected and have few shortcomings. Because they are based on CIS's indexing of congressional documentation other than the *Congressional Record*, however, material in the *Record* tends to receive only cursory coverage. CIS provides little information about important developments on the floor, and it does not distinguish between debates and important documentation inserted in the *Record*. For the Bankruptcy Reform Act of 1994, for example, CIS merely reports "House con-

sideration" on October 4, 1994. It does not indicate that a vital section-by-section description was inserted in that day's *Congressional Record.*

The CIS *Legislative Histories* entries vary somewhat in scope. About 10 to 15 percent of public laws are considered "major enactments" and receive a thorough treatment, including a list of bill versions, page references to debate in the *Congressional Record*, and full abstracts of hearings. The Religious Freedom Restoration Act history shown in Exhibit 8-9 includes these features. For most acts, the summaries include abstracts of the law and reports but no list of bills. The *Congressional Record* references simply list dates, and only the titles, dates, and classification numbers of hearings are indicated. For more information on these hearings, it is necessary to turn to the annual *Abstracts* volume.

CIS has only been publishing *Legislative Histories* volumes since 1984. *Abstracts* volumes from 1970 to 1983 include legislative history summaries for enacted laws, but these simply list the CIS numbers for relevant reports, hearings, and other materials. To find out the nature of these reports and hearings, it is necessary to find the appropriate abstracts in the annual volumes. These summaries are better than other sources available for this period because they are more thorough and include references to earlier Congresses, but they are far less convenient than the more recent *Legislative Histories* treatments.

Material in the *CIS/Index* is available on CD-ROM as *Congressional Masterfile II*. Earlier congressional materials, from the earliest available documents to 1969, are covered in *Congressional Masterfile I*. This index cumulates information from more than 100 volumes of CIS indexes covering reports, documents, hearings, and committee prints. The pre-1970 material does not include a legislative history component like that found in *CIS/Index*, but it does provide access to congressional material by subject.

Congressional Universe on the Web combines the features of the CIS indexes with full-text access to bills, reports, the *Congressional Record*, and other congressional documents. The site presents an impressive menu of ways to find information on bills and congressional publications. It includes indexing and legislative history information back to 1970, but full-text materials are only available beginning in the late 1980s.

Compilations

A compiled legislative history is one in which various congressional sources have been gathered in one publication. Just as *USCCAN*'s reprinting of selected re-

Public Law 103-141

107 Stat. 1488

Religious Freedom Restoration Act of 1993

November 16, 1993

Public Law

1.1 Public Law 103-141, approved Nov. 16, 1993. (H.R. 1308)

(CIS93:PL103-141   3 p.)

"To protect the free exercise of religion."

States the purposes of this act, to provide a claim or defense to persons whose religious exercise is substantially burdened by government, and guarantee application of the compelling interest test set forth in the Supreme Court decisions *Sherbert v. Verner* and *Wisconsin v. Yoder*.

Provides that no Federal, State or local government shall substantially burden a person's exercise of religion unless the burden is the least restrictive means of furthering a compelling governmental interest.

P.L. 103-141 Reports

103rd Congress

2.1 H. Rpt. 103-88 on H.R. 1308, "Religious Freedom Restoration Act of 1993," May 11, 1993.

(CIS93:H523-5   17 p.)
(Y1.1/8:103-88.)

Recommends passage of H.R. 1308, the Religious Freedom Restoration Act of 1993, to reinstate the legal standard for religious freedom cases providing that no Federal, State or local government shall substantially burden a person's exercise of religion unless the burden is the least restrictive means of furthering a compelling governmental interest.

Bill responds to Apr. 1990 Supreme Court decision in *Oregon Employment Division v. Smith*, holding that a law infringing on religious liberties may be held as Constitutional if it is shown to be a rational means of achieving a legitimate State objective.

Includes additional views (p. 14-17).

H.R. 1308 is similar to 102d Congress H.R. 2797.

2.2 S. Rpt. 103-111 on S. 578, "Religious Freedom Restoration Act of 1993," July 27, 1993.

(CIS93:S523-5   38 p.)
(Y1.1/5:103-111.)

Recommends passage of S. 578, the Religious Freedom Restoration Act of 1993, to reinstate the prior legal standard for religious freedom cases providing that no Federal, State or local government shall substantially burden a person's exercise of religion unless the burden is the least restrictive means of furthering a compelling governmental interest.

Bill responds to Apr. 1990 Supreme Court decision in *Oregon Employment Division v. Smith*, holding that a law infringing on religious liberties may be held as Constitutional if it is shown to be a rational means of achieving a legitimate State objective.

Includes additional views (p. 18-24).

S. 578 is similar to 102d Congress S. 2969 and 101st Congress S. 3254.

P.L. 103-141 Bills

101st Congress

HOUSE BILLS

3.1 H.R. 5377 as introduced.

SENATE BILLS

3.2 S. 3254 as introduced.

102nd Congress

HOUSE BILLS

3.3 H.R. 2797 as introduced.

3.4 H.R. 4040 as introduced.

SENATE BILLS

3.5 S. 2969 as introduced.

103rd Congress

ENACTED BILL

3.6 H.R. 1308 as introduced Mar. 11, 1993; as reported and passed by the House May 11, 1993.

COMPANION BILL

3.7 S. 578 as introduced Mar. 11, 1993; as reported by the Senate Judiciary Committee July 27, 1993.

P.L. 103-141 Debate

139 Congressional Record
103rd Congress, 1st Session - 1993

4.1 May 11, House consideration and passage of H.R. 1308, p. H2356.

4.2 Oct. 26, Senate consideration of S. 578, p. S14350.

EXHIBIT 8-9

ports can save some search time, a compilation that provides copies of reports, *Congressional Record* debates, bills, hearings, and other relevant documents can obviously be of great help.

A number of compiled legislative histories have been prepared at the request of congressional committees studying specific issues and are usually published as committee prints. Several such works on complex environmental legislation have been prepared recently by the Congressional Research Service for the Senate Committee on Environment and Public Works, including *A Legislative History of the Solid Waste Disposal Act, As Amended, Together with a Section-by-Section Index* (2 vols., 1991); *A Legislative History of the Safe Drinking Water Act Amendments, 1983-1992, Together with a Section-by-Section Index* (1993); and *A Legislative History of the Clean Air Act Amendments of 1990, Together with a Section-by-Section Index* (6 vols., 1993). Another useful example is the House Committee on Education and Labor's *Legislative History of Public Law 101-336, the Americans with Disabilities Act* (3 vols., 1990).

Other legislative history compilations are prepared by agencies charged with implementing a statute. For example, the National Labor Relations Board has published *Legislative History of the National Labor Relations Act* (2 vols., 1935); *Legislative History of the Labor Management Relations Act* (2 vols., 1948); and *Legislative History of the Labor-Management Reporting and Disclosure Act of 1959* (2 vols., 1959). (All three of these were reissued in commemorative editions, with larger type, on the agency's 50th anniversary in 1985.) A more extensive work is the Food and Drug Administration's *Legislative History of the Federal Food, Drug and Cosmetic Act and Its Amendments* (34 vols., 1979).

Federal Legislative Histories: An Annotated Bibliography and Index to Officially Published Sources (Greenwood Press, 1994), by Bernard D. Reams, Jr., provides a list of compilations published by the federal government between 1900 and 1991, with Superintendent of Documents and CIS numbers, summaries of contents, and indexes by name of act and public law number. The book also contains a 260-page index by bill number, which is twice as long as it should be due to a 128-page typographical error. (The entries on pages 335-463 are reprinted verbatim on pages 463-591.)

Commercial legal publishers, notably William S. Hein & Co., also produce a number of compiled legislative histories of significant acts. Recent Hein compi-

lations include *The Civil Rights Act of 1991: A Legislative History of Public Law 102-166* (7 vols., 1994) and *Federal Telecommunications Law: A Legislative History of the Telecommunications Act of 1996, Pub. L. No. 104-104, 110 Stat. 56 (1996), Including the Communications Decency Act* (21 vols., 1997). Another company, Legislative Histories OnDisc, has recently started publishing CD-ROM compilations, beginning with selected 1996 legislation. It provides searchable PDF versions of slip laws, committee reports, bills, and *Congressional Record* debates. Hearings are not included.

Sometimes legislative history compilations pop up unexpectedly with related material. *United States Code Annotated*, for instance, includes several legislative history documents for Titles 18 and 28, which were reenacted in 1948. The final volume for each title includes excerpts from committee reports, hearings, and remarks in the *Congressional Record*. In the case of Title 18, Crimes and Criminal Procedure, some of this material extends back to 1944. The *USCA* index includes no entries under "Legislative history," so features like this can only be found by happenstance or through working regularly with these titles.

Nancy P. Johnson's *Sources of Compiled Legislative Histories: A Bibliography of Government Documents, Periodical Articles, and Books* (Rothman, 1979-date) is a periodically updated listing of published compilations of legislative history documents, as well as sources that list and discuss these documents. Entries indicate the nature and scope of sources cited. For the Civil Rights Act of 1964, for example, several compilations are listed, including one published by the Equal Employment Opportunity Commission, as well as a journal article and a book chapter discussing the legislative history sources for the act. Entries are arranged chronologically by Congress and public law number, and the volume includes an index by name of act.

There is no guarantee that any legislative history compilation contains *every* relevant document. But most are trustworthy collections providing easy access to the needed material. Some, but not all, have the further advantage of indexing material by the sections of the act discussed. The Senate environmental compilations generally include such indexes, and the NLRB histories go further by indexing particular phrases within each section. Others, such as the FDA compilation, simply collect material chronologically, with no indexing other than lists of contents.

Information on Pending Legislation

Most of the discussion to this point has focused on sources useful in interpreting enacted legislation. Much research into legislative materials, however, concerns action now pending in Congress. These inquiries are not unrelated, as many of the same tables and electronic resources useful for earlier Congresses also carry information on proposed legislation. Because current congressional action is of interest to a wide range of researchers, several resources focus specifically on monitoring and tracking activity in Congress.

Current Awareness Sources

The first step in tracking current legislation is locating background information on the policy issues and the politics. Congressional action is guided as much by political concerns as it is by the issues directly involved in proposed legislation. News sources can explain which of the many bills introduced in Congress actually have a chance of passage, or why a particular piece of legislation is tied up in committee. No official documents would explain, for instance, that a bill was being delayed by a committee chairman as a tactical move to gain support for another bill on a completely unrelated topic.

For current information on Congress and national politics generally, one of the most thorough and highly respected sources is *CQ Weekly* (formerly *Congressional Quarterly Weekly Report*). Each issue summarizes activity on major legislation, providing references to bill numbers and committee reports, explaining the differences between similar bills covering the same subject, and analyzing the political climate for passage. "Boxscore" sidebars provide quick information on bill numbers, latest action, and report numbers, as well as references to earlier *CQ Weekly* coverage. Each issue includes tables of all House and Senate floor votes and a status table for major legislation. Detailed and thorough indexes to *CQ Weekly* are published quarterly.

Congressional Quarterly publishes several other information sources besides *CQ Weekly* and the several reference works already discussed in this chapter. A daily *Congressional Monitor* provides information about scheduled activities on the floor and in committees. *Congressional Quarterly Almanac* is an annual publication summarizing information from the year's *CQ Weekly* issues, and *Congress and the Nation* is a further consolidation discussing major legislation by subject, with each volume covering a four-year period. Much of CQ's reporting, including *CQ Weekly*, is available online through its Washington Alert service and on the Web for a fee <http://www.cq.com/>.

Other newspapers and magazines that focus on developments in Washington are also valuable for keeping on top of current developments. These include *Roll Call: The Newspaper of Capitol Hill* (twice weekly, available on the Web <http://www.rollcall.com> and on LEXIS-NEXIS as the ROLLCL file) and *National Journal* (weekly, accessible through Congressional Universe, LEGI-SLATE, and LEXIS-NEXIS). Newspapers such as the *New York Times* and the *Washington Post* include information on sponsors and committee action to provide a starting point, although they are less oriented to legislative research and rarely provide bill numbers or committee report numbers. The Library of Congress also provides quick access to numerous Web sites with congressional news and analysis <http://lcweb.loc.gov/global/legislative/news.html>.

A readily available official source of information on congressional activity is found in the *Congressional Record*'s "Daily Digest," which summarizes legislation introduced or acted on and committee actions taken. The "Daily Digest" provides a way to monitor current activities and can be browsed through THOMAS, with links to pages for debate and bill texts. GPO Access also has the "Daily Digest" but without links.

Bill-Tracking Resources

Once you have obtained some background information on pending legislation, the next step is to monitor the progress of relevant bills. For this purpose, a number of online systems and status tables are available. These are easiest to use with specific bill numbers, but most also have subject or keyword access.

Most of these resources can be used to research issues currently before Congress and to locate information on bills in previous terms. Their historical value, of course, depends on how many years they cover. GPO Access and THOMAS, for example, have few documents before 1993, but as their store of information grows, so will their value in retrospective research.

THOMAS is an excellent tool for following the path of current legislation. It features bill summary and status pages providing information about committee and floor actions, with links to bills, reports, and discussion in the *Congressional Record*. A search form with several ways to look for bill information is provided. One can simply enter a word or phrase, or search using the more than 10,000 subject terms in LC's Legislative Indexing Vocabulary (LIV). This vocabulary itself can also be browsed or searched to find appropriate subject terms. Searching is also possible by bill number, date, sponsor, or committee, as well as by designating which of 31 stages in the legislative process a bill has reached.

The commercial database systems also provide extensive information about congressional activity, including bill tracking. The LEXIS-NEXIS file BLTRCK (also available through Congressional Universe) and the WESTLAW database US–BILLTRK maintain up-to-date information on the progress of a bill through Congress, with backfiles to 1989 and 1991, respectively. CQ's Washington Alert has similar information, with such additional features as notes with floor remarks indicating the speaker's stand on the bill. LEGI-SLATE has files reviewing the legislative process for each bill and providing an overview of proposed legislation, with archived information back to 1979.

A number of print resources also track current legislation. One of the most commonly used is *Congressional Index* (CCH, weekly), which consists of two loose-leaf volumes, one for each house. *Congressional Index* includes indexes of bills by subject and author, brief summaries of each bill, and status tables showing actions taken. These status tables are thorough and up-to-date, although their value is sometimes hampered by the way they are supplemented. Instead of replacing the entire "Status of House Bills" and "Status of Senate Bills" tables each week, the publisher provides separate pages with supplementary "Current Status" tables and sometimes "Latest Additions" tables. This saves on paper and printing (and therefore on subscription cost), but it means that it may be necessary to check three separate places for information on a bill. *Congressional Index* also contains a variety of other information about Congress, such as committee assignments, lists of pending treaties, tables of voting records, and a weekly newsletter. It does not contain the text of bills or other documents. If available, older volumes of the *Congressional Index*, which began publication in 1938, can be used to find information on the progress of enacted laws and the status of bills in earlier Congresses.

If these electronic and commercial sources are unavailable, two congressional publications can also be of use in following the course of legislation. The "History of Bills and Resolutions" list in the *Congressional Record*'s fortnightly index covers bills that have been acted on within the preceding two weeks, identifying the committee to which each was referred and indicating committee report numbers, pages of consideration in the *Congressional Record,* and public law numbers of enacted legislation. If a bill is listed, all developments since its introduction are indicated. Because not every bill receives action during a given two-week period, it may be necessary to check earlier tables to find

an entry for a specific bill. As noted earlier, a cumulative version of this table is included in the final bound edition of the *Congressional Record* and provides a permanent record of the session's activities.

Another table of bill status appears in *Calendars of the United States House of Representatives and History of Legislation*, which is issued daily and lists bills in either House or Senate that have been reported out of committee. It does not include *all* bills, but it does cover those that are most likely to receive floor consideration. The House calendars for the 104th and 105th Congress are available on the Internet through GPO Access <http://www.access.gpo.gov/congress/cong003.html>.

Directories

Congress is a political institution responsible to an electorate and responsive to constituent concerns about its activities. Unlike the Supreme Court, which dispenses information only through its opinions, members of Congress regularly field questions about their activities. Their extensive staff can provide researchers with valuable insights about the status of pending legislation. The staff of the committee to which a bill has been assigned is often the best source of information about its status. The offices of individual representatives and senators can also be helpful, particularly about legislation that they have introduced.

The basic guide to Congress is the *Official Congressional Directory* (GPO, biennial). Its entries for senators and representatives include biographical sketches, committee assignments, and listings of key staff members. Information is also provided about committee staff and other congressional offices, and some historical information and maps are included. This is a useful directory, available in many libraries and through GPO Access <http://www.access.gpo.gov/congress/cong016.html>. But it is published more than six months after the start of the new term of Congress, so it is of little help at the beginning of the term, when the policy agenda is being shaped. The print version is only updated every two years, but the Internet version is modified during the term to reflect changes. Although the *Official Congressional Directory* is not the most thorough or current directory, it is widely available—and it has been published since 1809, so it is the major source for historical information on congressional organization.

More up-to-date and extensive information, along with more contact points, can be found in two commercial directories. *Congressional Staff Directory* (CQ Staff Directories, three times per year) has color-coded pages listing the staffs of Senate and House members, committees and staffs, and other congressional offices. Brief biographies of more than 3,200 staff members are included, and the volume is thoroughly indexed by name and keyword. It is available electronically on disk as part of *Staff Directories on CD-ROM* and online as CONDIR on LEXIS-NEXIS.

Congressional Yellow Book (Leadership Directories, quarterly) provides the most extensive lists of telephone numbers available, although it lacks the biographical information found in *Congressional Staff Directory*. Each representative has at least half a page, listing contact information (including e-mail and Web sites), committee assignments, and key aides and their areas of responsibility. Entries for committees include descriptions of issues within their jurisdiction, lists of members, and names and numbers of key staff members. The *Yellow Book* is indexed by name and subject. It is available online through WESTLAW as CONGYB.

If these works are unavailable, other directories of the federal government and Washington can provide contact points in Congress. *Washington Information Directory* (discussed in Chapter 6) may be the most useful because it is arranged by subject and indicates the committees and subcommittees with jurisdiction in particular areas. It focuses on organizations and institutions, and does not include as many names as the *Congressional Staff Directory* or *Congressional Yellow Book*.

Two directories that provide detailed information on members of Congress and their districts are *The Almanac of American Politics* (National Journal, biennial; available on LEGI-SLATE and LEXIS-NEXIS) and *Politics in America: Members of Congress in Washington and at Home* (Congressional Quarterly, biennial; available on Washington Alert). Both of these are descriptive works focusing on the members, with background information on their careers and voting records, as well as the states and districts they represent. Neither book provides extensive listings of staff members for further contact. CQ also publishes a smaller pocket guide, *Who's Who in Congress* (annual), with profiles, brief biographies, contact information, and committee assignments for each member.

For historical research, *Biographical Directory of the American Congress, 1774-1996* (CQ Staff Directories, 1997) provides brief entries on more than 11,000 legislators in the Continental Congress and the U.S. Congress. This is an update of a 1989 government publication, *Biographical Directory of the United States Congress, 1774-1989*, S. Doc. 100-34, that is less current but may be available in more libraries.

Guides for Further Research

A few guides focus specifically on sources of congressional research. One of the best is *A Research Guide to Congress: How to Make Congress Work for You* (LEGI-SLATE, 2d ed., 1991), by Judith Manion, Joseph Meringolo, and Robert Oaks. Although this work predates Internet access to congressional information, it includes valuable details on congressional processes and insider tips on obtaining difficult documents and understanding the quirks of the system. The book contains two major sections: "The Legislative Process," explaining procedures from the introduction of a bill to its passage; and "Legislative Research," including information on preparing a legislative history and research in specialized areas of congressional activity. Tables in appendixes list the coverage of *Statutes at Large* volumes and sessions of Congress.

Robert U. Goehlert and Fenton S. Martin's *Congress and Law-Making: Researching the Legislative Process* (ABC-Clio, 2d ed., 1989) contains some useful annotations on sources, but it is less helpful in understanding the idiosyncracies of the legislative process. Chapter 1, "The Legislative Process and How to Trace It," contains valuable insights into the congressional decision-making process and its various intricacies, but the rest of the work is a mixed bag. It is not clear why the chapter on federal legislation begins with discussion of the Federal Register System or why general sources such as PsycINFO or the *British Humanities Index* are included in a work with such a specific focus.

On the other hand, Goehlert and Martin have prepared an excellent and thorough bibliography, *The United States Congress: An Annotated Bibliography, 1980-1993* (Congressional Quarterly, 1995). Arranged by subject with a useful introduction and an extensive index, this work supplements Goehlert and John R. Sayre's unannotated *The United States Congress: A Bibliography* (Free Press, 1982). A 17-page introduction to the 1995 bibliography outlines resources available for studying Congress. This introduction has been expanded and published separately as *How to Research Congress* (Congressional Quarterly, 1996), and an abridged version appears in *Encyclopedia of the United States Congress* as the entry "Congress: Bibliographical Guide." A companion work by Goehlert, Martin, and Sayre, *Members of Congress: A Bibliography* (Congressional Quarterly, 1996), provides unannotated references to books, articles, and dissertations on individual legislators from 1774 through 1995.

CHAPTER 9
Federal Courts

The Supreme Court, undisputedly the most powerful and the most famous judicial body in the nation, decides fewer than 100 cases a year. At the same time thousands of cases every year are decided by lower courts. Each state has its own system of trial and appellate courts, and a federal system of courts sits in every state and territory of the United States.

These court systems serve two major purposes: They provide a forum for the resolution of disputes, and they establish a body of legal principles to guide future action. The Supreme Court's decisions cover areas of major public importance and are applied throughout the country, but there are many legal issues that the Supreme Court has never addressed. For guidance in these areas, we look to decisions of lower federal and state courts.

This chapter focuses on the federal courts, which, unlike state courts, comprise one national system. The federal courts face major issues under the U.S. Constitution and federal statutes, but they are not the place where most litigation takes place. Generally, if you are charged with a crime or sue your neighbor for making too much noise, the trial will take place in state court. Federal courts are courts of *limited jurisdiction*. They have power to hear only certain cases, such as those

involving interpretation of the U.S. Constitution or a federal statute (*federal question jurisdiction*), or those in which the parties are citizens of different states (*diversity jurisdiction*). If these jurisdictional requirements are not met, a case can only be heard in state court.

These rules have been established in part by Article III of the Constitution and in part by Congress. The only court created directly by the Constitution is the Supreme Court. The lower courts were created by Congress in response to the Constitution's charge that it "constitute Tribunals inferior to the supreme Court." Congress established the federal court system in the Judiciary Act of 1789, ch. 20, 1 Stat. 73, and has altered this system a number of times since then.

The Judiciary Act of 1789 created 13 districts—one for each of the 11 states that had ratified the Constitution plus Kentucky and Maine. The districts, except for Kentucky and Maine, were grouped into three circuits (Eastern, Middle, and Southern). The circuit courts, which sat in each district, consisted of the district judge and two Supreme Court justices. Unlike the modern courts of appeals, the circuit courts were principally trial courts. District courts heard mostly admiralty cases, and circuit courts handled diversity cases and major criminal proceedings. The structure of the court system changed over time, with the most significant development occurring in 1891 with the creation of the Circuit Courts of Appeals.

The general trial court in the federal system is the United States District Court. Each state and territory has at least one district, with many states divided geographically into two, three, or four districts. Whether a state is subdivided into more than one district does not depend entirely on population or geography. Oklahoma, with three districts, has considerably fewer people than Massachusetts, Minnesota, or New Jersey, each of which has one district. Alaska and Montana, two of the largest states geographically, have just one district apiece. In all, there are 94 district courts.

Congress determines the jurisdiction of the district courts, and it has enacted guidelines in Titles 18 and 28 of the *U.S. Code*. The three most prominent provisions are 18 U.S.C. § 3231, which gives the district courts jurisdiction over all offenses against the laws of the United States; 28 U.S.C. § 1331, which gives the district courts jurisdiction over civil actions arising under the Constitution, laws, and treaties of the United States; and 28 U.S.C. §1332, which governs suits between citizens of different states. Section 1332 is limited to cases above a minimum dollar amount in controversy; the amount was raised in 1988 from $10,000 to $50,000, and in 1996 to $75,000.

District courts generally operate with one judge presiding over a variety of trials. Three-judge district courts are convened under special circumstances determined by statute, but these are now limited to legislative apportionment cases.

Decisions of the district courts can be appealed to the United States Courts of Appeals, the successors to the Circuit Courts of Appeals created in 1891. The courts of appeals are divided into 11 numbered circuits, each covering several states; the District of Columbia Circuit, which hears appeals from not only the U.S. District Court for the District of Columbia but from numerous federal administrative agencies; and the Federal Circuit, a specialized court hearing appeals in particular subject areas, such as claims against the government, international trade, patents, and public contracts.

Maps of the federal circuits can be found in several sources. In law libraries, one of the most convenient locations is the frontispiece of each volume of the *Federal Reporter* and *Federal Supplement*, the major published sources of federal court opinions. These maps have appeared in every *Federal Reporter* and *Federal Supplement* volume published since 1929 (30 F.2d); the only major changes since that time have been

the split of the Fifth Circuit into the Fifth and Eleventh Circuits in 1980 and the creation of the Federal Circuit two years later. Current maps of the circuits are also available at several sites on the Internet, including the Federal Court Finder <http://www.law.emory.edu/FEDCTS/> and the Federal Court Locator <http://www.cilp.org/Fed-Ct/>. A map of the federal circuits and districts, from the Federal Judicial Center's booklet *Creating the Federal Judicial System*, appears here as Exhibit 9-1.

The courts of appeals generally hear cases in panels of three judges, who vote on the issues and write one or more opinions. Occasionally, all the judges in a circuit will rehear a case decided by a panel, if a *rehearing en banc* is granted. The Ninth Circuit, with 28 judges in nine western states and two Pacific territories, is so large that its *en banc* proceedings are conducted not by the full court but by panels of 11 judges.

The decisions of the courts of appeals are binding on all district judges in their circuit. Sometimes the circuits reach different conclusions about similar issues. Resolving such a conflict among the circuits and establishing national standards is a major reason the Supreme Court agrees to hear cases.

In addition to the district courts and courts of appeals, which exercise jurisdiction over a wide range of legal issues, there are several specialized federal courts.

- Each district has a United States Bankruptcy Court. These operate as adjuncts to the U.S. District Courts to decide cases arising under the Bankruptcy Code, with one or more specialized bankruptcy judges in each district. Bankruptcy court decisions generally are appealed to the district court.
- The United States Court of Federal Claims is a trial court hearing suits against the United States for damages, other than those related to torts or personal injuries. The Court of Federal Claims, established in 1982 (and until 1992 called the United States Claims Court), is the successor to the Court of Claims, which was first created by Congress in 1855 as an advisory body and achieved judicial status in 1863. Court of Federal Claims decisions can be appealed to the U.S. Court of Appeals for the Federal Circuit.
- The United States Court of International Trade, created in 1980 to succeed the Customs Court, acts as the trial court in customs disputes. Like the Court of Federal Claims, its decisions are appealed to the U.S. Court of Appeals for the Federal Circuit.
- The United States Tax Court, created in 1942 as the successor to the Board of Tax Appeals, has jurisdiction over controversies involving payment of

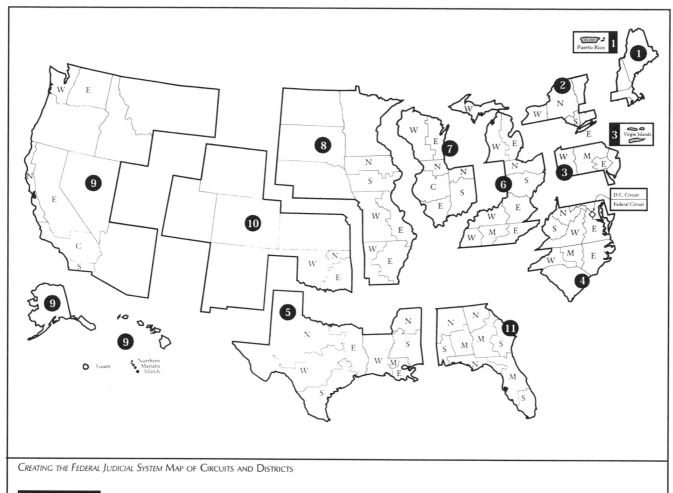

CREATING THE FEDERAL JUDICIAL SYSTEM MAP OF CIRCUITS AND DISTRICTS

EXHIBIT 9-1

taxes. Tax cases can also be heard in the district courts and the Court of Federal Claims, but suits in those courts require that the disputed taxes be paid first. Only in Tax Court can a challenge to a tax be brought before it is paid. Tax Court decisions can be appealed to the regional Courts of Appeals.

- The U.S. Court of Appeals for the Armed Forces (until 1994 known as the U.S. Court of Military Appeals) is the highest court in the military justice system. It reviews decisions of the Courts of Criminal Appeals for the Air Force, Army, Coast Guard, and Navy-Marine Corps, which in turn hear appeals from court-martial proceedings. Decisions of the Court of Appeals for the Armed Forces are final except for certiorari review by the Supreme Court.

- The U.S. Court of Veterans Appeals is one of the newest courts, created in 1988 to review administrative decisions from the Department of Veterans Affairs. Its decisions can be appealed to the Federal Circuit.

Finally, the federal court system has an administrative structure with three branches. The Judicial Conference of the United States, established in 1922 and given its present title in 1948, is the governing body of the court system and considers policy issues affecting the judiciary. The Administrative Office of the United States Courts, created in 1939, handles day-to-day coordination of court operations. The Federal Judicial Center, established in 1967, conducts research on the courts and the administration of justice.

REFERENCE SOURCES

General overviews of court systems and of the role of courts in American government and society have already been discussed in earlier chapters. Chapter 1 introduced several surveys of the legal system, and Chapter 3 covered several encyclopedic works with extensive treatment of the federal courts, particularly *Encyclopedia of the American Judicial System* (Scribner, 3 vols., 1987), edited by Robert J. Janosik. Reference works on constitutional law that were discussed in Chapter 7 can provide insights on the federal courts' consideration of constitutional issues as well as background on the creation and jurisdiction of the court system.

Understanding the Federal Courts, 2d ed. (Administrative Office of the U.S. Courts, 1996) is a 27-page booklet summarizing the organization and operation of the federal court system. It includes a map showing each circuit and district, an organizational chart of federal judicial administration, a directory indicating the number of judgeships authorized for each circuit and district, and a glossary of about 100 judicial terms. This information is also available on the Internet <http://www.uscourts.gov/understanding_courts/899_toc.htm>, although the graphic material is poorly scanned and barely legible.

Another booklet, *Creating the Federal Judicial System* (Federal Judicial Center, 2d ed., 1994), traces the growth of the judiciary from 1789 to the 1990s, with a series of 12 maps showing the allocation of states into circuits and districts over the years. Tables accompanying these maps show the number of circuits, districts, and judges along the way. This booklet is available as a PDF file <http://www.fjc.gov/FEDJUDHIS/creating/creating.pdf>. More extensive historical treatments are available in Erwin C. Surrency's *History of the Federal Courts* (Oceana, 1987) and in the historical appendix to "The Structure of the Federal Judicial System," 15 *Moore's Federal Practice* 100App.-1 to 100App.-42 (Bender, 3d ed., 1997).

Robert A. Carp and Ronald Stidham's *Judicial Process in America* (CQ Press, 4th ed., 1998) is a straightforward text explaining such matters as the history and organization of federal and state judicial systems, criminal and civil court processes, and judicial decision making. *The Federal Courts* (CQ Press, 3d ed., 1998) is an abridgement of this work, with slightly modified versions of 7 of its 12 chapters.

Two books that focus on caseload problems confronting the courts are Richard A. Posner's *The Federal Courts: Challenge and Reform* (Harvard University Press, 1996) and Thomas E. Baker's *Rationing Justice on Appeal: The Problems of the U.S. Courts of Appeals* (West Publishing, 1994). Both books summarize the organization and jurisdiction of the courts, explain the explosive growth of caseloads in recent years and the efforts to deal with it (including streamlining procedures by eliminating oral arguments and limiting publication of decisions), and discuss possible reforms, such as abolishing diversity jurisdiction or reevaluat-

ing the fundamental purpose of federal courts. Baker's book includes an extensive annotated bibliography of books and articles on the Courts of Appeals; this bibliography was reprinted, but in a far less useful format without annotations, as "A Bibliography for the United States Courts of Appeals," 25 Tex. Tech. L. Rev. 335 (1994).

Several law school texts cover the federal courts, focusing primarily on the scope and nature of federal jurisdiction. The classic work in this field, Charles Alan Wright's *Law of Federal Courts* (West Publishing, 5th ed., 1994), addresses these concerns and also provides a general overview of federal court procedures. Erwin Chemerinsky's *Federal Jurisdiction* (Little, Brown, 2d ed., 1994) focuses more specifically on such issues as justiciability, abstention, and review of state court actions. David P. Currie's *Federal Jurisdiction in a Nutshell* (West Publishing, 3d ed., 1990) is a shorter, more manageable introduction to these issues.

The far more extensive treatises on federal practice, Charles Alan Wright et al.'s *Federal Practice and Procedure* (West Publishing, 48 vols., 1969-date) and *Moore's Federal Practice* (Bender, 31 vols., 3d ed., 1997-date) include coverage of jurisdictional issues as well as procedures in trial and appellate courts. Both sets provide rule-by-rule commentaries on the major sets of procedural rules governing federal court actions, with copious notes on court cases interpreting these rules. *Federal Practice and Procedure* devotes 4 volumes to the Federal Rules of Criminal Procedure (1-3A), 19 volumes to the Federal Rules of Civil Procedure (4-12A), 15 volumes to jurisdiction and related matters (13-19), and 11 volumes to date to the Federal Rules of Evidence (21-31). *Moore's Federal Practice* devotes 14 volumes to the Federal Rules of Civil Procedure (1-14) and 5 to the Federal Rules of Criminal Procedure (24-28), as well as 4 volumes to jurisdiction (15-18), 3 to appellate practice (19-21), 2 to Supreme Court practice (22-23), and 1 to admiralty (29). Both treatises are available on CD-ROM; *Federal Practice and Procedure* is available through WESTLAW (FPP database), and *Moore's Federal Practice* is available through LEXIS-NEXIS (GENFED library, MOORES file).

Federal Procedure, Lawyers Edition (West Group [originally Lawyers Cooperative], 1981-date) is a substantial legal encyclopedia somewhat similar to *American Jurisprudence 2d* (*Am. Jur. 2d*) and *Corpus Juris Secundum* (*C.J.S.*), but dealing specifically with issues of federal practice. Because it focuses on the law in the federal system, rather than trying to summarize 50 separate state systems, it is much more practical and specific than the general encyclopedias. Eighty chapters, arranged alphabetically in 48 volumes, spell out procedures in district and appellate courts, as well as before federal administrative agencies. Both civil and criminal topics are covered. Useful "practice pointers" and other asides are included, as well as references to statutes, cases, and journal articles. *Federal Procedure* does not have the persuasive authority of scholarly treatises such as *Federal Practice and Procedure* or *Moore's Federal Practice*, but it is a clear and practical overview of real-life issues confronting federal litigants.

Directories

Court directories can be useful not only for contacting judges or court clerks. They can also outline the jurisdiction of specific courts and provide biographical information on judges.

The official source for contact information, and perhaps the most widely available in general libraries, is the *United States Court Directory* (Administrative Office of the United States Courts, annual). This is a serviceable directory with addresses and telephone numbers for judges, clerks, and other court personnel, but neither background nor biographical information. It is a substantial volume of more than 500 pages, primarily because it is arranged in a tabular format with lots of white space and few listings on each page. The directory is arranged by court and includes an alphabetical index of names.

Two commercial directories contain more extensive coverage of the federal courts. These are published as part of the familiar *Staff Directories* and *Yellow Books* series: *Judicial Staff Directory* (CQ Staff Directories, annual) and *Judicial Yellow Book* (Leadership Directories, semiannual). Each provides contact information for a wide range of personnel in the federal court system, not just judges but also court clerks, secretaries, staff attorneys, and law clerks, as well as telephone numbers and Web sites. The *Judicial Staff Directory* also has information on the Department of Justice and listings of U.S. attorneys and assistant U.S. attorneys for each district. The volume features 2,000 biographies of judges and staffers, and an index of all 15,000 listed individuals. Biographies are included for most, but not all, judges. The *Judicial Yellow Book* has a more convenient format, with biographical information accompanying listings rather than in a separate section. Photographs of a few judges are included. The *Judicial Yellow Book* contains less biographical information on personnel other than judges, but it does list educational institutions for most law clerks and some secretaries.

It also provides brief coverage of state appellate courts. The *Judicial Yellow Book* is available online through both LEXIS-NEXIS (YBJUD) and WESTLAW (JUDYB). The *Judicial Staff Directory* is part of *Staff Directories on CD-ROM* and is on LEXIS-NEXIS as the JUDDIR file.

The most thorough source for biographical information on federal judges is *Almanac of the Federal Judiciary* (Aspen Law & Business, 2 vols., updated semiannually). Volume 1 covers the district courts and specialized courts, while Volume 2 covers the Supreme Court and the courts of appeals. This set includes the basic data found in other sources, such as address, education, and work experience, but it also has descriptions of judges' noteworthy rulings and media coverage. The most interesting and controversial feature is lawyers' evaluations of the judges' ability and temperament. These evaluations are published anonymously, and some can be biting. Some judges are described as "unfit for service on the bench," "the worst you could ever imagine," or "the most pompous judge to sit on the federal bench." For a particular judge, one lawyer advises, "Spell out a great deal in your briefs—he needs a lot of help." Because few lawyers would lambaste a judge on the record, these anonymous evaluations provide rare insights into perceptions of judges and are often quoted in the press. Circuit Judge Alex Kozinski has referred to these "much-fretted-about" evaluations as a feature "which many judges pretend to ignore but in fact read assiduously"(*Standing Committee on Discipline v. Yagman*, 55 F.3d 1430, 1434 [9th Cir. 1995]). The evaluations appear only for court of appeals and district court judges, and many recent appointees are not evaluated until they have served for several years. The *Almanac of the Federal Judiciary* is available through WESTLAW as the AFJ database, but minus the media coverage and lawyers' evaluations sections.

Several directories cover both federal and state courts, and may be the first place to turn to locate a judge whose jurisdiction is not known. The most extensive of these, *The American Bench* (Forster-Long, biennial), is primarily a biographical work. Treatment of the federal judiciary is strangely bifurcated. Judges of appellate and specialized courts are included in a "United States Courts" section at the front of the volume, while district court judges are profiled separately under each state. Each jurisdictional section begins with a list of courts and judges, followed by alphabetically arranged biographies containing addresses and telephone numbers. An alphabetical name index at the front of the volume indicates the jurisdictions for all judges listed (but not the page numbers on which their biographies appear). Because information on federal judges is more conveniently available elsewhere, this comprehensive directory is more valuable for its coverage of state court judges.

Two shorter directories providing names and addresses are *WANT's Federal-State Court Directory* (WANT Publishing, annual) and *BNA's Directory of State and Federal Courts, Judges, and Clerks* (BNA, biennial). Of these, WANT provides more thorough information on federal courts, with address, telephone number, and date of appointment indicated for each judge; BNA's directory, which originally covered just state courts, simply provides one address for each circuit or district. Neither work includes biographical information. An abridged version of WANT's directory is available on the Internet <http://www.courts.com/directory.html>.

More comprehensive Internet coverage is accessible through Infospace <http://www.infospace.com>, or FindLaw <http://www.findlaw.com/casecode/dir/index.html>. These directories of courts, with information from Carroll Publishing Company, provide judges' names, addresses, and telephone numbers. These directories cover all levels of the federal court system, and include administrative offices and regional Department of Justice officials as well. The same directory information is also available from the FindLaw pages that cover individual courts.

West's Legal Directory, available through WESTLAW, includes coverage of judges and courts. The WLD-COURT and WLD-JUDGE databases contain contact information for court offices; WLD-JUDGE also provides biographical data on judges that is often more extensive than other sources, including lists of published works, representative cases, and classes taught. This information does not appear to be included in the Internet version of WLD <http://www.wld.com>.

Historical information on the federal bench can be found in such standard sources as the *Dictionary of American Biography* (Scribner's, 1928-date) or *Who Was Who in America* (Marquis, 1943-date). The Judicial Conference's *Judges of the United States* (GPO, 2d ed., 1983) includes brief biographical entries on more than 2,600 judges, but these are terse entries limited to standard data such as birth and death dates, education, and employment history. Coverage also tips heavily in favor of contemporary judges; just 15 lines of text profile John Jay, the first chief justice, but 144 lines profile Ruth Bader Ginsburg, who had just been

appointed to the court of appeals in 1980. The preface mentions changes planned for the third edition, but none has appeared.

One of the simplest and most readily available sources for identifying federal judges is a list that appears in the front of each volume of the *Federal Reporter* and *Federal Supplement*. These lists contain no contact information or biographical background, but they provide concise snapshots of the makeup of a court as of each volume's publication. Footnotes indicate changes and provide the dates of appointments, resignations, retirements, and deaths. These lists have been included in the reporter volumes since 1882 (12 Fed.). Up to 1992, every volume in both series lists both appellate and trial judges, but recent volumes (since 953 F.2d and 780 F. Supp.) limit coverage to one tier of the federal system. Judges of the courts of appeals are now listed in the *Federal Reporter* and district court judges in *Federal Supplement*. Judges of other specialized federal courts are generally listed in the front of reporters covering their work.

Information on nineteenth-century federal judges may be found in *Federal Cases*, West's compilation of pre-1880 opinions. Volume 1 includes a list of all judges, by court, indicating terms of service, and Volume 30 contains brief biographical sketches of each judge and reprints retirement tributes from the original reporter volumes. This tradition of printing tributes to departing judges, as well as memorials to departed judges, continues in the *Federal Reporter* and *Federal Supplement*. A note on a volume's spine indicates if it includes such proceedings or other special material.

Statistics

Several sources provide statistics on federal court activity. The Administrative Office of the United States Courts has been issuing an annual report since 1939-40, its first year in operation. Currently titled *Judicial Business of the United States Courts*, the annual report contains a narrative introduction and hundreds of pages of detailed tables providing information on cases commenced, pending, and terminated in the Supreme Court, courts of appeals, district courts, and bankruptcy courts. This report is most frequently found in a bound compilation along with *Reports of the Proceedings of the Judicial Conference of the United States* and *Activities of the Administrative Office of the United States Courts*. Some of the statistics are also printed in other Administrative Office series, including *Federal Judicial Caseload Statistics* (annual) and *Statistical Tables for the Federal Judiciary* (semiannual); even more information on specific districts is available in *Federal Court Management Statistics* (annual).

A wide variety of statistics on federal criminal law enforcement and other aspects of criminal justice are available in the Bureau of Justice Statistics' *Sourcebook of Criminal Justice Statistics*. The *Sourcebook* covers a range of matters, such as public attitudes toward crime and characteristics of persons arrested. Section 5, "Judicial Processing of Defendants," includes numerous tables on the activities of federal law enforcement agencies, United States attorneys, and the federal courts. The Bureau's homepage <http://www.ojp.usdoj.gov/bjs/> provides Internet access to the *Sourcebook* data and other statistics.

Statistics on nearly four million civil cases in federal district court are also available on the Internet <http://teddy.law.cornell.edu/questata.htm>. One can search this database by such criteria as subject matter, jurisdictional basis, or damages awarded. Searches are limited, however, to completed trials or to cases from one year at a time.

SOURCES FOR FEDERAL COURT DECISIONS

Most federal court opinions are not published in official reporters similar to *U.S. Reports*. The only official paper versions issued by the courts are individual slip opinions, which are not widely distributed and are rarely retained by libraries. Historically, researchers have relied on commercial publications and databases as the only available sources for lower federal court opinions. However, recent opinions are now available on the Internet directly from the government or through non-profit enterprises.

Federal Reporter and Federal Supplement

The most comprehensive published sources of lower court opinions are two sets of reporters from West Group (formerly West Publishing Company): *Federal Reporter* for court of appeals decisions and *Federal Supplement* for district court decisions. Even with increased use of electronic sources, these reporters are generally accepted as the standard repositories of these opinions.

In the nineteenth century, lower federal court opinions were published in dozens of separate series of reporters, most covering specific courts or geographic regions. In 1880, however, West began publishing the *Federal Reporter*, with cases from federal courts all over the country. Other commercial series, such as *Fed-*

eral Decisions (Gilbert Book Co., 30 vols., 1884-89) and *United States Courts of Appeals Reports* (Banks, 63 vols., 1893-99), were published around the same time, but only the *Federal Reporter* survived. In 1925, after 300 volumes, it began a second series (F.2d). Volume 999 of the second series in 1993 was followed by Volume 1 of the current third series (F.3d). Together, these three series contain more than 1,400 volumes of federal court decisions, with more than 30 volumes being added each year.

For more than 50 years, the *Federal Reporter* contained decisions from both the courts of appeals and the district courts. Then, in 1932, West launched a separate publication, *Federal Supplement* (F. Supp.), for the district court decisions. Although these opinions do not have as much precedential importance as court of appeals decisions, they can be persuasive on issues that the appellate courts have not addressed. They are also useful in understanding the factual and procedural background of cases. Only a small percentage of district court decisions are published, but the series still produces about 40 volumes a year. After 999 volumes, it began its second series (F. Supp. 2d) in 1998.

Federal Reporter and *Federal Supplement* are both published first in weekly paperback advance sheets, then in bound volumes cumulating the cases from two or more advance sheets. Because so many federal court decisions are issued, the advance sheets for these reporters can be sometimes be 1,000 pages or more.

Both reporters include with each case editorial material that is useful in legal research: one-paragraph synopses summarizing the holding, and numbered headnotes summarizing each point of law in the case. These features are shown in Exhibit 9-2, on the first pages of a court of appeals decision, *Davis v. City of Sioux City*, in a recent *Federal Reporter* volume. In the second page of Exhibit 9-2 are the conclusion of the court's opinion and the beginning of a separate opinion concurring in part and dissenting in part. Note in the last paragraph of the left column the bracketed and boldface **[3]**, which indicates that the discussion in this paragraph corresponds to the point of law summarized in headnote number 3 on the first page in Exhibit 9-2.

Even though *Federal Reporter* and *Federal Supplement* publish dozens of volumes every year, they don't include all federal cases. The volumes contain only judicial opinions on issues of law, not such other case outcomes as settlements or jury verdicts. Their purpose is not to serve as a comprehensive record of federal judicial business but to guide future courts and lawyers in resolving legal issues.

DAVIS v. CITY OF SIOUX CITY

1365

Cite as 115 F.3d 1365 (8th Cir. 1997)

Cheryl A. DAVIS, Appellee,

Thomas R. Davis, Plaintiff,

v.

CITY OF SIOUX CITY, Appellant.

No. 96–2194.

United States Court of Appeals,
Eighth Circuit.

Submitted Jan. 16, 1997.

Decided June 18, 1997.

Rehearing and Suggestion for Rehearing
En Banc Denied Aug. 11, 1997.*

Employee sued her former employer for retaliation and hostile environment sexual harassment in violation of Title VII. The United States District Court for the Northern District of Iowa, Donald E. O'Brien, J., entered judgment on jury verdict in favor of employee. Employer appealed. The Court of Appeals, Beam, Circuit Judge, held that: (1) employee's transfer to higher paying job after she complained of supervisor's sexual harassment was sufficiently adverse to support retaliation claim, but (2) instructions did not adequately and fairly submit issues to jury on hostile environment claim.

Affirmed in part and reversed in part.

Richard S. Arnold, Chief Judge, filed opinion concurring in part and dissenting in part.

1. Federal Courts ⊃822

Court of Appeals reviews District Court's jury instructions for abuse of discretion, considering whether, when taken as a whole, instructions fairly and adequately submitted issues to jury.

2. Civil Rights ⊃167, 371

In situation of quid pro quo sexual harassment by supervisor, where harassment results in tangible detriment to subordinate employee, liability under Title VII is imputed to employer but in cases alleging hostile environment sexual harassment by supervisor, employer is liable only if employer knew or should have known of hostile environment.

Civil Rights Act of 1964, § 701 et seq., as amended, 42 U.S.C.A. § 2000e et seq.

3. Master and Servant ⊃30(6.10)

Employee's transfer to higher paying position after she complained of supervisor's sexual harassment was sufficiently adverse to support retaliation claim; position lacked supervisory status, had fewer opportunities for salary increases, and offered little opportunity for advancement. Civil Rights Act of 1964, § 701 et seq., as amended, 42 U.S.C.A. § 2000e et seq.

———

James Raymond Villone, Sioux City, IA, argued, for appellant.

Robert L. Sikma, argued (Mayer Kanter, Sioux City, IA, on the brief), for appellee.

Before RICHARD S. ARNOLD, Chief Judge, ROSS and BEAM, Circuit Judges.

BEAM, Circuit Judge.

The City of Sioux City appeals from a jury verdict in favor of Cheryl Davis on her claims of retaliation and hostile environment sexual harassment. We affirm in part and reverse in part.

I. BACKGROUND

Cheryl Davis began working for the City of Sioux City (City) in the City Clerk's Office in 1977. In 1984, Davis became a Deputy Clerk. From 1982 to 1992, Bill Gross was the City Clerk and Davis's supervisor. Gross, in turn, reported directly to the City Council, which had sole responsibility for hiring, firing and disciplining him.

During the first nine years that Davis worked under Gross, Davis claims Gross engaged in some inappropriate behavior toward her. However, Davis did not feel that this behavior was sufficiently egregious to report. In January 1991, however, Gross suffered a heart attack. Following his return from medical leave, and especially in late 1991 and early 1992, Gross's inappropriate behavior

* Chief Judge Richard S. Arnold and Judge McMillian would grant the suggestion for rehearing en banc of appellee Cheryl A. Davis. Judge McMillian would also grant the suggestion for rehearing en banc of appellant City of Sioux City.

EXHIBIT 9-2

DAVIS v. CITY OF SIOUX CITY 1369
Cite as 115 F.3d 1365 (8th Cir. 1997)

case, the usual basis for a finding of agency will often disappear. *In such cases, the employer should not be held liable unless the employer itself has engaged in some degree of culpable behavior. For example, the employer could be held liable if it knew or should have known of the harassment and failed to take appropriate remedial action.*

Id. at 469 (citations and quotations omitted) (emphasis added).[7]

Therefore, we find that the district court abused its discretion in not instructing the jury on the knew or should have known employer liability standard. Consequently, we reverse and remand for a new trial on this issue. On retrial, the jury may well reach the same verdict, but must do so after being instructed on the appropriate liability standards.

B. Retaliation Claim

To prove unlawful retaliation, Davis must show that she complained of discrimination, the City took adverse action against her, and the adverse action was causally related to her complaint. *Marzec v. Marsh,* 990 F.2d 393, 396 (8th Cir.1993). At trial, Davis argued that her previous position as Deputy Clerk was eliminated, and her transfer to the less desirable property officer position was effectuated, in retaliation for filing her complaint about Gross. The jury agreed and awarded sizable damages. On appeal, the City argues that Davis's transfer was not sufficiently adverse to support the jury's verdict.

[3] On review of the jury's verdict, we view the evidence in the light most favorable to the prevailing party. *Elliott v. Byers,* 975 F.2d 1375, 1376 (8th Cir.1992). Applying this standard, we find that Davis's transfer was sufficiently adverse to support the jury's verdict on the retaliation claim. The City points to Davis's salary increase as evidence that the job transfer was not adverse. The jury apparently put more weight on Davis's evidence that the new position lacked supervisory status, had fewer opportunities for salary increases, and offered Davis little opportunity for advancement. The jury was free to credit this evidence and we will not disturb its verdict.

We have considered the remainder of the City's arguments and find them to be without merit.

III. CONCLUSION

Because the district court erred in instructing the jury on Davis's hostile environment sexual harassment claim, we reverse and remand that claim for a new trial. Finding no error in the jury's verdict for Davis on the retaliation claim, we affirm as to that claim. The case is remanded to the district court for proceedings consistent with this opinion.

RICHARD S. ARNOLD, Chief Judge, concurring in part and dissenting in part.

I agree with the Court that the judgment on the retaliation claim should be upheld, but I respectfully dissent from the Court's action on the harassment claim.

In my view, the District Court's instructions to the jury were correct. If we look to general "agency principles," *Meritor Savings Bank v. Vinson,* 477 U.S. 57, 72, 106 S.Ct. 2399, 2408, 91 L.Ed.2d 49 (1986), it was entirely proper to tell the jury that they could hold the city liable for Gross's conduct if that conduct was within the scope of his employment. Moreover, I do not believe that the "knew or should have known" language which the Court quotes from certain of our previous opinions was intended to establish a controlling rule of law in cases, like the present one, where the alleged harasser is a high-level supervisor. No such requirement is imposed in other kinds of tort cases, and I do not see why a special rule of law, particularly protective of corporate or governmental entities who are sued, should be fashioned for sexual-harassment cases.

I briefly restate the facts. Mr. Gross was the top person in the city clerk's office. He

---

7. *Meritor* suggests that another example of an employer's culpable conduct could be the absence of an anti-sexual harassment policy with a supervisor-bypass provision. 477 U.S. at 72, 106 S.Ct. at 2408. Because such a policy was in effect in this case, however, we need not address this issue.

EXHIBIT 9-2 (continued)

Furthermore, unlike the tightly controlled docket of the Supreme Court, the lower federal courts are swamped with cases that they must decide. More than 300,000 cases a year commence in federal district courts, and more than 50,000 appeals are filed in the courts of appeals. The Supreme Court need not repeatedly hear cases on the same issues, unlike the lower courts. To limit the amount of published case law, each court of appeals has rules establishing criteria for deciding whether opinions should be published. Generally, decisions are published if they establish or clarify rules of law, if they resolve or create conflicts with other decisions, or if they involve matters of public concern.

Traditionally, if a court of appeals opinion was not published in the *Federal Reporter*, it could not be cited as precedent. Today, however, many decisions that are not printed are available through electronic databases. With increased electronic dissemination, the rule against citation of "unpublished" opinions is gradually being displaced in several circuits. Such opinions are generally not considered binding precedent in subsequent cases, but they can be cited as persuasive authority. Some courts still prohibit citation of cases found only in electronic form, however, and rules vary dramatically between circuits. The Fifth Circuit has two distinct rules, one for citing cases decided before January 1, 1996, and the other for cases since that date. A recent law review comment, Kirt Shuldberg, "Digital Influence: Technology and Unpublished Opinions in the Federal Courts of Appeals," 85 Cal. L. Rev. 541 (1997), provides a thorough survey of the circuits' rules regarding unpublished opinions.

Other Published Reporters

Besides *Federal Reporter* and *Federal Supplement*, several other reporters offer access to lower federal court opinions. Some of these publish decisions of the courts of appeals and district courts that may not be included in those series, while others cover specialized courts. Several of these other reporters are published by West and contain the same editorial features as *Federal Reporter* and *Federal Supplement*.

Pre-*Federal Reporter* Cases

Federal court cases decided before the *Federal Reporter* began publication in 1880 were compiled by West in 1894 to 1897 in a 30-volume set, *Federal Cases*. This set contains more than 18,000 cases, arranged alphabetically, with a few cases that had been omitted from the main series included in an appendix. Although these cases are cited infrequently in modern court opinions, they are invaluable sources of legal history. Occasion-ally, they even contain human drama, as in *United States v. Holmes*, 26 F. Cas. 360 (C.C.E.D. Pa. 1842) (No. 15,383), in which crew members from a capsized ship kept an overcrowded lifeboat afloat by throwing some of the passengers overboard.

Specialized Topics

Federal Reporter and *Federal Supplement* are the only reporters containing decisions of the lower federal courts regardless of subject. A number of other reporters cover specialized areas, along with decisions from state courts and administrative agencies.

Federal Rules Decisions (*F.R.D.*) is a specialized reporter of district court decisions applying the Federal Rules of Civil Procedure and the Federal Rules of Criminal Procedure. It is published by West in monthly pamphlets and periodic bound volumes, and follows the same editorial format as *Federal Supplement*. The reporter began in 1940, two years after the Federal Rules of Civil Procedure were adopted. *F.R.D.* is an essential part of any collection of federal court decisions, but it is an odd little reporter because it by no means contains all decisions involving the application of the rules. Its volumes include a variety of other materials as well, such as articles and proceedings of judicial conferences.

Two other series of reporters on federal procedural issues are *Federal Rules Service* and *Federal Rules of Evidence Service*. *Federal Rules Service* began publication in 1939, a year before *Federal Rules Decisions*; *Federal Rules of Evidence Service* has been published since 1979. These series were formerly published by one of West's competitors (first Callaghan & Co., then Lawyers Cooperative), but now they too have the West Group imprint. They do not, however, have the same synopses and headnotes as other West reporters. They are edited not by West but by Pike & Fischer, Inc., with notes keyed to separate digests accompanying these sets. It is odd that one publisher issues two versions of the same decisions, with different editorial treatments.

Of the other specialized reporters, two (*West's Education Law Reporter* and *West's Social Security Reporting Service*) simply reprint decisions from West's other reporters, complete with the original pagination and editorial treatment. Most specialized reporters, however, are from other publishers; instead of West headnotes, they reflect a wide variety of editorial approaches. Many are published first as part of weekly or biweekly loose-leaf services, and then compiled in permanent binders or reissued in bound volumes. Table 9-1 presents a selected subject listing of these specialized reporters.

Exhibit 9-3 shows the first page of *Davis v. City of Sioux City* in a specialized reporter, *Fair Employment Practice Cases*. Note that the text of the decision is the same as that in Exhibit 9-2, but that the court opinion is preceded by a different set of headnotes prepared by the publisher, focusing specifically on sexual harassment issues.

Specialized Courts

The decisions of most specialized federal courts are published in separate series of reporters.

United States Bankruptcy Courts. *West's Bankruptcy Reporter* (1980-date) contains decisions of the U.S. Bankruptcy Courts, as well as bankruptcy decisions of the U.S. district courts. It also reprints bankruptcy cases from the Supreme Court and Courts of Appeals, but it retains the *Supreme Court Reporter* and *Federal Reporter* pagination for these cases. Other sources for decisions of bankruptcy courts include *Bankruptcy Court Decisions* (CRR Publishing Co., 1974-date), *Bankruptcy Law Reports* (CCH, 1948-date), and *Collier Bankruptcy Cases* (Bender, 1974-date).

United States Court of Federal Claims. West's *Federal Claims Reporter* (1982-date), originally titled *United States Claims Court Reporter*, contains decisions of this specialized trial court. Like *West's Bankruptcy Reporter*, it reprints appellate cases from the Court of Appeals for the Federal Circuit and occasionally from the Supreme Court. Decisions of the court's predecessor, the Court of Claims, appeared in the *Federal Reporter* from 1929 to 1932 and from 1960 to 1982, and in the *Federal Supplement* from 1932 to 1960. They

---

TABLE 9-1

SPECIALIZED REPORTERS, BY SUBJECT

Admiralty	*American Maritime Cases* (American Maritime Cases, Inc., 1923-date)
Antitrust and Trade Regulation	*Trade Cases* (CCH, 1948-date)
Commercial Law	*Uniform Commercial Code Reporting Service* (West Group [originally Callaghan & Co.], 1965-date)
Disabilities Law	*Accommodating Disabilities Decisions* (CCH, 1994-date)
	Americans with Disabilities Cases (BNA, 1993-date)
	Americans with Disabilities Decisions (West Group [originally Lawyers Cooperative Publishing], 1993-date)
	Individuals with Disabilities Education Law Report (formerly *Education for the Handicapped Law Report*) (LRP Publication, 1978-date)
	National Disability Law Reporter (LRP Publications, 1990-date)
Employee Benefits	*Employee Benefits Cases* (BNA, 1981-date)
Employment Rights	*Employment Practices Decisions* (CCH, 1971-date)
	Fair Employment Practice Cases (BNA, 1969-date)
	Individual Employment Rights Cases (BNA, 1987-date)
	Wage and Hour Cases (BNA, 1942-date)
Environmental Law	*Environment Reporter Cases* (BNA, 1970-date)
Intellectual Property	*Copyright Law Decisions* (CCH, 1981-date)
	United States Patents Quarterly (BNA, 1929-date)
Labor Law	*Labor Cases* (CCH, 1940-date)
	Labor Relations Reference Manual (BNA, 1937-date)
Native Americans	*Indian Law Reporter* (American Indian Lawyer Training Program, Inc., 1974-date)
News Media	*Media Law Reporter* (BNA, 1978-date)
Occupational Safety	*Occupational Safety and Health Cases* (BNA, 1974-date)
	Occupational Safety and Health Decisions (CCH, 1973-date)
Products Liability	*Products Liability Reports* (CCH, 1963-date)
Securities	*Federal Securities Law Reports* (CCH, 1945-date)
Taxation	*American Federal Tax Reports* (RIA [formerly Prentice-Hall], 1924-date)
	United States Tax Cases (CCH, 1937-date)
Telecommunications	*Communications Regulations* (formerly *Radio Regulation*) (Pike & Fischer, 1948-date)
Transportation	*Aviation Cases* (CCH, 1947-date)
	Federal Carriers Cases (CCH, 1940-date)
Utilities	*Public Utilities Reports* (Public Utilities Reports, Inc., 1915-date)

the EPA bars some of those claims, because each separate paycheck is a separate violation and some of plaintiff's claims arose more than two years before the filing of this complaint.

Plaintiff does not dispute that her "damages are limited to events which occurred within 300 days prior to filing the original charge of discrimination," a statement which responds not at all to defendant's arguments about the claims (as opposed to the damages). Plaintiff further asserts that, while the limitations period under the EPA is two years, it is two years from the date of the EEOC charge because she included the EPA claim in that charge.

Once again, neither party submitted legal authority for these positions in disregard for local rule CDIL 7.1(B), so once again I recommend that the motion on this issue be denied.

V. CONCLUSION

The motion should be allowed in part (punitive damages should be stricken from all prayers for relief) and denied in all other regards. The parties are advised that any objection to this Report and Recommendation must be filed in writing with the Clerk within ten (10) working days after service of this Report and Recommendation. Fed.R.Civ.P. 72(b); 29 U.S.C. §636(b)(1). Failure to object will constitute a waiver of objections on appeal. *Video Views Inc. v. Studio 21, Ltd.*, 797 F.3d 538 (7th Cir. 1986).

DAVIS v. CITY OF SIOUX CITY

U.S. Court of Appeals, Eighth Circuit

CHERYL A. DAVIS, Appellee, THOMAS R. DAVIS, Plaintiff v. CITY OF SIOUX CITY, Appellant, No. 96-2194, June 18, 1997; Rehearing denied August 11, 1997

CIVIL RIGHTS ACT OF 1964

1. Sexual harassment ►108.415909

Employer is not liable for hostile environment sexual harassment by supervisor unless it knew or should have known of harassment and failed to take appropriate remedial action.

2. Sexual harassment ►108.415925

Jury was entitled to find that female deputy city clerk whose position was eliminated after she filed sexual harassment complaint against male city clerk and who was transferred to less desirable property officer position suffered adverse action that was causally related to her complaint, even though city points to her salary increase, where jury was free to put more weight on her evidence that new position lacked supervisory status, had fewer opportunities for salary increases, and offered her little opportunity for advancement.

Appeal from the U.S. District Court for the Northern District of Iowa. Affirmed in part, and reversed and remanded in part.

James R. Villone, Sioux City, Iowa, for appellant.

Robert L. Sikma (Mayer Kanter, on brief), Sioux City, Iowa, for appellee.

Before RICHARD S. ARNOLD, Chief Judge, ROSS, Senior Circuit Judge, and BEAM, Circuit Judge.

Full Text of Opinion

C. ARLEN BEAM, Circuit Judge: — The City of Sioux City appeals from a jury verdict in favor of Cheryl Davis on her claims of retaliation and hostile environment sexual harassment. We affirm in part and reverse in part.

I. BACKGROUND

Cheryl Davis began working for the City of Sioux City (City) in the City Clerk's Office in 1977. In 1984, Davis became a Deputy Clerk. From 1982 to 1992, Bill Gross was the City Clerk and Davis's supervisor. Gross, in turn, reported directly to the City Council, which had sole responsibility for hiring, firing and disciplining him.

During the first nine years that Davis worked under Gross, Davis claims Gross engaged in some inappropriate behavior toward her. However, Davis did not feel that this behavior was sufficiently egregious to report. In January 1991, however, Gross suffered a heart attack. Following his return from medical leave, and especially in late 1991 and early 1992, Gross's inappropriate behavior toward Davis escalated. Such conduct included, but was not limited to: (1) spreading rumors that Davis was having extra-marital affairs; (2) following Davis to the restroom to make sure she was using the restroom and not talking to men instead; (3) calling the head of another department to see whether Davis was on the phone with men from that department; and (4) commenting that Davis's work attire was inappropriate, e.g., that her skirts were too short. Although Davis discussed this behavior with Gross, the situation did not improve and the behavior did not cease.

EXHIBIT 9-3

were also published by the government as *Court of Claims Reports* (231 vols., 1863-1982). The earliest decisions appear in *Reports from the Court of Claims Submitted to the House of Representatives* (18 vols., 1856-63). Federal claims cases are also published in *Contract Cases Federal* (CCH, 1944-date).

United States Court of International Trade. Decisions of the Court of International Trade are published by the U.S. Government Printing Office in the *U.S. Court of International Trade Reports* (1980-date), but the most convenient source is the *Federal Supplement*, where they appear along with district court decisions. Court of International Trade decisions are appealed to the Federal Circuit; these appellate decisions are also published by the government in *Cases Decided in United States Court of Appeals for the Federal Circuit* (1982-date), but again the more common source is the commercial reporter from West, *Federal Reporter*. Cases also appear in *International Trade Reporter Decisions* (BNA, 1980-date).

These reporters published by the government for the Court of International Trade and the Federal Circuit are successors to publications of these courts' predecessors, *United States Customs Court Reports* (85 vols., 1938-80) and *United States Court of Customs and Patent Appeals Cases* (69 vols., 1910-82). Volumes 17 through 59 of the latter series were published in two separate parts, one for customs cases and the other for patent cases.

United States Tax Court. The only major federal court for which West does not publish decisions is the United States Tax Court. Its decisions are officially published by the government in *Reports of the United States Tax Court* (1942-date; preceded by *Reports of the United States Board of Tax Appeals*, 47 vols., 1924-42). Official advance sheets are published, but the quickest sources for new decisions are the loose-leaf versions issued by the major tax publishers, CCH and RIA. The Tax Court also issues memorandum opinions, but it does not publish them in bound volumes. These opinions resolve factual disputes but do not normally interpret the tax code, and, thus, they have somewhat less precedential value than the regular decisions. They are published in *Tax Court Memorandum Decisions* (CCH, 1946-date) and *T.C. Memorandum Decisions* (RIA [formerly Prentice-Hall], 1928-date).

United States Court of Appeals for the Armed Forces. *West's Military Justice Reporter* (1978-date) contains decisions of the U.S. Court of Appeals for the Armed Forces, until 1994 known as the U.S. Court of Military Appeals, as well as selected decisions of the Courts of Criminal Appeals for the individual branches of the service. Decisions predating *West's Military Justice Reporter* were published in *Court-Martial Reports* (Lawyers Cooperative, 50 vols., 1951-75), with those of the Court of Appeals' predecessor also reprinted in a separate 23-volume series, *Decisions of the United States Court of Military Appeals*.

United States Court of Veterans Appeals. West's *Veterans Appeals Reporter* (1991-date) contains decisions of the U.S. Court of Veterans Appeals, as well as decisions on appeal in the Federal Circuit and the U.S. Supreme Court.

Free Electronic Access

Published volumes of reports are still the most widely available sources for most federal court decisions. Some commercial electronic sources are as comprehensive as the reporters, but they are not as readily or cheaply available to most researchers. Some decisions are available without charge on the Internet, but so far free access is limited to recent decisions. We will nonetheless examine free sites first, because they are the most easily accessible and because the value of these sites will increase as coverage expands.

Internet Sites

As recently as summer 1995 opinions from just three courts of appeals were posted on the Internet. Now every circuit is represented on the Web, some at more than one site. As of now, the prospects for district court opinions are less promising, but a growing number of courts are establishing Internet sites.

The first sites to post court of appeals decisions on the Web were operated by law schools, and these academic sites continue to provide most of the Internet access to the federal courts. Only the Fifth Circuit has its own official homepage with decisions and other court information. Although court decisions are government information, most of these sites are not official government Web sites but are instead law school-sponsored sites. Most circuits are hosted by an individual law school. The Second Circuit can be reached through two law schools, each of which provides a different method of searching decisions. The Tenth Circuit moved in 1997, so decisions from 1995 to 1997 are at one site, and more recent decisions are at another. Table 9-2 presents a list of Web sites for the United States Courts of Appeals, with dates of coverage.

Decisions on most of these sites are accessible by date, party name, or keyword, although some sites provide more sophisticated search methods with relevance ranking. Some access is rudimentary; Seventh Circuit decisions from 1993 and 1994, for example, are accessible only by docket number.

The sites for individual circuits can be reached in several ways, including online maps of the United States on which users click on the circuit of choice. Sites with maps are available at Emory University's Federal Court Finder <http://www.law.emory.edu/FEDCTS/>, the Center for Information Law and Policy's Federal Court Locator <http://www.cilp.org/Fed-Ct/>, and the Georgetown University Law Library's site <http://www.ll.georgetown.edu/Fed-Ct/>.

As it does with so many other aspects of legal information, the FindLaw site provides convenient access to decisions from all the circuits, both directly and through links to the above academic sites, <http://www.findlaw.com/casecode/courts/>. Useful features include an option to search its entire collection of courts of appeals decisions. This is an important feature because most federal law research involves looking for relevant decisions from any circuit. FindLaw also provides hot links to Supreme Court cases cited in opinions and a "highlight hits" option, which focuses on excerpts where search terms appear. In a few instances, FindLaw coverage extends further back in time than the law school sites. Most significant, it includes Ninth Circuit cases all the way back to the beginning of 1990.

Besides FindLaw, several other search engines cover all appellate court opinions on the Internet. Two of these are maintained by the law schools at Cornell and Washburn, but these valuable sites are frequently swamped with traffic and can be difficult to reach. (It may be more effective to run a quick search in an individual circuit, to find two or three relevant cases as

starting points.) The rather cumbersome direct addresses are <http://supct.law.cornell.edu/Harvest/brokers/circuit-x/fancy.query.html> and <http://topeka.wuacc.edu/Harvest/brokers/feds/query.html>, although these sites can be reached through links at numerous other Web sites. Both sites use Harvest system software to search, although Cornell provides a template for searching by keyword or party name. Law Journal Extra! also has a searchable database of court of appeals decisions since October 1994 <http://www.ljextra.com/cgi-bin/cir>.

A small but growing number of district courts are represented with Web sites, but few of these include comprehensive access to opinions. Two leading sites cover the district courts for the Northern District of Mississippi and the District of South Carolina. Both are maintained by law schools in their respective states <http://sunset.backbone.olemiss.edu/~llibcoll/ndms/> and <http://www.law.sc.edu/dsc/dsc.htm>. Both provide access to decisions chronologically, by party name, and through keyword searches. Unless the federal court system commits resources to official publication of opinions on Web sites, unofficial law school sponsorship will probably continue to be necessary to provide such access.

Most other district court Web sites provide notices and court rules rather than decisions. The court system's Web site maintains links to these sites <http://www.uscourts.gov/alllinks.html>, and some can be found through FindLaw <http://www.findlaw.com/casecode/district.html>. FindLaw's list is not comprehensive, and new sites continue to appear. On April 1, 1998, for example, Judge Susan Webber Wright's decision dismissing the *Jones v. Clinton* lawsuit appeared

---

TABLE 9-2

U.S. COURTS OF APPEALS INTERNET SITES

1st Circuit:	<http://www.law.emory.edu/1circuit/> (November 1995-date)
2d Circuit:	<http://law.touro.edu/2ndcircuit/> (January 1995-date),
	<http://www.law.pace.edu/lawlib/legal/us-legal/judiciary/second-circuit.html> (September 1995-date)
3d Circuit:	<http://www.cilp.org/Fed-Ct/ca03.html> (May 1994-date)
4th Circuit:	<http://www.law.emory.edu/4circuit> (January 1995-date)
5th Circuit:	<http://www.ca5.uscourts.gov/opinions.htm> (March 1993-date)
6th Circuit:	<http://www.law.emory.edu/6circuit> (January 1995-date)
7th Circuit:	<http://www.kentlaw.edu/7circuit> (January 1993-date)
8th Circuit:	<http://ls.wustl.edu/8th.cir/cindex.html> (November 1995-date)
9th Circuit:	<http://www.cilp.org/Fed-Ct/ca09.html> (June 1995-date)
10th Circuit:	<http://www.law.emory.edu/10circuit> (August 1995-September 1997),
	<http://lawlib.wuacc.edu/ca10/> (October 1997-date)
11th Circuit:	<http://www.law.emory.edu/11circuit> (November 1994-date)
D.C. Circuit:	<http://www.ll.georgetown.edu/Fed-Ct/cadc.html> (March 1995-date)
Federal Circuit:	<http://www.ll.georgetown.edu/Fed-Ct/cafed.html> (August 1995-date)

at the Eastern District of Arkansas Web site <http://www.are.courts.gov> before most researchers even knew the site existed.

The specialized federal courts are slower in catching up with the electronic age. One of the first to make its opinions available on the Internet is the U.S. Court of Appeals for the Armed Forces, with coverage beginning in October 1996 <http://www.armfor.uscourts.gov/Opinions.htm.> Some bankruptcy court homepages can be accessed through the judiciary site <http://www.uscourts.gov/allinks.html>, or FindLaw <http://www.findlaw.com/casecode/bankruptcy.html>.

Dial-In Bulletin Boards

The federal courts operate few Web sites, but most make their opinions available through electronic bulletin boards. These bulletin boards provide the text of opinions to the publishers and to the public. To log in to most bulletin boards requires direct dial-in access, registration, and a per-minute charge for use.

The courts of appeals' dial-in systems, known as ABBS (Appellate Bulletin Board System), allow access to other information, such as oral argument calendars, case dockets, local court rules, and other notices, as well as opinions. They are available for 11 of the 13 circuits. (The Fifth Circuit has an official Web site instead, and the Eleventh Circuit makes recent opinions available as compressed .zip files on the Internet <http://www.mindspring.com/~wmundy/opinions.html.>) Each of the circuits with bulletin boards has a local telephone number, and a few have toll-free numbers as well. More information on these programs is available from the Administrative Office of the United States Courts <http://www.uscourts.gov/PubAccess.html>.

Commercial Electronic Resources

The most thorough electronic resources for federal court opinions are commercial. These are generally not as freely available as the Internet sites, except to students at schools with institutional subscriptions, but their coverage extends much farther back than the mid-1990s.

LEXIS-NEXIS and WESTLAW

The most comprehensive sources for federal court opinions, in any medium, are the commercial online services LEXIS-NEXIS and WESTLAW. Both systems have every opinion published in the West reporters back to the beginning of the federal court system in the eighteenth century. In addition, LEXIS-NEXIS and WESTLAW feature a vast number of "unreported"

decisions that do not appear in the printed reporter volumes.

Even when found through the online systems, reported decisions are generally identified by their citations in the published volumes. Both LEXIS-NEXIS and WESTLAW also provide their own numbers for cases in their databases. The *Davis* case, for example, could be cited as either 1997 U.S. App. LEXIS 15197 or 1997 WL 329583. These citations are generally used, however, only if a decision is unreported or if it is too new to appear yet in the published sources.

Federal court decisions appear in a number of databases on both systems. Depending on the scope of inquiry, it is possible to search all available decisions or to restrict a search to a more specific court or jurisdiction. Table 9-3 shows the range of databases available on LEXIS-NEXIS and WESTLAW.

Both systems offer sophisticated search techniques, using either natural language or Boolean connectors. Retrieval can be restricted by date, and keyword searches can be limited to particular parts of documents, such as the names of the parties, judges, or attorneys in a case.

Other Commercial Internet Sources

Two somewhat more modest commercial services, V. and LOIS, provide access to court opinions on the Internet. These services are generally less expensive than LEXIS-NEXIS and WESTLAW, but their collections are also more limited. Both provide access to court of appeals decisions but hardly any coverage of decisions from the district courts and specialized federal courts. Coverage in V., a service of VersusLaw, Inc., <http://www.versuslaw.com>, goes back to 1930 for most of the circuits (1961 for the Fifth Circuit, 1941 for the Ninth Circuit, and 1950 for the D.C. Circuit). LOIS (Law Office Information Systems, Inc.) <http://www.pita.com> contains opinions from the courts of appeals back to 1971.

CD-ROMs

Case law on CD-ROM allows for electronic access and keyword searching without expensive online charges. Most legal CD-ROMs are nonetheless expensive. They are designed for lawyers who need access to case law on a daily basis, and are less often used by people who only occasionally do case research. Some CD-ROMs, however, may be available in academic or court law libraries open to the public.

The major publishers of case law on CD-ROM are also the suppliers of the comprehensive online data-

TABLE 9-3

LEXIS-NEXIS AND WESTLAW DATABASES FOR FEDERAL COURT OPINIONS

	LEXIS-NEXIS	WESTLAW
	(GENFED library)	
All federal cases	COURTS	—
All federal cases 1945-date	NEWER	ALLFEDS
All federal cases pre-1945	OLDER	ALLFEDS-OLD
All federal and state cases	MEGA	ALLCASES (1945-date), ALLCASES-OLD
All federal courts within a circuit	1ST, 2ND, . . .	FED1-ALL, FED2-ALL, . . .
	CADC, FED	FEDDC-ALL
U.S. Supreme Court	US	SCT (1945-date), SCT-OLD
U.S. Courts of Appeals	USAPP	CTA (1945-date), CTA-OLD
Specific circuits	1CIR, 2CIR, . . .	CTA1, CTA2, CTADC, CTAF;
	DCCIR, CAFC	CTA1-OLD, etc.
U.S. District Courts	DIST	DCT (1945-date), DCT-OLD
U.S. Bankruptcy Courts	BANKR	FBKR-BCT
U.S. Court of Federal Claims	CLAIMS	FEDCL
U.S. Court of International Trade	CIT	FINT-CIT
U.S. Court of Military Appeals	MLTRY	MJ
U.S. Court of Veterans Appeals	CVA	FMIL-VA
U.S. Tax Court	TCTCM	FTX-TCT

bases: West Group, producer of WESTLAW, and LEXIS-NEXIS, through its subsidiary the Michie Company. Both publishers offer extensive CD-ROM collections covering all the federal courts.

West's multi-disc CD-ROM products mirror the coverage in its *Federal Reporter* and *Federal Supplement*, with coverage starting in 1880 and staying current through monthly updates. West also offers CD-ROMs containing the decisions of individual circuits (e.g., *West's First Circuit Reporter*) and the district courts within a circuit (e.g., *West's Federal District Court Reporter: First Circuit*). These products, consisting of one to four discs apiece, generally provide coverage only back to 1925. *West's Federal Rules Decisions* is also available on CD-ROM.

Michie's Federal Law on Disc has separate discs for each circuit, with semiannual supplementation and retrospective coverage for most circuits beginning in the early 1890s. A separate *Michie's Federal Law on Disc: U.S. District Courts*, with dates of coverage varying from state to state, has one or two discs for the district courts in each circuit.

Other CD-ROM publications of federal case law include *LOIS Professional Library: U.S. Court of Appeals* (Law Office Information Systems, Inc.), with separate discs for each circuit and coverage beginning in 1971, and *Federal Appeals on Disc* (HyperLaw, Inc.), with cases since 1993 from all circuits on one disc.

Both are updated quarterly. These products are less expensive than the West and Michie versions, but subscriptions still run several hundred dollars per year.

Many topical reporters are also available on CD-ROM, including most of the CCH publications, as well as *American Maritime Cases on CD-ROM*, *Communications Regulation on CD-ROM*, and CD versions of the *Uniform Commercial Code Reporting Service* (*UCCSearch*) and *Public Utilities Reports* (*PURbase*). In some cases, electronic coverage extends back only a few years.

FINDING CASES BY NUMBER OR NAME

One can find federal court cases in several ways. Looking for cases by subject, through digests or electronic keyword searches, can be complicated. On the other hand, finding a case using the name of a party or a number associated with the case is relatively simple. Having this information, of course, requires learning of a particular decision from some other source, such as another case, a journal article, or a book.

Citations and Docket Numbers

Two basic numbers are associated with cases: citations and docket numbers. The citation is the number assigned to a particular opinion; it usually designates the volume and page number at which it can be found in a specific publication. The citation to *Davis v. City of Sioux City* (see Exhibit 9-2) is 115 F.3d 1365 (8th Cir. 1997). The docket number is the identifying number assigned to the case when the complaint or appeal is first filed in court. Each court has its own series of docket numbers. The docket number for the *Davis* case is 96-2194, a number also assigned to cases from the First and Fourth Circuits. Moreover, this number does not necessarily indicate the opinion issued on June 18, 1997. It is simply the number under which the clerk's office files all briefs and opinions in this litigation. Until a citation to this decision is available, however, it is the best available identifying number.

The simplest way to find court of appeals or district court cases is through citations to the *Federal Reporter* or *Federal Supplement*. Most legal literature provides these citations as a matter of course when discussing cases because lawyers and law students expect to be able to turn to the original primary sources. On the other hand, journals in other disciplines are not as consistent in providing legal citations, and newspapers and magazines rarely include them.

A citation to the *Federal Reporter* or *Federal Supplement* can also be used in most commercial electronic sources to retrieve the text of a particular case. On LEXIS-NEXIS, for example, typing *lexsee 115 f3d 1365* will retrieve the text of *Davis v. City of Sioux City*. The comparable feature on WESTLAW is called *Find*, as in *fi 115 f3d 1365*. Most CD-ROM products include templates for entering a case's citation.

Court opinions are public information, but *F.3d* and *F.Supp. 2d* citations are based on West Group's commercial series of reporters, in which the publisher vigorously asserts its copyright interests. To decrease reliance on one commercial source, the developing trend is to indicate court opinions by "public domain" citations assigned by the court. Under a public domain citation system, each opinion is numbered sequentially as it is issued. The first Fifth Circuit opinion from 1999, for example, would be "1999 5Cir 1." Because government information is not copyrighted, this number could be used by any publisher that wishes to issue the opinion, whether on the Internet, in CD-ROM, or in printed volumes.

Another component of public domain citations is that each paragraph in an opinion (or other document) is numbered, so that particular passages can be cited. These *pinpoint cites* are needed whenever language in an opinion is quoted or a specific part of a court's holding is discussed. With numbered paragraphs it would no longer be necessary to rely on West's page numbers. The paragraph numbers would be part of the official text and would remain the same no matter what format or source is used to retrieve and read it.

Public domain citations have received widespread endorsement from legal associations, including the American Bar Association. The Sixth Circuit has been assigning public domain citations to its published decisions since January 1994, but the Judicial Conference of the United States has thus far declined to approve systemwide implementation.

Docket numbers, the other major numbers associated with cases, are different from citations. They refer to the case file as a whole rather than a particular document. Some opinions in long-running matters, such as school desegregation litigation, may have docket numbers that were assigned years, or even decades, earlier. Each decision along the way has the same docket number. The desegregation case of *Davis v. East Baton Rouge Parish School Board*, for example, was filed in 1956 in the Eastern District of Louisiana. More than 40 years later the matter remains under court supervision. It has retained its original docket number through a move to the newly created Middle District of Louisiana in 1971, and through several trips to the Fifth Circuit and back in the past 40 years.

This can lead to confusion. Cases in the district courts often retain jurisdiction in pending matters while they are on appeal. In the appellate courts, on the other hand, each appeal is generally considered a separate case with one distinct set of questions to be decided. The *East Baton Rouge Parish* case, for example, has had at least 10 different docket numbers in the Fifth Circuit and 3 in the Supreme Court.

Even though docket numbers are not an ideal means of identifying particular documents, they may be all that is available for recent decisions if no public domain citations are assigned by the courts. It is therefore the number most frequently used for decisions on the Internet. Commercial sources add the West citation once a case is published in the advance sheets, but free Internet sites are less likely to edit documents once they appear online. On the Internet, therefore, docket numbers remain one of the key means of identifying decisions.

Names

Cases are normally identified by the names of their lead parties—the first named plaintiff (or appellant) and the first named defendant (or appellee). Footnotes in legal texts and journal articles generally lead from case names to citations, but references to cases are found in other sources as well. Books and articles in other scholarly disciplines generally include notes with case citations, but general interest magazines and newspapers rarely do. There, major decisions are discussed by name, without citations. To read the text of an opinion known by name, one must either use a printed table to find its citation or search an electronic database by party name.

Chapter 7 discussed digests covering Supreme Court decisions, including volumes containing tables of cases by name. Similar tables are published as part of West's series of *Federal Practice Digests*. The current edition, *West's Federal Practice Digest 4th*, covers cases back to the mid-1980s. Volumes 100 to 102 contain a "Table of Cases," listing decisions by their full names, beginning with the plaintiff or appellant, and Volumes 103 and 104 provide a "Defendant-Plaintiff Table of Cases." Only the "Table of Cases" includes information such as case history and the digest topics under which entries for a case appear, but both tables provide the citation needed to find the text of a case.

To cover the thousands of federal court cases, West has published several sets of federal digests, each covering a successive period of years. The first, *Federal Digest*, covers cases up to 1938. *Federal Digest* has been succeeded by *Modern Federal Practice Digest* and *West's Federal Practice Digest 2d* through *4th*. Each of these sets includes tables of cases and defendant-plaintiff tables for the time period covered.

It is usually important to know both parties' names to find a case because there is such a volume of federal court litigation. The *Federal Practice Digest 4th*, for example, contains more than 10 pages of listings under "Davis," and the "Defendant-Plaintiff Table of Cases" shows that the City of Sioux City has been sued by Charles J. Schenecker, Gene P. Scott, and Daniel J. Sicard as well as Cheryl A. Davis.

These tables are updated in annual pocket parts or pamphlets for each volume, and the "Table of Cases" is further supplemented in bimonthly pamphlets for the entire *Federal Practice Digest* set. These bimonthly tables do not cumulate, however, so it may be necessary to check more than one to find a recent case.

The supplementary pamphlets include a table indicating which reporter volumes they cover. To find recent cases, it is generally necessary to check the most recent bound volumes and advance sheets of the *Federal Reporter* or *Federal Supplement*. The bound reporter volumes have two separate tables of cases. All cases in the volume appear in one alphabetical table, listed under both plaintiff and defendant; jurisdictional tables list cases from each circuit, by plaintiff only. The advance sheets contain only the jurisdictional tables, so knowing a case's circuit can save considerable time.

Checking several volumes and advance sheets for a recent case name may seem like an onerous task, but it is not necessary to examine every single advance sheet. For example, the weekly advance sheet for July 1 may contain 199 F.3d pages 1200-1484, and 200 F.3d pages 1-200. This advance sheet will have two tables of cases in the front, one for the cases in each volume. The table for 199 F.3d is labeled "Cumulative Cases Reported" and includes cases in 199 F.3d that were printed in earlier advance sheets. New cases in the July 1 issue are listed in boldface type. If advance sheets more recent than July 1 are available, its 200 F.3d table can be ignored and a later, cumulative table checked instead. The spine of each advance sheet indicates the range of pages included, so it is easy to pick out the last pamphlet for each volume.

West publishes other digests covering federal cases. A series known as *Decennial Digests* covers the entire country, and individual state digests include coverage of federal cases arising from the district courts in each state. (Because these also provide access to state court decisions, they will be discussed separately in Chapter 12.)

Although the case tables in West's digests are the most comprehensive, almost all the specialized reporters include tables of the cases they print. Many of these, however, only cover a few volumes at a time, so it may be necessary to look through several tables to find a case if its date is not known.

Searching by name can be simplified, of course, by using an electronic resource. Most Internet case law sites provide an easy template for finding cases by party name, although the free sites are limited to recent cases. The more comprehensive commercial products, on CD-ROM and online, also offer searching by case name. On LEXIS-NEXIS, a search in the *name* segment, as in *name(davis and sioux city)*, will retrieve cases with specific party names. A similar search in WESTLAW uses the *title* field and can be typed as *ti(davis & "sioux city")*.

CASE RESEARCH

Several situations may require one to find cases by subject. Someone may mention a case but not know its name or citation. Finding how the courts have considered an issue may be an important part of a sociological or historical analysis. Most often, however, researchers need to find out what "the law" is in a particular jurisdiction.

Finding case law is one of the most complex aspects of legal research. While statutes are arranged by subject in codes, which are regularly revised so that they contain laws currently in force, court decisions are simply published chronologically in no particular subject arrangement. There is no compilation of case law in force. The original volumes in which the decisions are published are still used, even after decades or even centuries. Some decisions that are still valid parts of U.S. law were decided more than 400 years ago and were inherited from English law at the time of independence.

The relationship among cases is also complex. While some cases are expressly overruled by later decisions, many more are distinguished as presenting somewhat different questions. A famous example is *Brown v. Board of Education*, 347 U.S. 483 (1954), which did not overrule the doctrine in *Plessy v. Ferguson*, 163 U.S. 537 (1896), of "separate but equal" accommodation in public transportation. Instead, the Supreme Court in *Brown* held that the doctrine had no place in public education. Only gradually was the *Brown* holding extended to areas other than education. For 10 years, until passage of the Civil Rights Act of 1964, Pub. L. 88-352, 78 Stat. 241, the lower courts were divided on whether it was unconstitutional for businesses to refuse service to someone on the basis of race.

When faced with a new issue, a court may extend the reasoning of a prior decision, or it may decide that the earlier holding is limited to specific factual or legal issues. Unless they are expressly reversed or overruled, however, court decisions are still "the law." To confuse things further, even a case that has been overruled on one aspect of its holding may still be good law on another issue.

Several methods for finding relevant cases have already been discussed in earlier chapters. Legal encyclopedias summarize the law and provide footnote references to cases. Treatises and law journals focus on particular legal issues and cite cases extensively. Annotated statutory codes include notes of cases applying or interpreting specific code sections or constitutional provisions. Tools such as these are invaluable because they provide editorial expertise in finding the most important cases and in determining which cases are still valid statements of the law.

Four major resources are designed specifically for finding cases. These are complicated tools even in expert hands, but they are often essential in finding legal information.

1. **Digests** use classification systems that assign a specific topic and section number to each point of law in a case. Summaries of these points of law appear at the beginning of each case and are reprinted in classified order in the digest. The digest thus serves as an elaborate and detailed index to the case law.

2. *American Law Reports* **annotations** summarize the case law on particular topics. They organize the cases by fact situation and by holding, making it easier to find cases with issues similar to those being researched.

3. **Citators** track references to a case, including developments that may affect its status as good law. Because volumes of court reports are not updated to show which cases are still in force, citators are an essential tool in legal research. They also are used to find later cases that have cited a case in point, usually leading to more current case law on related issues.

4. **Electronic case databases** allow researchers to find cases using any specific combination of factual and legal terms. Available through a variety of media, including commercial databases, CD-ROMs, and the Internet, full-text searching has become the dominant method of finding cases. It is the most powerful means of sorting through millions of documents, but most experienced researchers use it in combination with resources in which scholars and editors have analyzed or classified cases by subject.

West's Federal Practice Digest

The traditional means for finding cases by subject is the digest, a publication that contains abstracts of court decisions and provides citations to reporter volumes. A digest is somewhat like a subject index, except it contains abstracts rather than just citations, providing a short description of each specific reference. A more important distinction is that a digest is based on a systematic classification of case law rather than a simple alphabetical arrangement of subject entries.

The only classification system covering court decisions on all subjects and from every jurisdiction is West Group's *key number system*. West uses this system in all its federal and state court publications. Most federal court research is conducted in *West's Federal Practice Digest 4th*, covering cases decided since the mid-1980s. This current edition is by far the most heavily used federal digest because recent decisions are the usual starting place in research. Earlier federal cases, however, are covered in four (not three!) earlier series: *Federal Digest* (1754–1939), *Modern Federal Practice Digest* (1939–61), *West's Federal Practice Digest 2d* (1961–75), and *West's Federal Practice Digest 3d* (1975 to mid-1980s). (The transition date from *FPD3d* to *FPD4th* varies, depending on the publication dates of the individual volumes.) Together these five sets comprise more than 350 volumes, providing access to thousands of volumes of court reports. The older digests, however, are used only in historical research or for the most comprehensive projects.

The current *Federal Practice Digest 4th* is updated by annual pocket parts. These are replaced by freestanding pamphlets once they grow too large to fit in the back of the volumes, and eventually the material is incorporated into revised volumes. The steady flow of reported cases has caused the set to swell from its original 105 volumes, published from 1989 to 1992, to more than 140 volumes. Half of these volumes have so many new cases that they are supplemented by pamphlets instead of pocket parts.

Between the annual supplements for each volume are bimonthly supplementary pamphlets covering the entire set. These pamphlets do not cumulate, and by the end of the year they total well over 10,000 pages of new references. Finally, the latest cases can be found through digests included in each reporter volume and advance sheet. Each year new references are incorporated into the annual supplements, and the updating begins anew.

Digest preparation begins usually with the publication of a case. Editors prepare headnotes summarizing the case's points of law and then assign these headnotes to particular sections of the digest. Some cases may have just one headnote, while others may have more than a hundred. Exhibit 9-2 shows the assignment of points of law in *Davis v. City of Sioux City* to three distinct topics: "Federal Courts," "Civil Rights," and "Master and Servant." The specific numbers within each of these topics assigned to the three headnotes indicate that the decision deals with the lower court's discretion in conducting the trial; sexual harassment and an employer's vicarious liability; and retaliation for an employee's exercise of rights. A person researching any of these issues could look in a digest and find references to the *Davis* case.

The West classification system includes more than 400 legal topics, each subdivided into specific numbered sections. The "Federal Courts" topic, for example, has more than 1,000 sections in nine volumes of *Federal Practice Digest 4th*, covering such matters as jurisdiction, venue, and the scope of appellate review. "Master and Servant" covers a broad range of issues in employment law, such as termination, discipline, compensation, and employer liability for injury to third persons.

Exhibit 9-4 shows a digest page containing a reprint of the text of headnote 3 in the *Davis* case, arranged by subject with other cases on "Master and Servant" issues. This page is taken from the table in Volume 115 of *F.3d* to show a somewhat broader range of issues than simply retaliatory discharge or discipline. This is such a rapidly developing area of law that section 30(6.10) alone occupies more than 50 pages in the latest supplement to *Federal Practice Digest 4th*. (*Federal Practice Digest 3d*, covering the early 1980s, contains just three pages; the section didn't even exist in *Federal Practice Digest 2d*.)

As the case law develops, the system gradually recognizes these changes. Key numbers are gradually expanded and changed, but only in response to the growing case law. Developments in a new area of law may be hard to find because there are not yet specific classifications. The retaliation headnote for the *Davis* case is bunched with notes from hundreds of other cases because the digest system does not yet differentiate among issues such as retaliatory discharge, demotion, or transfer.

Sexual harassment issues provide an example of how the digest adapts slowly to developments in the law. When the first sex discrimination cases reached the courts around 1970, there was no digest key number to cover such issues. They were therefore assigned to Civil Rights 1, "Nature of rights protected by civil rights laws." Once the amount of case law on sex discrimination started to grow, the "Civil Rights" topic was adapted to give sex discrimination its own key number in 1973. With every subsequent sex discrimination case assigned to that key number, it became overwhelmed in time by the volume of cases. A complete revision of the topic in 1989 resulted in nine separate key numbers for various aspects of sex discrimination, such as physical job requirements, comparable worth, and sexual orientation. Sexual harassment got its own key number, Civil Rights 167, which was assigned to the second headnote in the *Davis* case. This too has proved inadequate in dealing with the number of cases and the range of issues they present. Eventually there will be separate key numbers for sexual advances by supervisors and coworkers, hostile work environment, and same-sex sexual harassment.

⊶5 MASTER & SERVANT

administrative details incident to work; (2) source of instrumentalities of physician's work; (3) duration of relationship between parties; (4) whether hiring party has right to assign additional work or to preclude physician from working at other facilities; (5) method of payment; (6) physician's role in hiring and paying assistants; (7) whether work is part of regular business of hiring party and how it is customarily discharged; (8) provision of employee benefits; (9) tax treatment of income; and (10) parties' belief as to type of relationship.—Id.

⊶9.1. Apprentices.

C.A.3 (Pa.) 1997. Apprenticeship laws make reference to ERISA plans, so as to be preempted by ERISA, where approved apprenticeship programs need necessarily be ERISA plans; where apprenticeship laws are indifferent to the funding, and attendant ERISA coverage, of apprenticeship programs, they do not make reference to ERISA plans. Employee Retirement Income Security Act of 1974, § 514(a), 29 U.S.C.A. § 1144(a).—Ferguson Elec. Co., Inc. v. Foley, 115 F.3d 237.

(C) TERMINATION, DISCHARGE, AND DISCIPLINE.

2. DISCHARGE OR DISCIPLINE.

⊶30(6.10). —— In general.

C.A.11 (Ala.) 1997. Termination of employee who complained of supervisor's sexual harassment was neither retaliatory nor pretext for sex discrimination in violation of Title VII; employer made strenuous efforts to relocate employee to another position, and terminated her only when it became clear that employee would not return from leave nor accept any other available position. Civil Rights Act of 1964, § 701 et seq., 42 U.S.C.A. § 2000e et seq.—Farley v. American Cast Iron Pipe Co., 115 F.3d 1548.

C.A.11 (Fla.) 1997. To establish retaliation in violation of Title VII, employee must show that she engaged in protected activity, employer was aware of that activity, employee suffered adverse employment action, and there was causal connection between protected activity and adverse employment action. Civil Rights Act of 1964, § 704(a), as amended, 42 U.S.C.A. § 2000e–3(a).—Reynolds v. CSX Transp., Inc., 115 F.3d 860.

Temporary agency employee's failure to establish causal connection between her complaints of gender and racial harassment against supervisor and employer's replacement of all temporary employees in her department with permanent employees was fatal to her Title VII retaliation claim arising out of that replacement. Civil Rights Act of 1964, § 704(a), as amended, 42 U.S.C.A. § 2000e–3(a).—Id.

C.A.8 (Iowa) 1997. Employee's transfer to higher paying position after she complained of supervisor's sexual harassment was sufficiently adverse to support retaliation claim; position lacked supervisory status, had fewer opportunities for salary increases, and offered little opportunity for advancement. Civil Rights Act of 1964, § 701 et seq., as amended, 42 U.S.C.A. § 2000e et seq.—Davis v. City of Sioux City, 115 F.3d 1365.

⊶30(6.30). Refusal to perform wrongful act.

C.A.10 (Okl.) 1997. Oklahoma state law forbids employee's discharge for refusal to participate in illegal activity, when that discharge is coupled with showing of bad faith, malice or retaliation.—Mason v. Oklahoma Turnpike Authority, 115 F.3d 1442.

Under Oklahoma law, employee must present sufficient evidence from which jury could reason-

(128)

ably conclude that her discharge was significantly motivated by her refusal to violate the law, to submit to jury wrongful discharge claim based on refusal to violate the law.—Id.

⊶34.1. —— In general.

C.A.7 (Ill.) 1997. Analysis of employee's wrongful discharge claims required interpretation of collective bargaining agreement to determine validity of employee's arguments regarding railroad's retaliatory intent, and thus claims were preempted by RLA. Railway Labor Act, § 204, as amended, 45 U.S.C.A. § 184.—Monroe v. Missouri Pacific R. Co., 115 F.3d 514.

⊶43. —— Questions for jury.

C.A.11 (Fla.) 1997. Whether black female employee's complaints of gender and racial harassment against white male supervisor and her temporary replacement were causally connected, as required to support retaliation claim under Title VII, was for jury, where soon after she complained of harassing conduct, supervisor met with his superiors about unrelated error allegedly made by employee and contacted temporary employment agency that employed employee, agency replaced employee with another temporary worker, and supervisor commented that employee could no longer complain about sexual harassment. Civil Rights Act of 1964, § 704(a), as amended, 42 U.S.C.A. § 2000e–3(a).—Reynolds v. CSX Transp., Inc., 115 F.3d 860.

V. INTERFERENCE WITH THE RELATION BY THIRD PERSONS.

(A) CIVIL LIABILITY.

⊶341. Injury to servant by malicious procurement of discharge.

C.A.10 (Okl.) 1997. Under Oklahoma law, to support claim of tortious interference with employee's contractual relationship with employer, employee must present sufficient evidence from which jury could reasonably conclude that employer had contractual right which was interfered with, that interference was wrongful and malicious, interference was neither justified, privileged, nor excusable, and damages were proximately sustained as result of interference.—Mason v. Oklahoma Turnpike Authority, 115 F.3d 1442.

Under Oklahoma law, as predicted by Court of Appeals, corporate employees can be found liable for tortious interference with corporate contract. Restatement (Second) of Torts § 767.—Id.

MENTAL HEALTH

II. CARE AND SUPPORT OF MENTALLY DISORDERED PERSONS.

(A) CUSTODY AND CURE.

⊶51.20. —— Civil liabilities; actions and proceedings.

C.A.6 (Ky.) 1997. Under Maine law, as predicted by the Court of Appeals, any violation of duty of care by psychiatrist to adequately treat patient's mental affliction can, at most, engender liability only to patient himself or to specific other persons or classes of persons whom psychiatrist had reason to know are at special risk of violent injury at hands of patient.—Rousey v. U.S., 115 F.3d 394.

EXHIBIT 9-4

The digest system was originally developed more than 100 years ago, and topic names such as "Master and Servant" reflect its nineteenth-century view of the law. The system's continuity over the years lets researchers trace judicial doctrines back in time, but it grudgingly accommodates new perspectives on the shape of case law. Old topics such as "Action on the Case" and "Steam" remain, while new topics are only occasionally added. The topic "Federal Civil Procedure" was added in 1946, not long after the adoption of the Federal Rules, and "Federal Courts" joined the list in 1977 to focus on such issues as federal jurisdiction, venue, and standards of appellate review. Sometimes new issues are fitted into old structures. Cases under the federal crack-house statute, 21 U.S.C. § 856, enacted in 1986, can be found under the "Disorderly House" topic.

Under each key number in the federal digests, notes from decisions are arranged in hierarchical order: first the Supreme Court, then the courts of appeals arranged by state (not by circuit), then the district courts and other specialized federal courts. The *Federal Practice Digest 4th* covers cases in the *Supreme Court Reporter, Federal Reporter, Federal Supplement, Federal Rules Decisions, Bankruptcy Reporter, Federal Claims Reporter, Military Justice Reporter*, and *Veterans Appeals Reporter*. The specialized courts also have separate digests covering their specific areas; these include the *Bankruptcy Digest, United States Federal Claims Digest, West's Military Justice Digest*, and *West's Veterans Appeals Cumulative Key Number Digest*.

The topics in a digest are arranged alphabetically, from "Abandoned and Lost Property" to "Zoning and Planning," and each begins with a detailed outline of its contents. It is seldom easy, however, to begin by turning to a digest topic and finding an appropriate key number. Issues in the area of employment law, for example, are scattered through several topics, such as "Civil Rights," "Employers' Liability," "Labor Relations," "Master and Servant," and "Workers' Compensation." Child labor issues are found in the topic "Infants." Even if you can determine the right topic, you then have to look through the outline at the beginning of the topic to find the relevant section numbers.

An easier place to begin using the *Federal Practice Digest 4th* is the "Descriptive-Word Index" in Volumes 97 through 99. This index lists both legal and factual concepts, and indicates the topics and key numbers where they are covered in the digest. The "Descriptive-Word Index" includes entries for legal issues that arise in the *Davis* case, such as "retaliatory discharge" and "sexual harassment," with references to key numbers in the "Civil Rights" and "Master and Servant" topics. Sometimes the index is easy to use. As with any legal index, however, it may be necessary to follow several cross-references and to rethink the issues to find an appropriate entry. Sometimes the precise issues cannot be found, but a lead to the right area is provided; for example, even if the "Descriptive-Word Index" doesn't cover the specific aspects of sexual harassment law being researched, other entries in the "Civil Rights" topic show where related issues are covered.

An even more convenient way to approach a digest is to find a relevant case through other means and to examine its headnotes for appropriate research issues. From there it is an easy step to the digest volume containing a headnote's topic and key number. It is important to check the outline at the beginning of the topic to be certain that the key numbers are indeed relevant to the issues being researched. A headnote may discuss retaliation issues but be classified under "summary judgment," and other cases found at that key number would deal with this procedural issue regardless of the lawsuit's subject matter. Headnote 1 in the *Davis* case deals specifically with review of jury instructions, but it is grouped in the digest with other headnotes about the court's discretion in the conduct of a trial generally. Headnote 2 is assigned to two key numbers, one for sexual harassment issues and the other for cases dealing with vicarious liability under federal employment laws.

Once you find an appropriate topic and key number, it may still take some time scanning through pages of digest entries to find relevant headnotes. Although the system uses about 100,000 key numbers, some of them are still incredibly broad and include many irrelevant points. The digest has no text to explain which cases are the most important or to note which cases are consistently relied on and which have been ignored by subsequent decisions. Having to face 50 pages of headnotes on employer retaliation makes a strong case for using other sources before turning to the digest.

From the digest, it is necessary to turn to the cases themselves. Digest entries only summarize individual points of law and cannot be relied on to represent the cases' holdings. Some are based on asides or passing references in footnotes. A researcher looking for cases on seaworthiness would find the following headnote from *Houston Oilers, Inc. v. Harris County*, 960 F. Supp. 1202 (S.D. Texas 1997), in the *Federal Practice Digest 4th* under "Shipping": "Shipowners are entitled to rely on judgment of marine surveyors and rating agencies that vessel is 'seaworthy.'" This may be true, but the case deals with cancellation of a National Football

League game after the referee determined that the field was unsuitable for play. The judge simply noted an analogy between standards for playing fields and those for ships, but anyone reading the case would see that it has no bearing on the law of shipping.

Several other digests are available for finding court decisions, but each covers only a specialized area of the law. BNA's *Labor Relations Reporter*, for example, includes a digest covering employment discrimination issues from the cases published in *Fair Employment Practice Cases*. This resource provides a much more detailed treatment of the issues than West's system. Sexual harassment, for example, has just one West key number but is divided into 20 sections in the *FEP* digest. BNA employs a numerical system with decimal divisions that grow increasingly fine as the law develops. The *FEP* version of the *Davis* case, shown in Exhibit 9-3, has headnotes assigned to 108.415909, Employer liability, and 108.415925, Retaliation. This digest's scope is limited, but it can be invaluable for finding cases in this specific area of law.

ALR Federal

Another source for finding federal cases is *ALR Federal*, a publication containing articles known as *annotations*. *ALR Federal* was originally published by Lawyers Cooperative Publishing Company, a competitor of West, and provided an alternative to the digest system. Now that the companies have merged, it too is a West Group publication. An *ALR Federal* annotation gathers cases on a specific topic, sorts them according to their facts and their holdings, and provides a narrative overview of the law. An annotation can be much more informative than a digest, which contains no textual explanation.

ALR Federal is a hybrid publication that acts somewhat like a journal and somewhat like a legal encyclopedia. Like a journal, *ALR Federal* contains articles describing and analyzing cases on specific legal topics. Unlike many journal articles, however, *ALR Federal* annotations are written from a neutral perspective and do not criticize court decisions or advocate changes in the law. Its approach is more like that of a legal encyclopedia, but *ALR Federal* is not an encyclopedia because it is not organized by subject and its coverage is not comprehensive. For topics it treats, however, *ALR Federal* provides an extensive overview of case law.

An *ALR Federal* annotation provides a thorough summary of the case law in a particular area. It is divided into sections based on the underlying issues, relevant facts, and the courts' conclusions, making it possible to compare similar cases with different results. Exhibit 9-5, for example, shows the first page of an annotation on sexual harassment in 78 ALR Fed. 252 (1986). Its brief outline is arranged according to the type of conduct at issue (sexual advances or other conduct), whether supervisors or coworkers were involved, and whether the court held that there had been sexual harassment. Section 1, "Introduction," explains the scope of the annotation and provides references to other annotations on related topics. Section 2, "Summary," provides an overview of the case law and includes practice pointers. At the beginning of each annotation are additional references to legal encyclopedias, digests, law review articles, and other sources.

ALR Federal's treatment of sexual harassment issues demonstrates how it covers developments in the law. The first annotation on sex discrimination, 12 ALR Fed. 15 (1972), spanned more than 100 pages, but there were as yet no sexual harassment cases to discuss. The first harassment annotation appeared eight years later and focused on the topic of sexual advances by an employee's supervisor, 46 ALR Fed. 224 (1980). This was a much shorter annotation covering about a dozen cases. After another six years the annotation shown in Exhibit 9-5 was published. In the 1990s, annotations have appeared on sex discrimination in termination of employees, 115 ALR Fed. 1 (1993), constructive discharge due to sex discrimination, 116 ALR Fed. 1 (1993), individual liability of supervisors for discriminatory actions, 131 ALR Fed. 221 (1996), and same-sex sexual harassment, 135 ALR Fed. 307 (1996).

Each of these annotations is updated by annual pocket parts providing summaries of new cases and cross-references to newer annotations on related topics. This supplementation is one of the major features of *ALR Federal*, allowing even older annotations to remain useful guides to current legal developments. Eventually, however, these updates may prove inadequate to accommodate changes in the case law, and a new annotation is written that supersedes all or part of an earlier annotation. Thus, a brief annotation on the Marine Mammal Protection Act of 1972 in 43 ALR Fed. 599 (1979), discussing just six cases, was superseded 16 years later by a more extensive annotation at 124 ALR Fed. 593 (1995), with a far more detailed organization and analysis of more than 30 cases. The pocket part for the older *ALR Federal* volume provides a notice referring to the new superseding treatment.

Subject access is available through an *ALR Federal Quick Index*, a bound volume that is updated every few months with a new pocket part supplement. It

When is work environment intimidating, hostile, or offensive, so as to constitute sexual harassment in violation of Title VII of Civil Rights Act of 1964, as amended (42 USCS §§ 2000e et seq.)

TABLE OF COURTS AND CIRCUITS

Consult POCKET PART in this volume for later cases and statutory changes

§ 1. Introduction

[a] Scope

This annotation collects and analyzes the federal cases in which the courts have discussed or decided whether, or under what circumstances, a work environment is intimidating, hostile, or offensive, so as to constitute sexual harassment in violation of Title VII of the Civil Rights Act of 1964, as amended (42 USCS §§ 2000e et seq.). The annotation is limited to cases in which the court applies the guidelines set forth in 29 CFR § 1604.11(a)(3).

[b] Related matters

Right of complainant, under 42 USCS § 2000e-5(f)(1), to appointment of attorney in employment discrimination action. 75 ALR Fed 369.

Discoverability and admissibility of plaintiff's past sexual behavior in

EXHIBIT 9-5

covers annotations of Supreme Court cases in *Lawyers' Edition 2d* as well as *ALR Federal*. In addition, a six-volume *ALR Index* covers *ALR Federal* as well as other *ALR* publications covering state law topics. Both of these indexes are thorough and relatively easy to use, perhaps because they do not have to cover as much ground as the more comprehensive indexes for statutory codes or digests. The flip side is that there are many federal law issues that *ALR Federal* simply does not cover.

A three-volume *ALR Federal Tables* set lists all cases cited in the set, as well as statutes, regulations, and court rules. An entry simply indicates the annotation's volume and page number, but the tables of contents of all *ALR Federal* volumes are reprinted in the back of each *Tables* volume. This makes it relatively easy to determine whether it is worth pursuing an annotation listed under a particular case or statute.

ALR Federal, like the other more general *ALR* series, is available on CD-ROM and online through both LEXIS-NEXIS and WESTLAW. An electronic search for relevant annotations is usually most effective when it is limited to the titles of annotations. Unlike many law review articles, *ALR* annotations have thorough, descriptive titles, so there is less likelihood of missing a relevant document. Because annotations outline the factual and procedural backgrounds of cases even if not relevant to the particular issue being discussed, a full-text search usually retrieves a large number of documents. In most instances, many of these only make passing reference to the issues raised by the search terms.

Shepard's Citations

Another way of finding relevant cases is to use a citation index, which lists later documents that make reference to a particular known document. Citation indexing is represented in other disciplines by such tools as *Social Sciences Citation Index*, which tracks scholarly discussions. In law, the major citation index was developed as a way to verify the status of cases being relied on as precedent and is known as *Shepard's Citations*.

Shepard's Citations is a formidable-looking resource that serves two basic and useful functions. Before lawyers can rely on a decision as a statement of the law, they must make sure that it has not been reversed or overruled. *Shepard's* provides this information, as well as references to any other proceedings in the same case. But *Shepard's* is not limited to cases directly affecting a decision's validity. It also lists *any*

subsequent case that has cited the decision. Some of these later cases may distinguish their facts or limit the holding of the case they cite, while others follow its holding or apply it to new circumstances.

Shepard's thus allows a researcher to follow a judicial doctrine forward in time from a known case. It makes it possible to see how a doctrine has developed and how it is considered in recent cases. Tracing a doctrine back in time is done by consulting the cases cited as authority in a decision; tracing it forward is done by "Shepardizing" that decision to find new cases. *Shepard's Citations* is not the place to *begin* a research project because it requires having a case from which to work. But once a relevant case is found, *Shepard's* provides one of the most powerful and reliable means for finding other cases on the same issues.

Shepard's covers all published federal and state court decisions. For federal cases, the major resource is called *Shepard's Federal Citations*. It is available in a variety of formats—print, CD-ROM, online through LEXIS-NEXIS or WESTLAW, and on the Internet <http://www.bender.com>. The print product is the most cumbersome, and most lawyers now use one of the electronic versions. Not everyone has access to the electronic versions, however, while the printed publication is available in most law libraries. The main set consists of 21 volumes published in 1995; Volumes 1-15 cover *Federal Cases* and *Federal Reporter*, and Volumes 16-21 cover *Federal Supplement*, *Federal Rules Decisions*, and *Federal Claims Reporter* and its predecessors. These two components are supplemented by separate annual bound volumes, semiannual gold-covered pamphlets, monthly red-covered pamphlets, and biweekly blue-covered "Express" pamphlets. These various supplements cumulate, so only the most recent pamphlet of any given color is needed. To perform a comprehensive check for recent decisions that may cite a case or affect its validity, however, it is necessary to check the main volume and each supplementary volume and pamphlet.

Shepard's provides a substantial amount of information in a small space. For each case, listed by volume and page number in the reporter series, it indicates any parallel citations, subsequent history, and citing cases. Exhibit 9-6 shows a page from *Shepard's Federal Citations* covering decisions in Volumes 749 and 750 F.2d. The "Vol. 750" in the box at the middle of the page indicates the transition between the two volumes, and the individual cases are listed by their page numbers, between dashes, as in "—1576—" and "—1—". The first case listed, *H.F. Allen Orchards v. United*

States, 749 F.2d 1571, has been cited more than 100 times, but most of the other cases have much shorter listings. Note that the Supreme Court denied certiorari in *United States v. Wilson*, 750 F.2d 7, but affirmed the decision in *Schiavone v. Fortune*, 750 F.2d 15. This action is indicated by the lowercase "a" in the margin to the left of the first citation under *Schiavone*, 477US21. Cases in the next column show that the *Schiavone* case was followed, "f," and explained, "e," by subsequent District Court decisions.

These one-letter symbols will be cryptic to the new *Shepard's* user, but their meaning can be deciphered by checking a table in the front of each volume and pamphlet of *Shepard's Federal Citations*. Another prefatory table lists the abbreviations used for citing publications. It may be clear that "FS" and "FRD" refer to *Federal Supplement* and *Federal Rules Decisions*, but the meaning of "BRW" (*West's Bankruptcy Reporter*) might not be so readily apparent.

Another useful *Shepard's* feature is that references indicate the point of law for which a case is cited. To the left of the page number of most citing cases are small raised numbers. These indicate the number of the headnote in the cited case that summarizes the particular issue for which it is being cited. Of the five cases listed under *General Office Products Corp. v. M.R. Berlin Co. Inc.*, 750 F.2d 1, for example, the first discusses the legal issue noted in *General Office Products Corp.*'s second headnote and the other four discuss the point of law in its first headnote.

Shepard's editors work from slip opinions, and *Shepard's Federal Citations* covers citing references in recent court opinions that are not yet published in the *Federal Reporter* or *Federal Supplement*. If citations are not yet available, cases are listed by docket number. Docket number reference tables in the back of each pamphlet list case names, courts, and dates, so that cases can be found on the Internet, through an online database, or perhaps by checking the case tables in the latest reporter advance sheets.

Shepard's Federal Citations lists citations to federal court decisions in subsequent cases from both federal and state courts, as well as *ALR* annotations and selected other texts and periodicals. (Unfortunately, the publisher does not specify which texts and periodicals are included in the scope of coverage.) A separate *Shepard's Federal Law Citations in Selected Law Reviews* lists references in 19 major journals to cases from the Supreme Court and the lower federal courts (as well as to the U.S. Constitution and federal statutes). In addition, a number of specialized editions of *Shepard's Citations* provide coverage of decisions reported in topical reporters. *Shepard's Labor Law Citations*, for example, covers decisions in *Fair Employment Practice Cases*, providing parallel citations and references in later cases in both general and topical reporters.

The electronic versions of *Shepard's Federal Citations* have several advantages. Instead of providing fragmented coverage in several volumes and pamphlets, they offer one cumulative listing for each case. With no need to conserve page space, case treatments and names of publications can be spelled out in full rather than abbreviated. A search can be limited to those specific treatments or headnote numbers that are relevant in a particular situation. In addition, hypertext links lead directly from the *Shepard's* display to the text of a citing case or other document.

Electronic Resources

A number of sources offer electronic access to federal case law: the major commercial databases LEXIS-NEXIS and WESTLAW; CD-ROM products from several publishers; and a variety of Internet resources, both free and subscription-based. These resources vary greatly in scope. LEXIS-NEXIS and WESTLAW go back to the earliest federal court decisions, while free Internet coverage begins only in the mid-1990s for most circuits and contains hardly any district court decisions. An Internet site limited to decisions from the past three or four years is not yet a serious alternative to other means for extensive case research, but it may provide access to one or two relevant decisions that can then be tracked further using the West digests or *Shepard's Citations*.

Searching the full text of court opinions, whether through the commercial databases or the Internet, involves two general approaches: Boolean and natural language searching. Some sites only offer one or the other, but each can retrieve documents the other might miss.

Boolean searching uses keywords linked together with *and*, *or*, and proximity connectors. It retrieves only those documents that exactly meet the specifications of the search. Results are usually displayed in a sequence based on date of decision and hierarchy of court systems. In a Boolean search of all federal case law, for example, the first case displayed is the most recent Supreme Court decision matching the request. Older Supreme Court decisions follow, and then court of appeals decisions in reverse chronological order, and finally district court decisions in the same order. The number of documents retrieved depends on how well

Cir. 9	17ClC653	28FedCl 684	Cir. 1	—10—
629FS804	18ClC³466	28FedCl 765	656FS¹257	
Cir. 11	18ClC749	29FedCl 94	686FS972	Weil v
808F2d²1431	19ClC161	29FedCl 283		Retirement
	19ClC276	29FedCl 322	—7—	Plan
—1571—	19ClC394	29FedCl 359		Administrative
	19ClC496	29FedCl 528	United States	Committee
H.F. Allen	19ClC548	29FedCl 649	v Wilson	for Terson
Orchards v	20ClC11	29FedCl 724	1984	Company
United States	20ClC312	f 30FedCl 114		1984
1984	20ClC360	f 30FedCl³ 167	US cert den	
	20ClC388	30FedCl 266	in 479US839	s 913F2d1045
US cert den	20ClC426	30FedCl 428	in 107SC143	s 933F2d106
in 474US818	f 20ClC432	30FedCl 472	s 721F2d967	s 577FS781
in 106SC64	20ClC¹537	30FedCl 700	s 732F2d404	Cir. 2
s 4ClC601	21ClC493	30FedCl 738	s 571FS1422	773F2d1415
cc 618FS1030	21ClC631	31FedCl 284	s 586FS1011	853F2d1076
Cir. 3	21ClC60	31FedCl 312	Cir. 2	853F2d²1077
123FRD⁵525	21ClC208	31FedCl 329	885F2d²1006	e 112FRD62
Cir. 8	21ClC440	31FedCl 418	949F2d²1201	Cir. 3
823F2d264	21ClC⁴447	31FedCl 575	f 621FS867	q 828F2d151
Cir. 9	21ClC774	31FedCl 723	651FS1129	829F2d421
j 35F3d1344	22ClC18	31FedCl 730	691FS788	835F2d1021
Cir. Fed.	22ClC26	4UCR2d35	707FS703	854F2d1525
801F2d1297	22ClC⁴32		726FS1445	960F2d1182
856F2d1525	22ClC57		737FS847	d 640FS²530
877F2d960	22ClC420		824FS363	Cir. 4
886F2d324	22ClC528	—1576—	859FS739	764F2d243
j 886F2d1310	22ClC556		Cir. 4	Cir. 5
f 961F2d198	22ClC791	Amoco	750F2d¹1217	718FS¹1302
45F3d422	23ClC101	Oil Co. v	780F2d³1106	764FS1164
ClCt	23ClC203	United States	Cir. 5	f 764FS²1167
7ClC339	23ClC335	1984	757F2d¹1524	Cir. 6
7ClC714	23ClC537		Cir. 8	833F2d¹79
7ClC748	23ClC769	s 583FS581	833FS³754	769FS229
7ClC⁴751	24ClC664	CIT	Cir. 9	Cir. 10
f 8ClC365	24ClC839	647FS1579	874F2d1276	845F2d891
8ClC⁵602	25ClC319	651FS1445	f 889F2d¹852	100TCt230
9ClC485	25ClC360	10INT554	Cir. 11	e 100TCt233
10ClC309	25ClC405	10INT783	872F2d1514	
11ClC⁴2	25ClC514		872F2d²1519	—12—
11ClC298	25ClC526		738FS1407	
11ClC305	25ClC589	**Vol. 750**	738FS¹1414	Edwards
12ClC³20	25ClC601		Cir. DC	v Boeing
12ClC251	25ClC714	—1—	698FS³317	Vertol Co.
12ClC349	26ClC225		708FS397	1984
12ClC606	26ClC254	General Office	725FS³32	
13ClC⁵271	26ClC300	Products	25MJ479	s 717F2d761
13ClC458	26ClC746	Corp. v	31MJ877	cc 662F2d975
13ClC499	26ClC778	M.R. Berlin	91CR1660	cc 437FS1138
13ClC579	26ClC856	Co. Inc.	76ARF707n	Cir. 3
14ClC⁴236	26ClC996	1984	103ARF235n	24F3d468
14ClC341	26ClC1053		103ARF237n	723FS¹1033
14ClC355	26ClC1080	Cir. 1	103ARF246n	Cir. 11
15ClC130	26ClC1111	601FS²928	108ARF534n	17F3d360
15ClC597	26ClC1344	612FS¹311	112ARF366n	Fla
15ClC715	26ClC1412	631FS¹523		529So2d795
16ClC37	26ClC⁵1415	648FS¹835		
16ClC149	26ClC1441	657FS¹465		—15—
16ClC285	27FedCl 43			
16ClC508	27FedCl 170	—3—		Schiavone
16ClC657	27FedCl 213			v Fortune
17ClC98	27FedCl 261	Tremblay		1984
17ClC176	e 27FedCl 315	v Marsh		
17ClC³570	28FedCl 30	1984		a 477US21
17ClC³598	28FedCl 90			a 91LE18
	28FedCl 363	s 584FS224		a 106SC2379
	28FedCl 621			s 474US814

s 88LE45
s 106SC56
Cir. 1
f 108FRD⁴164
Cir. 2
869F2d²692
692FS²253
Cir. 3
886F2d²652
603FS¹328
603FS²329
635FS²214
f 647FS⁴1571
817FS¹441
e 105FRD87
123FRD²487
126FRD633
Cir. 4
774F2d1279
Cir. 5
638FS1324
Cir. 7
109FRD²660
111FRD⁵402
W Va
183 WV73
85McL1522
—19—
Emerick v
U.S. Suzuki
Motor Corp.
1984
Cir. 2
151FRD29
Cir. 3
852F2d⁵64
918F2d¹397
952F2d739
607FS¹896
623FS⁷14
637FS⁹1079
665FS⁴1145
752FS³193
774FS⁹944
791FS¹486
805FS³1230
113BRW878
Cir. 5
962F2d⁹451
Cir. 6
j 822F2d1431
Cir. 7
880F2d⁵911
N C
320 NC742
360 SE804
Pa
358 PaS136
516 A2d1219
53A3239s
98A3317s
35A4861s

Continued

293

EXHIBIT 9-6

the search is constructed and how commonly the terminology appears in court decisions.

Natural language searching eliminates the need to structure a careful Boolean search. It uses software that assigns greater weight to words that appear less frequently in the database and retrieves the documents that most closely match the request. The first case displayed is not the most recent but the most relevant—that case with the highest occurrence of heavily weighted search terms. Some cases may be retrieved even if they don't contain all the specified search terms.

Boolean searching is the preferred method for finding the latest cases on an issue or for pinpointing the uses of particular phrases or legal terminology. Natural language searching is a more reliable way to find cases with the most extensive discussion of an issue. A Boolean search for *summary judgment*, for example, would turn up thousands of documents, but the same search using natural language would retrieve only those cases in which the phrase appears over and over again—presumably those that discuss summary judgment at length.

Natural language searching and relevance ranking are rapidly becoming more sophisticated and widespread, and are used in many Internet search engines. The commercial databases of LEXIS-NEXIS, WESTLAW, and V offer the choice of Boolean or natural language, while LOIS thus far provides only for Boolean searching.

No matter what kind of search is performed, full-text searching doesn't organize things in the same manner as the digest system. Full-text searching finds cases according to the terminology the searcher selects, rather than the legal doctrines governing the decisions. Sometimes this can be invaluable, as when the digest scheme is slow in keeping up with developments. At other times, full-text search results are less than impressive, as when research involves interpretation of common legal concepts or when it is important to look at analogous situations to determine the relevant legal rules. In the area of employer retaliation, for example, cases may involve the exercise of employee rights protected under other federal statutes, such as the Americans with Disabilities Act or the Fair Labor Standards Act. A search limited to sexual harassment cases might miss important precedent.

Successful online searching requires a solid grasp of the terminology relevant to a particular legal issue. The major database systems have developed ways to help researchers by expanding search retrieval beyond the specific terms known to the researcher. WESTLAW,

LEXIS-NEXIS, and LOIS provide thesauri, which can suggest related terminology that may appear in relevant cases. For a term such as *retaliation*, for example, these thesauri can provide alternatives that may be useful, such as *reprisal*, *retribution*, or *revenge*.

In addition to the online thesaurus, LEXIS-NEXIS has a "related terms" feature listing words and phrases that are not synonymous but that frequently appear in close proximity to the search term. For *sexual harassment*, for example, the computer suggests such concepts as *supervisor*, *hostile*, *quid pro quo*, *retaliation*, and *termination*. Not all these would be relevant in a specific context, of course, but some may suggest new search approaches.

Another LEXIS-NEXIS feature called *.more* uses this related terms approach to prepare a new search based on a retrieved case. Concepts and phrases appearing in that case are automatically incorporated into a new search to find similar cases. A *.more* search based on the *Davis* case, for example, produces the following query: *harassment, supervisor, hostile, sexual, retaliation, imputed, harasser, "scope of employment," "sexual harassment," clerk, delegated, salary, usual, decision-making, instructing, inappropriate, "94 F.3d 463," "477 U.S. 57."* (The last two items are citations for cases cited in *Davis*. Another *.more* option searches for documents that cite the same cases cited in the original document.)

Another tool for powerful searching, available through most electronic resources, allows the user to restrict a query to particular parts of documents. A search for a party name is an obvious example. Some searches, such as those seeking opinions by a particular judge, are virtually impossible to conduct using printed resources, but a simple search for *ju(beam)* on WESTLAW or *opinionby(beam)* on LEXIS-NEXIS quickly retrieves all opinions written by Judge C. Arlen Beam, the author of the *Davis v. City of Sioux City* majority opinion. LOIS, but not V., also provides fields for searching by the names of judges. It is also possible, of course, to use Judge Beam's name in a full-text search, but that will retrieve all documents that use the word *beam,* not just those that he has written.

WESTLAW provides a powerful method of ensuring relevant retrieval by including headnotes, with topics and key numbers, in case databases. This is useful for several reasons. A full-text search will retrieve cases in which the search terms appear in a headnote as well as in the opinion itself, so some additional cases may be found. A WESTLAW search can include names of topics, as *to("civil rights")* or specific key numbers, as

78k167 for Civil Rights 167, along with other terms. Some key numbers have been used for hundreds of cases in recent years, so combining them with particular factual keywords is a highly effective way to focus in quickly on relevant cases.

In addition, it is possible to limit a WESTLAW search to terms appearing in the headnotes or in the synopsis, West's introductory paragraph summarizing the case's facts and holding. Sometimes a full-text search retrieves far too many documents, but searching only in the fields for these editorial summaries ensures that cases retrieved are directly on point. A search for *sy(sexual harassment and retaliation)* retrieves a few dozen cases focusing specifically on these issues, far fewer than the hundreds of cases retrieved with *sexual harassment and retaliation*. This powerful tool of limiting a search to synopses and headnotes is available only with Boolean searches.

One dramatic advantage of the more sophisticated electronic resources is the use of hyperlinks between cases and other documents, making it easy to move from one case to another that it cites, and perhaps from that case to the statute at issue or a law review article. LEXIS-NEXIS, WESTLAW and LOIS all provide links between cases. Such is not the case with V. or most free Internet sites.

Another valuable feature of LEXIS-NEXIS and WESTLAW is access to online citation services for verifying whether a case is good law and for finding related cases. LEXIS-NEXIS provides two major services that perform different parts of this function. One is the electronic version of *Shepard's Citations*, which provides the same information as that in the print product—except that it is updated more frequently, provides one cumulated listing, and can be more easily manipulated to narrow retrieval to particular jurisdictions or codes. The other LEXIS-NEXIS product, Auto-Cite, serves a more limited purpose. Instead of providing references to all citing cases, it focuses on developments that would affect a case's precedential value. Auto-Cite is the place to check, before submitting a brief, that all citations are correct and that the cases cited are still good law. As an aside, it includes references to any *ALR* annotations that cite the case being checked. (This feature was added when *ALR* and Auto-Cite were both products of Lawyers Cooperative Publishing. When Lawyers Cooperative and West Group merged, Auto-Cite was sold to LEXIS-NEXIS. The *ALR* publications stayed with the West Group, but to date these references remain part of Auto-Cite.)

For years, WESTLAW has also provided access to *Shepard's Citations*, but in 1997 it launched its own competing citation system, KeyCite. Like *Shepard's*, KeyCite lists other decisions in the same litigation and references to a case in other documents. *Shepard's* lists citing cases chronologically by jurisdiction, while KeyCite ranks them by how extensively they discuss the cited case. As in *Shepard's*, retrieval can be limited to specific headnotes. KeyCite enhances this feature by displaying the text of West's headnotes and indicating the number of citing documents for each specific point of law. It also expands on the scope of coverage offered by *Shepard's*, including citations found in thousands of unpublished opinions and in the hundreds of law reviews in WESTLAW databases.

KeyCite can be operated by entering a citation, but it is also incorporated into WESTLAW case displays through the use of flags and symbols. When a case that is not good law on some point is displayed, a red flag appears. A yellow flag means there is negative history of some sort, and a blue *H* indicates there is some direct history. Clicking on the flag or *H* leads to the KeyCite display. The absence of a flag or *H* doesn't mean that the case has no citations, simply that it has no negative or direct history citations.

Another way to find later cases that cite a particular decision is to enter the name or citation into any full-text system as a search term. This can provide information that is more up-to-date than that available through the citator systems, but it is not as thoroughly organized. This approach is most useful when searching for references to items that are not covered by the citators, such as texts or other documents.

OTHER INFORMATION ON COURTS AND THE JUDICIAL SYSTEM

Although judicial opinions are the focus of most research involving the federal courts, a number of other resources provide important information. Litigants need to know the procedures governing court actions and the forms for motions, briefs, and other documents; also, sometimes information is needed on a case that did not result in a published opinion.

Court Rules and Procedures

Federal court actions are governed by several sets of rules, depending on the nature of the proceedings. The Federal Rules of Civil Procedure and the Federal Rules of Criminal Procedure provide the basic structure for proceedings in the United States District Courts, and the Federal Rules of Appellate Procedure govern proceedings in the United States Courts of Appeals. These rules of general application were drafted by advisory committees of judges, pursuant to congressional authorization.

The Federal Rules of Evidence govern the introduction of evidence in both civil and criminal proceedings in federal court. The evidence rules were also drafted by judges initially, but they ended up being amended and passed by Congress because they were considered to exceed the rulemaking authority given to judges in the Rules Enabling Act, 28 U.S.C. § 2072. In effect, however, they operate in the same manner as the other court rules.

These various rules of national scope are supplemented by local rules in each court, covering specific procedures in greater detail. Local rules may govern such matters as the scheduling of discovery, required format for briefs and pleadings, and the use of cameras in courtrooms. Rules in each circuit establish the criteria by which it is decided which opinions are chosen for publication in the *Federal Reporter*.

The major sets of rules are printed with federal statutes in all three editions of the *United States Code*. Most court rules are printed after Title 28 (Judiciary and Judicial Procedure) in the official *U.S. Code* and *United States Code Annotated* (*USCA*), with the Federal Rules of Criminal Procedure appearing after Title 18 (Crimes and Criminal Procedure). *United States Code Service* (*USCS*) prints the rules in separate volumes at the end of its set, except for the Federal Rules of Evidence, which appear as an appendix to Title 28.

Advisory committee comments are included with all three versions, and *USCA* and *USCS* provide the same research aids that accompany statutes. Some rules are the subject of case annotations that are as extensive as statutes; the Federal Rule of Civil Procedure governing summary judgment, rule 56, is followed in both editions by several hundred pages of casenotes. These annotations can be vital clues in interpreting the scope of a rule's language.

The rules also appear in a variety of other publications, including pamphlets such as *Federal Civil Judicial Procedure & Rules* (West Group, annual) and *Federal Criminal Code & Rules* (West Group, annual). Extensive rule-by-rule discussion can be found in the major federal practice treatises, Wright & Miller's *Federal Practice and Procedure* and *Moore's Federal Practice*. Amendments to the rules are printed as House Documents and are reproduced in the advance sheets for each of West's federal court reporters as well as in

Lawyers' Edition, United States Code Congressional and Administrative News (*USCCAN*), and *USCS Advance*.

Rules of the Supreme Court and of the specialized federal courts are also included in the *U.S. Code* and its annotated editions. The rules of the Court of Federal Claims and the Court of International Trade appear after Title 28 in the *U.S. Code*, with those for other courts in appendixes to the titles with which they work (Court of Appeals for the Armed Forces after Title 10; Bankruptcy Courts, Title 11; Tax Court, Title 26; and Court of Veterans Appeals, Title 38). The rules of individual courts of appeals are not in the official *U.S. Code*, but they are included in *USCA* (in pamphlets shelved after Title 28) and *USCS* (like other rules, in separate volumes at the end of the set). Local district court rules are not included in these sources, but they are usually available in court rules pamphlets published for individual states. *Federal Local Court Rules* (West Group [originally Lawyers Cooperative], 5 vols., 2d ed., 1995-date) contains rules from all the courts of appeals and district courts, unannotated.

Even more detailed rules are prescribed by individual judges. *Directory of Federal Court Guidelines* (Aspen Law & Business, 2 vols., 1996-date) covers the requirements of judges on issues such as discovery, scheduling conferences, alternative dispute resolution, and jury practice. Information included is based on questionnaires sent to judges; those who did not answer the questionnaire are not represented.

Both LEXIS-NEXIS and WESTLAW have databases containing the rules that appear in their printed federal codes. In LEXIS-NEXIS's GENFED library, the RULES file contains rules found in *United States Code Service*; WESTLAW's US-RULES database has rules published in *United States Code Annotated*. In both cases, these include the Federal Rules of Civil Procedure, Federal Rules of Criminal Procedure, Federal Rules of Evidence, Federal Rules of Appellate Procedure, and rules for individual circuits and for specialized courts. LEXIS-NEXIS also has individual files for specific sets of rules (e.g., FRCP, FRAP, 1CRUL, VETRUL); WESTLAW does not provide as many separate databases, but a search can be limited to a particular set of rules by adding a *citation* field search term, as in *ci(frcp)* for the civil procedure rules.

Both systems include local rules for federal district courts in their databases covering state court rules, for example, the ALRULE or WYRULE file on LEXIS-NEXIS (in the CODES or STATES library), or the AL-RULES or WY-RULES database on WESTLAW. ALLRUL and RULES-ALL are comprehensive collections of state and local federal rules on LEXIS-NEXIS and WESTLAW, respectively.

A growing number of court rules are available on the Internet, posted by courts or bar associations. Most sites contain local rules for their own circuits or districts, and some include answers to frequently asked questions about filing requirements and trial procedures. The Federal Rules of Civil Procedure and Federal Rules of Evidence are available as hypertext publications from Cornell's Legal Information Institute <http://www.law.cornell.edu/rules/frcp/overview. htm> and <http://www.law.cornell.edu/rules/fre/ overview.html>. These and the other major sets of rules can also be downloaded from <http://home.att.net/ ~JSHABIB/> as a .zip file and then read as Windows 95 help files. A wide range of federal rules, including local rules, are available on CD-ROM in *Federal Court Rules on LawDesk* (West Group), updated quarterly.

Briefs and Other Court Filings

Briefs are filed in all cases in the United States Courts of Appeals, but they are not as widely available as briefs from Supreme Court cases. Microfiche editions are published for a few circuits, and one or more law libraries in most circuits maintain a collection of the original documents. Generally, however, it is necessary to go to the court itself for copies of briefs and other filings.

In district court actions, there is generally not one set of briefs as there is in appellate cases. Instead, there may be any number of written motions and memoranda on specific points of law that arise before, during, and after a trial. Some cases simply go to trial, result in a verdict, and produce no written submissions on points of law. Whatever documents are filed become part of the record of the case.

Case records are kept by the courts for several years and are then transferred to one of 14 regional Federal Records Centers. After 20 or 30 more years, they are transferred to regional branches of the National Archives and Records Administration. Depending on the age of the case materials sought, it may be necessary to contact one of these facilities. Most civil and criminal case records are not available by mail but must be obtained in person or through a record retrieval firm.

The Sourcebook of Federal Courts: U.S. District and Bankruptcy (BRB Publications, 2d ed., 1996) explains how to obtain case records from the trial courts. Case numbers, or docket numbers, are needed to get information about cases, so the first step is to determine the case number. Most courts have indexes by party name providing these case numbers. A docket sheet for each case lists the parties and the documents filed in the case. Most docket sheets are now kept electronically, although the documents themselves are usually available only on paper. The *Sourcebook* provides detailed information on document accessibility for each court, indicating methods by which cases are indexed and procedures for requesting information by mail, in person, or electronically. It also includes an extensive section providing information on the Federal Records Centers, including methods of indexing and procedures for obtaining copies.

Information on Verdicts, Settlements, and Pending Cases

Court opinions are widely available in libraries, and even unpublished opinions can be found through the online databases. Information on court actions that do not produce any opinions is harder to find. A case may be decided by summary disposition or tried to a verdict, or the parties may settle. Obtaining information on the case may require one to rely on news reports, to contact the attorneys, or to retrieve documents directly from the court.

If a case is settled and its record sealed, no information may be available. The sealing of cases involving sensitive personal information may be considered reasonable, but what about corporate litigation involving issues such as environmental pollution or products liability? In some cases, confidentiality is a condition of settlement that keeps other possible plaintiffs from benefiting from discovery in earlier litigation. For the past several terms of Congress, "Sunshine in Litigation Act" bills have been introduced that would require judges to consider "public health or safety" before sealing court files. Such a step would protect the public's interest in making public information gathered through court processes. So far none of these bills has received serious consideration, although several states have passed similar legislation.

Almost all federal courts report the status of pending cases through electronic bulletin boards. ABBS (Appellate Bulletin Board System) includes argument calendars, case dockets, and notices for the courts of appeals. Another system, PACER (Public Access to Court Electronic Records), covers cases pending in district and bankruptcy courts. Each court has a separate ABBS or PACER system, resulting in variations in procedures and in the scope of information provided. Most courts require registration and charge a per-minute fee for access to these services.

For some circuits, a voice system, AVIS (Appellate Voice Case Information System) provides limited information on cases—date opened, date closed, judgment—which can be retrieved by case number or party name. A similar program, VCIS (Voice Case Information System), is offered in most bankruptcy courts. Both services are free. Further information about these programs, as well as ABBS and PACER, is available on the Internet <http://www.uscourts.gov/PubAccess.html>.

A commercial Internet service, CourtLink, provides more convenient access to this information for a somewhat more substantial fee, <http://www.courtlink.com>. It requires a subscription fee and hourly access charges. Another commercial service, CaseStream, provides automatic monitoring of district court dockets.

Forms

In addition to the general sets of forms described in Chapter 3, several publications are designed specifically for federal practice. These provide the required format for pleadings, motions, and briefs, and address subjects likely to arise in federal litigation. The better and more extensive forms publications also include discussion of procedures and checklists.

One of the most useful of these publications, *Federal Procedural Forms, Lawyers' Edition* (West Group [originally Lawyers Cooperative], 32 vols, 1975-date) is a companion to *Federal Procedure, Lawyers' Edition*, and is organized in much the same manner. Sixty-eight chapters, on subjects such as consumer product safety and job discrimination, provide forms and discussion. Access is through an extensive two-volume index, which includes a table of cited statutes, regulations, and court rules.

West's Federal Forms (West Publishing, 19 vols., 1952-date) is arranged by court rather than subject, with separate volumes for the Supreme Court (2 vols.), courts of appeals (1 vol.), civil actions in district court (9 vols.), criminal actions in district court (2 vols.), bankruptcy (2 vols.), admiralty (2 vols.), and national courts, including the Court of Appeals for the Federal Circuit, (1

vol.; although the original set dates back to 1952, the average age of current volumes is about four years.) Other sets include *Bender's Federal Practice Forms* (Bender, 16 vols., 1951-date) and *Bender Forms of Discovery* (Bender, 20 vols., 1963-date), both published in loose-leaf binders for regular updating. A more specialized work, *Federal Local Court Forms* (West Group [originally Lawyers Cooperative], 3 vols., 1994-date) contains forms specifically designed for use in particular district courts, arranged by jurisdiction. Forms for specific courts of appeals are included in Volume 3.

In addition, there are publications containing model jury instructions, which can be adapted by judges in individual cases to explain the law to jurors. Model jury instructions can also provide useful summaries of legal doctrine in plain English. A criminal jury instruction, for example, may spell out the elements the government needs to prove guilt beyond a reasonable doubt. It may provide definitions of important legal concepts, drawn from court opinions as well as the text of the statutes.

One of the leading sets of jury instructions, Edward J. Devitt [1911-92] et al.'s *Federal Jury Practice and Instructions* (West Publishing, 3 vols., 4th ed., 1987-92), is available on WESTLAW (FED-JI database) as well as in print. The published version includes a general introduction of federal jury practice, followed by nearly two volumes of instructions in criminal cases and one volume for civil cases. Of competing publications, Josephine R. Potuto et al.'s *Federal Criminal Jury Instructions* (Michie, 2d ed., 3 vols., 1991-date) is limited to criminal trials and has not been updated since 1993, but Leonard B. Sand et al.'s, *Modern Federal Jury Instructions* (Bender, 5 vols., 1984-date) is comprehensive in scope and regularly supplemented. Several shorter collections of instructions have been compiled by committees of judges in particular circuits, and *Michie's Jury Instructions on CD-ROM* contains more than 7,000 model instructions for both federal and state jurisdictions. It is also available on LEXIS-NEXIS as the JURINS file in the 2NDARY and STATES libraries.

CHAPTER 10
Federal Administrative Law

Although Congress passes the laws that create the framework of federal law, and courts settle disputes and determine the scope of federal power, it is the executive branch of the federal government that is most involved in the daily activities of most Americans. Administrative agencies are responsible for enforcing the laws governing workplace safety and consumer protection; for regulating companies marketing drugs or issuing securities; and, of course, for collecting taxes.

Article II of the Constitution addresses the executive branch of government. It discusses the procedures for presidential elections at length but provides little direction about the scope of executive powers beyond military and foreign affairs and the responsibility to appoint ambassadors, judges, and federal officers. The executive branch's lawmaking function arises from the simple clause that the president "shall take Care that the Laws be faithfully executed." This requires the president, and by extension the subordinate officers he appoints, to adopt procedures for enforcing the laws. It has led to detailed regulations interpreting and applying the broad mandates of congressional acts.

The president has some inherent lawmaking power, but most legal actions of the executive agencies are based on express delegations of authority from Congress. Agencies are created by Congress and operate under specific mandates to administer matters within their field of expertise. Congress determines the standards under which an agency operates, sometimes in specific terms but more often in broad and vague language.

As the subjects of legislation have grown more technical and complex, so too has the necessity of administrative expertise. Thomas Jefferson saw the need for Congress to delegate tasks to the executive branch in 1787, when he wrote in a letter from Paris, "Nothing is so embarrassing nor so mischievous in a great assembly as the details of execution. The smallest trifle of that kind occupies as long as the most important act of legislation, and takes place of every thing else" (11 *Papers of Thomas Jefferson* 679 [Princeton University Press, 1955]). Over time Congress has come to agree and now leaves much of the detailed technical work to specialists.

Several administrative agencies were created early in the nation's history, including the Patent and Trademark Office and the Internal Revenue Service. More extensive administrative regulation began in 1887 with the creation of the Interstate Commerce Commission (which was abolished in 1995). Other major regulatory agencies, such as the Food and Drug Administration, were established early in the twentieth century. The rise of the modern administrative structure came with Franklin Roosevelt's New Deal. New Deal agencies still with us today include the Federal Deposit Insurance Corporation (1933), Securities and Exchange Commission (1934), Federal Communications Commission (1934), and National Labor Relations Board (1935). The third wave in the creation of administrative agencies was the increasing recognition of environmental and health concerns in the 1960s and 1970s, leading to the creation of the Environmental Protection Agency (1970), Occupational Safety and Health Administration (1970), and Consumer Product Safety Commission (1972).

These various offices are organized in two distinct manners: (1) within the departmental structure of the executive branch and (2) as independent agencies. Reporting directly to the president are 14 cabinet departments, each administering a broad area of activity. Some of the most familiar federal agencies are part of cabinet departments. The Food and Drug Administration, for example, is part of the Department of Health and Human Services, and the Internal Revenue Service is part of the Department of the Treasury. In addition, Congress has created dozens of independent agencies, such as the FCC and SEC, to deal with new or specialized concerns.

Many subjects of administrative agency regulation are highly technical and may appear to be of concern only to specialists in particular areas. The Federal Aviation Administration, for example, prepares airworthiness directives for specific aircraft models, and the Environmental Protection Agency mandates procedures for disposal of equipment with chlorofluorocarbons. The language of these regulations may be technical, but the general public feels the effect when an airplane lands safely or the rate of ozone depletion declines.

Other areas of administrative law are of more immediate concern to a wider population. For example, regulations from the Occupational Safety and Health Administration determine working conditions, and decisions of the National Labor Relations Board establish the scope of employees' collective bargaining rights. In all such instances, the administrative rules are based on the congressional acts in the *United States Code*, but the statutes are interpreted and articulated in much finer detail by the agencies.

REFERENCE SOURCES

To understand the workings of the executive branch, a necessary first step is to determine which agency regulates a particular area. It then helps to gain a background understanding of how the agency is organized and how it performs its work.

Guides and Bibliographies

The standard reference work on the federal government generally is the *United States Government Manual* (U.S. Government Printing Office, annual). The *Government Manual* provides information on each branch of government, with most of the volume devoted to executive branch agencies. Executive offices are discussed first, followed by the 14 cabinet-level departments and more than 50 independent agencies, boards, and commissions. The *Government Manual* includes descriptions of the agencies' functions and authority (including references to the enabling statutes under which they operate), organization charts, names of senior officials, and sources of agency information. Entries range in length from a few paragraphs to 70 pages for the Department of Defense. General mailing addresses and telephone numbers are provided, but the list of officials is not terribly current, and no contact information is provided for individuals listed.

Exhibit 10-1 shows a page from the *Government Manual* with information about the Bureau of Prisons, a division of the Department of Justice. It provides a brief overview of the Bureau's mission, its major divisions, and programs such as Federal Prison Industries and the National Institute of Corrections. Only one address and one telephone number are provided.

Charts in the *Government Manual* show the organization of each department and are useful in understanding the hierarchy and lines of authority of the government bureaucracy. In the Department of Justice, the Bureau of Prisons reports, just like the FBI, the Immigration and Naturalization Service, and several other offices, to the Deputy Attorney General.

The *Government Manual* includes three appendixes. Appendix A is a relatively brief listing of commonly used acronyms. Appendix B lists more than 1,000 agencies that have been terminated, transferred, or renamed since the beginning of Franklin D. Roosevelt's presidency in 1933. This is a convenient place to find out what happened to the Bureau of Outdoor Recreation (functions transferred in 1978) or the U.S. Metric Board (terminated in 1982 due to lack of funding). Appendix C, which also appears in every *Code of Federal Regulations* volume, indicates where each agency's regulations are published. The volume has indexes by name, agency, and subject.

The published version of the *Government Manual* is available in most academic and public libraries. It can also be found on the Internet through GPO Access at <http://www.access.gpo.gov/nara/nara001.html>. Entries can be located through keyword searches or by

350   U.S. GOVERNMENT MANUAL

of its investigative personnel are trained at the FBI Academy in Quantico, VA.

For further information, contact the Office of Public and Congressional Affairs, Federal Bureau of Investigation, J. Edgar Hoover F.B.I. Building, Ninth Street and Pennsylvania Avenue NW., Washington, DC 20535. Phone, 202–324–2727.

Bureau of Prisons

320 First Street NW., Washington, DC 20534. Phone, 202–307–3198

The mission of the Bureau of Prisons is to protect society by confining offenders in the controlled environments of prisons and community-based facilities that are safe, humane, and appropriately secure, and which provide work and other self-improvement opportunities to assist offenders in becoming law-abiding citizens.

The Executive Office of the Director provides overall direction for agency operations. In addition to typical administrative functions performed by an agency head, the Offices of General Counsel, Program Review, and Internal Affairs are within the Office and report to the Director.

The Administration Division develops plans, programs, and policies concerning the acquisition, construction, and staffing of new facilities, as well as budget development, financial management, procurement, and contracting.

The Correctional Programs Division is responsible for managing the correctional services (security) operations in Bureau institutions and case and unit management, as well as religious and psychological services, drug treatment programs, programs for special needs offenders, and inmate systems.

Federal Prison Industries (trade name UNICOR) is a wholly owned Government corporation whose mission is to provide employment and training opportunities for inmates confined in Federal correctional facilities. UNICOR manufactures a wide range of items— from executive and systems furniture to electronics, textiles, and graphics/ signage. Services performed by UNICOR's inmates include data entry, printing, and furniture refinishing. The corporation funds selected preindustrial,

vocational, and experimental training programs.

The Health Services Division has oversight responsibility for all medical and psychiatric programs; environmental and occupational health services; food and nutrition services; and farm operations.

The Human Resource Management Division provides personnel, training, and labor management within the agency. Its functions also include pay and position management and recruitment.

The National Institute of Corrections provides technical assistance, information services, and training for State and local corrections agencies throughout the country. It also provides technical assistance for selected foreign governments. The Institute's administrative offices, Prison Division, and Community Corrections Division are located in Washington, DC. Its Jails Division, Training Academy, and Information Center are located in Longmont, CO.

The Information, Policy, and Public Affairs Division encompasses the Bureau's Information Systems; Research and Evaluation; Security Technology; Office of Public Affairs; and Office of Policy and Information Resource Management.

The Community Corrections and Detention Division is responsible for program development and contracts relating to community-based and detention programs, as well as privatization and citizen participation.

The Bureau is subdivided into six geographic regions, each staffed with field-qualified personnel who are responsible for policy development and oversight, providing operational guidance to field locations, and providing support functions in areas such as auditing, technical assistance, budget, and personnel. Each regional office is headed by an experienced career Bureau manager who is a full member of the Bureau's executive staff.

For further information, contact the Public Information Officer, Bureau of Prisons, Department of Justice, Washington, DC 20534. Phone, 202–307–3198.

EXHIBIT 10-1

browsing the table of contents, and sections of the manual can be retrieved either as plain text or in PDF format duplicating the layout of the printed page.

Commercial databases such as LEXIS-NEXIS (USGM file, in several libraries) and WESTLAW (US-GOVMAN database) also provide access to the *Government Manual*, with fewer graphics but more sophisticated options, such as natural language searching. The *Government Manual* is also available in PDF format on CD-ROM from Solutions Software Corporation.

A commercially published work, *Federal Regulatory Directory* (Congressional Quarterly, 8th ed., 1997), is similar in ways to the *United States Government Manual* but offers several substantial improvements. Instead of evenhandedly treating the entire structure of the federal government, *Federal Regulatory Directory* focuses on those agencies that have the greatest impact on commercial activity and the general public. Thus, the Environmental Protection Agency (EPA), which receives a brief six-page entry in the *Government Manual*, gets about 25 pages in *Federal Regulatory Directory*. The Occupational Safety and Health Administration (OSHA) has an 18-page entry in *Federal Regulatory Directory* but only half a page in the *Government Manual* as part of its survey of the Department of Labor. On the other hand, agencies with little direct regulatory impact on the general public, such as the Bureau of Prisons, are only mentioned briefly. The only Department of Defense agency treated in *Federal Regulatory Directory* is the Army Corps of Engineers.

The *Federal Regulatory Directory* begins with a helpful overview of federal regulation and then treats 12 major regulatory agencies in depth. Most of these are independent agencies, but a few (such as the FDA and OSHA) are part of cabinet departments. Shorter articles examine 16 other independent regulatory agencies and more than 70 offices within the departments. The longer articles follow a standard format of introduction (summarizing the agency's responsibilities and providing a historical background and discussion of current issues); agency organization (biographies of commissioners or administrators, contact information for major divisions, an organization chart, and addresses of regional offices); congressional action (Senate and House committees with responsibility in the area, and an annotated list of the statutes that created the agency and that the agency is charged with administering); and information sources (Web sites, major telephone contacts, key offices, publications, and reference resources such as agency libraries). The shorter articles include a brief narrative background and information on key personnel, Web sites, publications, and key offices and telephone contacts. *Federal Regulatory Directory* tends to include more toll-free hot lines and information centers than the *Government Manual*; for example, it lists a dozen specialized EPA hot lines for topics such as asbestos, endangered species, and safe drinking water. It also provides more extensive listings of agency publications, including free brochures and books available through the Government Printing Office.

One of the most convenient sources for determining which federal agencies govern a particular area is the *Washington Information Directory* (Congressional Quarterly, annual). This directory is organized by subject, so it is not necessary to begin with any knowledge of governmental structure; it includes not only administrative agencies but relevant congressional committees and nongovernmental organizations. In the "Criminal Law" chapter, for example, a section on sentencing and corrections begins with a listing for the Bureau of Prisons, providing a one-paragraph summary of its duties as well as a mailing address, telephone and fax numbers, the name of the director, and a Web site address. This is followed by entries for a few specific offices within the Bureau, other Department of Justice offices in related areas, the U.S. Sentencing Commission; court offices, and organizations such as the American Correctional Association and Amnesty International USA. These may suggest contacts a researcher might not otherwise have considered.

A Historical Guide to the U.S. Government (Oxford University Press, 1998), edited by George T. Kurian, provides an excellent introduction to the departments, agencies, and commissions of the executive branch. It contains 183 alphabetically arranged articles, most written by historians and political scientists. About two dozen essays address broader issues on the nature of the federal bureaucracy, and more than 150 entries focus on specific agencies. They provide background information on the creation and development of each agency, as well as a discussion of its organization and activities. Most articles include bibliographies of books and articles for further information. Although the book offers a historical perspective, its emphasis is on agencies operating today. Those that no longer exist, such as the Bank of the United States or the National Recovery Administration, are generally mentioned only in passing. An appendix, "Basic Documents of Public Administration," provides the text of major congressional and presidential actions. A detailed index is included.

The only drawback to the *Historical Guide* is a matter of form, not substance, and that is its arbitrary approach to the alphabetization of entries in both the text and the index. Certainly it makes some sense for bureaus, departments, and offices to be listed under the substantive parts of their names, as in "Justice, Department of" or "Land Management, Bureau of." But the location of entries for agencies beginning with "Federal" or "National" is maddeningly inconsistent. Why would "Federal Communications Commission" and "Federal Trade Commission" be left intact, while "Election Commission, Federal" and "Maritime Commission, Federal" are moved elsewhere? Cross-references appear under the full names of these agencies, but in the acronym-heavy world of federal bureaucracy there is no sense in separating NASA and NLRB (both found under *N*) from NOAA ("Oceanic and Atmospheric Administration, National") and NTIS ("Technical Information Service, National").

An older work also useful for background and historical research is *Government Agencies* (Greenwood Press, 1983), edited by Donald R. Whitnah, with more than 110 signed articles discussing the origins and development of agencies, commissions, and departments (including several defunct agencies from the 1930s and 1940s). Appendixes trace the historical growth of agencies through a chronological list of agency creations and an alphabetical list of current agencies with their predecessors' names and dates of existence. Each article concludes with a "For Additional Information" section providing references to both official reports and secondary sources, but these are obviously now dated.

A number of reference sources on the executive branch focus specifically on the presidency. These address numerous facets of the institution and the men who have held the office. The most extensive, Leonard W. Levy and Louis Fisher's, *Encyclopedia of the American Presidency* (Simon & Schuster, 4 vols., 1994), contains more than 1,000 signed articles, including biographies of each president and vice president, discussion of presidential powers, relations with Congress, key legislation, and major Supreme Court cases. Articles cover a wide range of topics, from "Aircraft, Presidential" (explaining the type of airplane and tail numbers for various incarnations of *Air Force One*) to "Reorganization Power" (a mode of executive lawmaking in which presidential action took effect unless Congress expressly disapproved). Articles are generally straightforward and thorough, and conclude with short bibliographies containing references to selected articles and books. Appendixes include the text of the Constitution and tables with information on presidents, cabinets, and elections. An index of court cases and a general index round out the book.

The other major reference work is *Congressional Quarterly's Guide to the Presidency* (Congressional Quarterly, 2 vols., 2d. ed., 1996), edited by Michael Nelson. This work is similar to CQ's guides to the Supreme Court and Congress, and covers the origins, history, and processes of the presidency. It is arranged topically rather than alphabetically, with extensive discussion of major issues, such as presidential powers, the executive branch, and relations with Congress. For analysis of presidential lawmaking, the most important sections are Part 3, "Powers of the Presidency," which discusses the president's various roles and actions; and Part 6, "The Chief Executive and the Federal Government," which analyzes relations with Congress, the Supreme Court, and the federal bureaucracy. Chapter 29, "The Cabinet and Executive Departments," and Chapter 30, "Government Agencies and Corporations," serve as useful introductions to the offices of the executive branch, with historical background on the creation and development of each of the departments and independent agencies. In all, the work contains 37 chapters, each with footnotes and a selected bibliography providing leads for further research. Appendix A contains the texts of major documents and speeches, and Appendix B provides a variety of tabular and graphical data on the presidents and their cabinets. A thorough index is conveniently printed in both volumes.

Two shorter works, less comprehensive but perhaps accessible for a wider audience, are *The Presidency A to Z: A Ready Reference Encyclopedia* (Congressional Quarterly, 1992) and Richard M. Pious's *The Young Oxford Companion to the Presidency of the United States* (Oxford University Press, 1994). Each is part of a series that also covers Congress and the Supreme Court. Neither work goes into much detail, but both provide illustrated articles on presidents, other major political figures, policy issues, presidential powers, and significant historical events. *A to Z* has a bibliography at the end of the volume, while the *Companion* includes suggestions for further reading after each article. Both have appendixes containing tabular information about the presidency.

Several Internet sites provide background on the presidency. The Internet Public Library <http://www.ipl.org/ref/POTUS> has an extensive collection of materials, with separate pages for each president that provide links to historical documents, statistics, and biographical information on cabinet members. Grolier's "The American Presidency" site <http://www.grolier.com/presidents/> includes excerpts from three different encyclopedias, documentary features, and links to other presidential sites.

Two guides for more extensive research on the presidency have been written by Fenton S. Martin and Robert U. Goehlert. *How to Research the Presidency* (Congressional Quarterly, 1996) is a thin volume similar in scope and content to their other recent works on researching the Supreme Court and Congress. An older work, *The Presidency: A Research Guide* (ABC-Clio, 1985), is more extensive but now out of date. It includes coverage of official documents and secondary sources on the presidency as an institution, individual presidents, and presidential campaigns and elections. Martin and Goehlert have also prepared two unannotated bibliographies covering the Oval Office: *American Presidents* (Congressional Quarterly, 1987), listing material on individual officeholders, and *The American Presidency* (Congressional Quarterly, 1987), on the institution.

Bibliographic information on administrative agencies is less readily available. Robert Goehlert and Hugh Reynolds's *The Executive Branch of the U.S. Government: A Bibliography* (Greenwood Press, 1989) lists books and articles about cabinet-level departments, with a separate chapter for each department and more than 1,000 items in a "general studies" chapter. Each chapter, unfortunately, is simply an unannotated list arranged alphabetically by author. Except for a few early reports, coverage excludes materials published by the federal government itself. A detailed subject index provides some access to items on specific topics.

Several more general guides are available for assistance in finding and using federal government information. Works such as Edward Herman's *Locating United States Government Information: A Guide to Sources* (William S. Hein & Co., 2d ed., 1997); Joe Morehead's *Introduction to United States Government Information Sources* (Libraries Unlimited, 5th ed., 1996); and Jean L. Sears and Marilyn K. Moody's *Using Government Information Sources: Print and Electronic* (Oryx Press, 2d ed., 1994) discuss the wide range of information available from the government, including ways to find this information in depository libraries, through reference sources, and online.

Directories

Although the *U.S. Government Manual* and *Federal Regulatory Directory* provide major contact points for federal agencies, several directories provide much more in-depth information about specific offices and personnel. These are parts of series that also cover the other branches of the federal government, as well as state and local governments.

The two most comprehensive works are the *Federal Yellow Book* (Leadership Directories, quarterly) and the *Federal Staff Directory* (CQ Staff Directories, three times a year). *Federal Yellow Book* includes contact information for more than 38,000 people in the executive branch. For agency heads, it provides biographical information and photographs, and for some other administrators it includes brief notes on educational backgrounds. At the beginning of each agency's section is a listing of useful telephone numbers, including personnel locator and public information office, as well as Internet homepage address. The offices and divisions that follow are logically arranged, with a layout that illustrates the organizational structure and hierarchy. Listings for most agencies are extensive and include e-mail addresses for more than one-fifth of the people listed. An organization index, often the first place to look for a specific agency, is sandwiched between far more extensive subject and name indexes.

Federal Staff Directory covers more than 40,000 employees, with color-coded sections for executive offices, departments, independent agencies, and quasi-government offices. Although it does not generally provide Web site or e-mail addresses, it does include a section of biographical information on more than 2,600 people. The format is adequate for most purposes, with a larger type but less clear arrangement than the *Federal Yellow Book*. The volume includes a keyword index and a name index.

Both of these works are supplemented by companion volumes covering federal officials in offices outside the Washington, D.C., area. *Federal Regional Yellow Book* (semiannual) has been published since 1993 and is the old master in this area, with listings for 29,000 people in several thousand field offices, and several dozen pages of maps showing the regional organization of federal agencies. It includes indexes by location, name, and organization. In 1998, CQ Staff Directories introduced a new *Federal Regional Staff Directory* (semiannual), covering more than 40,000 people at regional offices and including biographies of 2,500 top staff members.

Carroll's Federal Directory (Carroll Publishing Co., bimonthly) covers the legislative and judicial branches as well as executive departments and agencies, with more than 35,000 officials listed with title, address, and telephone and fax numbers. Its listings are generally not as extensive as those in the *Federal Staff Directory* or *Federal Yellow Book*, but it is more frequently updated. The directory includes a keyword index. The publisher also issues *Carroll's Federal Regional Directory* (semiannual), as well as an annual combined edition in hardcover, *Carroll's Federal/Federal Regional Directory*.

These directories are also available in a variety of electronic formats, including CD-ROM. LEXIS-NEXIS has both the *Federal Yellow Book* (YBFED) and the *Federal Staff Directory* (FEDDIR) in several of its libraries, and both the *Federal Yellow Book* and *Federal Regional Yellow Book* are on WESTLAW (FEDYB, FEDREGYB). Carroll's directory information is available on the Internet through Infospace <http://www.infospace.com>, and FindLaw <http://www.findlaw.com/directories/government.html>. These sites include search forms for locating particular officials by name or title, and links to directories for federal and state government, including the executive branch and federal regional offices.

For most researchers, the choice among these titles is probably determined by which is most readily available. Generally, *Federal Yellow Book* and *Federal Regional Yellow Book* provide the clearest layout and the best coverage of e-mail addresses; both these and the Carroll titles include extensive listings of Web site addresses. *Carroll's Federal Directory* is the most frequently updated, so it may include new appointees not yet included in the other works. *Federal Staff Directory* and *Federal Regional Staff Directory* have the most biographical background of any of the directories. They are also the least expensive, so they may be easier to find than the other works.

Another directory, *Government Phone Book USA* (Omnigraphics, annual), provides extensive coverage of federal departments and agencies, in addition to state and local government offices. Each section includes a reference listing of frequently called numbers, but coverage is more cursory than the specialized federal directories, and individual names are not provided. At times it may be convenient to have federal and state information in one source, but at 1,700 pages, this is a rather cumbersome volume. The federal section has its own keyword index.

Agency Publications and Web Sites

The *United States Government Manual* and *Federal Regulatory Directory* provide a few leads to publications by federal agencies explaining the nature of the work they do. These range from tiny pamphlets, such as the Consumer Product Safety Commission's *Who We Are—What We Do for You!* (1997) and *The National Labor Relations Board and You: Unfair Labor Practices* (1990), to somewhat more substantial overviews of an agency's work, such as *All About OSHA* (1995) and *The Work of the SEC* (1994). Among the most informative works are those written specifically for a legal audience, such as *Basic Guide to the National Labor Relations Act* (1997), or those providing agency information contacts, such as *Access EPA* (1995) and *Information Seeker's Guide: How to Find Information at the FCC* (1997).

Many agencies publish annual reports, such as the Bureau of Prisons' *State of the Bureau: Accomplishments and Goals*. This publication provides a review of the year, statistics on staffing and inmate population, planning objectives, and a listing of Bureau facilities with maps, contact information, and population data.

One can locate these agency publications through library online catalogs or the GPO's *Monthly Catalog of U.S. Government Publications* (available in print, on the Internet back to January 1994 <http://www.access.gpo.gov/su_docs/dpos/adpos400.html>, and in CD-ROM versions from the government and from commercial sources). Also, browsing an agency's section of the shelves may provide a quick overview of what it publishes; depository libraries usually shelve materials by agency, using Superintendent of Documents classification numbers.

A wider and more up-to-date range of agency information is usually available from its Web site. Almost every federal agency now has a Web site with background information, links to departments or divisions, and documents such as press releases. Some sites, of course, are more comprehensive and sophisticated than others. The EPA site <http://www.epa.gov> includes extensive information for government officials, industry, and interested citizens. Numerous statistical databases are available, and various offices within the agency have their own homepages. Within the Office of Air and Radiation, for example, are dozens of specialized offices and programs. One of these, the Atmospheric Pollution Prevention Division, includes methane outreach programs, such as the Ruminant Livestock Efficiency Program, designed to reduce emissions of greenhouse gases from ranch animals' digestive systems. Each of these offices and programs provides information on its mission and links to more detailed information.

The Bureau of Prisons provides an example of a relatively simple but informative agency Web site <http://www.bop.gov>. Options include links to biographical information about the director, statistics about the prison system and its inmate population, instructions for obtaining information about federal inmates, several articles about Alcatraz, and a directory of BOP facilities and offices. The most extensive part of the site is a thorough compilation of program statements, providing detailed policies under which the bureau operates. Finally, the homepage provides a simple search engine and links to related sites (including related agencies and subdivisions, such as the Bureau Library's online catalog, the National Institute of Corrections, and Federal Prison Industries, and to the Corrections Connection <http://www.corrections.com>, which can lead one to state and local Web sites).

The amount of information available on the Internet is increasing exponentially, in part due to the Electronic Freedom of Information Act Amendments of 1996 (Pub. L. No. 104-231, 110 Stat. 3048). The amendments mandate that agencies make records that are subject to frequent information requests available electronically. They must also provide, on the Internet or through some other online means, indexes of the records that have been requested more than once and guides on how to request records. Finally, they must provide online access not only to material published in the *Federal Register* but to agency opinions, interpretations, policy statements, and staff manuals.

There are several convenient ways to locate government homepages on the Web. One simple approach, trying a commonsense acronym as an address, frequently works. Most agencies have straightforward URLs: <http://www.usda.gov> for the Department of Agriculture, <http://www.dot.gov> for the Department of Transportation, <http://www.sec.gov> for the Securities and Exchange Commission. The *.gov* domain reduces the competition for convenient Web addresses, but the results are nonetheless not always intuitive, e.g., the Department of Justice homepage is <http://www.usdoj.gov>, and the Federal Energy Regulatory Commission is <http://www.ferc.fed.us>.

When intuition fails, one can refer to several sites listing agencies and links to their homepages. Among the government agencies providing lists are the General Services Agency <http://www.info.gov/Info/html/executive.htm> and the Library of Congress <http://lcweb.loc.gov/global/executive/fed.html>. These sources are adequate for most purposes. As in many other areas of Internet development, however, academic and commercial sites have taken the lead in providing more thorough and accessible approaches to locating information.

Of the many Internet lists of government Web sites, two of the most useful are the Federal Web Locator <http://www.cilp.org/Fed-Agency/fedwebloc.html> from the Center for Information Law and Policy at Villanova Law School, and the Louisiana State University Libraries' U.S. Federal Government Agencies Page <http://www.lib.lsu.edu/gov/fedgov.html>. These may be the most comprehensive listings of federal sites. Both are arranged by agency, with executive offices first, followed by departments, independent establishments and government corporations, and miscellaneous boards, commissions, and committees. They are also both searchable, which is a handy feature for people who may not know, for example, that the National Oceanic and Atmospheric Administration is part of the Department of Commerce.

A few differences distinguish the CILP and LSU lists. CILP provides a quick list of acronyms at the top of the page, with jumps from these acronyms to the full listings, while LSU simply provides one alphabetical listing. The CILP list of acronyms may be intimidating to some but a quicker jumping-off point for those familiar with such acronyms as USDA, DOI, and FEMA. Both lists are updated frequently, and each includes a few agencies that do not appear on the other's list. The LSU list, based on the entries in the *U.S. Government Manual*, is also available from GPO Access <http://www.access.gpo.gov/su_docs/dpos/agencies.html>.

Federal Information Exchange, Inc. (RAMS-FIE), a company that links research organizations with the federal government, has a list <http://www.fie.com/www/exec.htm> that includes annotations for some sites, explaining the scope of an agency's work and the contents of its Web page. Not everything is annotated, however; the Department of Commerce listing, for instance, contains an extensive annotation for the Climate Prediction Center but nothing for the Bureau of the Census.

Although government information is increasingly available through the World Wide Web, some agencies still maintain electronic bulletin boards with information that is not on the Web. The most convenient access to most of these bulletin boards is through FedWorld, by telnetting to *fedworld.gov*, or by modem at (703) 321-3339. Bruce Maxwell's *How to Access the Government's Electronic Bulletin Boards* (Congressional Quarterly, annual) focuses on these resources, but with the increasing prevalence of Internet access, it is not clear whether this work will continue to be updated.

The Internet directories and guides discussed in Chapter 3 include extensive listings of government Web sites, although these are obviously not as up-to-date and convenient as online sources. Two publications focusing on federal resources are Bruce Maxwell's *How to Access the Federal Government on the Internet* (Congressional Quarterly, annual) and Greg R. Notess's *Government Information on the Internet* (Bernan Press, 1997). Both are arranged by subject rather than by agency.

Oversight Publications

One way to learn more about the functions of a particular agency is to examine the work of Congress in monitoring administrative activity. Because agencies administer congressional acts and use funds that Congress appropriates, the House and Senate take an active interest in how the agencies carry out their functions. Congressional oversight serves several purposes. It seeks to ensure that agencies comply with congressional intent (at least as interpreted by current members of Congress); that regulatory policies are being implemented effectively and fairly; and that the public interest, not just the interests of regulated industries, is reflected in agency policies.

The congressional oversight function is an inherent part of the relationship between the legislative and executive branches, but the Legislative Reorganization Act of 1946, ch. 753, § 136, 60 Stat. 832, spelled out the important role of congressional committees, specifying that each committee "exercise continuous watchfulness of the execution by the administrative agencies concerned of any laws, the subject matter of which is within the jurisdiction of such committee." The current provision, in 2 U.S.C. § 190d, is less strongly worded but still provides that each committee "shall review and study, on a continuing basis, the application, administration, and execution of those laws, or parts of laws, the subject matter of which is within the jurisdiction of that committee."

The oversight function is accomplished both by committees with jurisdiction over specific subject matters and by appropriations subcommittees in determining the amount of money to allocate to each agency. In either case, hearings are important sources of information. On April 9, 1997, for example, Bureau of Prisons director Kathleen Hawk testified at House appropriations hearings for the Department of Justice, along with the chair of the U.S. Sentencing Commission and the director of the U.S. Marshals Service. She discussed the Bureau's request for funds for inmate services, drug treatment programs, vocational training programs, and National Institute of Corrections services. Her testimony is published in a volume along with that of other Department of Justice officials, such as Attorney General Janet Reno and FBI director Louis Freeh. Hawk also testified before the House Judiciary Committee in June 1995 on various matters relating to the Bureau of Prisons, including overcrowding, privatization, and drug treatment issues, and in September 1996 on Federal Prison Industries, Inc. These hearings, published by the Government Printing Office and available in most federal depository libraries, can provide background information on the Bureau's activities and concerns.

Much oversight of agency action is performed by the General Accounting Office (GAO), a congressional support agency responsible for examining federal programs. The GAO was created in 1921, but its mandate was expanded considerably by legislation in the 1960s and 1970s. It examines agency operations, evaluating their effectiveness, looking for fraud or waste in the expenditure of funds, and recommending administrative reforms.

GAO officials frequently testify before congressional committees; in the 1995 House hearings on Bureau of Prisons issues, for example, the director of Administration of Justice Issues at the GAO delivered a statement summarizing his office's findings and recommendations on various challenges facing the BOP.

The GAO also publishes formal reports on specific issues, usually in response to requests from members of Congress. Reports generally begin with "results in brief" and "background" sections summarizing major issues, and recommend administrative reforms to reduce waste or improve procedures. Many use charts and graphs to present data and findings, and some include bibliographies and lists of related GAO reports.

In libraries, GAO reports are usually shelved according to the specific division or office responsible. The Health, Education and Human Services Division (HEHS) and the Resources, Community and Economic Development Division (RCED) usually cover issues of the most direct concern to the public. One of the many areas addressed by the General Government Division (GGD) is prison management, through such recent reports as *Federal Prison Expansion: Overcrowding Reduced but Inmate Population Growth May Raise Issue Again* (1993) and *Private and Public Prisons: Studies Comparing Operational Costs and/or Quality of Service* (1996).

The GAO publishes several guides to its reports and other documents. *Month in Review: Reports, Tes-*

timony, Correspondence and Other Publications provides abstracts of new studies, with instructions for obtaining free copies. These monthly issues cumulate in an annual *Abstracts of Reports and Testimony*, and a separate annual volume, *Indexes for Abstracts of Reports and Testimony*, contains a subject index with such extensive use of detailed headings that it occupies more pages than the abstracts. As a reminder to Congress and the agencies of work to be done, an annual *Status of Open Recommendations: Improving Operations of Federal Departments and Agencies* summarizes GAO recommendations that have not been fully implemented. This publication includes diskettes providing more information on recommendations.

All these publications are available on the GAO's Web site <http://www.gao.gov>, and GAO reports back to October 1994 are also available through GPO Access <http://www.access.gpo.gov/su_docs/aces/aces160.shtml>. The GAO Web site provides an order form for obtaining print copies of reports. A GAO Daybook listing new reports and testimony is available by fax, by e-mail subscription, or on the Internet <http://www.gao.gov/daybook/daybook.htm>. The Web version of the Daybook provides links to PDF versions of the reports if they are available electronically.

PRESIDENTIAL LAWMAKING

The president is involved in the lawmaking process in several capacities: by sending proposed legislation to Congress, by approving or vetoing bills that have passed both houses, and by supervising the executive branch of the government. This section focuses briefly on ways in which the president directly creates law, primarily through the use of *executive orders*. These are vehicles by which the president provides instructions for officers in departments and agencies, often pursuant to a specific statutory mandate.

In addition, the president issues *proclamations*, which are more general announcements of policy. Proclamations are most frequently used for ceremonial or commemorative purposes, such as the annual declaration of American Heart Month or National School Lunch Week, but a few have substantive importance. Proclamation 6907 of July 1, 1996, in response to an extended drought in the southwestern United States, declared a state of emergency and released feed grain from the disaster reserve. Proclamations are also used in the implementation of major trade agreements, such as the North American Free Trade Agreement (NAFTA). Most proclamations are less than a page in length, but

Proclamation 6763 of December 23, 1994, implementing General Agreement on Tariffs and Trade (GATT) trade agreements, included a 694-page annex of detailed tariff schedules.

Executive orders and proclamations are each issued in numbered series, with more than 13,000 executive orders and 7,000 proclamations to date. The use of executive orders has declined in recent decades, however; most years see from 100 to 150 proclamations and perhaps half that many executive orders.

Executive orders and proclamations are not the most frequently used documents of administrative law, but they are among the most widely available, perhaps because they constitute a discrete and relatively small body of material. Among the locations where they can be found are the *Federal Register*, *Code of Federal Regulations*, *Weekly Compilation of Presidential Documents*, and numerous Web sites.

The major official sources are the *Federal Register* and *Code of Federal Regulations*. Presidential documents are published in the daily issues of the *Federal Register* and cumulated at the end of the year into Title 3 of the *Code of Federal Regulations*. The annual volume also includes subject indexes and several tables. These tables list the year's proclamations, executive orders, and other presidential documents; note older presidential documents that were affected during the year; and list statutes cited as authority for presidential documents.

The Office of the Federal Register used to publish a *Codification of Presidential Proclamations and Executive Orders* every four years, reprinting in a subject arrangement those documents issued since 1961 that remained in force. These collections also included handy tables indicating the status of every proclamation and order issued since 1961. Unfortunately, no new edition has been published since 1989, so the value of this title is decreasing steadily.

Executive orders and proclamations are also printed, along with other presidential material, in the *Weekly Compilation of Presidential Documents*, which contains messages, transcripts of remarks and news conferences, and other statements. The *Weekly Compilation* includes quarterly, semiannual, and annual indexes, arranged by subject, name, and document category (including not just executive orders and proclamations, but addresses and remarks, bill signings, communications to Congress, and several types of documents). Most of the material in the *Weekly Compilation* is republished in a series of bound volumes known as *Public Papers of the Presidents*, but since 1989, executive orders and proclamations have simply been listed, with *Federal Register* citations, in an appendix.

Executive orders and proclamations are also reprinted in *United States Code Congressional and Administrative News* (*USCCAN*) (West Group), in both its monthly pamphlets and annual bound volumes back to 1941. *USCS Advance* (LEXIS Law Publishing) also includes executive orders and proclamations, but it is published only in temporary pamphlets and provides no permanent source.

Even though executive orders usually have more legal impact than proclamations, which are often ceremonial, only the latter documents are reprinted in *Statutes at Large*, the official compilation of federal session laws. This appears to be a matter of tradition, as proclamations have appeared in *Statutes at Large* since 1846 (volume 9), at a time when executive orders were viewed more as private communications between a president and cabinet officers.

Important executive orders and proclamations can also be found in the *U.S. Code*, *U.S. Code Annotated* (*USCA*), and *U.S. Code Service* (*USCS*), reprinted following code sections to which they relate. These can be located by number in each set through tables following the *Statutes at Large* cross-reference tables. The *USCS* tables are limited to those that are actually reprinted in the code. The tables in the *U.S. Code* and *USCA* are longer, including all documents mentioned in the code, including those that have been revoked or superseded.

The president also issues a variety of other significant legal documents that are not included in the executive order or proclamation series. These are also printed in the *Federal Register* and in the annual *CFR* cumulation of Title 3, and include such items as memoranda, notices, letters, and presidential determinations. Each year, for example, the president issues a determination of the number of refugees that will be admitted from various parts of the world. Another use of presidential determinations is to provide instructions for the secretary of state on most-favored-nation trade status for particular countries. These documents are also reprinted in *USCS Advance*, but not in *USCCAN*.

In the past, reorganization plans were a major mode of presidential executive action. These plans would reassign duties in the federal government and would take effect unless either house of Congress expressly disapproved. Reorganization Plan No. 3 of 1970, for example, created the Environmental Protection Agency, and the following plan created the National Oceanic and Atmospheric Administration. However, this type of "legislative veto" was ruled unconstitutional by the Supreme Court in *Immigration and Naturalization Service v. Chadha*, 462 U.S. 919 (1983); there have been no reorganization plans since. The statute governing the procedure, 5 U.S.C. §§ 901-912, was amended after *Chadha* to require express approval of plans by Congress. The sections remain in the *U.S. Code*, even though the reorganization power was not extended past 1984.

Although reorganization plans are no longer used, older plans may still have legal significance. They are printed in the annual *CFR* Title 3 volumes and reprinted in the *U.S. Code* and *USCA* as appendixes to Title 5. Plans that were disapproved or have been repealed are listed but not printed in full. Selected plans are also reprinted with the substantive statutes to which they relate, in *USCS* as well as in *U.S. Code* and *USCA*, with these locations indicated by numerical tables in each edition.

Presidential documents are indexed in several locations, including the *Weekly Compilation*, the official *Federal Register* index (under "Presidential Documents"), and the *CIS Federal Register Index* (discussed later in this chapter). The *CIS Index to Presidential Executive Orders and Proclamations* (22 vols., 1986-87), covering the years 1787 through 1983, indexes more than 75,000 presidential documents by subject, name, and date. The documents themselves are available from CIS on microfiche.

Executive orders, proclamations, and other presidential documents are widely available through electronic sources. WESTLAW has executive orders since 1936 and other presidential documents since 1984 in the PRES database, and LEXIS-NEXIS has all presidential documents since 1979 in the PRESDC file. On the Internet, the *Weekly Compilation of Presidential Documents* since 1995 is available from GPO Access <http://www.access.gpo.gov/nara/nara003.html>, and presidential documents are also available from the White House Virtual Library <http://library.whitehouse.gov>.

Court decisions and law review articles citing executive orders, proclamations, and reorganization plans can be found in *Shepard's Code of Federal Regulations Citations* (Shepard's, 2 vols., 1994, with monthly supplement). Coverage extends back to 1950 for cases and 1977 for law review articles.

REGULATIONS

The basic procedure by which most agencies govern their areas is issuance of rules and regulations. (The terms *rule* and *regulation* are used interchangeably when referring to sources of administrative law. Agencies *issue* or *promulgate* regulations, as opposed to elected legislatures, which *enact* or *pass* laws.)

The regulations from all federal agencies can be found in two major publications. The *Federal Register* is a daily gazette containing the text of all new regulations, and the *Code of Federal Regulations* is a subject arrangement of the rules in force. These two publications are the most important resources in federal administrative law.

The *Federal Register* and *Code of Federal Regulations* both began in the 1930s, as a direct result of the proliferation of administrative agencies during the New Deal. In the early years of Franklin Roosevelt's presidency, there was no central repository or publication from which people could determine what regulations existed. In 1934, several Texas oilmen were convicted of violating an administrative order that was no longer even in force. Their case made it all the way to the Supreme Court before the government discovered its error and quietly asked that it be dismissed. The motion was granted in a one-line note, *U.S. v. Smith*, 293 U.S. 633 (1934), but the significance of the development did not escape the notice of the justices, who at the time were not known for their support of New Deal programs. When the solicitor general appeared before them to argue another case two months later, they inquired at length about means of access to administrative rules and orders. The government's lawyer had to admit that there was no official publication in which they could be found.

The resulting publicity led to the enactment of the Federal Register Act in July 1935, ch. 417, 49 Stat. 500, and the first issue of the *Federal Register* was published on March 14, 1936. It did not take long to see that a simple chronological publication was insufficient for determining what regulations were in force, and a 1937 amendment to the Federal Register Act, ch. 369, 50 Stat. 304, created a subject compilation, the *Code of Federal Regulations*, which was first published in 1939.

The scope of the *Federal Register* increased substantially with the 1946 enactment of the Administrative Procedure Act, ch. 324, 60 Stat. 237, which created a system of rulemaking under which proposed regulations are announced and made available for public comment. Corporations, trade groups, local government agencies, and any other interested members of the public can submit comments, which the agency then considers in preparing its final rule for adoption.

Cornelius M. Kerwin's *Rulemaking: How Government Agencies Write Law and Make Policy* (CQ Press, 1994) provides a clear overview of the regulatory process, including chapters on the process of rulemaking, public participation, and oversight by Congress and the courts. Several tables illustrate such issues as the growth of rulemaking over the years and the influence of interest groups in agency rulemaking.

Code of Federal Regulations

Just as the *United States Code* is generally the starting point in statutory research, the *Code of Federal Regulations* is the place to begin an inquiry into administrative law. The *CFR* consists of 50 subject titles and more than 200 paperback volumes, which are revised and reissued each year.

To make this revision process ongoing, the cutoff date for inclusion of new regulations varies from title to title. Titles 1–16 contain regulations in force as of January 1; Titles 17–27 as of April 1; Titles 28–41 as of July 1; and Titles 42–50 as of October 1. At any given point in the year some volumes contain regulations up-to-date within two or three months, while the regulations in others are more than a year old. A list of volumes in a current *CFR* set is published in each Monday's issue of the *Federal Register*.

The scope of federal regulation has expanded considerably since the first *CFR* edition was published in 1939, but the basic structure of *CFR* titles has changed little. Titles 2 and 6, covering Congress and agricultural credit, are no longer used, and a handful of other titles have changed subject. Among these is Title 40, which originally covered prisons but became "Protection of Environment" in 1972.

Although both the *U.S. Code* and the *CFR* are divided into subject titles numbered from 1 to 50, the arrangement of the two works is not the same. The *U.S. Code* is truly arranged by subject, while the *CFR* is arranged by agency. Regulations of the Environmental Protection Agency, for example, are found in Title 40, even though they administer a variety of statutes found in several different titles of the *U.S. Code*.

In many instances, the statutes and regulations governing a particular area are in the same titles of the *U.S. Code* and *CFR*. For example, Title 8 in both sources covers immigration and nationality; Title 21, food and drug; Title 26, internal revenue; and Title 29, labor. But this is not always the case. Education regulations are in Title 34 of the *CFR*, rather than Title 20; and securities regulations are in Title 17, rather than Title 15. Title 50 of the *U.S. Code* concerns war and national defense, while Title 50 of the *CFR* deals with wildlife and fisheries.

Generally, each agency's regulations appear in one chapter, although there are exceptions. The Agricultural Marketing Service encompasses four chapters of Title 7 (Agriculture), while the Animal and Plant Health Inspection Service has chapters in both Title 7 and Title 9 (Animals and Animal Products). A "chapter" is not necessarily limited in length. The EPA's chapter in Title 40 runs to 22 volumes and more than 14,000 pages. (In 1972, the first year that EPA regulations appeared in Title 40, they covered just 415 pages in one volume.)

More than 300 distinct agencies are represented in the *CFR*. Regulations of related agencies are gathered in one title regardless of the departmental structure. Title 50, Wildlife and Fisheries, for example, includes regulations from the U.S. Fish and Wildlife Service (Department of the Interior), National Marine Fisheries Service (Department of Commerce), and Marine Mammal Commission (an independent agency). A list in the back of each volume (as well as in the *U.S. Government Manual*) indicates the titles and chapters in which agencies are represented. Those agencies that are part of cabinet departments (such as the Food and Drug Administration and the Occupational Safety and Health Administration) are listed both alphabetically and under their departments.

Regulations of the Bureau of Prisons are found in *CFR* Title 28, Chapter 5. This *CFR* title is updated every year as of July 1, and the revised volume is generally available by late September. Besides regulations of the Bureau of Prisons, Title 28 also includes regulations of various Department of Justice divisions in Chapter 1, Federal Prison Industries, Inc. in Chapter 3, and the Offices of Independent Counsel in Chapters 6 and 7. Other agencies within the Department of Justice are found elsewhere in the *CFR*, including the Immigration and Naturalization Service in Title 8 (Aliens and Nationality), and the Drug Enforcement Administration in Title 21 (Food and Drugs).

An agency's chapter is divided into subchapters by subject, and then into parts dealing with specific topics. For example, the Bureau of Prisons chapter is divided into four subchapters covering general administration; inmate admission, classification, and transfer; institutional management; and community programs and release. Part 540, the first page of which is shown in Exhibit 10-2, is part of the subchapter on institutional management, along with parts covering such topics as education, food service, religious programs, and medical services.

CFR parts are further subdivided, sometimes into subparts, and finally into individual sections. In a citation to an individual *CFR* section, the part number is followed by a period and the section number. (This is a separate number and not a decimal.) Thus, the provision governing special mail is cited as "28 CFR § 540.18," and these regulations as a whole can be cited as "28 CFR Part 540." Some sources refer to *CFR* sections and others to *CFR* parts; these are just ways to be more or less specific about the same material.

Following the outline of Part 540's contents are two valuable notes in small type. An *authority note* lists the laws under which the Bureau is making these regulations. For Part 540 this includes several sections of the *U.S. Code*, as well as an uncodified law in the *Statutes at Large* and the sections of the *CFR* (28 CFR 0.95-0.99) that outline the responsibilities of the Bureau within the Department of Justice organization. The authority note can be useful for determining the scope of an agency's power and the specificity of its congressional mandate. Some of the statutes listed deal directly with the issues addressed by the regulations, while others are simply enabling statutes creating the agency and giving it jurisdiction over its subject area.

The note following the heading for Subpart A in Exhibit 10-2, the *source note*, is even more valuable in administrative law research because it provides the reference to the location in the *Federal Register* at which the regulations were first published. This is important because the *Federal Register* generally provides more information about the regulation than is available from its text alone. Note that the source code here lists "50 FR 40108, Oct. 1, 1985, unless otherwise noted." The "otherwise noted" means that individual sections may have been added or amended since 1985, and additional source notes after these sections will provide further information.

The *CFR* is available in a number of electronic formats. The most widely available is on the Web from the Government Printing Office <http://www.access.gpo.gov/nara/cfr>. The GPO Access version is updated on the same basis as the paper version and can be searched in several ways. Specific sections can be retrieved by citation, and the entire current set can be searched by keyword. One can also limit searches to specific titles or volumes, which is quicker but requires knowing which agency is involved in a particular is-

Pt. 540   28 CFR Ch. V (7-1-97 Edition)

SUBCHAPTER C—INSTITUTIONAL MANAGEMENT

PART 540—CONTACT WITH PERSONS IN THE COMMUNITY

Subpart A—General

AUTHORITY: 5 U.S.C. 301, 551, 552a; 18 U.S.C. 1791, 3621, 3622, 3624, 4001, 4042, 4081, 4082 (Repealed in part as to offenses committed on or after November 1, 1987), 5006-5024 (Repealed October 12, 1984, as to offenses committed after that date), 5039; 28 U.S.C. 509, 510; Public Law 104-208, section 614 (110 Stat. 3009); 28 CFR 0.95-0.99.

Subpart A—General

SOURCE: 50 FR 40108, Oct. 1, 1985, unless otherwise noted.

§ 540.2 Definitions.

(a) *General correspondence* means incoming or outgoing correspondence other than *special mail. General correspondence* includes packages sent through the mail.

(1) *Open general correspondence* means general correspondence which is not limited to a list of authorized correspondents, except as provided in § 540.17.

(2) *Restricted general correspondence* means general correspondence which is limited to a list of authorized correspondents.

(b) *Representatives of the news media* means persons whose principal employment is to gather or report news for:

(1) A newspaper which qualifies as a general circulation newspaper in the community in which it is published. A newspaper is one of "general circulation" if it circulates among the general

450

sue. Sections retrieved can be viewed in plain text or PDF format.

The *CFR* is one of the major electronic products of the Government Printing Office, but, from the main GPO Access page, access to the *CFR* is hidden in the alphabetical listing under "National Archives and Records Administration's Office of the Federal Register." For Webless researchers, GPO Access is also accessible by Telnet at swais.access.gpo.gov (log in as *guest*) or by dial-in access at (202) 512-1661 (type *swais* and then log in as *guest*).

Subscription databases provide online access to more convenient versions of the *CFR* because they are updated on an ongoing basis to include new regulations. The *CFR* versions available through LEXIS-NEXIS (in the CODES or GENFED library) and WESTLAW are generally less than two weeks old. WESTLAW's *CFR* database provides even more current information by including "update" links to the *Federal Register* if a section is affected by new regulations that have not yet been incorporated. The LEXIS-NEXIS edition of the *CFR* is also available on the Web through CIS's subscription site, Congressional Universe <http://web.lexis-nexis.com/cis>. Other subscription databases providing access to regularly updated versions of the *CFR* include Law Office Information Systems (LOIS) <http://www.pita.com>, and LEGI-SLATE, which offers the most current *CFR* by providing the codified versions of new regulations the same day they are published.

Older editions of the *CFR* are sometimes needed to determine what regulations were in force at a particular time. The GPO Access site does not yet include many superseded versions, but it is keeping volumes on its site as they are replaced. Coverage starts with selected 1996 volumes. Individual titles and volumes can be searched, and older sections can be retrieved by number. The online databases also provide access to older editions of the *CFR*, back to 1981 (LEXIS-NEXIS), 1984 (WESTLAW), and 1988 (LEGI-SLATE).

The *CFR* is also available on CD-ROM from several publishers. *CFRplus on LawDesk* (West Group, monthly) may be the most powerful because it includes not only the currently codified regulations but background information from the *Federal Register*. A much less expensive version, *All 50 CFRs CD-ROM*, updated quarterly, is published by Solutions Software Corp.

Researchers using the *CFR* must remember two important points. First, except for the expensive online versions, the *CFR* is not updated between annual editions. Regulations change frequently, and it is necessary to check for changes by referring to a separate, specialized publication designed for this purpose, *LSA: List of CFR Sections Affected*. Second, no *CFR* format contains annotations of court decisions like *United States Code Annotated* or *United States Code Service*. Although regulations are cited in fewer cases than statutes, a court's interpretation of a *CFR* section can be an important consideration.

Federal Register

The most extensive source for regulatory information is the *Federal Register*, published daily by the U.S. government. It contains not just new regulations, but *proposed* regulations, notices of upcoming meetings, and other announcements. Each issue follows a standard format. A table of contents, arranged by agency, and a table of *Code of Federal Regulations* citations affected by new or proposed regulations appear in each issue. These are followed by separate sections containing new final rules, proposed rules, notices, and presidential documents.

At the end of each issue are "Reader Aids" pages providing telephone numbers for *Federal Register* customer service, as well as a list of *Federal Register* pages and dates for the month (useful for determining in which issue to find a particular citation). A cumulative table lists *CFR* parts affected since the beginning of the month and can be an important tool in checking the current status of a regulation.

The *Federal Register* is obviously the source for the text of newly adopted regulations that have not yet been incorporated into annual *CFR* volumes. In addition, it provides background information that never appears in the *CFR*. Preambles, designed to provide clear, straightforward explanations of the regulatory action, accompany proposed and final rules in the *Federal Register*. Under the rules governing publication of rules, the preamble should "inform the reader, who is not an expert in the subject area, of the basis and purpose for the rule or proposal" (1 CFR § 18.12[a]). As the Administrative Committee of the Federal Register explained in *its* preamble when it published this rule, even though "many problems addressed by Federal agencies are extremely complex and technical and therefore some regulations are necessarily complex and technical, . . . the need for, and intended effect of, even the most complex and technical regulation can be explained in words that can be understood by a person who is not an expert in the subject matter" (41 Fed. Reg. 56,623-56,624 [Dec. 29, 1976]).

Besides presenting an overview of the regulatory action, preambles include the names, addresses, and telephone numbers of agency personnel responsible for responding to inquiries. Preambles to final rules also provide agencies' analysis of comments received on the proposed rule.

Preambles are important documents because they may explain matters not apparent on the face of the regulation. They may also have legal significance. In establishing the rule in 1976, the Administrative Conference stressed that preambles are not simply reader aids but also serve a purpose similar to that of committee reports and other legislative history materials in interpreting statutes. The Administrative Conference noted that "normal rules of construction would apply. That is, the courts would follow the language of a regulation as long as it is clear and would look to materials, not included in the regulation, such as the preamble statement, only to clarify ambiguity."

An example of a *Federal Register* preamble is provided in Exhibit 10-3. In December 1997, the Bureau of Prisons revised its special mail procedures in instances where the mail may pose a threat of physical harm to the intended recipient. The Bureau had published a proposed rule in February 1996 and received eight comments on issues such as whether the revision was necessary and whether it provided the least restrictive method of achieving its goals. The proposed rule was modified somewhat in response to the comments, and it took effect in January 1998.

Sometimes the *Federal Register* preamble can explain apparent discrepancies between a statute and a regulation. For example, the Magnuson-Moss Warranty Act in the U.S. Code, at 15 U.S.C. § 2302, specifies that its provisions apply to consumer goods costing more than $5. The Federal Trade Commission raised this to $15 in its regulations at 16 CFR Part 701, but the codified regulations indicate no reason for this change. A quick glance at the source the *CFR* cites, however, 40 Fed. Reg. 60,188 (1975), reveals that the FTC originally proposed a $5 minimum for coverage but was convinced by the comments it received that a $15 minimum would be more in the public interest. Its explanation includes a discussion of whether it had the authority to raise this minimum, concluding, obviously, that it did.

Many proposed regulations are uncontroversial and do not elicit much response. On the other hand, the Fish and Wildlife Service received more than 160,000 comments when it proposed reintroducing wolves into Yellowstone National Park. The final rule outlining the history of this decision-making process is published at 59 Fed. Reg. 60,252 (1994).

The comments themselves are not generally published, but they are available in agency offices. Some are posted on the Internet. The FCC, for example, uses an Electronic Comment Filing System <http://www.fcc.gov/e-file/ecfs.html> through which comments can be submitted. Comments can also be searched by proceeding number, date, persons on whose behalf the comments are filed, law firm, and attorney name. The Department of Interior's Office of Surface Mining Reclamation and Enforcement has put collections of comments on its 1978 and 1982 proposed regulations on LEXIS-NEXIS (ENERGY library, REGCOM and COMNTS files).

The *Federal Register* is available on the Web from GPO Access <http://www.access.gpo.gov/su_docs/aces/aces140.html>, beginning with volume 59 (1994). It is searchable by keyword, and searches since 1995 can also be limited to specific sections of the *Federal Register* (such as final rules, proposed rules, or notices) or by date. Documents since 1995 can also be retrieved in PDF format to replicate the printed version.

LEXIS-NEXIS (FEDREG file of the CODES or GENFED library) and WESTLAW (FR database) provide online access to the *Federal Register* back to July 1980. The same material is available on the Internet from Congressional Universe <http://web.lexis-nexis.com/cis>. Services with less extensive backfiles include LEGI-SLATE (1985-date), DIALOG (File 669, 1988-date), and CQ Washington Alert (1990-date). Several CD versions are published, including editions by KR OnDisc (1990-date), West Group (1991-date), and Solutions Software Corp. (1994-date). Each of these is updated on a monthly basis.

For the faint at heart, WESTLAW includes a separate database containing just the table of contents, FR-TOC, even though a searcher can obtain the same result by limiting a search to the PRELIM (type of document, issuing agency, and affected *CFR* parts) and CAPTION (subject matter) fields. WESTLAW also has a regulation tracking database, US-REGTRK, from Information for Public Affairs, Inc., with summaries and status information about pending regulations. The US-REGTRK database includes the citations of *CFR* parts affected, contact information, comment deadlines, and effective dates, but not *Federal Register* citations.

Twice a year, the *Federal Register* publishes the government's Unified Agenda of planned regulatory actions. This document provides a summary of regulatory actions on which each agency is working, includ-

65184 Federal Register / Vol. 62, No. 237 / Wednesday, December 10, 1997 / Rules and Regulations

DEPARTMENT OF JUSTICE

Bureau of Prisons

28 CFR Part 540

[BOP–1048–F]

RIN 1120–AA48

Correspondence: Restricted Special Mail Procedures

AGENCY: Bureau of Prisons, Justice.
ACTION: Final rule.

SUMMARY: In this document, the Bureau of Prisons is amending its regulations on correspondence to provide for restricted special mail procedures in instances where the Warden has reason to believe that the special mail either has posed a threat or may pose a threat of physical harm to the intended recipient. Under these procedures, such special mail is subject to inspection, in the presence of the inmate, for contraband and, at the request of the intended recipient, may be read for the purpose of verifying that the special mail does not contain a threat of physical harm. These amendments are intended to provide for the continued efficient and secure operation of the institution and to protect the public.

EFFECTIVE DATE: January 9, 1998.

ADDRESSES: Office of General Counsel, Bureau of Prisons, HOLC Room 754, 320 First Street, NW., Washington, DC 20534.

FOR FURTHER INFORMATION CONTACT: Roy Nanovic, Office of General Counsel, Bureau of Prisons, phone (202) 514–6655.

SUPPLEMENTARY INFORMATION: The Bureau of Prisons is amending its regulations on correspondence (28 CFR part 540). A proposed rule on this subject was published in the **Federal Register** February 14, 1996 (61 FR 5846).

Provisions in § 540.18(c) previously stated that outgoing special mail may be sealed by the inmate and is not subject to inspection. The Bureau proposed a revised paragraph (c) to allow for restricted special mail procedures for special mail addressed to Federal court officials and members of Congress, and, if so requested, to other intended recipients. These restricted special mail procedures would apply in cases where the Warden (with the concurrence of the Regional Counsel) documents in writing that the inmate's special mail either has posed a threat or may pose a threat of physical harm to the intended recipient. Any inmate placed on restricted special mail status would be notified in writing by the Warden of the reason for being

so placed. The Warden is required to review an inmate's restricted special mail status at least once every 180 days and to notify the inmate in writing of the results of that review. The inmate may be removed from restricted special mail status if the Warden (with the concurrence of the Regional Counsel) determines that the inmate's special mail does not threaten or pose a threat of physical harm to the intended recipient. Such determinations are based on a comprehensive review of pertinent factors, such as the inmate's institutional adjustment, institution security level, and a current assessment of the conditions which led to the inmate's placement into restricted special mail status.

The Bureau received 8 comments on its proposed rule. Comment generally focused on the purported need for the proposed restrictions, possible infringement on the confidentiality of the attorney-client privilege, possible delay in handling mail being sent to courts, consideration of other means of dealing with the threat posed by such special mail (including duplicative security measures in place for recipients), ulterior motivation for the restrictions, and the general futility of preventing abuse.

With respect to the need for the regulation, the Bureau disagrees with suggestions that the rule misrepresents its intent. The rule is not intended to restrict an inmate s legal access. Instead, it is intended to help ensure institution security, discipline, and good order, and to protect the public. The Bureau notes that instances have occurred where special mail has caused, or has threatened physical injury to the recipient. While these instances may not constitute a widespread problem, neither do the procedures for restricted special mail status pose any change to the special mail privilege for the vast majority of inmates. Even so, for the purpose of assuring its commitment to the integrity of special mail, the Bureau has modified the proposed procedures to protect the special mail privilege to the extent practicable and commensurate with the need for the security, discipline and good order of the institution.

As previously proposed, the procedures apply only to inmates who have been placed on restricted special mail status (that is to say, those inmates whose special mail has been documented by the Warden, with the concurrence of the Regional Counsel, either to have posed a threat or which may pose a threat to the recipient). An inmate in this status must present all materials and packaging intended to be

sent as special mail to staff for inspection. Staff shall inspect the special mail material and packaging, in the presence of the inmate, for contraband. This last provision deletes the proposed phrase ''or the threat of physical harm'', as its intent is encompassed within the remaining provision of inspecting for contraband. This change addresses the concern of commenters that the proposed procedure infringes upon the confidentiality of the attorney-client privilege or access to the courts. As revised, the rule now states that staff reading of the correspondence is restricted to when the recipient of the special mail has so requested (the rule as proposed had assumed such permission with respect to Federal court officials and members of Congress). As revised, the procedure now more closely parallels the process for inspecting incoming special mail (see § 540.18).

Upon completion of the inspection, staff shall return the special mail material to the inmate if the material does not contain contraband or, when requested by the intended recipient, a reading determines that there is no threat of physical harm. The inmate must then seal the special mail material in the presence of staff. Special mail determined to pose a threat shall be forwarded to the appropriate law enforcement entity, and staff shall send a copy of the material, minus the contraband, to the intended recipient along with notification that the original of the material was forwarded to the appropriate law enforcement entity.

In response to comments, the Bureau does not expect this procedure to have much impact on the processing of special mail. The limited applicability of the rule and the general Bureau policy that mail be handled promptly should ensure that this mail is processed in a timely fashion.

In response to commenters who suggested that sufficient and less restrictive means were available to the intended recipients of special mail to address threats posed by the special mail, the Bureau believes its procedures are both prudent and unobstrusive. Visually observing the assembling of special mail serves to deter the actual transmission of dangerous materials and is compatible with the existing procedures for handling incoming special mail (see § 540.18). This protects both the intended recipient and other persons involved in the delivery or opening of the special mail. While the Bureau acknowledges, as one commenter noted, that this procedure may not be successful in preventing every possible instance of harm, the

EXHIBIT 10-3

ing regulations at the prerule stage, proposed rule stage, and final rule stage. It includes a detailed subject index.

In recent years, the Unified Agenda has appeared sometime between late April and mid-May, and again between late October and late November. The simplest way to find the Unified Agenda is to look for the fattest possible daily issue of the *Federal Register*. The October 29, 1997 issue, for example, occupies more than 1,500 pages in four separate pamphlets. This also is the only *Federal Register* publication of the Regulatory Information Service Center, so it can be found under the center's name in the monthly or annual *Federal Register Index*.

The fall Unified Agenda includes an annual Regulatory Plan, in which agencies provide narrative statements of their regulatory priorities and descriptions of the most significant actions they expect to issue in proposed or final form in the upcoming year. The Regulatory Plan covers about half as many agencies as the Unified Agenda.

Listings in the Regulatory Plan and Unified Agenda are predictions and don't create any legal obligations that the agencies accomplish their stated goals, but they are useful signposts of intended actions. The Bureau of Prisons rule shown in Exhibit 10-3, as published in the December 10, 1997, *Federal Register*, appeared in five editions of the Unified Agenda, back to Fall 1995. Originally it was listed as "Next Action Undetermined," and then its "Final Action" date was simply rescheduled, from September 1996, to December 1996, to July 1997, and finally to December 1997.

More information on the *Federal Register* is available in a pamphlet that is frequently shelved with recent issues, *The Federal Register: What It Is and How to Use It* (Office of the Federal Register, rev. ed., 1992). This pamphlet provides extensive examples of materials published in the *Federal Register* and explains how to use the various publications needed to find and update regulations.

Other Regulatory Sources

The *Code of Federal Regulations* and *Federal Register* are the only comprehensive sources for federal regulations, covering every department and agency. Other sources cover regulations from specific agencies or in particular subject areas.

A few agencies issue their own publications, containing regulations and other legal materials. Chief among these are the Federal Communications Commission and the Internal Revenue Service, each of which regularly publishes a record of its regulatory actions. The *FCC Record* (biweekly) is a truly voluminous publication, covering adjudications and licensing proceedings as well as rulemaking. Documents are simply reprinted, with no uniform typography and little indexing. More than 20,000 pages are churned out each year. The *Internal Revenue Bulletin* (weekly) is a more polished publication, professionally typeset and carefully organized. New regulations and rulings are published not simply in chronological order but according to the section of the Internal Revenue Code to which they relate. The *Internal Revenue Bulletin* also includes the text of new tax legislation and treaties, and reprints major congressional committee reports on tax laws. Twice a year the weekly *Bulletins* are superseded by *Cumulative Bulletin* volumes, which arrange six months of material by code section. Finding lists in both weekly and semiannual *Bulletins* make it possible to find IRS regulations (known as Treasury Decisions) and rulings by number.

Some agencies publish their regulations on CD-ROM. Agencies issuing CD-ROMs include the Health Care Financing Administration (*HCFA's Laws—Titles XI, XVIII, XIX; Regulations—Titles 42, 45; Manuals*, monthly) and the Occupational Safety and Health Administration (*OSHA CD-ROM*, quarterly). These generally provide the agency's regulations as well as supplemental materials, such as interpretations, directives, and program manuals. Although some of these are convenient products providing PDF documents and sophisticated searching, others are rather clunky, DOS-based packages.

Several agencies provide electronic access to their regulations through their Web sites. Although the same information is also available through GPO Access, the agency site may offer a more convenient way to integrate a search for regulations into other research. The EPA homepage, for example, provides direct access to Title 40 of the *CFR*, EPA *Federal Register* documents, and its Unified Agenda, as well as links to GPO Access's file. Regulations are available from the EPA in PDF format, as they are from GPO Access.

Commercial publishers also publish regulations in specific subject areas. *United States Code Service* and *United States Code Annotated* both reprint a limited number of regulations. *USCS* coverage extends only to consumer credit issues, while *USCA* includes about two dozen specific sets of regulations in such areas as banking, labor law, and patents. Most of these are rules governing practice before boards and commissions. The most extensive set is the Social Security

Administration's disability insurance regulations at 20 CFR Part 404, which *USCA* reprints in two volumes supplementing Title 42 of the statutes.

Tax regulations are published in annual volumes of *U.S. Code Congressional and Administrative News,* by West Group, and in the tax loose-leaf services *Standard Federal Tax Reporter* (CCH) and *United States Tax Reporter* (RIA). The latter works print the regulations, along with the Internal Revenue Code sections to which they relate, and include the text of proposed and temporary regulations. Other features include editorial commentary, notes of relevant decisions, and weekly updates of new developments. The context and editorial explanation can help to clarify regulations in a complicated area such as tax law.

Other loose-leaf services also reprint regulations in their subject areas. The major advantage they offer is more frequent updating than the annual *CFR* volumes, but some services are more helpful than others. *Federal Securities Law Reports* (CCH), like the tax services, prints regulations following related *U.S. Code* sections, accompanied by explanation and annotations of rulings and court decisions. Other services simply provide the text of the regulations without commentary. *Environment Reporter* (BNA) does this, in nine large, ungainly binders. The regulations in *Environment Reporter* are more frequently updated than they are in *CFR*, but they are no clearer. Some loose-leaf services use more than one approach. *Trade Regulation Reporter* (CCH) lists some regulations by subject and some in a separate "FTC Trade Rules and Guides" section. A finding list by *CFR* citation leads to the location of specific regulations in the set.

Commercial publishers also issue collections of subject regulations on CD-ROM. For example, two comprehensive (and expensive) CD-ROM products containing statutes, regulations, and other related materials in specialized areas are *Communications Regulation on CD-ROM* (Pike & Fischer, monthly), with the full text of 47 CFR, and *The Food and Drug Library* (IHS Regulatory Products, monthly), with FDA regulations as well as guides, manuals, press releases, and other material from the agency.

Finding Regulations

Finding the regulations of a particular agency is a fairly straightforward affair. One can search by agency, statute, or subject. In addition, tables and notes can provide references to regulations relating to particular statutes. As is often the case, the most difficult search is for regulations by subject or keyword.

Agency

As noted earlier, an alphabetical list of agencies appears in the back of each *CFR* volume, and the *U.S. Government Manual*, indicating which title and chapter of the *CFR* contains each agency's regulations. Offices within cabinet departments are listed both separately and under the department. This list is preceded in the *CFR* volumes by an outline of the entire set's titles and chapters. If an agency is represented in more than one title, the outline makes it easier to determine which subject is covered in each of its chapters.

New and proposed regulations from particular agencies are almost as easy to find. Even though the *Federal Register* is divided into separate sections for final rules, proposed rules, and notices, the table of contents in each issue is arranged alphabetically by agency name. This makes it easy to monitor activities by a specific agency. Agencies within departments are listed separately, but the table of contents includes cross-references from departments to any of its subdivisions represented that day. To assist alphabetization, agencies with names beginning with "Bureau of" or "Office of" are listed in an odd, inverted format: Land Management Bureau, Prisons Bureau, Thrift Supervision Office. (A recognizable format like "Prisons, Bureau of" would also serve this purpose but is not used.) This twisting of names does not extend to all agencies; those beginning with "Federal" or "National" are listed under their full titles.

Accompanying the *Federal Register* is a monthly index, which cumulates the daily tables of contents. It too is arranged by agency name, with cross-references from departments to more specific agencies. Each monthly index cumulates the entries from previous months, so the latest provides access to the entire *Federal Register* from the beginning of the calendar year. Rules, proposed rules, and notices are listed separately under each agency. Although this is a frustrating index for searches by subject, it can provide a useful, quick guide to activities by specific agencies.

Statute

Regulations under a specific statute can be found in several ways. The *CFR Index and Finding Aids* volume includes a "Parallel Table of Authorities and Rules," listing code sections that are cited as statutory authority for *CFR* parts. This table is simply a compilation of the authority notes provided by the agencies, with no editorial effort to coordinate the format, so there is some inconsistency in how statutory sources are cited. Most statutes are listed under *U.S. Code* citations, but some are listed as *Statutes at Large* and a few as Public Law numbers.

A more useful source of references to regulations from specific statutory provisions is the cross-references provided in the notes following sections in *United States Code Annotated* and *United States Code Service*. These link references to regulations with statutes on the same topic. Of the two annotated codes, *USCS* generally includes more *CFR* references. Bureau of Prisons regulations, for example, are noted in fewer than 10 sections in *USCA* but in more than three dozen sections in *USCS*. 18 U.S.C. § 4042, outlining the duties of the Bureau, includes only a general reference to 28 CFR Chapter V in *USCA*, while *USCS* mentions more than 20 distinct parts of the title. Like other features in *USCA* and *USCS*, these references are updated in the annual supplements.

Subject

Finding regulations by subject is not so easy. The *CFR Index and Finding Aids* volume contains a subject index, but its entries are rather general and finding appropriate entries can be frustrating. The index refers only to parts, not to specific sections. A page from this index is shown in Exhibit 10-4. Note under "Prisoners" that the only reference to Part 540 is under the subheading "Institutional management—Contact with persons in community."

A comparison with the index for the *U.S. Code* reveals the level of inadequacy of the *CFR* index in this regard. The *U.S. Code* index occupies seven volumes and nearly 9,000 pages; the *CFR* has more than twice as many sections as the *U.S. Code*, but its index is a mere 700 pages in one pamphlet. One sign of the lack of esteem with which this index is viewed is that GPO Access does not bother to include it in its Internet *CFR* coverage, even though it does provide the "Parallel Table of Authorities and Rules" from the same volume.

Despite its shortcomings, the *CFR Index and Finding Aids* is the most widely available subject index to the *CFR*. The present index is clearly inadequate, but it is still an improvement over the index that once accompanied the *CFR*. In 1976, an attorney sued to compel the government to produce a better index than the 164-page version that then covered 120 volumes (*Cervase v. Office of the Federal Register*, 580 F.2d 1166 [2d Cir. 1978]). The government reluctantly agreed to make improvements, but 700 pages is still rather pathetic, particularly when one considers that the index for the original 1939 edition of the *CFR*, covering just 17 volumes, was more than 500 pages.

A commercial *Index to the Code of Federal Regulations* (CIS, 4 vols., annual) contains more specific references to individual sections. The CIS index is much more thorough than the official index; under "Prison Inmates" are eight references to particular sections within Part 540, covering such topics as mail inspection, interviews with news reporters, and telephone calls. Volume 4 includes a geographic index and an administrative history of the *CFR*, noting changes since 1939 in the designation and contents of each title. This index is supplemented quarterly with coverage of new and revised regulations published in the *Federal Register*, indexed by subject and by *CFR* section.

As noted above, finding new regulations in the *Federal Register* by subject can be difficult. Because the official *Federal Register Index* is arranged by agency, rather than by subject, it is of little use to anyone who does not know what agency has jurisdiction over a particular issue. CIS, however, also publishes an extensive subject index to the *Federal Register*. CIS *Federal Register Index* (1984-date, weekly, with bound semiannual volumes) provides thorough, detailed coverage on a more current basis than the official index. It also includes indexes by *CFR* section and agency docket number.

A keyword search through the Internet or an online database, of course, may be the best way to find relevant regulations. Besides the separate *CFR* and *Federal Register* files, LEXIS-NEXIS provides a comprehensive ALLREG file, which combines the current *CFR* and *Federal Register* issues back to 1980. Even searched separately, the *CFR* and *Federal Register* are voluminous publications in which terms appear in many contexts, so searches must be carefully tailored to achieve useful results. Relevance ranking, such as that used by GPO Access, can help sort through a large retrieval. It is also important to remember that searches in the *CFR* retrieve individual sections; thus, it may be necessary to scan the chapters and parts in which sections are codified to get a better sense of their context.

Updating Regulations

An essential part of any legal research is determining if the relevant rules remain in force. For case law, this is done by looking for recent decisions that may have overruled or limited a case's holding. For statutes, annotated codes provide information about amendments and about judicial decisions interpreting provisions. Federal administrative law has its own updating process, one that can be confusing at first but is actually quite straightforward.

CFR Index   **Prisoners**

Price support programs

Agriculture Department, National Appeals Division procedure rules, 7 CFR 11

Commodity and conservation programs
   Commodity certificates, in kind payments, and other forms of payment, 7 CFR 1401

   Payments due persons who have died, disappeared, or have been declared incompetent, 7 CFR 707

Commodity Credit Corporation, trustee eligibility, rule of fractions, 7 CFR 1405

Cooperative marketing associations, 7 CFR 1425

Cotton, 7 CFR 1427

Dairy products, 7 CFR 1430

Export programs, terms and conditions for purchase of tobacco under export credit sales program, 7 CFR 1489

Grains and similarly handled commodities, 7 CFR 1421

Highly erodible land and wetland conservation, 7 CFR 12

Honey, 7 CFR 1434

Integrated farm management program option, 7 CFR 1414

Multiple programs, provisions applicable to, 7 CFR 718

Options pilot program, 7 CFR 1415

Parity prices determination, 7 CFR 5

Payment limitation, 7 CFR 795

Payment limitation and payment eligibility, 7 CFR 1400

Peanuts, 7 CFR 1446

Sugar, 7 CFR 1435

Tobacco, 7 CFR 1464

Voluntary production limitation program, 7 CFR 1416

Wheat, feed grains, rice, and upland cotton, production flexibility contracts, 7 CFR 1412

Wool and mohair, 7 CFR 1468

Printing

Acquisition regulations, required sources of supplies and services
   Agriculture Department, 48 CFR 408
   Energy Department, 48 CFR 908
   Environmental Protection Agency, 48 CFR 1508
   General Services Administration, 48 CFR 508
   Labor Department, 48 CFR 2908

National Aeronautics and Space Administration, 48 CFR 1808

Engraving and Printing Bureau, distinctive paper for U.S. currency and other securities, 31 CFR 601

Federal Acquisition Regulation, required sources of supplies and services, 48 CFR 8

Prisoners

Accident compensation for prison inmates, 28 CFR 301

Acquisition regulations, application of labor laws to Government acquisitions, Panama Canal Commission, 48 CFR 3522

Admission of inmates to institution, 28 CFR 522

Classification of inmates, 28 CFR 524

Community programs, 28 CFR 570

Computation of sentence, 28 CFR 523

Death sentences implementation in Federal cases, 28 CFR 26

Federal Acquisition Regulation, application of labor laws to Government acquisitions, 48 CFR 22

Functional literacy for State and local prisoners program, 34 CFR 489

General management and administration
   Costs of incarceration fee, 28 CFR 505
   General definitions, 28 CFR 500
   General management policy, 28 CFR 511
   Records access, 28 CFR 513
   Scope of rules, 28 CFR 501

Grievance procedures standards for inmates, 28 CFR 40

Indian country detention facilities and programs, 25 CFR 10

Inmate work programs, 28 CFR 345

Institutional management, inmates
   Administrative remedy, 28 CFR 542
   Contact with persons in community, 28 CFR 540
   Custody, 28 CFR 552
   Discipline and special housing units, 28 CFR 541
   Education, 28 CFR 544
   Food service, 28 CFR 547
   Grooming, nondiscrimination, smoking, family planning, organizations, contributions, manuscripts, polygraph tests, and pre-trial inmates, 28 CFR 551
   Inmate property, 28 CFR 553

EXHIBIT 10-4

Each month a pamphlet entitled *LSA: List of CFR Sections Affected* accompanies the *CFR*. This pamphlet lists any changes to regulations since the latest annual revision and indicates the *Federal Register* pages for these changes. It includes brief notes indicating the nature of the changes, such as "added," "removed," or "revised." An *LSA* page showing a reference under 28 CFR § 540.18 to the *Federal Register* rule in Exhibit 10-3 is shown in Exhibit 10-5.

LSA also includes references to proposed rules, although these are not as precise as those for actual changes. Proposed rule citations are listed separately at the end of each title, by part rather than by specific section. They also do not indicate the effect of a proposed change—whether it will amend the part slightly or replace it altogether. In Exhibit 10-5, a proposed change to Part 540 is listed at the bottom of the page. This turns out to be an amendment only to § 540.51, governing procedures for prison visits, but there is no way to know that without examining the *Federal Register* itself.

Because the titles of the *CFR* are revised throughout the year, the scope of coverage of each *LSA* pamphlet varies from title to title. The June *LSA*, for example, contains changes in Title 48 from the previous October through June, and in Title 26 only from April through June. In each instance, this is the coverage needed to bring the *CFR* provisions up-to-date from the latest revision through the month of the *LSA* pamphlet.

LSA covers all *Federal Register* items potentially affecting the *CFR*, including proposed rules, so the issues that cumulate 12 months of information form a permanent record for the year. Depending on the *CFR* title, this is a different monthly issue. Each year's June issue, for example, notes changes in Titles 28-41 from July 1 of the previous year through June 30. The Office of the Federal Register therefore advises libraries to retain the March, June, September, and December issues for their value in tracking regulatory developments. Some items in the *Federal Register*, such as temporary regulations that were adopted and then rescinded within a year, may never appear in the *CFR* itself.

Because *LSA* is not published until several weeks after the end of the month covered, there is still a gap in coverage. The next step is to consult the "CFR Parts Affected" table in the back of the last issue available for any month not covered by *LSA*. The tables in the daily *Federal Registers* cumulate entries for the entire month, so it is not necessary to check more than one issue per month. If, for example, the latest *LSA* avail-able is January and there are *Federal Register* issues through March 5, the issues to check are those for February 28 (or the last weekday in February) and March 5.

One situation requires the researcher to check more than one issue of *LSA*. If a *CFR* volume is more than a year old, updating its contents may require both the *LSA* issue covering 12 months of changes and a newer issue for subsequent changes. In September 1999, for example, to update a *CFR* volume current as of July 1, 1998, it is necessary to check the June 1999 *LSA* (with changes from July 1, 1998, to June 30, 1999), the August 1999 *LSA* (with changes during July and August), and the latest available September issue of *Federal Register*.

Significant differences characterize *LSA* and the "CFR Parts Affected" tables in the *Federal Register*. *LSA* indicates the specific *CFR* sections that are affected, while the *Federal Register* tables only list the more general *CFR* parts. The actions noted in a "CFR Parts Affected" table may not affect sections related to a research issue, but there is no way to tell without examining the individual *Federal Register* issues. Occasionally, in the case of long, frequently amended *CFR* parts, this may require checking several irrelevant citations. In addition, unlike *LSA*, the *Federal Register* table does not include explanatory notes, such as "amended" or "removed," indicating the nature of the change.

Usually lists of changes in the *CFR* are needed to bring a regulation up-to-date from the latest codification. They can also be used to track down an older reference in a case or article, as when a particular section of the *CFR* is cited, but the current version either has nothing at all or covers a completely different topic. This is not all that unusual because regulations are removed, superseded, and moved on a frequent basis. The most convenient place to begin tracking down what happened to the cited regulation is in the back of the current *CFR* volume, where lists indicate changes to sections in that volume for each year beginning in 1986. These provide one-word summaries of the changes and references to the *Federal Register* where the changes are published and explained. Earlier changes, from 1949 to 1985, are listed in a separate series of *List of CFR Sections Affected* volumes (1949-63, 1 vol.; 1964-72, 2 vols.; 1973-85, 4 vols.). Unlike *LSA*, these lists only cover rules that actually took effect, not proposed rules.

Updating regulations electronically can be a lot easier than using *LSA* and the *Federal Register* tables. Although GPO Access does not provide any convenient

CHANGES JULY 1, 1997 THROUGH JANUARY 30, 1998

NOTE: **Boldface page numbers indicate 1997 changes.**

EXHIBIT 10-5

updating method other than searching the *Federal Register* for a particular *CFR* part or section number, the commercial online databases are regularly updated to reflect new regulations. Even these versions, however, do not provide links from *CFR* sections to proposed changes that have not yet been adopted. To find these requires searching the full-text *Federal Register* database.

Because *LSA* and the *Federal Register* cover only administrative changes, the researcher must do one more thing before relying on a *CFR* provision as reflecting current law: Check for judicial decisions that may interpret a regulation or affect its validity. A court case might determine that a regulation is unconstitutional, but the unannotated *CFR* will not reflect this development unless the agency amends its regulation. For example, in 1989 a federal court threw out regulations in 45 CFR Part 1626 prohibiting the use of Legal Services Corporation funds for services to amnesty aliens, *California Rural Legal Assistance, Inc. v. Legal Services Corp.*, 727 F. Supp. 553 (N.D. Cal. 1989), *affirmed*, 917 F.2d 1171 (9th Cir. 1990). The invalidated regulations remained unchanged in the *CFR,* however, until they were finally amended in 1993.

In 1988, the Administrative Conference of the Federal Register proposed a requirement that agencies publish documents in the *Federal Register* when their regulations were affected by a court decision or an act of Congress (53 Fed. Reg. 29,990 [August 9, 1988]). Based on comments from agencies, however, the Conference decided not to impose this requirement due to confusion in how it would be interpreted and applied. It pointed out that "the requirement that the CFR contain documents having legal effect places responsibility on each agency to expeditiously amend its regulations whenever the regulations are rendered ineffective in whole or in part by a court decision or an Act of Congress" (54 Fed. Reg. 9,670 [March 7, 1989]).

Because agencies do not always act expeditiously, it is necessary to look elsewhere for judicial citations. The major printed source is *Shepard's Code of Federal Regulations Citations* (Shepard's, 2 vols., 1994, with monthly supplement), which lists court decisions and law review articles citing *CFR* sections. "Shepardizing" 28 CFR § 540.18, for example, leads to such cases as *Bieregu v. Reno*, 59 F.3d 1445 (3d Cir. 1995), in which the court found that prison officials' practice of opening legal mail outside of an inmate's presence violated the inmate's constitutional rights to free speech and court access. *Shepard's* also notes that other sections in 28 CFR Part 540, governing inmate receipt of publi-

cations, were considered by the Supreme Court in *Thornburgh v. Abbott*, 490 U.S. 401 (1989). Important cases are highlighted through the use of introductory signals such as *U* for "unconstitutional," or *V* for "void or invalid."

Regulations are frequently moved and amended, thus Shepardizing *CFR* citations can be tricky. To find relevant cases, it may be necessary first to trace the history of a *CFR* section. For example, Bureau of Prisons regulations governing general correspondence moved in 1985 from 28 CFR § 540.13 to § 540.14. A person looking under the current provision, § 540.14, would miss the reference to *Meadows v. Hopkins*, 713 F.2d 206 (6th Cir. 1983), which found these regulations to be constitutional. *Shepard's* provides some assistance by indicating the year of the *CFR* edition cited with an asterisk, as in "490US404*1988," or, if no specific *CFR* date is mentioned, the year of the citing reference with a delta, as in "C713F2d209 △ 1983." But these guides are only helpful to someone who knows the citation for a regulation in any given year.

Because relevant decisions can be easy to miss in *Shepard's*, it may be more fruitful to search the online databases for cases mentioning a particular agency and the subject of the specific regulation, perhaps in combination with a *CFR* part or section number.

Even a search this thorough may not turn up all relevant cases. The leading Supreme Court case on the handling of prisoners' correspondence, *Procunier v. Martinez*, 416 U.S. 396 (1974), was a constitutional challenge to California state prison regulations, and made no mention at all of the *CFR*. Yet its reasoning applies every bit as much to challenges to federal prison regulations. Such an occurrence shows why it is important to begin research with background texts or law review articles, which would discuss *Martinez* and provide the broader legal context for the specific regulations.

OTHER SOURCES OF ADMINISTRATIVE LAW

The *Code of Federal Regulations* fills more than 200 volumes, and every year the *Federal Register* prints thousands of new rules. Yet there is still considerable detail that these sources do not provide. The regulations establish the general procedures an agency follows, but implementation is also guided by more specific policy statements and interpretations. In addition, agencies determine how the statutes and regulations apply to particular cases through a variety of decision-making mechanisms from formal adjudications to informal advisory opinions.

Agency Policies and Manuals

Many agencies supplement their codified regulations with manuals and policy statements that provide more detail and illustrate the application of the regulations. When asked to determine whether an agency has properly followed its own rules, courts look to these other materials as well as to the codified regulations. The regulations published in the *Federal Register* and *CFR* carry more weight than subsidiary guidelines or policy statements, and would control if there were a discrepancy, but ambiguous regulations can be clarified by reference to other agency sources.

Agencies take pains to point out, however, that policy statements are for guidance only and do not have the force of law. The introduction to the Equal Employment Opportunity Commission's *EEOC Compliance Manual* notes, "The procedures and instructions set out in the EEOC Compliance Manual are not regulations but represent professional guidance to EEOC staff members. There may be instances when an office or program director may determine that a particular procedure or sequence of procedures is not applicable or should not be followed."

Policy statements and staff manuals are available to the public under the Freedom of Information Act, 5 U.S.C. § 552(a)(2), but only a few are officially published. Some are published commercially as a result of FOIA requests. The *Internal Revenue Manual*, providing guidelines for IRS personnel in administering tax collections and audits, is published by CCH in nine loose-leaf volumes and is available through both LEXIS-NEXIS (FEDTAX library, MANUAL file) and WESTLAW (FTX-IRM). The IRS itself does not publish the manual, but it does make parts available at its Web site in the "Tax Professional's Corner" of the "Tax Info for Business" subdirectory <http://www.irs.ustreas.gov/prod/bus_info/tax_pro/irm-part/>. The Internet version of the manual does not provide sections covering some of the agency's more controversial activities, such as Part 4, "Audit," and Part 9, "Criminal Investigations."

Under the Electronic Freedom of Information Act Amendments of 1996, 104 Pub. L. 231, 110 Stat. 3048, agencies must make policy materials available electronically, and not simply in response to individual requests. As a result, agency Web sites are becoming increasingly important sources of administrative information. This requirement applies, however, only to records created since November 1, 1996, and agency

compliance with E-FOIA requirements varies considerably.

The Bureau of Prisons is one agency that makes substantial amounts of material available through its Web page. Its regulations in 28 CFR are supplemented by extensive documents known as Program Statements, as well as by technical reference manuals providing guidelines, recommendations, and "how-to" information.

The BOP Program Statements on the Internet are divided into eight broad categories, such as general administration, personnel, and support services. The 5000 series, Inmate and Custodial Management, covers matters from compassionate release to hostage situation management. Included are rules governing inmate correspondence, with far more detail than the regulations in 28 CFR Part 540. For example, PS 5265.10 includes a section on special mail that reprints the regulation and adds comments on how wardens may treat mail that does not meet all the requirements of the rule for special mail handling. (The Program Statement numbering system, unfortunately, bears no relation to the corresponding sections of the *Code of Federal Regulations*.) Also included are lengthier files, such as a mail management manual, PS 5800.10, which can be downloaded in either WordPerfect or PDF format.

The amount of information available varies from agency to agency, as does the means of access. Some agency Web sites have thorough site indexes and comprehensive search options, while others are more rudimentary. This is changing gradually, as programs such as the Government Information Locator Service (GILS) seek to standardize electronic access to government information. Until standards are achieved, however, one must approach each Web site with an open mind and a willingness to experiment.

Decisions and Rulings

In addition to issuing regulations and guidelines for an entire industry or for the public at large, agencies also determine matters applicable to specific parties. The FCC licenses radio stations to use particular frequencies, and the EPA issues permits to private companies to transport hazardous wastes. Many agencies hold hearings to adjudicate disputed issues. Some have administrative law judges who hold quasi-judicial proceedings to decide such matters.

Unlike rulemaking, which follows a standard procedure in all agencies, decision-making processes vary greatly from agency to agency. Even the legal significance of these decisions is not uniform. Some agencies operate like courts in determining policy on a case-by-case basis. For example, the National Labor Relations Board has few regulations governing issues such as union representation and unfair labor practices, and relies instead on the adjudicative process to shape its policies over time. Other agencies specify that their decisions apply only to the particular circumstances and have no precedential authority in other matters.

Some agency decisions are advisory only and are not even binding as to the parties involved. The Antitrust Division of the Department of Justice, for example, issues business review letters in response to inquiries about planned mergers. The regulation governing these documents specifies that "a business review letter states only the enforcement intention of the Division as of the date of the letter, and the Division remains completely free to bring whatever action or proceeding it subsequently comes to believe is required by the public interest" (28 CFR § 50.6[9]). Business review letters, and similar documents, such as SEC no-action letters, are nonetheless of great interest to specialists as indications of an agency's views on complex issues.

Some agencies issue a range of documents with varying degrees of authority. The Internal Revenue Service's documentation follows a clearly defined hierarchy. *Revenue rulings*, which are published in the official *Internal Revenue Bulletin*, don't have as much force as regulations, but they may be used as precedent by taxpayers in similar situations. On the other hand, *private letter rulings*, in which the IRS advises taxpayers about the tax consequences of particular activity, are not published by the agency and, according to the tax code, "may not be used or cited as precedent" (26 U.S.C. § 6110[j][3]). These rulings are nonetheless available through commercial publications and databases. The IRS sought to prevent release of these rulings but lost in court (*Tax Analysts and Advocates v. IRS*, 362 F. Supp. 1298 [D.D.C. 1973], *modified*, 505 F.2d 350 [D.C. Cir. 1974]).

These various agency decisions are available in a number of formats because there is no comprehensive system of reporting similar to that for court decisions. About 15 agencies publish bound volumes of their decisions, similar to court reports, but these are few and growing fewer. These include major series such as *Decisions and Orders of the National Labor Relations Board* (1935-date) and *United States Securities and Exchange Commission Decisions and Reports* (1934-date). Others cover specialized areas, such as *Digest and Decisions of the Employees' Compensation Appeals Board* (1946-date) or the felicitously named *Administrative Decisions Under Employer Sanctions, Unfair*

Immigration-Related Employment Practices and Civil Penalty Document Fraud Laws of the United States (1988-date). This latter work is cited as OCAHO and contains the decisions of the Department of Justice's Office of the Chief Administrative Hearing Officer. Even Justice officials can't agree on the correct pronunciation of the acronym.

Some agency decisions are published only after seemingly unnecessary delay. Volume 26 of *Decisions of the Federal Maritime Commission*, covering July 1983 to June 1984, was not published until 1996. It's unclear what took so long because the volume contains no digest or index to provide subject access. By comparison, *National Transportation Safety Board Decisions* is a model of punctuality with a mere five-year delay.

A few agencies publish decisions individually or in pamphlets, but not in bound volumes. *Federal Mine Safety and Health Review Commission Decisions*, for example, are published monthly but not cumulated. *Agriculture Decisions* (1942-date) is a semiannual collection of three pamphlets arranging opinions according to the specific act of Congress at issue, with separate sections for such laws as the Animal Welfare Act, Horse Protection Act, and Packers and Stockyards Act.

Finding published decisions may require consulting several indexes. Some sources, such as the Department of Justice's *Administrative Decisions under Immigration & Nationality Laws* (1940-date), have thorough indexes in each volume. Other sources contain only tables of case names but have a separate series of indexes. *Indexes to Nuclear Regulatory Commission Issuances* (quarterly, with semiannual and five-year cumulations) includes indexes by cases, statutes, and regulations cited; subject; and facility. The National Labor Relations Board (NLRB) publishes a *Classified Index of National Labor Relations Board Decisions and Related Court Decisions* every three or four years, with lengthy summaries of decisions arranged according to a numerical classification system. Approaches vary dramatically from agency to agency; for some, indexing is inadequate or nonexistent.

Some agencies provide notices of their decisions but do not publish them in full. The Federal Election Commission's *Record* (monthly) includes digests of new advisory opinions, and its Web site <http://www.fec.gov> includes brief abstracts of compliance cases. The full texts are available in the Commission's Public Records Office or through a fee-based dial-in bulletin board.

Finally, some agency decisions are published in the *Federal Register*. This is where the Consumer Product

Safety Commission publishes settlement agreements, such as that with Binky-Griptight, Inc., charged with importing defective "Li'l Binks" pacifiers (63 Fed. Reg. 8,437 [Feb. 19, 1998]). International Trade Administration determinations on tariff disputes are published in the *Federal Register* as notices, even though some are lengthy. Final Determination of Sales at Less Than Fair Value: Fresh Cut Roses from Colombia, 60 Fed. Reg. 6,980 (Feb. 6, 1995) occupied 39 pages of the *Register*, and was immediately followed by another 24-page notice, Final Determination of Sales at Less Than Fair Value: Fresh Cut Roses from Ecuador, 60 Fed. Reg. 7,019 (Feb. 6, 1995).

Many agencies do not publish any official collections of their decisions, relying instead on commercial publications. Loose-leaf services provide thorough, up-to-date access to administrative decisions in several specialized areas. For example, *Trade Regulation Reports* (CCH) includes FTC orders and Department of Justice business review letters, some in summary form and some in full text. NLRB decisions are quickly reported in two major loose-leaf services, *Labor Relations Reporter* (BNA) and *Labor Law Reports* (CCH). Pike & Fischer publishes Federal Maritime Commission decisions in *Shipping Regulation Reports*, with a subject digest, about 12 years sooner than the commission issues its official volume.

Electronic dissemination of administrative decisions is growing, due in part to the Electronic Freedom of Information Act Amendments of 1996. The placement of decisions on Internet sites, however, follows no standard procedures, and some can be hard to find. Washburn University's Doc-Law has an annotated listing, Internet Administrative Decisions <http:/lawlib. wuacc.edu/washlaw/doclaw/admin25.html>, with links, instructions, and descriptions of site contents. From the dates of some "forthcoming" developments, however, the site does not appear to be updated regularly. A simpler list of decisions on the Web, more current but without annotations, is available from the University of Virginia Law Library <http://www.law.virginia.edu/Library/govadm.htm>.

The most comprehensive sources for administrative decisions are the commercial databases because they offer many decisions not available in any printed form and coverage extending much earlier than official Web sites. WESTLAW provides administrative decisions from more than 75 boards, agencies, and departments. Some of these, such as the Provider Reimbursement Review Board or the Board of Alien Labor Certification Appeals, are obscure enough (except to specialists in those areas) that they are not even mentioned in the *U.S. Government Manual* or *Federal Yellow Book*. LEXIS-NEXIS coverage is comparable, with a comprehensive file (GENFED library, FEDAGN file) combining decisions from more than 60 agencies.

Even though LEXIS-NEXIS and WESTLAW are available only to subscribers, they are the leading source of much government information that is otherwise available only upon request. Agency decisions are scattered through several topical areas of their databases. Table 10-1 may help locate major sources. It encompasses a variety of decisions and opinion letters but is not comprehensive, omitting more than a dozen contract appeals boards and several other specialized sources. For LEXIS-NEXIS, it lists only one topical library for each file, even though several agencies are represented in more than one library. The beginning dates for coverage are indicated in parentheses.

Perhaps the best way for the nonspecialist to learn about relevant administrative decisions is to rely on the notes in *United States Code Service*. Unlike its competitor *United States Code Annotated*, USCS includes administrative decisions in its annotations. It covers more than 50 commissions and boards, in 12 departments and 20 independent agencies. For example, annotations under the Flammable Fabrics Act, 15 U.S.C. §§ 1191-1204, include notes of Consumer Product Safety Commission advisory opinions as well as court decisions. Immigration laws provide references to the Board of Immigration Appeals, as do marine mammal protection laws to the National Oceanic and Atmospheric Administration. These agency decisions may well address issues that the courts have not yet considered. As the work of administrators with expertise in the subject area, they are often given significant weight by judges confronted with similar issues.

Just as statutes, court decisions, and regulations can be "Shepardized" to find more recent citing documents, so too can decisions from several agencies. The major source for Shepardizing is *Shepard's United States Administrative Citations* (1996, 4 vols., with bimonthly supplements), which covers a dozen major sources including the FCC, FTC and SEC. It lists citations to these decisions in later administrative proceedings, court cases, and law review articles, and also provides cross-references to the official citations from commercial loose-leaf reporters such as *Communications Regulation* or *Trade Regulation Reports*. Other *Shepard's* publications provide coverage of specialized administrative agencies. For example, *Shepard's Labor Law Citations* (1995, 19 vols., with monthly supplements)

TABLE 10-1

LEXIS-NEXIS AND WESTLAW DATABASES FOR FEDERAL ADMINISTRATIVE AGENCY DECISIONS

	LEXIS-NEXIS	**WESTLAW**
Commodity Futures Trading Commission	FEDSEC/CFTC (1976)	FSEC-CFTC (1976)
Consumer Product Safety Commission	TRADE/CONSUM (1980)	FATR-CPSC (1981)
Department of Agriculture	GENFED/AGDEC (1995)	USDA (1977)
Department of Commerce		
International Trade Commission	ITRADE/ITC (1979)	FINT-ITC (1975)
National Oceanic and Atmospheric Administration	ENVIRN/NOAA (1971)	FENV-ORW (1971)
Patent and Trademark Office	PATENT/COMMR (1981)	FIP-PTO (1987)
Department of Education		FED-ADMIN (1987)
Department of Energy		
Federal Energy Regulatory Commission	ENERGY/FERC (1977)	FEN-FERC (1977)
Department of Health and Human Services		FHTH-HHS (1974)
Department of Housing and Urban Development		FAIRHOUS (1989)
Department of the Interior	ENVIRN/INTDEC (1865)	INTDEC (1881)
Fish and Wildlife Service		FENV-ORW (1971)
Interior Board of Indian Appeals	ENVIRN/IBIA (1970)	FNAM-IBIA (1970)
Interior Board of Land Appeals	ENVIRN/IBLA (1970)	GFS (1970)
Department of Justice	GENFED/USAG (1791)	USAG (1791)
Antitrust Division	TRADE/DOJBRL (1984)	FATR-BRL (1975)
Board of Immigration Appeals	IMMIG/BIA (1940)	FIM-BIA (1940)
Office of the Chief Administrative Hearing Officer	IMMIG/OCAHO (1988)	FIM-OCAHO (1988)
Department of Labor		
Benefits Review Board	LABOR/DOLBRB (1993)	FWC-BRB (1984)
Board of Alien Labor Certification Appeals	IMMIG/BALCA (1987)	FIM-BALCA (1987)
Employees' Compensation Appeals Board		FLB-ECAB (1976)
Pension and Welfare Benefits Administration	EMPLOY/ERISA (1974)	FPEN-ERISA (1974)
Department of Transportation	TRANS/DOTAV (1980)	FTRAN-DOT (1979)
Federal Aviation Administration	TRANS/FAA (1989)	FTRAN-FAA (1989)
Surface Transportation Board	TRANS/STB (1996)	FTRAN-ICC (1996)
Department of the Treasury		
Customs Service	ITRADE/CUSBUL (1962)	FINT-CUSTB (1962)
Internal Revenue Service	FEDTAX/RELS (1954)	FTX-RELS (1954)
Office of the Comptroller of the Currency	BANKNG/OCCED (1977)	FFIN-OCCEA (1977)
Office of Thrift Supervision	BANKNG/OTSBUL (1964)	FFIN-OTS (1964)
Environmental Protection Agency	ENVIRN/ALLEPA (1974)	FENV-EPA (1974)
Equal Employment Opportunity Commission	LABOR/EEOC (1970)	FLB-EEOC (1969)
Federal Communications Commission	FEDCOM/FCC (1939)	FCOM-FCC (1965)
Federal Deposit Insurance Corporation	BANKNG/FDIC (1975)	FFIN-FDIC (1979)
Federal Election Commission	CMPGN/FECOPN (1991)	FEC (1987)
Federal Labor Relations Authority	LABOR/FLRA (1979)	FLB-FLRA (1979)
Federal Maritime Commission		FMRT-FMC (1984)
Federal Mine Safety and Health Review Commission		FLB-FMSHRC (1979)
Federal Reserve Board	BANKNG/FEDIL (1980)	FFIN-FRBIL (1928)
Federal Trade Commission	TRADE/FTC (1950)	FATR-FTC (1959)
General Accounting Office		
Comptroller General	GENFED/COMGEN (1921)	CG (1921)
Merit Systems Protection Board	LABOR/MSPB (1979)	FLB-MSPB (1979)
National Labor Relations Board	LABOR/NLRB (1972)	FLB-NLRB (1971)
National Mediation Board	LABOR/NMB (1935)	FLB-NMB (1935)
National Transportation Safety Board	TRANS/NTSBM (1966)	FTRAN-NTSB (1967)
Nuclear Regulatory Commission	ENERGY/NRC (1975)	FEN-NRC (1975)
Occupational Safety and Health Review Commission	LABOR/OSAHRC (1971)	FLB-OSRC (1971)
Office of Government Ethics	GENFED/OGE (1979)	FETH-OGE (1979)
Pension Benefit Guaranty Corporation	PENBEN/PBGC (1974)	FPEN-PBGC (1974)
Securities and Exchange Commission	FEDSEC/SECREL (1933)	FSEC-RELS (1933)
Social Security Administration	EMPLOY/SSRULE (1960)	FGB-SSR (1960)

includes citations to decisions and orders of the National Labor Relations Board, and *Shepard's Federal Occupational Safety and Health Citations* (1992, with quarterly supplements) covers the Occupational Safety and Health Review Commission and its administrative law judges. For researchers with access to commercial databases, full-text searches in the court and agency files may provide a more convenient way to trace the status of a decision or the development of agency doctrines.

PART 4
State Law

CHAPTER 11
State Legislation and Administrative Law

TOPICS COVERED

Multistate Reference Sources
  Surveys
  Directories
  Guides to State Web Sites
Constitutions
Statutes
  Published Codes
  Electronic Codes
  Session Laws
  Multistate Sources

Legislative Information
  Guides and Directories
  Current Information
  Legislative History
Administrative Law
  Other Agency Materials
  Decisions
  Executive Orders
  Attorney General Opinions
  Industry Standards
Counties and Cities

Federal law affects more people than the law of any one state, but it is state laws that determine most of the basic rules of society. State law governs such matters as contracts, criminal law, family law, landlord–tenant relations, wills, and intestate succession. The U.S. Constitution limits the powers of the federal government, in theory at least, and those powers not expressly delegated to the United States are reserved to the states under the Tenth Amendment. In practice, the scope of federal power is a hotly contested issue among politicians and in the courts.

The existence of 50 separate state legal systems does not necessarily mean that there are wide discrepancies among these systems. In some areas of law, particularly those related to such explosive issues as abortion or capital punishment, there are significant differences among the states. By and large, however, most differences are relatively minor. States look to each others' experiences in grappling with social issues. Similar concerns are addressed in each state, and often similar conclusions are reached. The difference is in the details. Every state has criminal laws against homicide, arson, and theft; only the penalties vary from state to state. Adverse possession exists in all jurisdictions, but the period after which ownership vests in the possessor can be as short as 2 years or as long as 60 years.

Researching state law is generally similar to researching federal law. It involves many of the same processes and similar tools—statutory codes, court reports, online databases, CD-ROMs, and Web sites. Federal law has been discussed first largely because it provides a uniform system nationwide. In contrast, the distinctions between states make generalizations difficult. For example, not all states still publish official court reports, and some states are more advanced than others in placing material on the Internet. Generally, however, state legal research follows the paradigm of federal legal research.

A first step in analyzing any legal issue is to determine which jurisdiction's laws apply: Is an issue one of federal or state law? The need to make this determination is one of the reasons to begin research in an encyclopedia or treatise, which can provide the necessary background information. Just as it is important to know whether federal or state law is involved (or both), it is sometimes necessary to decide which state's laws apply. This is usually obvious, it can sometimes be a thorny legal issue. If a contract was signed in one state and executed in another, which state's law governs interpretation of its terms? If a couple moves to a community property state shortly before they divorce, how is their marital property divided? Questions such as these have created a substantial body of legal doctrine, and literature, on conflict of laws.

Sooner or later one must find and understand the specific laws governing matters in a specific state, which is why general resources such as *American Jurisprudence 2d* or *Corpus Juris Secundum* are only starting points. The focus must be on the statutes, court decisions, and other laws of an individual state.

The amount of information available on state law can vary widely between jurisdictions. Large states with substantial lawyer populations have extensive libraries of treatises, specialized formbooks, practice guides, self-help books, and CD-ROMs, while smaller states may have only a few basic resources. Each state, nonetheless, has the same basic primary legal sources: a constitution, legislative acts, appellate court decisions, and administrative regulations.

MULTISTATE REFERENCE SOURCES

Materials from every state are generally available in larger law libraries, while smaller legal collections and general libraries tend to focus on materials for their home state. It is therefore helpful, particularly in trying to research the law of another state, to know about resources dealing with state laws throughout the country.

Surveys

Multistate resources are particularly valuable for researchers comparing the law in different jurisdictions. Often researchers need to determine how many states have a law specific to a particular topic. Checking each state's statutes may be necessary, but starting from scratch 50 times is a time-consuming pursuit. It can also be frustrating because states may use different terminology for similar purposes. Fortunately, several publications survey the laws in every state.

The best multistate survey publications summarize quickly and accurately the law in each jurisdiction, and also provide references that lead directly to the original statutes or other primary sources. The inclusion of these citations to primary sources is an important criterion in evaluating state law surveys because it makes the difference between a source that can be used as a springboard to further research and one that simply provides outdated conclusions. The inclusion of code citations ensures that a survey does not lose as much value over time. Laws change, but it is a much simpler matter to update citations than to begin a search in each code's subject index.

Surveys of state law are arranged either by jurisdiction, with several sections for each state covering a range of issues, or by subject, with lists or tables of state provisions collected for each topic. A state arrangement is more useful for someone needing information on one particular state, but a subject arrangement allows a quick comparison of an issue's treatment in several states.

The most comprehensive of these sources, *Martindale-Hubbell Law Digest* (Martindale-Hubbell, 2 vols., annual), is a companion to the *Martindale-Hubbell Law Directory*. It is arranged by state and provides detailed summaries of state statutory and common law rules, with citations to both code provisions and court decisions. The scope of the digests varies from state to state, from 24 pages for Vermont to 84 pages for Illinois, but each follows a standard format. About two dozen legal categories, such as "Business Regulation and Commerce," "Estates and Trusts," and "Family," contain specific entries on about 100 legal topics. The topics within each category are arranged alphabetically. (Before the 1998 edition, all the topics were in one alphabetical sequence.)

Individual entries range from a few words ("System does not obtain," for "Community Property" in several states; or "Abolished" for obsolete doctrines such as "Dower" and "Curtesy") to several pages for complex issues such as "Corporations" and "Taxation." The digests include sample forms for a variety of uses, such as liens, acknowledgments, deeds, and simple wills.

Each *Martindale-Hubbell* state digest is revised annually by specialists in the state's laws. A few digests are prepared by professors at law schools in the state, but most are handled by practicing lawyers at law firms—often one of the state's larger and more prestigious firms. Some entries provide helpful insider tips that may not be apparent from the face of the laws. The Louisiana digest notes, for example, that "no statutes authorize submission of controversy to court on agreed statement of facts but courts generally allow such submission."

The *Martindale-Hubbell Law Digest* is designed for attorneys needing quick information about other states It focuses on topics in commercial law and civil procedure of practical concern to out-of-state attorneys. Several issues of more general interest are covered as well. The rights and duties of children are outlined in the topic "Infants," and consumer issues arise in such topics as "Consumer Protection," "Landlord and Tenant," and "Motor Vehicles." The "Family" category includes such topics as "Marriage," "Divorce," "Guardian and Ward," and "Adoption." Exhibit 11-1 reproduces an excerpt from the Massachusetts section of the *Martindale-Hubbell Law Digest* providing a brief outline of the state's adoption law. Note that the digest includes references to relevant statutes and to a Massachusetts Supreme Judicial Court decision. (To save space, this decision is listed by citation only, without its parties' names.)

Some matters, however, are not covered in the *Martindale-Hubbell Law Digest* in much depth. Criminal law only gets a few paragraphs, focusing mostly on bail procedures. Important political and social issues, such as capital punishment, lesbian and gay rights, and abortion, are mentioned only in passing, if at all.

Most of the digest topics summarize legal doctrines, but a few entries provide useful information about the state's legal system. The "Courts and Legislature" category lists the appellate and trial courts, with explanations of their geographic and subject-matter jurisdiction; outlines the provisions for legislative sessions, as well as for initiative and referendum; and gives information about the state's court reports, digests, and code. The "Records" topic, in the "Documents and Records" category, includes information on location of court records and vital statistics.

Because the *Martindale-Hubbell Law Digest* is arranged by state, it is more convenient for checking a particular state's laws than for surveying differences between jurisdictions. The standardized format, however, makes it possible to turn to the same topic in each state's section for a summary of its laws. This is even easier to do electronically in the MARHUB library on LEXIS-NEXIS. A simple search for *topic(adoption)* retrieves 53 documents summarizing adoption law in each state, the District of Columbia, Puerto Rico, and the Virgin Islands. The *Martindale-Hubbell Law Digest* is not included with the CD-ROM or Internet versions of *Martindale-Hubbell Law Directory*.

Another work offering a quicker way to compare a particular topic across state lines is Richard A. Leiter's *National Survey of State Laws* (Gale, 2d ed., 1997). This resource contains tables providing information in 43 areas, arranged into 8 general categories (business and consumer, criminal, education, employment, family, general civil, real estate, and tax). Each table provides code citations as well as summaries of state legal doctrines. Unlike the *Martindale-Hubbell Law Digest* or other works designed specifically for lawyers, it does not limit its focus to commercial and business law but covers such issues as capital punishment, gun control, child abuse, the right to die, and stalking. Although a tabular format is used, entries are not limited to one or two words; some summaries, such as criteria for capital homicide, go on at some length as needed. The survey considers laws in force as of March 1, 1996, but because code citations are provided, this information can be updated relatively easily.

The *National Survey of State Laws* table on adoption laws, for instance, includes the code citation for the statutes in each state and information on who may be adopted, at what age a child's consent is required, who may adopt, and residency requirements. It also provides the names of state agencies administering adoption matters and courts with jurisdiction over adoptions, and indicates the time periods within which challenges to adoptions must be filed. For any given state, the *National Survey of State Laws* may not be as thorough or current a source as the *Martindale-Hubbell Law Digest*, but it is a much more convenient form for comparing state law provisions.

Other works provide extensive surveys of state statutes but not the citations that would facilitate further research. *Credit Manual of Commercial Laws* (National Association of Credit Management, annual) contains lengthy, informative discussions of issues of importance in business dealings, and it surveys state laws on about three dozen topics, such as statutes of limitations, liens, installment sales, and bad check laws. Only occasionally, however, does it include any citations. *Lawyer's Desk Book* (Prentice Hall, 10th ed., 1995, with 1997 supplement) covers maximum interest rates, usury penalties, inheritance taxes, and other issues. It has a few lists of state statutes, for arbitration, corporate indemnification, and blue sky laws, but otherwise few citations. A table indicates, for instance, whether a will is automatically revoked in each state by a subsequent marriage, divorce, or birth of a child, but cites no sources.

The Book of the States (Council of State Governments, biennial) provides a wide range of statistics on state government and state laws. It focuses on governmental structure and procedures, but contains a few tables listing state laws governing private activities. Chapter 7 includes tables listing minimum legal ages

MASSACHUSETTS LAW DIGEST

WILLS . . . *continued*

principal (c. 201D, §6), or physician's or health care facility's objections pursuant to c. 201D, §§14 and 15. However, health care proxy cannot permit suicide or mercy killing. (c. 201D, §12).

Health care proxy may be revoked by notifying agent or health care provider orally or in writing or by any other act evidencing specific intent to revoke. Proxy is automatically revoked upon execution of new proxy or divorce of principal if spouse is agent. Revocation must be recorded in principal's medical records. (c. 201D, §7).

Neither health care provider nor agent can be subject to criminal or civil liability if he acted in good faith while fulfilling his duty according to proxy. (c. 201D, §8).

If health care proxy has not been executed, health care provider may rely on informed consent of responsible parties acting on behalf of incompetent patient to extent permitted by law. Powers of attorney executed before this chapter was enacted Dec. 19, 1990 are valid to allow agent to make health care decisions for principal. (c. 201D, §16).

FAMILY

ADOPTION:

See generally c. 210; all citations, unless otherwise indicated, refer to said chapter. See also c. 119, §26(4), as amended effective Jan. 29, 1993, for authority of District and Juvenile Courts to terminate parental right to consent to adoption if in best interest of child based upon certain factors.

A person of full age (his spouse, joining) may (subject to certain exceptions) petition probate court in county where he (or if nonresident, where child) resides for leave to adopt as his child another person younger than himself (other than petitioner's spouse, brother, sister, aunt or uncle of whole or half blood). Minors may petition (or join spouse petition) for adoption of natural child of one of parties. (§1). Spouse must join petition for adoption. (§5A).

In any petition for adoption department of social services shall submit to court for verification that child is not registered with federal register for missing children and Massachusetts central register. (§5A).

Adoptive parents may sue for "wrongful adoption" based on misrepresentations made by adoption agency about child's pre-adoptive history. (421 Mass. 147, 653 N.E.2d 1104).

Consent Required.—Decree for adoption requires, inter alia, written consent of child if over 12; of child's spouse, if any; of lawful parents, may be previous adoptive parents, or surviving parent; or of mother alone if child born out of wedlock and not previously adopted. Such written consent may be executed no sooner than fourth day after birth of child to be adopted. It must be attested and subscribed before notary public in presence of two competent witnesses, one of whom must be selected by consenting person. Form of consent is set forth. Any consent or surrender outside commonwealth is valid if in accord with laws of state or country where executed. (§2).

Consent Not Required.—When petition for adoption filed by person having care and custody of child, Court may dispense with necessity of consent of persons named in §2 (other than child) if: (i) person to be adopted is at least 18 years old; or (ii) Court finds that allowance of petition for adoption is in best interest of child. Department of social services or any licensed child care agency may commence proceeding to dispense with need for consent to adoption of child in care or custody of such department or agency. (§3[a] and [b]). (On "care or custody" see c. 210, §3[b]; 25 Mass. App. Ct. 579, 521 N.E.2d 399.) If Department has only temporary custody of child, foster parents have standing to file adoption petition without consent of natural parents. (416 Mass. 791, 625 N.E.2d 1362). Such petition may be heard notwithstanding pendency of petition brought under c. 119 or c. 201 regarding same child. Justice may be assigned to hear

EXHIBIT 11-1

for marrying, making a will, buying alcohol, serving on a jury, leaving school, and driving a motor vehicle. The "Labor" section in Chapter 8 summarizes laws on workers' compensation, child labor, and minimum wages. Sources for the information in each table are listed, but no citations to statutes are provided.

Julius Fast and Timothy Fast's *The Legal Atlas of the United States* (Facts on File, 1997) is a colorful volume with more than 100 maps of the country illustrating various legal issues, with emphases on family law and criminal justice. Each chapter includes an introduction, but the inadequate cross-references make flipping back and forth between text and map a challenge. No references to state laws are provided, although a bibliography lists the source for each map.

The sources *The Legal Atlas of the United States* relies on, such as *Uniform Crime Reports 1991* and *The 1992 Information Please Almanac*, are not terribly current for a 1997 publication. No efforts appear to have been made to update data or to supply data missing from sources. Information from Florida and Iowa, for example, was omitted from a table in *Uniform Crime Reports 1991*, so they appear as blank areas on several maps. As both states are included in comparable tables in the 1990 and 1992 editions of the official source, why not use those data? Similarly, the map on laws governing sexual relations between consenting adults has data from only 26 states because that is all the particular source supplied.

The Legal Atlas of the United States is lacking as a basis for further study, but it still makes for fascinating browsing. Several of the maps reveal interesting regional patterns, as in the high DWI arrest rate in the Plains states or the greater restriction on smoking in public places found on the West Coast and in the North. Nevada stands out in several maps with the highest marriage rate, the highest divorce rate, and the highest arrest rate for prostitution.

Several more specialized resources survey state laws in particular fields. These can usually be found in online catalogs under the heading "[subject]—Law and legislation—United States—States," alongside general overviews and specific monographs.

The American Bar Association publishes a number of surveys, some covering specific topics. Most follow a standardized format for each state, making it easy to find information; some reprint excerpts from state statutes. One of the most useful of these surveys is *The Wills and Estate Planning Guide: A State and Territorial Summary of Will and Intestacy Statutes* (1995), prepared by officers of the Army Judge Advocate General Corps. More specialized works include John E. Floyd's *RICO State by State: A Guide to Litigation Under the State Racketeering Statutes* (1998) and *State by State Survey of the Economic Loss Doctrine in Construction Litigation* (1996). One of the ABA's most extensive surveys, *State Antitrust Practice and Statutes* (3 vols., 1990), is now rather out of date.

Another book that, unfortunately, has not been updated is *The State-by-State Guide to Women's Legal Rights*, by the NOW Legal Defense and Education Fund and Renée Cherow-O'Leary (McGraw-Hill, 1987). This survey provides a general introduction to major issues concerning women, and a survey for each state of rights in the home, school, workplace, and community. References to statutes and court cases are included, but the information obviously must be checked against more current laws.

Bureau of National Affairs, Inc. publishes several monographs summarizing state laws in specific areas of employment law. These follow a standard outline for each state, which usually involves a question-and-answer format. For example, Brian M. Malsberger's *Covenants Not to Compete: A State-by-State Survey* (2d ed., 1996) poses such questions as "What type of time or geographic restrictions has the court found to be reasonable? Unreasonable?" Answers include citations to relevant statutes, cases, and law review articles. Other BNA titles include Lionel J. Postic's *Wrongful Termination: A State-by-State Survey* (1994); Stewart S. Manela and Arnold H. Pedowitz's *Employee Duty of Loyalty: A State-by-State Survey* (1995); and Arnold H. Pedowitz and Robert W. Sikkel's *Trade Secrets: A State-by-State Survey* (1997). Some of these titles keep current with annual supplements.

Some surveys are prepared specifically to facilitate comparison of public policy issues between states. Ruth S. Musgrave and Mary Anne Stein's *State Wildlife Laws Handbook* (Government Institutes, 1993) thoroughly examines the laws in each state governing such issues as hunting and fishing, protected species, and habitat protection. It includes an introductory overview and a state-by-state discussion of administrative agencies' structure and duties as well as the substance of the laws. Citations to state codes are included. The volume also includes several tables providing convenient comparisons of state provisions.

Some state law summaries are designed not just for practical use in situations where quick glimpses of state laws are needed but for their reference value as well. For used car dealers, for example, *N.A.D.A. Title and Registration Text Book* (National Appraisal Guides, Inc., annual) summarizes motor vehicle laws and regulations for all 50 states and the District of Columbia on issues such as proof of ownership, registration, and licensing. It includes color photocopies of sample title and registration documents, as well as driver's licenses. The licenses include some interesting characters, such as Iama Sample License and Forfun C. Newjersey, but the book provides no citations to code sections.

State law surveys can also be found lurking in more general sources such as directories. Volume 2 of *Best's Directory of Recommended Insurance Attorneys and Adjusters* (A. M. Best Co., annual), for example, includes a "Digest of Insurance Laws" summarizing state laws. Like *Martindale-Hubbell Law Digest,* this digest is arranged by state and prepared by law firms in each state. It covers about three dozen insurance topics, such as agents and brokers, no-fault, and release, with citations to state codes. *The Adoption Directory* (Gale, 2d ed., 1995) includes quick summaries, without citations, of each state's laws on various aspects of adoption. These are combined, of course, with much other useful material, such as addresses of agencies and information about their services.

Finally, some state law surveys are produced by organizations with clearly defined interests. The Libel Defense Resource Center, for example, publishes two annual surveys of state law, *LDRC 50-State Survey: Current Developments in Media Libel Law* and *LDRC 50-State Survey: Media Privacy and Related Law.* Separate sections for each state, prepared by local attorneys, answer basic questions about media-related law and provide references to relevant case law and statutes. The LDRC comprises major media organizations, so there is no hint of impartiality in its coverage of these issues.

The National Abortion and Reproductive Rights Action League (NARAL) publishes *Who Decides?: A State-by-State Review of Abortion and Reproductive Rights* (annual). Sections for each state summarize selected statutes and regulations, with citations, and charts provide quick multistate comparisons. The NARAL guide is available on the Internet <http://www.naral.org/publications/whod98.html>, with links to analyses of recent and pending legislation in each state.

The Internet is a growing source of state law surveys. Many, like NARAL's, are prepared by special interest groups. The American Homebrewers Association <http://www.aob.org/legal/list.htm> presents a state-by-state summary of the statutory recognition of the home production of beer. Pages for each state summarize and cite relevant statutes, including full-text excerpts of relevant provisions, and provide contact information for agencies.

Some Internet surveys simply provide citations or reprint relevant statutory provisions, but even these can save considerable time for someone needing to compare state laws. The Kansas Elder Law Network <http://www.ink.org/public/keln/> includes several bibliographies prepared by law students, many with unannotated lists of code citations from each state. The Rutgers Animal Rights Law Center <http://www.animal-law.org/> includes surveys of state laws on such issues as anticruelty, hunter harassment, and product disparagement, providing citations and statutory text without commentary. A number of surveys, on the other hand, have quick summaries and plenty of commentary but no citations.

When using any survey, particularly one found on the Internet, it is necessary to be aware of the information's currency and the compilers' perspective. Some sites are regularly maintained by professional organizations, while others may have been prepared by individuals who have since lost interest or haven't had time to continue monitoring them. Abandoned sites can continue to float in cyberspace for years, so it is important to check the date of a site's most recent update.

One way to find Internet surveys in a specific area is to browse a legal subject index, such as FindLaw <http://www.findlaw.com/01topics/>. Under "Family law," for example, there are links to the Divorce Law Information Service Center <http://www.divorcelawinfo.com/statebystate.html>, explaining property division rules and residency requirements (without citations). AdoptioNetwork <http://www.adoption.org/legal/> summarizes state adoption laws (with code references and the full text of some states' laws).

An excellent series of bibliographies, *Subject Compilations of State Laws* (Greenwood Press [now Carol Boast and Cheryl Nyberg (Twin Falls, Idaho)], 13 vols., 1981-date), provides a more thorough guide to surveys on the Internet and in print. Earlier volumes in this series each covered several years, but supplements are now issued annually. Originally prepared by Lynn Foster and Carol Boast and now by Cheryl Rae Nyberg, these works list surveys and compilations in a wide variety of sources, including treatises, reference books, consumer guides, journals, and cases. Listings range from books reprinting laws in full to journal article footnotes listing citations. Each volume in the series begins with a helpful "Update on State Statutory Research," providing tips and comments on recent developments. It then lists the sources by subject under more than 200 topics, with cross-references under several hundred additional headings. The *Subject Compilations of State Laws* volumes do not cumulate, but the most recent supplement includes cross-references to earlier volumes for topics it does not cover.

The annotations for *Subject Compilations of State Laws* entries indicate the number of states covered, if fewer than 50; whether the source provides citations to code provisions; and whether the source provides full text, summaries, or citations only. Here, for example, are two *Subject Compilations of State Laws* entries on the subject of adoption:

Askin, Jayne. *Search: A Handbook for Adoptees and Birthparents.* 3d ed., Phoenix: Oryx Press, 1998. 352 pp. HV881 .A8 1998. 362.82'98. 98-22656.
> Pp. 239-309, "Appendix I, State-by-State Listings." Summaries. Some citations to codes. Covers age of majority, adoption records, inheritance rights of adopted children, and central registries.

Simon, Rita J.; Alstein, Howard. "The Relevance of Race in Adoption Law and Social Practice." *Notre Dame Journal of Law, Ethics & Public Policy* 11 (1997): 171-95.
> Pp. 173-74, fns. 9-14. Citations only. Cites to codes. Covers the eighteen states that mention race in their adoption laws.

Subject Compilations of State Laws is the type of tool that librarians appreciate but many researchers underutilize, perhaps because it is not an end in itself. One must follow three steps to find relevant laws: (1) look up a subject in *Subject Compilations of State Laws* and find a reference to a text, law review article, or Web site; (2) retrieve that item and turn to the survey or list; and (3) use the citations listed as a shortcut to the state statutes themselves to verify the current provisions. Although not an effortless process, it is still an invaluable time-saver for anyone doing multistate research.

A somewhat similar work by Jon S. Schultz, *Statutes Compared: A U.S., Canadian, Multinational Research Guide to Statutes by Subject* (William S. Hein & Co., rev. ed., 1992), is published in a loose-leaf format but has not been updated in several years. Unlike *Subject Compilations of State Laws,* it limits itself to surveys updated on a regular basis. It might therefore still be of some use as a guide to these sources. Despite the international scope of its title, most of the works it lists focus on state law. Those listing Canadian or multinational laws are marked with asterisks. Unfortunately, many of the entries in *Statutes Compared* refer to *Shepard's Lawyer's Reference Manual* (Shepard's/McGraw-Hill, 1983), a once useful work that has not been updated since 1988.

Directories

The researcher examining the legal system of a particular state will find one of the most useful sources to be a reference manual providing directory listings and background information on the state's government. Every state publishes a reference directory of some sort, but these vary widely in the amount of information they provide. Some include descriptions of state agencies, in a format similar to the *United States Government Manual,* while others focus on biographical information on legislators and department heads. Some are little more than government telephone directories. The Maryland State Archives' *Maryland Manual* (biennial) is one of the most informative, with discussions of the work of each agency and legislative committee. Missouri's *Official Manual* (biennial) has a 500-page list of all state personnel, including their home addresses and salaries. In addition to officially published directories, most states have commercial directories listing government offices and other resources.

All these works are listed in *State Reference Publications* (Government Research Service, annual). This useful annotated guide provides information on numerous directories and other resources on both legislative and executive branches of government. Each state has its own section listing Internet sites, general reference works, legislative manuals and handbooks, directories, statistical abstracts, and other reference sources. Prices, mailing addresses, and telephone numbers for acquiring each item are included. (Much of this information also appears in the publisher's other annual work, *State Legislative Sourcebook,* as Part 6, "General State Government Information," in each state's section.) An appendix contains an annotated listing of general state government reference books (such as *The Book of the States*), more than two dozen multistate government directories, and periodicals focusing on issues of state government.

Several directories cover all 50 states. These lack the background information available in an individual state's directory, but some include thorough telephone listings for state government officials. The most extensive multistate directories are published by the same companies that produce leading directories of the federal government.

Carroll's State Directory (Carroll Publishing Co., three times a year in paperback or annually in hardcover) covers the legislative, judicial, and executive branches of state government, listing more than 37,000 officials. It has five color-coded sections: reference information, including frequently used telephone numbers and state Web sites; an alphabetical listing of state executives; a state-by-state listing of major agencies; state legislatures; and state supreme courts. A keyword index provides topical access. Information from *Carroll's State Directory* is available on the Internet through Infospace, <http://www.infospace.com/>. FindLaw provides access to the same information <http://www.findlaw.com/directories/government.html>. Both sites include search forms for locating officials by name or title.

State Yellow Book (Leadership Directories, quarterly) contains separate sections providing coverage of executive and legislative branches. The executive branch section covers major departments, commissions, and agencies, with general contact information and some individual names; the legislative branch section includes listings of committees and staff. A one-page-per-state "State Profiles" section provides a brief survey of major demographic information. Indexes by subject and personnel are included. This directory is available on WESTLAW as the STATEYB database.

State Staff Directory (CQ Staff Directories, three times a year) was first published in 1997 and covers more than 40,000 state government officials. Its specialty, like the other *Staff Directories*, is its nearly 9,000 biographies, including every state legislator and more than 1,000 executive branch officials. Information on legislatures includes committees and their staff. An introductory page for each state features demographic information, an overview of state revenues and expenditures, important telephone numbers, and state Web site addresses. The directory is indexed by individual name and job function.

The Council of State Governments publishes three annual directories of state officials under the umbrella title *CSG State Directory* (formerly *State Leadership Directory*). *Directory I: Elective Officials* lists governors, elected executive branch officials, legislators, and supreme court justices by state; *Directory II: Legislative Leadership, Committees and Staff* lists officers, committee chairs, and legislative agencies; and *Directory III: Administrative Officials* lists state officials by function under more than 150 headings. This third directory may be the most valuable because, unlike most sources, it is arranged by function rather than by state. Thus, it is a useful source for concise listings of the names and addresses of governors, secretaries of state, lottery administrators, or state veterinarians. The three CSG directories are available on CD-ROM as well as in print.

Government Phone Book USA (Omnigraphics, annual) is a more general directory with more than 100,000 listings covering federal, state, and local government offices. The coverage of state governments includes a quick reference guide to governors, legislative information sources, and state supreme courts. Each section is indexed separately by keyword.

Other directories focus on agencies responsible for particular records and functions, rather than on state government generally. *Sourcebook of State Public Records* (BRB Publications, 3d ed., 1997) includes information on such agencies as secretaries of state, motor vehicle departments, and workers' compensation commissions, as well as lists of agencies involved in occupational licensing and business registration. It includes nearly 5,000 professional and business license addresses and telephone numbers.

David P. Bianco's *National Directory of State Business Licensing and Regulation* (Gale, 1994) covers more than 100 occupations and businesses licensed by state government, from accounting services to wrecking and demolition contractors. Every state regulates in some areas, such as aerial pest control services and donut shops, while only a few states regulate such businesses as tattoo parlors and travel agencies. Entries provide the addresses and telephone numbers of responsible state agencies and include brief overviews of licenses or permits required, general requirements, fees, and specific activities regulated. They also include useful references to state statutes or regulations, and discuss relevant federal licenses and permits. The volume features a listing of general business licensing agencies in each state and a geographic index. Another volume edited by Bianco, *Professional and Occupational Licensing Directory* (Gale, 2d ed., 1995), provides similar coverage of licensing procedures for about 500 occupations.

Guides to State Web Sites

Information on state government activity, including the text of legal sources, is increasingly available on the Internet. Approaches differ from state to state, of course, but most states now provide access to statutes, court decisions, and administrative material, as well as general background information and news of current developments.

State Internet information can be found either through comprehensive compilations or directly from general state homepages. The official addresses for state homepages vary, but each answers to the address <http://www.state.xx.us> (where *xx* is the two-letter postal code for the state). This works even for states that use other official addresses. The California homepage, for example, is <http://www.ca.gov>, but <http://www.state.ca.us> gets you in the door.

Getting to the state homepage is only the start, however. Once there, it is usually clear how to opt for government information rather than other choices such as tourism or economic development. Then it may be clear sailing to the full text of the state constitution, statutes, and administrative regulations. Some states, however, do not make the path so obvious. New York, for example, offers "Citizen's Access to Government," which leads to options for federal, state, and local government. The state link simply provides a long alphabetical list of agencies and offices. Finding legislative information requires the patience to look for "Senate" or "State Assembly" near the bottom of the list.

State idiosyncrasies can make the process frustrating, but several Web sites provide uniform access to resources from each state. Sites such as the following can simplify the procedure for hunting down information from an unfamiliar state government homepage.

- Piper Resources' State and Local Government on the Net <http://www.piperinfo.com/state/states.html> is one of the most thorough sources of information on state Web sites. Links to general state homepages and the legislative and judicial branches are included, but its strength is in listing executive departments, agencies, and boards, as well as counties and cities on the Web. The focus is on government offices, rather than the full text of statutes or other documents. It also provides links to territorial and tribal governments, regional commissions, and about two dozen national organizations active in state government, such as the Council of State Governments and the Council of State and Territorial Epidemiologists.

- The Legal Information Institute at Cornell Law School provides access to state legal materials <http://www.law.cornell.edu/statutes.html>. The focus is on the major primary sources of law. A standardized format for each state lists sources such as the constitution, statutes, recent session laws, bills and legislative information, judicial opinions, regulations, and state homepages. Links are included for those sources available at free sites, while other sources are listed but unlinked. This provides convenient access and makes it easy to survey the range of material available for each state. Cornell also provides access to state materials by subject, <http://www.law.cornell.edu/topics/state_statutes.html>.

- Washburn University's WashLaw site includes a StateLaw page <http://lawlib.wuacc.edu/washlaw/uslaw/statelaw.html> with links to state homepages, legislative information sites (including bill texts and bill tracking pages), courts, statute sites, and miscellaneous state information sites (including state agencies, local government, and state constitutions). Washburn's lists for each state include as many links as it can find to state and local government information. Besides major institutional sites, these links include homepages of individual legislators, both in Congress and in state legislatures, and a variety of historical documents and state organizations.

- Another major law school site, the Electronic Reference Desk at Emory Law Library, provides numerous links by state <http://www.law.emory.edu/LAW/refdesk/country/us/state/>. Sites with documents are sorted by category, including constitutions, bills, statutes, regulations, and cases, and links are provided to administrative agencies and other state organizations.

- FindLaw provides extensive coverage of state law <http://www.findlaw.com/11stategov/>. After choosing a state, clicking on "Primary Materials" leads to sources for the constitution, statutes, regulations, and court decisions. As at Cornell's site, items unavailable on the Internet are listed but not linked to any source. Other choices for each state include government information, courts, directories, bar associations, law schools, and law firms.

- "Full-Text State Statutes and Legislation on the Internet" <http://www.prairienet.org/~scruffy/f.htm> is an example of a private Web site providing a valuable perspective not readily available elsewhere. Part of the "scruffy home" site, which also features information on such topics as poodle schnauzers and a Japanese beer vending machine, this list is useful because it limits its coverage to sites providing the full text of state constitutions, statutes, and session laws. Sites are omitted if they have only summaries or incomplete documents, focus on single issues, or charge fees for access. The list is simple but notes variations in state site formats and provides helpful tips (e.g. "The other versions I have seen on the web are flawed"; "You may want to turn off your browser's graphics before you go to this site—it is larded with enormous graphic files").

Several print sources cover state Internet sites, although these are not as frequently or easily updated as resources on the Web itself. The state resources section of Don McLeod's *The Internet Guide for the Legal Researcher* (Infosources Publishing, 2d ed., 1997) devotes two pages to each state, with an introductory overview; descriptive summaries of major executive, legislative, and judicial sites; and notes on state bar associations, state libraries, and miscellaneous resources from a variety of law firms, law schools, and other providers. James Evans's *Government on the Net* (Nolo Press, 1998) provides an extensive listing for each state but not much commentary to explain the purpose and scope of the various sites listed. Most of its notes are simply copied from the sites themselves, making it difficult to distinguish between thorough, searchable resources and sketchy homepages with little useful information. Nonetheless, addresses are provided in the book and on the accompanying CD-ROM, *Law and Government on the Net*. Yvonne J. Chandler's *Neal-Schuman Guide to Finding Legal and Regulatory Information on the Internet* (Neal-Schuman, 1998) devotes separate chapters to judicial, legislative, and regulatory information, with annotated state-by-state listings in each chapter. A good basic list of major Web sites for each state appears, along with coverage of printed and CD-ROM sources, in Chapter 27, "State Legal Publications and Information Sources," of Kendall F. Svengalis's *Legal Information Buyer's Guide & Reference Manual* (Rhode Island LawPress, annual).

CONSTITUTIONS

Just as the United States Constitution establishes the responsibilities and powers of the national government and guarantees basic freedoms, each state has its own constitution, which is its fundamental law. The state constitution establishes the basic framework of state government and addresses areas untouched in the federal Constitution, such as education, local finance, and voter qualifications. Each state constitution also includes provisions comparable to the Bill of Rights, protecting the basic rights of its citizens, and covers a variety of other matters. Article 19, section 2 of the Arkansas constitution, for example, prohibits anyone participating in a duel from holding state office for 10 years.

The Supreme Court of the United States determines the scope of the protections offered by the U.S. Constitution; likewise, a state's supreme court is the final arbiter of its constitution. A state cannot deprive citizens of federal rights, but it can extend protections beyond those in the federal document. In recent years, the Supreme Court has limited federal constitutional protections for criminal defendants, but some state courts have interpreted comparable clauses in their own constitutions to provide more extensive rights. The Supreme Court has no jurisdiction to review a state court's interpretation of its constitution as long as "the state court decision indicates clearly and expressly that it is alternatively based on bona fide separate, adequate, and independent grounds" (*Michigan v. Long*, 463 U.S. 1032, 1041 [1983]).

State constitutions can be the basis of substantial rights unavailable under federal law. The Connecticut Supreme Court held in *Sheff v. O'Neill*, 238 Conn. 1, 678 A.2d 1267 (1996), that the state constitution required the integration of the school districts of Hartford and its suburbs. A year earlier, litigants in another case before the same court had claimed that the state had an obligation under its constitution to provide indigent citizens with a minimal level of subsistence, but the court disagreed. (*Moore v. Ganim*, 233 Conn. 557, 660 A.2d 742 [1995]). Each of these decisions examines sources of constitutional history more than 200 years old and spans nearly 150 pages (including a lengthy dissent in each case) in the *Connecticut Reports*.

Although state constitutions are similar in function to the U.S. Constitution, in some ways they are quite different. The U.S. Constitution is a venerable, concise document that has been amended only 27 times in more than 200 years. State constitutions tend to be much longer and more detailed, and they are amended and revised regularly. Twenty states still operate under their original constitutions, but most of these have been amended more than 100 times. It is far easier to put an amendment before the voters of a state than it is to seek approval by three-quarters of the states to amend the U.S. Constitution. (A popular vote is not even required in Delaware, where the constitution can be amended by the legislature.)

Even wholesale revision is a simpler matter at the state level. Some states have had several constitutions in their history, with Louisiana's 11 constitutions taking the lead. Since 1960, 10 states have adopted new constitutions. Many states have commissions that study constitutional issues and recommend needed changes, but the normal mode of revision is through a constitutional convention. A proposal to call a convention generally requires approval from the voters, and has been rejected recently in Arkansas (1995) and New York (1997).

The first chapter of *The Book of the States* provides a good comparative overview of state constitutions. Its first table contains information on the number of constitutions each state has had and the date each was adopted; for the present constitution, it indicates the effective date, approximate length, and number of amendments. The remaining tables in the chapter outline procedures for constitutional change and activities of constitutional commissions.

Current state constitutions are easy to find in several sources. Most are published in pamphlets by state governments, although these may not be widely available in other states. Some states have also published official guides to their constitutions, such as Gordon S. Harrison's *Alaska's Constitution: A Citizen's Guide* (3d ed., 1992), and Rob Williams et al.'s *A Citizens' Guide to the Kentucky Constitution* (1993).

Just as the U.S. Constitution is printed in the *U.S. Code* and its annotated editions, each state code includes a copy of its current constitution. Most are accompanied by annotations of court decisions, which are among the most important resources in understanding the constitutional provisions. Just as the U.S. Constitution cannot be read without considering how it has been interpreted by the Supreme Court, state constitutions must also be read in light of decisions by the state courts.

The state supreme court determines the meaning of its constitution, but the U.S. Supreme Court rules on conflicts between federal and state law. In *Torcaso vs. Watkins*, 367 U.S. 488 (1961), the Court ruled that a section of the Maryland constitution violated the First Amendment by barring atheists from holding public office. This case shows the importance of reading the annotations as well as the text of the constitution because the provision remains unchanged in the Maryland constitution nearly 40 years later (as do similar provisions in several other state constitutions). Cases citing particular constitutional provisions are also listed in *Shepard's* state citators, discussed later in this chapter.

The constitutions are included in most CD-ROM state law products, and they are available online on LEXIS-NEXIS and WESTLAW. LEXIS-NEXIS has individual files for each state constitution, such as ALCNST or AKCNST. Most, but not all, of these constitutions are annotated. The constitutions are also included in the code file for each state, and all 50 are in the ALLCDE file in the CODES or STATES library. There is no separate 50-state file for constitutions.

WESTLAW does not have separate constitution databases, but the state constitutions are included in both annotated (AL-ST-ANN, AK-ST-ANN) and unannotated (AL-STAT, AK-STAT) code databases, and in the multistate databases ST-ANN-ALL and STAT-ALL. WESTLAW also has a Table of Contents service making it possible to browse through a constitution's articles and sections. LEXIS-NEXIS has a similar feature for state statutes but not for constitutions.

Most states also provide the text of their constitutions at state Web sites. Direct links to constitutions are provided by several of the multistate sites listed earlier in this chapter. In FindLaw, for example, choosing "Primary Materials" for a state leads to a list of sources, beginning with the constitution; direct links to the available constitutions are collected at <http://www.findlaw.com/11stategov/indexconst.html>.

Most of the state constitutions on the Internet are part of official state Web sites, but a few are provided by law schools or commercial sites. Usually they provide the complete document but no annotations. The University of Mississippi's copy of the state constitution <http://www.olemiss.edu/depts/law_lib_research/laws/msconst.html> has only the Preamble and Article 3, with no explanation that its coverage is limited. A commercial site <http://www.mscode.com/> has the entire document, but searching is accessible only to subscribers.

Reference Guides to the State Constitutions of the United States, a series of volumes published by Greenwood Press, provides an excellent place to begin research in particular states' constitutions. This series began with Robert F. Williams's *The New Jersey State Constitution: A Reference Guide* (1990) and has continued through eight years and 30 state constitutions. A convenient list of volumes appears in the front of each new addition to the series, and most library catalogs list entries under the series title. The states *not* yet covered as of 1998 are Colorado, Delaware, Illinois, Kentucky, Maryland, Massachusetts, Minnesota, Missouri, Montana, New Hampshire, North Dakota, Ohio, Oklahoma, Oregon, Pennsylvania, Rhode Island, South Carolina, South Dakota, Virginia, and Washington.

Almost all volumes in the *Reference Guides* series have been written by leading constitutional scholars in the respective states. Most are political scientists, but the roster includes several law professors, some practicing attorneys, and two retired state supreme court justices. Not until the 29th volume was the job assumed by an outsider—*The Iowa State Constitution: A Reference Guide* (1998) was written by Jack Stark, assistant chief counsel of Wisconsin's Legislative Reference Bureau and author of *The Wisconsin State Constitution: A Reference Guide* (1997). Perhaps the states for which volumes have not yet been published lack any constitutional scholars willing to take on the project.

The books follow a standard format. Each begins with an overview of the state's constitutional history. The most extensive part is a section-by-section analysis of the constitution, reprinting the text of each section with a discussion of its background and judicial interpretations. Almost every volume also contains a bibliographical essay, with helpful recommendations and comments on sources for further study. Tables of cases and indexes round out the book. According to the general editor's notes, the series will eventually include a comprehensive index and a general volume covering themes common to all state constitutions.

The state *Reference Guides* provide a good introductory overview of a state's constitution, but they are not written for practical legal use. For a more focused analysis of the application of state constitutional law in civil and criminal litigation, the leading treatise is Jennifer Friesen's *State Constitutional Law: Litigating Individual Rights, Claims, and Defenses* (Michie, 2d ed., 1996, with annual pocket part supplement). This work focuses on the rights of privacy, equal treatment, freedom of religion, and freedom of expression; civil actions for violations of state constitutional rights; and the rights of the accused in investigative and criminal proceedings. A shorter, paperback introduction is Thomas C. Marks, Jr.'s *State Constitutional Law in a Nutshell* (West Publishing, 1988). Constitutional developments can be tracked through *State Constitutional Law Bulletin* (National Association of Attorneys General, 10 times per year), which summarizes new court decisions interpreting state constitutional provisions. The *Bulletin* is available online through LEXIS-NEXIS (LEGNEW library, AGSTCN file) and WESTLAW (NAAGSCLB database). A new Congressional Quarterly volume scheduled for publication in late 1998, Robert L. Maddex's *State Constitutions of the United States*, promises encyclopedic coverage of all 50 constitutions, including historical background, summaries of key points, and comparative charts on specific issues.

Constitutions of the United States: National and State (Oceana, 7 vols., 2d ed., 1974-date) is a collection of pamphlets reprinting all the current state constitutions, as well as those for several U.S. territories. Pamphlets are periodically replaced to keep the set up-to-date. Having the constitutions in one set facilitates multistate research, although it has no comprehensive index. Two topical indexes have been published, however, covering "Fundamental Liberties and Rights" (1980) and "Laws, Legislature, Legislative Procedure" (1982). Because constitutions change relatively infrequently, an earlier, more comprehensive *Index Digest of State Constitutions* (Legislative Drafting Research Fund of Columbia University, 2d ed., 1959, with 1971 supplement covering through 1967) may still be useful.

Older constitutions can be found in the annotated codes for some of the states. *West's Louisiana Statutes Annotated*, for example, includes nine earlier Louisiana constitutions (all but the 1861 constitution, which made no substantive changes and merely changed references to "United States of America" to "Confederate States of America"). Only about half of the codes for states with superseded constitutions include these earlier texts; the others limit their coverage to current documents.

Other, comprehensive sources provide information on older constitutions. A standard source, still found in many libraries, is Benjamin Perley Poore's *The Federal and State Constitutions, Colonial Charters, and Other Organic Laws* (GPO, 2d ed., 1878). This oversized two-volume set was updated a few decades later in a smaller but more voluminous seven-volume edition by Francis Newton Thorpe (GPO, 1909). Both of these editions have been reprinted, Thorpe most recently by William S. Hein & Co. in 1993.

A more modern publication, *Sources and Documents of United States Constitutions*, edited by William F. Swindler (Oceana, 11 vols., 1973–79), contains constitutions and other documents such as land grants and statehood acts, but most of these are simply photocopies from Poore's collection and other sources. Each state's entry contains a brief background note and a short bibliography. This publication includes useful tables for states with more than one constitution, comparing the location of various subjects in each document.

Just as the *Federalist* and other framers' writings may be useful in interpreting the terms of the United States Constitution, documents are available for studying the preparation of state constitutions. Among the most useful of these are the journals and proceedings of constitutional conventions. These are of varying quality, and some are compilations of newspaper reports rather than verbatim transcripts. Many of the earlier volumes are not indexed, so finding a discussion of a particular issue may require considerable patience.

References to the documents of constitutional conventions are available in a series of bibliographies. Cynthia E. Browne's *State Constitutional Conventions from Independence to the Completion of the Present Union, 1776-1959: A Bibliography* (Greenwood Press, 1973) has been supplemented by *State Constitutional Conventions, Commissions & Amendments, 1959-1978: An Annotated Bibliography* (CIS, 2 vols., 1981) and *State Constitutional Conventions, Commissions & Amendments, 1979-1988: An Annotated Bibliography* (CIS, 1989). The documents listed in these bibliographies are available from CIS on more than 10,000 microfiche.

STATUTES

The current subject compilation of a state's statutes is often the first place to find answers to state law questions. The statutes do not cover every aspect of state law because some areas remain matters of common law determined over the course of time by the courts. But state legislatures have enacted laws governing such broad areas that it is usually prudent to look first for relevant statutes.

Statutory language, however, is notorious for being either too sparse or too convoluted, which is why it is usually easier to begin with a secondary source that explains the law. Treatises and state encyclopedias outline legal doctrines and provide references to relevant statutes, and multistate reference works, such as those discussed earlier in this chapter, can provide quick summaries and access to the appropriate statutory provisions.

Collections of a state's statutes are among its most important legal publications, and they are usually available not only in law libraries but in most larger academic and public libraries as well. Statutes from other states are less widely available, but they too should be found in law school libraries. Under the American Bar Association's accreditation standards, one requirement of a core library collection is "at least one current annotated code for each state."

Published Codes

State statutes are published in forms similar to those used for federal statutes. Statutes in force are arranged by subject, assigned section or article numbers, and issued in compilations known as *codes*. Some states have officially published editions, like the *United States Code*. Most of these are published by the states themselves, but a few are published by West Group under official supervision.

General Statutes of Connecticut (16 vols., biennial)

Official Florida Statutes (5 vols., biennial, with interim supps.)

Illinois Compiled Statutes (West, 9 vols., biennial, with interim supps.)

Indiana Code (13 vols., quinquennial, with annual supps.)

Code of Iowa (5 vols., biennial, with interim supps.)

General Laws of Massachusetts (West, 17 vols., biennial, with interim supps.)

Minnesota Statutes (15 vols., biennial, with interim pocket parts)

Missouri Revised Statutes (9 vols., every 7 or 8 years, with annual supps.)

Oklahoma Statutes (West, 6 vols., every 10 years, with annual supps.)

Pennsylvania Consolidated Statutes (7 loose-leaf vols., updated semiannually)

Revised Code of Washington (9 vols., biennial, with interim supps.)

Wisconsin Statutes and Annotations (5 vols., biennial)

These publications are the official source of the statutes, but they are not the most useful versions because they do not include the extensive notes of court decisions found in annotated codes. Nonetheless, they may be the most widely available sources in general libraries within the state. Some of the annotated codes are both expensive and voluminous, and can be found only in larger libraries. But statutes in many states with official publications specify that copies be distributed without charge to college and public libraries, see, e.g., Ind. Code § 2-6-1.5-4; Mo. Rev. Stat. § 3.130. These statutes ensure that citizens have at least some access to their state's laws.

Besides these official publications, a few other states have commercial unannotated editions published to provide convenient desktop access to statutes. Because court decisions play such a vital role in interpreting statutes, however, the most important statutory publications are *annotated codes* combining the text of the statute with notes of court decisions and other information. At least one annotated code is published for each state.

Exhibits 11-2 and 11-3 show the publication of adoption statutes in the *Arkansas Code of 1987 Annotated* and *West's Revised Code of Washington Annotated*. These sample pages show some of the information provided by annotated state codes. In both instances, the actual text of the statutes is easy to pick out because it is in the largest type and not set in columns.

9-9-216. Appeal from and validation of adoption decree.

(a) An appeal from any final order or decree rendered under this subchapter may be taken in the manner and time provided for appeal from a judgment in a civil action.

(b) Subject to the disposition of an appeal, upon the expiration of one (1) year after an adoption decree is issued, the decree cannot be questioned by any person including the petitioner, in any manner upon any ground, including fraud, misrepresentation, failure to give any required notice, or lack of jurisdiction of the parties or of the subject matter unless, in the case of the adoption of a minor, the petitioner has not taken custody of the minor or, in the case of the adoption of an adult, the adult had no knowledge of the decree within the one-year period.

History. Acts 1977. No. 735. § 16: A.S.A. 1947, § 56-216.

Publisher's Notes. The Arkansas Supreme Court, in its per curiam of November 22, 1982, observed that some confusion exists among members of the bar as to the date of the final order for the purpose of appeal. The court stated: "In order to put an end to the confusion, we shall prospectively construe any decree of adoption to be a final decree, no matter whether it is interlocutory or final, if no subsequent hearing is required by the terms of that decree."

RESEARCH REFERENCES

Ark. L. Rev. Case Note, In re Adoption of Pollock: Arkansas Probate Court Jurisdiction — A Question of Policy, 41 Ark. L. Rev. 677.

CASE NOTES

Construction.

The one-year statute of limitations in subdivision (b)(1) of this section provides a special procedure which cannot be annulled by ARCP 41(a) or the savings statute, § 16-56-126, which allows an action dismissed without prejudice to be refiled within one year of the dismissal. In re Martindale, 327 Ark. 685, 940 S.W.2d 491 (1997).

Collateral Attack.

In a collateral attack on a foreign adoption former section setting the time upon which an adoption becomes final did not apply; where the parent was not given notice of the adoption proceeding; the section did not begin to run until the parent discovered the identity of the adopting parties. Olney v. Gordon, 240 Ark. 807, 402 S.W.2d 651 (1966) (decision under prior law).

A petition to determine heirship filed by deceased's collateral heirs was a collateral attack on the order of adoption, which was not subject to collateral attack. Williams v. Nash. 247 Ark. 135, 445 S.W.2d 69 (1969) (decision under prior law).

Probate court, in adoption proceedings, had no authority to grant visitation rights to grandmother and hence visitation portion of the adoption decree in excess of the court's authority or subject matter jurisdiction and was void and subject to collateral attack. Poe v. Case. 263 Ark. 488, 565 S.W.2d 612 (1978) (decision under prior law).

Finality of Decree.

Any decree of adoption is a final decree, no matter whether it is interlocutory or final, if no subsequent hearing is required by the terms of that decree. In re Adoption

EXHIBIT 11-2

sent to adoption of child by person with whom it has been placed by the agency, adoption is privilege, not right; and burden of proving that it is in best interests

of child to dispense with agency's consent is on would-be adoptive parents. In re Adoption of Doe (1968) 74 Wash.2d 396, 444 P.2d 800.

26.33.170.   When consent to adoption not required

An agency's, the department's, or a legal guardian's consent to adoption may be dispensed with if the court determines by clear, cogent and convincing evidence that the proposed adoption is in the best interests of the adoptee.

Enacted by Laws 1984, ch. 155, § 17, eff. Jan. 1, 1985. Amended by Laws 1988, ch. 203, § 1.

Historical and Statutory Notes

Laws 1988, ch. 203, § 1, inserted "by clear, cogent and convincing evidence"; and, at the end of the section, deleted "and that the refusal to consent to adoption is arbitrary and capricious".

Source:

Laws 1943, ch. 268, §§ 4, 5.

RRS §§ 1699–5, 1699–6.
Former §§ 26.32.040, 26.32.050.
Laws 1955, ch. 291, §§ 4, 5.
Laws 1973, ch. 134, §§ 3, 4.
Laws 1975–76, 2nd Ex.Sess., ch. 42, §§ 27, 28.

Library References

Adoption ⬅7.
WESTLAW Topic No. 17.
C.J.S. Adoption of Persons §§ 51 to 72.

Clear and convincing proof in civil cases, see Wash.Prac. vol. 5, Tegland, § 63.

Notes of Decisions

Agency   1

———

1. Agency

In cases where agency has become facilitator of child's adoption, one cannot simply select particular child in custodial care, obtain replacement report, pay filing fee, and become prospective adoptive parent with automatic entitlement to temporary placement of that child; custodian plays integral role in carrying out its legislatively mandated purpose of finding proper adoptive home. In re Dependency of G.C.B. (1994) 73 Wash.App. 708, 870 P.2d 1037, review denied 124 Wash.2d 1019, 881 P.2d 254.

Having been made legal custodian of child with express right to place child in prospective adoptive home and right to terminate such placement, Department of Social and Health Services (DSHS) has equal authority to withhold placement in first instance; nothing in legislation providing for preparation of postplacement

reports demonstrates any intent on part of legislature to take placement decisions away from custodial agency. In re Dependency of G.C.B. (1994) 73 Wash.App. 708, 870 P.2d 1037, review denied 124 Wash.2d 1019, 881 P.2d 254.

Issues as to petitioners' fitness as adoptive parents and the propriety of dispensing with a child-placing agency's consent to adoption may be determined in same hearing; for same evidence may go to qualifications of those desiring to be adoptive parents and reasonableness of approved agency's refusal to consent. In re Adoption of Doe (1968) 74 Wash.2d 396, 444 P.2d 800.

When "approved agency" refuses to file its written consent in adoption proceeding, full hearing on reasonableness of agency's action is contemplated, and if consent is withheld unreasonably, court, in its discretion, may enter order dispensing with consent of agency. In re Adoption of Reinius (1959) 55 Wash.2d 117, 346 P.2d 672.

EXHIBIT 11-3

Annotated state codes provide a variety of other valuable information besides the statutory text. Each section is followed by a note indicating the year and number of the session law in which it was enacted. If a section has been amended, the later session law is noted as well. In the Arkansas section shown in Exhibit 11-2, this note (marked "History") also provides the citation to this section in the earlier codification, *Arkansas Statutes Annotated 1947*. The Washington section in Exhibit 11-3 was amended in 1988, and the "Historical and Statutory Notes" explain exactly what change was made. The Washington notes go on to list previous, comparable provisions and amendments back to 1943.

Only some state codes, unfortunately, follow the practice of the *U.S. Code* in providing notes explaining the nature of each change in the statutory language. Some codes include extensive notes detailing each change over the course of several decades, while a few have explanatory notes on the most recent change only. Fully half of the state codes, however, provide nothing more than a list of session law references. If a statute in such a code was amended in 1993 and 1996, there is no way of telling how it read in 1994 without consulting the session laws.

These statutory references are followed by "Research References" or "Library References." Depending on the code, these provide citations to law review articles, state legal encyclopedias, practice treatises, and digests. In Exhibit 11-2, the LEXIS Law Publishing code for Arkansas has a reference to a law review article, while West's Washington code in Exhibit 11-3 includes references for use in its digests, legal encyclopedia (C.J.S.), and WESTLAW.

Finally, the code sections are followed by "Case Notes" or "Notes of Decisions." The scope and style of these case annotations vary. Some codes have numbered subdivisions, while others use boldface headings to sort material. No matter what format, these annotations provide references to court decisions applying and interpreting these particular sections.

Although the sample pages shown in Exhibits 11-2 and 11-3 both include annotations of court decisions, this is by no means true for every code section. Many state statutes have never been considered in published appellate court decisions. An example of a vital piece of legislation with no interpretive notes is the Georgia law, enacted in 1976, that prohibits anyone but the owner from gathering pecans that fall on public roadways during harvest season, (Ga. Code Ann. §§ 44-12-240 to 44-12-243). This law has been on the books for more than 20 years, but there are no notes of cases interpreting its scope or adjudicating its constitutionality.

Annotated codes vary considerably in size, ranging from a dozen volumes (Alaska) to more than 200 (California), and in the amount of editorial information they provide. Some are published under official sanction, while others are purely commercial ventures. Most are the work of two companies, LEXIS Law Publishing (which is gradually changing its imprint from Michie; 31 states), and West Group (25 states). Both publishers are represented in several of the larger states with competing code publications, much like West's *United States Code Annotated* (*USCA*) and LEXIS Law Publishing's *United States Code Service* (*USCS*). The only states not covered are Kansas and Montana (although West does publish annotated Kansas laws in selected areas such as civil procedure and probate).

Most state codes, like *USCA* and *USCS*, are published in bound volumes and supplemented by annual pocket parts, but a few codes are published in binders with loose-leaf supplements, and others have freestanding pamphlet supplements rather than pocket parts. In a few states where legislatures meet every other year, the codes have biennial pocket parts, but these are further supplemented in alternate years with pamphlets for new case annotations. Most codes are updated further between annual supplements by additional pamphlets. Almost all have softcover index volumes, which are replaced annually.

Table 11-1 indicates the current annotated codes published for each state, with the number of volumes and basic form of supplementation or frequency of replacement. Earlier titles and publishers are indicated for some codes to facilitate identifying these publications in online catalogs or other sources.

As is apparent, the names of codes vary from state to state. Some are called *Revised Codes*, some are *Revised Statutes*, and others are known as *Codified Laws* or *Consolidated Laws*. Some state code titles include a date, such as *Alaska Statutes 1962*, but these are simply the dates of the most recent recodifications. They linger in the titles of codes just to confuse people. (These dates are usually omitted in citations, but because they appear as part of titles in online catalogs they are left in to avoid further confusion.)

The abbreviation used for a state code may depend on the source in which it is cited. Law reviews, and academic literature generally, follow forms decreed in *The Bluebook: A Uniform System of Citation* (16th ed., 1996), but court decisions and other documents are not bound by *Bluebook* rules. The *Bluebook* demands that

TABLE 11-1

ANNOTATED STATE CODES

Code of Alabama 1975	(West [originally Lawyers Cooperative], 32 vols., annual pocket parts)
Michie's Alabama Code [formerly *Code of Alabama 1975*]	(LEXIS [originally Michie], 35 vols., annual pocket parts)
Alaska Statutes 1962	(LEXIS, 12 vols., biennial, with interim supps.)
Arizona Revised Statutes Annotated	(West, 50 vols., annual pocket parts)
Arkansas Code of 1987 Annotated	(LEXIS [originally Michie], 50 vols., biennial pocket parts)
Deering's California Codes Annotated	(LEXIS [originally Bancroft-Whitney], 197 vols., annual pocket parts)
West's Annotated California Codes	(West, 205 vols., annual pocket parts)
Colorado Revised Statutes	(Bradford, 13 vols., annual)
West's Colorado Revised Statutes Annotated	(West, 36 vols., annual pocket parts)
Connecticut General Statutes Annotated	(West, 47 vols., annual pocket parts)
Delaware Code Annotated	(LEXIS [originally Michie], 20 vols., biennial pocket parts)
District of Columbia Code Annotated	(LEXIS [originally Michie], 18 vols., annual pocket parts)
Harrison's Florida Statutes Annotated	(Harrison, 64 vols., annual pocket parts)
West's Florida Statutes Annotated	(West, 83 vols., annual pocket parts)
Code of Georgia Annotated	(Harrison, 81 vols., annual pocket parts)
Official Code of Georgia Annotated	(LEXIS [originally Michie], 45 vols., annual pocket parts)
Hawaii Revised Statutes	(State of Hawaii, 15 vols., annual pamphlet supps.)
Hawaii Revised Statutes Annotated	(LEXIS [originally Michie], 20 vols., annual pocket parts)
Idaho Code Annotated	(LEXIS [originally Bobbs-Merrill], 26 vols., annual pocket parts)
Illinois Compiled Statutes Annotated	(LEXIS [originally Michie], 56 vols., annual pocket parts)
West's Smith-Hurd Illinois Compiled Statutes Annotated	(West, 72 vols., annual pocket parts)
Burns Indiana Statutes Annotated	(LEXIS [originally Bobbs-Merrill], 43 vols., annual pocket parts)
West's Annotated Indiana Code	(West, 63 vols., annual pocket parts)
Iowa Code Annotated	(West, 63 vols., annual pocket parts)
Kansas Statutes Annotated	(State of Kansas, 14 vols., annual pamphlet supps.)
Baldwin's Kentucky Revised Statutes Annotated	(West [originally Banks-Baldwin], 16 loose-leaf vols., updated semiannually)
Kentucky Revised Statutes Annotated	(LEXIS [originally Michie], 33 vols., annual pocket parts)
West's Louisiana Statutes Annotated	(West, 113 vols., annual pocket parts)
Maine Revised Statutes Annotated 1964	(West, 38 vols., annual pocket parts)
Annotated Code of the Public General Laws of Maryland	(LEXIS [originally Michie], 39 vols., annual pocket parts)
Annotated Laws of Massachusetts	(LEXIS [originally Lawyers Cooperative], 81 vols., annual pocket parts)
Massachusetts General Laws Annotated	(West, 65 vols., annual pocket parts)
Michigan Compiled Laws Annotated	(West, 69 vols., annual pocket parts)
Michigan Statutes Annotated	(LEXIS [originally Callaghan], 68 vols., annual pocket parts)
Minnesota Statutes Annotated	(West, 73 vols., annual pocket parts)
Mississippi Code 1972 Annotated	(West [originally Harrison/Lawyers Cooperative], 26 vols., annual pocket parts)
Vernon's Annotated Missouri Statutes	(West, 65 vols., annual pocket parts)
Montana Code Annotated	(State of Montana, 12 vols., biennial, and 12 loose-leaf vols., updated biennially)
Revised Statutes of Nebraska 1943	(State of Nebraska, 14 vols., annual supps.)
Revised Statutes of Nebraska Annotated	(LEXIS [originally Michie], 25 vols., annual pocket parts)
Nevada Revised Statutes	(State of Nevada, 49 loose-leaf vols., updated biennially)
Nevada Revised Statutes Annotated	(LEXIS [originally Michie], 26 vols., biennial pocket parts)

TABLE 11-1 (continued)	
ANNOTATED STATE CODES	
New Hampshire Revised Statutes Annotated 1955	(LEXIS [originally Equity], 32 vols., annual pocket parts)
New Jersey Statutes Annotated	(West, 91 vols., annual pocket parts)
New Mexico Statutes 1978 Annotated	(LEXIS [originally Michie], 14 loose-leaf vols., updated annually)
McKinney's Consolidated Laws of New York Annotated	(West, 188 vols., annual pocket parts)
New York Consolidated Laws Service	(LEXIS [originally Lawyers Cooperative], 140 vols., annual pocket parts)
General Statutes of North Carolina	(LEXIS [originally Michie], 24 loose-leaf vols., updated annually)
North Dakota Century Code Annotated	(LEXIS [originally Smith], 24 vols., biennial pocket parts)
Baldwin's Ohio Revised Code Annotated	(West, 50 vols., annual pocket parts)
Page's Ohio Revised Code Annotated	(Anderson, 35 vols., annual pocket parts)
Oklahoma Statutes Annotated	(West, 72 vols., annual pocket parts)
Oregon Revised Statutes	(State of Oregon, 16 vols., biennial)
Oregon Revised Statutes Annotated	(LEXIS [originally Butterworth], 54 vols., annual pamphlet supps.)
Purdon's Pennsylvania Statutes Annotated and *Purdon's Pennsylvania Consolidated Statutes Annotated*	(West, 104 vols., annual pocket parts)
Laws of Puerto Rico Annotated	(LEXIS [originally Equity], 40 vols., annual pocket parts)
General Laws of Rhode Island 1956	(LEXIS [originally Bobbs-Merrill], 29 vols., annual pocket parts)
Code of Laws of South Carolina 1976 Annotated	(West [originally Lawyers Cooperative], 45 vols., annual pocket parts)
South Dakota Codified Laws [formerly *South Dakota Compiled Laws 1967*]	(LEXIS [originally Smith], 34 vols., annual pocket parts)
Tennessee Code Annotated	(LEXIS [originally Bobbs-Merrill], 32 vols., annual pocket parts)
Vernon's Texas Codes Annotated and *Vernon's Annotated Revised Civil Statutes of the State of Texas*	(West, 117 vols., annual pocket parts)
Utah Code Annotated 1953	(LEXIS [originally Smith], 27 vols., annual pocket parts)
Vermont Statutes Annotated	(LEXIS [originally Equity], 29 vols., annual pocket parts)
Virgin Islands Code Annotated	(LEXIS [originally Equity], 15 vols., annual pocket parts)
Code of Virginia 1950 Annotated	(LEXIS [originally Michie], 27 vols., annual pocket parts)
Annotated Revised Code of Washington	(LEXIS, 20 vols., annual)
West's Revised Code of Washington Annotated	(West, 77 vols., annual pocket parts)
West Virginia Code Annotated	(LEXIS [originally Michie], 27 vols., annual pocket parts)
West's Wisconsin Statutes Annotated	(West, 54 vols., annual pocket parts)
Wyoming Statutes Annotated	(LEXIS, 12 vols., biennial with interim supps.)

the section in Exhibit 11-3 be cited as "Wash. Rev. Code. § 26.33.170," but the Washington Supreme Court would instead cite it as "RCW 26.33.170." The court's abbreviation is more concise and is instantly recognizable to Washington attorneys, but it may be more difficult to decipher for a reader unfamiliar with local legal shorthand.

The arrangement of state codes also varies considerably. Most states have a division into titles and sections, in an arrangement similar to the federal statutes,

but several states have individual codes designated by subject rather than title number. California, for example, has 29 separate subject codes, such as the Family Code, Penal Code, and Revenue Code. A few states are in the process of recodifying their laws. Pennsylvania is creating its first official codification, with a numbering system similar to the unofficial one that has been in use. Until this project is completed, the Pennsylvania set has some unofficial *Pennsylvania Statutes* titles and some official *Pennsylvania Consolidated Statutes* titles—sometimes in the same volume and with the same title number. Maryland and Texas have both an older general sequence of numbered articles and a series of subject codes. Maryland's annotated code even has two distinct color bindings, black for the older articles and maroon for the newer subject codes. Michigan has a different problem, with two code publications using different numbering systems. Court rules require that both be cited.

Most states have a code commission or revisor of statutes who is responsible for compiling and editing the legislature's enactments into a coherent, systematic body of law, rearranging portions as needed, and correcting typographical errors and inconsistencies. In some states, revisors also work with legislators in drafting bills and assigning section numbers to proposed legislation. Minn. Stat. § 3C.04, perhaps drafted with an overbearing staffer in mind, specifies, "The revisor's office shall give members of the legislature advice concerning the legal effect of bills or proposed bills, but only at the request of the members."

The list above indicates how many volumes are in each set, but this number fluctuates regularly as replacement volumes are issued to accommodate new statutes and annotations. Some codes attempt to number each volume, which leads to some bizarre results, such as the volume of *Minnesota Statutes Annotated* numbered "32 to 34" or the *West's Florida Statutes Annotated* volumes "14A part 1," "14A part 2," and "14A part 3." There is always room in which to squeeze a new volume number; if volume 1 is followed by volume 1A, a new volume between them can be called volume 1½. The editors of several sets have recognized that trying to number volumes coherently is hopeless and rely instead on identifying volumes by title or section numbers. *New Hampshire Revised Statutes Annotated* started out with numbered volumes but gave up years ago, and only volume 4 (1983) remains in the current set.

Unlike a citation to the *U.S. Code*, in which the title number precedes the abbreviation, followed by the section number, as in "42 U.S.C. § 1983," most state codes are classified in one sequence of numbers and are simply cited by section number. The codes are divided into titles, but the section numbering frequently incorporates the title number. The Arkansas section in Exhibit 11-2, for example, is part of Title 9, Family Law, but it is cited as Ark. Code. Ann. § 9-9-216.

Differences in the arrangement of state codes are not simply a matter of classification. States can view similar issues in different contexts. In more than half the states, for instance, the topic of adoption is considered part of domestic relations or family law, but several states have titles or codes dealing specifically with children. Alabama uses the endearing title "Infants and Incompetents," combining two older legal terms for persons considered incapable of handling their own affairs. A few states put adoption among public welfare statutes, and some place it with other statutes on the jurisdiction of the probate courts. In New Jersey, adoption is part of an "Adoption, Apprenticeship and Indenture" subtitle of the "Children" title, even though the "Apprenticeship and Indenture" chapter was repealed in 1953.

The format of individual code provisions on adoption can vary widely as well. Some states have concise sections spelling out the law in plain English. Ark. Code. Ann. § 9-9-203 has just five words: "Any individual may be adopted." On the other hand, Tenn. Code Ann. § 36-1-111 takes more than 15 pages and nearly 8,000 words to address issues involving birthparents' consent.

Access to state codes is provided by indexes and tables similar to those for the *U.S. Code*. Each state code is accompanied by an extensive index of up to five volumes. These indexes are the main point of entry for finding statutes, although like the federal code indexes, they can be frustrating to work with. Some index volumes even include toll-free numbers for assistance and postcards inviting suggestions for improvement.

Almost every code is also accompanied by a set of tables providing valuable cross-references from session laws and from older codifications. These tables can be invaluable when trying to find the relevant statutory language at issue in a court decision. In 1992, Illinois adopted its first official recodification since 1874, completely changing the numbering system used for its statutes. To find a law cited in an earlier court decision, one must turn first to a table to determine its present location. Even in states that have not recodified their statutes, individual sections are frequently moved or replaced. Of the adoption statutes surveyed in early 1996 for the second edition of the *National Survey of State Laws*, for example, at least three have completely changed locations in their codes. These can be found through cross-references at the old location or through tables indicating the disposition of each of the older sections. Only if these sources fail is it necessary to turn to the subject index under "Adoption."

Because the depth and quality of annotated state codes vary, it may be useful to know of another means of finding materials citing state code provisions. Shepard's publishes a series of state citators, such as *Shepard's Alabama Citations* and *Shepard's Alaska*

Citations. These cover citations to both cases and statutes in court decisions, law review articles, and other sources. The law reviews covered for each state usually include any general interest reviews published in the state, as well as 19 leading law reviews that receive comprehensive coverage. As in *Shepard's Federal Statute Citations*, cases and articles discussing or citing code provisions are listed under the specific section or subsection cited. This should duplicate the coverage in the code annotations, but some cases and articles not cited in the code may appear. Most *Shepard's* state citators are updated monthly, and new cases may be listed before they are incorporated in code supplements.

In addition, the *Shepard's* citators include references to cases and articles citing other sources, such as the state constitution, uncodified laws, and court rules, as well as citations in the state's court decisions to the U.S. Constitution and federal statutes. They also claim to include references to legislative amendments to code provisions, but this coverage is glaringly inconsistent from state to state. Some states' amendments are noted within a year, while for others the coverage is several years out of date. The publisher does not differentiate between the states it keeps current and those it does not, so one must analyze carefully these listings before relying on them.

Shepard's citators for state statutes can be accessed through LEXIS-NEXIS as well as in print, and through the Internet <http://www.bender.com/>. Coverage for about 18 states is available through WESTLAW. One can achieve similar results by entering statutory citations as search terms in full-text databases of cases and journal articles. In the latter instance, a full-text search may turn up citing articles in journals not included within *Shepard's* rather narrow coverage.

Finally, although most legal research takes place in the current state code, older editions are often needed in historical research. This research may require not only superseded volumes from current annotated code sets but previous codifications dating as far back as the seventeenth century. Most major law libraries have these publications, in either microform or hard copy. The earliest "codes" were simply chronological compilations of statutes in force, but by the early nineteenth century most of the early states had subject arrangements of statutes. These were periodically revised as the old code grew outdated, leaving us a convenient trail of a state's statutory history. The indexes to the earliest codes are primitive, but over time indexing became more refined and thorough.

One way to approach older code volumes is to trace the references in a current provision back through history to determine their roots. In Exhibit 11-3, for example, the notes include citations to "Former §§ 26.32.040, 26.32.050," which could be found in a superseded volume of *West's Revised Code of Washington Annotated*, and to "RRS §§ 1699-5, 1699-6," references to an earlier codification, *Remington's Revised Statutes of Washington*. If related provisions on this topic go back further in time, it would be possible to turn to *Remington's Revised Statutes of Washington* and track down the older citations found in *its* statutory notes.

Older state codes are listed in most bibliographies and guides of legal resources for specific states. An extensive checklist of codes and compilations from all states appears in section 1 of *Pimsleur's Checklists of Basic American Legal Publications* (Rothman, 3 vols., 1962-date). This checklist provides only title, publisher, date, and number of pages or volumes, but it is a useful source for identifying early publications. References to codes can be found in online library catalogs, although the author is simply the name of the state and the same subject tracing ("Law—[state]") is used for a variety of general treatises and encyclopedias on state law.

Electronic Codes

State statutes are also available in several electronic formats. Most state codes are now accessible on the Internet, although a few states are still dragging their feet. Like the Internet versions of the *U.S. Code*, however, these free versions generally do not include important editorial additions such as notes of court decisions.

The easiest way to find state codes on the Internet is to go through one of the multistate Web sites described above because tracking them down from state homepages is not always a simple matter. Some are part of legislative information systems, while others are presented by code commissions, revisors of statutes, or private organizations.

Table 11-2 provides addresses for state codes available without charge on the Internet. Generally, these codes can be accessed through keyword searches by browsing through titles and sections, or by retrieving a particular section number. Most of the addresses listed in table 11-2 lead directly to the state codes, but in a few instances keyword searching and code tables of contents are presented at separate sites. In these instances, the addresses for legislative sites providing access to the various options are listed. Some state codes, unfortunately, are given much less prominence on these sites than such items as biographies of legis-

TABLE 11-2	
STATE CODE INTERNET SITES	

Alabama	*http://www.legislature.state.al.us/ALISHome.html*
Alaska	*http://www.legis.state.ak.us/folhome.htm*
Arizona	*http://www.azleg.state.az.us/ars/ars.htm*
Arkansas	
California	*http://www.leginfo.ca.gov/calaw.html*
Colorado	*http://www.intellinetusa.com/statmgr.htm*
Connecticut	*http://www.cslnet.ctstateu.edu/statutes/index.htm*
Delaware	*http://www.lexis/awpublishing.com/resources/resource_page.html*
Florida	*http://www.leg.state.fl.us/citizen/documents/statutes/*
Georgia	*http://www.ganet.org/services/ocode/ocgsearch.htm*
Hawaii	
Idaho	*http://www.state.id.us/legislat/legislat.html*
Illinois	
Indiana	*http://www.ai.org/legislative/ic/code/*
Iowa	*http://www.legis.state.ia.us/Code.html*
Kansas	*http://www.ink.org/public/statutes/statutes.html*
Kentucky	*http://www.lrc.state.ky.us/statrev/frontpg.htm*
Louisiana	
Maine	*http://janus.state.me.us/legis/meconlaw.htm*
Maryland	
Massachusetts	*http://www.state.ma.us/legis/laws/mgl/*
Michigan	
Minnesota	*http://www.leg.state.mn.us/leg/statutes.htm*
Mississippi	*http://www.sos.state.ms.us/MsCode/mscodeindex.html*
Missouri	*http://www.moga.state.mo.us/homestat.htm*
Montana	*http://www.mt.gov/leg/branch/laws.htm*
Nebraska	*http://unicam1.lcs.state.ne.us/folio.pgi/statutes.nfo?*
Nevada	*http://www.leg.state.nv.us/law1.htm*
New Hampshire	*http://www.199.92.250.14/rsa/*
New Jersey	*http://www.njleg.state.nj.us/*
New Mexico	*http://www.lexislawpublishing.com/resources/resource_page.html*
New York	*http://assembly.state.ny.us/cgi-bin/claws*
North Carolina	*http://www.ncga.state.nc.us/.html1997/statutes/statutes.html*
North Dakota	*http://www.state.nd.us/lr/centurycode.html*
Ohio	*http://www.conwaygreene.com/orc.htm* or *http://orc.avv.com/*
Oklahoma	*http://www.onenet.net/oklegal/index.html*
Oregon	*http://landru.leg.state.or.us/ors/*
Pennsylvania	
Rhode Island	*http://www.rilin.state.ri.us/Statutes/Statutes.html*
South Carolina	*http://www.lpitr.state.sc.us/code/statmast.htm*
South Dakota	*http://www.lexislawpublishing.com/resources/resource_page.html*
Tennessee	*http://www.lexislawpublishing.com/resources/resource_page.html*
Texas	*http://www.capitol.state.tx.us/statutes/statutes.html*
Utah	*http://www.le.state.ut.us/~code/code.htm*
Vermont	*http://www.leg.state.vt.us/statutes/statutes.htm*
Virginia	*http://leg1.state.va.us/000/src.htm*
Washington	*http://www.leg.wa.gov/www/ses.htm* or *http://www.mrsc.org/rcw.htm*
West Virginia	*http://www.legis.state.wv.us/Code/toc.html*
Wisconsin	*http://www.legis.state.wi.us/rsb/stats.html*
Wyoming	*http://legisweb.state.wy.us/titles/statutes.htm*

lators. Entries for several states are blank, but the number of these glaring omissions is decreasing with time.

Most of the sites listed are presented by state governments, but a few are commercial sites providing free access to unannotated statutes. The same Web site address is provided for Deleware, New Mexico, South Dakota, and Tennessee, all of which are available as Folio infobases from their publisher. Some states, such as Pennsylvania, have only selected statutes available.

Needless to say, the format of these Internet sites varies widely. Some are friendly and easily navigable. Others are primitive. Almost all are searchable, although idiosyncrasies exist. Kentucky's statutes can be searched, but only in four separate parts by section number. Only individual titles can be searched in North Dakota. Connecticut's site has no search option, but it provides access to the three-volume code index. There are no links from the index to code sections, so once a subject reference is found it is necessary to go back and click to the appropriate section. Utah's search engine, YeeHaw!, searches not only the code but all of the state government Web servers.

When using state codes on the Internet, it is important to note how current and how authoritative the information is. Some Web sites, even those directly from state legislatures, warn that their's is not the official text and that printed sources must be consulted if locating the exact text of the statute is critical. The Vermont site, for example, has a disclaimer that its version "was created for the use and convenience of the members and staff of the Vermont Legislature" and was not in any sense the "official" text enacted into law. Other sites can be more than a year out of date because it may take time for new amendments to be added to the database. Some Web sites are careful to notify users of limitations, but in other instances it may be necessary to hunt around for the date statutes were last updated.

The leading commercial sources for state statutes, as with other legal materials, are LEXIS-NEXIS and WESTLAW. Both have codes from all 50 states, as well as the District of Columbia, Puerto Rico, and the Virgin Islands. WESTLAW's collection is more thorough, with both annotated and unannotated versions of each state's statutes. The annotated edition uses the suffix "-ST-ANN" (AL-ST-ANN or WY-ST-ANN), and the unannotated edition uses "-ST" (AL-ST or WY-ST). Although access to annotations is important in statutory research, a full-text search in the annotated code may turn up hundreds of irrelevant documents in which the terms appear only in casenotes. A search in the unannotated database may focus retrieval more specifically on pertinent code sections. On the other hand, sometimes language in the annotations may help locate sections that would otherwise be missed because the statutory language is too obtuse.

LEXIS-NEXIS does not distinguish as clearly between annotated and unannotated statutes. Files with state statutes are found in the individual state libraries (from ALA to WYO), with the file name CODE. More comprehensive files combining the codes with the constitution and recent session laws can be retrieved from the CODES and STATES libraries by adding the word CODE to the state abbreviation (ALCODE, WYCODE). Although most of the LEXIS-NEXIS codes include annotations, at least 11 (Arizona, Colorado, Florida, Iowa, Louisiana, Maine, Minnesota, New Jersey, Oklahoma, Pennsylvania, and Texas) do not. Some of these do not even have history notes explaining when sections were enacted or amended, while others indicate only the year of the most recent amendment. Because the LEXIS-NEXIS file names do not differentiate between annotated and unannotated products, its code databases must be used with caution.

The importance of access to annotations in interpreting statutes cannot be overstated. Under Maine's sardine tax law, 36 Me. Rev. Stat. §§ 4692A-4700, for instance, LEXIS-NEXIS provides no casenotes or cross-references. WESTLAW's version, and the published code, provide cross-references to other statutes governing sardine packers and note that this law was upheld as constitutional in *State v. Stinson Canning Co.*, 161 Me. 320, 211 A.2d 553 (1965). Other cases are noted as well, including one defining *sardine* to include only whole fish and not "herring chunks" from which heads and tails had been removed (*State v. Milbridge Canning Corp.*, 159 Me. 1, 186 A.2d 789 [1963]). (The free Internet site from the Maine legislature also lacks these annotations but it still provides good value for the price.)

WESTLAW has other useful features for code research. Separate databases for code indexes (AL-ST-IDX, WY-ST-IDX) may help narrow a search that turns up too many documents in a full-text database. A more important feature is the display of an individual code section with links for its chapter and title, allowing one to scan the list of neighboring sections or chapters to get a better sense of a statute's scope and context. LEXIS-NEXIS does not have quick links from a section to the table of contents, but it has a *browse* feature for viewing adjacent code sections. Both systems also provide ways to find statutes by browsing the entire code's table of contents (TOC AL ST on WESTLAW, ALTOC on LEXIS-NEXIS).

Both systems also include notices with statutes that have been recently amended by slip laws too new to have been incorporated into the code database. WESTLAW's notice reads "This document has been amended. Use > Update," and LEXIS-NEXIS's note reads "Status: Consult slip laws cited below for recent changes to this document." Both provide convenient ways to link directly to the text of the new laws.

Finally, both WESTLAW and LEXIS-NEXIS maintain databases with superseded versions of the state codes for times when it is necessary to reconstruct the statute in force at a particular time. WESTLAW has individual year databases going back as far as 1986, depending on state (AL-STANN95), while the LEXIS-NEXIS files (AL1995) generally extend back to 1991.

Several other commercial sources offer online access to statutes. On the Internet, LOIS (Law Office Information Systems) <http://www.pita.com/> includes statutes for 18 of the states for which it provides court opinions, and V. <http://www.versuslaw.com/> is beginning to add statutes. Other commercial Web sites, such as LawNetCom, Inc. <http://www.mscode.com/>, focus on individual states.

Every state also has at least one CD-ROM product containing its statutes. Some of these are combined with court decisions, while others are simply the annotated versions of the statutes. As might be expected, the major multistate publishers of CD-ROMs are the same companies that produce the printed codes: LEXIS Law Publishing and West Group. Other publishers focus on individual states, with a variety of products. Although many of these are less expensive than those from the major publishers, most are nonetheless rather substantial investments. Only a few CD-ROMs providing unannotated codes, including several issued by state governments, are relative bargains. These CD-ROM products are listed by state in Chapter 27 of Kendall F. Svengalis's *Legal Information Buyer's Guide & Reference Manual* (Rhode Island LawPress, annual) and by title in *Directory of Law-Related CD-ROMs* (Infosources Publishing, annual). The latter work includes state code CDs in its index under the heading "Statutes—[state]."

Session Laws

State laws, like federal laws, are first published as individual slip laws and in chronological volumes of session laws. These volumes are not used as often as the codes in statutory research, but they can help determine the law in force at a particular date or analyze changes in the law. In some states, the session laws are also the authoritative version of the laws (like the *U.S. Statutes at Large*) and would be the controlling version if discrepancies were to be found in language between session law and code.

References to codes and session laws can sometimes be confused, particularly when they have such similar names. Many session laws are called *Acts*, but *General Laws of Massachusetts* and *Minnesota Statutes* are codes, while *General Laws of Mississippi* and *California Statutes* are session laws. Consulting the *Bluebook* for the citation forms for each state may help. Citations with section symbols (§) and decimals are most likely to codes, while citations beginning with a year rather than a volume number are usually to session laws.

Unlike the federal *Statutes at Large*, many state session law publications make it easy to find changes in statutory language by indicating additions and deletions in special typefaces. Entire sections are usually printed, with new material indicated in italics and deletions shown by the striking out of text. It is thus relatively easy to understand the nature of the amendments.

Slip laws are not widely distributed in most states, but the collected session laws are available in larger libraries either as bound annual volumes or in microform. A comprehensive microfiche set dating back to 1776, *Session Laws of American States and Territories*, is available from William S. Hein & Co. Section 2 of *Pimsleur's Checklists of Basic American Legal Publications* provides a comprehensive listing of published session laws for each state as far back as the 1660s. The earliest listings are the most interesting. The first Georgia law printed in 1735 was an act to prevent the importation and use of rum and brandies. The section for New Jersey notes that its legislature passed no laws at five consecutive sessions, between 1705 and 1708.

Before the official annual volumes are published, commercial publications in most states provide the text of new laws in pamphlet form. These are published by LEXIS Law Publishing (*[State] Advance Legislative Service*) and West Group (*[State] Session Law Service* or *[State] Legislative Service*) for most of the states for which they publish codes. They serve the same purpose as the *USCS Advance* pamphlets, providing access to recently enacted legislation.

Although older session laws are only available in print or microform, recent session laws are widely available electronically. Almost every state now provides access to recent legislation on its homepage. The simplest way to find this material is through one of the multistate sites listing state primary sources, as discussed earlier in this chapter. "State Laws on the Internet" <http://www.legalonline.com/statute2.htm> provides a regularly updated survey of session laws and bills on the legislatures' Web sites and other sources.

The commercial databases also provide comprehensive access to recent state session laws, albeit in different ways. On WESTLAW, databases such as AL-LEGIS or AK-LEGIS cover only the current legislative session, with older sessions in separate databases (AL-LEGIS-OLD or AK-LEGIS-OLD). LEXIS-NEXIS combines current and former sessions in files such as ALALS or AKALS (in several libraries, including CODES, LEGIS, and STATES). In both services, coverage of every state extends back at least to 1991; laws from as early as 1987 are available for some states.

Multistate Sources

A state code is the most important source for the statutes of any individual state. Several resources, however, contain statutes from several states. Like the multistate surveys discussed earlier in this chapter, these can provide easy access to state laws by topic. They also are useful in comparing state laws and in finding analogous provisions. A court that has not had to interpret a section of its state code will often look to other states to see how their courts have handled similar issues.

Although most laws vary from state to state, some are specifically designed to read the same way in each jurisdiction. Basing state statutes on the same model can simplify interstate commerce and ease conflicts in determining which state's laws apply in case of disputes. Formed in 1892, the National Conference of Commissioners on Uniform State Laws has drafted more than 200 *uniform laws* on a wide variety of subjects, many of which have been adopted in one or more states.

The National Conference has prepared a number of influential laws, including the Uniform Probate Code, the Uniform Child Custody Jurisdiction Act, and the Uniform Commercial Code. None of them has any force of law unless enacted by a state legislature. Each legislature is free to modify the text as it sees fit, although major changes would undermine the purpose of having a uniform law in the first place. Besides uniform laws, the Conference prepares *model acts* in areas in which uniformity between states is not a major concern, such as eminent domain and administrative procedure.

An enacted uniform law or model act appears in the state code. The state code is the official source, and it includes whatever changes or amendments were made by the state legislature. A national publication, *Uniform Laws Annotated* (West Publishing, 38 vols., 1968-date) is useful because it contains the text as approved by the National Conference, drafters' comments, and annotations to court decisions from jurisdictions that have adopted each act. Cases from another state are not binding precedent, but they can be persuasive in interpreting the same language. Some acts, such as the Uniform Commercial Code and the Uniform Controlled Substances Act, have several volumes of notes and annotations.

Each act in *Uniform Laws Annotated* is preceded by a list of states that have adopted it, with references to the session laws, effective dates, and code citations. State variations for each section are usually indicated, although a general note may specify that a state's version "departs from the official text in such manner that the various instances of substitution, omission, and additional matter cannot be clearly indicated by statutory notes." The laws are arranged by subject, with several volumes each of business and financial laws; estate, probate, and related laws; and matrimonial, family, and health laws. A handy pamphlet accompanying the set, *Directory of Uniform Acts and Codes; Tables—Index*, contains a directory listing the acts alphabetically, a table of jurisdictions listing the acts adopted in each state, and a brief general index to the acts. Each act has its own more extensive index in the back of its volume.

Another convenient source for uniform acts is Volume 2 of the *Martindale-Hubbell Law Digest* (annual), which includes the text of several dozen acts. It does not, however, include either the drafters' comments or annotations.

The National Conference has drafts of several uniform laws and model acts still under consideration on the Internet <http://www.law.upenn.edu/library/ulc/ulc.htm>, available in PDF, WordPerfect, or plain text versions. It does not, unfortunately, include the texts of older uniform acts that have been adopted by states. Several major acts, however, are available from Cornell's Legal Information Institute <http://www.law.cornell.edu/statutes.html>. This site includes the text of the Uniform Commercial Code, as well as lists for about 40 uniform acts of links to state Web sites where the adopted versions are found.

Uniform Laws Annotated is available online in WESTLAW as the ULA database, and the 2NDARY library in LEXIS-NEXIS includes separate files containing the UCC, with official comments, and more than two dozen other uniform and model acts as printed in the *Martindale-Hubbell Law Digest.*

Other organizations producing model state legislation include the American Law Institute (Model Penal Code), the American Bar Association (Model Business Corporation Act), and the Council of State Governments, which publishes an annual volume of *Suggested State Legislation.* Most of the acts in this last series are based on statutes passed by one state, and are published so that the states can benefit from each others' experiences. Each act is preceded by a brief explanatory introduction and a citation to the enacted legislation on which it is based. A cumulative index in each volume covers acts published in the series during the preceding 20 years.

Even when an issue is not the subject of a uniform or model act, state legislatures look to each other for inspiration on how to address matters of common concern. Five years after Georgia passed its 1976 legislation against unlawful pecan gathering, Mississippi enacted legislation with virtually identical language (Miss. Code §§ 69-33-1 to 69-33-9). (Some subjects, of course, are peculiarly local. The Maine sardine tax law discussed earlier in this chapter has not been replicated by any other state legislatures.)

Several sources make multistate research easier by reprinting state statutes on particular subjects. Chief among these are some of the major loose-leaf services. *Blue Sky Law Reports* (CCH) includes state security statutes, accompanied by relevant regulations and an overview for each state. The CD-ROM version of *Environment Reporter* (BNA) includes state laws on mining, solid waste, and air and water pollution. (These were formerly in the print version as well, but updating was discontinued in 1994.) *Labor Relations Reporter* (BNA) includes state laws on such issues as labor–management relations, employment practices, wage and hour regulation, and child labor. *Corporation, A Service* (Aspen Law & Business) contains corporation laws from every state, as well as case annotations and a practice guide.

Other compilations of state laws focus on narrower issues. *State Compensation Laws* (CCH, 1998) is a large paperback volume covering minimum wage, equal pay, child labor, and overtime laws. *Refusal of Treatment Legislation: A State by State Compilation of Enacted and Model Statutes* (Society for the Right to Die [now Choice in Dying], 1992-date, updated annually) includes introductory "highlights" for each state, followed by the unannotated text of the statutes. *Abortion in the United States: A Compilation of State Legislation* (William S. Hein & Co., 1991, 2 vols.), edited by Howard A. Hood, contains statutes arranged by state in Volume 1, and by topic in Volume 2. A 1992 supplement to this publication provided a few more recent enactments, but no further updates have been published. Several of the Internet surveys discussed earlier in this chapter also provide the full text of relevant statutes.

The broadest multistate coverage can be found through WESTLAW and LEXIS-NEXIS. Both have databases with all 50 states' codes and session laws. On WESTLAW, ST-ANN-ALL has annotated codes, STAT-ALL unannotated codes, and LEGIS-ALL session laws from the current legislative sessions. On LEXIS-NEXIS, the ALLCDE file has a combination of annotated and unannotated codes, while ALLALS provides access to several years' worth of session laws from each state. These databases can be useful for finding similar statutes in numerous states, but be aware that different legislatures can use different words to express the same concepts. One simple example is that 47 states have laws outlawing drug paraphernalia, but Georgia law uses the term "drug related objects" instead of "paraphernalia" (Ga. Code. Ann. §§ 16-13-32 to 16-13-32.2). A search for "drug paraphernalia" in the statutory text would miss these Georgia provisions, although the phrase does show up in the code's research references and annotations.

LEGISLATIVE INFORMATION

At the state level, current bills and reports on their status are readily available through commercial databases and official Web sites. Publications that would be useful in interpreting enacted legislation, however, can be difficult to obtain.

Guides and Directories

Legislative processes vary from state to state, so an important first step in studying legislative action is to learn the procedures for a particular jurisdiction. Most states publish introductory guides to the legislative process, including charts showing how bills become laws. Many of these guides are also available on state legislature Web sites. Florida's site <http://www.leg.state.fl.us/> includes an extensive "Citizen's Guide" providing a thorough introduction to the work of its legislature.

The leading national directory of available information sources is Lynn Hellebust's *State Legislative Sourcebook: A Resource Guide to Legislative Information in the Fifty States* (Government Research Service, annual). A separate chapter for each state provides information on legislative organizations and processes, with references to available published and online sources, including state Internet sites. A "best initial contact" is provided for each state, as well as information on bill status telephone numbers, bill tracking services, and legislative documents, such as session laws and summaries of legislation. Other topics covered include sources of information on individual legislators, study committees between legislative sessions, and lobbying. The 6-to-10 pages on each state make a convenient, thorough overview of available sources. An extensive appendix, "Resource Guide to Influencing State Legislatures," provides references to general resources on state legislation.

Several sources provide background information on legislative processes. *Encyclopedia of the American Legislative System* (Scribner, 3 vols., 1994), edited by Joel H. Silbey, provides a broad, scholarly analysis of legislative structures and procedures, with further research leads accompanying each article. William J. Keefe and Morris S. Ogul's *The American Legislative Process: Congress and the States* (Prentice Hall, 9th ed., 1997) is a more nuts-and-bolts overview of such topics as the ways in which committees operate, as well as political issues such as apportionment, elections, the roles of parties and interest groups in the legislative process, and the legislature's interaction with the executive and judicial branches. Both works provide extensive coverage of Congress as well as state legislatures.

Summary background information on state legislative procedures is available in Chapter 3 of *The Book of the States* (Council of State Governments, biennial), with several tables summarizing such topics as provisions governing legislative sessions, bill referral procedures, veto procedures, and effective date of enacted legislation. Other tables provide detailed information on such issues as leadership selection, compensation, and staffing.

Multistate coverage of legislatures is provided by general state directories, such as *State Yellow Book* and *State Staff Directory*, discussed earlier in this chapter. In the three-part *CSG State Directory, Directory I: Elective Officials* includes individual legislators and *Directory II: Legislative Leadership, Committees and Staff* focuses on organizational structure. Another focused source is *Handbook of State Legislative Leaders* (State Legislative Leaders Foundation, annual), with about five pages per state containing information on terms of office and length of legislative sessions, followed by brief biographies and contact information for senate presidents, house speakers, and party leaders. WESTLAW and LEXIS-NEXIS both provide access to a 50-state legislative directory from StateNet, a service of Information for Public Affairs, Inc. The LEGIS-DIR database on WESTLAW and the STLEG file on LEXIS-NEXIS (in the CODES, LEGIS, or STATES library) have contact information, committee membership, and legislator biographies for some states.

Older writing in this area can be found through Robert U. Goehlert and Frederick W. Musto's *State Legislatures: A Bibliography* (ABC-Clio, 1985). This is an unannotated listing of more than 2,500 books, articles, and dissertations since 1945. Part 1 lists general works under 25 subject areas, such as constitutional aspects and legislative structures; Part 2 lists materials for specific states. State documents, unfortunately, are generally not included.

Current Information

Information on pending bills in state legislatures is available through a number of electronic sources. Because access to up-to-date information in this area is essential, print resources are generally unsatisfactory and Internet dissemination has dramatically changed research processes.

Almost every state now has a Web site providing the text of bills and bill tracking information, similar to THOMAS on the federal level, and even those without strong Internet sites provide bill status information by telephone. *State Legislative Information* is an excellent source for determining what resources are available in each state, in print, by telephone, and on the Internet. The telephone numbers for obtaining bill status information in each state, available from the *State Legislative Directory*, can also be found on the Internet <http://www.piperinfo.com/state/hotline.html>.

Although many researchers have switched to electronic resources, most states continue to provide some sort of published notification of legislative developments. Some states mail out copies of all new bills to subscribers, while others only supply copies on request. A number of states publish bill digests or status summaries on a daily or weekly basis during the legislative session. Larger libraries usually receive the available documentation from their home state, unless it simply duplicates information available on demand through the Internet.

The state Internet sites can easily be found from general state homepages or through the general starting points discussed earlier in this chapter. MultiState

Associates, Inc. provides a "State Legislative Presence on the Internet" page <http://www.multistate.com/weblist.htm>, with links to each state legislature and an indication whether the state provides free access to the full text of bills and to bill tracking information. (Comparisons such as this may serve to shame those states for which the answer is "No" in either column to improve access to this important public information.) Brief reviews provide insider information on each site, from "Lots of info, easy to search—One of the very best state sites" to "Very disappointing—It can barely be called a home page."

The best state legislative Web sites provide full-text access to bills, searchable by keyword, sponsor, or bill number. Only a few do not yet provide the text of bills online, a situation that will presumably be remedied in the near future. In some states, one can even register to receive automatic e-mail notification when a particular bill is acted upon. Exhibit 11-4 shows the introductory bill-tracking screen for one of the more thorough and informative legislative homepages, the Minnesota State Legislature's Web site <http://www.leg.state.mn.us/leg/legis.htm>. Note that it includes the full text of bills, status information, bill summaries, committee information, and background documents on the legislative process and research.

The commercial databases also provide information on pending legislation in a standard format for every state. This is one area where there is little difference between LEXIS-NEXIS and WESTLAW because both get their data from StateNet. Each has databases, updated daily, providing the text of pending bills, monitoring the status of legislation, and combining the text and bill-tracking functions. Both services also provide multistate databases for monitoring legislation around the country on a particular topic. Table 11-3 shows the formats used for identifying these databases (LEXIS-NEXIS files are in the CODES, LEGIS, STATES, and individual state libraries).

These databases cover the current session only. Older bill tracking and texts are available, but here the systems' approaches differ somewhat. On WESTLAW, the BILLTRK-OLD, BILLTXT-OLD, and BILLS-OLD combine all previous years available and include material from Congress as well. LEXIS-NEXIS covers state legislation only, in separate files for each year back to TRCK90 and TEXT91.

The amount of information available from the Web sites and the commercial sources can vary. The 1995 Texas bill S.B. 1, which revised much of the state's Education Code, has a concise StateNet report, with just 12 bill-tracking entries and 6 versions of its text. The complete bill summary on the Texas Legislature Online site <http://www.capitol.state.tx.us/tlo/billnbr.htm>, on the other hand, includes references to 7 public hearings and more than 180 amendments passed on the floor of one chamber or the other (of nearly 400 introduced). Pity the poor researcher (or legislative staffer) who has to keep track of all these amendments, but for some purposes it may be important to know about them.

Legislative History

With the increase in electronic dissemination, information on current state legislation has blossomed. The search for documents useful in interpreting existing statutes, on the other hand, remains in a darker age. In most states, few publications like congressional committee reports or the *Congressional Record* exist to provide a record of legislative intent. Legislative journals generally just record actions and do not include transcripts of debates. Few states publish committee reports or hearings.

TABLE 11-3

LEXIS-NEXIS AND WESTLAW DATABASES FOR STATE LEGISLATIVE INFORMATION

	LEXIS-NEXIS	WESTLAW
Individual State		
Bill text	ALTEXT, WYTEXT	AL-BILLTXT, WY-BILLTXT
Bill tracking	ALTRCK, WYTRCK	AL-BILLTRK, WY-BILLTRK
Both	ALBILL, WYBILL	AL-BILLS, WY-BILLS
Multistate		
Bill text	STTEXT	ST-BILLTXT
Bill tracking	STTRCK	ST-BILLTRK
Both	STBILLS	ST-BILLS

Legislation and Bill Tracking

- **House Bills** -- Full text of House bills and searching of House bill status.
- **Senate Bills** -- Full text of Senate bills and searching of Senate bill status.
- **Unofficial Engrossments and Conference Committee Reports** -- House and Senate.
- **Special session bill text** -- House and Senate.
- **How to follow a bill**
- **Previous years' bills and bill tracking information**

More about bills

*Bill introductions -- House ▪ Senate
*Bill summaries -- House ▪ Senate

Laws and vetoes

*Bills sent to governor for signature; veto messages
*Session laws
*Act summaries
*Vetoes since 1939

More about actions on bills

*Journals -- House ▪ Senate
*Committees-- House ▪ Senate

Other information

*How a bill becomes law
*How to do legislative history
*How to research a legislative issue
*Getting bills from other states

Bills and status information are provided by the Office of Revisor of Statutes and are regularly updated.

 **Minnesota Legislative Information Service**

Legislature Home Page ▪ House ▪ Senate ▪ Legislation & Bill Tracking
Laws & Statutes ▪ Schedules ▪ General Information ▪ Links to the World

URL: http://www.leg.state.mn.us/leg/legis.htm

This page is maintained by the Minnesota Legislative Reference Library for the Minnesota Legislature (House, Senate, and joint legislative offices).

Last review or update: 3/20/98 (mm)

If you find errors in this page, please let us know at www@library.leg.state.mn.us

MINNESOTA STATE LEGISLATURE WEB SITE

EXHIBIT 11-4

One can perform state legislative history research, although the available documentation varies dramatically from state to state. The first step in looking for legislative information on a code section is to determine when the relevant language was enacted. Historical notes following a section may provide this information. Because many state codes simply provide a list of session law citations, it may be necessary to examine the session laws to find when the pertinent material was added or amended.

In many states, the various texts of a bill are a major source of legislative history information because they show the actual changes that occurred during consideration. From these changes it may be possible to draw inferences about the intent of the legislature. If a specific activity is included in a bill's coverage in an early version, but then removed, it would be plausible to argue that the legislature decided the bill would not cover that activity. Tracing amendments and changes in a bill's language, however, is not always enlightening or easy. Following the tortuous path of a bill that was amended dozens or hundreds of times may not be worth the necessary investment of time.

Other, more accessible sources are sometimes available. If a state adopts a uniform or model act, the comments of the committee that drafted the act were presumably considered by the legislature and would be persuasive in interpreting the text. Many states have law revision commissions, legislative research commissions, or interim study committees that analyze the need for legislation and submit recommendations to the legislature. Their reports can be important documents in evaluating a statute's scope and purpose. The first place to check for information from a drafting committee or commission is the annotated code, which should (but does not always) include excerpts from comments and reports after sections they discuss. Recent reports (since the mid-1990s) may be available on legislative Web sites.

Some states have other documents that can provide useful information. New York bills sent to the governor, for example, are accompanied by files known as "bill jackets" that contain such material as memoranda from sponsors and comments from study groups, agencies, and interested organizations. These bill jackets are available on microfilm back to 1921.

Some files of this sort are not so widely available. In Virginia, "legislative draft files" prepared by staff members who draft bills are available in the Division of Legislative Services library but have not been published or microfilmed. Files for bills introduced since 1989 are open to inspection, but earlier files can be seen only with the permission of the bill's sponsor. If the sponsor has died, the files are permanently closed. There are no files before 1960, and those for 1980-81 were accidentally discarded.

In some states, legislative history research may require listening to tape recordings. Minnesota committee hearings and floor sessions were taped starting in 1973, but there are no transcripts of these tapes. In Nebraska, on the other hand, hearings and debates since 1961 have been transcribed and are available on microfilm in several libraries around the state.

With such scant official documentation, it may be necessary to examine newspapers published during the legislative session to find comments from a bill's sponsor or other information about its consideration. This is easier done if the newspaper is available online in full text, but it is possible that a few hours of staring at microfilm could yield some useful information.

Publications such as *State Legislative Sourcebook* and state legal research guides provide information on legislative history resources available for particular states. Internet sites from several state legislatures or libraries include guides to legislative history research. A leading example is the tutorial "Compiling the Legislative History of a New York State Law," from the New York State Library <http://www.nysl.nysed.gov/leghist/>. José R. Torres and Steve Windsor's "State Legislative Histories: A Select, Annotated Bibliography," 85 Law Libr. J. 545 (1993), lists, state by state, books and articles that describe and discuss the available legislative sources. Some items listed focus specifically on legislative research, while others are general guides to state legal materials. A few are unpublished handouts by law libraries, updated forms of which may now be available on their Web sites.

Legislative history is just one of several factors to consider in attempting to interpret an unclear statute. Section 15 of the National Conference of Commissioners on Uniform State Laws' Model Statutory Construction Act, enacted by several states, provides a good overview of this and other possible considerations.

If a statute is ambiguous, the court, in determining the intention of the legislature, may consider among other matters:

(1) the object sought to be attained;

(2) the circumstances under which the statute was enacted;

(3) the legislative history;

(4) the common law or former statutory provisions, including laws upon the same or similar subjects;

(5) the consequences of a particular construction;

(6) the administrative construction of the statute; and

(7) the preamble.

This model act has been superseded by a new, less succinct Uniform Statute and Rule Construction Act, which was approved by the National Conference of Commissioners on Uniform State Laws in 1995 but has not yet been adopted in any jurisdiction.

ADMINISTRATIVE LAW

Each state, of course, has an extensive executive branch much like that in the federal government. Administrative departments and agencies promulgate regulations, issue opinions, and provide guidelines. Unfortunately, the publication of these administrative materials is not as thorough or regular as it is on the federal level. It became clear in the 1930s that the federal government needed to provide access to new regulations (*Federal Register*) and that it needed to publish a compilation of the regulations in force (*Code of Federal Regulations*). More than 60 years later, some state governments have yet to figure out that they should do the same.

Almost every state now has an administrative code, although few are as organized and accessible as the *CFR*. Some are simply compilations of material supplied by individual agencies. Some contain regulations of only a limited number of state agencies. A few do not even have general subject indexes. Even the best are generally published in loose-leaf format and require regular updating.

Just as the *Bluebook* mandates abbreviations for state statutes that can be different from those used in state documents and court opinions, citation forms for administrative codes can vary from source to source. The *Bluebook* says to cite the *Code of Maryland Regulations* as "Md. Regs. Code," but it is more commonly cited as "COMAR." Similarly, New York's administrative code is cited in law reviews as "N.Y. Comp. Codes R. & Regs.," and everywhere else as "NYCRR." These different forms can be confusing, but they are just alternate ways to refer to the same publications.

In addition to codes, almost every state publishes a periodical gazette akin to the *Federal Register* to provide notice of new or proposed regulations. Indeed, some do little more than publish notices, with information about contacting individual agencies for the full text of new regulations. Some include other materials, such as executive orders, synopses of administrative decisions, attorney general opinions, and court rules. Most of these registers are published on a weekly, bi-weekly, or monthly basis.

Most state administrative codes and registers are available in few libraries outside the state. The American Bar Association standards for law school accreditation, which require that the library's holdings include an annotated statutory code from every state, specify only that a core collection include the administrative code of the school's home state.

Retrieving state administrative regulations may require making several telephone calls, but a variety of resources can describe what materials are available for each state. These provide a quick introduction and can save considerable time and frustration in tracking down regulations.

The National Association of Secretaries of State publishes an annual *Administrative Codes and Registers: State and Federal Survey* with summary information about each publication, including the address and price for subscriptions. It uses a standard one-page, fill-in-the-blank and check-the-box format for each publication. For example, the survey indicates that the *Alabama Administrative Monthly* provides only notices, not full text, of newly proposed and adopted rules, and that it has no index.

BNA's Directory of State Administrative Codes and Registers: A State-by-State Listing (BNA Books, 2d ed., 1995), compiled by Kamla J. King and Judith Springberg, provides further information on administrative publications, including notes on available finding aids and search tips to find information. The directory notes electronic forms of access and provides contact information for those states without codes or registers. This overview for each state is followed by a listing of its code's contents, indicating the volume, title, and subtitle for the regulations of each agency. Information is also provided on the contents and indexing of the state registers. This is a useful directory, although its latest edition is getting outdated.

Even more detail on the contents of administrative codes is provided by the *William-Scott Guide to the Administrative Regulations of the States & Territories* (William-Scott, 2 vols., annual). This guide contains less background and fewer tips than the BNA directory, but it provides more comprehensive tables of contents for most states and is more frequently updated.

A growing number of administrative codes and registers are available on the Internet, although fewer states have regulations online than statutes. The Internet sites vary widely, of course. Most of the codes are searchable, but some can only be browsed by title. The Georgia site allows searching of individual titles, but not of the entire code. A few of the registers are searchable as well, but many are simply posted by date to provide current notice. An easy way to keep up on available Internet sites is through the National Association of Secretaries of State's "Administrative Codes and Registers" site <http://www.nass.org/acr/acrdir.htm>, which provide links to secretary of state homepages as well as full-text codes and registers.

Of the commercial databases, LEXIS-NEXIS provides the most extensive access to state regulations, with administrative codes from 34 states and registers from 18 states in its CODES and STATES libraries. For administrative codes, the file name is the two-letter postal code followed by ADMN (e.g. TXADMN), and for registers, the state abbreviation is followed by RGST (TXRGST). WESTLAW has codes from 26 states (TX-ADC) and registers from just 3 states (TX-ADR). LEXIS-NEXIS has a file combining all codes and registers (ALLADM), and WESTLAW has a combined database of all available state administrative codes (ADC-ALL).

Another commercial service, LOIS (Law Office Information Systems) <http://www.pita.com>, has regulations for 13 states, regularly updated with material from new issues of the register. LOIS provides exclusive access to an administrative code for its home state of Arkansas, with no counterpart in print.

Almost every state now has a CD-ROM containing its administrative code, usually in conjunction with other materials, such as statutes and court opinions. Two excellent guides to available sources are the "State Legal Publications and Information Sources" chapter of Kendall F. Svengalis's *Legal Information Buyer's Guide and Reference Manual* (Rhode Island LawPress, annual) and *Directory of Law-Related CD-ROMs* (Infosources Publishing, annual), indexed under "Regulations—[state]."

Table 11-4 indicates the codes and registers for each state, available in print, through LEXIS-NEXIS and WESTLAW, and on the Internet. Most of the electronic databases are updated at the same pace as the print versions. Some of the Internet sites provide only partial coverage to date, but most of these are gradually expanding. Publishers are indicated only for commercial publications, and CD-ROMs are included only for Arkansas and New Mexico, which have no printed administrative codes. Some of the registers have changed names or frequency of publication, but the earliest date and current frequency are indicated.

Even if state regulations as a whole are not available electronically, Web sites for numerous state government agencies provide access to their regulations.

Idaho, for example, has a convenient page <http://www.idwr.state.id.us/apa/agyindex.htm> with links to rules by agency, and the Wyoming secretary of state provides an indexed and searchable database <http://soswy.state.wy.us/rules/rules.htm>.

In addition, regulations from all 50 states in a few specialized areas are available through the commercial databases. Comprehensive coverage is available for environmental, health, and safety regulations (ENFLEX-AL for Alabama and ENFLEX-STATE for all states on WESTLAW; ENVIRN library, ALEVRG file for Alabama and STEVRG for all states on LEXIS-NEXIS), insurance regulations (ALIN-ADC and MIN-ADC on WESTLAW; INSURE library, ALREGS and STREGS files on LEXIS-NEXIS), and tax regulations (CCHTAX library, ALREG and CCHSTR files on LEXIS-NEXIS).

Finally, both LEXIS-NEXIS and WESTLAW provide access to StateNet's regulation tracking database. StateNet provides brief summaries of pending regulatory actions, with names and contact information for agency personnel, administrative code citations, proposal dates, comment deadlines, and times and places of public hearings. Entries include subject indexing to facilitate keyword searching. One can search by individual state (STATES / WYRGTR on LEXIS-NEXIS, or WY-REGTRK on WESTLAW) or all 50 states (STRGTR or ST-REGTRK).

Other Agency Materials

Codified and published regulations are not the only documentation from state administrative agencies. Some materials remain unpublished or available only in hard-to-find official compilations. The Virginia Department of Social Services notes in the introduction to its section of the *Virginia Administrative Code* that some of its regulations are available at its office and provides an address. The department also notes, "In addition to the regulations listed below, the department maintains loose-leaf financial assistance, social services, and administrative manuals of standards, policies and procedures for local departments of social services and public welfare, and issues frequent policy statements" (22 Va. Admin. Code 40). Much of this additional material may be available only upon request, by telephone or in person. Some agency manuals may require the filing of a state Freedom of Information Act request.

An increasing amount of state agency regulations, policies, and other information is available on the Internet. State tax administrators have found, for in-

TABLE 11-4

STATE ADMINISTRATIVE CODES AND REGISTERS

Alabama
Alabama Administrative Code (35 loose-leaf vols., updated quarterly)
Alabama Administrative Monthly (1982, monthly)

Alaska
Alaska Administrative Code (LEXIS, 8 loose-leaf vols., updated quarterly)[L, W]
    <http://www.legis.state.ak.us/cgi-bin/folioisa.dll/aac?>
Alaska Administrative Journal (1984, weekly)
    <http://www.legis.state.ak.us/cgi-bin/folioisa.dll/adjr?>

Arizona
Arizona Administrative Code (11 loose-leaf vols., updated quarterly)[L, W]
    <http://www.sosaz.com/Rules_and_regulations.htm> [partial]
Arizona Administrative Register (1976, weekly)

Arkansas
LOIS Professional Library, Arkansas Series (LOIS, CD-ROM, quarterly)
Arkansas Register (1977, monthly)

California
Barclays Official California Code of Regulations (Barclays, 38 loose-leaf vols., updated weekly)[L, W]
California Regulatory Notice Register (1974, weekly)
California Regulatory Law Bulletin (Barclays, 1993, weekly)[L]

Colorado
Code of Colorado Regulations (26 loose-leaf vols., updated monthly)
Colorado Register (1978, monthly)

Connecticut
Regulations of Connecticut State Agencies (14 loose-leaf vols., updated semiannually)[L, W]
Connecticut Law Journal (1935, weekly)[L]

Delaware
Code of Delaware Regulations (Weil, 14 loose-leaf vols., updated monthly)
Delaware Register of Regulations (1992, monthly)
    <http://www.state.de.us/research/dor/register.htm>
Delaware Government Register (Weil, 1996, monthly)

District of Columbia
District of Columbia Municipal Regulations (31 vols., irregular)
District of Columbia Register (1954, weekly)

Florida
Florida Administrative Code Annotated (Harrison, 26 loose-leaf vols., updated monthly)[L, W]
Florida Administrative Weekly (1975, weekly)[L]
    <http://election.dos.state.fl.us/faw/>

Georgia
Official Compilation: Rules and Regulations of the State of Georgia (22 loose-leaf vols., updated monthly)[L, W]
    <http://www.ganet.org/rules/>

Hawaii
Code of Hawaii Rules (Weil, 17 loose-leaf vols., updated monthly)
Weil's Hawaii Government Register (Weil, 1998, monthly)

Idaho
Idaho Administrative Code (8 vols., annual)[L, W]
Idaho Administrative Bulletin (1993, monthly)[L]
    <http://www.idwr.state.id.us/apa/bulletin/mstrtoc.htm>

Illinois
Illinois Administrative Code (18 loose-leaf vols., updated quarterly)[L, W]
    <http://www.sos.state.il.us/depts/index/code/title.html>

TABLE 11-4 (continued)

STATE ADMINISTRATIVE CODES AND REGISTERS

Illinois Register (1977, weekly)[L, W]
　　<http://www.sos.state.il.us/depts/index/register/register.html>

Indiana

Indiana Administrative Code (Conway Greene, 14 vols., quadrennial with annual supplements)[L, W]
　　<http://www.ai.org/legislative/iac/>
　　<http://www.conwaygreene.com/iac.htm>
Indiana Register (1978, monthly)

Iowa

Iowa Administrative Code (27 loose-leaf vols., updated biweekly)[L]
Iowa Administrative Bulletin (1978, biweekly)[L]

Kansas

Kansas Administrative Regulations (5 vols., triennial with annual supplement)[L, W]
Kansas Register (1982, weekly)

Kentucky

Kentucky Administrative Regulations Service (9 vols., annual)
　　<http://www.lrc.state.ky.us/kar/frntpage.htm>
Administrative Register of Kentucky (1974, monthly)

Louisiana

Louisiana Administrative Code (60 vols., irregular)
　　<http://www.state.la.us/osr/lac/lac.htm>
Louisiana Register (1975, monthly)
　　<http://www.state.la.us/osr/reg/register.htm>

Maine

Code of Maine Rules (Weil, 19 loose-leaf vols., updated monthly)
　　<http://www.state.me.us/sos/cec/rcn/apa/depts.htm>
Maine Government Register (Weil, 1991, monthly)[L]

Maryland

Code of Maryland Regulations (32 loose-leaf vols., updated irregularly)
Maryland Register (1974, biweekly)

Massachusetts

Weil's Code of Massachusetts Regulations (Weil, 26 loose-leaf vols., updated monthly)[L, W]
Massachusetts Register (1976, biweekly)[L]

Michigan

Michigan Administrative Code (3 vols., 1979, with annual supplement)
　　<http://www.state.mi.us/execoff/admincode/>
Michigan Register (1984, monthly)

Minnesota

Minnesota Rules (13 vols., biennial, with semiannual pocket parts)[L, W]
　　<http://www.revisor.leg.state.mn.us/arule/>
Minnesota State Register (1976, weekly)
　　<http://www.comm.media.state.mn.us/main3.htm>

Mississippi

Code of Mississippi Rules (Weil, 13 loose-leaf vols., updated monthly)
Mississippi Government Register (Weil, 1997, monthly)

Missouri

State of Missouri Code of State Regulations Annotated (12 loose-leaf vols., updated monthly)
Missouri Register (1976, semimonthly)

Montana

Administrative Rules of Montana (23 loose-leaf vols., updated quarterly)[L]
Montana Administrative Register (1973, semimonthly)

TABLE 11-4 (continued)

STATE ADMINISTRATIVE CODES AND REGISTERS

Nebraska
Nebraska Administrative Rules and Regulations (35 loose-leaf vols., updated monthly)

Nevada
Nevada Administrative Code (12 loose-leaf vols., updated irregularly)[L, W]
<http://www.leg.state.nv.us/law1.htm>
Register of Administrative Regulations (1997, monthly)
<http://www.leg.state.nv.us/law1.htm>

New Hampshire
Code of New Hampshire Rules (Weil, 15 loose-leaf vols., updated monthly)
New Hampshire Code of Administrative Rules Annotated (LEXIS, 4 vols., with quarterly supps.)
New Hampshire Rulemaking Register (1981, weekly)
New Hampshire Government Register (Weil, 1996, monthly)[L]

New Jersey
New Jersey Administrative Code (West, 33 loose-leaf vols., updated semimonthly)[L, W]
New Jersey Register (1969, semimonthly)[W]

New Mexico
Michie's New Mexico Administrative Code on CD-ROM (LEXIS, CD-ROM, quarterly)[L]
<http://www.lexislawpublishing.com/resources/resource_page.html>
New Mexico Register (1990, semimonthly)[L]

New York
Official Compilation of Codes, Rules and Regulations of the State of New York (West, 85 loose-leaf vols., updated semimonthly)[L, W]
New York State Register (weekly)

North Carolina
Barclays Official North Carolina Administrative Code (Barclays, 22 loose-leaf vols., updated monthly)[L, W]
North Carolina Register (1986, semimonthly)

North Dakota
North Dakota Administrative Code (19 loose-leaf vols., updated monthly)[L]

Ohio
Ohio Administrative Code (West, 17 vols., with annual supps.)[L, W]
<http://www.conwaygreene.com/oac.htm>
Ohio Monthly Record (West, 1977, monthly)

Oklahoma
Oklahoma Administrative Code (19 vols., with annual supps.)
Oklahoma Register (1983, semimonthly)

Oregon
Oregon Administrative Rules Compilation (15 vols., annual)[W]
<http://arcweb.sos.state.or.us/rules/OAR_1997_default.html>
Oregon Bulletin (1958, monthly)
<http://arcweb.sos.state.or.us/rules/bulletin_default.html>

Pennsylvania
Pennsylvania Code (58 loose-leaf vols., updated monthly)[L, W]
Pennsylvania Bulletin (1970, weekly)[L]

Rhode Island
Code of Rhode Island Rules (Weil, 23 loose-leaf vols., updated monthly)
Rhode Island Government Register (Weil, 1992, monthly)[L]

TABLE 11-4 (continued)

STATE ADMINISTRATIVE CODES AND REGISTERS

South Carolina
Code of Laws of South Carolina 1976 Annotated: Code of Regulations (West, 8 loose-leaf vols., updated annually)[L, W]
South Carolina State Register (1977, monthly)
   <http://www.lpitr.state.sc.us/regs.htm>

South Dakota
Administrative Rules of South Dakota (12 loose-leaf vols., updated annually)[L, W]
Register (1973, weekly)[L]
   <http://www.state.sd.us/state/legis/lrc/rules/register.htm>

Tennessee
Official Compilation: Rules and Regulations of the State of Tennessee (23 loose-leaf vols., updated monthly)
TAR: Tennessee Administrative Register (1975, monthly)

Texas
Official Texas Administrative Code (West, 20 vols., annual)[L, W]
   <http://lamb.sos.state.tx.us/tac/>
Texas Register (1976, weekly)[L, W]
   <http://lamb.sos.state.tx.us/texreg/>

Utah
Utah Administrative Code (LEXIS, 5 loose-leaf vols., updated quarterly)[L, W]
   <http://www.rules.state.ut.us/publicat/code.htm>
Utah State Bulletin (1973, semimonthly)
   <http://www.rules.state.ut.us/publicat/bulletin.htm>

Vermont
Code of Vermont Rules (Weil, 10 loose-leaf vols, updated monthly)
Vermont Government Register (Weil, 1991, monthly)[L]

Virginia
Virginia Administrative Code (West, 22 loose-leaf vols., updated semiannually)[L, W]
   <http://leg1.state.va.us/000/srr.htm>
Virginia Register of Regulations (1984, biweekly)
   <http://legis.state.va.us/codecomm/register/issfiles.htm>

Washington
Washington Administrative Code (12 vols., biennial with annual supps.)[L, W]
   <http://www.mrsc.org/wac.htm>
Washington State Register (1978, semimonthly)[L]

West Virginia
West Virginia Code of State Rules (11 loose-leaf vols., updated monthly)
West Virginia Register (1983, weekly)

Wisconsin
Wisconsin Administrative Code (23 loose-leaf vols., updated monthly)[L, W]
   <http://www.legis.state.wi.us/rsb/code/index.html>
Wisconsin Administrative Register (1956, monthly)[L]

Wyoming
Weil's Code of Wyoming Rules (Weil, 11 loose-leaf vols., updated monthly)
Weil's Wyoming Government Register (Weil, 1995, monthly)[L]

L=LEXIS-NEXIS; W=WESTLAW

stance, that the Web provides an inexpensive and convenient way to dispense literature; links to tax forms from almost every state are available from the Federation of Tax Administrators <http://www.taxadmin.org/fta/FORMS.html>. Collections of links to state agency Web sites include the Piper Resources, Washburn, and Emory sites discussed earlier in this chapter.

TABLE 11-5

STATE ATTORNEY GENERAL OPINION INTERNET SITES

California	*http://caag.state.ca.us/opinions/* (1997)
Colorado	*http://www.state.co.us/gov_dir/dol/ago/agoindex.htm* (1990)
Connecticut	*http://www.cslnet.ctstateu.edu/attygenl/agopin.htm* (1996)
Delaware	*http://www.state.de.us/attgen/opinion.htm* (1995)
Florida	*http://legal.firn.edu/opinions/* (1977)
Georgia	*http://www.ganet.org/ago/gaaopinions.html* (1994)
Hawaii	*http://www.state.hi.us/ag/optable/table.htm* (1992)
	http://hsba.org/Hawaii/Admin/Ag/agindex.htm (1987-92)
Idaho	*http://www2.state.id.us/ag/opinions/opinions.htm* (1990)
Illinois	*http://www.ag.state.il.us/opinion.htm* (1995)
Indiana	*http://www.ai.org/hoosieradvocate/html/cases/* (1997)
Iowa	*http://www.state.ia.us/government/ag/legal.html* (1996)
Kentucky	*http://www.law.state.ky.us/civil/opinions.html* (1993)
Maryland	*http://www.oag.state.md.us/Opinions/opinion.htm* (1997)
Michigan	*http://www.ag.state.mi.us/* (1997)
Minnesota	*http://www.ag.state.mn.us/library/index.htm* (1993)
Nevada	*http://www.state.nv.us/ag/agopinion/* (1992)
New York	*http://www.oag.state.ny.us/lawyers/opinions/opinion.html* (1995)
North Carolina	*http://www.jus.state.nc.us/Justice/opinion/agoopn.htm* (1993)
Ohio	*http://www.ag.ohio.gov/opinions/agopinio.htm* (1994)
Oregon	*http://www.doj.state.or.us/AGOffice/welcome4.htm* (1997)
Rhode Island	*http://www.riag.state.ri.us/civil/AOI.htm* (1995)
South Carolina	*http://www.scattorneygeneral.org/opinion.html* (1995)
South Dakota	*http://www.state.sd.us/state/executive/attorney/opinions/opinions.htm* (1989)
Texas	*http://www.oag.state.tx.us/WEBSITE/opengovt.htm* (1977)
Utah	*http://www.at.state.ut.us/Ophtm.htm* (1991)
Virginia	*http://www.state.va.us/~oag/opin/main.htm* (1996)
Washington	*http://www.wa.gov/ago/opinions/opinion_index.html* (1996)

Decisions

Many state administrative agencies in areas such as banking, insurance, public utilities, taxation, and workers' compensation issue decisions like their federal counterparts. Some of these are published in official series, and some are included in commercial publications such as *Public Utilities Reports* (Public Utilities Reports, Inc., 1915-date). LEXIS-NEXIS and WESTLAW include state agency decisions in the areas of environmental law, public utilities, securities, taxation, and workers' compensation, with databases for individual states and for all available states. Keep in mind that not all states are represented in these online collections.

Some administrative decisions are also available on the Internet. The Hawaii State Bar Association, for example, provides access to material from Hawaii's Civil Rights Commission, Corporation Counsel, Department of Labor & Industrial Relations, and other agencies <http://www.hsba.org/Hawaii/admin/admi.htm>.

Executive Orders

Many, but not all, governors have the power to issue executive orders. In most instances, these orders are published in the state registers, but in a few states they may only be available as individual documents. The National Association of Secretaries of State (NASS) and Bureau of National Affairs (BNA) guides to the registers discussed earlier indicate whether they include executive orders, and table 2-5 in *The Book of the States* summarizes the authorization (constitutional, statutory, or implied), scope, and procedures for these orders. Several governors include the text of executive orders on their Web sites, which can be accessed through the state government homepage or by links from the National Governors Association <http://www.nga.org/subtocgov.htm>.

Attorney General Opinions

State attorneys general operate in a wide range of areas, such as law enforcement and consumer protection, as outlined in *State Attorneys General: Powers and*

Responsibilities (BNA, 1990), edited by Lynne M. Ross. One important service attorneys general provide is the interpretation of state law through advisory opinions issued to state agencies or legislators. Although these opinions are not legally binding, they are given considerable weight by courts confronted with related issues. A few of the state editions of *Shepard's Citations* cover attorney general opinion citations to code provisions, and most (but not all) annotated codes include references to relevant attorney general opinions. *Maine Revised Statutes Annotated*, for example, indicates that the Maine attorney general issued an important opinion on the effect of can size and weight on the application of the state's sardine tax (1963-64 Me. Atty. Gen. Rep. 152).

Attorney general opinions appear in some state registers, and they are usually published in annual or biennial volumes. These volumes generally are indexed, but it may be necessary to check several as the indexes rarely cumulate. A valuable source for finding older attorney general opinions is section 3 of *Pimsleur's Checklists of Basic American Legal Publications*, which lists published volumes and provides a historical introduction for each state. Information on sources for current opinions is included as an appendix to *BNA's Directory of State Administrative Codes and Registers: A State-by-State Listing* (BNA Books, 2d ed., 1995).

Almost all attorneys general have Web sites, which can be found through links at the National Association of Attorneys General site <http://www.naag.org/aglinks.htm>. Not all include the text of opinions, however, and more than half of those that do simply list them chronologically with brief summaries. An increasing number of sites, however, allow searching either by keyword or through a subject index. Florida and Texas have the most thorough sites; both go back to 1977 and are searchable. Table 11-5 lists the sites with opinions, and the earliest dates covered.

LEXIS-NEXIS and WESTLAW provide more comprehensive access to attorney general opinions, with coverage in both systems beginning in 1977 for most states. There are a few exceptions. LEXIS-NEXIS, for example, doesn't include Maine opinions before 1984, while Mississippi goes back to 1951 and New Mexico all the way to statehood in 1912. Both systems have South Carolina opinions back to 1959. In LEXIS-NEXIS, these are in the file SCAG in either the individual state library or STATES, and in WESTLAW the database is SC-AG. Comprehensive databases for all 50 states are AG on WESTLAW, and ALLAG on LEXIS-NEXIS. On the Internet, the commercial site

LOIS has attorney general opinions for six states. In at least one instance (Oklahoma), LOIS coverage exceeds LEXIS-NEXIS and WESTLAW by several years.

Industry Standards

Many state (and local) agencies incorporate industry standards and codes by reference into their regulations and policies. Rules such as the Uniform Building Code, from the International Conference of Building Officials (ICBO), or the National Fire Prevention Code, from the Building Officials and Code Administrators International (BOCA), may have the force of law even if they are not published by a government agency. These codes are available in some libraries, and the agencies responsible for their enforcement should have copies, but otherwise they can be hard to find. Some are available on the Internet, although most sites for organizations promulgating standards simply provide information on purchasing copies. Neither BOCA, <http://www.bocai.org/>, nor ICBO <http://www.icbo.org/>, provides full text online. One of the most comprehensive collections of Web sites of organizations producing standards and codes, with more than 120 links, is available from Michael D. Leshner, P.E. & Associates, <http://www.erols.com/mlesh/standards.htm>. Tips on other, pre-Internet ways to obtain standards are provided in the column "Questions and Answers," 84 Law Libr. J. 409 (1992).

COUNTIES AND CITIES

Local laws govern a wide range of important issues, from day-to-day matters such as parking regulations and animal control to long-range concerns such as zoning and subdivision. *Charters* are the basic laws creating the structure of local government, in the same way that constitutions establish the powers of national and state governments; and *ordinances* are local enactments governing specific issues. Local laws are based on power delegated by the state legislature to adopt rules governing matters of local concern.

Local charters and ordinances can be among the most difficult primary legal sources to obtain. Many are published and accessible at libraries within the jurisdiction, but few of these collections are available beyond the city or county's borders. The leading publisher is Municipal Code Corporation, in Tallahassee, Florida, which has published codes for more than 2,500 cities and counties in 48 states. These are published in loose-leaf format for supplementation, but the updating schedule varies from locality to locality. Several other publishers have smaller, more regional clienteles.

A growing number of municipal codes are available on the Internet. The Seattle Public Library provides one of the most extensive sets of links to online municipal codes <http://www.spl.org/govpubs/municode.html>. Its collection continues to grow, covering hundreds of cities and counties in more than 40 states. A number of large cities, including Los Angeles, San Diego, and (of course) Seattle are included. Most states are represented only by a few localities, but as more local governments improve their Web sites, access to local codes will undoubtedly increase.

The Municipal Code Corporation provides free Internet access to part of its stable of city ordinances <http://www.municode.com/database.html>. More than 300 cities and counties are represented here as Folio infobases, which can be searched by keyword or viewed through tables of contents. More than half of these localities are in Florida, and some are rather small. The town of Medley, near Miami, has fewer than 700 inhabitants, and the city of Atlantis is not much bigger. But the Municipal Code Corporation site also covers five of the country's 15 largest cities (Houston, Indianapolis, Jacksonville, San Antonio, San Jose), as well as several other major cities such as Atlanta, Denver, and Miami.

Other sites within each state may provide further access. The Minnesota State Law Library, for example, has links to a growing number of local codes in its Minnesota Legal Resources page <http://www.courts.state.mn.us/library/mnlr.html>.

Even if cities have not put their ordinances on the Web, most have sites providing background information on local government in addition to business, culture, and tourism. Several guides to local Web sites are also available. One of the most systematic and convenient is the Harden Political InfoSystem <http://www.com/hpi/us50/index.html>. For counties <http://www.com/hpi/us50/ctyindex.html> and cities and towns <http://www.com/hpi/us50/munindex.html>, HPI provides a standardized form with basic information, such as addresses, census data, and elected officials, and includes links to homepages, if available. Either maps or lists can be used to find localities, and retrieval can be limited to localities with linked homepages.

The commercial databases offer few local law sources. Both LEXIS-NEXIS and WESTLAW include the New York City Charter and Code, but otherwise coverage is limited. LEXIS-NEXIS has Albuquerque

and Pittsburgh, while WESTLAW has Spokane—updated as of 1994. The options on CD-ROM are just as limited, with only a few of the largest cities represented by products such as *New York City Charter, Code and Rules on LawDesk* (West Group, quarterly) and *The Philadelphia Code and the Philadelphia Charter* (LocalLaw Publications, annual).

Whether published or online, sets of ordinances are rarely annotated with court decisions. Access to these decisions used to be available in *Shepard's Citations*, but for most states this feature has not been updated since about 1993—and has been omitted from newly recompiled volumes. (*Shepard's California Citations* is the exception, with ordinances still listed by jurisdiction and indexed by subject.) One way to find cases on the scope and application of local laws is through *Ordinance Law Annotations* (West Group [originally Shepard's], 15 vols., 1969-date, with annual supplements), a case digest focusing on issues of concern to cities and counties, with topics such as "Beauty Operators," "Florists," "Junk," and "Taxicabs." The annotations are by subject, but a table in Volumes 6A and 6B lists cases by state and locality.

Contact information for local governments throughout the country is available in several directories, published by the providers of information for federal and state governments as well. These include *Municipal Staff Directory* (CQ Staff Directories, semiannual), covering 3,000 cities with populations more than 10,000; *Municipal Yellow Book* (Leadership Directories, semiannual), covering both city and county governments; and *Carroll's Municipal Directory* and *Carroll's County Directory* (Carroll Publishing Co., both semiannual), covering nearly 8,000 cities and more than 3,000 counties, respectively. Each of these directories lists more than 30,000 local officials and provides other information, such as demographic data, finances, Web site addresses, and alphabetical name indexes. The *Municipal Staff Directory* includes biographical information on more than 1,000 mayors and city executives. The two Carroll directories are combined in an annual hardcover *Carroll's Municipal/County Directory*, and some of their information is available on the Internet <http://www/infospace.com> or <http://www.findlaw.com/directories/government.html>.

Two other sources for research on local law bear mentioning. *Municipal Year Book* (International City Management Association, annual) discusses trends in local government and features concise city and county directories, with names of major officials and a main telephone number. A "Sources of Information" bibliography provides research leads under several subject headings. *Index to Current Urban Documents* (Greenwood Press, quarterly) covers annual reports, management plans, and other publications of cities, counties, and regional organizations. It is indexed by locality (alphabetically, not by state) and subject, and is accompanied by a microfiche collection of materials listed.

CHAPTER 12
State Courts

Just as the federal courts interpret federal statutes and decide matters of federal common law, the state courts are the arbiters of issues of state law. They interpret the state's constitution and statutes, and have broad powers in developing common law doctrines through judicial decisions.

Also like the federal system, the courts in each state are arranged in a hierarchical format. Appellate courts decide points of law and establish rules binding throughout the state, while trial courts handle the bulk of judicial business and are the courts with which most people come in contact. In most states, these local courts not only handle litigation but maintain documents such as deeds and wills.

Trial courts go by different names in different states. Some states have circuit courts, some district courts or superior courts, and two states have courts of common pleas. Each state has trial courts with general jurisdiction to hear civil and criminal matters, but most also have courts of limited jurisdiction in specialized areas, such as probate, traffic, or small claims.

Every state has a court of last resort, which hears appeals and has the final word on interpretation of state law. This high court is called the Supreme Court in most states, but there are a few local variations. In Maine and Massachusetts, the court of last resort is called the Supreme Judicial Court, and in Maryland and New York it is called the Court of Appeals. (Just to confuse mat-

ters further, the Supreme Court in New York's court system is the general trial court.)

Only 10 states have a simple two-tiered judicial system with just trial courts and a supreme court. The others also have intermediate appellate courts, which generally handle most appeals from trial court judgments. Most states have procedures similar to the federal court system, with an automatic right of appeal to the intermediate level and discretionary review by the court of last resort. A few intermediate courts do not hear direct appeals but instead handle cases assigned to them by the state supreme court.

Intermediate appellate courts have existed for more than a century in a few states, but most have been established since the 1960s to relieve the crowded dockets of state supreme courts. The most recent states to add appellate courts are Nebraska (1991) and Mississippi (1993). North Dakota has a temporary Court of Appeals, established in 1987 and scheduled to dissolve on January 1, 2000. Kansas is on its second Court of Appeals, established in 1977; the first existed only from 1895 to 1901, and was abolished when the Kansas Supreme Court expanded from three to seven justices.

Several states have even more complicated court systems, with separate appellate courts for different subject matters. A few states have more than one intermediate appellate court, and Oklahoma and Texas each have two courts of last resort—a Supreme Court for civil matters and a Court of Criminal Appeals with exclusively criminal jurisdiction. Alabama and Tennessee also have Courts of Criminal Appeals, but in their systems these are intermediate appellate courts.

Structural differences are not the only distinctions among state court systems. Because states vary so dramatically in population and therefore in the amount of work their courts must handle, there are significant practical differences in the body of legal doctrine created by court decisions. State court research is different in large states with hundreds of judges than in states with just a few dozen judges. Because larger states have more courts and more litigation, they produce more cases to guide future disputes. In a smaller state, it is more often necessary to see how neighboring states have handled similar issues. For example, since 1945 the Nevada Supreme Court has cited California cases more than 1,000 times, while the California Supreme Court has such an extensive body of California case law with which to work that it only looks to its neighboring court once or twice a year. The amount of case law in the two states mandates different research approaches when confronted with new legal issues.

Large states produce not only more case law but a more extensive body of legal literature generally. Larger states have more law schools and therefore more law reviews. Their substantial lawyer population can support the publication of state legal encyclopedias, such as *California Jurisprudence 3d*, and extensive sets of specialized treatises and practice guides. Less populous states may have few secondary sources available. For the most part, this chapter examines basic resources available for all states.

REFERENCE SOURCES

Researchers often survey cases or court practices throughout the country. Even when study focuses on a specific jurisdiction, the procedures and decisions in other states can be highly influential. This section discusses resources providing broad access to information about state courts in general and surveys ways to find background information on courts in specific states. It focuses on guides explaining the structure and operation of courts, and directories with access information for trial and appellate courts in each state.

Guides

Because state court systems vary so much, familiarity with the structure and terminology used in a particular jurisdiction is important in understanding the nature and effect of its court decisions. Several reference tools provide charts for each state showing the jurisdiction of the various courts and the relationships among them.

The Court Statistics Project of the National Center for State Courts is the leading source for charts of state court structures. These charts appear in several sources, including *State Court Caseload Statistics* (National Center for State Courts, annual), *State Court Organization 1993* (U.S. Bureau of Justice Statistics, 1995), *Legal Researcher's Desk Reference* (Infosources Publishing, biennial), and *BNA's Directory of State and Federal Courts, Judges, and Clerks* (BNA, biennial). Slightly adapted versions appear in *WANT'S Federal-State Court Directory* and *Directory of State Court Clerks and County Courthouses* (WANT Publishing, annual).

State Court Organization 1993, the third edition of a work revised every six or seven years, provides the broadest range of information on the structure and jurisdiction of state court systems. The charts in Part 7 of this volume present for each state the different courts, the types of cases heard by each, and the routes of appeal. Exhibit 12-1 shows the chart on the structure of the Massachusetts court system. Information on each of several departments of the Trial Court of the Commonwealth includes the number of judges, a summary of case types, and a statement indicating whether or not jury trials are held. Coverage of the Appeals Court and Supreme Judicial Court shows the jurisdiction of each court and the number of judges each has. The arrows show that some appeals of trial court decisions go to the Appeals Court and some directly to the Supreme Judicial Court. (The higher court can take cases directly if they present novel questions of law or involve matters of constitutional interpretation or significant public interest.)

The rest of the *State Court Organization 1993* volume covers a range of other matters, such as selection of judges, court governance, trial and appellate court procedures, juries, and sentencing. Tables, usually based on survey responses, provide convenient comparisons of state procedures and policies. Table 32, for instance, examines rules governing the use of cameras in trial and appellate courts; entries for each court indicate its type (court of last resort, intermediate appellate court, general jurisdiction, limited jurisdiction), the dates experimental and permanent policies were established, and whether consent of the parties is required. Tables include footnotes with more detail on specific state variations. Each of the seven subject sections of the volume begins with an introductory overview and a bibliography of research sources.

MASSACHUSETTS COURT STRUCTURE, 1993

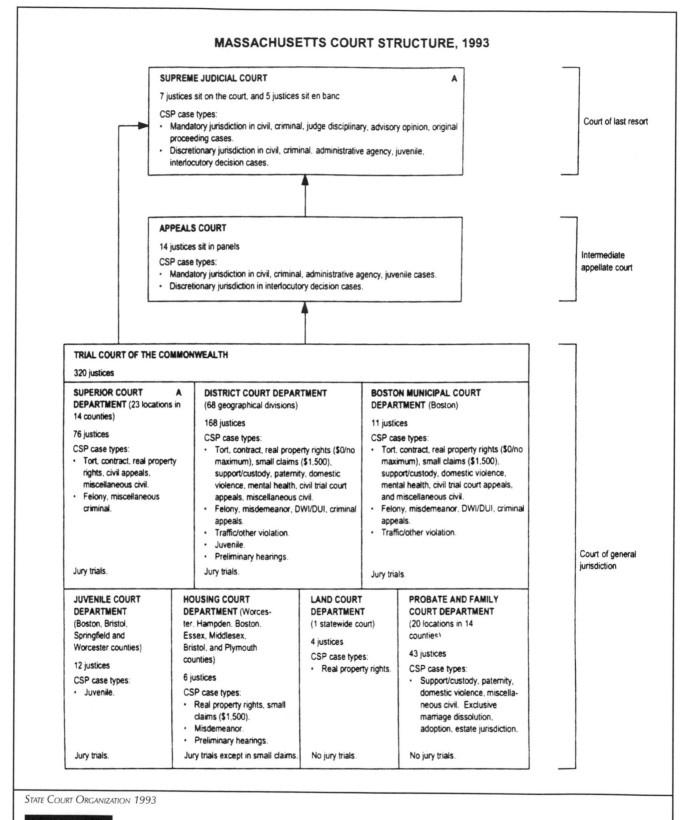

SUPREME JUDICIAL COURT   A

7 justices sit on the court, and 5 justices sit en banc

CSP case types:
- Mandatory jurisdiction in civil, criminal, judge disciplinary, advisory opinion, original proceeding cases.
- Discretionary jurisdiction in civil, criminal, administrative agency, juvenile, interlocutory decision cases.

Court of last resort

APPEALS COURT

14 justices sit in panels

CSP case types:
- Mandatory jurisdiction in civil, criminal, administrative agency, juvenile cases.
- Discretionary jurisdiction in interlocutory decision cases.

Intermediate appellate court

TRIAL COURT OF THE COMMONWEALTH

320 justices

SUPERIOR COURT A **DEPARTMENT** (23 locations in 14 counties)	**DISTRICT COURT DEPARTMENT** (68 geographical divisions)	**BOSTON MUNICIPAL COURT DEPARTMENT** (Boston)
76 justices	168 justices	11 justices
CSP case types: • Tort, contract, real property rights, civil appeals, miscellaneous civil. • Felony, miscellaneous criminal.	CSP case types: • Tort, contract, real property rights ($0/no maximum), small claims ($1,500), support/custody, paternity, domestic violence, mental health, civil trial court appeals, miscellaneous civil. • Felony, misdemeanor, DWI/DUI, criminal appeals. • Traffic/other violation. • Juvenile. • Preliminary hearings.	CSP case types: • Tort, contract, real property rights ($0/no maximum), small claims ($1,500), support/custody, domestic violence, mental health, civil trial court appeals, and miscellaneous civil. • Felony, misdemeanor, DWI/DUI, criminal appeals. • Traffic/other violation.
Jury trials.	Jury trials.	Jury trials.

JUVENILE COURT DEPARTMENT (Boston, Bristol, Springfield and Worcester counties)	**HOUSING COURT DEPARTMENT** (Worcester, Hampden, Boston, Essex, Middlesex, Bristol, and Plymouth counties)	**LAND COURT DEPARTMENT** (1 statewide court)	**PROBATE AND FAMILY COURT DEPARTMENT** (20 locations in 14 counties)
12 justices	6 justices	4 justices	43 justices
CSP case types: • Juvenile.	CSP case types: • Real property rights, small claims ($1,500). • Misdemeanor. • Preliminary hearings.	CSP case types: • Real property rights.	CSP case types: • Support/custody, paternity, domestic violence, miscellaneous civil. Exclusive marriage dissolution, adoption, estate jurisdiction.
Jury trials.	Jury trials except in small claims.	No jury trials.	No jury trials.

Court of general jurisdiction

STATE COURT ORGANIZATION 1993

EXHIBIT 12-1

Chapter 4 of *The Book of the States* (Council of State Governments, biennial), "The Judiciary," includes several tables outlining the structure and organization of state courts. Much of its focus is on the way judges are chosen, compensated, and removed from office, but it also lists the appellate and trial courts in each state and the number of judges sitting on each court. Most of its information is condensed from data in *State Court Organization 1993* and *State Court Caseload Statistics.*

Several sources provide a more general, narrative introduction to state courts. Harry P. Stumpf and John H. Culver's *The Politics of State Courts* (Longman, 1992) is an introductory text examining the hierarchy and organization of state court systems, politics of judicial selection, processes in civil and criminal proceedings, and appellate decision making. Charts on state court structures and caseloads are included, and each chapter includes a lengthy list of articles and books for further study. Robert A. Carp and Ronald Stidham's *Judicial Process in America* (CQ Press, 4th ed., 1998) is a more general work surveying many of the same issues, although much of its emphasis is on the federal courts. G. Alan Tarr and Mary Cornelia Aldis Porter's *State Supreme Courts in State and Nation* (Yale University Press, 1988) is a more focused study of the political role of the state judiciary, based on case studies of the supreme courts of Alabama, Ohio, and New Jersey. Extensive footnotes provide references to cases and other sources.

From time to time law reviews publish symposium issues on the role of state courts in the legal system. A recent example, with 10 articles and a panel discussion, is "The Future of State Supreme Courts as Institutions in the Law" in the May 1997 issue of the *Notre Dame Law Review* (volume 72, number 4). John B. Wefing's "State Supreme Court Justices: Who Are They?," 32 New Eng. L. Rev. 49 (1997), compiles statistical information on the men and women who staff the state courts of last resort, including gender, race, age, education, and prior judicial experience.

Works of national scope can only generalize on state court procedures, so it is usually helpful to find resources focusing on a specific court system. Several state governments have published guides to their court systems. Most of these are short pamphlets with history, charts showing court organization and the processes in civil and criminal proceedings, and perhaps a short glossary of legal terms. Examples include *A Guide to Arizona Courts* (Arizona Supreme Court, 1997); *I'll*

See You in Court: A Consumer Guide to the Minnesota Court System (Minnesota Supreme Court, annual); and *Citizen's Guide to Nebraska's Courts* (Nebraska Supreme Court, 1993). Useful guides are also prepared by professional or civil organizations, such as *A Resource Guide to Oklahoma Courts* (League of Women Voters of Oklahoma Citizen Education Fund, 1994).

Some resources formerly prepared for print distribution are now more widely available on the Internet, such as the New York State Bar Association's *The Courts of New York: A Guide to Court Procedures, with a Glossary of Legal Terms* <http://www.nysba.org/public/courts.html>, and *A Citizen's Guide to Washington's Courts* <http://198.187.0.226/courts/guide/home.htm> from the Office of the Administrator for the Courts for the Washington State Judiciary. More material such as this is becoming available from state court administrators. Some sites offer not only information on the courts but guides to the legal system, as well as instructions and forms for filing court actions. The Superior Court of Arizona, Maricopa County, has one of the most extensive and helpful sites <http://www.maricopa.gov/supcrt/supcrt.html>.

Links from general state homepages usually lead to descriptive information about each branch of government, including the courts. Some judiciary sites contain little information, but most explain the scope of each court's jurisdiction and provide historical and biographical information. New York's court system sponsors, with the *New York Law Journal*, an extensive "New York Courts and Law Guide" site <http://www.nylj.com/guide/> that contains links to more than 100 documents, such as the New York State Bar Association's *The Courts of New York*. Other documents, prepared by various private and governmental sources, include overviews of specific courts and guides to dozens of legal topics, such as adoption, employment discrimination, housing law, and estate planning.

Several collections provide access to state court Web sites. Some of these focus on sources for court opinions, but more general guides are provided by the National Center for State Courts <http://ncsc.dni.us/court/sites/courts.htm>; the Center for Information Law and Policy's State Court Locator <http://www.cilp.org/State-Ct/>; and Superior Information Services, Inc., a Web site development company <http://www.courts.net/>. Each of these sites provides links to state court systems and to individual courts throughout the country.

Directories

Courts are covered in most of the general state directories discussed in Chapter 11, but they are also the focus of several specialized resources. Directories of state courts serve several distinct purposes. Some focus on courts as policy-making institutions, with biographical information on appellate judges, while others provide contact information for people in search of court records. For example, trial court decisions are not published in most states, so it may be necessary to contact a court clerk's office to obtain copies of opinions or other documents.

The leading source for biographical information is *The American Bench* (Forster-Long, biennial). This thick tome covers judges throughout the country and at every court level. Each state has a separate section, which begins with a listing of courts, indicating the geographic and subject jurisdiction of each. These introductory sections list the names of the judges for each court, but provide no contact information. Maps of federal and state district boundaries follow, and then an alphabetical listing of judges providing addresses and telephone numbers. For perhaps half of the 18,000 judges listed, biographical information is also available. The biographies are supplied by the judges; most are rather short, but a few go on for two pages or more. An Alphabetical Name Index at the front of the volume indicates the state and court for all judges listed.

The *Judicial Yellow Book* (Leadership Directories, semiannual) is an excellent source for information on state appellate courts. It includes brief biographies for judges, with photographs of some, and lists judicial administrators, court staff, secretaries, and law clerks. The jurisdiction of each appellate court is noted, and contact information includes addresses of homepages. Judges are indexed by name and by law school. The *Judicial Yellow Book* is available online through both WESTLAW (JUDYB) and LEXIS-NEXIS (YBJUD).

West's Legal Directory includes information on courts that is accessible through WESTLAW (WLD-COURT database) and on the Internet <http://www.wld.com/>. The court listings can be found in the "Attorney Resources" section of the Internet site <http://www.wld.com/attorney/>. Contact information and an outline of the court's jurisdiction are provided. The WLD-JUDGE database on WESTLAW covers trial and appellate judges, and has biographical data, including lists of published works, representative cases, and classes taught. Another Internet source, InfoSpace, has information on appellate courts and court administrators from *Carroll's State Directory* <http://www.infospace.com> or through FindLaw <http://www.findlaw.com/11stategov/directories/courts.html>.

Tables in the front of court reports can be a valuable source for quickly identifying appellate court judges. West Publishing (now West Group) began providing this information in each of its series containing state court decisions in 1889. New appointments, retirements, and other changes in status are noted in footnotes. Court reports for individual states also list the judges whose opinions appear in the volume, and some go on to include lists of trial court judges, court administrators, and other officers such as attorneys general.

Other directories focus on the courts themselves rather than the judges. One of the most convenient and comprehensive is *BNA's Directory of State and Federal Courts, Judges, and Clerks* (BNA, biennial). Sections for each state begin with charts of the court structure and then list appellate, trial, and specialized courts. Court mailing addresses and Web sites are included, as are telephone numbers for each judge. The geographic coverage of each court is noted, but not the subject jurisdiction or the types of records held by the courts. A geographical jurisdiction index indicates the pages on which courts for particular counties appear, and a personal name index lists all judges and clerks in the volume.

WANT's Federal-State Court Directory (WANT Publishing, annual) includes versions of the useful charts showing the structure of each state's courts, but beyond that its directory information for states is slim. Each state is limited to one page (including the structural chart), listing the supreme court justices and the court administrator, and a few executive offices. The entries for state supreme courts are available on the Internet <http://www.courts.com/directory.html>.

Another WANT publication, *Directory of State Court Clerks and County Courthouses* (annual) is a better source for coverage of state courts. It lists the names, addresses, and telephone numbers of clerks of appellate and trial courts, and indicates the counties in each judicial circuit or district. It also covers county clerks, attorneys general, and state corporation commission offices, and includes instructions for obtaining vital statistics records, deed records, and probate information. The charts of each state's court structure are included here as well.

Other directories provide extensive information on obtaining court records. The leading publisher in this field is BRB Publications in Tempe, Arizona, which produces several guides to public and court records. Its basic guide is *The Librarian's Guide to Public*

Records (annual), which provides a good beginning overview. An introduction explains methods of searching for public records, with a quick summary of state and federal court organization and recordkeeping procedures. The main body of the guide is a state-by-state directory of records sources. For each state, an introductory page provides general help numbers and a list of major state Internet sites. This is followed by a list of statewide agencies with public records, and a county-by-county listing of courts and recording offices with addresses, telephone numbers, and office hours. A "What You Need to Know" page includes details of court structure, searching hints, and sources for online access. This book is also available under a different imprint, with only slight modifications, as *Find Public Records Fast: The Complete State, County, and Courthouse Locator* (Facts on Demand Press, rev. ed., 1998).

BRB Publications also issues several other more specific works on records sources. Its major state court directory, *Sourcebook of County Court Records* (4th ed., 1998), lists the same courts as *The Librarian's Guide to Public Records* but with more detailed entries. It includes information about the records available from each court and the form of payment accepted. *Public Records Online: The National Guide to Private and Governmental Online Sources of Public Records* (Facts on Demand Press, 1997) surveys electronic sources, and *Sourcebook of Local Court and County Record Retrievers* (BRB, 1998) indicates what records are available in each jurisdiction and provides information on companies that can retrieve these records for a fee. Information on these firms, most of which are members of the Public Record Retriever Network, includes address, telephone number, billing, and average turnaround time.

A similar work, *The Guide to Background Investigations: A Comprehensive Source Directory for Employee Screening and Background Investigations* (T.I.S.I., 8th ed., 1998), provides listings comparable to those in BRB's *Sourcebook of County Court Records*, with coverage of procedures for obtaining criminal and civil court documents as well as other records from state agencies. Dennis King's *Get the Facts on Anyone* (Macmillan, 2d ed., 1995), although not a directory, provides a thorough overview of an investigator's methods for finding information on individuals and organizations. Chapter 9, "Court Records," covers such topics as searching court indexes, studying case files, and obtaining criminal records.

Two court directories that may be useful but are not as regularly updated are Mark J. A. Yannone's *National Directory of Courts of Law* (Information Resources Press, 1991) and Elizabeth Petty Bentley's *County Courthouse Book* (Genealogical Publishing, 2d ed., 1995). The latter work includes some information on types of records held and procedures for obtaining copies.

A final directory, *National Directory of Prosecuting Attorneys* (National District Attorneys Association, biennial), focuses on officers of the court rather than the courts themselves. It lists the chief prosecutors in each state jurisdiction and includes an index by name. An appendix provides background information on each state's prosecutorial system, including the constitutional or statutory basis, organization, and scope of jurisdiction under which prosecutors operate.

Statistics

The major source for state court statistics is the National Center for State Courts Court Statistics Project. The project's annual report, *Examining the Work of State Courts*, analyzes the business of trial and appellate courts, with numerous charts and graphs showing trends in caseloads and filings in trial and appellate courts. Cases are examined by subject, with separate sections on tort, domestic relations, and criminal proceedings. The report is designed to present conclusions, not just raw data, and each section includes a thorough, straightforward discussion of major issues and findings.

The data are found in a separate annual supplement, *State Court Caseload Statistics*. In addition to extensive tables with caseload figures, this volume include some useful features, such as the state court structure charts found in *State Court Organization* and tables on jurisdiction and reporting practices in each state. Figure C, for instance, lists the maximum dollar amount and procedures for small claims courts, and Figure G lists the number of judges for the various components of each state's court system. Several of the charts, however, simply focus on the methods of counting cases for statistical purposes. A small sampling of NCSC statistics, *Caseload Highlights*, is available on the Internet <http://www.ncsc.dni.us/research.htm>.

More specialized statistics are also available. *Felony Sentences in State Courts* (U.S. Bureau of Justice Statistics, biennial) is a brief bulletin with about a dozen tables providing national totals and composites, but no information for individual states. Much of its data also appear in Section 5, "Judicial Processing of Defendants," in the Bureau's *Sourcebook of Criminal Justice Statistics* (annual). *Juvenile Court Statistics* (U.S. Office of Juvenile Justice and Delinquency Prevention, annual) provides information on juvenile cases by type, age, sex, and race. Its two major sections cover delinquency cases (criminal matters) and status offense cases (behavior that is an offense only when committed by a minor). An appendix lists the sources of data for each state, including a few annual reports but mostly unpublished data files.

Two databases of state court cases available on the Internet from the Inter-University Consortium for Political and Social Research make it possible to perform statistical analyses based on type of case, parties, disposition, and other factors. A civil cases database <http://teddy.law.cornell.edu:8090/questcvs.htm> covers a sample of about 30,000 tort, contract, and property cases terminated in 1992, while a civil trials database <http://teddy.law.cornell.edu:8090/questtrs.htm> is limited to about 6,500 cases that went to jury trial.

COURT DECISIONS

Local trial courts may be the judicial tribunals with which most people come in contact, but their role in creating legal doctrine is minimal. Juries decide cases on the basis of the facts before them. Trial judges must decide how to apply the laws, but their decisions rarely result in written opinions. Even fewer of these opinions are published and available to serve as guides in other proceedings, and those that are published have limited value as precedent.

Creating and refining the law, on the other hand, is a principal purpose of the appellate courts. Their decisions are available in published volumes, through commercial databases, and, to a growing extent, on the Internet.

In some ways, publication of court decisions has come full circle in the past 150 years. In the nineteenth century, courts published their own decisions, and each state had a series of reports similar to the *U.S. Reports* containing the case law of its supreme court. Efficient and timely commercial publication, however, caused several states to reconsider the expense of producing their own series of publications, and in the past 50 years 19 states have discontinued their official reports. With the growth of the Internet, however, many courts are once again disseminating their own opinions.

Printed Reports

Generally, state court opinions are published in two sources. One source is an official series of court reports published by or under the auspices of the state itself, and the other is part of a comprehensive report-

ing system covering cases from appellate courts in every state, West Group's National Reporter System. The same opinions appear in both sources, and the two versions are known as *parallel citations*. There are two exceptions to this rule, namely old cases and recent cases from some states. National Reporter System coverage for most states did not begin until the 1880s, so earlier cases appear only in the official state reports. In the past several decades, a number of states have discontinued publication of their official reports, so recent cases from those states may appear only in the National Reporter System.

The series of official state reports follow a standard format of designation and citation. The title page may have a long title such as *Reports of Cases Argued and Determined in the Supreme Court of the State of Vermont*, but the volume's spine is labeled *Vermont Reports* and the series is cited simply as "Vt." Exhibit 12-2 shows the first two pages of a decision in Volume 417 of *Massachusetts Reports*. The case, *Hamilton v. Ganias*, begins on page 666 and is therefore cited as "417 Mass. 666 (1994)." The opinion of the court begins near the bottom of page 666, following the name of the justice who wrote the opinion (WILKINS, J.).

Most states with intermediate appellate courts publish separate series of reports for those courts, such as *Massachusetts Appeals Court Reports*. These reports add the abbreviation "App." to the name of the state in a citation, as in "Mass. App." A few states combine the decisions of their supreme and appellate courts in one series, but a citation to an intermediate appellate court decision must identify the court either as part of the citation or in parentheses preceding the date of the decision. The abbreviation for the state, standing alone, means that the case is a decision of the state's court of last resort.

There are some oddities in official reports. *Arkansas Reports* and *Arkansas Appellate Reports* are bound together, so that the spine of each volume indicates two volume numbers, as in "328 Ark. / 57 Ark. App." This format undoubtedly simplifies the state's distribution of court reports, and it allows both courts to publish at the same time even though the Arkansas Court of Appeals generally issues fewer published opinions than the Arkansas Supreme Court. On the shelf, however, it makes the courts look like oddly conjoined twins.

Every state except Alaska has had an official series of reports, such as *Massachusetts Reports*, for most of its history, but, like the lower federal courts, a number of states now rely on commercial publication of their decisions. Despite this prevailing trend, new se-

666   417 Mass. 666

Hamilton *v.* Ganias.

JASON HAMILTON & another[1] *vs.* CHRIS GANIAS & others.[2]

Worcester. February 9, 1994. - May 4, 1994.

Present: WILKINS, ABRAMS, O'CONNOR, & GREANEY, JJ.

Negligence, Serving alcoholic liquors to guest. *Alcoholic Liquors*, Liability of host, Motor vehicle.

This court held that a social host had no duty to a nineteen year old underage drinker who became intoxicated by the voluntary consumption of alcohol and subsequently injured himself while negligently operating a motor vehicle. [666-668]

CIVIL ACTION commenced in the Superior Court Department on August 9, 1991.

A motion of the defendant Haglund for summary judgment was heard by *Elizabeth Butler*, J.; a motion of the defendant Ganias to dismiss was heard by *James P. Donohue*, J.; and separate and final judgments were entered by *Charles M. Grabau*, J., and *Donohue*, J., respectively.

The Supreme Judicial Court granted a request for direct appellate review and consolidated the cases.

Stephen M. CampoBasso (*Peter A. CampoBasso* & *Patrick R. Bunnell* with him) for the plaintiffs.

John A. Cvejanovich for Gary Haglund.

Joseph H. Caffrey for Chris Ganias.

WILKINS, J. In *Manning v. Nobile*, 411 Mass. 382 (1991), this court held that a social host had no duty to an adult guest who became intoxicated by the voluntary consumption

---

[1] Carol Hamilton, the mother of Jason Hamilton.

[2] Gary Haglund, John Carter, El Morocco Restaurant, Inc., Richard Aboody, Sr., and David Damato. Only the defendants Ganias and Haglund are before us in the plaintiffs' consolidated appeal from separate judgments ordered in favor of Ganias and Haglund.

417 Mass. 666   667

Hamilton v. Ganias.

of alcohol and subsequently injured himself while negligently operating a motor vehicle. The case now before us on direct appellate review presents the question whether the result should be different if the intoxicated guest who injured himself was a nineteen-year-old, underage drinker.

We hold that the reasons announced in the *Manning* case for denying social host liability to an intoxicated adult guest who injures himself apply to a nineteen year old who injures himself in similar circumstances.[3] We thus affirm the judgments dismissing the actions against Ganias and Haglund.

We decide this case on the broad principle that Jason Hamilton, although an underage drinker, was an adult (G. L. c. 4, § 7, Fiftieth [1992 ed.]), who was responsible for his own conduct and injured himself.[4] The Legislature has granted substantial rights to and has placed substantial obligations on people who are nineteen years old. Hamilton was old enough to vote (art. 3 of the Amendments to the Massachusetts Constitution), to make a valid will (G. L. c. 191, § 1 [1992 ed.]), to enter into valid contracts (G. L. c. 231, § 85O [1992 ed.]), to get married without parental consent (G. L. c. 207, §§ 7, 24, and 25 [1992 ed.]), to serve on a jury (G. L. c. 234, § 1 [1992 ed.]), to work on any job (G. L. c. 149, § 63 [1992 ed.]), for as many hours as he wished (G. L. c. 149, § 65 [1992 ed.]), to buy and carry a firearm (G. L. c. 140, §§ 131 and 131E [1992 ed.]), and to

---

[3] The record before the judges of the Superior Court, who respectively ordered judgments for Ganias and Haglund, did not disclose the ages of the defendants. We deny attempts by the defendants to supplement the record to show that they too were nineteen years old at the time of the events involved in this case.

[4] The facts do not indicate that either defendant before us acted in a "wilful, wanton, or reckless" manner. The Legislature has provided that a person or entity licensed to sell alcoholic beverages, or serving alcohol as an incident to its business, shall not be liable for the negligent serving of alcohol to an intoxicated person who injures himself "in the absence of wilful, wanton, or reckless conduct on the part of the licensee or such person or entity." G. L. c. 231, § 85T (1992 ed.). Because of this statement of public policy limiting the liability of a commercial server of alcoholic beverages to an intoxicated customer who injures himself, it is unlikely that this court would hold a social host to a stricter standard.

EXHIBIT 12-2 (continued)

ries continue to spring up. *Nebraska Appellate Reports* began publication in 1994 with the first decisions of Nebraska's new Court of Appeals.

The major commercial publisher of state court decisions is West Group, publisher of the *Supreme Court Reporter, Federal Reporter*, and *Federal Supplement*. Its National Reporter System dates back to the 1880s and covers the entire country with uniform editorial treatment. West publishes state cases in a series of seven *regional reporters*, each covering a section of the country. These reporters are: *Atlantic* (A.2d), *North Eastern* (N.E.2d), *North Western* (N.W.2d), *Pacific* (P.2d), *South Eastern* (S.E.2d), *Southern* (So.2d), and *South Western* (S.W.2d). Note that all these publications are in their second series, each of which began after the first 200 or 300 volumes. Two of the sets (*Pacific* and *South Western*) are fast approaching 1,000 volumes in their second series, and will probably soon become P.3d and S.W.3d. Exhibit 12-3 shows the first page of the *Hamilton v. Ganias* decision, as printed in West's *North Eastern Reporter 2d*. Note that it includes the same synopsis and headnote treatment as cases in West's reporters of federal court decisions.

Geographers and pollsters have tried for years to divide the country into identifiable regions, and none is ever entirely successful. Is Ohio, for example, in the East or the Midwest? West's regions were devised in the 1880s and may once have made some sense. In part, they were simply based on convenience. The *North Eastern Reporter* began publication in 1885, and includes Massachusetts, the largest of the New England states, along with Illinois, Indiana, Ohio, and New York. Decisions from the other New England states appear in the *Atlantic Reporter*, which began a year later and includes Delaware, Maryland, New Jersey, and Pennsylvania.

Virtually unchanged for more than a century, the West regions are simply arbitrary groups of states with no geographic meaning. Kentucky is in the *South Western Reporter*, and Kansas is in the *Pacific Reporter*. This makes about as much sense as putting the Atlanta Falcons and the Carolina Panthers in the Western Division of the National Football Conference, and ultimately it matters as little.

Also part of the National Reporter System are separate reporters for two of the states with the busiest court systems, *West's California Reporter* (Cal. Rptr. 2d) and *New York Supplement* (N.Y.S.2d). The decisions from these states would swamp their regional reporters, so their lower court cases are excluded from the *Pacific* and *North Eastern Reporters*. The *New York Supple-*

ment dates all the way back to 1888, but the *California Reporter* only began in 1959. Decisions of the California Supreme Court and the New York Court of Appeals appear in both regional and state reporters, so for these cases there are *three* parallel citations. Table 12-1 indicates current sources, with *Bluebook* abbreviations, for opinions from courts of last resort and intermediate appellate courts in each state.

In addition to the regional reporters, West also publishes what are known as *offprint reporters* containing the decisions of individual states but with regional reporter pagination. Thus, *West's Massachusetts Decisions* contains the text of *Hamilton v. Ganias* exactly as printed in the *North Eastern Reporter* (and as shown in Exhibit 12-3), including the N.E.2d volume and page numbers. *Massachusetts Decisions* may appear on library shelves, but it is never listed as a source for court decisions because it does not have its own numbering system. It is simply a way for Massachusetts lawyers to buy their own state's cases without having to fill their shelves with cases from Illinois and Indiana as well. Each volume of *Massachusetts Decisions* may contain cases from several *North Eastern Reporter 2d* volumes. These offprint reporters are published for more than 30 states. If a state has discontinued its official reports, the offprint series is the only published source limited to its case law. The opinion in *Hamilton v. Ganias,* for example, is the same in Exhibits 12-2 and 12-3.

In those states in which cases are published in both official and National Reporter System editions, the two versions should be identical with only different editorial headnotes. Case citations have traditionally included both the official reports and West's regional reporter so that researchers could find decisions no matter which source was available. References to cases in legal encyclopedias or texts generally include both of these parallel citations.

In recent years, however, this standard citation format has seen two changes. A change for the worse came in 1991, when the 15th edition of *The Bluebook: A Uniform System of Citation* decreed that law reviews should cite cases only to the regional reporter. A law review following this rule, as most do, would omit the *Massachusetts Reports* citation for *Hamilton v. Ganias*, even if it is published in Massachusetts and focuses on issues of state law. The *Bluebook's* edict has simplified the work of law review editors, but at the expense of people who use official state reports. (Another problem with this *Bluebook* rule is that inexperienced writ-

HAMILTON v. GANIAS

Cite as 632 N.E.2d 407 (Mass. 1994)

Mass. **407**

417 Mass. 666

|666Jason HAMILTON & another [1]

v.

Chris GANIAS & others.[2]

Supreme Judicial Court of Massachusetts, Worcester.

Argued Feb. 9, 1994.

Decided May 4, 1994.

Guest and his mother filed separate actions against social hosts, seeking recovery for personal injuries suffered by guest in motorcycle accident. The Superior Court Department, Worcester County, Elizabeth Butler and James P. Donohue, JJ., heard motions, and Charles M. Grabau and Donohue, JJ., entered separate and final judgments dismissing cases. Request for direct appellate review was granted and cases were consolidated for appeal. The Supreme Judicial Court, Wilkins, J., held that social hosts had no duty to 19–year-old underage guest who became intoxicated by voluntary consumption of alcohol and subsequently injured himself while negligently operating motor vehicle.

Judgments affirmed.

Intoxicating Liquors ⟶299

Social hosts had no duty to 19–year-old underage guest who became intoxicated by voluntary consumption of alcohol and subsequently injured himself while negligently operating motor vehicle, in light of broad principle that guest was adult who was responsible for his own conduct, and in light of lack of wilful, wanton or reckless conduct by social

hosts which would have been required to impose liability on commercial server of alcohol. M.G.L.A. c. 4, § 7, cl. 50; c. 231, § 85T.

Stephen M. CampoBasso, Leominster (Peter A. CampoBasso & Patrick R. Bunnell with him), for the plaintiffs.

John A. Cvejanovich, Springfield, for Gary Haglund.

Joseph H. Caffrey, Worcester, for Chris Ganias.

Before WILKINS, ABRAMS, O'CONNOR and GREANEY, JJ.

WILKINS, Justice.

In *Manning v. Nobile*, 411 Mass. 382, 582 N.E.2d 942 (1991), this court held that a social host had no duty to an adult guest who became intoxicated by the voluntary consumption |667of alcohol and subsequently injured himself while negligently operating a motor vehicle. The case now before us on direct appellate review presents the question whether the result should be different if the intoxicated guest who injured himself was a nineteen-year-old, underage drinker.

We hold that the reasons announced in the *Manning* case for denying social host liability to an intoxicated adult guest who injures himself apply to a nineteen year old who injures himself in similar circumstances.[3] We thus affirm the judgments dismissing the actions against Ganias and Haglund.

We decide this case on the broad principle that Jason Hamilton, although an underage drinker, was an adult (G.L. c. 4, § 7, Fiftieth [1992 ed.]), who was responsible for his own conduct and injured himself.[4] The Legislature has granted substantial rights to and

1. Carol Hamilton, the mother of Jason Hamilton.

2. Gary Haglund, John Carter, El Morocco Restaurant, Inc., Richard Aboody, Sr., and David Damato. Only the defendants Ganias and Haglund are before us in the plaintiffs' consolidated appeal from separate judgments ordered in favor of Ganias and Haglund.

3. The record before the judges of the Superior Court, who respectively ordered judgments for Ganias and Haglund, did not disclose the ages of the defendants. We deny attempts by the defendants to supplement the record to show that they

too were nineteen years old at the time of the events involved in this case.

4. The facts do not indicate that either defendant before us acted in a "wilful, wanton, or reckless" manner. The Legislature has provided that a person or entity licensed to sell alcoholic beverages, or serving alcohol as an incident to its business, shall not be liable for the negligent serving of alcohol to an intoxicated person who injures himself "in the absence of wilful, wanton, or reckless conduct on the part of the licensee or such person or entity." G.L. c. 231, § 85T (1992 ed.). Because of this statement of public policy

EXHIBIT 12-3

TABLE 12-1

STATE COURT REPORTS

Alabama	*Southern Reporter 2d* [So. 2d] (*Alabama Reports* ceased 1976)
Alaska	*Pacific Reporter 2d* [P.2d]
Arizona	*Arizona Reports* [Ariz.]
	Pacific Reporter 2d [P.2d]
Arkansas	*Arkansas Reports* [Ark.]; *Arkansas Appellate Reports* [Ark. App.]
	South Western Reporter 2d [S.W.2d]
California	*California Reports 4th* [Cal.4th]; *California Appellate Reports 4th* [Cal. App. 4th]
	Pacific Reporter 2d [P.2d]; *West's California Reporter 2d* [Cal. Rptr. 2d]
Colorado	*Pacific Reporter 2d* [P.2d] (*Colorado Reports* ceased 1980)
Connecticut	*Connecticut Reports* [Conn.]; *Connecticut Appellate Reports* [Conn. App.]
	Atlantic Reporter 2d [A.2d]
Delaware	*Atlantic Reporter 2d* [A.2d] (*Delaware Reports* ceased 1966)
Florida	*Southern Reporter 2d* [So. 2d] (*Florida Reports* ceased 1948)
Georgia	*Georgia Reports* [Ga.]; *Georgia Appeals Reports* [Ga. App.]
	South Eastern Reporter 2d [S.E.2d]
Hawaii	*West's Hawai'i Reports* [Haw.]
	Pacific Reporter 2d [P.2d]
Idaho	*Idaho Reports* [Idaho]
	Pacific Reporter 2d [P.2d]
Illinois	*Illinois Reports 2d* [Ill. 2d]; *Illinois Appellate Court Reports 3d* [Ill. App. 3d]
	North Eastern Reporter 2d [N.E.2d]
Indiana	*North Eastern Reporter 2d* [N.E.2d] (*Indiana Reports* ceased 1981)
Iowa	*North Western Reporter 2d* [N.W.2d] (*Iowa Reports* ceased 1968)
Kansas	*Kansas Reports* [Kan.]; *Kansas Court of Appeals Reports 2d* [Kan. App. 2d]
	Pacific Reporter 2d [P.2d]
Kentucky	*South Western Reporter 2d* [S.W.2d] (*Kentucky Reports* ceased 1973)
Louisiana	*Southern Reporter 2d* [So. 2d] (*Louisiana Reports* ceased 1972)
Maine	*Atlantic Reporter 2d* [A.2d] (*Maine Reports* ceased 1965)
Maryland	*Maryland Reports* [Md.]; *Maryland Appellate Reports* [Md. App.]
	Atlantic Reporter 2d [A.2d]
Massachusetts	*Massachusetts Reports* [Mass.]; *Massachusetts Appeals Court Reports* [Mass. App.]
	North Eastern Reporter 2d [N.E.2d]
Michigan	*Michigan Reports* [Mich.]; *Michigan Appeals Reports* [Mich. App.]
	North Western Reporter 2d [N.W.2d]
Minnesota	*North Western Reporter 2d* [N.W.2d] (*Minnesota Reports* ceased 1965)
Mississippi	*Southern Reporter 2d* [So. 2d] (*Mississippi Reports* ceased 1965)
Missouri	*South Western Reporter 2d* [S.W.2d] (*Missouri Reports* ceased 1965)
Montana	*Montana Reports* [Mont.]
	Pacific Reporter 2d [P.2d]
Nebraska	*Nebraska Reports* [Neb.]; *Nebraska Appellate Reports* [Neb. App.]
	North Western Reporter 2d [N.W.2d]

TABLE 12-1 (continued)

Nevada	*Nevada Reports* [Nev.]
	Pacific Reporter 2d [P.2d]
New Hampshire	*New Hampshire Reports* [N.H.]
	Atlantic Reporter 2d [A.2d]
New Jersey	*New Jersey Reports* [N.J.]; *New Jersey Superior Court Reports* [N.J. Super.]
	Atlantic Reporter 2d [A.2d]
New Mexico	*New Mexico Reports* [N.M.]
	Pacific Reporter 2d [P.2d]
New York	*New York Reports 2d* [N.Y.2d]; *Appellate Division Reports 2d* [A.D.2d]
	North Eastern Reporter 2d [N.E.2d]; *New York Supplement 2d* [N.Y.S.2d]
North Carolina	*North Carolina Reports* [N.C.]; *North Carolina Court of Appeals Reports* [N.C. App.]
	South Eastern Reporter 2d [S.E.2d]
North Dakota	*North Western Reporter 2d* [N.W.2d] (*North Dakota Reports* ceased 1953)
Ohio	*Ohio State Reports 3d* [Ohio St. 3d]; *Ohio Appellate Reports 3d* [Ohio App. 3d]
	North Eastern Reporter 2d [N.E.2d]
Oklahoma	*Pacific Reporter 2d* [P.2d] (*Oklahoma Reports* ceased 1953)
Oregon	*Oregon Reports* [Or.]; *Oregon Reports, Court of Appeals* [Or. App.]
	Pacific Reporter 2d [P.2d]
Pennsylvania	*Pennsylvania State Reports* [Pa.]; *Atlantic Reporter 2d* [A.2d]
Rhode Island	*Atlantic Reporter 2d* [A.2d] (*Rhode Island Reports* ceased 1980)
South Carolina	*South Carolina Reports* [S.C.]
	South Eastern Reporter 2d [S.E.2d]
South Dakota	*North Western Reporter 2d* [N.W.2d] (*South Dakota Reports* ceased 1976)
Tennessee	*South Western Reporter 2d* [S.W.2d] (*Tennessee Reports* ceased 1972)
Texas	*South Western Reporter 2d* [S.W.2d] (*Texas Reports* ceased 1962)
Utah	*Pacific Reporter 2d* [P.2d] (*Utah Reports 2d* ceased 1974)
Vermont	*Vermont Reports* [Vt.]
	Atlantic Reporter 2d [A.2d]
Virginia	*Virginia Reports* [Va.]; *Virginia Court of Appeals Reports* [Va. App.]
	South Eastern Reporter 2d [S.E.2d]
Washington	*Washington Reports 2d* [Wash. 2d]; *Washington Appellate Reports* [Wash. App.]
	Pacific Reporter 2d [P.2d]
West Virginia	*West Virginia Reports* [W. Va.]
	South Eastern Reporter 2d [S.E.2d]
Wisconsin	*Callaghan's Wisconsin Reports 2d* [Wis. 2d]
	North Western Reporter 2d [N.W.2d]
Wyoming	*Pacific Reporter 2d* [P.2d] (*Wyoming Reports* ceased 1959)

ers sometimes forget to identify the jurisdiction in parentheses, making the citation nearly meaningless.)

The exclusion of state reports in citations remains the rule in the current 16th edition (1996) of the *Bluebook*, but there has been an additional change. The preferred source is now a *public domain citation* if one is available. These citations, in which the court assigns each decision a number as it is issued, are now used in six states. The first of these, Louisiana, began citing its cases by docket number and date in 1994. Its format, as in "97-0956 (La. 05/01/98)," has not been duplicated in other jurisdictions. Instead, the five other states all follow a standard format using the state's postal code and sequential decision numbers. Under this approach, "1999 SD 1" represents the first decision issued in 1999 by the South Dakota Supreme Court. Besides South Dakota, which began using public domain citations in 1996, the other states adopting this format are Maine (1997), North Dakota (1997), Oklahoma (1997), and Montana (1998).

The other feature of cases using public domain citations is that each paragraph in a decision is numbered. Together, the numbered decisions and paragraphs mean that a particular discussion or quotation from a case can be cited from any print or electronic source and then found by someone using a different source or different medium, without reliance on a specific printed version.

The new public domain citations have the most significance for electronic retrieval of decisions, but they appear in the printed sources as well. West's regional reporters note the citations at the beginning of decisions from public domain states. Similarly, citations in official state reports are indicated at the beginning of some decisions in the regional reporters. Note in Exhibit 12-3 that the official citation, 417 Mass. 666, appears above the name of the case. Another feature shown in this exhibit is *star paging*, which indicates the exact page breaks in the official reports. Thus the symbol $\perp^{667}$ in the middle of the right-hand column shows the break between the text shown on the first page of Exhibit 12-2 and that shown on the second page of Exhibit 12-2 in the official reports.

The regional reporters include citations and star paging for fewer than half the states with official reports. A few states have citations at the beginning of decisions but no star paging, and others have no references at all. Some official reports are simply published too slowly for their citations to be included in the regional reporter. West's reporters, however, include the paragraph numbers in public domain citation states, and

for Louisiana, which cites to specific pages of its slip opinions instead of using paragraph numbers, the *Southern Reporter* indicates the page breaks in each slip opinion.

The official and regional reporters have several features in common. Most are published first in weekly advance sheets to provide current notice of new court decisions, and then several advance sheets are compiled into a bound volume. Both advance sheets and bound volumes include tables of the cases they contain; the regional reporters have an alphabetical table of all cases and separate tables for each jurisdiction. Every volume includes a digest or index to provide subject access to the cases. West's digests are based on its familiar key number system, while the state reports employ a variety of approaches. Some have extensive digests, while others have brief indexes with nothing but broad headings and strings of page numbers. In addition to an index, *Kansas Reports* includes a complete table of all cases ever overruled by the Kansas Supreme Court. *Ohio State Reports 3d* and *Ohio Appellate Reports 3d* include lists of opinions written by each judge.

While West's regional reporters follow a standard pattern, the official reports are a diverse lot. Some of these series are published by the states themselves, but several are issued under official sanction by commercial publishers. Many of these are published by West. For some states, the official and regional versions of cases appear identical, except for the number on each page. Other West series have the same synopses and headnotes as the regional reporter but a different layout, and a few series formerly published by other companies receive different editorial headnotes. These series may have headnotes keyed to case-finding publications for their specific states. Headnotes in California's and Wisconsin's reports are assigned section numbers from *California Digest of Official Reports* (West Group [originally Bancroft-Whitney]) and *Callaghan's Wisconsin Digest* (West Group [originally Callaghan]). Even though these are now West publications, they have retained their own editorial approaches to state case law. *North Carolina Reports*, which is published by the state, has headnotes keyed to the state legal encyclopedia, *Strong's North Carolina Index 4th* (West Group [originally Lawyers Cooperative]).

Having different editorial approaches in the state reports and the National Reporter System can be helpful at times. Some judicial opinions are straightforward and clearly delineate the scope of their holdings, but not every judge writes plainly and simply. Some opinions are deliberately vague because a court may rely on future cases to shape the law over the course of time. Just as two people may see a painting differently, two people may draw different conclusions from the same court opinion. The lack of an independent perspective in the state reports make it more likely that a West editor's interpretation will become the standard view of a case. To make matters worse, that interpretation extends beyond reports published by West to include some reports published by the states that now use West synopses and headnotes under license. Other states, however, continue to provide their own editorial embellishments. *Michigan Reports* and *Michigan Appeals Reports*, for example, have thorough, precise syllabi similar to those published in the *United States Reports*.

The syllabus and headnotes preceding an opinion, of course, are merely editorial features designed to make decisions easier to understand. The opinion itself is the law—except in Ohio, where the Ohio Supreme Court prepares an official syllabus to announce its holding. The syllabus controls if there are discrepancies between it and the opinion. The syllabus and opinion must be read together, of course, because the opinion provides the facts and discussion that explain the scope of the holding.

The state reports include other features not found in the National Reporter System. Even those published by West—including the offprint reporters—tend to include more extensive listings of judges than those in the National Reporter System. Some states simply list the appellate judges, but others also list every trial court judge in the state. *Montana Reports* includes court reporters, clerks, and city attorneys as well, and *North Carolina Reports* lists assistant attorneys general, district attorneys, and public defenders. Several state reports include lists of newly admitted attorneys, and some publish notices of disciplined attorneys. Other individual touches appear here and there. *West's Hawai'i Reports*, for example, includes the 'okina as the sixth letter in the state's name. (This symbol, which looks like an upside-down apostrophe, is actually a letter of the Hawai'ian alphabet and represents a glottal stop between vowels.)

Several reports include photographs of the justices. This may seem a trifle, but it can help considerably to humanize the decisions published in otherwise drab series of hundreds of identical volumes. *Michigan Reports* has included a color photograph of the assembled Michigan Supreme Court every two years since 1973, and the Ohio Supreme Court, looking cheerful and collegial, is featured in every three to five volumes of *Ohio State Reports. Georgia Reports* and *Georgia Appeals Reports* have individual black-and-white photographs of their jurists, but these are not as endearing as the group shots from Michigan and Ohio. The Wisconsin Supreme Court is photographed on the bench, sitting beneath a huge mural by Albert Herter of the signing of the U.S. Constitution. To take in the entire court and the painting, the photograph ends up with a row of tiny justices along its bottom margin.

While West's National Reporter System now covers all published appellate court decisions throughout the country, its oldest cases date from 1879. This leaves nearly a century of earlier decisions for which individual state reports are the only sources. Like the *U.S. Reports*, many of the state reports began as unofficial enterprises but were later taken over by the government. In 25 of the older states, the early volumes were once cited by the names of their reporters, like the early nominative Supreme Court reports. In 13 of these states, the nominative volumes were incorporated into the official numbering system, much like the volumes by Dallas, Cranch, and their successors were assigned *U.S. Reports* numbers. In the other 12 states, however, early nominative reports are still cited today by their reporters' names.

This is not a purely academic matter for legal historians. Just as *Marbury v. Madison*, 5 U.S. (1 Cranch) 137 (1803), is still read and cited as defining the scope of federal judicial power, state courts continue to look to their earliest decisions to aid in the resolution of current controversies. Some cases in the nominative reports remain a vital part of state common law. An Alabama Supreme Court decision in *Stewart & Porter's Reports* may still guide an Alabama court today. In *Gober v. Stubbs*, 682 So. 2d 430 (1996), Justice Gorman Houston quotes *Aldridge v. Tuscumbia C. & D.R.R.*, 2 Stew. & P. 199 (Ala. 1832), in which "this Court eloquently and succinctly defined a 'public use.'" It may seem odd from a modernist perspective to refer to a decision of "this Court" after 164 years, but it is indeed the same lawmaking body. A rule established in 1832 is still part of the law of the state.

Alabama had only four nominative reporters before the official series of *Alabama Reports* began. Some states, particularly New York and Pennsylvania, have a far more extensive and confusing roster of reports. In Vermont, the first reporter was Nathaniel Chipman (1752-1843), who also served as chief justice of the Vermont Supreme Court, U.S. district court judge, and U.S. senator. A few years later, he was followed by his younger brother Daniel Chipman, so their reports are cited as "N. Chip." and "D. Chip."

Finding these early nominative reports can be troublesome because abbreviations such as "N. Chip." are no longer familiar to many readers. A citation to a nominative reporter should, but does not always, indicate the jurisdiction and court in parentheses. Even if it does not, standard sources such as Mary Miles Prince's *Bieber's Dictionary of Legal Abbreviations* (William S. Hein & Co., 4th ed., 1993) or Donald Raistrick's *Index of Legal Citations and Abbreviations* (Bowker-Saur, 2d ed., 1993) can explain what the citations stand for and what jurisdictions they represent.

To place nominative reports into perspective among a state's court reports, several tables are published listing the reported case law from each state. The simplest and most convenient is found in Table 1 of *The Bluebook: A Uniform System of Citation*. For each appellate court, this table lists the sources with their dates of coverage and proper abbreviation forms. More extensive tables of early reports are published as appendixes in several legal research texts. These include Morris L. Cohen, Robert C. Berring, and Kent C. Olson's *How to Find the Law* (West Publishing, 9th ed., 1989); Miles O. Price and Harry Bitner's *Effective Legal Research* (Little, Brown, 1953) (but not later editions of this work); and Frederick C. Hicks's *Materials and Methods of Legal Research* (Lawyers Cooperative, 3d ed., 1942). Keith Wiese's *Hein's State Reports Checklist* (William S. Hein & Co., 2d ed., 1990-date) provides an extensive list of reports and includes reprints of several earlier compilations, including the Price/Bitner and Hicks lists.

Reports cited by the names of their reporters are a thing of the past, but legal tradition dies hard. Sixteen of the current series of state reports still indicate the names of the state reporters on the spine. A few even provide a volume number for both the series (e.g., 165 Vermont) and the reporter (e.g., 32 Abbott), even though nobody but the reporter's immediate family would use the latter citation. This tradition even extends to some of the offprint reporters. *West's Tennessee Decisions* has only S.W.2d page numbers, but a spine label identifies a recent volume as "316 Tenn. (Walkup 4)."

In most states, only decisions from courts of last resort and intermediate appellate courts are published, and these courts have been the focus of this discussion. In some states, however, decisions are also published from other courts. For example, a few states have additional reports for trial court decisions, such as *New York Miscellaneous Reports 2d* and *Ohio Miscellaneous Reports 2d*, and several states have reports from tax courts or other specialized tribunals. Several of Pennsylvania's counties have their own reporters for

trial court decisions. Whether decisions of these other courts are included within the scope of West's National Reporter System varies from state to state. Further information on decisions from these courts can be found in sources such as the *Bluebook* or *Hein's State Reports Checklist*.

Electronic Sources

While a law library's collection of printed volumes of court reports is the only comprehensive source for decisions dating back to the beginning of the state court systems, electronic sources provide more extensive coverage of modern decisions and are heavily used by researchers. Free Internet sites for recent decisions are available in most states, and commercial online and CD-ROM resources provide much deeper coverage.

Based on the wide availability of statutes, legislative information, and administrative codes on the Internet, one might assume that state courts would be turning to the Internet as a means of broadening access to their opinions. To date, however, developments are rather disappointing. Although nearly all state appellate courts have Web sites, some post no opinions. Others present recent opinions chronologically, but with no means of searching by subject. In some, the opinions must be downloaded because they cannot be viewed online. Even those sites with searchable databases generally do not begin coverage until the mid-1990s. This degree of access may be sufficient to begin a research project, but at this point it is inadequate for any serious investigation into state case law. The 1994 *Hamilton v. Ganias* case shown in this chapter is not available, let alone the cases from 1986 and 1991 on which it is based.

Those sites that simply provide access chronologically, or only by party name, are better than nothing, though, because they can provide the text of recent decisions cited in texts or articles. Several states, however, have sites that are worse than nothing because decisions are removed after just a few short weeks. A notice at Alaska's official court site, for example, states "Opinions are removed from this site once they are printed in Pacific Reporter, 2d, the designated official reporter of Alaskan appellate decisions." Idaho removes opinions after 60 days, and Washington after 90 days. Kentucky's web site has a few recent opinions that are accompanied by the following bizarre notice: "These opinions are not intended to be used for Legal Research. They are being provided for Informational Purposes only."

Considering the small investment required to store data electronically and maintain a Web site, these states are basically thumbing their noses at the public's right to learn about the workings of their government. The only people who can read decisions after 60 or 90 days are those with access to commercial databases or law libraries.

The best of the state court sites, by far, is the Oklahoma Supreme Court Network, which has decisions dating back to 1964. Several databases are available, including case law from Oklahoma and federal courts, statutes, court rules, attorney general opinions, and jury instructions. These can be searched separately or together, and results can be listed in chronological order or ranked for relevance. The search template for cases allows retrieval by citation, case name, court, author, or text.

A few other sites have some promising innovations. Mississippi only has decisions since 1996, but it is adding hypertext links to documents cited in its decisions. North Dakota has opinions since 1993 and allows searching by citation, party, trial judge, supreme court justice, and keyword. It also lists cases by topic under several dozen headings, with short summaries included for cases dating back to mid-1996. North Dakota also offers an e-mail notification service when new opinions are released.

Table 12-2 contains the addresses of Web sites providing free access to opinions from state courts of last resort. In some instances, these sites also provide access to decisions of intermediate appellate courts, but in several states those opinions are available at separate sites. Sites from which decisions are removed after a few weeks or months, or that are not being kept up-to-date, are excluded.

Any published list of Internet sites dates quickly, but several Internet resources for finding state court opinions are updated regularly.

- From FindLaw's State Resources page <http://www.findlaw.com/11stategov/>, "Courts" leads to court homepages (with or without opinions), and "Primary materials" leads to sites with opinions. The direct path to the list of statutes, cases, and other primary sources for a particular state is <http://www.findlaw.com/11stategov/xx/laws.html>, where *xx* is the state's postal abbreviation.
- Cornell's Legal Information Institute has a list of states <http://www.law.cornell.edu/opinions.html>, linking to a standardized form for each state indicating whether opinions are available from supreme courts and courts of appeals, as well as background and directory information for the state judiciary. The advantage of this approach is that the unlinked

entries clearly indicate when opinions from a particular court are *not* available.

- Piper Resources State Court Directory <http://www.piperinfo.com/pl03/statedir.html> focuses on sources for opinions, including subscription-based commercial sites. Each site includes scope of coverage (courts and dates) and notes on access restrictions and other material available.
- legal.online <http://www.legalonline.com/courts.htm> has a regularly updated guide to sites for federal and state courts, "Where to Find Court Opinions."
- Washburn University's State-Law page <http://lawlib.wuacc.edu/washlaw/uslaw/statelaw.html> leads to judicial sites rather than opinion sites, but it links to a State Courts Broker <http://cat.wuacc.edu/Harvest/brokers/courts/query.html> that searches more than two dozen sites with opinions.

The Internet court sites are most valuable as sources for obtaining the text of specific recent opinions known by name, date, or docket number. Searching for court opinions by subject, either from an individual state or through a multistate search engine such as Washburn's, may lead to a few relevant cases that can be used as beginning points in research, but it is no substitute for more comprehensive coverage in print or in online commercial databases.

For most states LEXIS-NEXIS and WESTLAW are the most comprehensive electronic sources for case law. Coverage varies significantly from state to state. WESTLAW has recently increased its retrospective coverage significantly, and now has the most extensive collection for most states. As competitors, however, both systems make sure that they keep up with each other's improvements in a particular market.

Both systems provide several means of access to state case law. One can search a particular state's courts or access a database combining those decisions with cases from the federal courts in the state. These more comprehensive databases may contain cases in which the federal courts apply or interpret state law, but they also include every Supreme Court case and every case from the U.S. Court of Appeals for the state. In most instances, it is probably best to limit research at first to state court cases. In addition, both LEXIS-NEXIS and WESTLAW have extensive and powerful databases with the decisions of all jurisdictions, either limited to state courts or combining all federal and state case law. These are huge databases with more than four million documents. Table 12-3 shows the format used for identifying these various databases.

TABLE 12-2	
STATE COURT OPINION INTERNET SITES	

Alaska	*http://www.touchngo.com/sp/sp.html* (1991)
Arizona	*http://www.supreme.state.az.us/opin/opinions.htm* (1997)
Arkansas	*http://www.state.ar.us/supremecourt/opinions/opmain.htm* (1996)
California	*http://california.findlaw.com/CA02_caselaw/slip.html* (1996)
Florida	*http://www.law.ufl.edu/suprcourt/opinions/* (1995)
Hawaii	*http://www.hsba.org/index/court/CASELAW.HTM*(1989)
Illinois	*http://www.state.il.us/court/* (1996)
Iowa	*http://www.iowabar.org/* (1992)
Kansas	*http://lawlib.wuacc.edu/kscases/kscases.htm* (1996)
Louisiana	*http://www.lasc.org/* (1996)
Maine	*http://www.courts.state.me.us/mescopin.home.html* (1997)
Maryland	*http://www.courts.state.md.us/* (1995)
Massachusetts	*http://www.socialaw.com/sjcslip/sjcslip.html* (1997)
Michigan	*http://www.icle.org/misupct/* (1995); *http://www.michbar.org/opinions/* (1997)
Minnesota	*http://www.courts.state.mn.us/library/archive/* (1996)
Mississippi	*http://www.mssc.state.ms.us/decisions/* (1996)
Missouri	*http://www.osca.state.mo.us/* (1997)
Montana	*http://www.lawlibrary.mt.gov/OPININS.HTM* (1997)
New Hampshire	*http://www.state.nh.us/courts/supreme/opinions.htm* (1995)
New Jersey	*http://www-camlaw.rutgers.edu/library/search.shtml* (1994)
New York	*http://www.law.cornell.edu/ny/ctap/overview.html* (1992)
North Carolina	*http://www.aoc.state.nc.us/www/public/html/opinions.htm* (1996)
North Dakota	*http://sc3.court.state.nd.us/court/opinions.htm* (1993)
Ohio	*http://www.sconet.ohio.gov/* (1992)
Oklahoma	*http://www.oscn.net/* (1964)
Pennsylvania	*http://www.courts.state.pa.us/* (1996)
Rhode Island	*http://www.ribar.com/ricases/casesrch.htm* (1997)
South Carolina	*http://www.law.sc.edu/opinions/opinions.htm* (1996)
South Dakota	*http://www.sdbar.org/opinions/index.htm* (1996)
Tennessee	*http://www.tsc.state.tn.us/intertst.htm* (1995)
Texas	*http://www.courts.state.tx.us/supreme/scopn.html* (1997)
Utah	*http://courtlink.utcourts.gov/opinions/* (1996)
Vermont	*http://dol.state.vt.us/www_root/000000/html/supct.html* (1993)
Virginia	*http://www.courts.state.va.us/opin.htm* (1995)
West Virginia	*http://www.state.wv.us/wvsca/opinions.htm* (1991)
Wisconsin	*http://www.courts.state.wi.us/WCS/sc_opinion_search.html* (1995);
	http://www.wisbar.org/Wis/index.html (1995)
Wyoming	*http://courts.state.wy.us/newopn.htm* (1996)

Two other commercial services also provide extensive access to court decisions on the Internet. These are LOIS (Law Office Information Systems) <http://www.pita.com>, and V. <http://www.versuslaw.com>. These systems offer different approaches to searching court opinions. LOIS has an extensive template in which citation, party name, docket number, court, date, judge, or attorney name can be entered, as well as a "search all fields" blank for full-text access. V. has a simpler approach limited to search terms and a specified date range, but it accepts more flexible, natural-language searches.

LOIS and V. are generally less expensive than LEXIS-NEXIS and WESTLAW. V. has a variety of pricing plans, including an option for unlimited access during a single 24-hour period. LOIS is generally available by annual subscription only, but it is possible to purchase a one-day visitor's pass up to three times a year. One of these temporary subscriptions may be the most cost-effective means of electronic searching for someone who does not regularly need access to legal materials.

Table 12-4 indicates the beginning dates of coverage for the courts of last resort of each state through the four commercial systems. LOIS, unlike its competitors, does not yet cover all 50 states. For each state the earliest date is highlighted in bold. The systems also provide access to decisions of intermediate appellate courts. In a few instances, coverage for these courts is not as extensive, but in most states intermediate appellate courts are covered since their inception.

CD-ROM is another format for electronic access to case law that is found in many law firms and in some public law libraries. A disc cannot match the comprehensiveness of LEXIS-NEXIS or WESTLAW's multistate databases, but it is well suited for locating the decisions of individual states. For research focusing on one particular state, CD-ROMs can be a powerful and effective resource. The coverage is often comparable to that online (which is not surprising because the same publishers provide the data in both formats), and there are no charges incurred each time a search is performed. Most state case law CD-ROMs, however, are designed for lawyers who need access to legal information on a daily basis, and cost several hundred dollars with monthly license fees.

Two thorough directories of state court CD-ROM products are Chapter 27, "State Legal Publications and Information Sources," of Kendall F. Svengalis's *Legal Information Buyer's Guide & Reference Manual* (Rhode Island LawPress, annual); and *Directory of Law-Related CD-ROMs* (Infosources Publishing, annual). Products are listed alphabetically by title in *Directory of Law-Related CD-ROMs*, but case law discs are indexed under "Court decisions—[state]."

CASE RESEARCH

Researching court decisions is a similar process for both federal and state law. The same types of tools are used—digests, annotations, citators, electronic databases—and the search procedures are comparable. This section focuses on some resources designed for finding cases from individual states, and some that allow comprehensive researching of courts throughout the country.

Generally, it makes sense to begin a research project by looking for case law from one state. On an issue of state law, only the decisions of the home state are binding precedent. Any other decision may or may not be persuasive, depending on a number of factors such as the similarity in fact, the authority and reputation of the court and judge, the age of the opinion, and its treatment in other court decisions.

When examining a decision, even from one's home state, one must consider the place of the deciding court within the structure of the court system. Most published decisions are from appellate courts and are generally binding on lower courts within the state, but some decisions are from trial courts or specialized courts and may have little bearing in subsequent cases.

In examining the following resources, we look at the issue confronted by the Massachusetts Supreme Judicial Court in *Hamilton v. Ganias*, the case presented in Exhibits 12-2 and 12-3. This is one of a series of decisions in which the court determined the scope of liability for a person who serves alcohol to someone who then causes an injury while intoxicated. The court first indicated in *McGuiggan v. New England Tel. & Tel. Co.*, 398 Mass. 152, 496 N.E.2d 141 (1986), that it would recognize a social host's liability to a third person injured by an intoxicated guest's negligent operation of a motor vehicle. In *Manning v. Nobile*, 411 Mass. 382, 582 N.E.2d 942 (1991), the court held that a social host was not liable for injuries an adult guest suffered as a result of consuming alcohol. The issue in the *Hamilton* case was whether this holding extended to an underage drinker. The court decided that the same reasoning should apply.

In these and related cases, the court has gradually defined the legal doctrine of social host liability in Massachusetts on the basis of specific cases presented to it. This is the way the common law operates. Whereas legislatures enact sets of rules at one time, a court develops the law on a gradual, case-by-case basis. This line of cases on social host liability can be found through several research methods.

State Digests

The official state reports have the answers to most questions of state law. The hard part, however, is finding those answers. Each volume of cases is usually indexed, but few states publish cumulative indexes providing access to more than one volume. Since the mid-1970s, every tenth volume of the *Illinois Reports 2d* has consisted of an index to the preceding nine volumes, but even this exception covers only a few volumes at a time—and it neglects decisions from the Illinois Appellate Court.

For comprehensive subject access to case law, researchers must turn to commercially published digests. A few states, such as California and Wisconsin, have their own unique digest systems, but the most widespread approach is the West key number digest system. Just as West Group publishes decisions of every state appellate court in its National Reporter System, it also publishes digests arranging the headnotes from these decisions by subject. Some of its digests cover a number of states, but the most convenient starting point is usually the digest for an individual state. These are published for every state but Delaware, Nevada, and Utah. The *Dakota Digest* and the *Virginia and West Virginia Digest* each covers two states, but the other 43 states have their own digests.

For some states, a single digest series covers all the decisions since the beginning of its reported case law, but many states have begun a second series for modern cases. Massachusetts is one of these states. *West's Massachusetts Digest 2d* (32 vols., 1986-date) supplements the original *Massachusetts Digest Annotated* (51 vols., 1933-84), which covers cases all the way back to 1761. New York has had four series, more than any other state, with cases since 1978 in *New York Digest 4th*. The site for most research is the current digest, with the older sets used only if nothing is found in the most recent set or if comprehensive historical research is needed.

Some states have digests that are called "second series," but have *replaced* rather than *supplemented* the earlier digests, and cover all reported case law in the state. Whether a state has one or two digests depends primarily on the amount of case law to be covered but it may also depend on consumer response to supplementary digests. Up until 1986, every digest which began a second series started coverage in 1930 or later. Since then, only *Michigan Digest 2d* in 1989 has taken this approach, and 15 other digests have published in second series with comprehensive retrospective coverage. Nineteen states still have their original digests, with individual volumes revised occasionally, but if these states publish new sets they will most likely be comprehensive.

Each of West's reporters uses the same key number system, and each of its state digests is organized in exactly the same manner. This minimizes differences in the structure of state law while allowing one to begin research in one state and expand it to others with ease. A state digest presents a comprehensive view of the case law of a particular state. In smaller jurisdictions without state legal encyclopedias and other specialized publications, the digest may be the most thorough and accessible summary of case law available.

West's digests have more than 400 topics, some broad ("Constitutional Law," "Criminal Law") and some narrow ("Abstracts of Title," "Cemeteries," "Party Walls"). A few old topics have been weeded out and a few new topics added, but the basic outline has changed little in more than 100 years. The classification schemes used for individual topics have been expanded and revised over time, but as the law changes, coverage of new issues is generally inadequate for several years. The law of social host liability has developed considerably in recent years, but cases on this issue appear together in the digest's "Intoxicating Liquors" topic under the key number for "Civil damage laws—Persons liable—In general." The 1986 volume of *West's Massachusetts Digest 2d* had no cases at all under this number. A decade later its pocket part had more than a dozen. Exhibit 12-4 shows a reference to the *Hamilton* case, as well as several other recent decisions, in the *Massachusetts Digest*.

In addition to cases from Massachusetts courts, *West's Massachusetts Digest 2d* covers cases from the U.S. District Court in Massachusetts, cases in the U.S. Court of Appeals for the First Circuit originating in Massachusetts, and cases in the U.S. Supreme Court from Massachusetts state or federal courts. These federal cases can be useful even in state law research because federal courts must often apply and interpret state law. Although guided by state court decisions, they must often address issues on which the state courts have not yet ruled. In Exhibit 12-4, the first two notes are from a U.S. District Court decision applying Massachusetts law.

TABLE 12-3

LEXIS-NEXIS AND WESTLAW DATABASES FOR STATE COURT OPINIONS

	LEXIS-NEXIS	**WESTLAW**
Massachusetts state cases	MASS or STATES / MACTS	MA-CS
Massachusetts state and federal cases	MASS or STATES / MAMEGA	MA-CS-ALL
All state courts	STATES / COURTS	ALLSTATES (1945-date)
		ALLSTATES-OLD (pre-1945)
All state and federal courts	MEGA or STATES / MEGA	ALLCASES (1945-date)
		ALLCASES-OLD (pre-1945)

In the state libraries on LEXIS-NEXIS, it is also possible to search individual courts (MASS for the Supreme Judicial Court, APP for the Appeals Court).

TABLE 12-4

SCOPE OF COVERAGE IN COMMERCIAL DATABASES OF STATE COURT OPINIONS

	LEXIS-NEXIS	WESTLAW	LOIS	V.
Alabama	1954	**1887**		1955
Alaska	**1959**	**1959**	1991	1960
Arizona	1898	**1866**	1925	1930
Arkansas	1943	**1886**	1924	1957
California	**1850**	1883	1997	1930
Colorado	**1864**	**1864**	1924	1930
Connecticut	1936	**1885**	1899	1950
Delaware	1945	**1886**		1950
Florida	**1886**	**1886**	1948	1950
Georgia	1936	**1887**	1939	1940
Hawaii	**1847**	**1847**	1989	1996
Idaho	1944	**1881**	1997	1965
Illinois	1885	**1884**	1996	1985
Indiana	1934	**1884**	1970	1935
Iowa	1944	**1879**		1995
Kansas	1945	**1882**	1949	1982
Kentucky	1944	**1886**		1945
Louisiana	**1887**	**1887**	1949	1980
Maine	1965	**1885**		1996
Maryland	1937	**1885**	1949	1950
Massachusetts	**1884**	1885	1925	1930
Michigan	**1879**	**1879**		1930
Minnesota	1898	**1879**		1930
Mississippi	1943	**1886**		1994
Missouri	1923	**1886**	1949	1960
Montana	1964	**1881**		1993
Nebraska	1965	**1879**	1949	1965
Nevada	1945	**1882**		1996
New Hampshire	1965	1885	**1874**	1930
New Jersey	**1885**	**1885**		1950
New Mexico	1945	**1883**		1930
New York	**1877**	1885		1955
North Carolina	1944	1887	**1778**	1945
North Dakota	1926	**1867**		1930
Ohio	**1821**	**1821**		1992
Oklahoma	1942	**1890**	1949	1994
Oregon	1945	**1853**		1950
Pennsylvania	**1885**	**1885**		1950
Rhode Island	1965	1885	**1828**	1950
South Carolina	1964	**1887**	1900	1996
South Dakota	1966	**1867**		1965
Tennessee	1944	**1886**		1950
Texas	**1886**	**1886**		1950
Utah	1945	**1881**		1950
Vermont	1963	**1885**		1930
Virginia	**1730**	1887		1930
Washington	1898	**1854**		1940
West Virginia	1964	**1887**		1991
Wisconsin	1936	**1879**	1939	1945
Wyoming	1959	**1883**		1993

Note: The earliest date in each state is highlighted in bold.

The most important part of many digest volumes is the annual pocket part supplement, which provides access to the recent cases. For newly developing areas of law, such as social host liability, this may be the place where *all* relevant cases are found. Supplements too bulky to fit in the back of the volume are issued as freestanding pamphlets, and eventually the material may be recompiled and republished as two separate volumes. Each digest is further updated between annual supplements by an additional pamphlet issued every few months, and the latest cases can be found through digests in recent reporter volumes and advance sheets.

Researchers can access state digests in two ways. The first is through the "Descriptive-Word Index," shelved at either the beginning or the end of the set. This index, usually occupying three or four volumes, lists factual and legal concepts appearing in the digest. The basic format is the same from state to state because the indexes are based on digest topics and key number definitions, rather than state case law. Even if a state has no cases on a particular issue, it remains in the index. Guardian and Ward key number 5, "Guardians in Socage," has had cases from only four states, and from just one state since 1900. Yet it remains in every digest and an entry under "Socage" appears in every state digest's descriptive-word index.

The descriptive-word indexes are not always responsive to developments in state case law. Whether "Social host" appears in the index varies from state to state, but its inclusion seems to have little relation to whether the state has cases on the issue. Georgia and Pennsylvania both have cases on social host liability, but neither index includes an entry under "Social host." The index volumes are updated with annual pocket parts, but these are invariably scrawny supplements that do not even attempt to keep track of state case law developments. Occasionally a specific entry will appear, such as "Shopping center—Injuries to child jumping over trench near loading dock," but generally and unfortunately the indexes are the neglected backwaters of the digests.

A simpler and more reliable method to find cases in the digest bypasses the index. If other research approaches are used to find a relevant case, its headnotes can be used to determine appropriate digest topics and key numbers. A person researching social host liability in Massachusetts, for example, might read a law review article that discusses the *McGuiggan v. New England Tel. & Tel. Co.* and *Manning v. Nobile* cases cited earlier in this chapter. Those cases, as published in the *North Eastern Reporter* or on WESTLAW, contain headnotes classified to Intoxicating Liquors 299 and can lead directly to other cases, such as *Hamilton v. Ganias,* discussed earlier.

Each state digest also includes a "Table of Cases," listing decisions by plaintiff's name, and a "Defendant-Plaintiff Table." Both provide citations to regional and official reports, if available. The "Tables of Cases" list the key numbers under which case abstracts are found and indicate if there were any subsequent developments in the case such as an affirmance or reversal by a higher court. These tables are updated in annual pocket parts, but only the "Tables of Cases" are further updated in the interim supplements. For recent cases, it may also be necessary to check the "Cases Reported" tables in the reporter volumes and advance sheets. The regional reporter advance sheets list cases by jurisdiction, or by plaintiff only, but the bound volumes also include a table listing all cases alphabetically under both parties' names.

Another feature that may be of occasional use is the "Words and Phrases" table, generally found in a volume at the end of the set. Unlike the more general publication *Words and Phrases*, discussed in Chapter 2, this table does not reprint definitions but simply gives the names and citations of the cases (including the page on which the definition appears). It is not, therefore, as convenient a place to study the meaning of a term, but it is a handy research source because it is limited to a specific jurisdiction. Like the case tables, this feature is updated in pocket parts, supplements, and recent reporter volumes and advance sheets.

Multistate Digests

It may be necessary to expand research beyond an individual state for a number of reasons. Perhaps no cases on point can be found in the state's courts, making it necessary to look for relevant case law from other jurisdictions. Or perhaps the ruling case law from the state is old and seems ripe for reconsideration. More modern cases from other jurisdictions may persuade a state supreme court to reconsider its earlier position.

For research into the law of more than one state, the uniform editorial treatment of the West system is invaluable. It is a simple matter to transfer research from one state to another, or to resources covering all states at once.

Besides the digests for individual states, West Group publishes several digests with broader coverage of state courts. A series of regional digests match the coverage of West's regional reporters, while *Decennial*

15 Mass D 2d—13   **INTOXICATING LIQUORS** ⟐299

evidence of negligence. M.G.L.A. c. 138, § 69.—Bennett v. Eagle Brook Country Store, Inc., 546 N.E.2d 174, 28 Mass.App.Ct. 35, review granted 548 N.E.2d 887, 406 Mass. 1102, reversed 557 N.E.2d 1166, 408 Mass. 355.

⟐288. —— **Injuries to person.**
D.Mass. 1994. Wilful, wanton, or reckless standard, rather than negligence standard, applies under Massachusetts law to claims against person or entity that serves alcohol to intoxicated person who then injures himself or herself. M.G.L.A. c. 231, § 85T.—Griffith v. U.S., 858 F.Supp. 278.

"Wilful, wanton, or reckless conduct" for which person or entity may be held liable under Massachusetts law for serving alcohol to intoxicated person who then injures himself or herself is intentional conduct, by way either of commission or omission when there is duty to act, that involves high degree of likelihood that substantial harm will result to another. M.G.L.A. c. 231, § 85T.—Id.

Mass.App.Ct. 1993. Victims of assault by tavern patron had no cognizable claim against tavern for negligently serving patron, as evidence, including patron's consumption of approximately eight beers over period of about two hours, would not support inference that tavern was put on notice that it was serving alcohol to intoxicated person; there was no evidence that patron's conduct in tavern was aggressive, troublesome, or even loud and vulgar. M.G.L.A. c. 138, § 69.—Kirby v. Le Disco, Inc., 614 N.E.2d 1016, 34 Mass.App.Ct. 630.

⟐291. —— **Proximate cause of injury.**
C.A.1 (Mass.) 1989. Mere violation of Massachusetts statute making it illegal to serve person known by bartender to have been drunk within previous six months can serve as premise for tort duty and establish actual cause of harm, but while it is some evidence of negligence, it is insufficient by itself to show negligence and proximate causation. M.G.L.A. c. 138, § 69.—Swift v. U.S., 866 F.2d 507.

⟐295. —— **Contributory act or negligence.**
Mass. 1996. Where licensee serves alcohol to intoxicated minor, licensee's liability would not be precluded by statute providing that, in absence of willful, wanton, or reckless conduct on part of licensee, intoxicated person who was served by licensee may not maintain action against licensee for injuries that person causes to himself; statutory provisions regulating serving of alcohol refer to two classes of persons, intoxicated persons and minors, service to whom is subject of special concern and basis of regulatory action or liability. M.G.L.A. c. 231, § 85T.—Tobin v. Norwood Country Club, Inc., 661 N.E.2d 627, 422 Mass. 126.

Contributory negligence of minor who was killed when she was struck by car after consuming alcohol in defendant club would reduce damages recoverable in both suit on behalf of her estate, and on her parents' claim for minor's wrongful death. M.G.L.A. c. 231, § 85.—Id.

⟐299. —— **In general.**
D.Mass. 1994. Under Massachusetts law, social host is not liable to third party for damages caused by intoxicated guest unless host himself served or provided alcohol.—Daugherty v. Elmcrest, Inc., 853 F.Supp. 561.

Under Massachusetts law, for purposes of determining liability for damages caused by intoxicated person, commercial establishment is not analogous to social host.—Id.

Mass. 1996. Commercial establishment that supplies alcoholic beverages owes duty of care to minors if evidence shows that establishment knew or reasonably should have known that it was furnishing alcohol to minors, even if there was no "hand to hand" furnishing or selling of alcohol to minors.—Tobin v. Norwood Country Club, Inc., 661 N.E.2d 627, 422 Mass. 126.

Mass. 1994. Social hosts had no duty to 19-year-old underage guest who became intoxicated by voluntary consumption of alcohol and subsequently injured himself while negligently operating motor vehicle, in light of broad principle that guest was adult who was responsible for his own conduct, and in light of lack of wilful, wanton or reckless conduct by social hosts which would have been required to impose liability on commercial server of alcohol. M.G.L.A. c. 4, § 7, cl. 50; c. 231, § 85T.—Hamilton v. Ganias, 632 N.E.2d 407, 417 Mass. 666.

Mass. 1994. Employer did not furnish alcohol to employee and thus, under doctrine of host liability, employer owed no duty of care to protect members of general public from consequences of employee's intoxication, even if employer made no attempt to stop employee from drinking and knew or should have known that employee left work while intoxicated.—Kelly v. Avon Tape, Inc., 631 N.E.2d 1013, 417 Mass. 587.

Mass. 1993. Commercial vendor of alcoholic beverages may be liable to third person who was injured in motor vehicle accident negligently caused by customer after vendor sold alcohol to someone who vendor knew or reasonably should have known was intoxicated.—Mosko v. Raytheon Co., 622 N.E.2d 1066, 416 Mass. 395.

Employer that neither furnished nor controlled alcohol served at employer-sponsored party could not be held liable for injuries caused by employee's intoxicated driving; any benefit employer realized from hosting or sponsoring employee party did not justify departing from principle that host's duty of care derived from control over liquor supply.—Id.

Mass. 1993. In determining whether social host liability for tortious acts of motorists exists basic question is whether, in circumstances depicted by evidence, common-law duty of negligence is to be imposed on defendant for protection of travelers on highway.—Cremins v. Clancy, 612 N.E.2d 1183, 415 Mass. 289.

Friend did not have social host liability for injuries caused by intoxicated motorist who brought beer to friend's house and consumed it, while teenager provided setting and atmosphere.—Id.

Mass. 1991. Social host had no duty to protect motorcyclist from negligent driving of intoxicated guest who drank alcohol which he brought to host's party; even though host allowed underaged guest to continue drinking after observing guest in visibly intoxicated condition, host did not serve or make any of his own alcohol available to guest.—Ulwick v. DeChristopher, 582 N.E.2d 954, 411 Mass. 401.

Social host's violation of statutes prohibiting person in control of premises from allowing use of premises for illegal keeping of alcohol and prohibiting underage persons from possessing alcoholic beverages did not constitute breach of duty to protect motorcyclist from negligent driving of intoxicated guest. M.G.L.A. c. 138, § 34C; c. 139, § 20.—Id.

Mass. 1991. Statute protecting party licensed to serve alcohol from liability for injuries caused by negligent serving of alcohol to intoxicated person applied to owner of hotel in which alcohol was served to guest at private party although hotel owner did not directly serve alcohol to guest. M.G.L.A. c. 231, § 85T.—Manning v. Nobile, 582 N.E.2d 942, 411 Mass. 382.

By using word "serve" in statute protecting parties licensed to serve alcohol from liability for injuries caused by negligent serving of alcohol to intoxicated person, Legislature did not intend to restrict statute's scope to cases in which defendant or his employees visibly dispenses alcohol to plaintiff. M.G.L.A. c. 231, § 85T.—Id.

EXHIBIT 12-4

Digests contain references to cases from the entire country, including both federal and state courts.

West publishes digests covering four of its regional reporters—*Atlantic, North Western, Pacific,* and *South Eastern.* It has discontinued digests covering the other three regions, *North Eastern, South Western,* and *Southern.* The digests for the *Atlantic, North Western,* and *South Eastern* regions are in second series, covering back to the 1930s, and the *Pacific Digest* is in five separate series with the most recent beginning coverage in 1978.

The valuable service the *Atlantic* and *Pacific Digests* provide is coverage of court decisions from Delaware, Nevada, and Utah, the states omitted from West's roster of state digests. For states other than these three, the value of these sets is marginal if other digests are available. Federal cases, even on topics of state law, are not included, and the grouping of states is based on the artificial boundaries of the West reporters. A Kansas researcher has access in the *Pacific Digest* to cases from Alaska and Oregon, but not cases from Missouri or Nebraska. It makes more sense either to focus on Kansas law or to use a comprehensive digest that does not draw arbitrary distinctions among other states.

West's comprehensive digest is a truly mammoth publication known as the *American Digest System.* This set of publications covers every case West publishes from the federal and state courts, as well as cases in other reporters before West began its publications. It consists of three distinct publications: the *Century Digest, Decennial Digests,* and *General Digests.*

The *Century Edition of the American Digest,* or *Century Digest* (50 vols., 1897-1904), covers decisions from "the earliest times" to 1896. This is a valuable source for historical research, but it is little used in modern legal research. The *Century Digest* uses a somewhat different classification system from the key numbers used in later digests, but cross-references are provided to it from its successor, the *First Decennial Digest.*

From 1897 to 1976, eight *Decennial Digests* each compiled 10 years' worth of headnotes. These grew increasingly cumbersome, and now *Decennial Digests* appear every five years. The *Tenth Decennial Digest, Part 2* is the most recent installment, covering cases from 1991 to 1996. Even at five-year intervals, these are still massive sets with dozens of volumes. The topic "Criminal Law" covers more than nine volumes in the 1991-96 compilation, with some individual key numbers spanning more than 100 pages. Criminal Law 1134(3), "Scope of review—Questions considered in general," occupies 156 pages, with most states represented by dozens or hundreds of cases for this five-year period alone. Intoxicating Liquors 299, the key number shown in Exhibit 12-4, takes up about seven pages in this digest, with 116 cases from courts in 31 states.

The latest *Decennial Digest* is supplemented by *General Digest* volumes, published every three or four weeks to provide access to new cases. Each *General Digest* gathers the digest references from the advance sheets in West's federal and regional reporters into one sequence of about 1,200 pages. The individual volumes do not cumulate, and over the course of five years 70 or more volumes are published. These are then compiled into a new *Decennial Digest,* which is published gradually over the course of a year or two.

To ease the burden of checking dozens of recent volumes for a specific key number, *General Digest* volumes include a "Table of Key Numbers" listing the volumes in which each number appears. These tables cumulate over the course of 10 volumes and then start over. After 37 *General Digest* volumes, for example, it would be necessary to check these tables in volumes 10 (covering 1-10), 20 (11-20), 30 (21-30), and 36 (31-37). Intoxicating Liquors 299 appears in about half the volumes, but some numbers may appear in one or two volumes or not at all.

Hunting for cases in several *Decennial Digest* and *General Digest* volumes may not be painless, but these sets will continue to serve a purpose until everyone has access to comprehensive full-text databases. Until then, they are the most extensive sources of case information available to the public in most law libraries.

In *Decennial* or *General Digests,* abstracts under each key number are printed in the same order by jurisdiction. Federal cases are first, starting with the Supreme Court and then the courts of appeals and the district courts. These are followed by state cases, beginning with the Alabama Supreme Court, in chronological order with the most recent first; Alabama appellate courts; Alaska Supreme Court; and on to the Wyoming Supreme Court at the end of each listing. It is thus possible to isolate cases from a particular state in the *Decennial* and *General Digests* if the state digest is not available. The advantage of a state digest is that references spanning 50 years or more are gathered in just two places: a volume and its pocket part. New cases in the state digests are cumulated into pocket part supplements every year, while dozens of *General Digest* volumes remain uncumulated until the end of a five-year period.

As the law develops, the digests gradually change to accommodate new issues and new legal doctrines. When state digests are issued in revised volumes, headnotes under the older numbers are actually reclassified to where they would be under the new system. The *Decennial Digests*, however, are not revised once they are published, and tracking an issue backward in time may require consulting cross-references to find earlier classifications. As an example, the topic "Chemical Dependents" was introduced in the *Ninth Decennial Digest, Part 1* (1976-81); for earlier cases, a table provides references to the older topic "Drunkards" and to selected portions of "Drugs and Narcotics."

Occasionally, when new topics are introduced, the *Decennial Digests* include retrospective coverage of cases in the area. When the topic "Mental Health" was added in the *Sixth Decennial Digest* (1946-56), it included notes of cases dating back to *Ex Parte Drayton*, 1 S.C. Eq. (1 Des.) 144 (1787). The same procedure has been followed for several other added topics, including "Zoning and Planning" 10 years later and "Securities Regulation" in 1976. This approach is not always used, however; when the topic "Racketeer Influenced and Corrupt Organizations" debuted in 1991, only cases from the preceding five-year period were listed.

Like other West digests, the *Decennial Digests* are accompanied by descriptive-word indexes. These are generally no better or worse than the indexes for the state digests. The 1986-91 index has no entry for "Social host," but includes "Socage," even though there have been no cases assigned to its key number since 1956. The *General Digests* have short and unhelpful descriptive-word indexes, in which the same few entries keep appearing volume after volume.

Among the *Decennial* and *General Digests*' more valuable features are their comprehensive tables of cases. If a case is mentioned without reference to its jurisdiction (or its citation), finding it may require checking these tables. It helps to have some idea of its date because it may otherwise be necessary to check several *Decennial* installments. Only the oldest and the most recent tables cumulate. The cases in the *Century Digest* and the *First Decennial Digest* are listed in a combined five-volume table covering all cases through 1906, and *General Digest* tables cumulate in every tenth volume.

The tables in older *Decennial Digests* and in *General Digest* volumes list cases by plaintiff only, but *Decennial Digests* since 1976 include defendant-plaintiff tables as well. One useful purpose for tables such as these is finding cases involving particular corporate defendants, although it is important to remember that digest coverage is limited to reported cases and by no means represents a comprehensive list of lawsuits.

Although the *Decennial* and *General Digests* are huge, unwieldy publications, they represent an enormous effort to analyze and classify millions of court decisions. This may seem increasingly archaic in an age of electronic dissemination and full-text access, but digests still handle some research queries better than computers can. The resolution of legal issues often requires consideration of rules applied in analogous situations, even if the same search terms do not necessarily appear. A tool that gathers legally similar cases by subject serves a valuable purpose.

WESTLAW users can have it both ways by combining full-text access and keyword searching with the digests' editorial enhancements. WESTLAW incorporates the digests into its online system in several ways. The most significant is by including in the case databases the headnotes and digest classifications for cases published in West reporters. As a result, the terms appearing in the headnotes, as well as digest topics and key numbers, can be incorporated into searches. Topics can be searched by name, as in *topic("intoxicating liquors")*, while key number searches combine numbers for the topic and section. "Intoxicating Liquors" is topic 223, so a search for *223k299 and underage* would lead directly to the *Hamilton* case discussed earlier.

Case headnotes displayed by WESTLAW are linked to the digests themselves. Clicking on the number next to the name of a topic or one of its subdivisions leads to a choice of exploring the digest outline or incorporating the classification into a new search. This search is run not in the full-text cases but in a database of just headnotes. For most purposes, full-text databases provide more flexibility and greater power, but these databases limited to case headnotes are worth mentioning for one reason. Because they are based on the digest entries, not the cases themselves, they are more comprehensive than the full-text files. The full-text MA-CS database goes back to 1885, but the MA-HN database includes the earliest reported colonial cases from Massachusetts. Links are provided from digest entries to the full text of cases available online.

WESTLAW also has databases combining headnotes from every state (ALLSTATES-HN) and state and federal courts (ALLCASES-HN). The headnotes include the names of the cases, making these the most comprehensive sources for finding cases involving specific parties and a valuable resource for historians and genealogists. A search in ALLCASES-HN for *ti(smith)* retrieves more than 250,000 documents, while *ti(exxon)* finds just under 5,000. Be aware, however, that these numbers represent the number of headnotes and not the number of cases involving these parties. Each headnote is a separate document, and most cases are represented by several entries. A search for *ti(oryx)* retrieves 146 documents, but these represent just 16 cases.

American Law Reports (ALR)

Another means of access to opinions from courts around the country is *American Law Reports: Cases and Annotations (ALR)*, which contains articles summarizing cases on particular topics. *ALR* was published for decades by Lawyers Cooperative Publishing Company, but it is now a West Group product. *ALR* has been published in several series since it began in 1919; its current fifth series began in 1992. (A separate series covering issues of federal law, *ALR Federal*, has already been discussed in Chapter 9.)

ALR fills a unique niche in legal research literature because it is somewhat like a legal encyclopedia, somewhat like a digest, and somewhat like a law journal. Like an encyclopedia, it provides a broad overview of legal doctrine. Like a digest, it contains extensive summaries of cases and serves primarily as an aid in finding relevant case law. Like a journal, it is published periodically with no particular order to its contents. Each annotation includes one illustrative case, as a vestige of *ALR*'s origin as a selective case reporter. Until the beginning of *ALR5th*, the cases were printed before each annotation, but now they appear in a separate section at the back of the volume.

Some *ALR* annotations are on rather narrow topics, such as "Liability for Injuries Caused by Cat," 68 ALR4th 823 (1989), while others are relatively broad. Recent annotations on the liability of landlords for failure to protect tenants from criminal acts, 43 ALR5th 207 (1996), and for repairs authorized by tenants, 46 ALR5th 1 (1997), have run several hundred pages apiece. One of the lengthiest annotations, "Propriety of Execution of Search Warrant at Nighttime," 41 ALR5th 171 (1996), occupies almost 600 pages.

On issues of social host liability, *ALR* has published two substantial annotations. "Social Host's Liability for Injuries Incurred by Third Parties as a Result of Intoxicated Guest's Negligence," 62 ALR4th 16 (1989), has been followed by "Social Host's Liability for Death or Injuries Incurred by Person to Whom Alcohol was Served," 54 ALR5th 313 (1997). The latter annotation collects decisions from 22 states on this issue, sorts them according to the theories of liability on which they are based and particular circumstances affecting the decisions, and summarizes the holdings. Liability can be based, for example, on common law negligence, reckless misconduct, intentional tort, or violation of statutes. The ages of the host and the guest can be important factors, as can their behavior. Did the host induce a state of intoxication or fail to assist a guest in need? Did the guest knowingly decide to ride in a vehicle with an intoxicated driver?

Under each of these circumstances, decisions in some cases have held the host subject to liability, and others have not. These diverging results are indicated by the division of most sections of the annotation into "[a]" and "[b]" subsections. Comparing the cases provides an opportunity to analyze how a court might consider particular circumstances. Exhibit 12-5 shows a summary of *Hamilton v. Ganias* under § 22[b], as an example of a case where the court considered the age of the guest as a factor and decided not to impose liability. Note that this summary is more extensive than a digest entry, with background on the facts of the case and the reasoning behind the court's decision.

Several other features make this *ALR* annotation a useful research source. A page of "Research References" at the beginning provides leads to other publications, including legal encyclopedias, digests, and law review articles. The electronic search queries that were used to find cases on point are also included. This is followed by a detailed alphabetical index of specific factual and legal issues discussed, such as "Absence of homeowners from premises" and "Adult guest still under legal drinking age," and by a jurisdictional table listing the cases discussed as well as statutes in issue. Under Massachusetts, the two cases listed are *Hamilton* and *Manning v. Nobile*. Several of these editorial features were expanded and improved for the current *ALR5th* series. Earlier annotations, for example, lack references to digests and online searches, and their tables of jurisdictions simply list the section numbers at which cases from each state appear, omitting the names and citations of the cases.

The social host liability annotation begins with a summary of its scope and a list of other *ALR* annotations on related topics. This list can be useful in suggesting analogous situations. In this instance, it includes not only the earlier work on social host liability but annotations on such topics as the liability of colleges or fraternities for injuries incurred during initiation ac-

§ 22[a]   ALCOHOL—SOCIAL-HOST LIABILITY   54 ALR5th
54 ALR5th 313

years of age and an adult on the day preceding his 21st birthday. On appeal, however, the court declared this determination to be erroneous, explaining that the common-law rule was not applicable in the case before it. It is common knowledge, the court observed, that when an individual is requested to provide identification at a liquor store or bar, alcohol will be served to him or her only if he or she shows proof of being 21. In enacting 18 Pa Cons Stat § 6308, which provides that a person "less than 21 years of age" commits a crime if he or she attempts to purchase, purchases, possesses, or consumes alcohol, continued the court, the legislature intended that it be interpreted in accordance with the commonly accepted and practiced method for determining the legal age for the purchase and consumption of alcohol, and a common-law rule cannot be utilized to override the reasonable intent of the legislature in enacting a statute. Accordingly, the court concluded, the decedent was a minor on the day preceding his 21st birthday, and his parents could maintain a cause of action based upon his roommates' negligent furnishing of alcohol to him.

[b] Social host not subject to liability

The court in the following case indicated that a social host could not be held liable for the injuries or death of a guest who was over the legal age of majority but under the legal drinking age.

Affirming the judgment below, the court in Hamilton v Ganias (1994) 417 **Mass** 666, 632 NE2d 407, summary op at (Mass) 22 MLW 1793, held that a 19-year-old underage drinker could not recover damages from two social hosts for personal injuries he sustained in a motorcycle accident. The court noted that in Manning v Nobile (1991) 411 **Mass** 382, 582 NE2d 942, § 11, it was held that a social host had no duty to an adult guest who became intoxicated and subsequently injured himself while negligently operating a motor vehicle. For the same reasons stated in Manning, the court declared, the result is no different where the guest is a 19-year-old. Although under the legal drinking age, observed the court, a 19-year-old is an adult who is responsible for his own conduct. He is old enough to vote, to make a valid will, to marry without parental consent, to serve on a jury, to work at any job, to carry a firearm, and to be treated as an adult in the criminal justice system, noted the court. Accordingly, the court concluded, the plaintiff's voluntary consumption of alcohol foreclosed the existence of any duty owed to him by the social hosts.

§ 23. Guest's decision to drive a vehicle after consuming alcohol

In the following case, the court held that the fact that an intoxicated party guest voluntarily drove his automobile on a public highway served

372

EXHIBIT 12-5

tivities, proof of causation of intoxication, and products liability for alcoholic beverages. Scanning these annotations might raise issues that might not otherwise have come to mind.

Section 2[a] of the annotation then goes on to provide a general overview of the topic, integrating as best as possible the conclusions drawn from case law in two dozen jurisdictions. Section 2[b] notes several "practice pointers" for counsel bringing or defending a cause of action for social host liability. The rest of the annotation summarizes and analyzes the individual cases, as shown in Exhibit 12-5. Unlike a digest, which simply consists of individual abstracts, *ALR* attempts to coordinate the various cases into a reasonably coherent picture of the state of the law.

A major advantage of *ALR* is that each annotation is supplemented after publication by notes of new cases and references to more recent annotations on related topics. Modern annotations (since 1965) in *ALR3d*, *ALR4th*, and *ALR5th* are updated with annual pocket parts in each volume. Pre-*ALR3d* annotations are less frequently used and have different updating systems. Volumes in the *ALR2d* series (100 vols., 1948-65) had no flaps for pocket parts, so they are updated with separate *Later Case Service* volumes, each of which covers up to four *ALR2d* volumes; these in turn have pocket parts for recent developments. The first series of *ALR* (175 vols., 1919-48) is rarely used today except for long-settled areas such as property law. Many of its annotations have been superseded by more recent treatments in later series, but some continue to be updated through an annual *ALR Blue Book of Supplemental Decisions,* which simply lists the citations of more recent cases. One set of *Blue Book* volumes covers the entire set of 175 *ALR* volumes. Of course, these older annotations may be useful for historical research, as may their predecessors in *American Decisions* (Bancroft, 100 vols., 1878-88), *American Reports* (Parsons, 60 vols., 1871-88), *American State Reports* (Bancroft-Whitney, 140 vols., 1888-1911), and *Lawyers' Reports Annotated* (Lawyers Cooperative, 146 vols., 1888-1918).

When using an *ALR* annotation, it is always important to check the latest supplement, not only for notification of the most recent cases but also for cross-references. From time to time, older annotations are superseded or supplemented, and the pocket part or supplement simply provides a cross-reference to the newer treatment instead of noting new cases. (This information is noted as well in an "Annotation History Table" in the final volume of the *ALR Index*.)

The *ALR* sets are accompanied by two indexes providing subject access. The more comprehensive is a six-volume *ALR Index,* covering *ALR2d* through *5th*, *ALR Federal,* and *Lawyers' Edition 2d,* with quarterly pocket parts. (An *ALR First Series Quick Index* covers the little-used first series.) A separate *ALR Quick Index*, covering *ALR3d, ALR4th,* and *ALR5th*, is an annual paperback which may be more convenient. Its typeface is smaller, but the entire alphabet is contained in one volume. These indexes are fairly easy to navigate, perhaps because they do not have to be as comprehensive as the indexes to digests or statutes. There is no entry under "Social host," but "Social guest" provides a cross-reference to "Guests, invitees, or licensees," where the social host annotations can be found under the subheadings "Driving while intoxicated" and "Intoxicating liquors."

Shelved near the *ALR Index*, and possibly subject to confusion with it, is a separate set of 18 volumes labeled *ALR Digest to 3d, 4th, 5th and Federal*. This set classifies the annotations and cases printed in *ALR* by topic, in a manner similar to West's digest series. There is no separate index to this set, so the main means of access is from the headnotes *ALR* provides for the cases it publishes. Because *ALR* is an alternative to the digest system, it is hard to imagine much reason for the *ALR Digest*'s existence. Perhaps it may be of occasional use in placing an issue covered by *ALR* in a broader context.

ALR3d through *5th* are also available on CD-ROM and on WESTLAW (ALR database), and coverage in LEXIS-NEXIS (ALR library, ALR file) goes all the way back to the beginning of *ALR2d*. Online searches may be more effective if they are limited to the titles of annotations. Because the facts of each case are summarized, whether or not they are pertinent to the topic of the annotation, a full-text search may retrieve a large number of annotations on completely unrelated issues. A search for *title(social host)* retrieves the two annotations specifically on point, while a full-text search for *social host* retrieves several dozen documents, including annotations on insurance company insolvency, admissibility of hospital records, and applicability of strict liability rules to injury from electrical current escaping from power lines.

In addition to the *ALR Index*, several other legal publications provide access to annotations. Many state codes include references to *ALR* annotations, and the citators to be discussed in the following section include annotations among the material they list citing cases.

Shepard's Citations and KeyCite

The producers of both LEXIS-NEXIS and WESTLAW offer comprehensive resources listing cases and other documents citing decisions from the state courts. *Shepard's Citations* (formerly published by Shepard's, Inc., but now owned by Reed-Elsevier) is available in print as well as in CD-ROM, through both LEXIS-NEXIS and WESTLAW, and on the Internet <http://www.bender.com/>. KeyCite is available only electronically, through WESTLAW or on the Internet <http://www.keycite.com/>. A third service, Auto-Cite, provides more limited information and is available only through LEXIS-NEXIS.

Shepard's Citations and KeyCite are powerful tools for checking the status of a case and for finding more recent cases on related issues. Both work from citations of cases, so they are not places to begin research or to find cases by subject. Once a relevant case has been found, however, they can provide a broad range of information.

The simplest and most straightforward function of *Shepard's* and KeyCite is to verify the accuracy of a citation and to supply its parallel citation, if one is available. Finding the parallel citation is valuable for someone with a regional reporter citation who needs the official citation for a brief, or for someone with an official citation who needs to find a case in a library with only regional reporters. Parallel citations are not available for all cases; the West reporters do not cover cases before the 1880s, and 19 states no longer publish official reports.

The parallel citations are followed by references to other documents, some of which represent different stages of the same litigation and some of which cite the case. These are important resources for determining a case's value as precedent. A case's status can be affected in several ways, including reversal by a higher court or a later overruling by the same court. Later cases may either limit a decision's holding to narrowly defined facts or apply its reasoning to other situations. Someone looking for information on *McGuiggan v. New England Tel. & Tel. Co.* in *Shepard's Citations* or KeyCite would find references to *Manning v. Nobile* and *Hamilton v. Ganias*, which distinguish its reasoning in cases of injuries to third parties from cases in which an intoxicated guest has injured himself or herself. This information is presented in different ways in the two systems.

Exhibit 12-6 shows a page from *Shepard's Northeastern Reporter Citations*, including the citation for *McGuiggan*, 496 N.E.2d 141. *Shepard's* arranges cases chronologically by jurisdiction, with Massachusetts cases listed first. Note that the citations for several cases are preceded by one-letter abbreviations such as "d" or "f." A table at the front of each *Shepard's* volume explains these abbreviations, noting that "d" stands for "distinguished" and "f" for "followed." In the *McGuiggan* listing, the *Hamilton v. Ganias* reference, 632 N.E.2d 408, is one of several that distinguish their circumstances from those in *McGuiggan*. Other recent cases, however, follow *McGuiggan* or explain its holding ("e"). The *Hamilton* reference is followed by a federal case from the First Circuit and by cases from several other states.

Shepard's publishes two separate citators covering Massachusetts cases: *Shepard's Massachusetts Citations* and *Shepard's Northeastern Reporter Citations*. Either source can be used to determine if a case has been reversed or overruled. There are, however, differences between the two publications. The most significant is in their scope of coverage of citing material. Both include later cases from Massachusetts, as well as federal court decisions and *ALR* annotations. Only the regional *Shepard's* (including *Shepard's California Reporter Citations* and *Shepard's New York Supplement Citations*) have references to cases from other states, however, and only the state *Shepard's* provide any references to law review articles and other sources such as attorney general opinions. This means that a thorough search for documents citing a particular case may require checking both *Shepard's Massachusetts Citations* and *Shepard's Northeastern Reporter Citations*. (For cases before the start of the National Reporter System, and therefore without regional reporter citations, *Shepard's* does list cases from other states under official citations in the state volumes. If a state has discontinued its official reports in recent years, it is still necessary to check both the state and regional *Shepard's* units, but all information is listed under the regional citation.)

Shepard's presents different information based on the citation used. Only *Shepard's Massachusetts Citations* lists cases under their official *Massachusetts Reports* citations, with references to later cases in the same set of volumes. *Shepard's Massachusetts Citations* also contains a section listing cases under their *North Eastern Reporter* citations, with citations in later cases in that reporter series. This duplicates much of the coverage in *Shepard's Northeastern Reporter Citations* but omits the cases from other states. There may be differences between the references listed under these two reporter citations. Some citing references, including

NORTHEASTERN REPORTER, 2nd Series — Vol. 496

—49—

Harrison
v Indiana
1986

cc 575 NE642
501 NE[12]449
501 NE1037
501 NE[7]1040
502 NE[11]103
502 NE[12]103
507 NE[13]973
508 NE[12]797
534 NE[6]1109
11A2870s
14A4227s

—53—

Allen v Indiana
1986

j 519 NE1282
539 NE[1]939
557 NE[1]669
557 NE[2]669
562 NE724
567 NE[1]865
580 NE224

—55—

Von Almen
v Indiana
1986

512 NE[3]876
519 NE[10]142
519 NE[12]142
532 NE[4]1164
567 NE[4]112
582 NE401
598 NE[11]1047

—60—

Wright v
Indiana
1986

548 NE[1]841
637 NE[1]829
Mich
455 NW724
459 NW90
475 NW338
S D
417 NW405
57A2302s

—61—

McKinney
v Indiana
1986

504 NE1013
510 NE657

—63—

Arnold v
Melvin
R. Hall Inc.
1986

s 478 NE696
s 481 NE409
532 NE[6]27
546 NE[4]1229
546 NE[5]1230
579 NE[6]128
Cir. 7
856F2d[3]822
884F2d[6]969
j 884F2d972

—67—

Hadley v
Indiana
1986

499 NE[12]1125
500 NE[4]156
503 NE[12]409
509 NE[4]814
511 NE446
515 NE[5]1380
516 NE[4]30
f 529 NE[4]327
534 NE[8]724
f 540 NE[8]594
540 NE[4]606
543 NE633
547 NE[8]1049
563 NE[8]105
619 NE289
622 NE[8]472
Cir. 7
748FS[5]684
73A2769s

—75—

Mers v Indiana
1986

496 NE[3]579
496 NE[15]581
j 497 NE1058
505 NE[10]824
j 508 NE23
512 NE[9]857
512 NE[10]857
528 NE[4]1145
539 NE[11]20
f 540 NE1181
542 NE[5]552
544 NE[8]160
e 563 NE[1]96
587 NE[6]740
67A2245s

—84—

Chaffee v Clark
Equipment Co.
1986

s 480 NE236
s 519 NE574
533 NE[1]1211
622 NE[2]1324
95A3541s

—87—

Phillips v
Indiana
1986

503 NE[5]1244
509 NE[4]881
519 NE[4]566
523 NE[2]413
523 NE[5]426
524 NE[7]784
526 NE[3]980
549 NE[6]1033
f 551 NE[3]1157
f 562 NE[3]1312
563 NE[3]614
567 NE[6]123
578 NE348
588 NE[4]1300
593 NE[3]196
598 NE523
f 637 NE[3]830
638 NE1322
j 638 NE1325
26MJ718
Ill
530 NE[3]1365
532 NE547
579 NE[4]354
Ala
504 So2d351
518 So2d866
545 So2d148
548 So2d1087
571 So2d383
Ariz
753 P2d1173
760 P2d545
Md
527 A2d342
Va
358 SE592
79A314s

—90—

Kaufman
v Indiana
1986

535 NE[1]496

—91—

Scott County
School District
2 v Dietrich
1986

s 499 NE[1]1170
509 NE[1]1142

—93—

Ray v Indiana
1986

s 466 NE1389
s 512 NE841
542 NE[10]564
562 NE1320
578 NE[1]384
590 NE[5]637
593 NE[7]185
f 627 NE[10]824

—103—

Geller v Meek
1986

586 NE[2]937

—111—

M & K
Corp. v
Farmers
State Bank
1986

j 505 NE473
509 NE255
517 NE[1]432
519 NE[1]159
535 NE[3]571
Cir. 7
874F2d478
Mass
524 NE[2]393
Ga
361 SE532

—115—

Orr v Turco
Manufacturing
Company Inc.
1986

v 512 NE151
s 484 NE1300
f 505 NE[3]811
510 NE[3]741
513 NE677
q 534 NE756

—119—

Kordick v
Merchants
National Bank
and Trust
Company of
Indianapolis
1986

505 NE[7]466
505 NE[8]466
540 NE[8]28
549 NE769
569 NE[8]758
584 NE[7]587
587 NE668
591 NE[8]647
612 NE[2]141
612 NE[3]141
f 625 NE[6]1262
625 NE[5]1263
f 625 NE[8]1263
625 NE[10]1263
636 NE[8]171
Cir. 1
807FS[6]854
Cir. 7
845F2d[2]729
887F2d[8]824
732FS[8]952
Ill
j 529 NE33
529 NE[6]33
Mo
805 SW354
Tex
788 SW184

—125—

Bremen Public
Schools
v Varab
1986

j 504 NE344
548 NE[2]837

—128—

Umbarger
v Bolby
1986

514 NE[1]648
95A212s

—129—

Chase
Manhattan
Bank v
Lake Tire
Company Inc.
1986

505 NE[2]459

516 NE1097
529 NE381
533 NE168
Cir. 8
836FS657

—135—

Yaney v
McCray
Memorial
Hospital
1986

516 NE[2]55
532 NE[2]1194
570 NE290
570 NE[2]969
597 NE317
627 NE[1]447
Cir. 7
f 791FS1341

—141—

McGuiggan v
New England
Telephone and
Telegraph Co.
1986

(398Mas152)
d 495 NE[1]847
d 495 NE[2]848
509 NE[2]1201
514 NE[1]102
520 NE[1]1285
j 520 NE1287
528 NE151
531 NE[1]603
550 NE[2]902
557 NE1169
563 NE[2]233
582 NE945
d 582 NE[2]947
d 582 NE[2]956
582 NE958
612 NE[2]1185
f 612 NE1187
e 622 NE[2]1067
d 632 NE408
Cir. 1
905F2d[3]523
Ill
586 NE[2]374
Ind
519 NE[2]1227
Ohio
524 NE[2]174
Colo
815 P2d950
Haw
788 P2d162
La
524 So2d52
N C
438 SE431

1385

EXHIBIT 12-6

several listed under *McGuiggan* in Exhibit 12-6, include small numbers indicating which *McGuiggan* headnote's point of law is being discussed. If the official reports use different systems of headnotes than the regional reporters, these numbers will not be the same in the two sources. *McGuiggan,* for example, has four headnotes in *Massachusetts Reports,* and three in the *North Eastern Reporter.* When searching for cases on a particular topic, it is important not to get these headnote numbers mixed up.

Exhibit 12-7 shows a KeyCite display for *McGuiggan.* The arrangement of the citing cases is not based on date or jurisdiction but on (1) whether their effect on *McGuiggan* can be seen as negative, and (2) the extent to which they discuss the case. The negative cases are listed first. These may not necessarily affect the strength of *McGuiggan* as precedent. They may be decisions from other states that decline to follow its rules in their jurisdictions or decisions that choose not to extend the *McGuiggan* rationale to other situations. These are followed by "positive cases," or cases that do not criticize or limit *McGuiggan.* Cases listed first examine the case at length, followed by those that discuss it and merely cite it. In Exhibit 12-7, *Hamilton* is number 11, listed among the cases that cite *McGuiggan.* Quotation marks after some of the cases listed (not *Hamilton*) indicate that they quote directly from the language of the *McGuiggan* opinion.

Both *Shepard's Citations* and KeyCite can be used to find later citing cases. The results are similar, but arranged differently and with different editorial features. Only *Shepard's* notes cases that follow or explain a holding, but it simply lists the Hawaii and Indiana cases while KeyCite notes that they decline to follow the *McGuiggan* rationale. Each has some information about later cases that the other lacks.

Both services also provide references to journal articles citing cases, but here *Shepard's Citations* is no match for KeyCite. *Shepard's* claims to list articles from major journals in a court's home state as well as 19 national law reviews, but it does not even cover comprehensively this small group. KeyCite's coverage of law reviews, based not on a list of selected journals but on the articles in WESTLAW's databases, is far more thorough. For *McGuiggan v. New England Tel. & Tel. Co.,* *Shepard's* lists five articles. KeyCite has only one of these, the 1988 *Boston University Law Review* note listed at the bottom of Exhibit 12-7, but it adds articles from 20 other journals—including several that *Shepard's* claims to cover, such as *Cornell Law Review,* *Harvard Law Review,* and *Northwestern Univer-*

sity Law Review. Generally, the only articles listed in *Shepard's* but lacking in KeyCite are those too old to be included in WESTLAW's full-text online databases.

The Internet sites for both *Shepard's Citations* and KeyCite are fee-based, with a charge incurred for each citation checked. The *Shepard's* site has one advantage, in that no fee is charged until information on a specific citation is requested. The preliminary part of this process, finding the appropriate citation, is free. A citation can be entered, and the name and date of the case and its parallel citation display. Even more valuable is the ability to find cases by party name. The search *hamilton* in Massachusetts cases retrieves a list of 98 cases, including *Hamilton v. Ganias.* Party name searches cannot be run in the entire national database, but must be limited to particular state or regional databases.

Other resources provide some of the information available from *Shepard's Citations* and KeyCite. West publishes a series of *National Reporter Blue Book* volumes (7 vols., 1928-89, with annual pamphlet supplement) with cross-reference tables for finding parallel citations. These are updated in tables printed at the front of regional reporter volumes and advance sheets. Auto-Cite, a citator service on LEXIS-NEXIS, provides parallel citations and references to any subsequent cases that affect the validity of a case as precedent, but it does not list all citing cases. For *McGuiggan,* it lists no later cases. It does, however, include references to *ALR,* so it may be a convenient method for finding relevant annotations.

RULES AND PROCEDURES

Anyone needing to deal directly with a court rather than simply study its decisions must have access to the rules governing its procedures. These rules take different forms in different states. Although a number of states base their rules on federal models, such as the Federal Rules of Civil Procedure, the Federal Rules of Criminal Procedure, and the Federal Rules of Evidence, other states have their own unique systems. Some state court procedures are governed by statutes or procedural codes, and some are a mix of statute and court rules.

State court rules are available in a number of printed and electronic sources. The simplest sources are pamphlets published by the states themselves, but these are usually limited to one particular set of rules and are not often updated. Commercial paperback compilations provide a much broader range of rules and related procedural statutes. Publications such as *Massachusetts*

Citations to the Case: limited to Headnotes = 2, Highest Court, Law Reviews
(Showing 37 of 60 documents)

Negative Cases

Declined to Follow by

1 Johnston v. KFC Nat. Management Co., 788 P.2d 159, 162+, 71 Haw. 229, 234+ (Hawai'i Feb 27, 1990) (NO. 13446) ★ ★

2 Gariup Const. Co., Inc. v. Foster, 519 N.E.2d 1224, 1227 (Ind. Mar 02, 1988) (NO. 75S03-8803-CV-288) ★ ★

Declined to Extend by

3 Ulwick v. DeChristopher, 582 N.E.2d 954, 956+, 411 Mass. 401, 404+ (Mass. Dec 16, 1991) (NO. 5644) ▼▼ ★ ★ ★ ★

Positive Cases

★ ★ ★ ★ Examined

4 Cremins v. Clancy, 612 N.E.2d 1183, 1185+, 415 Mass. 289, 291+ (Mass. May 17, 1993) (NO. 6130)

5 Manning v. Nobile, 582 N.E.2d 942, 945+, 411 Mass. 382, 386+ (Mass. Dec 11, 1991) (NO. 5573) ▼▼

★ ★ ★ Discussed

6 Vickowski v. Polish American Citizens Club of Town of Deerfield, Inc., 664 N.E.2d 429, 432+, 422 Mass. 606, 610+ (Mass. May 07, 1996) (NO. 06998) ▼▼

7 Tobin v. Norwood Country Club, Inc., 661 N.E.2d 627, 632+, 422 Mass. 126, 134+ (Mass. Feb 22, 1996) (NO. SJC-06919)

8 Mosko v. Raytheon Co., 622 N.E.2d 1066, 1067+, 416 Mass. 395, 397+ (Mass. Nov 10, 1993) (NO. M-6116)

9 Alioto v. Marnell, 520 N.E.2d 1284, 1285+, 402 Mass. 36, 38+ (Mass. Mar 29, 1988) (NO. N-4538) ▼▼

★ ★ Cited

10 Burroughs v. Com., 673 N.E.2d 1217, 1220, 423 Mass. 874, 878 (Mass. Dec 09, 1996) (NO. SJC-07083)

11 Hamilton v. Ganias, 632 N.E.2d 407, 408, 417 Mass. 666, 668 (Mass. May 04, 1994) (NO. W-6294, W-6371)

12 O'Gorman v. Antonio Rubinaccio & Sons, Inc., 563 N.E.2d 231, 233, 408 Mass. 758, 761 (Mass. Dec 05, 1990) (NO. 5352)

13 Bennett v. Eagle Brook Country Store, Inc., 557 N.E.2d 1166, 1169, 408 Mass. 355, 359 (Mass. Aug 16, 1990) (NO. 5290)

14 Dhimos v. Cormier, 509 N.E.2d 1199, 1201, 400 Mass. 504, 507 (Mass. Jul 14, 1987) (NO. M-4388)

15 Langemann v. Davis, 495 N.E.2d 847+, 398 Mass. 166+ (Mass. Aug 06, 1986) (NO. BARN-3967)

16 Hickingbotham v. Burke, 662 A.2d 297, 301+, 140 N.H. 28+ (N.H. Jul 24, 1995) (NO. 93-237) ▼▼

17 Ferreira v. Strack, 652 A.2d 965, 969 (R.I. Jan 24, 1995) (NO. 93-381-APPEAL) ▼▼

★ Mentioned

18 Charlton v. Kimata, 815 P.2d 946, 951 (Colo. Jul 15, 1991) (NO. 90SA118)

Non-Cases

19 WHEN THE PARTY'S OVER: McGUIGGAN v. NEW ENGLAND TELEPHONE AND TELEGRAPH CO. AND THE EMERGENCE OF A SOCIAL HOST LIABILITY STANDARD IN MASSACHUSETTS, 68 B.U. L. Rev. 193+ (1988)

Rules of Court and *Nebraska Court Rules and Procedure* (both West Group, annual) are designed to provide quick access to the text of the rules. Some of these paperbacks contain rules for both state courts and local federal courts; others have local federal rules in a separate volume. The official comments of the committees or reporters who drafted the rules are usually included, but not annotations of subsequent cases in which the rules are applied. These paperbacks are designed for lawyers who are familiar with the rules, and, thus, they do not provide much explanation or background information.

More thorough editions of court rules are generally published as part of state codes, sometimes in bound volumes updated by pocket parts and sometimes as softcover volumes replaced annually. These versions provide more in-depth coverage of the rules in a format similar to that used for statutes. The text of each rule is accompanied by annotations of court decisions in which it has been applied and interpreted. *Massachusetts General Laws Annotated*, for example, includes three volumes of annotated rules governing civil procedure, criminal procedure, and appellate procedure. Some annotated collections of rules, such as *Virginia Rules Annotated* (LEXIS Law Publishing, annual) are published separately rather than as part of state codes.

The most extensive and informative sources for information on court rules are practice treatises, which combine the text of the rules with commentary and discussion of cases. Like *Federal Practice and Procedure* or *Moore's Federal Practice*, these works explain the background and application of the court rules and discuss any relevant cases. Practice treatises may not be available for every state, but they are published for most of the larger states. In Massachusetts, for example, two extensive rule-by-rule commentaries are James W. Smith and Hiller B. Zobel's *Rules Practice* (West Publishing, 4 vols., 1974-81, with annual pocket parts) and Edward M. Swartz et al.'s *Massachusetts Pleading and Practice: Forms and Commentary* (Bender, 7 vols., 1974-date, updated annually). Other works, such as Joseph R. Nolan's *Civil Practice* (West Publishing, 2 vols., 2d ed., 1992, with annual pocket parts) and Kent B. Smith's *Criminal Practice and Procedure* (West Publishing, 2 vols., 2d ed., 1983, with annual pocket parts) take a broader view of procedural issues.

Two other print sources for information on court rules are worth noting. The advance sheets to most court reports, including the West regional reporters, contain the text of new amendments to court rules. *Shepard's Citations* includes coverage of court rules following

statutes in its state publications, providing another way to find cases and other citing documents.

Court rules from all states are available online through LEXIS-NEXIS (for Massachusetts, the MARULE file in the MASS, CODES, and STATES libraries) and WESTLAW (MA-RULES). LOIS, on the Internet <http://www.pita.com/> has a growing collection of court rules covering more than a dozen states.

A number of court systems have posted rules on their Internet sites, although these can be harder to find than other primary sources. Checking court homepages through the multistate sites listed earlier in this chapter may lead to online court rules, as well as to other features, such as answers to frequently asked questions about filing procedures. Washburn University's State-Law <http://lawlib.wuacc.edu/washlaw/uslaw/statelaw.html> is one of the few multistate collections that includes links to court rules as well as to statutes and case law. For some states, rules may also be available at commercial sites. Rules for the New York Court of Appeals, for example, are posted by the *New York Law Journal* <http://www.nylj.com/rules/ctapindex.html>.

States usually have official forms prepared for use in specific situations, such as filing complaints or responding to summonses, which are included in sources for court rules. More extensive collections, with a wider range of forms, are also available for most states. Publications for Massachusetts, for example, include *Massachusetts Pleading and Practice: Forms and Commentary*, cited above; Paul G. Garrity and James A. Frieden's *Massachusetts Standardized Civil Practice Forms* (Little, Brown, 4 vols., 1986); and Robert M. Rodman's *Procedural Forms Annotated* (West Publishing, 4 vols., 5th ed., 1990, with annual pocket parts). One way to find these publications is to check online catalogs under headings such as "Forms (law)—[state]" or "Civil procedure—[state]—Forms." Law libraries usually carry sets for their home states but rarely have forms for other jurisdictions.

Each state also has model jury instructions for use in preparing the explanation of the law with which the judge guides jurors' deliberations. Because jury instructions are designed to make sense to nonlawyers, they can provide useful summaries of legal doctrine in plain English. These are available online for a few states, through LEXIS-NEXIS (California, Florida, and Virginia), WESTLAW (California, Illinois, and Washington), and LOIS (Arkansas, Colorado, Nebraska, and Oklahoma). Publications for more than 30 states can be found in *Legal Looseleafs in Print* (Infosources Publishing, annual) under the index heading "Jury instructions," and online catalogs generally list them under the subject heading "Instructions to juries." A comprehensive state-by-state list published in the *Legal Reference Services Quarterly* several years ago is still useful. Cheryl Rae Nyberg and Carol Boast's "Jury Instructions: A Bibliography. Part I: Civil Jury Instructions," 6(1/2) Legal Reference Services Q. 5 (Spring/Summer 1986) was followed by Cheryl Rae Nyberg, Jane Williams, and Carol Boast's "Jury Instructions: A Bibliography. Part II: Criminal Jury Instructions," 6(3/4) Legal Reference Services Q. 3 (Fall/Winter 1986). Part 2 of the bibliography includes a cumulative list of acronyms, useful for determining the jurisdiction for mysterious references such as BAJI (California) or CRIMJIG (Minnesota).

State appellate courts have briefs similar to those filed with the U.S. Supreme Court, but these are not as widely available. A pair of articles by Gene Teitelbaum in *Legal Reference Services Quarterly* surveyed library holdings as of the mid-1980s. "State Courts of Last Resort's Briefs and Records: An Updated Union List," 5(2/3) Legal Reference Services Q. 187 (Summer/Fall 1985) was followed by "Intermediate Appellate State Courts' Briefs and Records: An Updated Union List," 8(1/2) Legal Reference Services Q. 159 (1988). According to these surveys, a few states do not distribute their briefs to libraries, but in most states they are available at the state library and one or more law schools. For some states, briefs are also available on microfiche. In Massachusetts, for example, microfiche copies of Supreme Judicial Court and Appeals Court briefs can be found at a dozen libraries around the state, including four law schools and six local trial court libraries open to the public.

Information on matters such as jury verdicts and settlements is often hard to find. A number of newsletters known as *verdict reporters* report these developments, but they are not widely distributed. These newsletters provide brief summaries of cases, indicating the nature of the complaint, the jury verdict, and the names of the attorneys and expert witnesses for each side. Most, such as *New England Jury Verdict Review and Analysis* (Jury Verdict Review Publications, monthly) and *The Ohio Trial Reporter* (Judicial Advisory Services, monthly), cover specific states or regions. Two publications of national scope are *The National Jury Verdict Review and Analysis* (Jury Verdict Review Publications, monthly) and *Verdicts, Settlements & Tactics* (West Group, monthly). Several of these publications are available through LEXIS-NEXIS (VERDCT library) and a few through WESTLAW (separate data-

bases for individual publications, including VST for *Verdicts, Settlements & Tactics*). Using a simple search string such as "chairlift and California," for example, turns up attorneys who have represented people suing California ski resorts for injuries caused by faulty chairlift equipment, as well as attorneys defending the ski resorts, experts for each side on design and medical issues, and the outcome of each case.

LAWYER CONDUCT

A final area of state court activity is the regulation of lawyers, not only through malpractice litigation but through the enforcement of professional standards. In most states, the supreme court has jurisdiction over the admission and discipline of lawyers, although in many instances these matters are delegated to boards of bar overseers or state bar associations. Materials governing the ethics and discipline of lawyers are found in rules, court decisions, and ethics opinions.

Lawyers' actions in most states are regulated by versions of the Model Rules of Professional Conduct, prepared by the American Bar Association in 1983. A few states continue to use rules based on the ABA's earlier codification, the Model Code of Professional Responsibility (1969), and California has its own rules based on neither ABA model. The rules for a particular state are usually published with other court rules in paperback compilations such as West's *Massachusetts Rules of Court*. The rules governing lawyers can be hard to find because they are sometimes buried amid other rules promulgated by the court of last resort. The Massachusetts Rules of Professional Conduct, for example, are Supreme Judicial Court Rule 3:07. State codes usually provide annotations of court decisions applying the rules, but cases can also be found through the court rules section of a state's *Shepard's Citations*. The rules for all states, in unannotated versions, appear in the *National Reporter on Legal Ethics and Professional Responsibility* (University Publications of America, 4 loose-leaf vols., 1982-date).

The *Annotated Model Rules of Professional Conduct* (ABA Center for Professional Responsibility, 3d ed., 1996), although not keyed to any specific jurisdiction, is a convenient research source. It includes comments, legal background, and notes of decisions from jurisdictions that have adopted the rules. The *Annotated Model Rules* is available from WESTLAW as the ABA-AMRPC database. The CODES file in the ETHICS library on LEXIS-NEXIS has the Model Rules and official comments, but no annotations.

The *ABA/BNA Lawyers' Manual on Professional Conduct* (BNA, 2 loose-leaf vols., 1984-date) is another useful multistate resource. One volume is a reference manual treating major ethical and disciplinary issues, with each one divided into a "Practice Guide" summarizing the area, "Background" explaining the history and scope of state rules, and "Application" discussing cases under the rules. The other volume, "Current Reports," contains biweekly newsletters with information about court decisions, ethics opinions, disciplinary proceedings, and other developments. The *Lawyers' Manual* is also available on WESTLAW as the ABA-BNA database.

While court decisions on issues such as lawyer discipline and disbarment are published like any other cases, advisory opinions from state and local bar associations can be much harder to find. Some state bars do not publish their opinions in full, but include digests of ethics opinions in their bar journals. Obtaining the full text may require contacting the bar. The *National Reporter on Legal Ethics and Professional Responsibility* provides access to opinions from 42 states. Besides the four loose-leaf volumes covering the current year, annual transfer binders contain older opinions dating back to 1981. Each year has its own subject index. LEXIS-NEXIS provides access to the opinions published in the *National Reporter* in the ETHICS library, ETHOP file. WESTLAW has ethics opinions from 18 states, accessible separately or combined as the METH-EO database.

Most state bars and disciplinary agencies now have Web sites, with some information about procedures for filing complaints and resolving problems with lawyers. The "Lawyer Discipline in Massachusetts" Web site <http://www.state.ma.us/obcbbo/>, for example, includes the Massachusetts Rules of Professional Conduct, other relevant rules, and explanations of complaint procedures and sanctions. Legalethics.com <http://www.legalethics.com/> provides the most extensive collection of Internet resources in this area. Its "EthicSites Index" <http://www.legalethics.com/states.htm> has links to state bar associations, rules, and available ethics opinions. Not all organizations are accessible electronically, but the list includes addresses and telephone numbers. The ABA Center for Professional Responsibility also provides a directory of lawyer disciplinary agencies <http://www.abanet.org/cpr/disciplinary.html> listing contact information for the agency in each state responsible for fielding and handling complaints.

Index

Compiled by Debbie Lindblom